VISIONS OF POLITICS

The third of three volumes of essays by Quentin Skinner, one of
the world's leading intellectual historians. This collection includes
some of his most important essays on Thomas Hobbes, each of
which has been carefully revised for publication in this form. In a
series of writings spanning the past four decades Professor Skinner
examines, with his customary perspicuity, the evolution and character of Hobbes's political thought. An indispensable work in its own
right, this volume also serves as a demonstration of those methodological theories propounded in volume 1, and as an appositional
commentary on the Renaissance values of civic virtue treated in
volume 2. All of Professor Skinner's work is characterised by philosophical power, limpid clarity and elegance of exposition. These
essays, many of which are now recognised classics, provide a fascinating and convenient digest of the development of his thought.

QUENTIN SKINNER is Regius Professor of Modern History in the
University of Cambridge and a Fellow of Christ's College. He has
been the recipient of several honorary degrees, and is a Fellow
of numerous academic bodies including the British Academy, the
American Academy and the Academia Europea. His work has
been translated into nineteen languages, and his many publications
include *The Foundations of Modern Political Thought* (two volumes,
Cambridge, 1978), *Machiavelli* (Oxford, 1981), *Reason and Rhetoric in
the Philosophy of Hobbes* (Cambridge, 1996) and *Liberty before Liberalism*
(Cambridge, 1998).

VISIONS OF POLITICS

Volume 3: Hobbes and Civil Science

QUENTIN SKINNER

Regius Professor of Modern History, University of Cambridge

CAMBRIDGE
UNIVERSITY PRESS

PUBLISHED BY THE PRESS SYNDICATE OF THE UNIVERSITY OF CAMBRIDGE
The Pitt Building, Trumpington Street, Cambridge, United Kingdom

CAMBRIDGE UNIVERSITY PRESS
The Edinburgh Building, Cambridge CB2 2RU, UK
40 West 20th Street, New York, NY 10011-4211, USA
477 Williamstown Road, Port Melbourne, VIC 3207, Australia
Ruiz de Alarcón 13, 28014 Madrid, Spain
Dock House, The Waterfront, Cape Town 8001, South Africa

http://www.cambridge.org

First published 2002

Printed in the United Kingdom at the University Press, Cambridge

Typeface Baskerville Monotype 11/12.5 pt   *System* LaTeX 2ε   [TB]

A catalogue record for this book is available from the British Library

ISBN 0 521 81368 9 hardback
ISBN 0 521 89060 8 paperback

Contents

VOLUME 3
HOBBES AND CIVIL SCIENCE

General preface

Several of the chapters in these volumes are appearing in print for the first time. But most of them have been published before (although generally in a very different form) either as articles in journals or as contributions to collective works. Revising them for republication, I have attempted to tread two slightly divergent paths at the same time. On the one hand, I have mostly allowed my original contentions and conclusions to stand without significant change. Where I no longer entirely endorse what I originally wrote, I usually indicate my dissent by adding an explanatory footnote rather than by altering the text. I have assumed that, if these essays are worth re-issuing, this can only be because they continue to be discussed in the scholarly literature. But if that is so, then one ought not to start moving the targets.

On the other hand, I have not hesitated to improve the presentation of my arguments wherever possible. I have corrected numerous mistranscriptions and factual mistakes. I have overhauled as well as standardised my system of references. I have inserted additional illustrations to strengthen and extend a number of specific points. I have updated my discussions of the secondary literature, removing allusions to yesterday's controversies and relating my conclusions to the latest research. I have tried to make use of the most up-to-date editions, with the result that in many cases I have changed the editions I previously used. I have replied to critics wherever this has seemed appropriate, sometimes qualifying and sometimes elaborating my earlier judgements. Finally, I have tinkered very extensively with my prose, particularly in the earliest essays republished here. I have toned down the noisy polemics I used to enjoy; simplified the long sentences, long paragraphs and stylistic curlicues I used to affect; taken greater pains to make use of gender-neutral language wherever possible; and above all tried to eliminate overlaps between chapters and repetitions within them.

I need to explain the basis on which I have selected the essays for inclusion in these volumes. I have chosen and grouped them – and in many cases supplied them with new titles – with two main goals in mind. One has been to give each volume its own thematic unity; the other has been to integrate the volumes in such a way as to form a larger whole.

The chapters in volume 1, *Regarding Method*, are all offered as contributions to the articulation and defence of one particular view about the reading and interpretation of historical texts. I argue that, if we are to write the history of ideas in a properly historical style, we need to situate the texts we study within such intellectual contexts and frameworks of discourse as enable us to recognise what their authors were *doing* in writing them. To speak more fashionably, I emphasise the performativity of texts and the need to treat them intertextually. My aspiration is not of course to perform the impossible task of getting inside the heads of long-dead thinkers; it is simply to use the ordinary techniques of historical enquiry to grasp their concepts, to follow their distinctions, to recover their beliefs and, so far as possible, to see things their way.

The other volumes are both concerned with leading themes in early-modern European political thought. In volume 2, *Renaissance Virtues*, I focus on the fortunes of republicanism as a theory of freedom and government. I follow the re-emergence and development from the thirteenth to the sixteenth century of a theory according to which the fostering of a virtuous and educated citizenry provides the key to upholding the liberty of states and individuals alike. My concluding volume, *Hobbes and Civil Science*, examines the evolution and character of Thomas Hobbes's political thought, concentrating in particular on his theory of the state. I consider his views about the power of sovereigns, about the duties and liberties of subjects and about the grounds and limits of political obedience. I attempt in turn to relate these issues to Hobbes's changing views about the nature of civil science and its place in his more general scheme of the sciences.

While stressing the unity of each volume, I am anxious at the same time to underline the interrelations between them. I have attempted in the first place to bring out a general connection between volumes 2 and 3. As we turn from Renaissance theories of civic virtue to Hobbes's civil science, we turn at the same time from the ideal of republican self-government to its greatest philosophical adversary. Although I am mainly concerned in volume 3 with the development of Hobbes's thought, much of what he has to say about freedom and political obligation can also be read as a critical commentary on the vision of politics outlined in volume 2.

The linkage in which I am chiefly interested, however, is the one I seek to trace between the philosophical argument of volume 1 and the historical materials presented in volumes 2 and 3. To put the point as simply as possible, I see the relationship as one of theory and practice. In volume 1 I preach the virtues of a particular approach; in the rest of the book I try to practise what I preach.

As I intimate in my general title, *Visions of Politics*, my overarching historical interest lies in comparing two contrasting views we have inherited in the modern West about the nature of our common life. One speaks of sovereignty as a property of the people, the other sees it as the possession of the state. One gives centrality to the figure of the virtuous citizen, the other to the sovereign as representative of the state. One assigns priority to the duties of citizens, the other to their rights. It hardly needs stressing that the question of how to reconcile these divergent perspectives remains a central problem in contemporary political thought. My highest hope is that, by excavating the history of these rival theories, I may be able to contribute something of more than purely historical interest to these current debates.

Full contents: Volumes 1–3

Acknowledgements

I remain deeply obliged to the large number of colleagues who supplied me with detailed comments on the original versions of the chapters in these volumes, and I am very glad of the chance to renew my thanks to them here. This is also the moment to single out a number of friends who have given me especially unstinting support and encouragement in my work over the years. I list them with the deepest gratitude: John Dunn, Clifford Geertz, Raymond Geuss, Fred Inglis, Susan James, John Pocock, John Thompson, Jim Tully. My debt to them can only be described – in the words of Roget's indispensable *Thesaurus* – as immense, enormous, vast, stonking and mega.

I also owe my warmest thanks to those friends who have helped to give the individual volumes in this book their present shape. For advice about the argument in volume 1 I am particularly grateful to Jonathan Lear, Kari Palonen, Richard Rorty and the late Martin Hollis. For numerous discussions about the themes of volume 2 I am similarly indebted to Philip Pettit and Maurizio Viroli. As will be evident from my argument there, I also learned a great deal from chairing the European Science Foundation workshop 'Republicanism: A Shared European Heritage'. Special thanks to Martin van Gelderen and Iain Hampsher-Monk for many instructive and enjoyable conversations, and for helping to make our meetings such a success.[1] For advice about volume 3 I owe an overwhelming debt to Kinch Hoekstra, Noel Malcolm and Karl Schuhmann, all of whom have shown a heartwarming readiness to place at my disposal their astounding knowledge of early-modern philosophy. A number of my recent PhD students have likewise helped me by commenting on individual chapters or on my project as a whole. My thanks to David Armitage, Geoffrey Baldwin, Annabel Brett, Hannah Dawson, Angus

---

[1] The papers read and discussed at our meetings have now been published in two volumes: *Republicanism: A Shared European Heritage*, ed. Martin van Gelderen and Quentin Skinner (Cambridge University Press, 2002).

Gowland, Eric Nelson, Jürgen Overhoff, Jonathan Parkin and Richard Serjeantson.

As well as receiving so much assistance from individual scholars, I owe at least as great an obligation to the institutions that have sustained me throughout the long period in which I have been working on the materials presented here. The Faculty of History in the University of Cambridge has provided me with an ideal working environment throughout my academic career, and I have benefited immeasurably from my association with Christ's College and Gonville and Caius College. I never cease to learn from my colleagues and from the many brilliant students who pass through the Faculty, and I owe a particular debt to the University for its exceptionally generous policy about sabbatical leave. This is the first piece of work I have completed while holding my current post as a Leverhulme Senior Research Fellow. I hope that other publications will follow, but in the meantime I already owe the Leverhulme Trust my warmest thanks for its support.

I need to reserve a special word of appreciation for the owners and custodians of the paintings and manuscripts I have examined. I am indebted to the Marquis of Lansdowne for permission to consult the Petty Papers at Bowood, and to the Duke of Devonshire and the Trustees of the Chatsworth settlement for allowing me to make extensive use of the Hardwick and Hobbes manuscripts at Chatsworth. I am similarly grateful for the courtesy and expertise I have encountered in the manuscript reading rooms of the Bibliothèque Nationale, the British Library, the Cambridge University Library, the Bodleian Library and the Library of St John's College Oxford. I am likewise grateful for the friendly helpfulness of the custodians of the Cappella degli Scrovegni in Padua and the Palazzo Pubblico in Siena.

For permission to reproduce photographs my thanks are due to Alinari (Florence), the Warburg Institute (University of London) and Dost Kitavebi (Ankara). For permission to make use of material that originally appeared in their pages I am grateful to the following journals and publishers: Blackwells and Co., The British Academy, *Comparative Studies in Society and History*, *Essays in Criticism*, Europa Publications, *The Finnish Yearbook of Political Thought*, *The Historical Journal*, *History and Theory*, *History of Political Thought*, *The Journal of Political Philosophy*, *The Journal of the Warburg and Courtauld Institutes*, Macmillan and Co., *New Literary History*, *Politics*, *Prose Studies*, The Royal Historical Society, Stanford University Press and The University of Pennsylvania Press.

I have benefited from an extraordinary amount of patient and re-sourceful assistance in the final stages of preparing these volumes for the Press. Richard Thompson amended the quotations in several articles in which I had originally modernised the spelling of early-modern texts. Alice Bell devoted an entire summer to checking transcriptions and references with wonderful meticulousness. Anne Dunbar-Nobes undertook the enormous labour of assembling the bibliographies, rewriting them in author-date style, reformatting all the footnotes and checking them against the bibliographies to ensure an exact match.

While these volumes have been going through the Press I have received a great deal more in the way of technical help. Anne Dunbar-Nobes agreed to serve as copy-editor of the book, and saw it into production with superb professionalism as well as much good cheer. Philip Riley, who has for many years acted as proofreader of my work, generously agreed to perform that task yet again, and duly brought to bear his matchless skills, patience and imperturbability.

I cannot speak with sufficient admiration of my friends at Cambridge University Press. One of my greatest pieces of professional good fortune has been that, throughout my academic career, Jeremy Mynott has watched over the publication of my books with infallible editorial judgement. Richard Fisher has likewise been a pillar of support over the years, and has edited the present work with characteristic enthusiasm, imagination and unfaltering efficiency. My heartfelt thanks to them both, and to their very able assistants, for so much goodwill and expertise.

I cannot end without acknowledging that, if it were not for Susan James and our children Olivia and Marcus, I could not hope to manage at all.

Conventions

Abbreviations. The following abbreviations are used in the footnotes:

BL: British Library
BN: Bibliothèque Nationale
DNB: Dictionary of National Biography
OED: Oxford English Dictionary

Bibliographies. These are simply checklists of the primary sources I have actually quoted and the secondary authorities on which I have relied. They make no pretence of being systematic guides to the ever-burgeoning literature on the themes I discuss. In the bibliographies of printed primary sources I list anonymous works by title. Where a work was published anonymously but its author's name is known, I place the name in square brackets. In the case of anonymous works where the attribution remains in doubt, I add a bracketed question-mark after the conjectured name. The bibliographies of secondary sources give all references to journal numbers in arabic form.

Classical names and titles. I refer to ancient Greek and Roman writers in their most familiar single-name form, both in the text and in the bibliographies. Greek titles have been transliterated, but all other titles are given in their original language.

Dates. Although I follow my sources in dating by the Christian era (CE and BCE), I have had to make some decisions about the different systems of dating prevalent in the early-modern period. The Julian Calendar ('Old Style') remained in use in Britain, whereas the Gregorian ('New Style') – ten days ahead of the Julian – was employed in continental Europe from 1582. When quoting from sources written or published on the Continent I use the Gregorian style, but when quoting from

British sources I prefer the Julian. For example, I give Hobbes's date of birth as 5 April rather than 15 April 1588, even though the latter date is technically correct from our point of view, given that the Gregorian calendar was adopted in Britain in the eighteenth century. A further peculiarity of early-modern British dating is that the year was generally taken to start on 25 March. I have preferred to follow the continental practice of treating the year as beginning on 1 January. For example, I treat Hobbes's translation of Thucydides – entered in the Stationers' register with a date of 18 March 1628 – as entered in 1629.

Gender. Sometimes it is clear that, when the writers I am discussing say 'he', they do *not* mean 'he or she', and in such cases I have of course followed their usage rather than tampered with their sense. But in general I have tried to maintain gender-neutral language as far as possible. To this end, I have taken full advantage of the fact that, in the British version of the English language, it is permissible for pronouns and possessives after *each, every, anyone,* etc. to take a plural and hence a gender-neutral form (as in 'to each their need, from each their power').

References. Although I basically follow the author-date system, I have made two modifications to it. One has been rendered necessary by the fact that I quote from a number of primary sources (for example, collections of Parliamentary debates) that are unattributable to any one author. As with anonymous works, I refer to these texts by their titles rather than by the names of their modern editors and list them in the bibliographies of primary sources. My other modification is that, in passages where I continuously quote from one particular work, I give references so far as possible in the body of the text rather than in footnotes. Except when citing from classical sources, I generally give references in arabic numerals to chapters from individual texts and to parts of multi-volume works.

Transcriptions. My rule has been to preserve original spelling, capitalisation, italicisation and punctuation so far as possible. However, I normalise the long 's', remove diphthongs, expand contractions, correct obvious typographical errors and change 'u' to 'v' and 'i' to 'j' in accordance with modern orthography. When quoting in Latin I use 'v' as well as 'u', change 'j' to 'i', expand contractions and omit diacritical marks. Sometimes I change a lower-case initial letter to an upper, or vice versa, when fitting quotations around my own prose.

Introduction: Hobbes's life in philosophy

I

With this third and concluding volume, I turn from Renaissance theories of self-government to their leading philosophical opponent, Thomas Hobbes. As we shall see, Hobbes was nurtured in the humanist ideals with which I was chiefly concerned in volume 2. But he went on to repudiate his upbringing and, in developing his theories of freedom, obligation and the state, he sought to discredit and supersede some of the most fundamental tenets of humanist political thought. Reacting above all against the Renaissance predilection for self-governing city-republics, he constructed a theory of absolute sovereignty grounded on a covenant specifically requiring that each one of us 'give up my Right of Governing my selfe'.[1] The aim of this Introduction will be to trace the process by which Hobbes arrived at these anti-humanist commitments, to examine the resulting elements in his civil science and to consider their place in his more general scheme of the sciences.

II

To begin at the beginning. Thomas Hobbes was born on 5 April 1588 in Westport, a parish adjoining the town of Malmesbury in Wiltshire.[2] He was the second son of another Thomas Hobbes,[3] curate of the neighbouring and all too aptly named parish of Brokenborough.[4] The elder Hobbes appears to have found his life altogether too much for him. A

---

[1] Hobbes 1996, ch. 17, p. 120.   [2] Aubrey 1898, vol. 1, pp. 323, 327.
[3] Aubrey 1898, vol. 1, pp. 323 and 324–5 notes that Edmund, brother of Hobbes *père*, was his elder by two years.
[4] Aubrey 1898, vol. 1, p. 323 wrongly describes Hobbes's father as vicar of Westport. Malcolm 1996, pp. 14, 38 corrects the mistake. Malcolm also notes (p. 14) that Brokenborough was one of the poorest livings in the area. Malcolm's article is of exceptional value and I am greatly indebted to it.

man of little education who could barely read the church services,[5] he
played cards all night, fell asleep during the sermon,[6] became notorious
for drunken and quarrelsome behaviour[7] and eventually fled to London
in 1604 after picking a fight with another local clergyman.[8] It is not
known whether his famous son ever saw him again.

Hobbes's father was succeeded in the curacy of Brokenborough by
a man in his late twenties called Robert Latimer,[9] who was destined
to play a more formative role in shaping the young Hobbes's life than
his own father ever seems to have done. A graduate of Magdalen Hall,
Oxford,[10] Latimer had arrived at Westport directly from university in
the mid-1590s to run a small private school.[11] Hobbes attended this
establishment from about the age of ten,[12] and it is a fact of great importance in Hobbes's intellectual development that Robert Latimer was
able to provide him with an excellent grounding in the humanistic curriculum then typical of the Elizabethan grammar schools.[13] This training mainly centred on the study of the classical languages, and the
young Hobbes duly succeeded (as we shall see in chapter 2) in acquiring
an extraordinarily high level of proficiency in Latin and Greek. But
the study of classical rhetoric would also have formed a significant part
of his education, and this too is important (as we shall see in chapter 3)
in relation to explaining the evolution of his thought. Hobbes makes no
mention of Latimer in either of his autobiographies,[14] but he undoubtedly owed his schoolmaster a major intellectual debt.

---

[5] So says Aubrey 1898, vol. 1, p. 323, who also speaks of his 'ignorance and clownery'.

[6] Aubrey 1898, vol. 1, p. 387.

[7] Aubrey 1898, vol. 1, p. 387. Cf. Malcolm 1996, p. 15.

[8] See Aubrey 1898, vol. 1, p. 387 for the incident and Malcolm 1996, p. 15 for the date.

[9] Malcolm 1996, p. 16 has established this fascinating fact. I infer Latimer's age at the time from the
fact that, according to Aubrey 1898, vol. 1, p. 328, Latimer was 'a young man of about nineteen
or twenty' when Hobbes began attending his school in the late 1590s. But Latimer may have
been older than Aubrey supposed. Foster 1891–2, vol. 3, p. 884 records that Latimer took his BA
at Magdalen Hall as early as 1591, proceeding to an MA at Magdalen College in 1595.

[10] Foster 1891–2, vol. 3, p. 884. Cf. Malcolm 1996, p. 16.

[11] Aubrey 1898, vol. 1, p. 328.

[12] This can be inferred from the fact that, as Aubrey 1898, vol. 1, p. 328 informs us, after finishing
his 'petty' training at the church school in Westport at the age of eight, Hobbes attended a school
run by the minister in Malmesbury before moving to Latimer's establishment.

[13] For this curriculum see Skinner 1996, pp. 19–65.

[14] It will be best to say a word about Hobbes's autobiographies at the outset, given that they provide
such important insights into his career, and will be frequently cited not merely in the present
Introduction but in several later chapters. Hobbes tells us in Hobbes 1839b, p. xcix, line 375
that he wrote his verse *Vita*, much the longer of his two autobiographical sketches, at the age
of eighty-four – that is, in 1672. Hobbes MSS (Chatsworth) MS A. 6 is Hobbes's corrected
manuscript copy, and provides a more authoritative text than Hobbes 1839b, the version printed
by Molesworth. I have therefore preferred to quote from the Chatsworth manuscript, although

As a younger son, Hobbes may have been intended for the church,[15] and this may help to explain how it came about that his father's elder brother, a childless and prosperous glover, agreed to pay for Hobbes to be sent to university.[16] No doubt as a result of Latimer's advice, Hobbes followed in his teacher's footsteps and went to Magdalen Hall Oxford, where he took his bachelor's degree in 1608.[17] But instead of seeking ecclesiastical preferment he immediately followed the no less time-honoured path of joining an aristocratic household. As soon as he graduated, he entered the service of William Cavendish, a Derbyshire landowner who became the first Earl of Devonshire in 1618. Hobbes's initial duties were those of tutor and companion to Cavendish's son, the future second earl, who also bore the name William Cavendish.[18] Subsequently, Hobbes went on to act as secretary to the younger Cavendish,[19] but reverted to his tutorial role soon after the second earl's sudden death in 1628.[20] The third earl – yet another William Cavendish – was barely eleven years old at the time,[21] and Hobbes was asked to take charge of his education, a task that occupied him for seven painstaking years (as he put it in his verse *Vita*) until Cavendish attained his majority in 1638.[22]

It is important to underline the extent to which, as this sketch already indicates, Hobbes was a product of the literary culture of humanism. As we shall see in chapter 2, the values of the *studia humanitatis* largely underpin the syllabus he worked out for the instruction of the third earl in the 1630s. Hobbes himself draws attention to the point when referring to his tutorial labours in his verse *Vita*. Although he mentions that he taught the young earl some logic, arithmetic and geography,[23] he stresses that they mainly concentrated on the three basic elements of the *studia humanitatis*: grammar, rhetoric and poetry. They began 'by learning the meaning of the speech used by the Romans, and how to join Latin words

---

my page references are to the Molesworth edition. Tricaud 1985, pp. 280–1 has established that Hobbes's shorter prose *Vita* was partly drafted in the 1650s and given its final form only a few months before his death in 1679.

[15] A point helpfully made in Malcolm 1996, p. 15.   [16] Aubrey 1898, vol. 1, p. 324.

[17] Aubrey 1898, vol. 1, p. 330. It is not known exactly when Hobbes matriculated. See Malcolm 1996, p. 39. But Aubrey 1898, vol. 1, pp. 328, 330 is probably correct in stating that Hobbes entered the university at the beginning of 1603.

[18] Malcolm 1994c, pp. 807–8.

[19] See Hobbes MSS (Chatsworth) MS 73Aa, flyleaf, where Hobbes identifies himself as 'secretary to ye Lord Cavendysh'. Hobbes also refers to himself on the title-page of Hobbes 1629 as 'Secretary to ye late Earle of Devonshire'.

[20] Malcolm 1994c, p. 815.

[21] Malcolm 1994c, p. 815 notes that the third earl was born in 1617.

[22] Hobbes 1839b, p. lxxxix, line 103. Cf. Malcolm 1994c, pp. 808–9 and 815–17.

[23] Hobbes 1839b, p. lxxxix, lines 99–101.

together in the proper way'.[24] Then they went on to consider 'how poetry is composed' and at the same time 'how orators write, and by means
of what art rhetoricians are accustomed to deceive the uninitiated'.[25]
As Hobbes adds in his prose *Vita*, what he provided for his pupil was
thus an education *in literis*, the traditional humanistic ideal of 'good
letters'.[26]

A similar preoccupation with rhetoric and poetry is apparent in
Hobbes's own earliest works. One of the tasks he set himself while tutoring the third earl was to produce a Latin paraphrase of Aristotle's
Art of Rhetoric, an English version of which was published anonymously
as *A Briefe of the Art of Rhetorique* in c.1637.[27] Although Hobbes professed to
despise Aristotle as a philosopher of nature, and declared him to be 'the
worst teacher that ever was, the worst politician and ethick', he nevertheless acknowledged that his *Rhetoric* was 'rare'.[28] One sign of its impact on
Hobbes's thinking has frequently been remarked upon. When Hobbes
turns to examine the character of the 'affections' in chapters 8 and 9
of *The Elements of Law*, he enunciated a number of his definitions in the
form of virtual quotations from Aristotle's analysis of the emotions in the
opening chapters of Book 2 of the *Rhetoric*.[29] But a further and connected
use of Aristotle's *Rhetoric* in *The Elements* has been little discussed. When
Hobbes asks himself in chapter 9 – and again in chapter 6 of *Leviathan* –
about the nature of the emotions expressed by the peculiar phenomenon
of laughter, he proceeds to outline a theory of the ridiculous that closely
resembles that of Aristotle in the *Rhetoric*. I offer a survey in chapter 5
of this Aristotelian tradition of thinking about the laughable, and ask at

[24] Hobbes 1839b, p. lxxxviii, lines 95–6:

> Hunc Romanarum sensus cognoscere vocum;
> Jungere quoque decet verba Latina modo.

[25] Hobbes 1839b, p. lxxxviii, lines 97–8:

> Fallere quaque solent indoctos rhetores arte;
> Quid facit Orator, quidque Poeta facit.

[26] Hobbes 1839a, p. xiv.

[27] For the Latin paraphrase see Hobbes MSS (Chatsworth) MS D. 1, pp. 1–143. It contains numerous
corrections in Hobbes's hand and must in substance be Hobbes's work. [Hobbes (?)] 1986, an
English translation of this manuscript, has always been credited to Hobbes as well. But a number
of anomalies and misunderstandings in the translation have led Karl Schuhmann to the dramatic
but convincing conclusion that, while the Latin paraphrase is by Hobbes, the English translation
is not.

[28] Aubrey 1898, vol. 1, p. 357.

[29] See Aristotle 1926, II. 1. 8 to II. 11. 7, pp. 172–246, and for discussions of the parallels see Strauss
1963, pp. 36–41; Zappen 1983; Skinner 1996, pp. 38–9.

the same time why that tradition appears to have mattered so much to Hobbes.

Hobbes's next work reflected an even keener interest in the other basic element in the *studia humanitatis*, the art of poetry. Around the year 1627[30] Hobbes composed a Latin poem of some five hundred hexameters, *De Mirabilibus Pecci, Carmen*, which he presented as a gift to the second earl and subsequently published in c.1636.[31] But by far the most important product of Hobbes's so-called 'humanist period'[32] was his translation of Thucydides's history, which he published as *Eight Bookes of the Peloponnesian Warre* in 1629.[33] Hobbes's introductory essay, *Of the Life and History of Thucydides*, is a thoroughly humanist text. As I seek to demonstrate in chapter 2, it is wholly constructed according to the precepts laid down in classical handbooks of rhetoric for the presentation of persuasive arguments, as well as being founded on the humanist assumption that 'the principal and proper work of history' is 'to instruct and enable men, by the knowledge of actions past, to bear themselves prudently in the present and providently towards the future'.[34]

III

During the 1630s Hobbes began to direct his intellectual energies along new paths. He began to turn away from – and against – his humanist allegiances, and to take an increasingly professional interest in the study of mathematics and the natural sciences. Hobbes's correspondence from this period suggests that his scientific curiosity was quickened as a result of his acquaintance with the Earl of Devonshire's cousins, the Earl of Newcastle and his younger brother Sir Charles Cavendish, both of whom were conducting experiments at the earl's principal residence, Welbeck Abbey in Nottinghamshire.[35] By 1636 we find Hobbes writing confidently to Newcastle on a variety of scientific themes. He offers an opinion about local motion and its relation to heat, about Galileo's theory of colour and light, and more generally about the nature of scientific proof.[36] He also discusses the optical experiments being carried out at

[30] Aubrey 1898, vol. 1, p. 360 supplies the date.
[31] Aubrey 1898, vol. 1, p. 360. Wood 1691–2, p. 479 adds that the poem was first 'printed at *Lond.* about 1636'.
[32] For this concept see Strauss 1963, p. 30; Reik 1977 and especially Schuhmann 1990.
[33] Hobbes 1629.   [34] Hobbes 1975a, p. 6.
[35] See Malcolm 1994c, pp. 801–5 and pp. 812–15.
[36] Hobbes 1994, Letter 19, pp. 33–4 and Letter 21, pp. 37–8.

Welbeck by Robert Payne, who soon became a close friend.[37] Payne was employed by Newcastle nominally as his chaplain, but devoted much of his time in the mid-1630s to studying the phenomenon of refracted light, a subject that rapidly attracted Hobbes's attention as well.[38]

Hobbes's shift from the humanities to the sciences appears to have happened rather suddenly. So it seems natural to ask whether the moment of conversion can be pinpointed with any accuracy. Hobbes himself supplies a very precise date. Accused of plagiarism at one point in his bruising controversy with Descartes in 1641, he retorted that he had first articulated his theories about 'the nature and production of light, sound and all phantasms or ideas' in the presence of 'those most excellent brothers William Earl of Newcastle and Sir Charles Cavendish' as early as the year 1630.[39] It seems to have been this declaration that prompted Ferdinand Tönnies to attribute to Hobbes, and to date to the year 1630, an anonymous manuscript to which Tönnies gave the title *A Short Tract on First Principles*.[40] The authorship of the *Short Tract* has of late been a subject of intense debate,[41] but it is certainly clear that the ideas it contains are at least partly those of Hobbes.[42] Although it includes some claims that Hobbes was subsequently to repudiate,[43] it is written in his familiar demonstrative style and contributes to his long-standing ambition to outline a purely mechanistic conception of nature.

The *Short Tract* appears to have been completed in 1632–3.[44] Soon after this, Hobbes's scientific interests deepened as a result of various contacts he made on a visit to France and Italy with the third Earl of Devonshire between 1634 and 1636.[45] The most important friendship he struck up in this period was with Marin Mersenne, who acted as the convenor of regular scientific meetings at the Convent of the Annunciation in Paris, where he lived as a member of the Minim Friars.[46] Hobbes indicates in his

---

[37] Hobbes 1994, Letter 16, pp. 28–9.   [38] On Payne see Malcolm 1994c, pp. 872–7.

[39] Hobbes 1994, Letter 34, p. 108.   [40] Tönnies 1969a, Appendix I, p. 193.

[41] For a critical edition of the text see [Hobbes (?)] 1988. Bernhardt 1988, pp. 88–92 insists on Hobbes's authorship, while Zagorin 1993 and Schuhmann 1995 advance powerful arguments in favour of it. But Malcolm 1994c, p. 874 remains unconvinced, observing that the *Short Tract* is in Robert Payne's handwriting and inferring that the work 'can plausibly be attributed' to him. Raylor 2001 outlines the debate, concluding that the tract was indeed written by Payne, but that its ideas are at least in part those of Hobbes.

[42] Schuhmann 1995 and Raylor 2001 make this clear beyond doubt.

[43] For example, about the nature of light and its propagation. See Prins 1996, pp. 129–32 and cf. Hobbes 1998.

[44] Schuhmann 1995, p. 26.

[45] See Malcolm 1996, p. 23 for details of Hobbes's itinerary.

[46] Dear 1988, p. 14. Cf. Hobbes 1985, p. 351.

prose *Vita* that Mersenne first welcomed him into this circle in 1635, and that thereafter they 'communicated daily about my thoughts'.[47] These meetings appear to have aroused in Hobbes an almost obsessional desire to understand the laws of physics, and above all the phenomenon of motion. In his verse *Vita* he recalls that, after setting out for Italy with the young earl in the autumn of 1635,[48] 'I began to think about the nature of things all the time, whether I was on a ship, in a coach, or travelling on horseback.'[49] He makes it clear that his thinking was based on a rejection of the Aristotelian assumption that the truth about the world must be closely connected with its appearance. On the contrary, Hobbes tells us, 'it seemed to me that there is only one thing in the whole world that is real, although it is falsified in a number of ways'.[50] This single reality is motion, 'which is why anyone who wishes to understand physics must first of all devote themselves wholeheartedly to studying what makes motion possible'.[51]

Back in England at the end of 1636, Hobbes began to elaborate this basic insight as a claim about three types of bodies. 'The whole *genus* of philosophy', he came to believe, 'contains just three parts: *Corpus, Homo, Civis*, body, man and citizen.'[52] Armed with these fundamental categories, he found himself able, he reports, 'to move from the various types of motion to the variety of things, that is, to different species and elements of matter,

---

[47] Hobbes 1839a, p. xiv: 'cogitatis suis cum Reverendo Patre Marino Mersenno ... quotidie communicatis'. This is confirmed in Blackbourne 1839, p. xxviii. See also Hobbes 1839b, p. xc, line 127, which speaks of communicating with Mersenne 'anew' on returning to Paris in 1636 after wintering in Italy. Hobbes 1994, Letters 12 to 16, pp. 22–30 make it clear that Hobbes was in Paris for at least a year between autumn 1634 and 1635. See Jacoby 1974, pp. 62–3 and for a classic discussion of the importance of this visit see Brandt 1928, pp. 149–60.

[48] Hobbes 1994, Letter 16 (25 August 1635) pp. 28–9, shows Hobbes still in Paris. Hobbes 1994, Letter 17 (16 April 1636) pp. 30–1, sent from Florence, speaks of having arrived there after a stay in Rome.

[49] Hobbes 1839b, p. lxxxix, lines 109–10:

> Ast ergo perpetuo natura cogito rerum,
> Seu rate, seu curru, sive ferebar equo.

[50] Hobbes 1839b, p. lxxxix, lines 111–12:

> Et mihi visa quidem est toto res unica mundo
> Vera, licet multis falsificata modis:

[51] Hobbes 1839b, p. lxxxix, lines 119–20:

> Hinc est quod, physicam quisquis vult discere, motus
> Quid possit, debet perdidicisse prius.

[52] Hobbes 1839b, p. xc, lines 137–8:

> Nam philosophandi
> Corpus, Homo, Civis continet omne genus.

and from there to the internal motions of men and the secrets of the heart, and from there, finally, to the blessings of Sovereignty and Justice'.[53] With this outline firmly in mind, he goes on, 'I decided to write three books on these issues, and started to collect my materials every day.'[54]

By the end of the 1630s Hobbes had made considerable progress with this tripartite scheme. Admittedly there is little evidence that he had made much headway with the first of his projected volumes, *De Corpore*, which he finally managed to publish only in 1655. But by 1640 he had finished a major Latin manuscript treatise on optics,[55] the subject of the opening half of his second projected volume, *De Homine*, which eventually appeared in 1658.[56] And in May 1640 he completed the manuscript of *The Elements of Law, Natural and Politic*, the latter part of which consists of a polished sketch of his promised third volume on the blessings of sovereignty and justice.[57]

Soon after circulating this manuscript Hobbes begin to fear for his
. safety in consequence of the worsening political crisis in England. Forced to reconvene Parliament in 1640 after a gap of eleven years, King Charles I found himself obliged to stand by while his advisers were arrested and his regime denounced. Among those sent to the Tower by parliamentary order was Roger Maynwaring, who had preached as royal chaplain in favour of the absolute power of kings.[58] Hobbes told John Aubrey that he

---

[53] Hobbes 1839b, p. xc, lines 133–6:

> Motibus a variis feror ad rerum variarum
> Dissimiles species, materiaeque dolos;
> Motusque internos hominum, cordisque latebras:
> Denique ad Imperii Justitiaeque bona.

[54] Hobbes 1839b, p. xc, lines 139–40:

> Tres super his rebus statuo conscribere libros;
> Materiemque mihi congero quoque die.

[55] BL Harl. MS 6796, fos. 193–266. The date of this manuscript has been established in Malcolm 1994b, pp. liii–lv, where it is shown that it was transcribed in 1640 for Sir Charles Cavendish. As Hobbes's correspondence indicates, he was spurred to write by the appearance of Descartes's *Dioptrique*, the essay on optics published as an appendix to the *Discours de la méthode* in 1637. Hobbes must have been one of Descartes's earliest English readers. Hobbes 1994, Letter 27, p. 51 shows that he received a copy of the *Discours* as early as 4 October 1637.

[56] Hobbes 1839d, chs. 2 to 9, pp. 7–87. As Robertson 1886, p. 59n. first noticed, these chapters are virtually identical with those on vision in BL Harl. MS 3360 fos. 73ʳ–173ʳ, the English manuscript treatise on optics which Hobbes completed early in 1646.

[57] As Tönnies 1969a, pp. v–viii first recognised, *The Elements* is the work described in Hobbes 1840d, p. 414 as the 'little treatise in English', of which 'though not printed, many gentlemen had copies'. The standard edition is Hobbes 1969a, but it contains so many transcription errors that I have preferred – in this and in subsequent chapters – to quote instead from BL Harl. MS 4235, arguably the best surviving manuscript, although my page references are to the 1969 edition.

[58] Sommerville 1992, pp. 18–19.

regarded Maynwaring's doctrines as essentially the same as his own,[59] and feared that he might suffer a similar fate.[60] The upshot, Aubrey reports, was that 'then thought Mr. Hobbes, 'tis time now for me to shift for my selfe, and so withdrew into France and resided at Paris'.[61]

IV

Hobbes lived in France for the next eleven years, continuing to work on his physics and on the application of his scientific principles to civic life. He made his first task that of completing the sketch of his political theory he had already circulated. The outcome was the appearance of *Elementorum Philosophiae Sectio Tertia De Cive* at Paris in 1642.[62] The full title signals the intended place of the work in Hobbes's tripartite division of philosophy, but the delays attending the completion of his trilogy proved so protracted that, when this final section was reissued in two further editions at Amsterdam in 1647, it appeared instead under its shorter and more familiar title as *De Cive*.[63]

One striking feature not merely of *De Cive* but of Hobbes's earlier sketch in *The Elements of Law* is the vehemence with which he repudiates the values of the rhetorical culture in which he had originally been nurtured. One of his principal purposes in both these works is to challenge and overturn the central tenets of Renaissance civil science and replace them with a new conception of *scientia civilis* founded on authentically scientific premises. In chapters 3 and 4 I seek to illustrate these claims at greater length. In chapter 3 I begin by laying out the classical assumption that a civil science must be founded on a union of reason and rhetoric, and hence of science and eloquence. I then show how Hobbes sought to discredit and replace this approach by disjoining the science of politics from any connection with the rhetorical arts. In chapter 4 I turn to consider the fundamental rhetorical assumption that all moral questions are susceptible of being debated *in utramque partem*, on either side of the case. I seek to establish that one of Hobbes's leading aims as a moral philosopher was to undermine and supersede this style of argument by fixing the definitions and implications of moral terms in a purportedly scientific way.

After the publication of *De Cive* in 1642, Hobbes reverted to working on his philosophical system in the order in which he had originally conceived

[59] Aubrey 1898, vol. 1, p. 334.
[60] This is especially clear from Hobbes 1994, Letter 35, pp. 114–15.
[61] Aubrey 1898, vol. 1, p. 334.   [62] See Hobbes 1642 and cf. Hobbes 1983a.
[63] For these two further editions see Warrender 1983a, pp. 8–13.

it. The first important piece of writing to which this gave rise was a lengthy critical examination of Thomas White's treatise *De Mundo*.[64] 'The most learned Mr White', as Hobbes called him,[65] was an English Catholic priest and a fellow exile well known to Hobbes,[66] whose *De Mundo* had been published in September 1642.[67] Hobbes drafted his reply during the winter of 1642 and spring of 1643,[68] producing a massive if somewhat diffuse manuscript in which he discussed, among many other things, several of the questions eventually handled in *De Corpore*, including such topics as place, cause, motion, circular motion and the behaviour of heavenly bodies.[69]

After sketching this outline of his natural philosophy, Hobbes turned to the business of working it out in detail. An early outcome was *Of Liberty and Necessity*, which he composed in the form of a letter to the marquis (as he had become) of Newcastle in the summer of 1645, having conducted a debate on the subject with John Bramhall in Newcastle's presence in Paris earlier in the same year.[70] Pursuing an argument already implicit in the *Short Tract*,[71] and further developed in the analysis of deliberation in his *Critique* of White,[72] Hobbes provides an elegant solution to the problem of how to render metaphysical determinism compatible with the idea of free action. I examine his solution – which he subsequently incorporated into his civil philosophy – in the course of chapter 7.[73]

The main project to which Hobbes devoted himself after finishing his critique of *De Mundo* was the completion of the opening volume in his projected trilogy.[74] Recalling this period in his verse *Vita*, he remembered it as a time when 'I thought night and day for four years about the form of my book *De Corpore* and how it should be written'.[75] It soon became clear, however, that the task he had set himself was even harder than he

---

[64] For the manuscript see Bibliothèque Nationale, Fonds Latin MS 6566A. For the dating see Jacquot and Jones 1973, pp. 12–13, 43–5.
[65] Hobbes 1840a, p. 236.
[66] On White and Hobbes see Southgate 1993, pp. 7–8, 28–9.
[67] Southgate 1993, p. 7.   [68] Jacquot and Jones 1973, pp. 43–5.
[69] Hobbes 1839c, chs. 7, 9, 15–16, 21–2, 25–6. Cf. Hobbes 1973, chs. 4, 7, 14, 22, 30.
[70] These facts are established in Lessay 1993b, pp. 31–8. On Newcastle's circle in Paris see Jacob and Raylor 1991, pp. 215–22.
[71] [Hobbes (?) 1988], Section 1, Conclusions 11–13, pp. 20–2.
[72] BN Fonds Latin MS 6566A, fos. 349^v–351^v. Cf. Hobbes 1973, chapter 30, sections 26 to 30, pp. 360–2.
[73] For further discussion of the debate with Bramhall see Overhoff 2000, pp. 134–41.
[74] This is made clear in Hobbes 1839b, p. xci, lines 159–60.
[75] Hobbes 1839b, p. xci, lines 159–60:

Inde annis quatuor libri *De Corpore* formam,
Qua sit scribendus, nocte dieque puto.

had initially supposed. As he explained to friends who expressed anxiety about the lengthening delays, his main difficulty stemmed from his belief that in *De Cive* he had demonstrated all the leading propositions he had put forward. He was now trying, as he put it in a letter to Samuel Sorbière in June 1646, 'to achieve in metaphysics and physics what I hope I have achieved in moral theory, so that there may be no room left for any critic to write against me'.[76] As he lamented in a subsequent letter, however, this was exactly the outcome that continued to elude him. 'It is not the effort of finding out the truth but that of explaining and demonstrating it which is holding up publication.'[77]

One of Hobbes's stumbling blocks was that, as his *Critique* of White's *De Mundo* had already made painfully clear, he was unable to make up his mind about the character of a demonstrative science.[78] He opens his *Critique* by arguing that the process of acquiring demonstrative knowledge is a matter of identifying causes and their necessary consequences.[79] But he attempts at the same time to hold fast to the contrasting belief (already enunciated in *The Elements of Law*) that the 'steps of science' instead consist of tracing the implications of the meanings and definitions of terms.[80] A still more intractable problem was that, even when Hobbes felt confident about the kinds of demonstrations he needed, he found it almost impossible to supply them to his own satisfaction, to say nothing of the satisfaction of his mathematical colleagues. He appears to have encountered this difficulty above all in Part 3 of *De Corpore*, and especially in chapter 18, which presents two alleged equations between straight and parabolic lines.[81] As late as 1649 he was still vainly wrestling with the proofs he had rashly committed himself to supplying in order to make good this part of his argument.[82]

At some stage Hobbes decided to stop banging his head against this particular wall and returned to the study of civil science. The outcome – the magnificent yet ironic outcome – was that his stay in Paris failed to culminate in the long-promised completion of the opening section of his tripartite scheme of philosophy. Instead it culminated in the publication of *Leviathan*, a new version of the section he had already published as *De Cive*. Hobbes finished *Leviathan* in the opening months of 1651, and it

[76] Hobbes 1994, Letter 42, p. 133.   [77] Hobbes 1994, Letter 61, p. 177.
[78] See Malcolm 1990, esp. pp. 154–7 and cf. Malcolm 1996, p. 29.
[79] BN Fonds Latin MS 6566A, fo. 6ᵛ, esp. para. 3. Cf. Hobbes 1973, I. 3, p. 107.
[80] Hobbes 1969a, pp. 24–6.   [81] Hobbes 1839c, pp. 227–30.
[82] Cavendish to Pell, 5 October 1649, BL Add. MS 4278, fo. 291ᵛ: Hobbes is still hoping 'to finde a right line aequall to a parabolick line'. He never found it to anyone's satisfaction – not even his own, as John Wallis ruthlessly pointed out in Wallis 1662, pp. 125–8.

was published in London by the firm of William Crooke. It appeared in late April or early May,[83] and within a matter of weeks it seems to have been widely available. Writing to Samuel Hartlib from Amsterdam on 18 July, William Rand was able to report that 'I have a booke entitled Liviathan or of a Commonwealth, made by one Hobbs'. The book, Rand adds, is full 'of fine cleare notions, though some things too paradoxicall & savouring of a man passionately addicted to the royall interest'.[84]

Hobbes's *Leviathan* is often viewed as a continuation – even a vulgarisation – of a number of themes already present in *De Cive* and *The Elements of Law*. If we focus, however, on the central concept in each of these works – that of civil science itself – we come upon a sharp discontinuity. The earlier recensions of Hobbes's political theory had been grounded on the assumption that reason possesses an inherent power to persuade us of the truths it finds out, and thus that the arts of eloquence have no necessary place in civil science. In *Leviathan*, by contrast, we are told that 'the Sciences are small Power', and that they cannot hope to persuade us of the findings they enunciate.[85] Hobbes now accepts in consequence that, if reason is to prevail, we shall need to supplement and enforce its findings by means of the rhetorical arts.[86] This represents one of the most abrupt shifts of perspective in the evolution of his civil philosophy, and it forms the subject of chapter 3.

To say all this, however, is by no means to say (as some commentators have done) that *Leviathan* must be accounted a work of rhetoric as opposed to a work of science.[87] Although Hobbes undoubtedly came to believe that the findings of civil science have little hope of being implemented or even credited without the aid of the rhetorical arts, he never abandoned his aspiration to construct what he describes in *Leviathan* as 'the science of Vertue and Vice'.[88] His later statements of his political theory in consequence retain several elements of his earlier hostility to the basic tenets of classical and humanist *scientia civilis*. As I stress in chapter 4, he continues to speak out against the predilection of rhetoricians for generating moral ambiguity, and he responds with the same 'scientific' solution to the problem he had originally put forward in *De Cive*. He likewise continues to repudiate what he had initially identified

---

[83] Hobbes 1996, Epistle, p. 4 is signed 'Paris. *Aprill* 15/25. 1651'. See 'Illustrations' 1848, p. 223 for a letter of 6 May 1651 from Payne to Sheldon reporting that 'I am advertised from Oxf[ord] that Mr Hobbes' book is printed and come thither: he calls it Leviathan.'

[84] Rand to Hartlib, 18 July 1651, Hartlib Papers (Sheffield) 62/30/3B.

[85] Hobbes 1996, ch. 10, p. 63.   [86] Hobbes 1996, Conclusion, pp. 483–4.

[87] See for example Taylor 1965, p. 35.   [88] Hobbes 1996, ch. 15, p. 111.

in *The Elements of Law* as the confusions inherent in the humanist vision of history as a teacher of wisdom.[89] As I point out in chapter 8, his later political writings not only embody a number of heterodox arguments about English constitutional history, but are grounded on the still more heterodox assumption that historical arguments have no legitimate place in a science of politics at all. Hobbes summarises this commitment in *Behemoth*, his dialogues on the civil wars,[90] when he insists that, even if we study the forms of ancient commonwealths in detail, we can never hope 'to derive from them any argument of Right, but onely examples of fact'.[91]

To these considerations we need to add that, at some moments in *Leviathan*, Hobbes repudiates the ideals of classical and Renaissance political theory with even greater ferocity than in his earlier works. Perhaps the most important of these attacks is directed against the republican ideal of 'free states' and a number of associated arguments of a constitutionalist character. As we saw in volume 2 chapter 14, Renaissance political writers had begun to describe self-governing communities as *states*, *stati* or *états*, and more specifically as *stati liberi* or free states. They tended as a result to equate the powers of the state with the powers of its citizens when viewed as an *universitas* or corporate body of people. As we shall see in chapter 6, Hobbes dramatically reverses this understanding, arguing that it is only when we perform the act of instituting a sovereign to represent us that we transform ourselves from a multitude of individuals into a unified body of people. He accordingly reserves the term *civitas* or state for the name of the artificial person we bring into existence when we authorise a sovereign both to represent us and to impersonate (or 'bear the Person of') the state or commonwealth.[92]

Hobbes had already spoken in *The Elements of Law* and *De Cive* of the *civitas* as an artificial person.[93] As I shall argue in chapter 6, however, it is only in *Leviathan* that he formulates his theory of authorisation and makes the concept of 'bearing a person' the fulcrum of his theory of

---

[89] For Hobbes's account of these alleged confusions see Skinner 1996, pp. 260–2.

[90] Hobbes 1969b remains the standard edition. The editor, Ferdinand Tonnies, used as his copy-text a manuscript fair-copied by Hobbes's amanuensis, James Wheldon. (See St John's College MS 13 and cf. Tonnies 1969b, pp. ix–x.) But Tonnies (or his amanuensis) altered Hobbes's spelling and punctuation and made numerous transcription mistakes. When citing from *Behemoth* I have therefore preferred to quote from the St John's MS, although my page references are to Tonnies's edition.

[91] Hobbes 1969b, p. 76.   [92] Hobbes 1996, Introduction, p. 9.

[93] Hobbes 1969a, pp. 108, 173–4 and Hobbes 1983a, VII. XIV, p. 155; XII. VIII, p. 190; XIII. III, pp. 195–6.

sovereignty.[94] Part 1 of *Leviathan*, 'Of Man', analyses the natural powers of persons, and culminates in the chapter entitled 'Of Persons, Authors, and things Personated'. This pivotal section examines the various ways in which we can represent ourselves under different guises – thereby adopting different *personae* – as well as permitting ourselves to be represented by other persons whose actions we authorise. This analysis leads directly into Part 2, 'Of Commonwealth', in which Hobbes goes on to explain the sovereign rights of the artificial person we bring into existence when we covenant as a multitude to choose a representative to act on our behalf, thereby instituting 'that great LEVIATHAN called a COMMON-WEALTH, or STATE'.[95] As we saw in volume 2 chapter 14, it would scarcely be an exaggeration to say that, by placing the concept of artificial personality at the heart of his civil science, Hobbes closes one chapter in the history of the modern theory of the state and opens another and more familiar one. Arguably he is the earliest political writer to maintain with complete self-consciousness that the legal person lying at the heart of politics is neither the person of the sovereign nor the person constituted by the *universitas* of the people, but is rather the artificial person of the state.

Underlying Hobbes's attack on the ideal of free states is an idiosyncratic analysis of freedom itself. As we have seen, Hobbes had already presented his views on the metaphysics of freedom in his tract *Of Liberty and Necessity* in 1645. It is only in the pages of *Leviathan*, however, that he fully pursues the political implications of his account. As we saw in volume 2 chapter 12, Roman and Renaissance theorists of the *civitas* had argued that one insidious way of producing unfreedom is by encouraging conditions of social and political dependence. The only way to avoid this predicament, they had argued, is to ensure that each and every citizen is given an equal voice in government. As Hobbes himself observes in *The Elements of Law*, one crucial implication of the argument is thus that individual liberty is possible only under conditions of self-rule: 'noe man can partake of Liberty, but onely in a Popular Commonwealth'.[96]

I argue in chapter 7 that one of Hobbes's aspirations in *Leviathan* is to demolish this entire structure of thought, and with it the theory of equality and citizenship on which humanist civil science had been raised. Hobbes's response is rooted in his basic principle to the effect that nothing is real except matter in motion. The only sense we can assign to the idea

---

[94] Zarka 1985 excellently emphasises these developments.
[95] Hobbes 1996, p. 9.   [96] Hobbes 1969a, p. 170.

of being unfree is therefore that it names the condition of a body whose movements have been obstructed or compelled. In the natural condition of mankind the ties capable of acting as such impediments are bonds or chains that literally prevent us from doing or forbearing at will. In the artificial condition of life within a Commonwealth we are further tied or bound by the artificial chains of the law, which prevent us by fear of evil consequences from acting anti-socially. For Hobbes, accordingly, the limits on our personal liberty are nothing to do with living in conditions of domination and dependence. They are simply the products of coercion: physical coercion by actual bonds in our natural state, moral coercion by the bonds of law in Commonwealths. For Hobbes there is nothing more to be said about the concept of individual liberty.

V

Throughout his period of exile from 1640 to 1652, Hobbes moved between his speculations about natural bodies and the reconsideration of his civil philosophy. It remains to ask how he apportioned his time between these two pursuits. Hobbes himself furnishes an unambiguous answer in the two autobiographies he composed in the 1670s. As we have seen, his verse *Vita* informs us that he began by thinking for four years about the details of *De Corpore*. He goes on to add, however, that in the summer of 1646 a number of events conspired to interrupt his train of thought. The young Prince of Wales and his retinue arrived at Paris in July, and soon afterwards Hobbes found himself called upon to act as tutor in mathematics to the prince.[97] Hobbes recalls that the exiled courtiers brought shocking news about the victories of Parliament in England and the growing disposition of the roundheads to regard their successes as a sign of God's providence. 'I could not bear', Hobbes declares 'to hear so many crimes attributed to the commands of God', and decided that 'although I had intended to write my book *De Corpore*, for which all the materials were ready, I would have to put it off'.[98] The highest priority, he now felt, was 'to write something that would absolve

---

[97] Cavendish to Pell, 7 December 1646, BL Add MS 4278 fo. 265ᵛ: Hobbes's intended departure from Paris has been 'staied' because he is now 'imploied to reade Mathematickes to oure Prince'.
[98] Hobbes 1839b, p. xcii, lines 187–90:

> Tunc ego decreram *De Corpore* scribere librum,
> Cuius materies tota parata fuit.
> Sed cogor differre; *pati tot tantaque foeda*
> *Apponi iussis crimina, nolo, Dei.*

the divine laws'.[99] He accordingly began to compose the treatise which, 'under the name of *Leviathan*, now fights on behalf of all kings and all those who under whatever name bear the rights of kings'.[100] His prose *Vita* reiterates that, apart from the hours he spent tutoring his future king, this was the moment at which he began to devote himself full-time to the composition of *Leviathan*.[101]

There is certainly some truth in Hobbes's later recollection that he shifted from natural to civil science in the course of 1646. During the previous winter he had still been fully occupied with his physical specu-lations, and specifically with completing his English treatise on optics.[102] Of the two sections into which this manuscript is divided,[103] the first was finished and fair-copied by the beginning of November 1645,[104] but the second was only completed in the spring of 1646.[105] With this task out of the way, Hobbes undoubtedly turned his attention once more to political philosophy. The move was prompted by Samuel Sorbière, who came forward with the idea of a second edition of *De Cive*, offering to see a revised version through the press with the Amsterdam firm of Elzevir.[106] Hobbes responded to Sorbière's invitation in two ways.[107] He composed a new *Praefatio*, publicising for the first time his proposed philosophical trilogy;[108] and he inserted a large number of annotations into his text with the intention – as the *Praefatio* puts it – 'of amending, softening and ex-plaining anything that may have seemed erroneous, hard or obscure'.[109] Hobbes had already entered some of these corrections in his working copy of the 1642 edition,[110] and it seems to have taken very little time to

---

[99] Hobbes 1839b, p. xcii, line 191:

> Divinas statuo quam primum absolvere leges.

[100] Hobbes 1839b, p. xcii, line 200–2: Hobbes speaks of the book which, 'nomine *Leviathan*',

> Militat ille Liber nunc Regibus omnibus, et qui
> Nomine sub quovis regia iura tenent.

[101] Hobbes 1839a, p. xv.
[102] See Prins 1996, pp. 145–6 for a discussion of this manuscript.
[103] BL Harl. MS 3360, fos. 1–193.
[104] Cavendish to Pell, 11 November 1645, BL Add. MS 4278, fo. 223^r includes a postscript saying of Hobbes's English treatise on optics that 'he hath done half of it, & M^r: Petit hath writ it faire; it is in english at my brothers request'. 'Mr Petit' must be William Petty, who according to Aubrey 1898, vol. 1, p. 368 'assisted Mr. Hobbes in draweing his schemes for his booke of optiques'.
[105] This can be inferred from the fact that BL Harl. MS 3360 is signed (fo. 1^r) 'Thomas Hobbes at Paris 1646' and from the fact that, when Hobbes refers to the work in a letter of 1 June 1646, he implies that it has been completed for some time. See Hobbes 1994, Letter 42, p. 133.
[106] Hobbes 1994, Letters 40 and 41, pp. 125–30.   [107] Warrender 1983a, pp. 40–3.
[108] Hobbes 1983a, *Praefatio ad Lectores*, pp. 77–84.
[109] Hobbes 1983a, *Praefatio ad Lectores*, p. 84: 'si quae erronea, dura, obscurave esse viderentur, ea emendarem, mollirem atque explicarem'.
[110] So says Gassendi in a letter to Sorbière of April 1646 in Gassendi 1658, vol. 6, p. 249, col. 2.

finish and copy them out. Writing to Sorbière on 16 May, he was already able to thank him for a letter praising the completed work.[111] Although it took longer than expected for the second edition of *De Cive* to see the light,[112] Hobbes's active role in the project appears to have come to an end at this point.

Beyond this moment, however, such evidence as survives from the 1640s tends to contradict Hobbes's own later account of the gestation of *Leviathan*, and to do so in a rather astonishing way.[113] Having finished the revisions of *De Cive*, Hobbes seems to have returned at once to his interrupted labours on the opening section of his intended trilogy. His letter to Sorbière of 16 May 1646 announces his imminent withdrawal from the distractions of Paris in the hope, he says, of devoting himself with greater freedom 'to finishing off the first part of my Elements'.[114] By October he was giving his friends the impression that the treatise was well advanced. Charles Cavendish felt able to assure John Pell that, although Hobbes 'reades mathematickes sometimes to our Prince', he neverthe-less 'hath spare time enough besides to goe on with his philosophie'.[115] Sorbière wrote to Gui Patin[116] around the same time to say that 'I am avidly expecting the Elements of his entire philosophy and I am urging him to send me the whole work.'[117]

Sorbière's expectations were destined to be disappointed, for in the course of the next twelve months Hobbes's life fell into one of its deepest troughs. He must already have been in difficulties in December 1646, for we find Cavendish announcing in a further letter to Pell that he now expected Hobbes to take at least another year even to finish his physics.[118] By the summer of 1647 things had gone from bad to worse, and Hobbes was forced by illness to stop work altogether. Mersenne wrote to Sorbière in early November to say that Hobbes had been contending with death for two or three months,[119] while Hobbes later recalled in his verse *Vita* that 'I was prostrated by illness for six months, and prepared myself for

---

[111] Hobbes 1994, Letter 40, p. 126.   [112] Hobbes 1994, Letter 50, p. 153.

[113] I have been much helped in arriving at this interpretation by the chronology in Schuhmann 1998.

[114] Hobbes 1994, Letter 40, p. 127. See also Cavendish to Pell, 19 July 1646, BL Add. MS 4278, fo. 259^r: 'M^r: Hobbes is goeing out of towne to a more retired place for his s[t]udies.'

[115] Cavendish to Pell, 12 October 1646, BL Add. MS 4278, fos. 263^{r-v}.

[116] Patin became well acquainted with Hobbes in Paris. See, for example, the letter from Patin to Sorbière (1 December 1646) in Mersenne 1980, p. 660.

[117] Tönnies 1975, p. 57: 'Elementa totius philosophiae avide expecto et ut ad me transmittat urgeo.' For the date of this letter (October 1646) see Tönnies 1975, p. 367.

[118] Cavendish to Pell, 7 December 1646, BL Add. MS 4278, fo. 265^v: 'I doute M^r: Hobbes will not finish & publish his phisickes this twelvmonth.'

[119] Mersenne to Sorbière, 5 November 1647 in Mersenne 1983, pp. 522–5, at p. 524: 'Hobbius per duos aut tres menses . . . cum morte contendit.' Cf. Hobbes 1983a, Letter 26, p. 314.

the approach of death'.[120] Although he began to recover at the end of 1647,[121] he never seems to have been the same man again. It was around this time, according to Aubrey, that he first began to suffer from 'the shaking palsey in his handes', a condition that left him virtually unable to write for the last two decades of his life.[122]

As soon as Hobbes started to recover, he returned to working on *De Corpore*, the completion of which he soon began to talk about with renewed confidence. 'If the disease had not intervened', he told Sorbière in November 1647, 'I should, I think, have completed the first part of my philosophy', but 'as things now are, you can expect to receive that part about Whitsun'.[123] In August 1648 a further bulletin from Cavendish to Pell included a similar note of assurance. 'M^r: Hobbes hath nowe leasure to studie & I hope wee shall have his [philosophy] within a twelve-month.'[124] By 14 June 1649 we find Hobbes writing to Sorbière that 'I think I am close enough to the end of the first part (which is both the largest part and the part which contains the deepest speculations) that I shall be able, God willing, to finish it before the end of this summer'.[125] He now felt so sure of attaining his goal that he started to have engravings made of the geometrical figures he needed for some of his proofs.[126] A further letter from Cavendish to Pell in October 1649 implied that Hobbes's book was virtually done, and would actually be in print by the spring of the coming year.[127]

It may be that these references amount to nothing more than a smoke-screen, and that Hobbes decided to keep the generation of his great

---

[120] Hobbes 1839b, p. xcii, lines 195–6:

> Dein per sex menses morbo decumbo, propinquae
> Accinctus morti.

[121] Hobbes 1994, Letter 56, p. 164. Cf. Hobbes 1839b, p. xcii, line 195.
[122] Aubrey 1898, vol. 1, p. 352. Hobbes 1994, Letter 94, p. 324 makes it clear that Hobbes was using an amanuensis as early as 1656. Aubrey 1898, vol. 1, p. 352 remarks that Hobbes's letters after the mid-1660s were barely legible.
[123] Hobbes 1994, Letter 56, p. 164.
[124] Cavendish to Pell, 2 August 1648, BL Add. MS 4278, fo. 273^r.
[125] Hobbes 1994, Letter 61, p. 177.
[126] See Pell to Cavendish, 26 May 1649, BL Add. MS 4280, fo. 136^r: Sorbière has just told him 'that the most of the figures and diagrams, belonging to Mr Hobbes his Philosophy, are already graven in Copper at Paris'. It would seem that Hobbes did in fact have some of the plates engraved in advance of publication. As Beal 1987, p. 578 observes, Hobbes MSS (Chatsworth) MS A. 5 contains, in a scribal hand, some material eventually published in chapters 2 and 3 of *De Homine*, including six engraved geometrical diagrams.
[127] Cavendish to Pell, 5 October 1649, BL Add. MS 4278, fo. 291^v: 'I received a letter latelie from M^r: Hobbes which puts me in hope wee shall have his philosophie printed the next springe.' For a discussion see Hervey 1952, pp. 85–6.

Leviathan a secret even from his closest friends.[128] But most of the evidence suggests that, between 1646 and 1649, Hobbes continued to labour on *De Corpore*, and that he made a sudden decision in the autumn of 1649 to return as a matter of urgency to his work on civil science. The astonishing implication is that *Leviathan* must have been completed in less than eighteen months.

If this is the correct reading of the evidence, there must have been some extraordinary development towards the end of 1649 to spark off such a correspondingly extraordinary outburst of creative energy on Hobbes's part. Hobbes informs us in *Leviathan* that he intended his work for a specifically English audience,[129] to which he adds in his verse *Vita* that his reason for writing it in his mother tongue was to make its relevance to his fellow-citizens as clear as possible.[130] What could have given him such a sense of urgency about the need to address himself to the immediate political predicament of his native land?

The answer, I believe, is that after the execution of Charles I in January 1649, and the subsequent abolition of the monarchy and the House of Lords, surviving royalists found themselves faced with two acute and closely related cases of conscience. They naturally viewed the regicide government as little better than a conquering power. One question that accordingly arose was whether they could legitimately enter into negotiations with the Council of State for the recovery of their estates (as Sir Charles Cavendish decided to do in 1649) or whether such a decision would commit them to acknowledging the legitimacy of the new regime when they ought to be questioning it at all costs.[131] The other and still more pressing difficulty arose in October 1649, and it must I think have been this development that prompted Hobbes to reach for his pen. On 11 October Parliament called on virtually the entire literate population to swear the so-called Oath of Engagement, requiring them to be 'true and faithful to the Commonwealth of England, as it is now established, without a King or House of Lords'.[132] To take such an oath was obviously to concede that, although the regicide government may originally have lacked a just title to rule, it ought nevertheless to be obeyed on the grounds

---

[128] This is the argument put forward in Skinner 1996. For prompting me to reconsider the evidence I am indebted to Malcolm 1996, p. 31 and Schuhmann 1998.

[129] Hobbes 1996, Epistle, p. 3 and Conclusion, pp. 482, 490.

[130] Hobbes 1839b, p. xcii, lines 197–8.

[131] Malcolm 1994c, pp. 804–5.

[132] *An Act for Subscribing the Engagement* 1986, p. 357. On the oath see Wallace 1964, p. 386 and for its extension see *Constitutional Documents 1625–1660*, p. 391. As Wallace 1964, p. 387 notes, it was repealed in January 1654.

that it had succeeded in bringing about a peaceful settlement. The grand case of conscience raised by the events of 1649 was accordingly whether the capacity of the new regime to offer peace and protection should be taken to constitute a sufficient reason for swearing allegiance to it.[133]

Hobbes believed that in *Leviathan* he had articulated a theory of political obligation capable of offering comfort to surviving royalists and all other waverers on these very points. As I argue in chapter 9, the essence of his theory is that 'the Obligation of Subjects to the Soveraign, is understood to last as long, and no longer, than the power lasteth, by which he is able to protect them'.[134] The application of this principle, Hobbes maintains, will serve in the first place to resolve the question of whether it is lawful to compound for one's estates. If a subject is 'protected by the adverse party for his Contribution', he should recognise that, since 'such contribution is every where, as a thing inevitable, (not withstanding it be an assistance to the Enemy,) esteemed lawfull; a totall Submission, which is but an assistance to the Enemy, cannot be esteemed unlawful'. To which he adds the ingenious claim that those who refuse to compound, and consequently forfeit their estates, do more harm to the loyalist cause than those who submit. This is because 'if a man consider that they who submit, assist the enemy with but part of their estates, whereas they that refuse, assist him with the whole, there is no reason to call their Submission, or Composition an Assistance; but rather a Detriment to the Enemy'.[135]

Of more importance, Hobbes goes on, is the fact that his basic argument serves to settle the question of whether it is lawful to 'engage'. As I emphasise in chapter 9, Hobbes informs us in his Review and Conclusion that the writing of *Leviathan* was 'occasioned by the disorders of the present time' and undertaken 'without other designe, than to set before mens eyes the mutuall Relation between Protection and Obedience'.[136] One aspect of this reciprocity is that, if you are no longer protected by your lawful sovereign, then your obligations are at an end. The corollary is that, if you are offered peace and protection – even by mere conquerors – you have a sufficient reason for paying allegiance as a true subject. Hobbes's fundamental principle, as he states it in chapter 21, is that 'The end of Obedience is Protection; which, wheresoever a man

[133] For an excellent discussion of the relevance of these events see Sommerville 1996, pp. 263–4.
[134] Hobbes 1996, ch. 21, p. 153 and Conclusion, p. 491.
[135] Hobbes 1996, Conclusion, pp. 484–5.   [136] Hobbes 1996, Conclusion, p. 491.

seeth it, either in his own, or in anothers sword, Nature applyeth his obedience to it, and his endeavour to maintaine it.'[137]

My thesis is thus that the theory of political obligation developed in *Leviathan* makes that work (among many other things) the greatest of the numerous tracts in favour of 'engagement' that appeared in the wake of the parliamentary resolution of October 1649. I begin to present this thesis in chapter 7, and proceed to lay out different facets of my argument in chapters 8, 9 and 10. In chapter 7 I concentrate on the distinctive view of political liberty underpinning Hobbes's claim that in certain circumstances the act of yielding to a conqueror can be freely performed, and can therefore give rise to genuine bonds of allegiance. In chapter 8 I focus on the use made by the writers in defence of *de facto* powers of historical evidence about the rights of conquerors. In chapter 9 I go on to consider the place of the engagement controversy in the broader ideological context in which Hobbes's theory of political obligation was formed. And in chapter 10 I discuss the engagement controversy itself, ending with an account of Hobbes's distinctive contribution to it.

VI

When Edward Hyde, the future earl of Clarendon, visited Hobbes early in 1651, Hobbes showed him some proof-sheets of *Leviathan*.[138] Hyde later recalled asking Hobbes in shocked tones 'why he would publish such doctrine', to which Hobbes answered, '*The Truth is, I have a mind to go home.*'[139] Clarendon sought to make this admission a matter of grave reproach after the Restoration of 1660,[140] and Hobbes's implacable enemy John Wallis went so far as to argue that *Leviathan* 'was written in defence of Oliver's title, or whoever, by whatsoever means, can get to be upmost'.[141] But Hobbes always insisted that his work was an exercise in loyalism, and in his *Considerations* of 1662 he responded to Wallis's taunts by declaring that he had published *Leviathan* 'in the behalf of those many and faithful servants and subjects of his Majesty, that had taken his part in the war' and had consequently been forced 'to promise obedience for the saving

---

[137] Hobbes 1996, ch. 21, p. 153.   [138] Clarendon 1676, p. 7.

[139] Clarendon 1676, pp. 7–8. Cf. Malcolm 1996, p. 31. Clarendon's phrase echoes a letter of 21 October 1651 from Henry Hammond to Matthew Wren printed in 'Illustrations' 1850, p. 295: 'having now a mind to return hither, [Hobbes] hath chosen his way by this book'.

[140] Clarendon 1676, p. 5, in speaking of Oliver Cromwell's rule, maintains (as does Wallis) that Hobbes 'defended his Usurpation'.

[141] Wallis 1662, p. 5. For the fact that several of Hobbes's arguments in *Leviathan* are directed against Hyde and his associates see Sommerville 1996, pp. 264–7.

of their lives and fortunes'. His sole concern, he declared, had been to show that they 'had done all that they could be obliged unto', and could never be fairly accused of treachery.[142]

The fact remains that Hobbes was correct in assuming that, in the political climate of 1651, the eirenic message of *Leviathan* was likely to be warmly received by supporters of the Rump. Writing to Gilbert Sheldon in May 1651, Robert Payne somewhat sorrowfully observed that Hobbes 'seems to favour the present Government'.[143] William Rand likewise remarked in a letter to Samuel Hartlib immediately after reading *Leviathan* in July 1651 that 'I conceive he is comeing over to the parliament side'.[144] As I argue in chapters 6 and 9, there is nothing specifically royalist about Hobbes's final version of his civil science.[145] His conception of sovereignty explicitly allows for the artificial person of the state to be 'personated' by a council rather than by an individual sovereign, while his theory of political obligation is based not on legitimist principles but on the assumption of a strictly mutual relationship between protection and obedience.

Hobbes may have had reasons of his own for wanting to go home,[146] but in the event he was forced to leave France by a campaign of vilification launched against him by various factions within the exiled Court.[147] His verse *Vita* complains that, after the publication of *Leviathan*, a number of Charles's advisers 'led him to believe that I should be seen as a member of the adverse party' and made Charles issue a command 'to absent myself in perpetuity from the royal residence'.[148] There is evidence too that the violence of Hobbes's attack on the papacy and the Catholic church in Books 3 and 4 of *Leviathan* scandalised the priestly entourage of the Catholic Queen Mother.[149] Sir Edward Nicholas went so far as to suggest in a letter of January 1652 that the Catholic courtiers 'were the

[142] Hobbes 1840d, pp. 420–1.   [143] 'Illustrations' 1848, p. 223.
[144] Rand to Hartlib, 18 July 1651, Hartlib MSS (Sheffield), 62/30/4A.
[145] Sommerville 1996, pp. 259–60.
[146] Malcolm 1996, p. 32 points to the death of Mersenne in 1648, which evidently left Hobbes feeling intellectually as well as personally isolated in Paris. See also Hobbes 1994, Letter 62, p. 178 in which Hobbes tells Gassendi, a year later, that he is now looking forward to returning to England if possible.
[147] See Knachel 1967, pp. 71–3, and for full references to the contemporary evidence see Schuhmann 1998, pp. 125–6, 128–9.
[148] Hobbes 1839b, p. xciii, lines 219–20:

> Creditur; adversis in partibus esse videbar;
> Perpetuo iubeor Regis abesse domo.

That this is what happened is confirmed in Nicholas 1886, p. 284.
[149] Malcolm 1996, p. 33.

chief cause that that grand atheist was sent away',[150] to which Hobbes himself adds in his prose *Vita* that it was fear of ill-treatment at the hands of the local clergy that finally made him leave.[151]

After a bad journey – the ways deep and the weather sharp – Hobbes arrived in London early in 1652, where he duly found a warm welcome.[152] A letter of late February from Sir Edward Nicholas to Lord Hatton reports in tones of evident resentment that 'Mr Hobbes is at London' where he is 'much caressed' by the supporters of the new regime 'as one that hath by his writings justified the reasonableness and righteousness of their arms and actions'.[153] Hobbes makes no mention of his reception, merely informing us in his verse *Vita* that, 'I was judged worthy of a pardon by the Council of State, after which I immediately retired in complete peace to apply myself to my studies as before.'[154] As we have seen, the eventual outcome of this new period of seclusion was the publication, after years of doubt and delay, of the two remaining sections of his tripartite system of philosophy, the *De Corpore* in 1655 and the *De Homine* in 1658.

Although Hobbes never went on his travels again, he managed to keep in touch with his friends abroad for many years. The significance of these personal and intellectual links forms the subject of chapter 11. Of all Hobbes's correspondents from this later period, by far the most faithful was François du Verdus, the 'candid friend' to whom Hobbes's verse *Vita* is addressed.[155] A member of an old land-owning family in Bordeaux, Du Verdus initially came to Paris in the early 1640s to study mathematics with Gilles de Roberval,[156] whom Hobbes knew and greatly admired.[157] Du Verdus's first surviving letter to Hobbes is dated 4 August 1654,[158] after which they appear to have written regularly to each other for the next twenty years, although Hobbes's side of the correspondence has not survived.[159]

---

[150] Nicholas 1886, p. 285.   [151] Hobbes 1839a, p. xvii.
[152] For details of his journey see Hobbes 1839b, p. xciii, lines 227–8.
[153] Sir Edward Nicholas to 'Mr Smith' [Lord Hatton] in Nicholas 1886, pp. 286–7.
[154] Hobbes 1839b, p. xciii, lines 230–2:

> *Concilio Status* conciliandus eram.
> Quo facto, statim summa cum pace recedo,
> Et sic me studiis applico, ut ante, meis.

[155] Hobbes 1839b, p. xcix, line 369.   [156] Malcolm 1994c, pp. 904–5.
[157] Cavendish to Pell, 11 May 1645, BL Add. MS 4278, fo. 205^r notes that 'M^r: Hobbes commends M^r: Roberval extreamelie.'
[158] Hobbes 1994, Letter 67, pp. 186–8.
[159] Du Verdus wrote his last surviving letter to Hobbes in March 1674. See Hobbes 1994, Letter 196, pp. 736–9. Malcolm 1994c, p. 912 has established that Du Verdus died in the following year.

It is perhaps unfortunate that du Verdus should have been the most indefatigable of Hobbes's correspondents, for he was a person of marked eccentricity. His first surviving letter strikes a typical note, offering effusive but misplaced congratulations to Hobbes on having got married at last.[160] Later he pestered Hobbes with some embarrassing effusions in Italian verse, including what he described as a 'philosophical night poem' and 'a sort of short opera'.[161] He became subject to fits of paranoia, writing that his enemies were poisoning him and casting spells to make him seem insane.[162] Worst of all, he conceived the ambition of translating *Leviathan* into French, a project that led him to bombard Hobbes with page after page of queries that leave one feeling relieved that the work never appeared.[163]

Fortunately Hobbes's other admirers were less unbalanced, and their letters provide some fascinating glimpses (as I seek to show in chapter 11) into Hobbes's growing reputation in the *république des lettres* by this time. Some of the most interesting were written in the late 1650s by the obscure but impressive figure of François Peleau, who raises some shrewd questions about Hobbes's views on the political virtues and the allegedly anti-political aspects of human nature.[164] Most impressive of all are two glowing tributes from the young Leibniz in the early 1670s. One of them congratulates Hobbes on being the first philosopher to use 'the correct method of argument and demonstration' in political philosophy.[165] The other ends by announcing that 'I know of no other writer who has philosophized as precisely, as clearly, and as elegantly as you have – no, not excepting Descartes with his superhuman intellect.'[166] Perhaps these words did something to compensate Hobbes for the brutally condescending treatment he had suffered at Descartes's hands in their altercation over the *Dioptrique* almost thirty years before.[167]

VII

Hobbes admits in his *Considerations* that, after the publication of *Leviathan*, Charles II was undoubtedly displeased with him.[168] So when Charles was

---

[160] Hobbes 1994, Letter 67, p. 186.   [161] Hobbes 1994, Letter 168, p. 625.

[162] Hobbes 1994, Letter 170, p. 651, Letter 180, p. 698 and Letter 196, p. 742.

[163] See Hobbes 1994, Letter 100, pp. 344–58 and Letter 108, pp. 397–412.

[164] Hobbes 1994, Letter 90 (enclosure), pp. 307–10 and Letter 110, pp. 424–5.

[165] Hobbes 1994, Letter 195, p. 733.

[166] Hobbes 1994, Letter 189, p. 720. For a discussion see Tönnies 1975, pp. 151–67.

[167] For Descartes's responses to Hobbes's criticisms see Hobbes 1994, Letter 32, pp. 86–9, Letter 33, pp. 94–7 and Letter 36, pp. 116–17.

[168] Hobbes 1840d, p. 424.

restored to his throne in 1660 Hobbes may have suffered a momentary qualm. If so, he was quickly reassured, for the king turned out to be in forgiving mood. Aubrey as usual has the story. 'It happened, about two or three dayes after his majestie's happy returne, that, as he was passing in his coach through the Strand, Mr Hobbes was standing at Little Salisbury-house gate (where his lord then lived).' When the king caught sight of Hobbes, he 'putt of his hatt very kindly to him, and asked him how he did', after which 'order was given that he should have free accesse to his majesty, who was always much delighted in his witt and smart repartees'. Having been forbidden the royal presence ten years before, Hobbes now found that, as Aubrey quaintly puts it, the king's favours 'were redintegrated to him'.[169] He was even awarded a royal pension, although it seems to have been erratically paid.[170]

Hobbes may have proved acceptable to his former pupil in mathematics, but he proved far less acceptable to the professional mathematicians and other scientists of the Restoration age. He first incurred their scorn when he appended to the English translation of *De Corpore* a lengthy pamphlet entitled *Six Lessons to the Professors of the Mathematics*, in which he unwisely sought to impugn the work of John Wallis, the Savilian Professor of Geometry at Oxford.[171] Wallis replied at once in his *Due Correction for Mr Hobbes*, concentrating on the most vulnerable sections of *De Corpore*, especially the chapters in Part 3 on the dimensions of circles and the alleged equations between straight and parabolic lines.[172] Hobbes retorted partly by shifting his ground, broadening his attack to encompass a critique of the experimental method as practised by the scientists then banding together to form the Royal Society. He first published these doubts in his *Dialogus Physicus* in 1661, which opens by speaking somewhat petulantly about the nascent Society and attempts to dismiss Robert Boyle's classic experiments on the elasticity of the air as nothing more than dreams and fantasies.[173] Boyle issued a devastating rejoinder in the second edition of his *New Experiments* in 1662,[174] while Wallis took the opportunity to re-enter the fray on his own account as well as in defence of Boyle

[169] Aubrey 1898, vol. 1, p. 340.
[170] Hobbes 1839b, p. xcviii, lines 359–60. Later Hobbes had to petition for its renewal. See Hobbes 1994, Letter 210, pp. 774–5.
[171] Hobbes 1845j, pp. 181–356. See Jesseph 1999 for a very fine analysis of the ensuing debate between Wallis and Hobbes.
[172] [Wallis] 1656, pp. 79–118 (on Hobbes's account in chapters 15 and 16 of motion and acceleration) and pp. 125–8 (on Hobbes's account in chapters 18, 19 and 20 of parabolic lines, angles of incidence and the dimensions of circles).
[173] Hobbes 1985, esp. pp. 350–2 and 377.
[174] Boyle 1662. For an excellent discussion see Shapin and Schaffer 1985, pp. 169–207.

in his *Hobbius Heauton-timorumenos* of 1662. Wallis not only vindicated the importance of Boyle's experiments[175] but offered a further and still more contemptuous restatement of his earlier objections to Hobbes's views about such issues as angles of contact, parabolic lines, the doctrine of infinities and the dimensions of circles.[176]

By this stage Hobbes and his formidable antagonists had begun to exchange insults as much as arguments, and any possibility of an amicable settlement was finally lost. As I suggest in chapter 12, the attitude of Hobbes's opponents is perhaps best symbolised by their refusal to make him a Fellow of the Royal Society after it received its charter in 1662. Hobbes's own former pupil, the third earl of Devonshire, was inscribed a Fellow as early as December 1660,[177] but in spite of the fact that Hobbes continued to write on scientific and mathematical topics until 1678, he was never able to persuade the Society to publish any of his alleged findings,[178] nor was he ever elected a Fellow or formally recognised in any other way.

I argue in chapter 12 that Hobbes's exclusion is best explained in mainly personal terms. He was perceived by many of the active Fellows – not without some justification – as an absurdly tenacious and ill-tempered dogmatist. When I originally highlighted these purely personal factors, I did so as part of a wider argument designed to question the assumption that the early Royal Society can usefully be viewed as a professional academy of a recognisably modern kind. I sought to challenge the belief that the founding Fellows were pursuing a distinctive research programme, and that their rejection of Hobbes was best explained by invoking either his purported amateurism or his repudiation of their theoretical approach to the problems of natural philosophy.

I still think that this general claim about the early Royal Society is an important one. For lack of taking it seriously, some historians have not only misconstrued Hobbes's relations with the original Fellowship but the character of the Society itself.[179] I now accept, however, that my argument as presented in chapter 12 is overstated. This is not to say that I endorse Shapin and Schaffer's revival of the suggestion that it was Hobbes's philosophical programme, and specifically his so-called 'anti-experimentalism', that 'gave grounds for his exclusion'.[180] But I am now persuaded that Hobbes's exclusion was probably due – as Noel Malcolm

175 Wallis 1662, pp. 152–4.   176 Wallis 1662, pp. 88–120.   177 Malcolm 1994c, p. 817.
178 Shapin and Schaffer 1985, pp. 135–6.
179 These points have been excellently elaborated in Hunter 1979, 1981 and 1982.
180 Although the evidence and arguments in Shapin and Schaffer 1985, pp. 131–9 are impressive.

has suggested – to a desire on the part of the Fellows to distance themselves and their mechanistic explanations of nature from a writer whose
scientific studies were often closely akin to theirs, but whose alleged
atheism made him too dangerous an ally to acknowledge. Malcolm summarises by saying that, confronted as they were by charges of heterodoxy
similar to those levelled at Hobbes, and fearing a similar notoriety, the
early Fellows 'reacted in a preemptive and diversionary way'.[181] This explanation is not of course incompatible with my argument in chapter 12,
but it offers a better account of why the personal animosities that a
number of Fellows undoubtedly felt towards Hobbes were allowed to
prevail.

VIII

John Aubrey tells us that, in the years following the Restoration, Hobbes
spent most of his time living in one of the houses owned by the Devonshire
family in London.[182] Samuel Sorbière visited him there in the summer of
1663 and found him scarcely altered after an interval of fourteen years.[183]
Certainly Hobbes's energies remained undimmed at this time, and the
mid-1660s proved to be among the most intellectually fertile periods of
his entire life. Aubrey implies that Hobbes's renewed burst of activity
may have been partly due to personal anxieties, for he mentions that
'there was a report (and surely true) that in parliament, not long after the
king was setled, some of the bishops made a motion to have the good old
gentleman burn't for a heretique'.[184] The parliamentary record points to
a date in October 1666 when a committee was set up to consider a 'Bill
against Atheisme Prophaneness and Swearing' and specifically to receive
information about Hobbes's *Leviathan*.[185] Hobbes reacted by turning
himself into an expert on the law of heresy, and went on to write a number
of works in which the unlawfulness of persecution for this alleged crime
figured as a central theme. He opened his campaign with his *Dialogue
between a Philosopher and a Student of the Common Laws of England*, in which
Sir Edward Coke's views about the nature of heresy, as well as various
statutes on the subject, are discussed at length.[186] The draft of this treatise

[181] Malcolm 1996, p. 35. Cf. also Malcolm 1988. Malcolm's argument has been valuably developed
in Parkin 1999.
[182] Aubrey 1898, vol. 1, p. 341.   [183] Sorbière 1664, p. 65.   [184] Aubrey 1898, vol. 1, p. 339.
[185] Malcolm 1994a, p. xxv.
[186] Hobbes 1971c, pp. 122–32, the fifth of the seven sections into which the dialogue is divided, is
entitled 'Of Heresie'.

probably dates from the mid-1660s,[187] although Hobbes never allowed it to be printed[188] and left it to be posthumously published in William Crooke's collection of his *Tracts* in 1681.[189] By 1668, however, Hobbes had completed a separate manuscript on the laws of heresy,[190] as well as his *Historical Narration concerning Heresy, and the Punishment thereof*, which he circulated as early as June 1668, although it remained unpublished until 1680.[191] Finally, the year 1668 saw the publication of the Latin edition of *Leviathan*, in which Hobbes included a new appendix consisting of three dialogues,[192] the second of which examined the meaning of heresy yet again.[193] The Hobbesian figure of B responds to A's innocent enquiries with a robust statement of the claim – already adumbrated in chapter 42 of the English edition – that to speak of heresy is merely to speak of holding a contested belief, and that to hold a contested belief can scarcely be regarded as a crime.[194]

It would be absurd, however, to imply that Hobbes's period of intense activity in the mid-1660s was solely motivated by renewed fears about his personal safety. Besides writing on heresy, he made substantial additions to two long-standing areas of his interests. He kept up his diatribes against John Wallis and other practitioners of algebraic geometry at Oxford, and in publishing his *De Principiis et Ratiocinatione Geometrarum* in 1666 he confronted them with a new line of attack. Previously he had been content to assume that, as he puts it in *Leviathan*, geometry is the one science that God has given mankind, since its findings are not only precise but constitute true knowledge.[195] But he now made a

---

[187] Aubrey 1898, vol. 1, p. 341 states that he first attempted to persuade Hobbes to study the law in 1664. Hobbes replied that he doubted whether he would live long enough to undertake the task, but 'afterwards' changed his mind and wrote his treatise *De Legibus*. Schuhmann 1996, p. 157 takes 'afterwards' to mean later in the same year, and concludes that the *Dialogue* was drafted between 1664 and 1665. But Aubrey 1898, vol. 1, p. 394 also states that Hobbes 'haz writt a treatise concerning lawe, which 8 or 9 yeares since I much importuned him to doe'. If 'haz writte' means has *now* or *recently* written, this would point to a completion date in the early 1670s.

[188] For Hobbes's refusal to publish, see Hobbes 1994, Letter 208, p. 772, a letter to Aubrey in which he makes it clear that he regards the work as unfinished.

[189] Macdonald and Hargreaves 1952, pp. 73–4.

[190] This manuscript was first published in Mintz 1968. Mintz dated it (p. 409) to 1673, forgetting that Charles II's reign was reckoned to begin in 1649, not 1660. Willman 1970 pointed out the slip and proposed a date of c.1661, but Lessay 1993a, pp. 59–61 convincingly argues for a date between 1666 and 1668.

[191] See Hobbes 1840c. For the circulation of this treatise in manuscript form see Hobbes 1994, Letter 181, p. 699; for its publication see Macdonald and Hargreaves 1952, pp. 72–3.

[192] Hobbes 1841a, *Appendix ad Leviathan*, pp. 511–69.

[193] Hobbes 1841a, *Appendix ad Leviathan*, cap. 2, *De Haeresi*, pp. 539–59.

[194] See Hobbes 1841a, pp. 541, 547 and cf. Hobbes 1996, pp. 398–402.

[195] Hobbes 1996, ch. 4, p. 28.

sharp distinction between the science itself and the unscientific conduct
of those who practise it. The new generation of geometers argue with
so much arrogance, he now maintains,[196] that 'their writings are no less
afflicted by uncertainty and falsity than those of the writers on Physics
and Ethics'.[197]

Of greater importance is the fact that Hobbes added significantly at
this period to the corpus of his writings on civil science. The first and
most substantial addition took the form of *Behemoth*, his four dialogues
on the causes and course of the English civil wars between 1640 and
1660. Hobbes appears to have finished a draft of this text as early as the
summer of 1666,[198] after which he revised it with a view to publication
in 1668.[199] Unfortunately he failed to persuade Charles II to license its
printing,[200] and the work remained unpublished until a pirated edition
appeared in 1679.[201]

Hobbes next turned his attention to the Latin edition of *Leviathan*. We
learn from a letter he sent to his publishers – the Amsterdam firm of
Johan Blaeu – that in the latter part of 1667 he began to devote two
hours a day to working on the translation, aiming to finish by Easter of
the following year.[202] He must more or less have met his own deadline,
for as we have seen his treatise was duly published by Blaeu in the course
of 1668.[203]

The differences between the two versions of *Leviathan* are considerable,
and are only beginning to be properly examined. One rather poignant
difference is that, whereas the original version is one of the great monuments of English prose, the Latin *Leviathan* is poorly written, containing
many Anglicisms and many outright mistakes. This is one of several signs
that Hobbes may have allowed his Latin to become somewhat rusty in

---

[196] See Hobbes 1845b, pp. 385, 390, announcing his campaign 'against the arrogance of the
Professors of Geometry' ('Contra fastum Professorum Geometricae').

[197] Hobbes 1845b, p. 385: 'incertitudinem falsitatemque non minorem inesse scriptis eorum, quam
scriptis Physicorum et Ethicorum'.

[198] Schuhmann 1996, p. 155 suggests that, when Du Verdus refers in his letter to Hobbes of 13
April 1668 to 'vostre Epitome de vos Troubles', he is speaking of the troubles of Hobbes's native
land and is thus referring to *Behemoth*. (It is certainly suggestive that Hobbes 1996, ch. 29, p. 225
describes the upheavals of the 1640s as 'the late troubles of *England*'.) Schuhmann infers that
Behemoth 'existed in a more or less finished version already in mid-1666'.

[199] Schuhmann 1996, pp. 155–6.

[200] Hobbes 1994, Letters 206 and 208, pp. 771–2 inform us of this failure.

[201] Macdonald and Hargreaves 1952, pp. 64–5. For Hobbes's displeasure at this unauthorised
printing see Hobbes 1994, Letter 208, p. 772.

[202] Hobbes's letter has not survived, but Johan Blaeu refers to it and to Hobbes's schedule of writing
in his reply of 9 December 1667. See Hobbes 1994, Letter 179, p. 693.

[203] Hobbes 1841a.

his old age. We already find Lodewijck Huygens reporting, as early as 1652, that Hobbes insisted on speaking English to foreign guests, his conversational Latin having evidently dried up.[204]

A comparison between the two versions of *Leviathan* also reveals some important changes of emphasis. Hobbes deleted a large number of passages in the course of translating his text, especially those in which he had incautiously spoken in mockery of the Christian mysteries and the Catholic church.[205] But he also inserted a substantial amount of new material and reconsidered several of his arguments. One problem of political obedience that had always worried him arose from the conflict between aristocratic values and the duty of all subjects to obey the law. He already complains in the English *Leviathan* that the rich and powerful too readily presume 'that the punishments ordained by the Lawes, and extended generally to all Subjects, ought not to be inflicted on them'.[206] The Latin version shows that these feelings of resentment increased with age, especially when he contemplated the aristocratic code of honour and the associated practice of duelling.[207] The English *Leviathan* merely admonishes the aristocracy to avoid the practice by recalling the Aristotelian principle that a magnanimous man will treat petty insults as beneath his notice.[208] But the Latin version instead denounces the code of duelling as straightforwardly criminal, on the grounds that 'the State wishes its public words – that is, the laws – to have greater force among its citizens than the words of any individual man'.[209] It is perhaps suggestive that, during the intervening years, Pascal had reached the same conclusion in the seventh letter of *Les Provinciales*, in which the argument culminates in the claim that those who tolerate duelling are simply encouraging criminal acts.[210]

By far the most substantial of Hobbes's additions to *Leviathan* took the form of the three dialogues he printed as an appendix to the Latin text. As we have already seen, the second contains his final thoughts on the meaning of heresy and the absurdity of treating it as a crime.[211] Of the other two, the first examines the contents of the Nicene Creed, emphasising

---

[204] Schuhmann 1998, pp. 129–30.

[205] For this pattern of deletions see Skinner 1996, pp. 403–25.

[206] Hobbes 1996, ch. 27, p. 205 and for similar sentiments see Hobbes 1996, ch. 30. pp. 233, 237–8.

[207] Thomas 1965, pp. 194–6 was the first to stress this addition and its significance.

[208] Hobbes 1996, ch. 27, pp. 206–7.

[209] Hobbes 1841a, p. 215: 'Civitas verba publica, id est leges, apud cives plus valere vult, quam verba hominis singularis.'

[210] Pascal 1960, p. 738. For a comparison of Hobbes's and Pascal's views on power see Zarka 1995, pp. 268–84.

[211] Hobbes 1841a, cap. 2: *De Haeresi*, pp. 539–59.

the small number of propositions that Christians are commanded to believe,[212] while the third responds to various objections levelled against the theological arguments put forward in the English edition of 1651.[213] Hobbes provides further evidence in favour of his earlier contentions about incorporeal substances and the nature of God, but at the same time he withdraws his notorious and (as he puts it) negligent suggestion in chapter 42 that Moses must have been one of the three Persons of the Trinity.[214]

Hobbes brought this period of intense activity to a close in the spring of 1668, when he finished *An Answer to a Book Published by Dr Bramhall*.[215] Bramhall had issued *The Catching of the Leviathan* in 1658,[216] but Hobbes affects never to have heard of it at the time, 'so little talk there was of his Lordship's writings'.[217] Hobbes notes that Bramhall attacks his religious as well as his political views, but without managing in either case to produce 'any refutation of any thing in my *Leviathan* concluded'.[218] The sole reason for replying, he goes on, is that Bramhall has also accused him of atheism and impiety, words so defamatory as to require some response. Hobbes thereupon presents a vigorous and highly rhetorical restatement of his views not merely about God, the Trinity and the Bible but about such strictly political matters as the dictates of nature and the character of civil law.

The completion of all these projects seems to have left Hobbes prostrated. He had suffered a similar experience in 1651, becoming seriously ill and almost suicidally depressed immediately after the publication of *Leviathan*.[219] He fell ill again in the course of 1668, and according to Aubrey was thought on this occasion 'like to die'.[220] Although he recovered, he began to think of withdrawing from the hurly-burly of London, and Aubrey tells us that he finally took his leave of the capital in 1675 in

[212] Hobbes 1841a, cap. 1: *De Symbolo Niceno*, pp. 511–39.

[213] Hobbes 1841a, cap. 3: *De quibusdam Objectionibus contra Leviathan*, pp. 559–69.

[214] Hobbes 1841a, p. 563. Cf. the discussion *Of the Trinity* in Hobbes 1996, ch. 42, pp. 339–41.

[215] That Hobbes wrote his *Answer* immediately after completing his translation of *Leviathan* is established by the fact that, in the course of the *Answer*, he refers to 'my *Leviathan* converted into Latin, which by this time I think is printed beyond the seas'. See Hobbes 1840b, p. 317. That the *Answer* was finished by the middle of 1668 is established by the fact that Hobbes sent a manuscript of the work to Joseph Williamson with a covering letter dated 30 June 1668. See Hobbes 1994, p. 699 and cf. Schuhmann 1996, pp. 159–60. The *Answer* remained unpublished until 1682. See Macdonald and Hargreaves 1952, pp. 39–40.

[216] For Bramhall's attack on Hobbes see Mintz 1962, pp. 110–23.

[217] Hobbes 1840b, p. 282.   [218] Hobbes 1840b, p. 282.

[219] So says Gui Patin in a letter to André Falconet of September 1651. See Patin 1846, Letter 398, vol. 2, pp. 593–4.

[220] Aubrey 1898, vol. 1, p. 350.

order to live out the remainder of his days 'in contemplation and study' at the Devonshire mansions in Derbyshire.[221]

Despite the contempt of the Royal Society, these contemplations continued to embrace the study of mathematics and natural philosophy. Hobbes published two further attacks on John Wallis: his *Rosetum Geometricum* of 1671, in which he expanded his criticisms to encompass Wallis's theory of motion,[222] and his *Lux Mathematica* of 1672, in which he rehearsed once more his opposition to Wallis's views about points, lines and the dimensions of circles.[223] Hobbes brought this aspect of his work to an end with the publication of *Principia et Problemata Aliquot Geometrica* in 1674, a final restatement of his views about the character of mathematical reasoning and a number of specific issues, including the study of angles and, yet again, the dimensions of circles.[224] His last work of all, the *Decameron Physiologicum* of 1678, similarly rounded off his work on physics, presenting in a series of ten dialogues his final thoughts on such topics as the vacuum, the lodestone, the causes of heat and a number of other favourite themes.[225]

The closing years of Hobbes's life also saw him reverting to the humanistic studies of his youth. According to Aubrey he had never ceased to read his Homer and Virgil,[226] and in the early 1670s he decided to make a translation of Homer into English verse. At first he concentrated on the *Odyssey*, publishing a version of the last four books as *The Travels of Ulysses* in 1673.[227] Thereafter he completed – in little more than a year – a rendering of the entire *Iliad* and *Odyssey* into rhymed pentameters.[228] To this he added a Preface entitled *Concerning the Virtues of an Heroic Poem*, in which he defended the neo-classical aesthetic of 'discretion' in terms of which his translation had been conceived.[229] Hobbes ends his Preface by asking himself why he undertook the work at all. 'Because I had nothing else to do.' But why publish it? 'Because I thought it might take off my adversaries from showing their folly upon my more serious writings, and set them upon my verses to show their wisdom.'[230] Hobbes had lost none of his aggression when he wrote these words in his mid-eighties.

---

[221] Aubrey 1898, vol. 1, pp. 346, 350.
[222] Hobbes 1845c, pp. 1–88. The 'censure' of Wallis's *De Motu* occupies pp. 50–88. For the date of publication see Macdonald and Hargreaves 1952, p. 56.
[223] Hobbes 1845d, pp. 89–150. The work is dedicated (pp. 91–2) to the Fellows of the Royal Society. For the date of publication see Macdonald and Hargreaves 1952, p. 57.
[224] Hobbes 1845e, pp. 151–214. For the date of publication see Macdonald and Hargreaves 1952, p. 63.
[225] Hobbes 1845h, pp. 89–95 (the vacuum), pp. 117–28 (causes of heat and cold) and pp. 155–68 (the lodestone).
[226] Aubrey 1898, vol. 1, p. 349.   [227] Hobbes 1844b.   [228] Hobbes 1844c.
[229] Hobbes 1844a, p. iii.   [230] Hobbes 1844a, p. x.

Although there is no evidence that Hobbes had planned to say anything further about civil science, he suddenly found himself drawn back into the fray in 1679 with the eruption of a constitutional crisis in which the Devonshire family became deeply implicated. The heir to the third earl – yet another William Cavendish – started to play an increasingly active role in Parliament after the discovery of the alleged Popish Plot in October 1678. He served on a committee to enquire into the plot itself, and later helped to draft a bill protesting against the growth of popery. This brought him into contact with the radical plans being promoted by the Earl of Shaftesbury to exclude Charles II's younger brother, the Catholic James Duke of York, from the succession to the throne. When Parliament met in March 1679, Shaftesbury delivered a violently anti-Catholic philippic in the House of Lords on the religious and constitutional perils allegedly facing Scotland, England and Ireland. A copy of his speech, written out by Hobbes's amanuensis James Wheldon, appears to have been made for Hobbes's use, and contains a number of small corrections in Hobbes's shaky hand.[231] Shaftesbury's speech opens with the warning that 'Popery and Slavery like two Sisters goe hand in hand'.[232] He illustrates his dictum from the recent history of Scotland, speaking in terms remarkably reminiscent of the *Two Treatises of Government* which his own secretary, John Locke, began to draft shortly afterwards.[233] The Scots, Shaftesbury maintains, have already seen 'their Lives Liberties and Estates Subiect to the Arbitrary will & pleasure of those that govern'.[234] This offers a grim reminder not merely of the dangers posed by popery in England, but of the far graver risks arising from the fact that so many members of the Court remain imbued with the slavish principles of the Catholic faith. 'We must be still upon our guard', recognising that 'those men are still in place and Authority haveing the Influence upon the mind of our excelent Prince that he is not nor cannot bee that to us which his own Nature & goodness inclines him too'.[235]

Shaftesbury's campaign gained so much momentum that a Bill was duly introduced into the House of Commons on 15 May 1679 to exclude

---

[231] Hobbes MSS (Chatsworth) MS G. 2. Beal 1987, p. 584 states that this manuscript is 'in an unidentified hand, with corrections in a second hand'. But comparisons with other manuscripts copied for Hobbes by James Wheldon (for example, Hobbes MS D. 5) suggest that the hand is definitely Wheldon's, while comparisons with corrections made by Hobbes to other manuscripts copied for him by Wheldon (for example, St John's MS 13) suggest that the second hand (e.g., at p. 1 line 26 and p. 2 line 26) is that of Hobbes himself.

[232] Hobbes MSS (Chatsworth) MS G. 2, p. 1.

[233] For the fact that Locke began to write his *Two Treatises* at this juncture see Laslett 1988, pp. 35–7, 51, 61, 65–6.

[234] Hobbes MSS (Chatsworth) MS G. 2, p. 2.   [235] Hobbes MSS (Chatsworth) MS G. 2, p. 2.

James from the throne.[236] Hobbes appears to have followed this part of
the argument as well, for his papers include a version of the Commons
resolution headed, again in James Wheldon's hand, 'A Copy of the Bill
concerning the D: of York'.[237] Charles II prorogued Parliament in haste
two weeks later, but not before holding a series of meetings with his
ministers to consider how best to protect the Protestant religion while
securing the succession of his brother at the same time.[238]

The young William Cavendish was later to be one of the grandees
instrumental in summoning William of Orange to displace James II
from the throne, a service for which he was rewarded with a dukedom in
1694. But in 1679 he appears to have taken up a middle position between
the exclusionists and the strict protagonists of hereditary right. Since he
was clearly much puzzled about the constitutional issues involved, it is a
matter of some significance that a document (again in James Wheldon's
hand) survives among Hobbes's papers in which the question of whether
the heir to a throne can lawfully be excluded is explicitly raised.[239]

The manuscript in question is endorsed 'Questions relative to Hereditary Right. Mr. Hobbes' and it reads, in full, as follows:

> If you allow that a king does not hold his title by divine Institution, as indeed 'tis
> absurd to say he does, then I suppose you will admitt that his title to Governe
> arises from his protecting those that are govern'd. My next Question therefore is
> this, If a Successour to a Crown, be for some reason or other which is notorious,
> incapable to protect the people, if the Government should devolve upon him,
> is not the Prince in possession oblig'd to put him by, upon the request of his
> subiects?
>
> Here agen you mistake me. I deny not but a King holds his Title by Divine
> right. But I deny that any Heir apparent does so. Nor did I mention the word
> *Institution*; nor do I know what you mean. But I will shew you what I mean
> by Example. If a Constable lay hands upon me for misdemeanor, I aske him
> by what right he meddles with me more then I with him. He will answer me,
> *Iure Regio* (i) by the right of the King. He needs not say, because you are a Theefe.
> For perhaps I might truly say as much of him. Therefore that which is said to be
> done *Iure Devino* in a King is said to be done by Warrant or comission from God;
> but that I had no commission. Law and Right differ. Law is a command. But
> Right is a Liberty or priviledge from a Law to some certaine person though it
> oblige others. Institution is no more but Enthroneing, Proclameing, Anointing,
> Crowning &c. Which of all humane, and done *Iure Regio*. But tis not so of Heirs

---

[236] Kenyon 1972, p. 156.
[237] Hobbes MSS (Chatsworth) MS G. 3, p. 1. The endorsement is in James Wheldon's hand, but
the copy of the Bill is not, and I have not been able (nor has Beal) to identify the copyist.
[238] Kenyon 1972, p. 157.
[239] Hobbes MSS (Chatsworth) MS D. 5. The text is on the first two pages of two quarto leaves.

apparent. For God[240] is no Heir[241] to any King. Nor has any inheritance to give away.

You say the Right of a King depends upon his protecting of the people. I confesse that as the King ought to protect[242] his people so the people ought to obey the King. For it is impossible for the best King in the world to protect his people, except his Subjects furnish him with so much money as he shall judge sufficient to doe it.

To your next question, whether the King in Possession[243] be not obliged to put by his next Heir in case of notorious incapacity to protect them. I answer that if the incapacity proceed from want of money, I see no reason, though he can, why he should do it. But if it proceed from want of naturall reason the King in possession may do it, but is not obliged thereunto. Therefore I will speake of that Subject no more till we have such a weak King. But in case the King in possession may lawfully disinherit his diseased Heir and will not; you have not yet answered me to the question, Who shall force him for I suppose the sound King living cannot be lawfully deposed by any person or persons that are his Subjects; because the King dying is *ipso facto* dissolved; and then the people is a Multitude of lawlesse men relapsed into a condition of warr of every man against every man. Which by making a King[244] they intended to avoid.

I have elsewhere discussed my discovery of this manuscript and commented on it at length.[245] Here I need only underline the fact that the specific question to which Hobbes was asked to reply is whether a king can be obliged to exclude a notoriously unsuitable heir. Applying one of the basic principles of his civil science, he responds that, while a king undoubtedly possesses such a power of disinheritance, he can never be forced to exercise it by his own subjects. To which he adds with a characteristic note of caution that he will 'speak of that subject no more till we have such a weak king'.[246]

This was to be Hobbes's last word on politics, the scientific study of which he claimed to have invented.[247] The tone of his response is distinctly irritable, but he was clearly in full possession of his faculties at the time of writing it. A few months later, however, he was 'suddainly striken with a dead Palsie which stupified his right side from head to foote, and took away his speech, in truth I think his reason and sense too'. These are the words of Justinian Morse, the Earl of Devonshire's

[240] One word crossed out after 'God'; 'is' inserted in Hobbes's hand.
[241] Two or three words crossed out after 'Heir'.   [242] Two words crossed out after 'protect'.
[243] One word crossed out after 'possession'.
[244] One word crossed out after 'King'. 'They' inserted above the line in Hobbes's hand.
[245] Skinner 1965.
[246] Chatsworth: Hobbes MS D. 5, [p. 2] (marked 'p. 10' on MS).
[247] Hobbes 1839e, p. ix.

secretary, who adds that Hobbes died within a week.[248] The death occurred at Hardwick Hall on 4 December 1679, when Hobbes was only four months short of his ninety-second birthday. A true humanist at the last, he composed a Latin epitaph for himself[249] in which he placed his main emphasis on his probity as a gentleman and the widespread fame he had gained from his works.[250]

IX

The rest of the chapters in this volume are all concerned with Hobbes's civil science and its place in his general philosophy. It is worth underlining Hobbes's preference for speaking of 'civil science'[251] rather than politics or political philosophy, the terms preferred by so many of his modern commentators. It is true that in *Leviathan* Hobbes takes himself to be engaged in what he calls 'the study of the Politiques', and thus in that form of science which examines the rights and duties of sovereigns and subjects.[252] He speaks, however, of providing his readers not with one but two 'prospective glasses' to enable them 'to see a farre off the miseries that hang over them', and these twin telescopes are said to be 'Morall and Civill Science'.[253] Civil science, as he explains, is concerned with 'Consequences from the Accidents of *Politique* Bodies'.[254] But moral science is concerned with one particular set of 'Consequences from the Accidents of Bodies Naturall', in that it takes as its theme the question of 'what is *Good*, and *Evill*, in the conversation, and Society of man-kind'.[255]

I have tried in the chapters that follow to say something about both these components of Hobbes's thought. As I have indicated, my first four chapters take up a number of topics in his moral philosophy, focusing in particular on what he understood by 'the science of Vertue and Vice'.[256] Chapter 6 shifts from natural to artificial persons, concentrating on the rights and duties of the person of the state. Subsequent chapters go on

---

[248] Pritchard 1980, pp. 182, 183–4. See Aubrey 1898, vol. 1, pp. 382–3 for an account of Hobbes's final days written by his amanuensis, James Wheldon.

[249] The epitaph, which can still be seen on Hobbes's tomb in the parish church of Hault Hucknall in Derbyshire, is reproduced in Blackbourne 1839, p. lxxx.

[250] Blackbourne 1839, p. lxxx.

Vir probus, et fama eruditionis
Domi forisque bene cognitus.

[251] Hobbes 1996, ch. 18, p. 129.   [252] Hobbes 1996, ch. 30, p. 242.
[253] Hobbes 1996, ch. 18, p. 129.   [254] Hobbes 1996, ch. 9, p. 61.
[255] Hobbes 1996, ch. 9, p. 61; ch. 15, pp. 110–11; ch. 31, p. 254.
[256] Hobbes 1996, ch. 15, p. 111.

to examine other aspects of the artificial world that we choose to inhabit when we covenant to establish that great Leviathan, the king of the proud.[257] Chapter 7 discusses the liberties (and thus the rights) of subjects, after which I turn in chapters 8, 9 and 10 to their duties, and hence to the concept of political obligation, the core of the strictly 'politique' aspect of Hobbes's civil science. I accordingly end by emphasising what Hobbes himself always liked to emphasise most of all, the supreme importance of recognising and protecting the rights of the state.

[257] Hobbes 1996, Introduction, p. 9; ch. 28, pp. 220–1.

2

Hobbes and the studia humanitatis

I

Hobbes's philosophical ideas, we are frequently told, were 'formed' by the scientific revolution spanning the seventeenth century.[1] I shall argue that this orthodoxy rests to a misleading extent on emphasising the period in which Hobbes began to put into print his ideas on the natural and moral sciences, beginning with his first major treatise, *De Cive*, in 1642. We need to remember that, by the time he made his public debut as a writer on *scientia civilis*, Hobbes was already in his early fifties. By the standards of the age he already had a lifetime of study behind him. If we turn, moreover, to examine the nature of his studies during the first half of his long life, a picture in strong contrast with the prevailing orthodoxy begins to emerge. Hobbes is revealed not as a product of the scientific culture to which he later contributed so extensively, but rather as a student and exponent of the predominantly literary culture of humanism.

A number of commentators have already noted that Hobbes's intellectual development passed through a 'humanist period' before he turned to the sciences, natural and moral, in the course of the 1630s.[2] Little attempt has been made, however, to explore the extent to which his earlier studies may be said to conform to the ideal of the *studia humanitatis*, and thus to the distinctively 'humanist' range of genres and disciplines.[3] And no attempt at all has been made to examine how far the works

---

This chapter is a revised and extended version of an essay that originally appeared under the title 'Thomas Hobbes and the Renaissance *Studia humanitatis*' in *Writing and Political Engagement in Seventeenth-Century England*, ed. Derek Hirst and Richard Strier (Cambridge, 2000), pp. 69–88.

[1] See, for example, Sorell 1986, p. 1. But I should add that, while I disagree with Sorell on this point, his study is an exceptionally valuable one.

[2] Strauss 1963, p. 30; Reik 1977, pp. 25–34; Johnston 1986, pp. 3–25; Tuck 1989, pp. 1–11.

[3] But the situation is beginning to change. Schuhmann 1990, p. 332 stresses the 'broadly humanistic direction' of Hobbes's work after 1615 and begins to trace (pp. 332–6) the relations between Hobbes's early studies and the Renaissance *studia humanitatis*. Paganini 1999 explores the humanist origins and orientation of several key topics in Hobbes's thought.

he published prior to *De Cive* embody an authentically humanist understanding of how philosophical texts should be organised and presented
to maximise their argumentative force. These are the gaps I hope to fill in
the existing literature, although I can only hope to do so in a preliminary
and promissory way.[4]

II

According to Renaissance pedagogical theory, the first and basic element
in the five-fold syllabus of the *studia humanitatis*[5] was grammar, the study
of the classical languages.[6] John Aubrey's biography makes clear that
Hobbes acquired an exceptional mastery of these linguistic skills at an
early age. As we saw in chapter 1, Hobbes was sent at about the age
of ten to a school run by a young man called Robert Latimer, whom
Aubrey describes as 'a good Graecian'.[7] Aubrey tells us that Latimer
'delighted in his scholar, T. H.'s company, and used to instruct him, and
two or three ingeniose youths more, in the evening till nine a clock'.[8]
The young Hobbes 'so well profited in his learning', Aubrey goes on,
'that at fourteen yeares of age, he went away a good schoole-scholar
to Magdalen-hall, in Oxford'.[9] As proof of the high level of proficiency
in Greek and Latin that Hobbes had by then attained, Aubrey adds in
admiring tones that 'it is not to be forgotten, that before he went to
the University, he had turned Euripidis Medea out of Greeke into Latin
iambiques, which he presented to his master'.[10]

These literary interests must have been sadly interrupted by the
scholastic curriculum that Hobbes was obliged to follow at Oxford, a
curriculum that he recalls in his verse *Vita* with unmixed contempt.[11]
But he seems to have had the idea of returning to his humanistic studies
as soon as he left Oxford in 1608.[12] As we saw in chapter 1, he immediately joined the household of William Cavendish, later the first earl of
Devonshire. Hobbes was employed as tutor to Cavendish's son, the future
second earl, who also bore the name William Cavendish.[13] Hobbes and

---

[4] The argument that follows draws on chapter 6 of Skinner 1996, although I have revised and
greatly extended my earlier analysis, in particular by the use of various manuscript sources not
previously exploited.
[5] See Kristeller 1979.
[6] Charlton 1965, pp. 116–19; Grafton and Jardine 1986, pp. 143–5.
[7] Aubrey 1898, vol. 1, p. 329.   [8] Aubrey 1898, vol. 1, p. 328.
[9] Aubrey 1898, vol. 1, p. 328.   [10] Aubrey 1898, vol. 1, pp. 328–9.
[11] Hobbes 1839b, pp. lxxxvi–lxxxvii, lines 33–50.   [12] Aubrey 1898, vol. 1, p. 330.
[13] Hobbes 1839b, p. lxxxvii, lines 63–5.

his charge began by removing to the University of Cambridge, where the young Cavendish was awarded the degree of Master of Arts in July 1608, while Hobbes was incorporated (by virtue of his Oxford degree) as a member of St John's College.[14] The choice of college is interesting in view of the fact that St John's had been a leading centre for the study of the humanities ever since Roger Ascham and Sir John Cheke had begun teaching there in the 1530s.[15] However, this particular educational scheme appears not to have worked out. We learn from the account book kept by Cavendish *père* that Hobbes was paid twenty shillings in November 1608 for hiring a coach to take the young Cavendish back to his father's estates in Derbyshire after what appears to have been only a single term of residence.[16] So far as studying at Cambridge was concerned, that was that.

After this failed experiment, Hobbes tells us that he abandoned his studies more or less completely. 'During the year that followed, I spent almost the whole of my time with my master in the city, as a result of which I forgot most of the Latin and Greek I had ever known.'[17] After returning from a trip to France and Italy with the young Cavendish in 1615, however, Hobbes seems to have settled down once more to a scholarly mode of life.[18] He informs us that 'my master provided me with leisure throughout the ensuing years, and supplied me in addition with books of all kinds for my studies'.[19] As he makes clear, moreover, his reading largely centred on the five canonical disciplines of the *studia humanitatis*: grammar, rhetoric, poetry, history and moral philosophy.

Hobbes tells us in his prose *Vita* that he began by setting himself a course of study specifically designed to recover and extend his mastery of the classical tongues. 'As soon as I got back to England, I started carefully to read over the works of a number of poets and historians,

---

[14] Malcolm 1994c, pp. 855–6.   [15] Charlton 1965, pp. 142, 159; Simon 1979, pp. 203–9.

[16] Hardwick MSS (Chatsworth) MS 29, p. 38; cf. Malcolm 1994c, p. 856 note.

[17] Hobbes 1839a, p. xiii: 'Anno sequente, cum domino suo in urbe perpetuo fere degens, quod didicerat linguae Graecae et Latinae, magna ex parte amiserat.'

[18] Hobbes 1839a, p. xiii. Note that Hobbes and Cavendish left only in 1614 (not in 1610 as is usually stated). See Skinner 1996, pp. 218–19 and cf. Peck 1996.

[19] Hobbes MSS (Chatsworth) MS A. 6, lines 75–6 (cf. Hobbes 1839b, p. lxxxviii, lines 73–4):

> Ille per hos annos mihi praebuit otia, libros
> Omnimodos studiis suppeditatque meis.

Hobbes MSS (Chatsworth) MS A. 6 is a fair copy of Hobbes's verse *Vita* in the hand of his last amanuensis, James Wheldon, with corrections by Hobbes. Since this is in some places a better text than the one printed by Molesworth (Hobbes 1839b), I have preferred to use it when quoting from the *Vita*, although I have also given references to Molesworth's edition in brackets.

together with the commentaries written on them by the most celebrated grammarians.'[20] He adds that 'my aim was not to learn how to write floridly, but rather to learn how to write in an authentically Latin style, and at the same time how to find out which particular words possessed the meaning best suited to my thoughts'.[21] He must have begun to recover his knowledge of Greek in the same period, Lucian being one of the authors on whom he seems to have concentrated. Lucian is praised in the Appendix to the Latin *Leviathan* as an excellent writer of Greek[22] and Hobbes exhibits a knowledge of his writings in several different works. He is mentioned in the *Critique* of Thomas White's *De Mundo*[23] as well as in *Lux Mathematica*[24] and the *Historia Ecclesiastica*,[25] while in *Leviathan* he is cited (although without acknowledgement) at several points. The story in chapter 8 about the learned madness of the people of Abdera is taken from Lucian's account of how to write history,[26] while the description of human law in chapter 21 is presented as a commentary on Lucian's version of the fable of Hercules.[27]

No doubt as part of this process of re-educating himself in the classics, Hobbes appears to have renewed acquaintance with the ancient theorists of rhetoric at the same time, and thus with the second element in the *studia humanitatis*. He must have made a close study of Aristotle's *Art of Rhetoric* at this juncture or in the early 1630s, given that his Latin paraphrase of the text was translated into English and printed by c.1637.[28] He must also have read, or more probably re-read, the major treatises on Roman rhetorical theory in the course of the 1620s. Previous studies of Hobbes's intellectual development have tended to leave the impression that his detailed knowledge of ancient eloquence may have been confined to Aristotle's *Rhetoric*.[29] But in the introduction to his translation of Thucydides, which he published in 1629, Hobbes makes it clear that he was familiar with a number of leading works of Roman rhetorical thought. He not only refers to Cicero's *Orator, De Optimo Oratore* and

---

[20] Hobbes 1839a, pp. xiii–xiv: 'Itaque cum in Angliam reversus esset, Historicos et poetas (adhibitis grammaticorum celebrium commentariis) versavit diligenter.'

[21] Hobbes 1839a, p. xiv: 'non ut floride, sed ut Latine posset scribere, et vim verborum cogitatis congruentem invenire'.

[22] See Hobbes 1841a, p. 540 on Lucian as 'bonus author linguae Graecae'.

[23] Hobbes 1973, p. 329.   [24] Hobbes 1845d, p. 148.   [25] Hobbes 1845g, p. 361, line 438.

[26] Hobbes 1996, ch. 8, p. 56. The reference is duly picked up by Tricaud in Hobbes 1971a, p. 73.

[27] Hobbes 1996, ch. 21, p. 147; cf. Lucian 1913, p. 65. For this invocation of Lucian see also below, chapter 7 section III.

[28] For this work see above, chapter 1 section I, and cf. notes 79 and 108–9 below.

[29] Strauss 1963, pp. 35, 41–2; Shapiro 1980, pp. 148–50.

De Oratore but also quotes from each of these texts.[30] Finally, it seems likely that it was during the same period that he immersed himself in Quintilian's *Institutio Oratoria*, a treatise to which he makes explicit reference in several of his later works.[31]

There is plentiful evidence that Hobbes was also much preoccupied in the 1620s with the third element in the *studia humanitatis*, the study of classical poetry. He tells us in his verse *Vita* that he read a great deal of ancient drama and poetry at this period, specifically mentioning Horace, Virgil and Homer among the poets, together with Euripides, Sophocles, Plautus and Aristophanes among the dramatists.[32] John Aubrey confirms that, although Hobbes in later life possessed relatively few books, his visitors could always expect to find copies of Homer and Virgil on his table.[33] Both these poets are invoked on numerous occasions in Hobbes's later works, and there are direct quotations from Virgil's *Aeneid* in the *Critique* of White's *De Mundo*, in *Leviathan* and (although unacknowledged) in *De Corpore*.[34] Hobbes's verse *Vita* adds that this was a time when he also read many other ancient poets.[35] One of these must have been Statius, to whom he alludes in chapter 12 of *Leviathan*.[36] Another must have been Martial, one of whose epigrams is quoted in *De Cive*.[37] Another must have been Lucan, whose *Pharsalia* Hobbes cites in his essay on heroic poetry and praises for having achieved 'the height of Fancie'.[38] Yet another must have been Ovid, whom Hobbes might have been expected to include in the list of his favourite ancient writers, especially as he modelled his verse *Vita* on the autobiography that Ovid included in his *Tristia*.[39] But of all the ancient poets, Horace was unquestionably Hobbes's favourite,

---

[30] Hobbes 1975b, pp. 10, 18–19, 26–27. As Lessay points out in Hobbes 1993, p. 139n., Hobbes's reference to the *De Oratore* is inaccurate. The passage he cites comes from *Orator*, IX. 32.

[31] See the allusions in Hobbes 1971b, esp. pp. 49–51; various references in Hobbes 1996 (e.g., the definition of laughter in ch. 6, p. 43) and the invocation of Quintilian's judgement on Lucan in Hobbes 1844a, p. viii.

[32] Hobbes 1839b, p. lxxxviii, lines 77–8.   [33] Aubrey 1898, vol. 1, p. 349.

[34] See, respectively, Hobbes 1973, p. 121 and note; Hobbes 1996, ch. 38, p. 312; Hobbes 1839c, p. 414: 'Densum ergo idem est quod frequens, ut densa caterva; rarum idem quod infrequens, ut rara acies, rara tecta.' Virgil 1999–2000, vol. 2, p. 66 (*Aeneid* VIII, 98–9) has 'rara domorum/tecta vident', while Virgil 1999–2000, vol. 2, p. 146 (*Aeneid* IX, 508) has 'rara est acies'.

[35] Hobbes 1839b, p. lxxxviii, line 79.

[36] Duly noted by Tricaud in Hobbes 1971a, p. 105 and note.

[37] Hobbes 1983a, XV. XV, p. 227; cf. Martial 1919–20, VIII. XXIV, vol. 2, p. 18.

[38] Hobbes 1844a, p. vii; cf. Hobbes 1971a, p. 46.

[39] As I note in Skinner 1996, p. 233, note 145, Hobbes not only imitates Ovid's elegiac couplets but even echoes some turns of phrase. Compare, for example, Ovid 1988, line 20 with Hobbes 1839b, line 28; Ovid 1988, line 56 with Hobbes 1839b, line 154; Ovid 1988, line 132 with Hobbes 1839b, line 369.

with references to the *Epistles* in particular being sprinkled throughout his later works.[40]

It is evident from Hobbes's autobiographies that he also devoted himself after his return to England in 1615 to the fourth of the five elements in the *studia humanitatis*, the study of history.[41] He informs us that 'in my early years I was drawn by my natural bent to the historians no less than to the poets',[42] and he explains that this made him turn 'to our own historians as well as to those of Greece and Rome'.[43] He does not tell us which English historians he read, but he emphasises that, among the Greeks, 'it was Thucydides who pleased me above all the rest'.[44] Aubrey reveals that, among the historians of Rome, Hobbes chiefly admired Caesar, and particularly his *Commentarii*.[45] He adds that Hobbes never abandoned these early interests, and that in later life it was not uncommon to find him reading 'some probable historie'.[46]

Hobbes must in addition have made a close study of several other classical historians at this time. This is evident from *The Elements of Law* and *De Cive*, both of which reveal a detailed knowledge of Sallust's *Bellum Catilinae*.[47] It is also evident from *Leviathan*, in which Hobbes not only

---

[40] The reference in Hobbes's *Elements of Law* to 'an oderunt peccare in the unjust' alludes to Horace, *Epistles*, I. XVI, line 52. See Horace 1929, p. 354 and cf. Hobbes 1969a, p. 83. The remark in *De Cive*, 'qui consulta patrum, qui leges iuraque servant' is quoted (except that *servant* should read *servat*) from Horace, *Epistles*, I. XVI, line 41. See Horace 1929, p. 354 and cf. Hobbes 1983a, XIII. XII, p. 200. (The quotation recurs in *Leviathan*. See Hobbes 1996, ch. 4, p. 26.) The phrase 'quis vir bonus' from the *Critique* of Thomas White's *De Mundo* alludes to Horace, *Epistles*, I. XVI, line 40. See Horace 1929, p. 354 and cf. Hobbes 1973, p. 414. (In *De Corpore* Hobbes converts the allusion into a quotation. See Hobbes 1839c, p. 26.) A further allusion to Horace's *Epistles* occurs in *Leviathan* chapter 42. See Horace 1929, I. XVIII, line 15, p. 368 and cf. Hobbes 1996, ch. 42, p. 339. We also find a reference to the *Satires* in chapter 21 of *Leviathan*. See Horace 1929, I. I, line 81, p. 10 and cf. Leviathan 1996, ch. 21, p. 146.

[41] On humanism and history in early seventeenth-century England see Woolf 1990.

[42] Hobbes 1839a, p. xx: 'Natura sua, et primis annis, ferebatur ad lectionem historiarum et poetarum.'

[43] Hobbes MSS (Chatsworth) MS A. 6, lines 77–8 (cf. Hobbes 1839b, p. lxxxviii, lines 75–6):

Vertor et ad nostras, ad Graecas, atque Latinas
Historias.

[44] Hobbes 1839a, p. xiv; see also Hobbes MSS (Chatsworth) MS A. 6, line 82 (cf. Hobbes 1839b, p. lxxxviii, line 80):

Sed mihi prae reliquis Thucidides placuit.

[45] Aubrey 1898, vol. 1, p. 331. But if this was so, it seems strange that Hobbes never makes any reference or even (so far as I am aware) any allusion to the *Commentarii* in his later works.

[46] Aubrey 1898, vol. 1, p. 349.

[47] Hobbes 1969a, pp. 175–6; Hobbes 1983a, XII. XII, pp. 192–3. Hobbes also quotes Sallust in Hobbes 1973, p. 424.

refers to Plutarch's life of Brutus[48] but also puts the life of Solon to elegant though unacknowledged use.[49] The same point emerges still more clearly from the translation of Thucydides. One of the distinctive features of Hobbes's edition was his attempt to locate the place-names mentioned in Thucydides's text. Hobbes explains in his opening address that he was able to discover their location 'by travel in Strabo, Pausanias, Herodotus, and some other good authors'.[50] His index confirms that he made extensive use of all these authorities, besides reading a number of other historians with the same purpose in mind. One was Appian, whose account of the Roman civil wars he mentions at several points.[51] A second was Polybius, whose *Histories* he refers to with some frequency.[52] But the most important was Livy, whose authority he invokes on dozens of occasions, drawing his information from at least ten different books of the history.[53]

During the period of reading that followed his return to England in 1615, Hobbes also seems to have taken a special interest in the fifth and culminating element in the *studia humanitatis*, the study of moral and civil philosophy. His reading must at least have encompassed Justus Lipsius's *De Doctrina Civili*, which he quotes in the Introduction to his translation of Thucydides,[54] as well as Francis Bacon's *Essays*, several of which he helped to translate into Latin.[55] He must have known Thomas More's *Utopia* and Jean Bodin's *Six livres de la République*, both of which he mentions in *The Elements of Law*, the latter in tones of considerable respect.[56] We learn in addition from one of his letters to the Earl of Newcastle that he began reading John Selden's *Mare Clausum* as soon as it was published

[48] Duly noted by Tricaud in Hobbes 1971a, p. 18 and note. Several anecdotes in *De Cive* also appear to be taken from Plutarch. See Hobbes 1983a, V. V, p. 133; VII. XVI, p. 157; X. XV, p. 179.
[49] The discussion of cobweb laws in chapter 27 of *Leviathan* is taken from Plutarch's life of Solon, evidently in North's translation. See Hobbes 1996, ch. 27, p. 204 and cf. Plutarch 1579, p. 89. That Hobbes read Plutarch at an early stage is clear from the fact that he already refers to this passage in the discourse *Upon the Beginning of Tacitus* published in *Horae Subsecivae* in 1620. See [Cavendish and Hobbes] 1620, p. 272. Cf. also [Hobbes 1995 (?)], p. 49. (It is from this latter edition that all subsequent quotations from the *Discourses* will be taken.) For Hobbes's alleged authorship of this *Discourse* (and of two others) see below, note 70.
[50] Hobbes 1975a, p. 9.   [51] See, for example, Hobbes 1629, Sig. b, 2ᵛ.
[52] Hobbes 1629, Sig. c, 1ʳ; Sig. c, 2ʳ; Sig. c, 3ʳ.
[53] For full details see Skinner 1996, p. 236, note 167. Hobbes later alludes to Livy's history at several points in *Leviathan*. See Hobbes 1996, ch. 12, p. 82 (the story of Numa) and Hobbes 1996, ch. 14, p. 99 (the example of an oath). He also refers to Livy by name on two occasions. See Hobbes 1996, ch. 7, p. 49 and ch. 33, p. 261.
[54] Hobbes 1975b, p. 27.   [55] Aubrey 1898, vol. 1, p. 331.
[56] Hobbes 1969a, pp. 30, 172. Hobbes had earlier mentioned *Utopia* in his discourse *Of Lawes*, one of the anonymous contributions he appears to have made to *Horae Subsecivae* in 1620. See [Hobbes 1995 (?)], p. 106 and for Hobbes's alleged contributions to the *Horae* see below, note 70.

in 1635,[57] and from references in *The Elements of Law* that by 1640 he had mastered a number of classical texts in moral and civil philosophy including Aristotle's *Politics* and the works of Cicero and Seneca.[58]

Hobbes also worked in close collaboration with Cavendish on a number of projects arising from their study of this final element in the *studia humanitatis*. No doubt encouraged and helped by Hobbes, Cavendish undertook an ambitious exercise in humanist moral theory when he composed his *Discourse Against Flatterie*, which he published in 1611. Although the *Discourse* appeared anonymously, it was known to the booksellers as Cavendish's work,[59] and was dedicated to his father-in-law, Lord Bruce of Kinloss.[60] After returning from his travels in 1615, Cavendish continued to read and write on similar themes. The first outcome was a set of ten short pieces[61] to which he gave the Baconian title of *Essayes*, and which he presented to his father in the form of a bound manuscript volume.[62] Hobbes must have been acting as Cavendish's secretary by this time, for the volume is actually in Hobbes's hand,[63] although it includes corrections by Cavendish and his signature claiming the work as his own.[64] The state of the manuscript suggests that he and Hobbes must have worked closely together on the production of the final text.[65]

William Cavendish's final contribution to the moral sciences took the form of a volume of essays entitled *Horae Subsecivae*, 'Leisure Hours'. This collection was first published anonymously in 1620,[66] but when the firm of Legatt and Crooke registered it for republication in 1637 they described it as 'Lord Cavendishes *Essaies*'.[67] The first half of the *Horae* contains twelve short pieces entitled 'Observations', and consists of a slightly extended version of the manuscript volume already presented by

---

[57] Hobbes 1994, letter 18, vol. 1, p. 32. Hobbes and Selden were fellow members of Magdalen Hall, Oxford, and became friends towards the end of Selden's life. See Aubrey 1898, vol. 1, p. 369.

[58] Hobbes 1969a, pp. 170, 174, 177.   [59] Jaggard 1941, p. 169.

[60] [Cavendish] 1611, Sig. A, 2^r.

[61] Malcolm 1981, p. 321 suggests that these were probably drafted before 1610, although later revised to take account of Cavendish's foreign travels, including as they do the Discourse describing Rome.

[62] Hobbes MSS (Chatsworth), MS D. 3.

[63] Correctly noted in Strauss 1963, p. xii and note, and more recently in Wolf 1969 and Harwood 1986, p. 26 and note.

[64] Hobbes MSS (Chatsworth) MS D. 3 has corrections at pp. 5, 13, 15, 22, 48, 58, *et passim*, and Cavendish's signature at p. vi.

[65] Wolf 1969, pp. 113–31 claims that the essays are Hobbes's work, but this seems to go beyond the evidence.

[66] [Cavendish and Hobbes] 1620.

[67] *Registers of the Company of Stationers of London 1554–1640*, vol. 4, p. 362.

Cavendish to his father.[68] The second half is given over to four longer *Discourses*, the individual titles of which are *Upon the beginning of Tacitus, Of Rome, Against Flattery* and *Of Lawes*.[69]

Of these longer essays, the third is a revised and abbreviated version of Cavendish's *Discourse Against Flatterie* of 1611. But the other three, according to a recent computer analysis,[70] are the work not of Cavendish but of Hobbes.[71] A dramatic finding. If we accept the ascription, we alter by over twenty years the date at which Hobbes first embarked on the publication of his civil science. But should the ascription be accepted? Despite the authority of computers in our culture, there remain grounds for doubt. As well as the questionable status of the statistical methods employed,[72] there is the disconcerting fact that the three *Discourses* are often conventional in content and pedestrian in style. In particular, the one entitled *Of Rome* is an undistinguished example of the kind of report that any dutiful young aristocrat on the Grand Tour might have composed for the edification of his parents at home.

Nevertheless, it seems very probable that Hobbes at least had a considerable hand in these texts. As we have seen, he and his former pupil undoubtedly worked together on Cavendish's earlier essays, and it would not be surprising if they had subsequently agreed to collaborate in a more extended way. There are, in short, some independent reasons for thinking it likely that the computer analysis is correct. Given these reasons, it seems appropriate to assume, at least provisionally, that the three *Discourses* singled out by the computer are indeed by Hobbes. The implications with respect to the place of the *studia humanitatis* in his intellectual development are of great interest, and one of my aims in what follows will be to try to draw them out.

---

[68] The two pieces added to the earlier collection of ten 'Essayes' in Hobbes MSS (Chatsworth) MS D. 3 are entitled 'Of a Country Life' and 'Of Religion'.

[69] [Cavendish and Hobbes] 1620, pp. 223–324; 325–417; 419–503; 505–41.

[70] See the computer analysis reported in Reynolds and Hilton 1993, pp. 366, 369 and Fig. 6, Appendix 3, p. 378. Cf. also Reynolds and Saxonhouse 1995, pp. 12–19.

[71] Reynolds and Hilton 1993, p. 366 state the outcome of their computer analysis with precision when they conclude that what it shows is that 'these texts are statistically indistinguishable from uncontested Hobbes texts'. Later they state that 'we conclude that Hobbes wrote these three Discourses' (p. 369). They also state (p. 369) that the analysis establishes that Hobbes was *not* the author of the fourth Discourse – the one on flattery – which now appears almost certainly to have been written by Cavendish, though no doubt with the advice of Hobbes.

[72] Martinich 1997 disquietingly notes that the stylometric form of statistical analysis used to establish Hobbes's authorship of the three *Discourses* has also been used to establish that the Book of Mormon was written not by Joseph Smith in the nineteenth century but by a number of different authors (one of whom was an angel) at a much earlier date.

III

So far I have concentrated on Hobbes's humanistic studies during the period of his service to the second earl of Devonshire. This period came to an unexpected end in 1628 when the earl suddenly died and was succeeded by his eleven-year-old son, yet another William Cavendish.[73] These developments at first caused Hobbes to lose his position in the Devonshire household, but he regained it in 1631 when the second earl's widow invited him to return as tutor to her young son.[74] There then ensued what Hobbes describes in his verse *Vita* as 'seven painstaking years'[75] in the course of which he served as teacher and travelling companion to the son of his former pupil, continuing in these roles until the third earl attained his majority in 1638.

Hobbes's verse *Vita* includes a revealing account of the syllabus he drew up in his renewed tutorial capacity. He mentions that he taught the young William Cavendish some logic, arithmetic and geography,[76] and it is evident from other sources that he also gave him some instruction in geometry.[77] As the *Vita* makes clear, however, he took his principal duty to be that of inculcating the main elements of the *studia humanitatis*. He accordingly started his pupil off with Latin grammar, his aim being to instil 'an understanding of the meaning of the speech used by the Romans, and of how to join Latin words together in the proper way'.[78] Some evidence of Hobbes's method of teaching this basic skill can be seen in one of William Cavendish's surviving exercise books at Chatsworth. From this it appears that Hobbes dictated in Latin, subsequently going over his pupil's version and pointing out his mistakes. One of the texts on which they worked together in this way was Aristotle's '*Art*' of *Rhetoric*. Cavendish's exercise book contains Hobbes's Latin paraphrase of Aristotle's text, with numerous marks to suggest that it may have been dictated to him in short sections, and with a large number of corrections and additions in Hobbes's hand.[79]

---

[73] Malcolm 1994c, pp. 808–9.   [74] Malcolm 1994c, pp. 808–9.
[75] Hobbes 1839b, p. lxxxix, line 103.   [76] Hobbes 1839b, p. lxxxix, lines 99–101.
[77] Hobbes MSS (Chatsworth), MS D. 2, exercise book in the hand of the third earl of Devonshire. This contains thirty geometrical proofs, twelve of which are initialled by Hobbes ('T. H.'), presumably to show that he had checked them. The first ten proofs have marginal comments added by Hobbes, who supplies corollaries in the case of 10, 13, 14, 25, 26, 27, 29 and 30.
[78] Hobbes MSS (Chatsworth) MS A. 6, lines 98–9 (cf. Hobbes 1839b, p. lxxxviii, lines 95–6):

Hunc Romanarum sensus cognoscere vocum,
Iungere quoque decet verba Latina modo.

[79] See Hobbes MSS (Chatsworth) MS D. 1. Robertson 1886, p. 29 first identified this manuscript as the third earl's dictation book. One of the items it contains (pp. 160–54 *rev.*) is a series of extracts

After this, Hobbes's verse *Vita* explains, they moved on to the second element in the *studia humanitatis*, the study of rhetoric. Hobbes's account implies that he was following a recognised scheme of instruction at this juncture, rather than teaching what he might ideally have wished to impart, since his description of the *Ars rhetorica* is far from neutral in tone. What he taught the young earl, he observes, was 'how Orators write, and by means of what art Rhetoricians are accustomed to deceive the uninitiated'.[80] As we have seen, Hobbes's method of conveying this additional skill took the form of combining it with the teaching of grammar, concentrating on a number of texts capable of serving both pedagogical purposes at once. This had been the usual method of instruction in the grammar schools of Hobbes's youth, in which the rules of composition had generally been taught from a study of the best authors together with handbooks of rhetorical style.

There is considerable evidence that Hobbes paid no less attention in his teaching to the other three elements in the *studia humanitatis*. He mentions in his verse *Vita* that he taught the young Cavendish 'what a Poet does',[81] and it is clear that they also spent a good deal of time on ancient history. Among the texts on which they worked together was Florus's epitome of Livy's history of Rome. One of Cavendish's exercise books shows that he copied out a number of extracts from this source, including notes on Romulus, Camillus, Tarquin and Junius Brutus.[82] A further text on which he and Hobbes worked together was Valerius Maximus's *Factorum et Dictorum Memorabilium Libri Novem*. Another of Cavendish's exercise books shows that he turned into English an impressively large number of anecdotes taken from this popular compilation.[83] A hundred

---

from Florus's epitome of Livy. But the main item (pp. 1–143) is the Latin version of the *Briefe* of Aristotle's *Rhetoric* eventually published in English in 1637. For further discussion see above, chapter 1 note 27 and cf. Harwood 1986, pp. 1–2 and Malcolm 1994c, p. 815. The dictation book is signed 'W. Devonshire' twice on the inside covers and frequently elsewhere. It is also signed 'Thomas Hobbes' inside the back cover, although not in Hobbes's hand. The book is in the third earl's handwriting, with headings, corrections and additions by Hobbes.

[80] Hobbes MSS (Chatsworth) MS A. 6, lines 100–1 (cf. Hobbes 1839b, p. lxxxviii, lines 97–8):

> Fallere quaque solent indoctos Rhetores arte;
> Quid facit Orator . . .

[81] Hobbes MSS (Chatsworth) MS A. 6, line 101 (cf. Hobbes 1839b, p. lxxxviii, line 98):

> Quid facit Orator, quidque Poeta facit.

[82] See Hobbes MSS (Chatsworth) MS D. 1, pp. 160–54 *rev.*, with notes on Tarquin and Brutus (p. 157), Camillus (p. 156) and Romulus (p. 155). I am greatly indebted to Karl Schuhmann for identifying Florus as the source.

[83] Hardwick MSS (Chatsworth) MS 70, exercise book in hand of third earl of Devonshire. Here too I am greatly indebted to Karl Schuhmann for establishing that all Cavendish's translations are taken from Valerius Maximus. I have been unable to determine which edition Hobbes used.

and twenty of these extracts survive, reflecting various stages in the development of Cavendish's handwriting, and it is striking that a majority of them concern the early history of republican Rome. A number discuss the military leaders from the era of the Punic wars: there are extracts on Publius Claudius, Lucius Paullus, Quintus Metellus and Marcus Regulus in addition to a series of ten extracts on the Scipio family. A still larger number celebrate the heroes of the early republic: there are extracts on Lucius Brutus, the liberator of the Roman people from their kings; on the severity of Camillus and Postumius as Censors; on Gaius Flaminius and Tiberius Gracchus as leaders of the plebs; on the elder Cato, who carried into extreme old age 'a youthfull courage in defending the Commonwealth';[84] and on the military greatness of Publius Rutilius and Fabius Flaccus, the first of whom 'begot in the legions a more subtle way of avoiding and of giving strokes', while the second discovered the value of using nimble velites against cavalry.[85]

The humanist handbooks of Tudor England had invariably emphasised that an education in the *studia humanitatis* should culminate in the study of moral philosophy. As Sir Thomas Elyot had explained in *The Book Named the Governor*, 'by the time that the child do come to seventeen years of age, to the intent that his courage be bridled with reason, it were needful to read unto him some work of philosophy; specially that part that may inform him unto virtuous manners, which part of philosophy is called moral'. By way of embarking on this final stage of the syllabus, Elyot goes on, 'there would be read to him, for an introduction, two of the first books of the work of Aristotle called *Ethicae*, wherein is contained the definitions and proper significations of every virtue'.[86]

Hobbes appears to have followed these humanist precepts to the letter. As a way of introducing the third earl to the rudiments of moral philosophy, he seems to have commissioned the production of a Greek and Latin manuscript, found among his papers, which is headed *Aristotelis Parva Moralia, sive de Ethicis virtutibus*.[87] Hobbes's choice of

---

Valerius was one of the most popular Roman writers in the Renaissance, with some twenty printed editions appearing in the fifteenth century after the *editio princeps* at Strasburg in 1470. During the sixteenth century at least fifty more editions appeared, while the opening decades of the seventeenth century saw about a dozen more.

[84] Hardwick MSS (Chatsworth) MS 70, *sub* 'Of the elder Cato'. Cf. Valerius 1966, VIII. VII. 1, p. 384.

[85] Hardwick MSS (Chatsworth) MS 70, *sub* 'Of Publius Rutilius and Gaius Mallius [*sic*] Consuls' and *sub* 'Of the Uses of the Velites first found out'. Cf. Valerius 1966, II. III. 2, p. 67 and II. III. 3, pp. 67–8.

[86] Elyot 1962, p. 39.

[87] Hobbes MSS (Chatsworth) MS A. 8 (1). Due to a modern mis-binding, the *Parva Moralia* MS is no longer first in order in the volume in which it appears (MS A. 8, *Three Digests*). I have followed

author is perhaps surprising, given that he was later to denounce Aristotle as 'the worst teacher that ever was'.[88] But the explanation is perhaps that he again saw himself as following an approved pattern of instruction rather than his own inclinations at this point. Certainly the contents of the *Parva Moralia* are largely Aristotelian in character. The title is not of course the name of any authentic work by Aristotle, but it was doubtless intended to recall the best known of the post-Aristotelian epitomes, the *Magna Moralia*, which continued to be printed as part of the Aristotelian corpus in sixteenth-century editions of his works.

The Hobbesian *Parva Moralia* manuscript is mainly devoted to considering the specific virtues discussed by Aristotle in Books 3 to 6 of *Nicomachean Ethics*, together with a number of the apparent virtues discussed in Books 2 and 7. The Latin terms conventionally used to translate Aristotle's vocabulary are used throughout, the individual chapters being entitled *De Prudentia, De Temperantia, De Modestia et Magnanimitate, De Fortitudine, De Iustitia Particulari, De Liberalitate et Magnificentia, De Comitate et Urbanitate, De Mansuetudine* and *De Veritate & Veracitate*.[89] To these are added, again in Aristotelian vein, the virtues 'improperly so-called', the first being *De Verecundia* and the rest *De Indignatione, De Continentia, De Tolerantia* and *De Heroica Virtute*.[90] The manuscript contains a large number of marginal references to the sources of its arguments, all of which correspond to the chapters in which Aristotle had discussed the same issues in *Nicomachean Ethics*. While Aristotle's arguments are supplemented as well as truncated and rearranged, the manuscript undoubtedly offers a basically Aristotelian account of 'the definitions and proper significations of every virtue' in exactly the manner recommended by Sir Thomas Elyot in *The Book Named the Governor*.

It would seem, however, that Hobbes principally taught the young Cavendish the elements of moral philosophy in the more homely manner also recommended by the humanist writers of advice-books on good conduct. His method appears, that is, to have been to turn to the moralists and historians of antiquity as sources of sententious maxims and

Beal in assuming that the manuscript was 'probably made by Hobbes for his pupil, the third Earl of Devonshire'. See Beal 1987, p. 582. However, some of the philological points made in the manuscript are so detailed that it is hard to think of them as part of an elementary course of instruction in moral science. The manuscript has been little studied, and many puzzles about its provenance and character remain to be solved.

[88] Aubrey 1898, vol. 1, p. 357.

[89] Hobbes MSS (Chatsworth) MS A. 8 (1). These chapters are preceded by a longer discussion entitled *De Virtute Generatim Spectata* (pp. 1–11) and occupy pp. 12–32.

[90] Hobbes MSS (Chatsworth) MS A. 8 (1), p. 33: *De Virtutibus improprie dictis et primo de Verecundia*. The other four chapters occupy pp. 34–9.

instructive anecdotes. The exercise book in which his pupil translated the edifying stories collected by Valerius Maximus includes a great deal of material of this kind. From Pomponius Rufus, for example, Valerius recounts the tale of Cornelia, the mother of the Gracchi, who was shown some precious jewels and ornaments by a guest. According to Cavendish's translation, she waited for her children to return home from school, 'and these, saith shee, are my ornaments'. The moral is said to be that 'Certainly hee hath all things, who desireth nothing.'[91] Cavendish similarly translates Valerius's version of the story from Cicero's *De Oratore* about Simonides, who was called away from a banquet just before the roof collapsed and caused the deaths of everyone else present. The moral drawn by Valerius in this case is even more high-flown. As Cavendish renders it, 'What is more rich than this happinesse, Which neither, the Sea nor the Land raging was able to destroy.'[92]

As well as repeating these improving tales – and a great many others in similar vein – Cavendish was clearly encouraged to treat the historical figures about whom he read as exemplars of particular virtues and vices. Hobbes appears to have accepted the conventional view that the lives of the philosophers provide the most instructive examples. The life of Solon reminds us about the importance of industriousness.[93] Diogenes's conduct towards Alexander the Great illustrates the value of independence and continence.[94] Socrates's willingness to begin playing a musical instrument in old age suggests that it is never too late to learn.[95] Carneades, who wonderfully addicted himself to learning for ninety years, exemplifies the value of a life committed to the pursuit of wisdom.[96] And so on. It seems, in short, that Hobbes's method of instruction was based on the typically humanist assumption that history and moral philosophy can be taught together, since history serves as the light of truth[97] and hence as philosophy teaching by examples.

---

[91] Hardwick MSS (Chatsworth) MS. 70, *sub* 'Of Cornelia'. Cf. Valerius 1966, IV. IV, Introd., pp. 187–8. Cavendish follows Valerius in noting that the story is taken from Pomponius Rufus.

[92] Hardwick MSS (Chatsworth) MS 70, *sub* 'Of Simonides'. Cf. Valerius 1966, I. VIII. ext. 7, pp. 52–3.

[93] Hardwick MSS (Chatsworth) MS 70, *sub* 'Of Solon'. Cf. Valerius 1966, VIII. VII. ext. 14, p. 393.

[94] Hardwick MSS (Chatsworth) MS 70, *sub* 'Of Diogenes'. Cf. Valerius 1966, IV. III. ext. 4, pp. 186–7.

[95] Hardwick MSS (Chatsworth) MS 70, *sub* 'Of Socrates a Philosopher'. Cf. Valerius 1966, VIII. VII. ext. 8, p. 391.

[96] Hardwick MSS (Chatsworth) MS 70, *sub* 'Of Carneades a philosopher'. Cf. Valerius 1966, VIII. VII. ext. 5, pp. 389–90.

[97] Cicero 1942, II. IX. 36, vol. 1, p. 224. On history and 'the light of truth' in Renaissance England see Woolf 1990.

IV

Throughout his three decades of service as tutor and secretary to the Devonshire family, Hobbes was continually occupied in studying and teaching the *studia humanitatis*. But of even greater significance is the fact that his own writings from this period are overwhelmingly humanist in character. If we turn to consider the works he published prior to the appearance of *De Cive* in 1642, we not only find that he contributed to all five of the recognised humanist disciplines; we also find that his published works were wholly confined to these distinctively humanist genres.

The most obvious way of demonstrating a mastery of the primary element in the *studia humanitatis*, the *ars grammatica*, was by making translations of classical texts. This in turn helps to explain why the art of translation attained such an unparalleled degree of prestige and prominence in the era of the Renaissance. If we reflect on Hobbes's scholarly activities in the 1620s, it becomes evident that he was much influenced by this humanist scale of values. He initially worked as a translator of English into Latin, a skill he exercised at some stage in the early 1620s as secretary to Francis Bacon.[98] It is not clear how this secondment from the Devonshire household arose, but it must have occurred at some time between Bacon's dismissal from the Lord Chancellorship in May 1621 and his death in April 1626.[99] One of Bacon's projects during these years was to rewrite his earlier vernacular works in Latin. He published an extended version of *The Advancement of Learning* as *De Dignitate et Augmentis Scientiarum* in 1623, and at the same time he began to translate some of his *Essays* into Latin. For this latter undertaking he needed some help, and according to Aubrey it was Hobbes who supplied it. Aubrey not only records that 'The Lord Chancellour Bacon loved to converse' with Hobbes, but that Hobbes 'assisted his lordship in translating severall of his Essayes into Latin, one, I well remember, is that *Of the Greatnes of Cities*'.[100]

Hobbes made a much more important contribution to the study of the classical languages when he published his translation of Thucydides's history as *Eight Bookes of the Peloponnesian Warre* in 1629.[101] Hobbes

---

[98] Blackbourne 1839, p. xxv. On Bacon and the Cavendishes see also Gabrieli 1957 and Malcolm 1984, pp. 47–54.

[99] Jardine and Stewart 1998, pp. 459–60, 502.   [100] Aubrey 1898, vol. I, p. 331.

[101] Henry Seile, the publisher, entered the book in the Stationers' Register on 18 March 1629. See *Registers of the Company of Stationers of London 1554–1640*, vol. 3, p. 161.

concedes in his opening address that Thucydides's text has already been rendered into English, and that he has seen a copy of this earlier version, which Thomas Nicolls had issued in 1550.[102] But Hobbes objects that Nicolls's rendering is not only full of inaccuracies, but offends against a more fundamental tenet of humanism by failing to use the best available text. Nicolls had been content to work from a French translation (published by Claude de Seyssel in 1527) which in turn derived from Lorenzo Valla's Latin edition of the 1450s.[103] By contrast, Hobbes stresses, he has worked directly from Thucydides's original Greek, using the newly corrected edition of Aemilius Portus[104] and supplementing Portus's text with an up-to-date scholarly apparatus, 'not neglecting any version, comment, or other help I could come by'.[105] The outcome, Hobbes proudly announces, is a version as free as possible from errors, for 'I can discover none, and hope they be not many.'[106]

Soon afterwards Hobbes made a contribution to the second discipline in the *studia humanitatis* when his paraphrase of Aristotle's *'Art' of Rhetoric* was published. Hobbes had first encountered the editor of the *Rhetoric*, Dr Theodore Goulston, as a fellow-member of the Virginia company in the early 1620s.[107] But it appears to have been as part of his duties as tutor to the third earl of Devonshire in the early 1630s that Hobbes made a close study of Goulston's Greek text.[108] As we have seen, he began by translating sections of it into Latin, dictating them to his pupil as a series of comprehension exercises.[109] This version was then turned into English and anonymously published as *A Briefe of the Art of Rhetorique* in c.1637.[110] This was the first English translation of Aristotle's *Rhetoric* to be printed. Hobbes may not have been the author of this version, but his success in truncating, reshaping and supplementing Aristotle's text in order to create his Latin paraphrase[111] enabled a useful translation to

---

[102] Hobbes 1975a, p. 8; cf. Schlatter 1975, pp. xi–xii.   [103] Schlatter 1975, pp. xi–xii.
[104] Not 'Porta', the form in which the name appears in Schlatter's edition. See Hobbes 1975b, p. 8, but cf. Schuhmann 1984, p. 177n. Portus's edition was published at Frankfurt in 1594.
[105] Hobbes 1975a, p. 8.   [106] Hobbes 1975a, p. 8.
[107] *Records of the Virginia Company of London*, vol. 2, pp. 340–1, 533–4.
[108] For the evidence that Hobbes used Goulston's text see Harwood 1986, pp. 21–2, 50, 99–100.
[109] Hobbes MSS (Chatsworth) MS D. 1. For this manuscript see above, note 79, and cf. Robertson 1886, p. 29.
[110] See [Hobbes (?)] 1986. Hobbes's authorship of this translation of his Latin paraphrase has never been doubted, but Karl Schuhmann has arrived at the dramatic but convincing conclusion that, while the Latin paraphrase is Hobbes's work, the English translation is not. For details see above, chapter 1 note 27.
[111] On these changes see Harwood 1986, esp. pp. 7, 13, 17, 19–20; Rayner 1991, pp. 87–91.

be produced, and it went through three editions before the end of the century.[112]

During his first period of service to the Devonshires Hobbes also made an ambitious contribution to the third element in the *studia humanitatis*, the study and imitation of classical verse. He presented to the second earl, around the year 1627, a poem of some five hundred Latin hexameters entitled *De Mirabilibus Pecci, Carmen*, a description of the 'wonders' of the Peak District in Derbyshire.[113] The most striking feature of the poem, which Hobbes published a few years later, is its continual use of themes and motifs derived from classical epic verse.[114] The poem centres on the Homeric idea of a memorable journey, describing a trip from the Earl of Devonshire's seat at Chatsworth to the neighbouring town of Buxton and its surrounding countryside. Recounting seven wonderful episodes, Hobbes permits himself copious use of the classical trope to the effect that he cannot hope to do justice to his experiences. He nevertheless attempts to describe them, and in doing so repeatedly ornaments his verses with Virgilian echoes and references. The groves of Chatsworth are cooler than Virgil's beeches;[115] the fountains in its gardens are finer than the sacred fount of Callirhoe;[116] the descent into the vaporous depths of Elden Hole is similar to Aeneas's visit to the underworld;[117] the robber's cave visited at the end of the journey is reminiscent of the Gorgon's lair.[118]

Throughout the early part of his career, Hobbes also took an active interest in the fourth of the humanistic disciplines, the writing of history. We find him displaying considerable historical erudition in his edition of Thucydides, particularly in the footnotes and marginal glosses appended to the text. There are references to the patterns of alliances at the outbreak of the Peloponnesian war, the nature of Greek religious observances, the methods of waging the war itself, and so forth.[119] As his introductory essays make clear, moreover, Hobbes decided to make more widely available this masterpiece of ancient historiography for reasons of a pre-eminently humanist kind. One reason was his wish to show that Thucydides had discharged 'the principal and proper work of history'

---

[112] Macdonald and Hargreaves 1952, pp. 7–9.
[113] Hobbes MSS (Chatsworth) MS A. 1 is a fair copy in 14 folio pages, of which lines 233 to 319 (pp. 7–9) are in Hobbes's hand.
[114] Wood 1691–2, vol. 1, p. 479 states that the poem was 'printed at *Lond.* about 1636'.
[115] Hobbes 1845f, p. 325, line 16.   [116] Hobbes 1845f, p. 326, line 31.
[117] Hobbes 1845f, p. 334, lines 298–9.   [118] Hobbes 1845f, p. 339, lines 503–4.
[119] Hobbes 1975a, pp. 576, 577, 578, 581, 583.

more effectively than anyone else, that of seeking 'to instruct and enable men, by the knowledge of actions past, to bear themselves prudently in the present and providently towards the future'.[120] A further reason was the hope that we can learn something of importance from the fact that Thucydides 'least of all liked the democracy'.[121] Thucydides shows that any community dependent on large assemblies for its processes of decision-making will be liable to suffer dangerously from 'the emulation and contention of the demagogues for reputation and glory of wit'. With their continual 'crossing of each other's counsels', they will be sure to undermine any concern for the public good and eventually cause the dissolution of the commonwealth.[122]

Of even greater importance as a contribution to the study of history is the discourse entitled *Upon the beginning of Tacitus* which, we are now assured, Hobbes contributed to *Horae Subsecivae* in 1620. Following the typically humanist method of quoting key passages from a classical text and commenting on them, a large part of the essay is given over to narrating the rise of the Emperor Augustus to power and his successful conversion of Rome from a republic into a principality.[123] Hobbes first invokes Tacitus's authority to explain 'the means Augustus used in acquiring and confirming to himself the supreme and Monarchical authority'.[124] He then adds an extensive account, again in the form of glosses on Tacitus's text, of how Augustus thereafter managed to perpetuate his imperial authority 'and derive it to posterity'.[125]

Reflecting on this narrative, Hobbes adds in typically humanist vein that a number of general lessons can be drawn from it, especially in view of the fact that Augustus followed 'the best order that can be, to assure a new sovereignty'.[126] The situation in which Augustus found himself was that of a usurper seeking to impose the 'restraint and pressure of Monarchical rule' upon a people only recently 'weaned from liberty'.[127] He thus found himself facing the very predicament which, as Machiavelli had notoriously argued in *Il Principe*, is above all fraught with danger for a new prince.[128] This makes it particularly instructive, Hobbes suggests, to observe what courses of action Augustus followed: how he never engaged in policies that 'a new Prince ought to avoid', how he concentrated

---

[120] Hobbes 1975a, p. 6.   [121] Hobbes 1975b, p. 13.   [122] Hobbes 1975b, p. 13.
[123] See [Hobbes (?)] 1995, in which this theme is first taken up at p. 42 and thereafter occupies the whole of the *Discourse*.
[124] [Hobbes (?)] 1995, p. 31.   [125] [Hobbes (?)] 1995, p. 49.   [126] [Hobbes (?)] 1995, p. 44.
[127] [Hobbes (?)] 1995, pp. 63–4.   [128] Machiavelli 1960, ch. 5, p. 29.

with exemplary skill on the lines of conduct 'best for a new prince'.[129]
Watching Augustus in action, we can hope to learn from 'a master in the
Art of government'.[130]

The early part of Hobbes's career culminated in the production of two
major treatises of civil philosophy, traditionally the fifth and final element
in the *studia humanitatis*. Hobbes explains in the Preface to *De Cive*[131] that
'a few years before the civil war broke out, my country started to seethe
with questions about the right of Sovereignty and the obligations of
citizens to obedience', in consequence of which he felt it a matter of
urgency to put his thoughts on these matters into publishable shape.[132]
He began by circulating *The Elements of Law, Naturall and Politique*,[133] which
he completed in May 1640,[134] and shortly afterwards he issued *De Cive*,
which first appeared in Paris in April 1642.[135]

As we have seen, however, it appears that Hobbes had already published a work of civil philosophy over twenty years earlier, for we are now
informed that he contributed the discourse *Of Lawes* to *Horae Subsecivae* in
1620. It is certainly striking that, although this essay makes no pretence
of presenting its arguments in the form of scientific proofs, its conclusions
not infrequently resemble those which Hobbes was later to claim to have
demonstrated with certainty in *De Cive* and *Leviathan*. We are already
told in *Of Lawes* that reason prescribes complete obedience, since we 'are
rather bound to obey, than dispute; Laws being, as it were, the Princes we
ought to serve, the Captains we are to follow'.[136] We are likewise told that
'common reason' is at once 'engrafted in our natures' and is at the same
time 'a Law, directing what we are to doe, forbidding the contrary'.[137]
Here the verbal parallels with *Leviathan* are close, for Hobbes there in-
structs us that a law of nature 'is a Precept, or generall Rule, found out
by Reason, by which a man is forbidden to do, that, which is destructive
of his life'.[138] The need for complete obedience is confirmed in *Of Lawes*
with the reflection that any attempt to live together without law would
bring so much confusion 'that the differences of Right and wrong, Just
and unlawful, could never be distinguished'.[139] Here too there are verbal

---

[129] [Hobbes (?)] 1995, pp. 43–4.   [130] [Hobbes (?)] 1995, p. 65.
[131] Hobbes added this *Praefatio* when he reissued *De Cive* in 1647. See Warrender 1983a, pp. 8–13.
[132] Hobbes 1983a, *Praefatio*, p. 82: 'patriam meam, ante annos aliquot quam bellum civile exarde-
sceret, quaestionibus de iure Imperii, & debita civium obedientia'.
[133] This is the form in which the title appears in the two best MSS. See BL Harl. MS 4235 and cf.
Hobbes MSS (Chatsworth) MS A. 2. B (except that the latter reads 'Elementes').
[134] Hobbes 1969a, p. xvi is signed 'May ye. 9th 1640'.
[135] Warrender 1983a, pp. 5–8.   [136] [Hobbes (?)] 1995, p. 105.   [137] [Hobbes (?)] 1995, p. 115.
[138] Hobbes 1996, ch. 14, p. 91.   [139] [Hobbes (?)] 1995, p. 106.

parallels with *Leviathan*, in which Hobbes insists that 'the notions of Right and Wrong, Justice and Injustice have there no place' where there is no law.[140]

V

I began by suggesting that, if we are to lend precision to the suggestion that Hobbes's early intellectual allegiances were predominantly humanist in character, two main questions need to be addressed. The first is whether his early studies conformed to the Renaissance ideal of what it means to contribute to the humanistic disciplines. We have now seen that this can be answered with a resounding affirmative. But there remains the second and arguably more significant question: whether Hobbes's early writings were presented and 'disposed' in an authentically humanist style.

Before considering this issue, we need to recall the leading assumptions about the organisation of literary texts that the humanists of Tudor England had inherited from their classical authorities and put into general currency. The most important was that all public utterances must conform to one of three rhetorical genres. That this contention became so widely accepted was undoubtedly due in large part to the fact that, as Quintilian had noted, almost every ancient rhetorician had repeated the list of *genera* originally put forward by Aristotle in his *Art of Rhetoric*.[141] Aristotle had laid it down that – in the words of the translation attributed to Hobbes – 'there are three kinds of *Orations; Demonstrative, Judicial, Deliberative*'.[142] The pseudo-Ciceronian *Rhetorica ad Herennium* opens by repeating Aristotle's categories,[143] while Quintilian later takes over the same classification, commending Aristotle at the same time 'for establishing this tripartite division of oratory into the judicial, the deliberative and the demonstrative'.[144]

The ancient rhetoricians had almost invariably begun by discussing the *genus demonstrativum*. Aristotle declares (in the translation attributed to Hobbes) that the proper office of such epideictic orations is '*Praysing* and *Dispraysing*', while their proper end is to point out what is '*Honourable*, or

---

[140] Hobbes 1996, ch. 13, p. 90.   [141] Quintilian 1920–2, III. IV. 1, vol. 1, p. 390.

[142] [Hobbes (?)] 1986, p. 41.

[143] *Ad C. Herennium* 1954, I. II. 2, p. 4: 'tria genera sunt causarum . . . demonstrativum, deliberativum, iudiciale'.

[144] Quintilian 1920–2, II. XXI. 23, vol. 1, p. 366: 'Aristoteles tres faciendo partes orationis, iudicialem, deliberativam, demonstrativam.'

Dishonourable'.[145] He stresses that things as well as persons can be commended or condemned, and lists among the things most worthy of praise 'Monuments' and, more generally, 'things that excell'.[146] When offering such laudations, we should bear in mind that 'to praise the Worke from the Vertue of the Worker, is a circular Proofe', and instead concentrate on 'declaring the magnitude' of the work concerned.[147] Among Roman rhetoricians, Quintilian particularly takes up this analysis, agreeing that our praises can properly encompass animals, inanimate objects, cities, public works and 'every other kind of thing'.[148] If we are praising a city, we should remember that 'antiquity brings with it a great deal of authority';[149] if we are praising specific buildings or public works, we must emphasise 'not merely their honourable character but their beauty and usefulness'.[150]

This inclusive understanding of the *genus demonstrativum* was enthusiastically revived by the rhetorical theorists of the Renaissance, many of whom exhibit a special interest in re-establishing the genus of panegyric both in prose and verse.[151] As we saw in volume 2 chapter 2, one resulting development was the emergence of a sub-genre specifically devoted to praising the *magnalia* or signs of greatness in cities. The most celebrated was Leonardo Bruni's *Laudatio Florentinae Urbis* of 1403–4,[152] but a number of much earlier examples survive. These include the anonymous poem in praise of the city of Lodi, *De Laude Civitatis Laudae*, which was probably written as early as the 1250s,[153] and Bonvesin della Riva's panegyric on Milan, *De Magnalibus Mediolani*, which was completed in 1288.[154] Quintilian's further suggestion that almost anything can in principle be praised was also much developed by the Tudor humanists. Richard Rainolde, for example, in his *Foundacion of Rhetorike* of 1564 – a widely used textbook in the Elizabethan grammar schools[155] – assures us that 'All thynges that maie be seen, with the iye of man, touched, or with any other sence apprehended' can equally well be commended or

---

[145] [Hobbes (?)] 1986, p. 41.   [146] [Hobbes (?)] 1986, p. 53.   [147] [Hobbes (?)] 1986, p. 54.

[148] Quintilian 1920–2, III. VII. 6, vol. 1, p. 466; III. VII. 26–7, vol. 1, p. 476 and III. VII. 27, vol. 1, p. 478 on 'rerum omnis modi'.

[149] Quintilian 1920–2, III. VII. 26, vol. 1, p. 476: 'multum auctoritatis adfert vetustas'.

[150] Quintilian 1920–2, II. VII. 27, vol. 1, p. 476 on 'honor, utilitas, pulchritudo'.

[151] On this development see Skinner 1996, pp. 42–3. On epideictic oratory in the Renaissance see Hardison 1962 and McManamon 1989.

[152] See Bruni 1968.

[153] See *De Laude* 1872 and for the suggested dating see Hyde 1965, p. 340.

[154] See Riva 1974 and for a similar though later celebration of Milan (dated c.1316 in Hyde 1965, p. 340) see Alessandria 1890.

[155] Charlton 1965, pp. 111–12; Skinner 1996, pp. 29–30.

condemned: 'as Manne. Fisshe. Foule. Beaste. Orchardes. Stones. Trees. Plantes. Pettals. Citees. Floodes. Castles. Toures. Gardeins. Stones. Artes. Sciences'.[156]

The second form of utterance to which the classical rhetoricians had addressed themselves was the *genus deliberativum*. Aristotle had laid it down in the *Rhetoric* that (in the words of the Hobbesian translation) the office of such speeches is '*Exhortation* and *Dehortation*', and that their proper end is 'to proove a thing *Profitable*, or *Unprofitable*'.[157] He goes on to explain that 'an Orator in *exhorting* always propoundeth *Felicity*, or some part of *Felicity* to be attained by the actions he exhorteth unto', to which he adds that 'by *Felicity*, is meant commonly, *Prosperity with vertue*, or *a continuall content of the life with surety*'.

The implication that an orator who deliberates must in effect be counselling was subsequently taken up by the leading Roman writers on the rhetorical arts.[158] They also accept that, as the *Ad Herennium* puts it, the purpose of offering such counsel will normally be *suasio et dissuasio*, to persuade someone to act or dissuade them from acting in some particular way.[159] The only moment at which they express any doubts about Aristotle's analysis is in considering his claim that the goal of deliberative oratory is to indicate which of various possible actions should be treated as especially advantageous or profitable. As Cicero observes in his *De Inventione*, 'whereas Aristotle is content to regard *utilitas* as the aim of deliberative oratory, it seems to me that our aim should be *honestas et utilitas*, honesty allied with advantage'.[160]

The last form of utterance discussed by the classical and Renaissance rhetoricians was the *genus iudiciale*. Once again they generally take their definitions from Aristotle's *Rhetoric*, in which the office of judicial oratory had been described (in the translation attributed to Hobbes) as that of '*Accusation* and *Defence*' and its goal as that of discovering in some particular instance what is '*Just*, or *Unjust*'.[161] It follows that 'the thing to be prooved is, that *Injury* has beene done'.[162] Among the Roman writers, Cicero provides the fullest restatement of these categories. He agrees that the *genus* takes the form of accusation and defence; he agrees that

[156] Rainolde 1564, fo. xxxvii[r].   [157] [Hobbes (?)] 1986, p. 41.
[158] See, for example, *Ad C. Herennium* 1954, III. II. 2–3, pp. 158–60.
[159] *Ad C. Herennium* 1954, I. II. 2, p. 4. Cf. Cicero 1949, II. IV. 12, p. 176 and Quintilian 1920–2, III. VIII. 6, vol. 1, pp. 480–2.
[160] Cicero 1949, II. LI. 156, p. 324: 'In deliberativo autem Aristoteli placet utilitatem, nobis honestatem et utilitatem.' Cf. Cicero 1949, II. LV. 166, p. 332 and Quintilian 1920–2, III. VIII. 22, vol. 1, p. 490. The author of the *Ad Herennium* reverts to a more Aristotelian position. See *Ad C. Herennium* 1954, III. II. 3, p. 160.
[161] [Hobbes (?)] 1986, p. 41.   [162] [Hobbes (?)] 1986, p. 54.

'the question at issue is always what is equitable'; and he speaks at length of the need to establish whether some injury has in fact been suffered in order to ensure that equity and justice are upheld.[163]

VI

If we now return with the above considerations in mind to Hobbes's early writings, we find that they fall into two strongly contrasting categories. By the time he came to draft *The Elements of Law* and *De Cive*, he was in full revolt against the literary culture of humanism. In both these texts he explicitly repudiates the ideal of rhetorical organisation in favour of what he takes to be the canons of science. But if we turn instead to the works that Hobbes allowed to appear in print before the publication of *De Cive*, we find him confining himself entirely to the accepted rhetorical genres.

Among these early writings are two contributions to the *genus demonstrativum* so conventional as to count as little more than rhetorical exercises. One is the Latin poem of 1627, *De Mirabilibus Pecci, Carmen*. Hobbes takes especially seriously Aristotle's injunction that, if we are praising monuments or other such works, we must concentrate on their sheer magnitude. The first 'wonder' Hobbes describes is Chatsworth, which he commends for its fame and size.[164] The second is the Peak itself, which he praises for its grandeur and frightening appearance.[165] The third is Mam Tor, the 'maimed rock', which he admires in the same way for its mighty scale.[166] And so on.

If Hobbes was indeed the author of the discourse *Of Rome* from *Horae Subsecivae*, then he had earlier penned a yet more conventional exercise in the *genus demonstrativum*. The essay is an instance of one of the most popular forms of *Laudatio* revived in the Renaissance, that in which a city is praised for its signs of greatness. It is true that Hobbes's account is in part a *vituperatio* as well, since he ends by pointing to the corrupting implications of the fact that Rome is nowadays 'wholly subject to the Pope, which he holds as a temporal prince'.[167] Hobbes criticises the leaders of the church in exactly the manner prescribed by ancient theories of rhetoric, stressing their lack of *honestas* and their consequent failure to follow a virtuous way of life. He particularly concentrates on the extent to which their conduct is founded on the worst of all the vices, the sin of pride. Fascinatingly,

---

[163] Cicero 1949, I. V. 7, p. 16 and II. IV. 12, p. 176.   [164] Hobbes 1845f, p. 325, lines 4–5.
[165] Hobbes 1845f, p. 330, lines 179, 183.   [166] Hobbes 1845f, p. 332, line 238.
[167] [Hobbes (?)] 1995, p. 94.

in view of his long polemic against Cardinal Bellarmine in *Leviathan*, he specifically exempts Bellarmine from these charges, stressing that he is chiefly noted for his learning and his modest way of life.[168] If, however, we consider the pope and the rest of the cardinals, 'it is strange to see their pride'.[169] They 'violently desire honor, and superfluity in wealth'; they are 'proud, seditious and covetous'; they have nothing to teach us apart from 'ambitious thoughts, and unsatisfied desires after the wealth and glory of this world'.[170] We can safely conclude that 'the sumptuousness of the Pope, and the pride of his government, is one token of the falsity of their doctrine'.[171]

Apart from this concluding *vituperatio*, Hobbes's essay consists entirely of what he himself describes as a 'Laudatory' to Rome.[172] As we have seen, Aristotle had argued that monuments are particularly susceptible of being effectively praised. Hobbes duly informs us that he will concentrate on the city's 'Ethnic Antiquities', 'Christian Monuments', 'modern Buildings, Gardens, Fountaines, etc' as well as on its 'Colleges, Churches, and Religious Houses'.[173] Aristotle had gone on to propose that, in praising monuments, we should focus on their sheer magnitude, to which Quintilian had added that we should seek to commend their antiquity and if possible their beauty and usefulness. Hobbes duly begins by observing that Rome remains unchallenged for antiquity as well as greatness, and subsequently illustrates his claim by emphasising the great age and size of the amphitheatre, the 'wonderful great compass' of Diocletian's baths, the 'great length' of St Peter's basilica, and so on.[174] He speaks too of 'the singular use and profit that may be gathered' from an understanding of these antiquities, and continually draws attention to their beauty and elegance.[175] Rome's many statues are choice and lifelike; her triumphal arches are of great height and exquisitely engraved; her ancient temples are singular and rare; St Peter's is remarkable and magnificent.[176] Finally, Aristotle had added that we should speak of 'things that excel', thereby couching our praises in the form of superlatives. Hobbes duly assures us that Rome's 'Statues, and other Antiquities' have 'exceeded all that went before'; that her ancient temples have ever afterwards 'beene esteemed the best'; and that the Cathedral of St Peter not only possesses 'the most goodly *Facciata*, or forefront of the world', but has now been ornamented 'by the most famous Painter and Statuist

---

[168] [Hobbes (?)] 1995, pp. 96–7.   [169] [Hobbes (?)] 1995, p. 96.
[170] [Hobbes (?)] 1995, pp. 97–8.   [171] [Hobbes (?)] 1995, p. 97.   [172] [Hobbes (?)] 1995, p. 80.
[173] [Hobbes (?)] 1995, pp. 72–3.   [174] [Hobbes (?)] 1995, pp. 71, 77, 78, 84.
[175] [Hobbes (?)] 1995, p. 80.   [176] [Hobbes (?)] 1995, pp. 76–8, 82, 85–6.

in the World, Michelangelo'.[177] The entire city, in short, is 'in every kind
Superlative'.[178]

Hobbes's early publications also include two contributions to the *genus
deliberativum* in which he offers advice – again in exactly the manner
prescribed by the classical theorists of eloquence – about how political
leaders should conduct themselves if they wish to obtain honour and advantage. This furnishes the main theme of the discourse *Upon the beginning
of Tacitus*, which draws from the political career of Augustus a number
of general lessons about how new princes should act 'to assure a new
sovereignty' and give the people 'the sweetness of ease, and repose'.[179]
Hobbes's other contribution to this *genus* is his discourse *Of Lawes*, which
follows the prescriptions of the classical rhetoricians even more closely.
As we have seen, they had argued that, when counselling someone to
act in some particular way, we should try to persuade them that the
line of conduct we are proposing will at once prove virtuous and profitable, and will bring them not merely surety but continual contentment
of life. Seeking to persuade us in the discourse *Of Lawes* that it will always be better to obey, Hobbes attempts to establish his point in exactly
this way. He begins by arguing that the rule of law brings 'a double
benefit', since it guarantees 'the general good and government of the
State' and at the same time 'the quiet, and peaceable life of everyone in
particular'.[180] He goes on to describe laws as 'the people's bulwarks, and
defenses, to keep them in safety, and peace', to which he adds that the
equal administration of justice 'is the true knot that binds us to unity and
peace'.[181] A constant willingness to obey the law brings honour to kingdoms and safety to kings, while enriching and securing their subjects.[182]
The laws can thus be described as 'the true Physicians and preservers of
our peaceable life, and civil conversation', and as the means of 'sowing
peace, plenty, wealth, strength, and all manner of prosperity amongst
men'.[183]

Hobbes's early writings culminate in a notable contribution to the
genus iudiciale, widely regarded as the most important of the rhetorical
genres. His essay *Of the Life and History of Thucydides*, published in 1629
as the Introduction to his translation of the history, takes the form of a
classical forensic oration in defence of Thucydides's achievement. As we
have seen, the ancient rhetoricians had argued that the aim of writing in

---

[177] [Hobbes (?)] 1995, pp. 81, 82, 84.   [178] [Hobbes (?)] 1995, p. 82.
[179] [Hobbes (?)] 1995, p. 44.   [180] [Hobbes (?)] 1995, p. 105.
[181] [Hobbes (?)] 1995, pp. 105–6.   [182] [Hobbes (?)] 1995, pp. 108–9.
[183] [Hobbes (?)] 1995, p. 111.

this *genus* should be to establish that some injury has been done, thereby enabling a verdict to be reached in line with the requirements of equity and justice. Hobbes duly assures us that a grave injury to Thucydides's reputation has been perpetrated by a number of envious detractors, especially Dionysius of Halicarnassus, who 'hath taken so much pains, and applied so much of his faculty in rhetoric, to the extenuating of the worth' of Thucydides's masterpiece.[184] Developing the case for the defence, Hobbes follows with almost mechanical exactitude the rules for the correct 'disposition' of a forensic speech as laid down by the classical theorists of eloquence.[185]

As the classical textbooks had explained, any such formal oration must begin with an *exordium* calculated to put the listener in a receptive frame of mind. The best approach, according to the *Ad Herennium*, is to speak as simply and directly as possible.[186] Hobbes duly takes the lesson to heart, for his *exordium* merely affirms that 'two things are to be considered' in Thucydides's writings, his elocution and his truthfulness.[187] Before proceeding further, however, Hobbes duly pauses (as Cicero had particularly advised) to add an observation of the highest sententiousness.[188] 'For in *truth* consisteth the *soul*, and in *elocution* the *body* of history. The latter without the former, is but a picture of history; and the former without the latter, unapt to instruct.'[189]

Hobbes then turns to his *narratio* of the facts, the second element in the proper *dispositio* of any formal utterance. The relevant facts about Thucydides's truthfulness are that his veracity has never been impugned, that he had no motive for lying, and that he possessed all the necessary means to find out the truth.[190] The facts about his *elocutio* – which Hobbes arranges in logical sequence as the *Ad Herennium* had advised[191] – are said to be of two kinds: those concerned with method and those concerned with style. The relevant facts about Thucydides's method are that he employed a strict narrative form, interspersing it with orations in the deliberative mode, while the most salient fact about his style is that the best judges have always commended it.[192]

Next Hobbes passes to the third element in the classical theory of *dispositio*, the *divisio* or statement of points of agreement and disagreement with his adversaries.[193] He acknowledges one important point of

---

[184] Hobbes 1975b, p. 19.   [185] Here I draw on my fuller account in Skinner 1996, pp. 244–9.
[186] *Ad C. Herennium* 1954, I. VII. 11, p. 20.   [187] Hobbes 1975b, p. 16.
[188] Cicero 1949, I. XVIII. 25, pp. 50–2.   [189] Hobbes 1975b, p. 16.
[190] Hobbes 1975b, p. 17.   [191] *Ad C. Herennium* 1954, I. IX. 15, p. 26.   [192] Hobbes 1975b, p. 17.
[193] *Ad C. Herennium* 1954, I. X. 17, p. 30.

agreement between himself and Dionysius, which stems from the fact that the latter is willing to recognise the purity and propriety of Thucydides's style.[194] Hobbes's main concern, however, is with the other side of the *divisio*, and thus with the places where he remains in disagreement with Dionysius's judgement. Here again he pays close attention to the classical rules, providing us with a *confirmatio* and a *confutatio* in which he lays out Dionysius's criticisms and dismisses them at the same time.[195]

First Hobbes considers Dionysius's claim that Thucydides failed to choose a satisfactory theme, and that Herodotus ought on those grounds to be preferred. Herodotus's theme, Hobbes retorts, was such that he constantly found himself obliged 'to write of those things, of which it was impossible for him to know the truth', whereas Thucydides invariably wrote from first-hand knowledge.[196] Next Hobbes addresses Dionysius's objection that Thucydides ought not to have placed the responsibility for starting the war so squarely on the shoulders of his fellow-countrymen. Hobbes answers by reminding us of Thucydides's other and higher obligation: he wrote, as an historian must, 'not as a lover of his country but of truth'.[197] Dionysius's third criticism is that Thucydides's strictly narrative approach is hard to follow. To this Hobbes replies that it is nevertheless the most natural approach, and is unlikely to confuse any moderately attentive reader.[198] Lastly Hobbes responds to Dionysius's suggestion that Thucydides ought to have discussed the real causes of the war before considering the pretexts given for it, answering that 'the reprehension is absurd', for 'without a pretext, no war follows'.[199]

After this *confutatio*, Hobbes summarises in exactly the manner recommended by the *Ad Herennium*.[200] He asks himself, that is, what *ratio* or justifying motive Dionysius could have had for criticising Thucydides so unrelentingly. His answer offers a fine example of the kind of withering rebuttal most admired by the classical theorists of eloquence:

What motive he had to it, I know not; but what glory he might expect by it, is easily known. For having first preferred Herodotus, his countryman, a Halicarnassian, before Thucydides, who was accounted the best; and then conceiving that his own history might perhaps be thought not inferior to that of Herodotus: by this computation he saw the honour of the best historiographer falling on himself. Wherein, in the opinion of all men, he hath misreckoned. And thus much for the objections of Denis of Halicarnasse.[201]

---

[194] Hobbes 1975b, p. 18.   [195] *Ad C. Herennium* 1954, I. X. 18, p. 32.
[196] Hobbes 1975b, pp. 19–20.   [197] Hobbes 1975b, p. 21.   [198] Hobbes 1975b, pp. 22–3.
[199] Hobbes 1975b, p. 23.   [200] *Ad C. Herennium* 1954, I. XVI. 26, p. 50.
[201] Hobbes 1975b, p. 26.

The calculated bathos of the closing sentences points to the absurdity of trying to undermine Thucydides's fame.

The final element in any rhetorically organised argument was the formal *peroratio*. The writers of textbooks such as the *Ad Herennium* had popularised the view that in rounding off a speech one must be sure to invoke the wisest experts on one's side.[202] Here again Hobbes faithfully follows the classical rules. Among ancient experts he calls on Demosthenes, Cicero and Lucian, while among contemporary witnesses he singles out Justus Lipsius, declaring that 'the most true and proper commendation' of Thucydides is to be found in Lipsius's *De Doctrina Civili*.[203] Hobbes focuses in particular on Lipsius's observation that 'Thucydides, who hath written not many nor very great matters, hath perhaps yet won the garland from all that hath written on matters both many and great.'[204] A neat antithesis, and with it Hobbes rests his case.

VII

Hobbes's early rhetorical writings stand in astonishing contrast with the self-consciously scientific approach adopted in *De Cive*, in which he proceeds by framing definitions and pursuing their implications in a purportedly demonstrative style. The suddenness and completeness of this change of front have not perhaps been sufficiently recognised. Hobbes provides us with one of the most dramatic instances of a major philosopher in the midst of whose intellectual career we encounter what the French like to call a *rupture*. It was followed in Hobbes's case by a virtual reversal of his previous literary and to some degree his intellectual allegiances. Hobbes the humanist, careful to follow the precepts of the *ars rhetorica*, was supplanted by the more familiar figure of Hobbes the geometer, determined to present his conclusions in the form of demonstrative proofs.[205]

---

[202] See *Ad C. Herennium* 1954, II. XXX. 48, p. 146 on the need to appeal to *hominibus sapientissimis*.
[203] Hobbes 1975b, pp. 26–7.   [204] Hobbes 1975b, p. 27.
[205] But never completely supplanted. As noted in chapter 1, Hobbes's *Leviathan* is a profoundly rhetorical text, and in old age Hobbes returned to his youthful enthusiasm for the *studia humanitatis* when he devoted himself to translating Homer's *Iliad* and *Odyssey* into English verse.

3

Hobbes's changing conception of civil science

I

When Hobbes pauses to characterise his own contributions to political theory, he generally describes himself as engaged in the writing of *scientia civilis* or civil science. In the Epistle Dedicatory to his first work on politics, *The Elements of Law* of 1640, he promises to explain 'the true and only foundation of such Science'.[1] In the 1647 Preface to *De Cive* he begins by speaking of his treatise as a contribution to *scientia civilis*, adding that this is the most valuable of all the sciences.[2] In the *Leviathan* of 1651 he reiterates that his aim is to demonstrate the benefits of 'Morall and Civill Science',[3] and in the revised Latin edition of 1668 he speaks of the dangers incurred by those who lack the *scientiae* needed for appreciating the duties of citizenship.[4]

By the time Hobbes began his formal schooling in the 1590s, the humanist educational theorists of Elizabethan England had put into widespread currency a distinctive view about the nature of civil science.[5] The sources from which they principally drew their understanding were the major rhetorical treatises of ancient Rome, especially Cicero's *De Inventione* and *De Oratore*, together with Quintilian's great summarising work of the next century, the *Institutio Oratoria*. These treatises chiefly

---

This chapter is partly based on my essay '*Scientia Civilis* in Classical Rhetoric and in the Early Hobbes' in *Political Discourse in Early-Modern Britain*, ed. Nicholas Phillipson and Quentin Skinner (Cambridge, 1993), pp. 67–93.

[1] Hobbes 1969a, p. xvi.
[2] Hobbes 1983a, pp. 77–8. Despite claims to the contrary in Warrender 1983b, pp. 4–8, the English version of *De Cive* was not made by Hobbes himself. Malcolm 2000 has identified the translator as the poet Charles Cotton. Unfortunately Cotton's version is misleadingly free at many crucial points, so I have preferred to make my own translations.
[3] Hobbes 1996, ch. 18, p. 129. See also Hobbes 1996, ch. 9, p. 61, Hobbes's diagram of the sciences, in which he initially subdivides the basic category of science into natural and civil elements.
[4] Hobbes 1841a, p. 140.
[5] For an outline of this aspect of humanist culture in England see Skinner 1996, esp. pp. 19–40, 66–110.

offered expositions of *inventio, dispositio* and *elocutio*, the basic techniques necessary for speaking and writing in the most persuasive style.[6] But they also embodied an explanation of why the acquisition of these rhetorical arts should be regarded as a matter of social and cultural importance. The influence of this explanation upon those who, like Hobbes, began their education in the grammar schools of Elizabethan England can hardly be overestimated.

To be an Elizabethan grammar school pupil was to receive an intensive training in the two primary elements of the classical 'humanistic' syllabus.[7] First came the study of grammar, the goal of which was to memorise the vocabulary and structure of Latin and (sometimes) Greek in sufficient detail to be able to read these languages with fluency. Then came rhetoric, the principal subject taught in the senior classes. Pupils were expected to master the leading classical handbooks on the art of rhetoric in conjunction with learning to imitate the best classical authors, the goal in this case being that of learning not merely to read but to write Latin – in verse as well as prose – in the best and most eloquent style.[8]

To study the art of rhetoric meant studying the undisputed masters of the ancient *Ars rhetorica*, Cicero and Quintilian. While their works were often merely expounded by schoolmasters or read in the form of extracts and digests, a number of Elizabethan grammar school statutes make it clear that serious pupils were expected to read some at least of these texts for themselves.[9] As a consequence, any grammar school pupil of Hobbes's generation would have studied the views of Cicero and Quintilian on the nature of *scientia civilis* more closely than those of anyone else. As Hobbes himself was later to insist in his own works on civil science, the impact of this classical education on the moral and political sensibility of his generation was at once overwhelmingly strong and, he came to believe, largely detrimental to the public good.[10]

---

[6] For a discussion of these elements in the classical theory of written eloquence see Skinner 1996, esp. pp. 40–51.

[7] On the five-fold character of the *studia humanitatis*, and its individual elements as grammar, rhetoric, poetry, history and moral philosophy, see Kristeller 1979. The standard work on the Elizabethan grammar school curriculum remains Baldwin 1944. See also Charlton 1965; Simon 1979; and Skinner 1996, pp. 26–40.

[8] For the overwhelming concentration on these linguistic skills see Charlton 1965, pp. 116–19, Grafton and Jardine 1986, pp. 143–5. For a survey of grammar and rhetoric teaching in this period see Percival 1983.

[9] See, for example, the 1566 statutes of Norwich Grammar School printed in Saunders 1932, p. 147.

[10] For an excellent discussion of Hobbes's later hostility to classical education and its allegedly subversive implications see Dzelzainis 1995, esp. pp. 3–7.

Cicero had initially articulated his views about *scientia civilis* at the start of *De Inventione*, which opens with an account of the founding of cities that was destined to be endlessly repeated by the humanists of the Renaissance. Cicero begins by assuming that individuals, the substance or *materia* out of which cities are constructed, must come together in a union of an honourable and mutually beneficial kind if they are to realise their highest potentialities.[11] He further assumes that, at some determinate moment, some mighty leader must have recognised this fact and resolved to force the available human material into just such a unified shape.[12] This leads him to ask about the nature of the talents required by those who aspire to advise their fellow-citizens on how to live together in friendship and peace. To put the same question the other way round, he asks about the character of *scientia civilis* or civil science.

It goes without saying that for Cicero a good citizen is always and necessarily male. His thesis is that such men are distinguished by the possession of three linked qualities necessary and jointly sufficient for the effective practice of civil science. We must be capable in the first place of instructing our fellow-citizens in the truth, and must therefore be persons of *sapientia* or wisdom, the primary talent required of those who aspire to advise or teach. When reflecting on the origins of cities, Cicero declares that wisdom is the key quality that every founding father and lawgiver must undoubtedly have possessed.[13] Next, we must acquire a proper knowledge of the subjects on which we propose to speak, and must therefore be possessed of *ratio*, the power to reason and comprehend aright. Cicero declares in his account of the origins of cities that reason must therefore be of even greater significance than wisdom, since it can only have been through the highest reasoning faculties that founding fathers were able to counsel their fellow-citizens and legislate wisely on their behalf.[14]

Cicero's further and contrasting argument is that civil science can never be a matter of wisdom and reason alone. If we wish to discharge the highest duties of citizenship – pleading successfully for justice in the lawcourts and beneficial policies in the assemblies[15] – it will never

---

[11] See Cicero 1949, I. II. 2, pp. 4–6 on the need for men as the *materia* of cities to congregate *in unum locum* and act together in a manner at once *utilis* and *honestus* if they are to realise their highest *opportunitas*.

[12] See Cicero 1949, I. II. 2, pp. 4–6 on how some *magnus vir* must have *compulit* this *materia*.

[13] Cicero 1949, I. II. 2, p. 4.

[14] Cicero 1949, I. II. 2, pp. 4–6. Cf. Cicero 1942, I. XXXVI. 165, vol. 1, pp. 112–14.

[15] On these activities as the highest duties of citizenship and at the same time as the characteristic abilities of the orator see Skinner 1996, pp. 66–87.

be sufficient to reason wisely about the issues involved. It will always be necessary to move or impel our hearers to accept our arguments. This in turn means that, besides being a wise man capable of reasoning aright, the good citizen must be a man of the highest eloquence, capable of arousing his listeners and persuading them by the sheer force of 'winning' speech to acknowledge the truths that reason brings to light.

The ideal citizen is accordingly seen as the possessor of two pre-eminent qualities: reason to find out the truth and eloquence to make his hearers accept it.[16] This is the essence of the civic ideal and the conception of civil science put forward at the start of *De Inventione*. As we saw in volume 2 chaper 10, Cicero concedes that 'eloquence in the absence of wisdom is frequently very disadvantageous and never of the least advantage to civil communities'.[17] But he insists that, since 'wisdom in itself is silent and powerless to speak', wisdom in the absence of eloquence is of even less use.[18] What is needed 'if a commonwealth is to receive the greatest possible benefit' is *ratio atque oratio*, powerful reasoning allied with powerful speech.[19] We can thus be sure that 'cities were originally established not merely by the reason of the mind but also, and more readily, by means of eloquence'.[20]

As a result, Cicero goes on, 'a large and crucial part' of *scientia civilis* must be occupied by the art of eloquence, and especially by 'that form of artistic eloquence which is generally known as rhetoric, the function of which is that of speaking in a manner calculated to persuade, and the goal of which is that of persuading by speech'.[21] Cicero's further contention, in short, is that rhetoric is the key to eloquence. If we are to plead or deliberate effectively, we must learn the techniques of the *Ars rhetorica*, above all the technique of 'ornamenting' or 'adorning' the truth in such a way as to arouse our listeners to accept it. As Crassus puts it in Book 3 of *De Oratore*, 'the greatest praise for eloquence is reserved

---

[16] On the Ciceronian ideal of a union between reason and eloquence, and the revival of this ideal in the Renaissance, see Seigel 1968.

[17] Cicero 1949, I. I. 1, p. 2: 'civitatibus eloquentiam vero sine sapientia nimium obesse plerumque, prodesse nunquam'.

[18] Cicero 1949, I. I. 1 and I. II. 3, pp. 2 and 6: *sapientia* is *tacita*, so that 'sapientiam sine eloquentia parum prodesse civitatibus'.

[19] See Cicero 1949, I. II. 3, p. 6 on *ratio atque oratio* and cf. I. IV. 5, p. 12 on how, if *eloquentia* is added to *sapientia*, 'ad rem publicam plurima commoda veniunt'.

[20] Cicero 1949, I. I. 1, p. 2: 'urbes constitutas . . . cum animi ratione tum facilius eloquentia'.

[21] See Cicero 1949, I. V. 6, p. 14: on *civilis scientia* and the fact that 'Eius quaedam magna et ampla pars est artificiosa eloquentia quam rhetoricam vocant', and that 'Officium autem eius facultatis videtur esse dicere apposite ad persuasionem finis persuadere dictione.'

for the amplification of argument by means of *ornatus*'.[22] The addition
of such 'adornment' provides the best means 'either of conciliating the
minds of our hearers or else of exciting them'.[23] And the capacity to
arouse the emotions in this way is what enables us to win our hearers
over to the cause of justice and truth.

Why are Cicero and Quintilian so insistent that, in the absence of these
rhetorical arts, even the wisest reasoning can never hope to carry us to
victory in the lawcourts and assemblies? They regard the answer as particularly obvious in the case of 'deliberative' oratory. The aim of writing
or speaking in the deliberative mode[24] is to counsel or advise the adoption
of a certain policy, a policy at once honourable and advantageous to the
commonwealth. The speaker's aim is to reason in such a way as to
persuade his fellow-citizens to follow one course of action rather than
another. But Cicero and Quintilian both adopt what philosophers nowadays like to call the 'Humean' view that, even if I succeed in presenting
you with good reasons for acting in some particular way, I can never hope
by force of reason alone to motivate you so to act. Cicero gives powerful
expression to this dilemma at the start of *De Inventione* when praising the
founding fathers of cities. The wisdom of these visionary figures enabled
them to perceive 'that there was an opportunity for men to achieve the
greatest things'[25] if only they would abandon their lawless reliance on
natural ferocity in favour of learning 'to keep faith, to recognise the need
to uphold justice and be ready to submit their wills to others'.[26] As he
adds, however, it is impossible to believe that such legislators could ever
have induced uncivilised multitudes to change their settled habits simply
by reason and argument. We can be sure that 'at first they cried out
against such unfamiliar plans', even though it was undoubtedly in their
interests to accept them.[27]

This reminds us why counsellors and lawgivers must be masters of
the rhetorical arts. They need to call on something more powerful than
'mute and voiceless wisdom' if they are to alter our behaviour;[28] they

---

[22] Cicero 1942, III. XXVI. 104, vol. 2, p. 82: 'Summa autem laus eloquentiae est amplificare rem
ornando.'

[23] Cicero 1942, III. XXVII. 104, vol. 2, p. 82: 'vel cum conciliamus animos vel cum concitamus'.

[24] For an account of the *genus deliberativum* see Skinner 1996, pp. 41–4, 93–5, 114–15 and references
there.

[25] See Cicero 1949, I. II. 2, pp. 4–6 on the 'magnus videlicet vir et sapiens' who recognised 'quanta
ad maximas res opportunitas in animis inesset hominum'.

[26] Cicero 1949, I. II. 3, p. 6: 'fidem colere et iustitiam retinere discernunt et aliis parere sua voluntate
consuescerent'.

[27] Cicero 1949, I. II. 2, p. 6: 'primo propter insolentiam reclamantes'.

[28] See Cicero 1949, I. II. 3, p. 6 on *sapientia* as *tacita* and *inops dicendi*.

need to supply us in addition with a desire to act rationally. But the only means of empowering wisdom in this way is to lend it the force of eloquence. 'Eloquence', as Cicero repeats, 'is essential if men are to persuade others to accept the truths that reason finds out.'[29] This is why 'I find that many cities have been founded, and even more wars have been ended, while the firmest alliances and the most sacred friendships have been established not simply by rational argument but also, and more readily, by means of eloquence'.[30]

The rhetoricians add that it is not merely when speaking in the deliberative mode that orators will find it necessary to deploy the rhetorical arts. They will encounter the same necessity even when their sole concern, as in forensic oratory, is to persuade their hearers to accept the justice of some particular verdict.[31] This is because the force of reason is not merely insufficient to motivate action; it is also insufficient in a large number of cases to induce belief. We can readily see why this is so, the rhetoricians explain, as soon as we reflect on the subject matter of forensic and deliberative speech. An orator performing in the lawcourts will be engaged in prosecuting or defending in circumstances in which it will often be possible for a skilful adversary to mount a no less plausible argument on the other side. An orator advising an assembly will similarly be attempting to show that some particular course of action ought to be followed in circumstances in which it will often be no less reasonable to propose a contradictory policy. In such situations there will be no possibility of demonstrating beyond question that one side is in the right. As Quintilian puts it, these are the sorts of cases 'in which two wise men may with just cause take up one or another point of view, since it is generally agreed that it is possible for reason to lead even the wise to fight among themselves'.[32] These are instances, in other words, in which 'the weapons of powerful speech can always be used *in utramque partem*, on either side of the case'.[33] By the time Cicero came to write his *De Oratore*, he was ready to insist that the subject matter of oratory makes the capacity to speak *in utramque partem* the most important skill of all. The figure of Crassus summarises in Book 3 by proclaiming that 'we ought to have

[29] See Cicero 1949, I. II. 3, p. 6 on the need for 'homines ea quae ratione invenissent eloquentia persuadere'.

[30] Cicero 1949, I. I. 1, p. 2: 'multas urbes constitutas, plurima bella restincta, firmissimas societates, sanctissimas amicitias intelligo cum animi ratione tum facilius eloquentia comparatas'.

[31] For an account of the *genus iudiciale* see Skinner 1996, pp. 41–5, 95–7, 116–17 and refs. there.

[32] Quintilian 1920–2, II. XVII. 32, vol. 1, p. 338: 'duos sapientes aliquando iustae causae in diversum trahant (quando etiam pugnaturos eos inter se, si ratio ita duxerit, credunt)'.

[33] Quintilian 1920–2, II. XVI. 10, vol. 1, p. 322: 'in utramque partem valet arma facundiae'.

enough intelligence, power and art to speak on either side of the case' on all the leading commonplaces: 'on virtue, duty, equity, goodness, dignity, benefit, honour, ignominy, reward, punishment and all the rest'.[34]

Once again, the moral is said to be that it will never be sufficient to reason wisely in order to win over an audience. Given that we can always hope to speak with plausibility *in utramque partem*, it will always be necessary in addition to have mastered the art of rhetoric, and thus to have learned how to deploy its techniques of adornment to allure or impel our audience round to our side. It is true that these considerations are not thought to apply in the natural as opposed to the moral sciences. As the figure of Scaevola concedes at the start of *De Oratore*, 'we can pass over the mathematicians, the grammarians and the followers of the muses, with whose arts this capacity for powerful speaking has no connection at all'.[35] But Scaevola's main contention is that, in cases where we cannot look for certainty – as in most of the arguments characteristic of civic life – the need for eloquence becomes paramount, and with it a need for a mastery of the rhetorical arts. You cannot do without these skills 'if you want the case you are pleading in the courts to seem the better and more plausible one, or if you want the speeches you deliver in the assemblies to have the greatest persuasive force, or if you merely want your utterances to appear truthful to the uninstructed and skilful to the wise'.[36] If, in short, your arguments fall in any way within the purview of civil science, you will always find it necessary to supplement your reasoning with the moving force of eloquence.

II

When Hobbes reissued his *De Cive* in an expanded version in 1647, he inserted a new Preface outlining his philosophical method and summarising what he believed himself to have achieved.[37] He begins by stressing that, like the sages of antiquity, he is primarily concerned with the concept of civil science,[38] and he names Cicero among 'the philosophers

---

[34] Cicero 1942, III. XXVII. 107, vol. 2, pp. 84–6: 'de virtute, de officio, de aequo et bono, de dignitate, utilitate, honore, ignominia, praemio, poena similibusque de rebus in utramque partem dicendi animos et vim et artem habere debemus'.

[35] Cicero 1942, I. X. 44, vol. 1, p. 32: 'Missos facio mathematicos, grammaticos, musicos, quorum artibus vestra ista dicendi vis ne minima quidem societate contingitur.'

[36] Cicero 1942, I. X. 44, vol. 1, pp. 32–4: 'ut in iudiciis ea causa, quamcumque tu dicis, melior et probabilior esse videatur; ut in concionibus et sententiis dicendis ad persuadendum tua plurimum valeat oratio; denique ut prudentibus diserte stultis etiam vere dicere videaris'.

[37] Warrender 1983a, pp. 8–13; cf. Hobbes 1983a, pp. 77–84.

[38] Hobbes 1983a, p. 77.

of Greece and Rome' who took pride in the contributions they made to 'what is unquestionably the most valuable of all the sciences'.[39] He follows their account of its subject matter, arguing as Cicero had done that civil science is chiefly concerned with the doctrine of public duties or *officia*,[40] and can therefore be described (in Cicero's own words) as a science of justice.[41] He also endorses the classical view that such a science must be purposive in character.[42] He marks a sharp distinction, that is, between civil and natural science, although he allows that both are capable of amounting to genuine sciences. The aim of natural science is to understand the behaviour of physical bodies, and in this case we need to adopt a purely mechanistic approach. But the aim of civil science is to understand the behaviour of one particular type of artificial body, the body of the commonwealth. The peculiarity of such bodies stems from the fact that men are at once their artificers and their material.[43] And this means, for Hobbes no less than for Cicero, that we cannot avoid asking about the purposes for which they are brought into existence.[44]

When Hobbes turns to ask about these purposes, he again voices his agreement with the classical point of view. Cities are founded primarily 'in order to preserve life', and more specifically to enable us, by reasoning firmly about our common concerns, to follow 'the royal road to peace'.[45] This is why we are justified in singling out the exceptional utility of civil science. 'For nothing could be more useful than to find out how this can be done.'[46] Finally, Hobbes reiterates the classical belief that what a student of civil science needs above all to comprehend is the nature and range of the qualities that enable men, the material of cities, to mould themselves successfully into those particular shapes.[47] We need 'rightly to understand the character of human nature, what makes men either

---

[39] See Hobbes 1983a, p. 77 on 'Cicero, caeterique Philosophi Graeci, Latini' and cf. pp. 77–8 on *scientia civilis* and on this form of *scientia* as 'dignissima certe scientiarum'.

[40] See Hobbes 1983a, pp. 77–8 on *scientia civilis* as a *doctrina officiorum*. Cf. the title of Cicero's major treatise on moral philosophy, *De Officiis*.

[41] See Hobbes 1983a, pp. 77–8 on *scientia civilis* as a *scientia iustitiae*.

[42] This aspect of Hobbes's argument has largely been overlooked by recent commentators, who have generally assumed that for Hobbes all sciences must take the same anti-teleological form. For a valuable corrective see Malcolm 1990, pp. 145–57. I am tempted to go even further than Malcolm and add that Hobbes's Baconian conception of *scientia propter potentiam* gives a purposive orientation to his view of the natural sciences as well.

[43] On men as the *materia* of cities see Hobbes 1983a, p. 79, para. 9. See too the title of the Latin *Leviathan* (Hobbes 1841a) with its allusion to men as the *materia* of *civitates*.

[44] Hobbes 1983a, pp. 79–80; cf. Malcolm 1990, esp. pp. 147, 149, 151–2.

[45] See Hobbes 1983a, pp. 78–9 on *civitates* being founded *vivendi causa* (para. 4) and in order to enable us, by means of right reasoning, to follow the *via regia pacis*.

[46] Hobbes 1983a, p. 79: 'qua re utilius nihil excogitari potest'.

[47] On the *materia* and *forma* of cities see Hobbes 1983a, p. 79.

fit or unfit to bind themselves together into a commonwealth, and how far men need to agree among themselves if they wish to form such a unity'.[48]

There is a sense in which Hobbes continues to uphold these classical allegiances when he turns to enquire into the nature of the qualities required. He fully agrees that, as Cicero had put it at the start of *De Inventione*, among the attributes we must possess if we are to succeed in bringing people together in civic unity are wisdom and the powers of reasoning to which it gives rise.[49] Beyond this point, however, Hobbes suddenly parts company with, and turns violently against, the presuppositions of classical and humanist civil science. The rest of his analysis, not merely in *De Cive* but in his earlier *Elements of Law*, takes the form of a frontal assault on the further assumptions about the character of *scientia civilis* put forward by the most revered humanist authorities.

The attack is launched at the outset of *The Elements of Law*,[50] the manuscript of which Hobbes completed and circulated in May 1640.[51] As we have seen, one of the two governing assumptions of humanist civil science had been that reason possesses no inherent power to persuade. Hobbes's superbly confident Epistle Dedicatory responds with the lie direct. His own ambition, he retorts, is to construct a science of justice and policy on the basis of right reason alone: 'to reduce this doctrine to the rules and infallibility of Reason'.[52] The possibility of creating such a science arises from the fact that there are 'two principall parts of our Nature'.[53] One is admittedly passion; but the other is reason, 'which', as he later adds in discussing the laws of nature, 'is noe lesse of the nature of man than passion, and is the same in all men', since 'God Almighty hath given reason to a man, to be a light unto him'.[54] This being so, there need be no barrier in principle to our employing our reason to lay the foundations for a science of civil life which, 'Passion not mistrusting, may not seek to displace'.[55] As a result, we can hope to produce a form of learning, even in matters of justice and policy, that will finally be 'free from controversies and dispute'.[56]

---

[48] Hobbes 1983a, pp. 79–80: 'qualis sit natura humana, quibus rebus ad civitatem compaginandam apta vel inepta sit, & quomodo homines inter se componi debeant, qui coalescere volunt, recte intelligatur'.

[49] See Hobbes 1983a, p. 81 on the indispensability of following the dictates of *ratio*.

[50] For an excellent analysis, concentrating on this aspect of *The Elements*, see Johnston 1986, pp. 26–65, an account to which I am much indebted.

[51] Hobbes 1969a, p. xvi is signed 'May ye. 9th 1640'.

[52] Hobbes 1969a, p. xv.   [53] Hobbes 1969a, p. xv.   [54] Hobbes 1969a, pp. 75, 99.

[55] Hobbes 1969a, p. xv.   [56] Hobbes 1969a, p. xv.

Hobbes presses home his attack in the body of *The Elements*. Against the view that reason is impotent in the absence of powerful speaking, he insists in chapter 17 that reason is capable of dictating conclusions, of obliging us to follow particular arguments.[57] To this he adds in the opening chapter of part 2 that 'reason teacheth us' about such matters as the value of government.[58] But he has already explained in chapter 13 that to teach is to beget in the minds of others a conception which they will have no inclination to dispute.[59] What he is again affirming is that reason is capable of producing conclusions beyond controversy or doubt. He insists, moreover, that these 'dictates' of reason are such that even those of the meanest capacity can hope to follow them without difficulty.[60] He accordingly repudiates with considerable asperity the rhetorical assumption that we must always make a special effort, as Quintilian had advised, to win the attention and benevolence of our audience.[61] Reversing the usual argument, Hobbes declares that 'if reasoning aright I winne not Consent (which may very easily happen) from them that being confident of their owne Knowledge weigh not what is said, the fault is not mine but theirs'. This is because 'as it is my part to show my reasons, so it is theirs to bring attention'.[62]

Hobbes is no less vehemently opposed to the other governing assumption of humanist civil science, the assumption that no moral or political conclusion can ever be established with demonstrative certainty, since there will always be room to mount a plausible argument on either side of the case. To these contentions he responds even more polemically. The polemics in this case begin with his title, *The Elements of Law*. This is surely intended to recall *The Elements of Geometry*, the title given to Euclid's great treatise by Sir Henry Billingsley when he published the first English translation in 1571.[63] Hobbes's initial move is thus to associate his own treatise in the minds of his readers with one of the most celebrated works of deductive and demonstrative reasoning ever written.

The Epistle Dedicatory to *The Elements* continues in no less polemical vein. Hobbes is explicit in claiming that he has discovered the principles of a fully demonstrative science 'of Justice & Policy', and that he will be able to explain for the first time 'the true and only foundation of such Science'. He concedes that anyone writing about these matters will be dealing with issues in which he 'compareth Men, & medleth with

[57] Hobbes 1969a, pp. 89, 92.   [58] Hobbes 1969a, p. 116.
[59] Hobbes 1969a, p. 64.   [60] Hobbes 1969a, pp. 22, 66.
[61] Quintilian 1920–2, VI. II. 13–19, vol. 2, pp. 422–6.
[62] Hobbes 1969a, pp. 1–2.   [63] See Euclid 1571.

their Right & Profitt'. But there is no reason to leave the study of civil science in its present state, in which 'they that have written of Justice & Policy in generall do all invade each other, & themselves, with contradiction'. We can hope to proceed in a genuinely scientific manner, thereby arriving at conclusions that are 'not slightly proved'. We can hope in consequence, simply by force of scientific reasoning, to build up a set of political principles that, as Hobbes revealingly puts it, will be 'inexpugnable' – incapable of being challenged or dislodged by an opposing force in the manner usually assumed to be inevitable.[64]

This second line of attack is likewise kept up in the body of the text. Hobbes's opening chapter begins by reaffirming that, when we are told that 'true knowledge' is impossible to acquire in matters of justice and policy, this merely reveals 'that they which have heretofore written thereof have not well understood their owne subject'.[65] The fact is that we can lay down 'necessary and demonstrable rules' about how to produce good and peaceful government.[66] We can hope in consequence to construct 'that Science in particular from which proceed the true and evident conclusions of what is right and wronge, and what is good and hurtfull to the being and welbeing of mankinde'.[67] We are not condemned to follow those who have merely 'insinuated their opinions, by eloquent Sophistry'; we can hope to write 'concerning morallity and policy demonstratively'.[68] Unlike the rhetoricians, whose art depends on insinuations and emotional appeals, we can hope to ground our arguments on principles of truth.

If we turn from _The Elements_ to _De Cive_, first published two years later, we encounter a yet more confident effort to challenge and supersede the presuppositions of humanist civil science. Hobbes is even more emphatic that the methods of right reason carry with them an inherent power to persuade and convince, and thus that the idea of an alliance between reason and rhetoric is an irrelevance. He first assures us in his Epistle Dedicatory – in a direct allusion to the rival rhetorical doctrine – that he aims to persuade his readers 'not by any outward display of _oratio_ but rather by the firmness of _rationes_'.[69] He speaks at several subsequent points about the 'dictates' of right reason and its power to order, command and enforce particular conclusions upon us.[70] And in examining the duties

---

[64] Hobbes 1969a, pp. xv–xvi.   [65] Hobbes 1969a, p. 1.   [66] Hobbes 1969a, p. 171.
[67] Hobbes 1969a, p. 176.   [68] Hobbes 1969a, p. 183.
[69] Hobbes 1983a, p. 76: 'neque specie orationis, sed firmitudine rationum'.
[70] See Hobbes 1983a, II. II, p. 100 and XV. IV, p. 221 on 'dictamina rectae rationis'; III. XIX, p. 115 on how 'ratio iubet'; III. XXVII, p. 118 and XV. XIV, p. 227 on how 'ratio dictat'; XV. XV, p. 229 on how 'ratio imperat'.

of sovereigns in chapter 13 he adds that 'the opinions they need to insert into the minds of men' can and ought to be inserted 'not by commanding but by teaching, not by fear of penalties but by perspicuity of reasons'.[71] The implication is unmistakable: if reason is sufficient to insert opinions into the minds of men, there is no place for the techniques of persuasion associated with the art of eloquence.

Hobbes likewise reiterates his earlier denunciation of the connected belief that, in matters of civil science, we can only hope to discuss the issues in a 'probable' way, since it will always be possible to mount a plausible case *in utramque partem*. The Epistle Dedicatory to *De Cive* begins by identifying, as the position to be overcome, the view that in discussions about justice an effective argument 'can always be sustained on either side of the case'.[72] Hobbes mentions that orators habitually 'fight with contrary opinions and speeches',[73] and alludes to the view that in politics (as Quintilian had conceded) we can only reach conclusions 'worthy of being debated'.[74] He retorts that, so long as we follow the methods of science, we can argue 'in such a way that no space is left for contrary disputes'.[75] We can reach conclusions capable not merely of being defended as probable but of being systematically proved.[76] And this, he claims, is what he has achieved. By contrast with all previous writers on civil science, 'I have followed a proper principle of teaching', as a result of which 'it seems to me that I have succeeded in this brief work in demonstrating the character of moral virtue and the elements of civic duties by connecting them in a completely self-evident way'.[77]

Soon afterwards Hobbes underlined this categorical distinction between the methods of rhetoric and of science in his *Critique* of Thomas White's *De Mundo*, the manuscript of which he drafted in the winter of 1642 and spring of 1643.[78] White, like Hobbes, wished to distinguish between two kinds of philosopher. On the one hand, White asserted, 'there are those who truly philosophise, that is, proceed by a certain

---

[71] Hobbes 1983a, XIII. IX, p. 198: 'opiniones non imperando, sed docendo, non terrore poenarum, sed perspicuitate rationum animis hominum inseruntur'.

[72] See Hobbes 1983a, *Epistola Dedicatoria*, p. 75 on the claim that such an argument can always be 'utraque pars . . . tueatur'.

[73] Hobbes 1983a, X. XII, p. 178: 'contrariis sententiis orationibusque pugnant'.

[74] See Hobbes 1983a, XII. X, p. 191, speaking of topics 'ad disserendum'.

[75] See Hobbes 1983a, II. I, p. 98 on the methods 'qui locum contra disputandi non relinquunt'.

[76] Hobbes is very emphatic that his conclusions in *De Cive* are not merely probable but demonstrated. See for example Hobbes 1983a, VII. IV, p. 152 and XV. I, p. 219.

[77] Hobbes 1983a, *Epistola Dedicatoria*, pp. 75–6: 'commodo usus sit docendi principio . . . inde virtutis moralis officiorumque civilium Elementa, in hac opella, evidentissima connexione videor mihi demonstrasse'.

[78] For this manuscript and its date of composition see Jacquot and Jones 1973, pp. 12–13, 43–5.

way and the fixed route of demonstration'.[79] On the other hand, 'there are those who merely make a show of philosophy, but in fact confine themselves to logic, that is, exercise the faculty of debating *in utrumque* when dealing with philosophical material'.[80] Hobbes in reply pounces on what he takes to be White's confusion between logic and rhetoric. 'The fact is', Hobbes retorts, 'that "the capacity to proceed by a certain way and the fixed route of demonstration" belongs entirely to logic; by contrast, the ability to debate *in utramque partem* arises out of the discipline of rhetoric.'[81] Having reaffirmed this distinction, Hobbes takes the opportunity to insist once more that the methods of rhetoric must be avoided. 'Certainly', he concludes, 'everything I have said seems to me to have been demonstrated.'[82]

Hobbes summarises his comprehensively anti-rhetorical stance in a passage of magnificent effrontery in chapter 12 of *De Cive* when discussing the dissolution of commonwealths. He returns to the idea that wisdom can be acquired simply 'by contemplating things as they are in themselves', and 'by gaining an understanding of words in their true and proper definitions' thereby ensuring that our statements of belief are founded on principles of truth.[83] If we follow this route, we shall be able to produce 'an expression of any propositions or conceptions in our mind which is at once perspicuous and elegant'.[84] As a consequence, we shall be able to express ourselves not merely with wisdom but with true eloquence.[85] This ability to speak with eloquence, and thereby offer an explication of our beliefs at once elegant and perspicuous, was of course exactly what the theorists of rhetoric had always promised those capable of mastering the techniques of *inventio*, *dispositio* and *elocutio*. But Hobbes insists that the key to elegance and perspicuity lies not in studying the art of rhetoric but in following the methods of science. With this contention

---

[79] BN, Fonds Latin MS 6566A, fo. 451ʳ (cf. Hobbes 1973, ch. 39, para. 7, p. 432): 'eos *qui vere philosophantur*, id est, *eos qui certa via et fixo demonstrationis tramite incedunt*'.

[80] BN, Fonds Latin MS 6566A, fo. 451ᵛ (cf. Hobbes 1973, ch. 39, para. 7, p. 432): 'eos *qui philosophiam prae se ferunt sed vere tantummodo logicam, hoc est in utrumque disserendi facultatem in materia philosophica exercent*'.

[81] BN, Fonds Latin MS 6566A, fo. 451ᵛ (cf. Hobbes 1973, ch. 39, para. 7, p. 432): 'Nam *"incedere via certa & fixo demonstrationis tramite"*, id solius logicae est; disserere autem in utramque partem posse, id a rhetoricae disciplina oritur.'

[82] BN, Fonds Latin MS 6566A, fo. 452ʳ (cf. Hobbes 1973, ch. 39, para. 7, p. 433): 'Certe ego, etsi omnia quae dixerim viderentur mihi demonstrata esse.'

[83] See Hobbes 1983a, XII. XII, p. 192 for the claim that *sapientia* 'oriturque partim a rerum ipsarum contemplatione, partim a verborum in propria & definita significatione acceptorum intelligentia'.

[84] Hobbes 1983a, XII. XII, p. 192: 'sententiae & conceptuum animi perspicua & elegans'.

[85] Hobbes 1983a, XII. XII, p. 192.

he completely turns the tables on the rhetoricians and their assumptions about the need to adorn the truth. He willingly accepts their central contention that eloquence is indispensable to civil science. But he maintains that genuine eloquence arises from 'the Art of logic, not the Art of rhetoric'.[86] When we acknowledge the indispensability of eloquence, we are merely saying that it is necessary to reason logically; we are not in the least saying that it is necessary to call on the artificial aids associated with 'that form of powerful eloquence which is separated from a true knowledge of things'.[87]

A number of recent commentators have interpreted Hobbes's drive towards demonstrative certainty in the moral sciences as a response to the growing popularity of Pyrrhonian scepticism and associated arguments of a supposedly relativist kind.[88] I have been arguing, by contrast, that his project is best understood as a reaction not to scepticism as an epistemological doctrine but to the modes of argument characteristic of the rhetorical culture of humanism. Hobbes is seeking to replace the dialogical and anti-demonstrative approach to moral reasoning encouraged by the humanist assumption that there are two sides to any question, and thus that in civil science it will always be possible to argue on either side of the case. He is chiefly reacting, in short, against what the English version of *De Cive* calls the 'rhetorication' of moral philosophy.[89] One of his fundamental purposes is to transcend and supersede the entire rhetorical structure on the basis of which the humanist conception of civil science had been raised. To understand his own vision of civil science as he first articulated it, we need to see it as framed in large part as an alternative to prevailing humanist orthodoxies, and as an attempt to replace them with a theory of politics based on authentically scientific premises.

III

After the publication of *De Cive* in 1642 Hobbes resumed his interrupted researches in the natural sciences. As we have seen, the first significant

---

[86] See Hobbes 1983a, XII. XII, p. 193 on true *Eloquentia* as a product of mastering the *Ars logica*, not the *Ars rhetorica*.

[87] Hobbes 1983a, XII. XII, p. 193: '*eloquentia potens*, separata a rerum scientia'.

[88] For suggestions about the influence of epistemological scepticism on the development of Hobbes's thought see Pacchi 1965, pp. 63–9, 97–100, 179–83; and Battista 1966, pp. 22, 53, 135, 145, 172–5. The argument has been much taken up by more recent commentators. See Battista 1980; Missner 1983; Sarasohn 1985; Kahn 1985, pp. 154, 181; Tuck 1989, pp. 64, 93, 102; Hampsher-Monk 1992, pp. 4–6; Hanson 1993, 644–5; Flathman 1993, pp. 2–3, 43–7, 51–2. But for an excellent corrective see Sorell 1993.

[89] Hobbes 1983b, p. 26.

piece of writing to which this gave rise was his examination of White's *De Mundo*, the massive manuscript treatise he finished in the spring of 1643. Thereafter he settled down to complete his *De Corpore*, the first of three projected volumes into which he had decided to divide his general system of philosophy. He continued to labour on this text throughout most of the 1640s,[90] returning to his work on civil science only after the constitutional crisis in England reached its resolution with the execution of Charles I and the abolition of the monarchy in 1649. Spurred into action by the new and intractable problems raised by the establishment of the Commonwealth, Hobbes stopped work on *De Corpore* and, in less than eighteen months, completed what he described in a letter to his friend Robert Payne in 1650 as a new 'trifle', his theme being 'Politique in English'.[91] Within a year Payne was able to report that Hobbes's trifle had arrived in the bookshops of Oxford and that 'he calls it *Leviathan*'.[92]

It is commonly said that the political theory of *Leviathan* is 'substantially the same' or 'almost exactly the same' as in *The Elements of Law* and *De Cive*, the changes between the earlier and later texts being 'relatively minor' and 'of secondary importance'.[93] This seems an orthodoxy well worth challenging.[94] If we focus on Hobbes's account in *Leviathan* of the concept of civil science itself, what we find is not a new version of his earlier theory but a new and contrasting theory, evidently motivated by a desire to reappropriate much of what he had earlier cast aside. *The Elements* and *De Cive* had been based on the conviction that civil science must transcend and repudiate the purely persuasive techniques associated with the art of rhetoric and the 'adornment' of truth. By contrast, *Leviathan* reverts to the humanist assumption that, if the truths of reason are to be widely believed, the methods of science will need to be supplemented and empowered by the moving force of eloquence.

As I stressed in chapter 1, it would be a mistake to infer that *Leviathan* should be accounted a work of rhetoric as opposed to a work of science. While it reflects a remarkable change of mind on Hobbes's part about

---

[90] He paused only in 1646 to make some revisions and additions to *De Cive*, the second edition of which appeared in 1647.

[91] 'Illustrations' 1848, p. 172. Cf. Greenslade 1975, p. 310.

[92] 'Illustrations' 1848, p. 223.

[93] For these claims see respectively Tuck 1989, p. 28; Raphael 1977, p. 13; Rogow 1986, p. 126; Warrender 1957, p. viii. For similar suggestions see Hampton 1986, p. 5; Baumgold 1988, pp. 3, 11.

[94] It has already been challenged in Johnston 1986 and Sorell 1986, two important books to which I am much indebted. I must also emphasise my debt to several valuable articles on contiguous themes, especially Whelan 1981, Barnouw 1988, Condren 1990 and Rayner 1991.

the proper relations between reason and rhetoric, it also embodies a continuing conviction that civil philosophy can and ought to aspire to demonstrative certainty. In chapter 5 of *Leviathan* Hobbes reaffirms that what it means to master 'the Science of any thing' is to possess the capacity to 'demonstrate the truth thereof perspicuously to another'.[95] In chapter 15 he applies his general argument to the case of civil science, repeating that moral and civil philosophy must take the form of 'the Science of what is *Good*, and *Evill*, in the conversation, and Society of mankind'.[96] He brings Book 2 to a resounding close by declaring that he has in fact 'put into order, and sufficiently or probably proved all the Theoremes of Morall doctrine', and has thereby articulated the principles of 'the Science of Naturall justice'.[97]

What Hobbes undoubtedly abandons in his later work, however, is his previous confidence in the unaided powers of demonstrative reasoning to alter people's beliefs and behaviour.[98] The first published hint of this new scepticism occurs in one of the Annotations to the 1647 edition of *De Cive*.[99] Describing what we can hope to discover by the light of reason alone, Hobbes now lays a sombre emphasis on the fact that most people 'are either not accustomed to, or else not capable of, or else not interested in arguing properly'.[100] He subsequently enlarges on this insight in analysing the concept of reason in chapter 5 of *Leviathan*. First he observes that even those who understand how to argue properly are highly fallible and prone to self-deceit:

And as in Arithmetique unpractised men must and Professors themselves may often erre and cast up false; so also in any other subject of Reasoning the ablest, most attentive and most practised men may deceive themselves and inferre false conclusions; Not but that Reason it selfe is alwayes Right Reason, as well as Arithmetique is a certain and infallible Art: But no one mans Reason, nor the Reason of any one number of men makes the certaintie; no more than an account is therefore well cast up because a great many men have unanimously approved it.[101]

---

[95] Hobbes 1996, ch. 5, p. 37; cf. Hobbes 1841a, p. 39: 'perspicue demonstrare'.
[96] Hobbes 1996, ch. 15, p. 110.   [97] Hobbes 1996, ch. 31, p. 254.
[98] A point excellently made in Missner 1983, pp. 419–21. For analogous points see Whelan 1981, p. 71; Johnston 1986, pp. 98, 101–4; Condren 1990, pp. 703–5.
[99] But the seeds of Hobbes's later doubts can be traced to his account of the distinction between reason and right reason in chapter 30 of his *Critique* of Thomas White's *De Mundo*, where he concedes that 'it is to be doubted whether the reason of any one man can always be right, although everyone thinks their own reasoning alone is right'. See BN, Fonds Latin MS 6566A, fo. 348ᵛ (cf. Hobbes 1973, ch. 30, para. 22, p. 359): 'dubitatur an ullius hominis ratio recta semper esse possit, putantque singuli suam solam rectam esse'.
[100] Hobbes 1983a, XIV. XIX, Annotatio: 'qui recte ratiocinari non solent, vel non valent, vel non curant'.
[101] Hobbes 1996, ch. 5, p. 32.

To this he adds, even more despondently, that most people have no understanding of right reasoning at all. At this juncture he revives a complaint
not uncommon among scientific writers of the previous generation to
the effect that ordinary people are actually afraid of the sciences. John
Dee had lamented in his Preface to Billingsley's translation of Euclid that
anyone who devotes himself to mathematics is liable to be denounced
as a 'conjurer'.[102] Hobbes makes exactly the same point, declaring that
most people are so far from understanding science 'that they know not
what it is', the most obvious instance being that 'Geometry they have
thought Conjuring' – 'a magic art', as the Latin *Leviathan* adds.[103]

Hobbes also speaks in a new tone of frustration of what follows from
this devaluation of reason and science. The most obvious outcome is
that people fall 'vehemently in love with their own new opinions (though
never so absurd,)' and become 'obstinately bent to maintain them'.[104]
A further consequence, as he later observes in discussing miracles, is
that 'such is the ignorance and aptitude to error generally of all men,
but especially of them that have not much knowledge of naturall causes'
that they are susceptible of being deceived 'by innumerable and easie
tricks'.[105] Worst of all, as he adds in his critique of demonology, 'wee see
daily by experience in all sorts of People, that such men as study nothing
but their food and ease, are content to beleeve any absurdity, rather than
to trouble themselves to examine it'.[106]

Given this ever-deepening scepticism about the capacity of reason to
win assent, Hobbes found himself obliged in *Leviathan* to confront a new
set of questions about the nature of *scientia civilis*, a set of questions he had
earlier seen no reason to ask. If the findings of science possess no inherent
power to convince, how can we hope to empower them? How can we
hope to win attention and consent, especially from those whose passions
and ignorance lead them to repudiate even the clearest scientific proofs?

These were exactly the questions that the classical and Renaissance
theorists of eloquence had always addressed. As we have seen, Cicero in
particular had argued that, in the quest for wise and peaceable government, the faculty of unaided reason *parum prodesse* – can scarcely hope to
have much effect.[107] He had inferred that, if reason is to be of any use,

[102] Dee 1571, Sig. A, 1ᵛ.
[103] Hobbes 1996, ch. 5, p. 36; cf. Hobbes 1841a, pp. 37–8 on geometry as an 'ars magica'.
[104] Hobbes 1996, ch. 7, p. 48.   [105] Hobbes 1996, ch. 37, p. 304.
[106] Hobbes 1996, ch. 45, p. 454.
[107] See Cicero 1949, I. I. 1, p. 2 on *ratio* and how it 'sine eloquentia parum prodesse civitatibus'.

it will need to be empowered by the *vis* or moving force of eloquence, and thus by the rhetorical techniques of 'adorning' and 'amplifying' the truth.[108] Developing the same line of thought, Quintilian had underpinned Cicero's mechanistic imagery by arguing that, if the claims of justice and truth are to be vindicated, it will always be necessary to use the force of eloquence to pull or draw – *trahere* – our fellow-citizens towards accepting them.[109] He had thus been led to identify the ideal citizen with the perfect orator, the figure whose rhetorical prowess enables him to arouse and attract us to the truth by way of adorning it.[110]

Returning in *Leviathan* to the humanist roots from which he had cut himself off in *The Elements* and *De Cive*, Hobbes not only arrives at the same conclusions but expresses them in terms that echo with fascinating closeness these classical formulations of the case. He first hints at this new commitment in analysing the concept of power in chapter 10. 'The Sciences are small Power', he now concedes, but 'Eloquence is Power', and must indeed be numbered among the most eminent faculties of the human mind.[111] He develops the argument in chapter 25, in the course of which he introduces the play on words lying at the heart of the classical and Renaissance theory of rhetoric. The reason why eloquence is so powerful, he now explains, is that those who listen to eloquent speakers find themselves 'moved' to endorse their side of the argument.[112] The effect of eloquence can thus be described by saying – and here he actually invokes Quintilian's terminology – that it 'drawes' our hearers into accepting our point of view.[113]

A remarkable passage in the Conclusion to *Leviathan* points the moral for the proper conduct of civil science. Hobbes begins by associating the argument he now wishes to put forward with the two leading *genera* of rhetorical utterance: the *genus iudiciale*, here described as 'Pleadings', and the *genus deliberativum*, here described as 'Deliberations'.[114] He closely follows the language used by the rhetoricians in the accounts they had given of the skills required for speaking with success in either of these genres. As we have seen, they had begun by acknowledging that the possession of *ratio* is indispensable. As Hobbes now expresses their claim,

---

[108] Cicero 1949, I. I. 1, p. 2: 'urbes constitutas . . . cum animi ratione tum facilius eloquentia'.
[109] Quintilian 1920–2, V. XIV. 29, vol. 2, p. 364.
[110] Quintilian 1920–2, Proemium, 10, vol. 1, p. 10: 'vir ille vere civilis . . . non alius sit profecto quam orator'. See also Cicero 1942, I. VIII. 34, vol. 1, p. 26.
[111] Hobbes 1996, ch. 10, p. 62; cf. Hobbes 1996, ch. 9, p. 61.
[112] Hobbes 1996, ch. 25, p. 181.   [113] Hobbes 1996, ch. 25, p. 181.
[114] Hobbes 1996, Conclusion, p. 483.

'the faculty of solid Reasoning, is necessary: for without it, the resolutions of men are rash, and their sentences unjust'.[115] But the rhetoricians had added that, while *ratio* is necessary, it will never be sufficient to win round an audience. This is because, as Hobbes expresses their further claim, 'if there be not powerfull Eloquence, which procureth attention and Consent, the effect of Reason will be little'.[116] Here Hobbes echoes their language with particular closeness. When he remarks that, in the absence of eloquence 'the effect of reason will be little', he offers a virtual translation of Cicero's *ratio parum prodesse*. And when he infers that reason will need to be supplemented with 'powerfull eloquence', he similarly alludes to Cicero's image of the *vis* or power of eloquent speech.

Turning to reconsider this humanist understanding of civil science, Hobbes first observes that a number of writers have rejected it on the grounds of its apparent incoherence. The specific objection he mentions is exactly the one he had earlier voiced himself in *The Elements* and *De Cive*. As he now states it, the alleged difficulty is that, if we call on solid reasoning as well as powerful eloquence, we shall be founding our civil science on 'contrary Faculties'. This is because the faculty of reasoning is 'grounded upon principles of Truth', whereas the faculty of persuasion, and hence the art of eloquence, depends 'upon Opinions already received, true, or false; and upon the Passions and Interests of men, which are different and mutable'.[117]

As we have seen, Hobbes had initially drawn the conclusion that this does indeed render the humanist account incoherent, and that any civil science worthy of the name must therefore hold itself aloof from the art of rhetoric and the distorting influence of eloquence. Now, however, his ruminations on the *genus iudiciale* and *genus deliberativum* lead him in the opposite direction, and thus to a startling rapprochement with the rhetorical tradition he had earlier sought to discredit and supersede. The right response, he now declares, is to recognise that 'these are indeed great difficulties, but not Impossibilities: For by Education, and Discipline, they may bee, and are sometimes reconciled'.[118] The basis for this reconciliation, he goes on, lies in accepting the fundamental principle on which the classical rhetoricians had always insisted:

---

[115] Hobbes 1996, Conclusion, p. 483.
[116] Hobbes 1996, Conclusion, p. 483. For commentary on this passage see Shapiro 1980, p. 157; Whelan 1981, p. 71; Johnston 1986, pp. 130–2; Barnouw 1988, pp. 3–4; Cantalupo 1991, pp. 20–3, 241–9; Prokhovnik 1991, pp. 120–2.
[117] Hobbes 1996, Conclusion, p. 483.   [118] Hobbes 1996, Conclusion, p. 483.

Reason, and Eloquence, (though not perhaps in the Naturall Sciences, yet in the Morall) may stand very well together. For wheresoever there is place for adorning and preferring of Errour, there is much more place for adorning and preferring of Truth, if they have it to adorn.[119]

He now endorses, in short, the very conclusion he had earlier denied: that the technique of adding rhetorical 'adornment' to the truth can after all be made compatible with the methods of right reasoning, and can thus be employed to lend persuasive force to the findings of science.

Announcing this change of mind, Hobbes mirrors the language he had previously used to mount the opposite case. He had declared in *The Elements* that, so long as his readers 'bring attention', it ought to be sufficient for him 'to show my reasons' to win their assent.[120] He now acknowledges that the only way to win 'attention and consent' will be to write with powerful eloquence.[121] In *The Elements* he had concluded that, because rhetoricians 'derive what they would have to be believed from somewhat believed already' and in doing so 'must have Aide from the passions of the Hearer', the art of rhetoric must be outlawed from civil science.[122] In *Leviathan* he concludes that, although it is true that rhetoricians rely 'upon Opinions already received, true or false; and upon the Passions and Interests of men', a science of politics can never-theless be founded on an alliance between reason and these apparently contradictory faculties.[123]

Hobbes continues to allow that eloquence is 'not perhaps' suited to the natural sciences,[124] although even here his tone is so tentative as to imply that some rapprochement with the art of rhetoric may be possible. But his principal contention is that, in the moral if not in the natural sci-ences, the ornamentation of truth should be attempted wherever possible. Drawing this last and crucial inference in the Conclusion to *Leviathan*, Hobbes reverts once more to the language he had earlier used to mount the opposite case. He had argued in *The Elements* that the art of rhetoric is almost inherently treasonous, and had emphasised 'how want of wise-dome, and store of Eloquence, may stand together'.[125] Now he not only affirms that reason and eloquence 'may stand very well together', but adds the purely Ciceronian thought that, in the moral sciences, we should aim to adorn the truth 'wheresoever there is place' for such adornment.[126]

---

[119] Hobbes 1996, Conclusion, pp. 483–4.   [120] Hobbes 1969a, p. 2.
[121] Hobbes 1996, Conclusion, p. 483.   [122] Hobbes 1969a, p. 177.
[123] Hobbes 1996, Conclusion, p. 483.   [124] Hobbes 1996, Conclusion, p. 483.
[125] Hobbes 1969a, pp. 175–6.   [126] Hobbes 1996, Conclusion, p. 484.

None of this implies that Hobbes ever came to feel any positive admiration for the art of eloquence. On the contrary, it is clear from many observations in *Leviathan* that he largely retained his earlier anxieties about its irrational and potentially subversive character.[127] What he eventually felt obliged to acknowledge, however, was that the methods of science will need to be supplemented by the techniques of rhetoric if they are to have any beneficial effects. We cannot hope after all to outlaw the art of eloquence from the domain of civil science.

---

[127] See Hobbes 1996, ch. 17, pp. 119–20 on the dangers posed by rhetoric to civil peace. See also Hobbes 1996, ch. 19, p. 132 and ch. 25, p. 181 on the irrational impact of orators in public assemblies.

4

Hobbes on rhetoric and the construction of morality

I

Towards the end of *The Elements of Law*, which he completed in 1640, Hobbes launched the first of many assaults on the state of moral philosophy in his time. Those who talk about 'right and wronge, good and bad',[1] he complains, are largely content to adopt the opinions 'of such as they admire, as Aristotle, Cicero, Seneca, and others of like authority'. But these writers have failed to provide us with anything approaching a genuine understanding of virtue and vice. They have merely 'given the names of right and wrong as their passions have dictated; or have followed the autority of other men, as we doe theires'.[2]

One of Hobbes's principal aspirations is to overcome this kind of reliance on authority[3] and to formulate what he describes in *Leviathan* as 'the science of Vertue and Vice'.[4] In his later writings he insists with increasing confidence that he has in fact attained his goal. He declares in chapter 26 of *Leviathan* that his conclusions in that treatise 'concerning the Morall Vertues' are 'evident Truth'.[5] Five years later, we find him speaking with still greater assurance in *De Corpore* of the contrast between his own knowledge of moral theory and the mere opinions held by ancient philosophers on the same subject.[6] There were 'no philosophers natural or civil among the ancient Greeks', even though

---

This chapter is a revised version of an article that originally appeared under the title 'Thomas Hobbes: Rhetoric and the Construction of Morality' in the *Proceedings of the British Academy* 76 (1991), pp. 1–61.

[1] Hobbes 1969a, p. 177. Cf. BL Harl. MS 4235, fo. 132ᵛ, which shows that, in a moment of exasperation, Hobbes initially added 'everythinge' at this point but then crossed it out.

[2] Hobbes 1969a, p. 177.

[3] On Hobbes's wish to transcend such authority see Danford 1980.

[4] Hobbes 1996, ch. 15, p. 111.   [5] Hobbes 1996, ch. 26, p. 191.

[6] The Latin version first appeared in 1655, the English translation in 1656. See Macdonald and Hargreaves 1952, pp. 41–2. Cf. the complaints in Hobbes 1839e, p. 10 about 'the want of moral science'.

'there were men so called'. If we think of civil philosophy as a genuinely scientific subject, then it is 'no older . . . than my own book *De
Cive*'.[7]

It has been a valuable feature of recent scholarship on Hobbes and
his contemporaries to insist that, in advancing such claims about the
scientific standing and evident truth of their conclusions, they were
pitting themselves against a prevalent form of scepticism.[8] It is ar-
guable, however, that the nature of the sceptical challenge they took
themselves to be facing has been characterised in an oversimplified way.
It tends to be assumed that their basic concern was with the doubts
increasingly expressed about the status of the sciences following the rediscovery of Sextus Empiricus's manuscripts in the latter part of the
sixteenth century.[9] Sextus had not only outlined the familiar contentions
of academic scepticism, but also the more radical doubts associated
with Pyrrho and the school of Alexandria. The Pyrrhonians had suggested that, because conflicting evidence can always be assembled for
and against any proposition, it will always be rational to suspend belief.[10]
It was against this new threat to the idea of truth that the systematic philosophers of the scientific revolution are said to have pitted themselves.

There seems no doubt that the wish to counteract Pyrrhonism does
much to explain the epistemology of the period. As a number of scholars
have shown, it is against this background that we need to read the anti-
sceptical arguments of Descartes, as well as the 'mitigated scepticism'
associated with Gassendi and Mersenne.[11] To equate the challenge of
scepticism with that of Pyrrhonism, however, is to overlook a quite different range of sceptical arguments that proved at least as troublesome to
those whose principal ambition – as in the case of Hobbes – was to create
a science of morality. These further doubts arose not within the domain
of philosophy but rather within the neighbouring discipline of rhetoric,
the assumptions and procedures of which attained a new importance in
the latter part of the sixteenth century.

The earliest group of English vernacular treatises on the *Ars rhetorica*
appeared in the 1550s, by which time the study of rhetoric had already

---

[7] Hobbes 1839e, p. ix.
[8] For discussion of this claim, and a bibliography, see above, chapter 3, section II.
[9] See for example Curley 1978, pp. 12, 16; Popkin 1979, p. 214; Missner 1983, p. 408; Tuck 1989,
pp. 7, 14.
[10] For this characterisation of Pyrrhonism see Popkin 1979, pp. xiv–xvi and cf. Dear 1984, p. 192.
[11] On Descartes see Curley 1978 and Popkin 1979, pp. 172–92. On Gassendi and Mersenne see
James 1986–7. On Gassendi see also Bloch 1971, pp. 110–47 and on his 'modified scepticism'
Sarasohn 1982. On Mersenne see also Lenoble 1943, pp. 190–5 and 321–8 and Dear 1984.

established itself as an integral part of the linguistic training provided by the English grammar schools. As we saw in chapter 3, it was a training that could scarcely have been less hospitable to the idea of reducing moral philosophy to a science. Students of rhetoric were encouraged to argue not in a demonstrative but in a forensic style, part of their skill being to show that a plausible case can always be constructed even out of the most unpromising dialectical materials. Still more threatening to the idea of a moral science was the fact that they were also expected to master a number of techniques for persuading an audience that any normative question can always be debated *in utramque partem*, on either side of the case. Most threatening of all was the fact that these techniques included a *figura* known to rhetoricians as *paradiastole*,[12] the precise purpose of which was to show that any given action can always be redescribed in such a way as to suggest that its moral character may be open to some measure of doubt.

These considerations bring me to the thesis I shall seek to develop in what follows. It is against this rhetorical background, I shall argue, that Hobbes's concern to establish a science of virtue needs to be understood. To a large extent, what Hobbes was doing in laying out his moral theory was addressing himself to this particular brand of rhetorical scepticism and seeking to demonstrate that it can be overcome. It follows that, if we wish to understand the role of scepticism in Hobbes's thought, as well as the shape and character of his own arguments about civil science, we have no option but to start by setting off across the rugged and ill-charted terrain of Renaissance rhetorical theory.[13] In particular, we need to begin by examining the *figura* of paradiastole, the main device employed by practitioners of the *Ars rhetorica* to indicate the shifting and ambiguous character of virtue and vice.

---

[12] The *figura* of paradiastole was until recently little studied. But I am much indebted to Cox 1989, pp. 53–5 and Whigham 1984, pp. 40–2, 204–5.

[13] Howell 1956 provides a large-scale map, but even he has nothing to say about the use of specific rhetorical techniques. But for an excellent outline (concentrating on the Italian background) see Monfasani 1988, and for valuable introductions see Vickers 1988; Vickers 1989, pp. 254–93; and Rhodes 1992. On the importance of *elocutio* see also Vickers 1981, and for a list of figures and tropes see Vickers 1989, pp. 491–8 (a list which does not, however, include *paradiastole*). Commentaries on Hobbes (some of my own included) have been woefully insensitive to the importance of this rhetorical background, but the position is now beginning to improve. Zappen 1983 discusses Hobbes's supposed Ramism; Kahn 1985 his use of dialogue; Sacksteder 1984, Johnston 1986, Mathie 1986 and Rayner 1991 his changing attitudes to rhetoric; Sorell 1986, pp. 133–7 and 1990a and 1990b his use of persuasive devices. But even these scholars fail to address what I take to be the central question: what impact the Renaissance understanding of the *partes rhetoricae* had upon the character and presentation of Hobbes's civil science. For an attempt to answer this question, however, see Skinner 1996, pp. 215–437.

II

The history of the word *paradiastole* begins with a curious irony. The word itself is obviously Greek, and its literal meaning can perhaps be conveyed by saying that it describes the rhetorical act of going beyond a certain distinction, and hence of putting together dissimilar things. But no ancient Greek text appears to have survived in which the term is mentioned, still less defined.[14] For a definition, and for an attempt to illustrate the precise rhetorical technique to which the term refers, we need to shift our attention from Greece to Rome. Specifically, we need to turn to the earliest Roman adaptations of the hellenistic theory of rhetoric within which the word seems initially to have been coined.[15]

The earliest surviving attempt at a definition is provided by Publius Rutilius Lupus, who published a treatise entitled *De Figuris Sententiarum et Elocutionis* in about 20 CE. Rutilius's *De Figuris* is an early example of a rhetorical genre that became widely popular in the Renaissance, a genre in which the entire discussion centres on the topic of *elocutio*, and more specifically on the figures and tropes of speech. Rutilius's text as it has come down to us consists of forty-one sections arranged in two books. Each section is devoted to one of the figures, the names of which are given in transliteration from the Greek together with brief definitions and a number of illustrations in each case. Book I, section 4 is headed *Paradiastole*. This *schema* can be defined, Rutilius says, as 'that which separates two or more things which may appear to have the same force, and teaches us how far they are distinct from each other'.[16] It is an instance of paradiastole, for example, when you attempt to show 'that you should be recognised as wise rather than cunning, or courageous rather than overconfident, or careful rather than avaricious in your family affairs, or severe rather than malevolent'.[17]

When Quintilian turned his attention to the same *schema* in his *Institutio Oratoria* a generation later, he largely contented himself with repeating Rutilius Lupus's account. Quintilian admittedly exhibits some hesitation over whether the technique should be classified as a *schema* at all. When he first addresses this question, he suggests that its rhetorical importance is

---

[14] This I infer from the absence of any references to the word in Greek texts in the standard databases.

[15] That the term is hellenistic in origin is suggested by the fact that its first occurrence postdates Aristotle's *Art of Rhetoric*. On the other hand the concept, even if not the word, was well known to Thucydides, as I indicate below.

[16] Rutilius Lupus 1970, I. 4: 'Hoc schema duas aut plures res, quae videntur unam vim habere, disiungit et quantum distent docet.'

[17] Rutilius Lupus 1970, I. 4: 'te pro astuto sapientem intelligenti, pro confidente fortem, pro inliberali diligentem rei familiaris, pro malivolo severum'.

such that it ought perhaps to be classified instead as a general method of amplification.[18] He later observes, however, that 'when an act of temerity is called *courage*, or when luxury is called *liberality*, some writers want to say that these are instances of catachresis', as a result of which they treat the device as one of the tropes.[19] But he explicitly adds that he dissents from this judgement, since it is only proper to speak of catachresis when we adapt a neighbouring term to describe something for which no term exists at all.[20] Quintilian's own final suggestion is accordingly that the device ought probably to be grouped among the *schemata* after all. He adds that those who argue for this classification generally agree that the name to be given to the figure is Παραδιαστολή,[21] a term he renders into Latin as *distinctio* and defines as 'the figure by means of which similar things are distinguished from each other'.[22]

It was this final suggestion that came to be most widely accepted. This is not to say that Quintilian's analysis was universally endorsed by later Roman writers on the rhetorical arts. Julius Rufinianus, for example, whose glossary *De Figuris Sententiarum & Elocutionis* appeared in the course of the fourth century, offers a strongly contrasting account.[23] To a large extent, however, it was Rutilius Lupus's understanding of the concept that prevailed. This appears to have been due in part to the influence of the late-Roman rhetorical treatise entitled *Carmen de Figuris vel Schematibus*. The *Carmen*, whose author has never been identified, discusses some sixty figures of speech, the thirty-eighth of which is given in Greek as Παραδιαστολή and in Latin as *subdistinctio*. We have an example of paradiastole, the *Carmen* adds, 'when someone who is insanely reckless is called courageous, or when a prodigal is called a good fellow, or when an infamous person is called illustrious'.[24]

An even more important conduit for transmitting the same understanding appears to have been Isidore of Seville's *Etymologiarum sive Originum Libri XX*, perhaps the most widely used encyclopaedia of late antiquity. Isidore opens his treatise with a survey of the liberal arts,

---

[18] Quintilian 1920–2, VIII. IV. 1–14, vol. 3, pp. 262–70.
[19] Quintilian 1920–2, VIII. VI. 36, vol. 3, p. 320: 'Illa quoque quidam catachresis volunt esse, cum pro temeritate *virtus* aut pro luxuria *liberalitas* dicitur.'
[20] Quintilian 1920–2, VIII. VI. 34, vol. 3, p. 320. For an analysis of Quintilian's discussion see Parker 1990.
[21] Quintilian 1920–2, IX. III. 65, vol. 3, p. 482: 'cui dant nomen παραδιαστολή . . . Cum te pro astuto sapientem appeles, pro confidente fortem, pro illiberali diligentem.' On paradiastole as a *figura* see Kowalski 1928.
[22] See Quintilian 1920–2, IX. III. 65, vol. 3, p. 482 on *distinctio*, 'qua similia discernuntur'.
[23] Rufinianus 1533, fo. 31ʳ.
[24] *Carmen de Figuris* 1863, p. 67: 'Dum fortem, qui sit vaecors, comemque vocat se / Quom sit prodigus, et clarum qui infamis habetur.'

devoting Book 1 to grammar and Book 2 to rhetoric and dialectic. His discussion of rhetoric includes a survey of the figures of speech, and among these he duly mentions the *schema* of paradiastole. He begins by putting forward a new definition, claiming that 'we have an instance of paradiastole whenever we have to grasp what we say by interpretation'.[25] But in turning to illustrate this somewhat vague claim he draws his examples almost verbatim – as he duly acknowledges – from Rutilius Lupus's account. 'It is a case of paradiastole', he maintains, 'when, as Rutilius Lupus says, book 1 section 4, you call yourself wise rather than cunning, or courageous rather than heedless, or careful rather than parsimonious.'[26]

As well as trying to define the meaning of the term, a number of Roman rhetoricians sought to illustrate how the technique of paradiastole can be put to effective use in moral or forensic argument. The earliest surviving attempt to carry the discussion forward in this way can be found in the treatise generally known as the *Rhetorica ad Herennium*. The author of this work – who seems to have been a near contemporary of Cicero's – has never been conclusively identified.[27] But his treatise was very widely used as a textbook of rhetoric, and his analysis of paradiastole had a marked impact on subsequent discussions of the concept, including that of Quintilian himself.

The author of the *Ad Herennium* describes the technique at the start of Book 3, the opening sections of which are devoted to the theme of deliberative oratory. A deliberative speech, we are first reminded, has as its characteristic aim the procuring of some *utilitas* or advantage.[28] The main problem in deliberative oratory is accordingly that of finding the best means to establish that we are in the right, while at the same time placing our opponents at a disadvantage. One of the principal techniques recommended for achieving these results is that of paradiastole. We must seek to ensure that the virtues – those qualities of action which show that we are in the right – 'are amplified if we are recommending them, but attenuated if we are proposing that they be ignored'.[29] The author

---

[25] Isidore 1911, I. XXI. 9, vol. 1, Sig. H, 1ʳ: 'Paradiastole est, quotiens id, quod dicimus, interpretatione discernimus.'

[26] Isidore 1911, I. XXI. 9, vol. 1, Sig. H 1ʳ: 'Paradiastole est... (cf. Rutil. Lup. I, 4): "cum te pro astuto sapientem appellas, pro inconsiderato fortem, pro inliberali diligentem".'

[27] Until Raphael Regius convinced the learned to the contrary in the 1490s, the *Ad Herennium* had generally been supposed to be by Cicero himself. On its date and authorship see Caplan 1954, pp. vii–xiv.

[28] *Ad C. Herennium* 1954, III. II. 3, p. 160: 'Omnem orationem eorum qui sententiam dicent finem sibi conveniet utilitas proponere.'

[29] *Ad C. Herennium* 1954, III. III. 6, p. 166: 'partes sunt virtutis amplificandae is [*sic*; *recte* si] suadebimus, adtenuandae si ab his dehortabimur'.

proceeds to offer a remarkably forthright illustration of what he has in mind:

We must try if possible to show that what our opponent designates as justice is really cowardice, and a lazy and corrupt form of liberality; what he calls prudence we shall speak of as foolish, indiscreet and offensive cleverness; what he speaks of as temperance we shall speak of as lazy and dissolute negligence; what he names courage we shall call the heedless temerity of a gladiator.[30]

By the time this advice was being put forward, the technique of speaking paradiastolically had come to occupy a prominent place in Roman public debate. This is attested by most of the leading historians of the period. Almost all of them point to the extreme potency of the device in moral and political argument, while a number of them display an interest in analysing and further exploring the nature of the technique itself.

The first major Roman historian to concern himself with paradiastole is Sallust in his *Bellum Catilinae*. The main passage in which he illustrates the device in action is the one in which he describes the debate in the Senate following the first discovery of Catiline's plot. Most speakers concentrated on what should be done with those already arrested, but Marcus Cato called for strong measures to forestall any further extortion or violence. Cato is represented as conceding that 'at this point someone is sure to ask instead for mildness and clemency'.[31] But such a response, he is made to say, will simply be an instance of the pervasive corruption already introduced into public affairs by the use of paradiastolic speech. 'The truth is that by now we have lost the true names of things. It is due to the fact that the squandering of other people's goods is nowadays called liberality, while audacity in wrong-doing is called courage, that the republic has been reduced to its present extremity.'[32]

Slightly later in date, but very similar in tone, is Livy's invocation of paradiastole in his *History*. He illustrates the technique in the course of his celebrated description in Book 22 of the delaying tactics adopted by the Roman dictator, Quintus Fabius Maximus, in the face of Hannibal's advance on Rome. We are told that Fabius's campaign was almost

---

[30] *Ad C. Herennium* 1954, III. III. 6, pp. 166–8: 'si quo pacto poterimus, quam is qui contra dicet iustitiam vocabit, nos demonstrabimus ignaviam esse et inertiam ac pravam liberalitatem; quam prudentiam appellarit, ineptam et garrulam et odiosam scientiam esse dicemus; quam ille modestiam dicet esse, eam nos inertiam et dissolutam neglegentiam esse dicemus; quam ille fortitudinem nominarit, eam nos gladiatoriam et inconsideratam appellabimus temeritatem'.
[31] Sallust 1931, LII. 11, p. 102: 'Hic mihi quisquam mansuetudinem et misericordiam nominat.'
[32] Sallust 1931, LII. 11, p. 102: 'Iam pridem equidem nos vera vocabula rerum amisimus: quia bona aliena largiri liberalitas, malarum rerum audacia fortitudo vocatur, eo res publica in extremo sita est.'

undermined by his own master of horse, who was 'more enraged even than Hannibal was by these prudent measures'.[33] Evidently a rhetorician as well as a soldier, the master of horse is represented as seeking to discredit his commander-in-chief by way of offering a paradiastolic redescription of his dogged refusal to join battle. As Livy puts it, 'fierce and hasty in his judgements, and with an ungovernable tongue, he spoke of his superior at first among a few, and then openly among the troops, not as a man of deliberation but simply as lacking in energy, and not as cautious but rather as timorous'.[34]

To this account Livy adds an observation about the nature of paradiastole which was later to be much repeated, and which certainly offers a clearer explication of the concept than most of the rhetoricians had managed to provide. He points out – in a discussion reminiscent of Aristotle's doctrine of the mean[35] – that the capacity to speak paradiastolically depends on the fact that some of the vices are 'neighbours' of the virtues.[36] This in turn gives rise to the perpetual possibility of 'exalting' or 'disparaging' particular actions by way of redescribing them. On the one hand, as Ovid was later to put it in a phrase that became proverbial, 'vice is often able to hide itself by its proximity to virtue'.[37] And on the other hand, as Livy himself remarks in the case of Fabius's subordinate, even the most virtuous lines of conduct can always be disparaged 'by fabricating vices that lie in the neighbourhood of the person's virtues'.[38]

Of all the Roman historians, however, it is Tacitus who shows himself most interested in the phenomenon of paradiastolic speech. As he remarks at the beginning of the *Agricola*, he felt himself to be living 'in times harsh and inimical to the virtues'.[39] He was, moreover, a man of sceptical and even cynical temperament, someone who delighted in showing that – in the words of the *Historiae* – leading political figures can generally expect to find their vices reinterpreted as virtues.[40] So it is perhaps

---

[33] Livy 1929, XXII. XII. 11, p. 240: 'Sed non Hannibalem magis infestum tam sanis consiliis habebat quam magistrum equitum.'

[34] Livy 1929, XXII. XII. 12, pp. 240–2: 'Ferox rapidusque in consiliis ac lingua immodicus primo inter paucos, dein propalam in volgus pro cunctatore segnem pro cauto timidum.'

[35] Since writing this essay I have come to see that Aristotle's doctrine of the mean in fact occupies a crucial place in discussions about paradiastole. See Skinner 1996, pp. 153–61.

[36] See Livy 1929, XXII. XII. 12, p. 242 on how some vices are *vicinae* to some virtues.

[37] Ovid 1979, II, line 662, p. 110: 'Et lateat vitium proximitate boni.' Among English rhetorical theorists of the Renaissance, Francis Bacon and Philip Sidney both treat Ovid's sentiment as proverbial. See Bacon 1857, p. 677 and Sidney 1912, p. 26.

[38] Livy 1929, XXII. XII. 12, p. 242: 'adfingens vicina virtutibus vitia'.

[39] Tacitus 1970, I. 4, p. 28: 'saeva et infesta virtutibus tempora'.

[40] Tacitus 1925, I. 52, p. 90 describes how 'vitia pro virtutibus interpretabantur'. Tacitus also recognises that paradiastole has potentially wider uses. For example, something closely akin to the device is at work in the oft-cited epigram from *Agricola* in Tacitus 1970, 30. 5, p. 80:

not surprising to find him offering so many instances of the rhetorical technique by which these reinterpretations were generally carried out.

There are two moments in particular in the *Historiae* where, with a characteristic shrug, Tacitus points to the technique in play. The first is in recounting the death of the emperor Galba in 69 CE. Tacitus makes it painfully clear that he wholly dissents from the high opinions voiced at the time about Galba's capacities. 'Everyone', as he puts it in a much-cited epigram, 'would have judged him worthy to rule if only he had not ruled.'[41] 'Nevertheless', he adds, 'Galba's high birth, together with the general terror of the times, served to guarantee that his sheer inertia was hailed as wisdom.'[42] The other moment at which Tacitus speaks in similar vein is in recording the ignominious end of Vitellius, Galba's immediate successor on the throne. Of this emperor, whom Tacitus views with unmitigated contempt, he first observes that 'without restraint and without judgement he not only gave away his own property but also squandered that of others'.[43] But in spite of this, he adds in a formula strikingly reminiscent of Sallust, 'his vices were duly reinterpreted as virtues', and 'his partisans redescribed his conduct as an example of good fellowship and generosity'.[44]

By this stage, the prevalence of paradiastolic speech had begun to attract the attention of the moralists, who tended to underline the sense of unease with which the historians had already described the technique. This disquiet is especially evident in Seneca, who speaks with grave concern at a number of points in his *Epistulae Morales* about the subversive implications of paradiastolic speech. In Letter 92 he laments the fact that, prone as we are to measure the standards of virtue by our own natures, we end up (as Sallust had already remarked) 'by imposing the name of virtue upon our vices'.[45] But it is in Letter 45, in which he discusses the sophistries of rhetoric, that he particularly insists on the need to ensure that we 'stamp everything with identifying marks that cannot possibly be disputed'.[46] Unless we do so, we shall find that 'we embrace evil

---

'auferre trucidare rapere falsis nominibus imperium, atque ubi solitudinem faciunt, pacem appellant'.

[41] Tacitus 1925, I. 49, p. 82: 'omnium consensu capax imperii nisi imperasset'.

[42] Tacitus 1925, I. 49, p. 82: 'Sed claritas natalium et metus temporum obtentui, ut, quod segnitia erat, sapientia vocaretur.'

[43] Tacitus 1925, I. 52, pp. 88–90: 'sine modo, sine iudicio donaret sua, largiretur aliena'.

[44] Tacitus 1925, I. 52, pp. 88–90 claims that 'ipsa vitia pro virtutibus interpretabantur' and that 'ita comitatem bonitatemque faventes vocabant'.

[45] Seneca 1917–25, Epistola 92. 25, vol. 2, p. 462: 'vitiis nostris nomen virtutis inponimus'. Cf. Sallust 1931, LII. 11, p. 102.

[46] Seneca 1917–25, Epistola 45. 7, vol. 1, p. 294: 'His certas notas inprime.'

things in the place of good'.[47] Above all, we shall find that 'vices creep up on us under the name of virtues, with temerity hiding under the title of courage, moderation being called cowardice, and timidity being accepted as cautiousness'.[48] 'And once this happens', Seneca concludes, 'we are straying into great danger.'[49]

At the same time, Seneca is greatly interested in understanding the basis of paradiastolic speech, and especially in understanding how it comes about that a rhetorical redescription of a good or evil action can often be made to look so plausible. He addresses the question directly in Letter 120, the theme of which is how we acquire our knowledge of the good, and arrives at the same Aristotelian answer as Livy had done. The explanation is simply that 'there are as you know a number of vices that are close neighbours of virtues'.[50] This is why, 'extraordinary as it may seem', we sometimes find that 'evil things present themselves to us in the guise of virtue, while the good shines forth out of its opposite'.[51] One example Seneca cites is that 'a prodigal man can deceive us into thinking him liberal'.[52] A second is that 'negligence can be made to look like sheer good nature'.[53] And a third (already mentioned in the *Ad Herennium*) is that 'temerity can be made to look like courage'.[54]

With these allusions to Livy and Sallust as well as to the *Ad Herennium*, Seneca may be said to furnish a summary of how the concept of para-diastole had by that stage come to be understood. This is not to say that a completely unambiguous concept had by then been acquired. Some-times the technique is still described as a matter not of offering redescrip-tions but rather of proposing new meanings for the terms denoting virtue and vice. This still appears, for example, to be part of Quintilian's un-derstanding of the concept in his *Institutio Oratoria*. After putting forward his definition and examples in Book 9, he adds that 'I am not sure that

---

[47] Seneca 1917–25, Epistola 45. 6, vol. 1, p. 294: 'Pro bonis mala amplectimur.'

[48] Seneca 1917–25, Epistola 45. 7, vol. 1. p. 294: 'Vitia nobis sub virtutum nomine obrepunt, temeritas sub titulo fortitudinis latet, moderatio vocatur ignavia, pro cauto timidus accipitur.' Note that the last of these formulae quotes – while reversing – the formula in Livy 1929, XXII. XII. 12, p. 242.

[49] Seneca 1917–25, Epistola 45. 7, vol. 1, p. 294: 'in his magno periculo erramus'.

[50] Seneca 1917–25, Epistola 120. 8, vol. 3, pp. 384–6: 'Sunt enim, ut scis, virtutibus vitia confinia.' Cf. Livy 1929, XXII. XII. 12, p. 242.

[51] Seneca 1917–25, Epistola 120. 8, vol. 3, p. 384: 'quod mirum fortasse videatur: mala interdum speciem honesti optulere et optimum ex contrario enituit'.

[52] Seneca 1917–25, Epistola 120. 8, vol. 3, p. 386: 'sic mentitur prodigus liberalem'.

[53] Seneca 1917–25, Epistola 120. 8, vol. 3, p. 386: 'Imitatur neglegentia facilitatem.'

[54] Seneca 1917–25, Epistola 120. 8, vol. 3, p. 386: 'Imitatur ... temeritas fortitudinem.' Cf. *Ad C. Herennium* 1954, III. III. 6, pp. 166–8 on the capacity to make *fortitudo* appear as *temeritas*.

this device can really be classified as a figure of speech'.[55] His reason is that, instead of using language in a non-standard way, the technique is such that 'everything is made to depend upon the definition of terms'.[56]

As a number of earlier writers had pointed out, however, the technique of arguing paradiastolically is not in the least dependent on suggesting new definitions of familiar terms. Rather it takes the form of claiming that a given evaluative term, in virtue of its agreed meaning, can properly be applied as a description of a given action or state of affairs in a case where this may not at first sight seem conceivable. That this is the character of the rhetorical technique is brought out with admirable clarity in the discussion of definition in Book 4 of the *Ad Herennium*.[57] The author considers how one might try to establish of a given action that, although it may have been described (and hence commended) as an instance of carefulness, it ought to be redescribed (and hence condemned) as an instance of avarice. We are advised to begin by referring to commonly accepted definitions, observing that 'carefulness takes the form of an earnest conservation of one's own goods, whereas avarice involves the wrongful covetousness of the goods of others'.[58] We must then seek to show that, although the action in question may have been classified as carefulness, it ought instead to be acknowledged that it involved an element of wrongful covetousness, and thus that 'it is not in truth an instance of carefulness, but rather of avarice'.[59]

A second example makes the point even more clearly. We are asked to consider how an act described as courageous might be redescribed as mere temerity. Again, the first step is to cite the ordinary definitions of the evaluative terms involved. 'Courage is contempt for labour and danger in a case where the purpose is useful and the advantages have been duly weighed, whereas temerity involves incurring dangers with a gladiatorial kind of endurance and without any consideration of the risks.'[60] The suggestion is that, by insisting on *temerity* rather than *courage* as the more perspicuous description of the action concerned, we can hope to persuade our audience that there may indeed have been something

---

[55] Quintilian 1920–2, IX. III. 65, vol. 3, p. 482: 'an figura sit dubito'.
[56] Quintilian 1920–2, IX. III. 65, vol. 3, p. 482: 'Quod totum pendet ex finitione.'
[57] See the discussion of *definitio* in *Ad C. Herennium* 1954, IV. XXV. 35, p. 316.
[58] *Ad C. Herennium* 1954, IV. XXV. 35, p. 316: 'diligentia est adcurata conservatio suorum, avaritia iniuriosa appetitio alienorum'.
[59] *Ad C. Herennium* 1954, IV. XXV. 35, p. 316: 'Non est ista diligentia, sed avaritia.'
[60] *Ad C. Herennium* 1954, IV. XXV. 35, p. 316: 'fortitudo est contemptio laboris et periculi cum ratione utilitatis et conpensatione commodorum, temeritas est eum inconsiderata dolorum perpessione gladiatoria periculorum susceptio'.

heedless about it after all, and thus that the less favourable term ought instead to be applied – in virtue of its accepted meaning – as a way of describing and hence condemning the action previously praised.

As the author of the *Ad Herennium* also recognises, this understanding of what is meant by speaking paradiastolically further implies that the technique can always be used in one of two contrasting ways. On the one hand there is the use that mainly preoccupies Sallust and Seneca: that of seeking to excuse or justify disgraceful actions by covering them with the names of neighbouring virtues. As the *Ad Herennium* expresses it, in these cases we seek to 'amplify' the character of the action involved.[61] But on the other hand there is the use that Livy prefers to emphasise: that of seeking to discountenance virtuous actions by arguing that they are really instances of some neighbouring vice. In these cases, as the *Ad Herennium* adds, we seek to 'attenuate' the action by claiming that 'the virtue in question consists in qualities other than those exhibited by the action under review'.[62]

III

Of all the ancient rhetoricians, it was undoubtedly Quintilian who gave the fullest and most authoritative survey of the figures and tropes of speech. But the sections of the *Institutio Oratoria* in which he had dealt with this topic were lost at some stage in late antiquity, and were only returned to circulation after Poggio Bracciolini unearthed a complete copy of the *Institutio* at St Gallen in 1416.[63] As a result, it was only in the course of the *quattrocento* that some of the more arcane *schemata* explicated by Quintilian, including the *schema* of paradiastole, began to resurface once again in textbooks on the rhetorical arts.

One of the earliest treatises on *elocutio* to make full use of Quintilian's re-discovered text was Antonio Mancinelli's *Carmen de Figuris*, which was first printed in 1493.[64] Mancinelli's impressive survey begins by describing a number of purely grammatical *schemata*, after which he turns to the *tropi* and finally the *schemata* or figures of speech. His discussion of paradiastole, which he places almost at the end of his book, is presented mainly in the

---

[61] The verb is *amplificare*. See *Ad C. Herennium* 1954, III. III. 6, p. 166.

[62] *Ad C. Herennium* 1954, III. 111. 6, p. 166 suggests that one way in which we can hope *adtenuare* is by claiming 'in contrariis potius rebus quam in his virtus constare quae ostendantur'.

[63] For Poggio Bracciolini's rediscovery of the complete text see Sabbadini 1967, vol. 1, p. 78, and cf. vol. 1, p. 13 on the lacunae in other MSS, in books 8 to 12. On the general theme of the Renaissance 'recovery' of rhetoric see Vickers 1990.

[64] On Mancinelli (1452–1515) see Murphy 1981, pp. 198–9.

form of illustrative examples. One of these we have already encountered in Seneca: the case of a prodigal man who seeks to redescribe himself as liberal.[65] A second had made an even earlier appearance in the *Ad Herennium*, and had subsequently been much repeated: the case of someone seeking to have their sheer temerity recognised as courage.[66] But the rest of Mancinelli's analysis, as he himself admits, is drawn entirely from Book 9 of Quintilian,[67] including his two other examples of paradiastolic speech. One is 'when you call yourself wise rather than cunning'; the other is 'when you call yourself courageous rather than overconfident'.[68]

The fullest discussion of paradiastole in a Renaissance rhetorical text can be found in Johannes Susenbrotus's *Epitome Troporum ac Schematum*. First published in c.1535,[69] the *Epitome* quickly established itself as one of the most popular textbooks on *elocutio* of the sixteenth century.[70] Although Susenbrotus explicitly refers to Mancinelli,[71] the definition of paradiastole he offers at the outset of his discussion appears to be all his own. 'It is an instance of paradiastole', he explains, 'when, by means of a courteous interpretation, we give a favourable representation either to our own vices or to the vices of others by speaking of them in a flattering style.'[72] 'In short', as he later adds, we have a case of paradiastole 'whenever vices display themselves under the guise of virtue'.[73]

It is perhaps unfortunate that this definition came to be so widely adopted, especially among English rhetoricians of the Renaissance. For Susenbrotus's understanding of paradiastole is obviously somewhat one-sided. Relying as he evidently does on Mancinelli's examples, all of which happened to be instances of using the device to excuse rather than denigrate, Susenbrotus infers that the figure can actually be defined by its concern with mitigation or excuse.[74] This not only excluded the

---

[65] Mancinelli 1493, Sig. H. 1ʳ: 'sic prodigum dicam liberalem'.

[66] Mancinelli 1493, Sig. H. 1ʳ: 'sic . . . temerarium fortem'.

[67] Mancinelli 1493, Sig. H. 1ʳ: 'Paradiastole sit teste Fabio libro nono [est] quum . . . '

[68] Mancinelli 1493, Sig. H. 1ʳ: 'quum te pro astuto sapientem appellas: pro confidente fortem'.

[69] See Murphy 1981, p. 280 for the probable date of the *editio princeps*. According to Murphy, the first English printing (London 1562 – the edition I use) was the fifth to appear. On Susenbrotus's text see also Brennan 1960.

[70] For its use in English schools during the latter part of the sixteenth century see Baldwin 1944, vol. 1, pp. 356, 382, 405–6, 413, 664–5.

[71] See the reference to 'Mancin.' in Susenbrotus 1562, p. 46.

[72] Susenbrotus 1562, p. 46: 'Paradiastole, Παραδιαστολή, est cum civili interpretatione nostris aut aliorum vitiis assentando blandimur.'

[73] Susenbrotus 1562, p. 46: 'Breviter, cum vitia sub virtutis specie sese ostendant.'

[74] Susenbrotus 1562, p. 78: 'huic pertinet mitigandi sive extenuandi locutiones'. Drawing on the explications furnished by Susenbrotus and his English followers, the OED is led to suggest a similarly one-sided definition. See OED, *sub* Paradiastole: 'A figure in which a favourable turn is given to something unfavourable.'

possibility – which most Roman rhetoricians had emphasised – that the figure can equally well be used to display virtue under the guise of vice;[75] it also led to some confusion between the concept of paradiastole and that of meiosis or *diminutio*, the 'understating' figure of speech.[76]

Despite this weakness, Susenbrotus's analysis proved extremely valuable. One of its strengths lay in the fact that it offered a clear restatement of the originally Aristotelian explanation of how it comes about that paradiastolic redescriptions can often be made to look so plausible. Susenbrotus stresses in particular the kinship between a number of virtues and their seeming opposites, in consequence of which 'we are often able to elevate a vice by placing it under the name of a neighbouring virtue'.[77] But the main value of his analysis stemmed from its unusually wide range of examples. After laying out his definition, Susenbrotus goes on to offer no fewer than nine instances of paradiastolic speech. The first three are familiar from Quintilian: 'when you call yourself wise rather than cunning, or courageous rather than overconfident, or careful rather than parsimonious'.[78] The next two appear to be taken from Seneca: 'when we say of a prodigal man that he is liberal, or a man of sheer temerity that he is courageous'.[79] But the last four, although partly reminiscent of the *Ad Herennium*, are largely new: 'when we say of an avaricious man that he is merely frugal, or of a haughty man that he is magnanimous, or describe a sycophant as a companion, or a dependant as a friend'.[80] Finally, in his later and partly overlapping discussion of meiosis, Susenbrotus adds several more examples that again appear to be all his own. These include 'describing a cruel man as somewhat too severe', 'describing an imprudent man as somewhat ingenuous' and 'describing a city corrupted by licence as enjoying liberty'.[81]

It was largely from these continental textbooks, and from the Roman authorities on which they relied, that the analysis of paradiastolic speech passed into the vernacular treatises on *elocutio* that first began to appear

---

[75] See, for example, *Ad Herennium* Book 3, in which all the examples given had been of attempts to denigrate virtue.

[76] Susenbrotus 1562, pp. 46, 77–8 gives some of his examples of paradiastole *sub* meiosis, others *sub* paradiastole.

[77] Susenbrotus 1562, p. 78: 'Quoties vitium nomine vicinae virtutis elevamus.'

[78] Susenbrotus 1562, p. 46: 'Ut cum pro astuto sapientem appellas: pro confidente, fortem: pro illiberali, diligentem.'

[79] Susenbrotus 1562, p. 46: 'cum item prodigum dicimus liberalem, temerarium fortem'.

[80] Susenbrotus 1562, p. 46: '[cum dicimus] avarum frugalem, fastidiosum magnanimum, adulatorem comem, assertorem amicum'.

[81] Susenbrotus 1562, p. 78: 'cum crudelem appellamus paulo severiorem: imprudentem simpliciorem: . . . corruptam licentia civitatem liberam'.

in England during the second half of the sixteenth century. The earliest English work in which the concept of paradiastole is distinguished from meiosis and separately defined is Henry Peacham's *The Garden of Eloquence*, the original version of which was published in 1577.[82] The rector of a parish in Lincolnshire, Peacham was much concerned, as Thomas Wilson had been before him, with employing the *Ars rhetorica* to improve the quality of preaching and more generally to assist in the cause of reformation.[83] One way in which this ambition is reflected is in Peacham's choice of examples, several of which have a distinctly puritanical cast. Apart from details of this character, however, Peacham's definition of paradiastole is largely taken (although without acknowledgement) from Susenbrotus's account. Under the heading *Paradiastole* we read as follows:

It is when by a mannerly interpretation, we doe excuse our own vices, or other mens whom we doe defend, by calling them vertues, as when we call him that is craftye, wyse: a covetous man, a good husband: murder a manly deede: deepe dissimulation, singuler wisdome: pryde cleanlynesse: covetousnesse, a worldly or necessarye carefulnesse: whoredome, youthful delight & dalyance: Idolatry, pure religion: glotony and dronkennesse, good fellowship: cruelty severity. This figure is used, when vices are excused.[84]

This is basically a translation of Susenbrotus's list, with the addition of some puritan asides – notably the mention of how readily the vices of pride and whoredom are liable to be excused. There is one further addition, however, which can hardly fail to catch the attention of any reader of Shakespeare: the suggestion that someone might try to excuse an act of murder by redescribing it as a manly deed. 'When you durst do it then you were a man' is exactly the redescription that Lady Macbeth offers Macbeth in her speech encouraging him to kill Duncan.[85]

After Henry Peacham's *Garden of Eloquence*, the next important discussion of paradiastole by an English rhetorician appeared in *The Arte of English Poesie*, the final section of which contains a more sophisticated survey of *elocutio* than any that had hitherto appeared.[86] The *Arte* has generally been attributed to George Puttenham, a nephew of Sir Thomas Elyot, and was first published in 1589.[87] Puttenham's discussion of paradiastole is notable for introducing a new way of describing the technique,

---

[82] See Peacham 1971, Sig. N, iiii^v and cf. Murphy 1981, p. 220 for its printing history.
[83] On this aspiration see Wildermuth 1989.   [84] Peacham 1971, sig. N, iiii^v.
[85] Shakespeare 1988, *Macbeth*, I. VII. 49, p. 981.
[86] For this section, entitled 'Of Ornament', see Puttenham 1970, pp. 137–308.
[87] On the question of authorship see Willcock and Walker 1970, pp. xi–xliv.

one that was later to be much repeated. When our words 'tend to flattery, or soothing, or excusing', he explains, 'it is by the figure *Paradiastole*, which therefore nothing improperly we call the *Curry-favell*, as when we make the best of a bad thing, or turne a signification to the more plausible sence'.[88]

As we saw in volume 2 chapter 10, Puttenham's definition invokes a metaphor drawn from the grooming of horses.[89] After this preliminary flourish, however, his examples are almost entirely derivative, most of them being taken directly from Susenbrotus's and Peacham's accounts.[90] It is a case of paradiastole, Puttenham goes on, when we 'call an unthrift, a liberall Gentleman: the foolish-hardy, valiant or couragious: the niggard, thriftie: a great riot, or outrage, an youthfull pranke, and such like termes: moderating and abating the force of the matter by craft, and for a pleasing purpose'.[91]

By the end of the sixteenth century, as a result of the wide availability of Susenbrotus's writings and those of his English followers, the concept of paradiastole had come to be thoroughly assimilated into English discussions of the rhetorical arts. Almost every textbook of the period refers familiarly to the concept, usually defining it in the way that Susenbrotus had originally proposed.[92] A similar definition can be found, for example, in the new and much expanded edition of *The Garden of Eloquence* issued by Peacham in 1593,[93] while an even closer adaptation of Susenbrotus's analysis appears in the treatise on tropes and figures appended by Angel Day to the 1592 edition of his letter-book, *The English Secretary*.[94]

The English rhetoricians of this period also refer in a familiar way to the problem of how paradiastolic speech is possible. They generally make the point by way of a brief allusion to the idea that certain virtues and vices are 'neighbours', but in some cases they consider the question

---

[88] Puttenham 1970, pp. 184–5.
[89] On this usage see further above, volume 2 chapter 10, section II.
[90] But in two of his examples (those of alleged liberality and thrift) he follows Wilson's phraseology. See Puttenham 1970, pp. 184–5 and cf. Wilson 1554, fo. 67^r. The point is worth making in view of the fact that Puttenham's editors fail to mention Wilson in their appendix on 'The Sources of the *Arte*' in Puttenham 1970, pp. 319–22.
[91] Puttenham 1970, p. 185.
[92] This generalisation applies only to rhetorical writings of broadly neo-Ciceronian allegiances. Although a number of Ramist rhetorics – including Fenner 1584, Fraunce 1950 and Butler 1629 – circulated in England during the closing decades of the sixteenth century, none made any reference to paradiastole.
[93] Peacham 1593, pp. 168–9.
[94] Day's account is a partial translation of Susenbrotus. See Day 1967, p. 84 (second pagination) and cf. Susenbrotus 1562, p. 46. For the many editions of Day's book, which first appeared in 1586, see Murphy 1981, pp. 108–9.

at greater length. Perhaps the most interesting of these considerations is that of Francis Bacon, who examines the issue in the fragment entitled *Of the Colours of Good and Evil* which he appended to the original edition of his *Essays* in 1597 and eventually incorporated into the section on the foundations of rhetoric in his *De Augmentis* of 1623.[95] Bacon's discussion is couched in the form of a set of answers to various rhetorical 'sophisms', the fourth of which states that 'what is remote from good is evil, and what is remote from evil is good'.[96] Repudiating this contention, Bacon not only reiterates the classical explanation of what makes paradiastolic redescription plausible, but also quotes the formula that Ovid had made proverbial:

It is not merely because of their partnership and similarity of nature that things come together and congregate. For evil also – especially in civil affairs – takes refuge in good in order to hide and be protected by it. Just as malefactors seek sanctuaries, so vice seeks admission under the shadow of virtue. 'Vice is often able to hide itself by its proximity to virtue.'[97]

The final sentence, quoting Ovid's *Ars Amatoria*, brings us full circle to the seminal discussions mounted by the poets and moralists of ancient Rome.

IV

From the time when the classical rhetoricians first began to analyse the concept of paradiastole, the enormous rhetorical power of the device had always been recognised. The point is one that their Renaissance followers make with even greater emphasis. By this means, Susenbrotus remarks in an allusion to 2 Corinthians, 'even Satan himself can be transformed into an angel of light'.[98] Among English rhetoricians, George Puttenham similarly stresses the value of the device as a means of 'moderating' and

95 See *Exempla Colorum Boni et Mali*, Appendix 1 to the chapter (book 6, ch. 3) entitled *De Fundamentis, et Officio Rhetoricae* in Bacon 1857, pp. 674–88. For the *De Augmentis* Bacon revised his earlier account as well as translating it into Latin. For his earlier account see Bacon 1859. Jardine 1974, p. 221 notes that Bacon points to Aristotle as the inspiration for his discussion of 'colours'. Briggs 1989, pp. 72–9 notes in addition the alchemical background to the emphasis on tinctures and colouring.
96 Bacon 1857, p. 676: 'quod vero remotum est a bono, malum; quod a malo, bonum'.
97 Bacon 1857, p. 677: 'nam non solum res coeunt et congregatur propter consortium et naturae similitudinem, sed etiam malum (praesertim in civilibus) confugit ad bonum, ut lateat et protegatur. Itaque scelerati homines petunt asyla Divorum, et vitium ipsum se in virtutis umbram recipit: Saepe latet [*recte* lateat] vitium proximitate boni.' The final clause quotes Ovid 1979, II, line 662, p. 110.
98 Susenbrotus 1562, p. 46: 'Nam & ipse Satanas transfiguratur in Angelum lucis.' The allusion is to 2 Corinthians 11.14.

hence 'abating' the statement of hard truths.[99] He particularly notes
that in many cases 'it may commendably be used by Courtiers', who
are especially liable to find themselves speaking and acting in circumstances in which – as a contemporary advice-book delicately put it – they
'must sometimes use, as they say, words of silke'.[100] Faced with such a
predicament, Puttenham suggests, an ability to speak paradiastolically
may amount to nothing less than a condition of survival.

Given the recognised power and usefulness of the device, it is not
surprising that, once it came to be properly understood, it was very
widely put to work. We find this happening above all in two characteristic genres of Renaissance moral and political theory, in each case with
increasingly challenging results. One group of writers who became especially interested in paradiastole were those concerned with the so-called
rhetorical paradoxes. These formed a part of epideictic or demonstrative oratory, in which the aim is to induce an audience to share an attitude either of admiration or contempt for some particular subject.[101] As
Hobbes was to observe in discussing these 'Orations of Prayse' and
'Invectives' in chapter 8 of *Leviathan*, their goal 'is not truth, but to Honour or Dishonour'.[102] One of the standard exercises in speaking demonstratively was the *laudatio*, in which the speaker was expected to put
together everything that could possibly be said in favour of some chosen
theme.[103] It was this exercise – together with its contrary, the *vituperatio* –
which lent itself so readily to paradoxical treatment. A speaker or writer
who aspired to produce a paradoxical *laudatio* sought to develop a case in
favour of something not generally thought to be commendable at all.[104]

Sometimes the resulting *encomia* simply dealt with states of affairs normally felt to be disagreeable or unfortunate.[105] The classic example in
the rhetorical literature of the English Renaissance is Anthony Munday's
translation of Ortensio Lando's *Paradossi*, which Munday issued in 1593

---

99 See Puttenham 1970, p. 184 on the use of paradiastole in 'moderating and abating the force of
   the matter by craft, and for a pleasing purpose'.
100 Puttenham 1970, p. 184; cf. [Béthune] 1634, p. 73.
101 See, for example, the characterisation of epideictic oratory in *Ad C. Herennium* 1954, III. VI. 10
    to III. VIII. 15, pp. 172–84. For further discussion see Hardison 1962, pp. 24–42.
102 Hobbes 1996, ch. 8, p. 51.
103 *Ad C. Herennium* 1954, III. VI. 10, pp. 172–4; cf. Quintilian 1920–2, III. VII. 1–18, vol. 2, pp.
    464–72.
104 As Colie 1966, pp. 5–6 notes, however, Renaissance rhetorical theorists admitted that, if un-
    praiseworthy actions can be praised, then they were not unpraiseworthy in the first place, so
    that rhetorical paradoxes are not strictly paradoxes.
105 Colie 1966, pp. 1–4. There is no implication that the device could not be used in wholly serious
    ways. On the contrary, a standard motive for speaking paradoxically was to uncover some
    allegedly deeper truth. For an exemplification see Vickers 1968.

under the title *The Defence of Contraries*. Munday undertakes to vindicate such propositions as that 'it is better to be poore than Rich', 'it is better to be fowle than fair', and so forth.[106] But in some cases – and it was here that the technique of paradiastole came into play – a more daring attempt was made to plead for the reconsideration of some widely criticised vice, the most celebrated instance in Renaissance moral theory being Poggio Bracciolini's early *quattrocento* dialogue in defence of avarice.[107]

The first part of Poggio's *De Avaritia* takes the form not of a paradiastolic but a directly paradoxical *apologia* for avaricious behaviour. This is put into the mouth of the humanist Antonio Loschi, who speaks in particular of those 'who desire more than enough' and accumulate money 'far beyond their needs'.[108] He concedes that such behaviour must be described as avaricious, but seeks to prove 'that such avarice ought not to be condemned'.[109] If we dispassionately consider the conduct of such people, we shall be forced to recognise that they alone are in a position 'to exercise some of the most splendid virtues'.[110] Without their lust for gain, 'ordinary people would find themselves deprived of mercy and charity, for no one would be able to serve as a benefactor or to act with liberality'.[111] Moreover, their avarice frequently brings 'great ornament and elegance to their communities', since 'it is their money that builds magnificent houses, outstanding villas, temples, colonnades and hospitals'.[112]

Antonio's oration is succeeded, in accordance with the rhetorical convention of arguing *in utramque partem*, by a *vituperatio* or denunciation of avarice. This is pronounced by a theologian, Andrea of Constantinople, who chiefly devotes himself to a point-by-point refutation of Antonio's case. Andrea prefaces his attack, however, with a very different line of argument. He first suggests that, while avarice is undoubtedly a detestable sin, the forms of behaviour described by Antonio ought not to be viewed as instances of avarice. The sin of avarice, Andrea begins by reminding us – in a passage strongly reminiscent of the *Ad Herennium* – involves 'a greed for gain that goes beyond anything decent or just' and

---

[106] Munday 1593, I. XVII. 23. The title-page carries no name, but the Dedication is signed (Sig. A. 2ʳ) 'Anthony Mundy'. Cf. Sidney 1912, p. 26 on how 'a playing wit' can succeed in praising such misfortunes as 'the jolly commodities of being sicke of the plague'.
[107] Bec 1967, p. 379 gives November 1428 as its date of completion.
[108] Bracciolini 1964–9, vol. 1, p. 13: 'quin cupiat plus quam sit satis . . . [et] ultra quam existat satis'.
[109] Bracciolini 1964–9, vol. 1, p. 12: 'non est avaritia vituperanda'.
[110] See Bracciolini 1964–9, vol. 1, p. 13 on their 'usus gratissimarum virtutum'.
[111] Bracciolini 1964–9, vol. 1, p. 13: 'Tollet . . . populo misericordiae videlicet, & charitas, nullus erit neque beneficus, neque liberalis.'
[112] Bracciolini 1964–9, vol. 1, p. 15: 'magnum ornamentum & decorum suis civitatibus . . . magnificae domus, egregiae villae, templa, porticus, hospitalia avarorum pecuniis constructa'.

'a vehement cupidity which is at once inordinate and includes a thirst for stealing other people's goods'.[113] But the behaviour of those who greatly value money and seek to accumulate more than they strictly require does not necessarily involve them in any such acts of theft or injustice. They are simply displaying 'one of the natural forms of desire that are free from blame'.[114] So their behaviour, Andrea concludes, ought not to be condemned as avaricious; it ought rather to be accepted as an instance of 'the sort of moderate and temperate desire that no one holds to be reprehensible'.[115] It is essential to the ironic structure of Poggio's dialogue that, by means of this paradiastolic redescription of the avaricious behaviour discussed by Antonio, Andrea is made to support a large part of Antonio's case while appearing to reject it.[116]

By the end of the sixteenth century we encounter a similar treatment of the rhetorical paradoxes in English moral thought. The most remarkable instance is Lazarus Piot's *The Orator*, a version of Alexander Sitvayn's collection of 'a hundred several discourses in form of Declamations' issued by Piot in 1596.[117] Most of Piot's examples are concerned in a relatively straightforward fashion with the question of what can be said for and against some particular judgement. His ninety-fifth Declamation, for instance, examines the striking case of 'a Jew, who would for his debt have a pound of the flesh of a Christian'.[118] The judge pronounces that, if he takes more or less than exactly a pound, his own life shall be forfeit. We first hear the Jew's declamation against the justice of his sentence, and then a rival speech from the Christian in which the Jew's arguments are overturned.[119]

In a number of cases, however, Piot relies less on the presentation of arguments for and against some particular action and more on a paradiastolic redescription of the action itself. This is the method he adopts, for example, in his second Declamation, in which he examines

---

[113] Bracciolini 1964–9, vol. 1, p. 18: 'cupiditas habendi ultra quam deceat, plus quam oporteat. Cupiditas vehemens quae excedit modum, & est cum siti auferendi'. Cf. *Ad C. Herennium* 1954, IV. XXV. 35, p. 316.

[114] Bracciolini 1964–9, vol. 1, p. 18: 'Sunt enim qu[a]edam naturales cupiditates . . . quae absunt a culpa.'

[115] Bracciolini 1964–9, vol. 1, p. 18: 'Nil habet haec reprehensionis cupiditas modica & temperata.'

[116] This is not to say that Poggio Bracciolini directly endorses Antonio's case, as Bec 1967, p. 379 implies in describing the dialogue as 'libelle en faveur de l'esprit de lucre'. The effect of the use of paradiastole is, rather, to leave the reader to ponder two contrasting ways of thinking about what Antonio has said.

[117] Piot 1596, Epistle to the Reader, Sig. A, iv^r, stresses that his concern is with 'Rhetoricke to inforce a good cause, and art to impugne an ill'.

[118] Piot 1596, p. 400.   [119] Piot 1596, pp. 400–6.

the conduct of one of the earls of Flanders. The earl's son bought fruit from a woman who came to his palace, but he kept her waiting so long for her payment that, when she returned home, 'she found her child dead for want of the teat'.[120] The woman appealed to the earl, who caused his son to be hanged. The people thereupon complained to the king that the earl had exhibited 'very cruelty', and that he ought to be punished for his 'detestable' and 'very odious' deed, since 'there is no vice thought more unbeseeming a man then crueltie'.[121] But the earl is represented as managing to defend himself by insisting that his behaviour ought rather to be redescribed as an act of 'justice joined with wisdom', and thus that he cannot 'be taxed of crueltie' after all.[122] To have spared his son, he declares, would have been an instance of 'pittie without justice', and this would in turn have been 'follie or rather iniquitie', a manifest danger to the commonwealth.[123]

Of even greater importance was the other body of literature in which the possibilities of paradiastolic redescription were explored in the course of the Renaissance. This was the literature of advice-books for princes and other public figures in which they were counselled on how to discharge their duties in the most effective way. This genre was also linked with classical rhetoric, and especially with the ideal of deliberative oratory, the aim of which is to persuade an audience of the expediency of acting in some particular way. The results in this case were even more unsettling, especially as the genre was one in which the lines of demarcation between *honestas* and *utilitas*, virtue and 'policy', were increasingly held up for scrutiny in a self-consciously rhetorical and questioning style.

Of all those who published such handbooks of 'counsel' in the course of the sixteenth century, it was Niccolò Machiavelli in *Il Principe* who succeeded in putting the technique of paradiastolic redescription to the most sensational use. Machiavelli's account of the code of conduct that any ruler must follow if he wishes 'to maintain his state' has of course been intensively analysed by modern commentators. But the extent to which he employs the techniques of classical rhetoric in order to persuade his readers of his novel and subversive conclusions has only recently begun to be recognised.[124] It is evident, however, that he makes use of a number of standard rhetorical devices, among which that of paradiastole is assigned a crucial role.

[120] Piot 1596, p. 9.   [121] Piot 1596, pp. 9–10.   [122] Piot 1596, p. 13.
[123] Piot 1596, p. 15.
[124] See Garver 1980 and the valuable analysis in Tinkler 1988. Cox 1997 offers a critique of the latter and an exceptionally perceptive analysis of deliberative rhetoric in *Il Principe*. Viroli 1998 also lays particular emphasis on Machiavelli's rhetorical practices.

Machiavelli resorts to the technique throughout his notorious sequence of chapters on 'how a prince should conduct himself towards
his subjects or allies'.[125] His investigation first involves him in reconsidering the ideal of princely liberality, the subject of chapter 16. He prefaces
his discussion by conceding that liberality is undeniably one of the most
laudable of the virtues; a ruler who is miserly will always be blamed.[126]
He then declares that much of the conduct of 'those who are usually held
to be liberal' ought rather to be redescribed as ostentatiousness.[127] To
this he adds – closely echoing Sallust – that those who seek to uphold a
reputation for liberality will inevitably find themselves driven into 'doing
everything they possibly can to gain money for themselves'.[128] With these
redescriptions, Machiavelli paves the way for the basic argument of his
chapter: that princes ought not to worry so much about being described
as miserly or parsimonious.

His next chapter reconsiders the ideal of clemency in a similar way. He
begins by acknowledging that cruelty is of course a vice. 'Every prince
ought to want to be viewed as merciful and not cruel.'[129] But he then insists that many of the actions usually celebrated as instances of clemency
ought rather to be redescribed in far less favourable terms. For example,
the avoidance of cruelty for which the Florentines congratulated themselves when they refused to punish the leaders of the uprising at Pistoia
ought really to be seen as an instance of over-indulgence.[130] Likewise, the
clemency for which Scipio Africanus became famous in his campaigns
against Hannibal was really an example of laxity.[131] As before, these redescriptions pave the way for the main argument of the chapter: that
'a prince ought not to worry too much about acquiring a reputation for
being a cruel man'.[132]

Machiavelli develops a comparable argument in chapter 18, in the
course of which he discusses how far princes should honour their word.

---

[125] Machiavelli 1960, p. 64: 'quali debbano essere e' modi e governi di uno principe con sudditi o
con li amici'. For a translation of the passages with which I am concerned see Machiavelli 1988,
pp. 54–63.

[126] See Machiavelli 1960, p. 65, acknowledging that it is 'laudabilissima' to possess this quality.

[127] See Machiavelli 1960, p. 66 on the 'suntuosità' of those generally 'tenuto liberale'.

[128] Machiavelli 1960, p. 66: 'sarà necessitato alla fine, se si vorrà mantenere el nome del
liberale . . . fare tutte quelle cose che si possono fare per avere danari'.

[129] Machiavelli 1960, p. 68: 'ciascuno principe debbe desiderare di esser tenuto pietoso e non
crudele'.

[130] See Machiavelli 1960, p. 69, claiming that it was really a case of 'troppa pietà'.

[131] See Machiavelli 1960, p. 71, claiming that it was really a case of a 'natura facile'.

[132] Machiavelli 1960, p. 69: 'Debbe per tanto uno principe non si curare della infamia di
crudele.'

Again he begins by acknowledging the conventional point of view. 'Everyone agrees how laudable it is for a prince to uphold his promises, and to live a life of integrity rather than deceit.'[133] He then argues that much of what is normally described as deceit is indispensable if princes are to defend themselves in advance against the treachery of others. Picking up one of Quintilian's examples, he concludes that such *astuzia* ought therefore to be redescribed as prudence, and recognised without demur as one of the forms of behaviour to be expected of any wise prince.[134] Once again, the subversive conclusion depends on the use of the same rhetorical technique, that of paradiastolically redescribing the apparently disgraceful action in such a way as to exhibit it as worthy of being commended or at least excused.

These conclusions immediately caused Machiavelli to be hailed as a figure of diabolical wickedness. The point is pressed with the greatest intensity in the most famous of the many 'anti-Machiavel' treatises of the sixteenth century, that of Innocent Gentillet. First issued in 1576, Gentillet's diatribe appeared in English as *A Discourse* 'against Nicholas Machiavell the Florentine' in 1602.[135] Gentillet specifically targets Machiavelli's attempts to redescribe the forms of behaviour for which princes are usually condemned, claiming that Machiavelli's entire argument rests on nothing more than an attempt 'to call injustice by the name of justice', 'crueltie by the name of clemencie' 'night by the name of light' and other such paradiastolic sleights of hand.[136]

Despite such fulminations, the same period also witnessed the publication of a number of humanist works of 'counsel' in which the technique of paradiastolic redescription was put to work in a broadly Machiavellian style. Perhaps the most important was Justus Lipsius's treatise on the political virtues, first published in Latin in 1589 and issued in English as *Sixe Bookes of Politickes or Civil Doctrine* in 1594. One crucial point at which Lipsius employs the device is in his chapter on 'mixed prudence' in Book 4, the chapter in which he specifically remarks that 'some kinde of persons rage too much against Machiavell'.[137] Lipsius admits that mixed prudence – 'where there is deceipt' – has usually been described and condemned as an instance of dishonest guile.[138] He points out, however, that although such actions are 'commonly reputed dishonest', they still

---

[133] Machiavelli 1960, p. 72: 'Quanto sia laudabile in uno principe mantenere la fede, e vivere con integrità e non con astuzia, ciascuno lo intende.'
[134] See Machiavelli 1960, p. 72 for the claim that 'astuzia' will inevitably form part of the conduct of 'uno signore prudente'.
[135] On the original edition see Skinner 1978a, pp. 250–1. For the translation see [Gentillet] 1602.
[136] [Gentillet] 1602, p. 215.   [137] Lipsius 1594, p. 114.   [138] Lipsius 1594, p. 112.

have as their goal 'the societie and benefit of men'.[139] But if this is so, they deserve to be redescribed and commended as instances of genuine prudence. 'So doth prudence not change her name, albeit a fewe drops of deceipt be mingled therewith.'[140] Later, Lipsius employs the same device in the course of discussing what he calls 'military prudence' in Book 5. The question he raises at this juncture – much discussed by humanists ever since Erasmus and More – is whether it is proper to seek victory in war by means of trickery and deceit.[141] As Lipsius notes, it is commonly said that we ought to 'abhorre from these subtilties', since we owe it to our enemies to meet them in open fight.[142] But this again, he complains, is to describe the issue in the wrong way. Like the ancient Romans, we ought to recognise that such alleged 'subtiltie' is better described 'under the name of pollicie', a name which in turn helps us to see that the behaviour in question seems 'rather to deserve commendation then blame'.[143]

If we turn to the English political literature of the same period, we encounter several instances of a similar willingness to view the device of paradiastole as an indispensable weapon of 'politic' government. One exceptionally forthright treatment can be found in Richard Beacon's dialogue of 1594, *Solon his Follie.*[144] Beacon devotes much of his second book to investigating 'the art and skill of perswading', focusing in partic-ular on the question of 'how to winne, moove and dispose the affections of the people'.[145] The character of Epimendes in the dialogue praises Solon for having seen so clearly that one of the most efficacious tech-niques of persuasion will always be that of paradiastole. Epimendes offers the reminder in the course of praising Solon's achievement as a lawgiver:

> You clothed things bitter and unpleasant with pleasing names; calling taxes, contributions; garrisons, gardes; prisons, houses; and such like: by the which pollicie, you made even things odious pleasing and acceptable to the people, and easily thereby persuaded the embracing thereof.[146]

Here the technique of rhetorical redescription is explicitly recom-mended, as in Lipsius, as a helpful and hence a justifiable aspect of 'policy'.

The most important English writer of the period to experiment with paradiastole in this 'politic' vein was Francis Bacon, whose main

---

[139] Lipsius 1594, p. 113.   [140] Lipsius 1594, p. 114.   [141] For a full analysis see Adams 1962.
[142] Lipsius 1594, p. 175.   [143] Lipsius 1594, pp. 175, 177.
[144] For a full discussion see Peltonen 1995, pp. 75–102. See also Anglo 1990 on Beacon's sources and Canny 1987, pp. 167–73 on the 'Machiavellian' context of the work.
[145] Beacon 1594, pp. 29–31.   [146] Beacon 1594, p. 32.

observations about the technique can be found in the second appendix to his account of the *Ars rhetorica* in the *De Augmentis*.[147] Bacon's appendix takes the form of a long list of concepts – including a large number of virtues and vices – which he discusses *pro* and *contra* in such a way as to produce 'Examples of Antitheses'.[148] The resulting arguments are mainly of a straightforwardly paradoxical kind. For example, he shows how one might commend the vice of ingratitude by suggesting that it merely recognises the true motives for which benefits are conferred; by contrast, he shows how one might criticise the virtue of temperance by arguing that it reflects a state of innocence rather than any positively virtuous quality.[149] In several instances, however, he relies not on paradox but on paradiastole. One of his arguments in favour of cruelty is that, if an action condemned as cruel can be shown to have proceeded from a sense of danger, then it ought to be redescribed (and hence commended) as an instance of prudence.[150] Similarly, one of his arguments against courage is that the alleged virtue ought really to be redescribed (and hence condemned) as a species of prodigality, since it presupposes a willingness to be careless of one's own life and at the same time to endanger the lives of others.[151]

Of all the moralists of this period, however, it is Michel Montaigne in his *Essais* who makes the most daring use of paradiastole as a means of probing and questioning the conventional moral assumptions of the age. With the publication of John Florio's magnificent translation of the *Essais* in 1603, these observations entered the mainstream of English moral thought, with consequences for the understanding of paradiastole that proved of lasting importance.[152] Montaigne makes his most significant use of the device in his longest and perhaps most famous essay, his *Apology* for the Spanish theologian Raymond Sebond. Sebond had argued in his *Natural Theology* that all the truths of Christianity are susceptible of being demonstrated from the evidence of nature. Montaigne's 'defence' takes the paradoxical form of insisting that human reason is too weak a guide to lead us to any such definite conclusions about anything.[153] One way in which he presses the point is by emphasising the variety

[147] For a discussion of this Appendix see Jardine 1974, pp. 219–24.
[148] Bacon 1857, p. 689.   [149] Bacon 1857, pp. 694, 697.   [150] Bacon 1857, p. 695.
[151] Bacon 1857, p. 697.
[152] My quotations are taken from this translation. See Montaigne 1892–3. On the role of rhetoric in the presentation of Montaigne's moral outlook see Kritzman 1980, pp. 21–33, 95–105; Kahn 1985, pp. 115–51.
[153] On Montaigne and Sebond's text see Skinner 1978b, pp. 279–80. For an attempt to dispel the paradoxical air of Montaigne's defence see Gray 1974.

of human customs and laws. So extreme is their changeability that we cannot think of our own society as the embodiment of any absolute standards of goodness or truth. To do so would be to accept as goodness 'that which but yesterday I saw in credit and esteeme, and to morrow, to have lost all reputation'; similarly, it would be to accept as truth 'that which these Mountaines bound, and is a lie in the world beyond them'.[154] To underline his scepticism, Montaigne examines a number of our own most cherished customs and observances, adopting from Herodotus the tactic of considering how they might be viewed from an alien culture or a different historical period. The effect is to suggest that even our most exalted religious and social practices can always be redescribed in such a way as to challenge the evaluations we unhesitatingly place on them.

Montaigne's first example is that of the behaviour we think proper in the face of a father's death. We think it essential that our fathers should receive Christian burial. To this commitment, however, Montaigne opposes the outlook of those ancient tribes who instead regarded it as an act of 'abomination and cruelty' to 'cast the carcases of their parents into the corruption of the earth'.[155] He proceeds to examine their reasons for redescribing the act of burial in such unfamiliar terms. They believed that their most important duty was in some way to preserve their fathers among them. They believed in consequence that they ought to eat their fathers, thereby giving them 'the worthiest and most honourable sepulchre'.[156] We are left confronting the fact that an action of which we are bound to say that 'nothing can be imagined so horrible' can nevertheless be redescribed and commended as 'a testimonie of pietie and good affection'.[157] By contrast, we are forced to recognise that Christian burial, which we take to be a sacred duty, can nevertheless be redescribed and condemned as an indication of cruelty and disrespect.

The other example Montaigne considers in the same passage relates to our ideal of 'civility'. He first notes that, as part of the 'ceremonies' we associate with this ideal, we seek to restrain the public pursuit of various forms of behaviour – especially sexual behaviour – which we nevertheless regard as 'both lawful and honest, being done in secret'.[158] We describe these forms of concealment as instances of 'reservation and circumspection', thereby holding them up as 'parts of estimation' and commendable elements in a civilised life.[159] Montaigne contrasts this emphasis on gravity and decorum with the attitude of those ancient

---

[154] Montaigne 1892–3, vol. 2, p. 303.   [155] Montaigne 1892–3, vol. 2, p. 304.
[156] Montaigne 1892–3, vol. 2, p. 304.   [157] Montaigne 1892–3, vol. 2, p. 304.
[158] Montaigne 1892–3, vol. 2, p. 308.   [159] Montaigne 1892–3, vol. 2, p. 308.

philosophers who followed 'Nature's first image as a pattern', rather than 'the common-beaten path'.[160] These sages took the view that any attempt at 'concealing and disclaiming what nature, custome and our desire publish and proclame' must be regarded as a form of deceit, and in consequence 'deemed to be a vice'.[161] It follows that, if we were to confront these philosophers with the very forms of behaviour that we commend as *honnesteté*, they would be certain to condemn them as *sottise*.[162] As Florio's translation puts it, they would dismiss the very actions we admire for their civility as instances of folly or stupidity.[163]

V

As the technique of paradiastole was put to these increasingly provocative uses in the course of the sixteenth century, there was a corresponding revival among conservative moralists of the fear that the device had always aroused. It seemed to conjure up a world of complete moral arbitrariness, a world without any possibility of agreement about the application of moral terms, nor any possibility in consequence of avoiding a state of unending confusion and mutual hostility.

This anxiety was as old as the art of rhetoric itself. As we have seen, the historians and moralists of ancient Rome had viewed the technique with unmixed hostility, Livy going so far as to denounce it as 'the most infamous of all the arts'.[164] But similar anxieties had already been voiced at an even earlier date. Thucydides includes a withering denunciation of the evils of paradiastolic speech in Book 3 of his *History*, although he gives no name to the rhetorical technique involved. This may well have been one of the aspects of his political outlook that encouraged Hobbes to decide, when brooding about the impending political crisis of his own age, that the best means of instructing his fellow-countrymen would be to issue an English translation of Thucydides's *History*. Hobbes's version, originally published in 1629,[165] provides an unsurpassable rendering of the passage in which Thucydides describes how the cities of Greece fell into sedition, in the course of which 'the received value of names imposed for signification of things was changed into arbitrary'.[166] As a result, 'inconsiderate boldness was counted true-hearted manliness: provident

[160] Montaigne 1892–3, vol. 2, p. 307.   [161] Montaigne 1892–3, vol. 2, p. 308.
[162] Montaigne 1946–7, II. 12, vol. 3, p. 373.   [163] Montaigne 1892–3, vol. 2, p. 308.
[164] Livy 1929, XXII. XII. 12, p. 242 speaks of 'pessima ars'.
[165] Macdonald and Hargreaves 1952, p. 1.
[166] Hobbes 1975a, p. 222. The passage was frequently invoked by Renaissance writers interested in paradiastole. See, for example, Montaigne 1892–3, vol. 1, p. 118; Lipsius 1594, p. 69.

deliberation, a handsome fear: modesty, the cloak of cowardice: to be wise in every thing, to be lazy in every thing'. So great was the resulting corruption of public life that anyone who 'could outstrip another in the doing of an evil act, or that could persuade another thereto that never meant it, was commended'.[167]

With the revival of the *Ars rhetorica* in the Renaissance, these ancient fears burst forth with renewed vehemence. In England this happened almost as soon as the theory of *elocutio* began to be widely taught in the latter part of the sixteenth century. When Humfrey Braham, for example, published his somewhat nostalgic account of *The Institucion of a Gentleman* in 1555, he drew particular attention to 'the sayinge of the wyse Romayne Salust', who took note of 'the mysgovernaunce of many yonge gentylmen in Rome, whiche used to wrest the names of good thinges into the names of vices'.[168] We too, according to Braham, are losing 'the trew names of thinges', for with us too 'the givyng away of other mens goodes is called liberalitie, & unshamefastnes in noughty thinges, is called high or gentle courage'.[169]

Six years later, Sir Thomas Hoby's translation of Baldassare Castiglione's *Il Libro del Cortegiano* lent weighty support to these anxieties. Speaking at the outset of the debate about the qualities of the perfect courtier, the figure of the Count is made to complain that it is becoming 'almoste unpossible' to gain agreement about what sort of a person should be admired, 'and that by reason of the varietie of judgementes'.[170] Drawing specifically on the characterisation of paradiastole that Livy had put into currency, the Count goes on to explain that the problem arises because everyone is ready to 'prayse or dysprayse accordynge to hys fansye, always coverynge a vyce with the name of the next vertue to it, and a vertue with the name of the nexte vice'.[171] The Count underlines his point with a number of examples, two of which suggest that he may have been a student of Quintilian. Nowadays we find people calling 'him that is sawcye, bolde: hym that is sober, drie: hym that is seelye, good: hym that is unhappye, wittie, and lykewyse in the reste'.[172]

The same complaint was carried a step further when George Pettie and Bartholomew Young issued their translation of Stefano Guazzo's *La Civile Conversazione* in the early 1580s. According to the figure of Guazzo in the dialogue, the technique of denigrating people's behaviour by redescribing it in unfavourable terms has not only corrupted public

---

[167] Hobbes 1975a, pp. 222–3.   [168] [Braham] 1555, Sig. B iii[v].
[169] [Braham] 1555, Sig. B iv[r].   [170] Castiglione 1994, p. 37.
[171] Castiglione 1994, p. 37.   [172] Castiglione 1994, p. 37.

life, but is undermining the pleasure of civil conversation itself. 'The malice of men', Guazzo laments, has of late become 'so great that they spare not the honour of whosoever it bee, whether Prince or private person, and thinke sinisterly and preposterously of all the good deedes which are wrought'.[173] He specifically alludes to the technique of paradiastole as one of the means by which this malice is expressed. 'If you addict your selfe to devotion, and the exercise of charitie, you are taken for an hypocrite'; similarly, 'if you be affable and courteous, you shalbe called a flatterer'.[174]

In the generation immediately following, even fiercer denunciations of paradiastole began to appear. It was during this period that the subversive implications of the technique, as practised in particular by Machiavelli, first began to be widely recognised. The effect upon the more conservative moralists of late Elizabethan and early Stuart England was at once to revive their interest in the device, and at the same time to give them an even stronger sense of the need to counsel against its use.

A striking example can be found in the writings of Henry Peacham. As we have seen, Peacham issued his *Garden of Eloquence* in two very different forms, the first in 1577, the second in 1593.[175] In the original edition he contented himself with a conventional definition of paradiastole,[176] but in the revised version he went on to attack the use of the figure in violent terms. He now describes it as 'a vice of speech', which 'opposeth the truth by false tearmes, and wrong names, as in calling dronkennesse good felloship, insatiable avarice good husbandrie, craft and deceit wisdome and pollicie'.[177] It is no better than an 'instrument of excuse, serving to selfe-love, partiall favour, blinde affection, and a shamelesse person, which for the better maintenance of wickednesse useth to cover vices with the mantles of vertues'.[178]

A similar though immeasurably more eloquent denunciation of the technique can be found in Ben Jonson's *Catiline*, which was first performed and published in 1611.[179] The Chorus brings Act 4 to a close with an assault on Cicero's detractors which ends by calling on Rome, exactly as Cato had done in Sallust's *Bellum Catilinae*, to abandon the disgraceful and dangerous practice of paradiastole in favour of calling things by their proper names:

---

[173] Guazzo 1925, vol. 1, p. 38.   [174] Guazzo 1925, vol. 1, p. 38.
[175] See respectively Peacham 1971 and Peacham 1593. Javitch 1972, pp. 876–7 remarks on the difference between the two editions in their handling of paradiastole.
[176] Peacham 1971, Sig. N, iiii^v.   [177] Peacham 1593, pp. 168–9.   [178] Peacham 1593, p. 169.
[179] See Barton 1984, p. 154 and cf. pp. 157–9 on Jonson's use of Sallust.

What age is this, where honest men,
Plac'd at the helme,
A sea of some foule mouth, or pen,
Shall over-whelme?
And call their diligence, deceipt;
Their vertue, vice;
Their watchfulnesse, but lying in wait;
And bloud, the price.
O, let us plucke this evill seede
Out of our spirits;
And give, to every noble deede,
The name it merits.[180]

The honest are being overwhelmed not merely by the increasing tendency to excuse the vices but also by the direct disparagement of the virtues.

Of all the English moralists of this period, however, it is Hobbes who offers by far the fullest and most systematic critique of paradiastole, and it is within this context that his analysis needs to be placed if its significance is to be understood. Hobbes first considers the device in chapter 5 of *The Elements of Law*, where he treats it as one of the two major sources of confusion bedevilling the use of evaluative terms. It is worth beginning, as Hobbes himself does, by making a sharp distinction between the two types of ambiguity he singles out, if only because they have so often been conflated by his modern commentators, with the result that the importance of paradiastole in his moral and political theory has remained unrecognised.

One source of moral confusion stems from the fact that so many evaluative terms lack a univocal meaning. Hobbes examines this problem at the start of chapter 5, the main topic of which is the application of names. Many names 'are not of Constant Signification, but bringe into our mindes other thoughts, than those for which they were ordayned'.[181] Indeed, 'there is scarce any word that is not made Equivocall by divers Contexture of speech'.[182] By way of example Hobbes considers the word *faith*. It 'sometymes signifieth the same with belief', but sometimes it 'signifieth particularly that belief which maketh a Christian' and sometimes it instead 'signifieth the keepinge of a Promise'.[183]

---

[180] Jonson 1937, p. 526.   [182] Hobbes 1969a, p. 20.   [183] Hobbes 1969a, pp. 20–1.
[183] Hobbes 1969a, p. 20. Hobbes gives other examples at pp. 38 and 83.

In the final section of the chapter Hobbes turns to the other source of confusion, which he explicitly contrasts with the problems resulting from 'unconstant' definitions of terms. This further difficulty stems from the fact that the application of all evaluative terms will always be 'diversified by Passion'.[184] Due to their varying temperaments, different individuals will always be prone to assess particular actions and states of affairs from disparate points of view. As a result, they will tend to apply different evaluative terms – whose meanings need not be in dispute – as rival descriptions of the same set of circumstances. The upshot is that we can hardly hope to find 'scarce two men agreeing, what is to be called good, and what evill'.[185] Hobbes goes on to offer two specific examples to underline his point. Both are classic instances of paradiastolic redescription, and both had already been singled out by a number of earlier writers – especially Susenbrotus and his English disciples[186] – as standard examples of the technique. One is that of someone who redescribes a liberal action as a case of prodigality; the other is that of someone who redescribes an act of valour as a case of temerity.[187]

Hobbes's chief purpose in identifying these two sources of linguistic confusion is to emphasise the social conflicts that inevitably flow from them.[188] He initially speaks of these dangers in purely general terms, stressing the incommodities that arise from the fact that 'the Invention of names' has so often 'precipitated men into Errour'.[189] But when he comes to the political section of his argument, he mainly concentrates on the dangers of paradiastolic speech. He first makes the point in the course of analysing the laws of nature in chapter 17. Even if men agree about the content of these laws, and hence about the range of the moral virtues, their differing passions will make it difficult for them 'to understand by what actions, and Circumstances of Actions, those Lawes are broken'.[190] But if people cannot agree about the actions that ought and ought not to be characterised as virtuous, then 'there must needes arise many great Controversies about the interpretation thereof, by which the peace must needes be dissolved'.[191] The final chapter on the dissolution of commonwealths puts the same argument even more bluntly. 'Where

---

[184] Hobbes 1969a, ch. 5, p. 23. Hobbes enlarges on the point in ch. 7, p. 29, and repeats it in ch. 17, pp. 93–4.

[185] Hobbes 1969a, p. 23.

[186] The same examples can already be found in Susenbrotus 1562, p. 45; Puttenham 1970, pp. 184–5; Day 1967, p. 84 (second pagination).

[187] Hobbes 1969a, p. 23.

[188] See the valuable discussion in Whelan 1981, pp. 73–4.

[189] Hobbes 1969a, p. 22.   [190] Hobbes 1969a, p. 90.   [191] Hobbes 1969a, p. 90.

every man is his owne Judge, and differeth from other concerning the names and appellations of thinges', we shall inevitably find that from those differences 'arise quarrells, and breach of Peace'.[192]

Soon after circulating *The Elements of Law*, Hobbes revised and expanded the political section of his manuscript, issuing the resulting treatise as *De Cive* in 1642. One of the many concepts he examines more fully in this first published version of his civil science is that of paradiastole. Not only does *De Cive* offer a more extensive explanation of how the phenomenon of paradiastolic speech arises; it also expresses an even keener sense of anxiety about the dangers attending its use.

Hobbes presents his new analysis in the course of chapter 3, the principal aim of which is to demonstrate that the laws of nature and the traditional moral virtues are one and the same. Towards the end of his discussion he addresses the question of how we can hope to persuade someone that a given action ought to be described with the name of a virtue. He concedes that this raises a serious difficulty, the source of which he begins by identifying in terms that recall and extend the argument of *The Elements of Law*:

The words *good* and *evil* are names imposed on things in order to indicate either the desire or the aversion of those by whom the things in question are named. However, the desires of men are diverse, depending as they do on the diversity of their temperaments, their customs and their attitudes. This is particularly so, moreover, in the things that pertain to life's public activities, where we not only find one person *commending* (that is, calling *good*) something that another person *denounces* (that is, calls *evil*); in many cases we even find the same person at different times *praising* and *censuring* the very same thing.[193]

Hobbes next turns to examine the resulting difficulty, again echoing and elaborating his earlier account. 'It may be that everyone agrees to speak in praise of the virtues of which we have spoken.'[194] It may be, that is, that everyone agrees about the meanings, and hence the evaluative direction, of such terms as 'modesty, equity, good faith, humanity, pity' and so forth.[195] 'Nevertheless', Hobbes concludes, 'people may still disagree

---

[192] Hobbes 1969a, p. 188.
[193] Hobbes 1983a, III. XXXI, p. 119: '*bonum & malum* nomina esse rebus imposita ad significandum appetitum vel aversionem eorum a quibus sic nominantur. Appetitus autem hominum pro diversis eorum temperamentis, consuetudinibus, opinionibusque, diversi sunt ... sed multo magis, in iis rebus quae pertinet ad actiones vitae communes, ubi quod hic *laudat*, id est, appellat *bonum*, alter *vituperat* ut *malum*; immo saepissime idem homo diversis temporibus idem & *laudat* & *culpat*.'
[194] Hobbes 1983a, III. XXXII, p. 120: 'consentiant omnes in laude dictarum virtutum'.
[195] See Hobbes 1983a, III. XXXI, p. 120, listing *modestia, aequitas, fides, humanitas, misericordia*.

about their nature, and about the sort of thing in which each of these qualities may be said to reside.'[196] They may disagree, that is, as to whether or not some particular action or state of affairs deserves to be described by the name of one of the virtues.

Hobbes later enlarges on the point, with rather greater clarity, in the course of discussing the concept of civil law in chapter 14. 'There may be general agreement that certain forms of behaviour, such as *theft, adultery* and the like, are to be described as *sins*.'[197] We may agree, that is, about the meanings of those particular terms, and hence agree 'that they can only be taken in a bad sense' and employed to censure whatever courses of actions they are used to describe.'[198] As Hobbes stresses, however, 'we are not asking whether theft is a sin; we are asking what is to count as a case of theft'.[199] Even if we agree, that is, about the meaning and evaluative use of the term, we may still disagree as to whether it is legitimate to apply it in some particular case in order to describe (and hence condemn) the action involved.

It is when Hobbes turns in chapter 3 to explain why this problem is ineliminable that he specifically alludes to the device of paradiastole. He considers the case of 'a good action performed by someone which is displeasing to someone else'.[200] Citing the precondition of paradiastolic redescription which, as we have seen, Livy in Aristotelian vein had particularly emphasised, he points out that it will always be open to such a critic 'to impose upon the action in question the name of some neighbouring vice'.[201] By the same token, 'disgraceful actions which please people can similarly be redescribed with the name of a virtue'.[202] It is because of this 'neighbourly' relationship between so many of the virtues and the vices, Hobbes concludes, 'that one and the same action can always be praised by some, and described as a virtue, while others censure it and convert it into a vice'.[203]

---

[196] Hobbes 1983a, III. XXXII, p. 120: 'tamen dissentiant adhuc de earum natura, in quo nempe, unaquaeque earum consistat'.

[197] Hobbes 1983a, XIV. XVII, p. 214: 'Possunt quidem convenire in generalia quaedam, veluti *furtum, adulterium,* & similia, esse *peccata*.'

[198] Hobbes 1983a, XIV. XVII, p. 214 uses the phrase 'in malam partem accipi'.

[199] Hobbes 1983a, XIV. XVII, p. 214: 'Sed non quaerimus an furtum sit peccatum; quaerimus quid furtum dicendum sit.'

[200] Hobbes 1983a, III. XXXII, p. 120 speaks of a *bona actio* which *cuiquam displicet*.

[201] Hobbes 1983a, III. XXXII, p. 120: 'ei actioni imponitur nomen alicuius vitii vicini'.

[202] Hobbes 1983a, III. XXXII, p. 120: 'similiter nequitiae quae placent, ad virtutem aliquam referuntur'.

[203] Hobbes 1983a, III. XXXII, p. 120: 'Unde evenit eandem actionem ab his laudari & virtutem appellari, ab illis culpari & vitio verti.'

Hobbes's discussion in chapter 3 culminates in a demonstration of the intense danger of employing the device. As we have seen, his chief purpose in this chapter is to show that the traditional list of the moral virtues can be equated with the laws of nature. But the laws of nature, he has already argued, are the names of those theorems that must indispensably be accepted if we are to succeed in preserving civic peace.[204] It follows that, if we cannot agree about the lines of conduct that are properly to be described as virtuous, civic peace will inevitably be jeopardised. Hobbes draws the inference even more grimly than in *The Elements of Law*. 'Wherever *good* and *evil* are measured by the mere diversity of present desires, and hence by a corresponding diversity of yardsticks, those who act in this way will find themselves still in a state of war.'[205]

When Hobbes reverts to the problem of paradiastole in *Leviathan*, he largely reiterates – and at some points even abridges[206] – these earlier accounts. His discussion in *Leviathan* is notable, however, for introducing a new range of examples. As in *The Elements of Law*, Hobbes places his account of paradiastole at the end of his chapter on speech and its abuses. As before, he begins by noting that the problem of 'different naming' can arise even when 'the nature of that we conceive, be the same'.[207] The basic reason, he again stresses, lies in the fact that we all have 'different constitutions of body, and prejudices of opinion'.[208] These in turn are bound to affect our sense of how best to describe any given action or state of affairs. The moral is that 'in reasoning, a man must take heed of words; which besides the signification of what we imagine of their nature, have a signification also of the nature, disposition, and interest of the speaker'.[209] This is particularly evident in the case of 'the names of Vertues, and Vices'. For 'one man calleth *Wisdome*, what another calleth *feare*; and one *cruelty*, what another *justice*; one *prodigality*, what another *magnanimity*; and one *gravity*, what another *stupidity*, &c.'[210]

Of these examples, two had already been widely cited as paradigm cases of paradiastolic speech. The possibility of excusing a cruel action by redescribing it as strict justice or mere severity had been one of Susenbrotus's leading illustrations, and had already been taken up by

---

[204] Hobbes 1983a, II.I–III, pp. 98–100.
[205] Hobbes 1983a, III. XXXI, p. 119: 'Sunt igitur tamdiu in statu belli, quam *bonum* & *malum* prae appetituum praesentium diversitate, diversis mensuris metiuntur.'
[206] There is no mention in *Leviathan* of the 'neighbourly' relationship between certain vices and virtues invoked in *De Cive* to explain the phenomenon of paradiastolic speech.
[207] Hobbes 1996, ch. 4, p. 31.   [208] Hobbes 1996, ch. 4, p. 31.   [209] Hobbes 1996, ch. 4, p. 31.
[210] Hobbes 1996, ch. 4, p. 31.

several of his English followers, including both Wilson and Peacham.[211] The example of excusing a prodigal action by redescribing it as liberal or magnanimous was even more familiar. As we have already seen, it occurs in Seneca and Tacitus, again in Susenbrotus, again in several of his English admirers, including both Puttenham and Day,[212] and again in Hobbes's own earlier discussion of paradiastolic speech in *The Elements of Law*.

These examples point to Hobbes's familiarity with the standard rhetorical literature of his age. But his other two instances are of even greater interest, for in these cases it seems possible to identify a specific source. First he considers the case of someone redescribing, and hence dismissing, an act of wisdom or prudence as an instance of mere timorousness or fear. This is not an example to be found in any of the Renaissance discussions of paradiastole, nor in any of the classical guides to the *Ars rhetorica* from which they were largely derived. As we have seen, however, this was exactly the example that Livy had given in describing how Fabius Maximus's master of horse had sought to challenge his tactics in the war against Hannibal. The implication is that Hobbes's illustration may well be taken directly from Livy, especially as he alludes to the same passage from the *History* in discussing the concept of paradiastole in *De Cive*.[213]

Hobbes's last example is that of someone redescribing a grave or measured form of behaviour as an instance of mere dullness or stupidity. This memorable illustration is without precedent in any of the rhetorical textbooks we have examined, whether from the classical or the Renaissance period. As we have seen, however, Montaigne considers it at length in the course of his remarks about the ambiguities of moral description in his *Apology* for Sebond. We are left with the fascinating possibility that, during his exile in France, at some point between the publication of *De Cive* in 1642 and *Leviathan* in 1651, Hobbes may have made a study of Montaigne's *Apology* for the first time.[214]

---

[211] See Susenbrotus 1562, p. 45; Wilson 1554, fos. 66ᵛ, 67ʳ; Peacham 1971, Sig. N, iiiiᵛ.

[212] See Puttenham 1970, pp. 184–5; Day 1967, p. 84 (second pagination).

[213] Hobbes 1983a, VII. XVI, p. 157.

[214] There are independent reasons for thinking this plausible. Hobbes MSS (Chatsworth) MS E. 1. A, the Chatsworth library catalogue of the 1630s, contains no copy of any work by Montaigne, suggesting that Hobbes may not have had access to Montaigne's works before the 1640s. But in *Leviathan* there are several allusions to Montaigne's *Essais*. For example, the joke about everyone being contented with their own share of wisdom in Hobbes 1996, ch. 13 p. 87 can be found in Montaigne 1946–7, II. 17, vol. 4, p. 84. Likewise, the contemptuous reference to scholars behaving like birds in Hobbes 1996, ch. 4, p. 28 resembles Montaigne 1946–7, I. 25, vol. 1, pp. 190–1.

Hobbes's analysis of paradiastole in *Leviathan* is also notable for the even greater pessimism with which he confronts the dangers of using the device. He makes the point in high rhetorical style in concluding his survey of the laws of nature in chapter 15. 'Morall Philosophy', he declares, 'is nothing else but the Science of what is *Good*, and *Evill*, in the conversation, and Society of man-kind.' But this science is threatened by the fact that '*Good*, and *Evill*, are names that signifie our Appetites, and Aversions; which in different tempers, customes and doctrines of men, are different'. The implications of these differences are as grave as possible. So long as 'private Appetite is the measure of Good, and Evill', we shall find ourselves living 'in the condition of meer Nature'.[215] And this condition, as Hobbes has already demonstrated in chapter 13, is nothing other than a state of war of all upon all.[216]

Hobbes's engagement with the problem of paradiastole is one of the most extensive in the political literature of the seventeenth century. Having first addressed the topic in his translation of Thucydides in 1629, he only says his final word on the subject in the Latin *Leviathan* of 1668.[217] Moreover, his analysis constitutes one of the last serious treatments of the issue in English moral and political thought. Towards the end of the seventeenth century the popularity of neo-classical rhetoric in England appears to have fallen into a sharp decline,[218] as a result of which the study of moral philosophy quickly lost any contact with the rhetorical assumptions and vocabulary in terms of which a number of meta-ethical issues, including that of paradiastole, had previously been discussed. By the early eighteenth century the word had fallen completely out of use, and most of the stock examples of the phenomenon had similarly passed into oblivion.[219] Among moral theorists of that period, we already find the topic of evaluative redescription being handled in an idiom far more reminiscent of modern philosophical debates about the so-called problem of 'moral realism'.[220]

---

[215] Hobbes 1996, ch. 15, p. 111.   [216] Hobbes 1996, ch. 13, pp. 88–9.

[217] Hobbes's own translation (and extensive revision) of *Leviathan* was published in the edition of his Latin works issued by Johan Blaeu, Amsterdam 1668.

[218] Although historians of rhetoric have yet to investigate the reasons for this decline, the printing histories of the leading English rhetorical textbooks of the second half of the seventeenth century leave little doubt that there was a precipitate loss of popularity after the 1680s. Consider, for example, Farnaby 1970 (first published 1625), Blount 1971 (first published 1656), or Smith 1969 (first published 1657). The first reached a fifteenth edition in 1696, the second a sixth edition in 1683, the third a fifth edition in 1688, but thereafter none was republished until the twentieth century. See Murphy 1981, pp. 50, 143–4, 271–2.

[219] Here I rely on the OED, which treats the word as obsolete, giving 1706 as the last date at which a definition was attempted.

[220] For an excellent survey of types of 'realism' in contemporary moral philosophy see Railton 1986.

During the last quarter of the seventeenth century, however, there was one further English writer who made a contribution of major importance to the analysis of paradiastolic speech. This was Dr Robert South, Canon of Christ Church and Prebendary of Westminster, who delivered and subsequently published an entire series of sermons on the subject in 1686.[221] A writer of deeply conservative temperament,[222] South declares at the outset that the danger which concerns him – that of 'the fatal imposture and force of words' – has of late become more threatening than ever before.[223] This is due to the popularity of two contrasting ways of thinking about the issue of paradiastolic speech, both of which South begins by stigmatising as false and absurd. The first he evidently associates with Montaigne, since his exposition includes a number of disapproving allusions to the *Apology* for Sebond.[224] The other he definitely associates with Hobbes, since he identifies him as 'the infamous author of the *Leviathan*' and denounces him for his 'lewd, scandalous and immoral' views about the relationship between virtue and vice.[225]

South then turns to consider the phenomenon of paradiastole anew. He begins by stressing the peculiarity which, as we have seen, practically every writer on the topic had emphasised: the fact that there is a 'similitude, neighbourhood and affinity' between 'vice and virtue, good and evil, in several notable instances of each'.[226] He then mentions a range of cases in which a danger of 'promiscuous confusion' can easily arise from these misleading similarities.[227] Most of his examples are familiar, indeed hackneyed: they include the difficulty of distinguishing 'between liberality and prodigality'; between 'an act of courage and an act of recklessness'; and between 'an act of pusillanimity and an act of great modesty or humility'.[228] More interestingly, however, he rounds off his list by repeating the example that Hobbes had perhaps found in Montaigne. 'Nay, and some have had the good luck to have their very dullness dignified with the name of gravity, and to be no small gainers by the mistake.'[229]

South is not primarily interested, however, in offering a new analysis of paradiastolic speech. As the above account indicates, he is largely

[221] South (1634–1716) delivered four sermons on 'this vast and even immense subject' (South 1823f, p. 285). For the first sermon see South 1823a. The other three are collected in South 1823b at pp. 103–34, 235–64, 265–88. For a discussion see Reedy 1992, pp. 93–102.
[222] It was he who delivered the oration denouncing the Royal Society at the dedication of the Sheldonian Theatre in July 1669. See below, chapter 12 section III.
[223] South 1823a, p. 108.   [224] South 1823a, pp. 113–14.   [225] South 1823a, p. 115.
[226] South 1823a, p. 129.   [227] South 1823a, p. 130.   [228] South 1823a, p. 130.
[229] South 1823a, p. 130.

content to lay out the issues in conventional style. His main purpose is to emphasise the dangerous and subversive character of the device. Here at least he and Hobbes stand together. With a command of rhetoric not unworthy of the infamous author of *Leviathan*, South repeatedly inveighs against the 'verbal magic' of paradiastole and the 'enchantment' to which it gives rise.[230] The effect is that people are 'ushered to their destruction with panegyric and acclamation' in a shameful display 'of the absurd empire and usurpation of words over things'.[231] So seriously does South view the device that, by the end of his concluding sermon, he has managed to convince himself that 'most of the miseries and calamities which afflict mankind, and turn the world upside down, have been conceived in, and issue from, the fruitful womb of this one villainous artifice'.[232]

VI

If the technique of paradiastole represents such a dangerous threat to the moral basis of political life, how can the threat be neutralised? How can the boundaries of moral description be fixed and a stable moral order guaranteed? These are the questions to which the writers we have been considering next address themselves, and in working towards an answer they generally place their faith in two connected lines of argument.

They usually begin by appealing, implicitly or explicitly, to the fundamental principle that the moral order must be treated as an aspect of the order of nature. This is the basic assumption, for example, with which Gentillet confronts Machiavelli's attempt to redescribe the lines of conduct normally proscribed in public life. Gentillet puts the point most directly in the course of discussing Machiavelli's maxim that 'a prince neede not care to be accounted cruell'.[233] Gentillet responds that this is not just 'to praise that which is to be despised and detested'. It is 'to overthrow the order which God and nature have established in the distinction of good and evill things'.[234]

Benjamin Whichcote draws on the same assumption in the sermon he preached specifically against the dangers of paradiastolic speech. He asks how we can hope to counter what he describes as the sin of *'eluding one's own Judgement'* by 'pretending to Difference, when there is

---

[230] South 1823a, pp. 126, 128.
[231] South 1823a, p. 128. Cf. also South 1823b, pp. 204–6, 235–6 on the mischievous, direful and even fatal effects of employing the device.
[232] South 1823b, p. 286.   [233] [Gentillet] 1602, p. 199.   [234] [Gentillet] 1602, p. 215.

none'. We must ensure, he replies, that we are 'severe and impartial; not giving our selves leave to comply with our *own* Humours'. This may be emotionally arduous, but it is a matter of no great intellectual difficulty. We merely need to pay sufficient attention to 'the great *Notices* of Reason and Nature; the Measures of Vertue and Vice', which show us that the differences between such terms are created not '*by Will*; but by the Reason of the thing'.[235]

The same assumptions likewise underlie Robert South's sermon in denunciation of Montaigne and his followers. We need to recognise, South insists, that 'good and evil, honest and dishonest' are not 'founded in the opinions of men concerning things'. They are 'qualities existing or inherent in things themselves'.[236] Such actions as 'murder, adultery, theft, fraud' are equally evil at all places and all times, and no amount of redescription can possibly render them good.[237] The reason, South grandiloquently concludes, is that 'the nature of good and evil, as to the principal instances of both, spring from that essential habitude, or relation, which the nature of one thing bears to another by virtue of that order which they stand placed in, here in the world, by the very law and condition of their creation'.[238]

These writers recognise, however, that it is only half the battle to be able to insist that the terms denoting the virtues and vices are at the same time the names of inherently good and evil qualities. We still need to be able to establish, in the case of any action whose moral quality may be in doubt, that one or other of the terms we normally use to describe the virtues and vices can indisputably be applied as the right description of the action concerned. Unless we can somehow fasten our evaluative language unambiguously onto the world of social behaviour, the threat of paradiastolic redescription will not have been eliminated.

It is at this juncture that most of the writers we have been considering turn to their second strand of argument. They go on to claim that the question of whether it is justifiable to apply a particular appraisive term will always in effect be a factual one. Among those who defend this thesis in detail – for example, Robert South – it is generally possible to distinguish two separate steps in their reasoning. First, they insist on the need to clarify at the outset what South calls 'the general natures and definitions' of the terms we employ to mark off good and evil behaviour.[239] This is the indispensable step we must take if we eventually wish to be able to say

[235] Whichcote 1698, pp. 80–1.   [236] South 1823a, p. 113.   [237] South 1823a, p. 116.
[238] South 1823a, p. 121.   [239] South 1823a, p. 129.

with confidence that a given action is properly to be described as liberal rather than prodigal, courageous rather than reckless, and so forth. If we fail to begin by grasping the correct definitions of such appraisive terms, and instead remain content to 'take names and words as they first come', we shall find ourselves unable to speak with any confidence about individual cases. Without a preliminary understanding of definition, we can never hope 'to draw the line nicely and exactly between vice and virtue, and to adjust the due limits of each'.[240]

South's point had already been foreshadowed by a number of classical writers on paradiastole. Recall, for example, the discussion in the *Ad Herennium* about whether the behaviour of gladiators can be described as truly courageous. To arrive at the answer, according to the *Ad Herennium*, we must first remind ourselves of the full and exact definition of the term *courage*. We need to recollect, that is, that the meaning of the word is such that it can only be applied in circumstances in which someone has faced a danger, and in which we feel confident in adding that 'the purpose is useful and the advantages have been duly weighed'.[241]

The second step, according to the writers we are considering, must then be to examine the exact circumstances of the action or state of affairs to be appraised. South makes this further point by way of invoking the visual metaphor that pervades so many of these discussions about how to make our moral language fit the world. We must learn 'to discern the real good and evil' that comes before our eyes. We must seek above all 'to consider and weigh circumstances, to scatter and look through the mists of error, and so separate appearances from realities'.[242]

As before, the suggestion that we can hope to 'see' how any given action requires to be described is one that classical discussions of paradiastole had always emphasised. Consider again the example of the gladiators in the *Ad Herennium*. Does their behaviour deserve to be regarded as truly courageous? We begin by reminding ourselves that courage involves facing a danger where 'the purpose is useful and the advantages have been duly weighed'. We then ask ourselves whether the facts about gladiatorial contests answer to this definition. Reflecting on this question, we are bound to recognise that gladiators fight for no useful purpose, and 'without any consideration of the risks'.[243] This being so, we are bound to conclude that they cannot be said to exemplify genuine

---

[240] South 1823a, p. 130.
[241] *Ad C. Herennium* 1954, IV. XXV. 35, p. 316: 'cum ratione utilitatis et conpensatione commodorum'.
[242] South 1823a, p. 130.
[243] *Ad C. Herennium* 1954, IV. XXV. 35, p. 316: 'cum inconsiderata dolorum'.

courage. They can only be described as exhibiting 'a kind of reckless temerity'.[244]

By now it will be clear why these lines of reasoning were widely held to neutralise the dangers of paradiastole. They issue in the conclusion that any given action can always be truly described, and in consequence truly appraised. By lining up definitions with facts, we can always hope, as South insists, to arrive at 'a full discovery of the true goodness and evil of things'.[245] But if this can genuinely be done, then the possibility of paradiastolic redescription will be automatically ruled out. If we now attempt, for example, to redescribe the behaviour of the gladiators as a case of genuine courage, we shall stand convicted of misapprehending and in consequence falsely describing the facts of the case.

This conclusion was explicitly drawn by almost every English rhetorician who addressed the problem of paradiastole in the era of the Renaissance. Henry Peacham declares that any paradiastolic redescription simply 'opposeth the truth by false tearmes and wrong names'.[246] George Puttenham agrees that the essence of the technique consists of describing an action with 'a terme more favorable and of lesse vehemencie then the troth requires'.[247] Francis Bacon likewise admits that, whenever we engage in the exercise of producing 'antitheses', we always seek 'to exaggerate or depreciate the facts with the full force of human ingenuity in a fashion that is not only unfair but is altogether beyond the truth'.[248]

Among moral philosophers of the same period, the implications of the argument were usually stated in very similar terms. Consider, for example, the upshot of the attack mounted by Gentillet on Machiavelli for having claimed that 'Crueltie which tendeth to a good end is not to be reprehended'.[249] Gentillet concedes that cruel actions can often be 'coloured with some pretext or shew of good'; even murderers sometimes manage to 'call themselves abbreviators of justice'.[250] But in spite of any such 'pallations & shewes', we cannot doubt that, with 'their maske or visard taken from them, murder will always bee found murder, and theft, theft'.[251] To describe such actions in any other terms will simply be 'to call things with contrarie names'.[252]

---

[244] See *Ad C. Herennium* 1954, IV. XXV. 35, p. 316 for the claim that exposing oneself to danger 'cum inconsiderata dolorum perpessione gladiatoria' can only be described as *temeritas*.

[245] South 1823a, p. 131.   [246] Peacham 1593, p. 168.   [247] Puttenham 1970, p. 220.

[248] Bacon 1857, p. 688: 'eosque ultimis ingenii viribus, et tanquam improbe et prorsus praeter veritatem, attolli et deprimi'.

[249] [Gentillet] 1602, p. 227.   [250] [Gentillet] 1602, p. 228.   [251] [Gentillet] 1602, p. 228.

[252] [Gentillet] 1602, p. 215.

Robert South's criticism of Montaigne and his followers issues in the same conclusion: paradiastolic redescriptions are simply untrue to the facts. They amount to 'a misrepresentation of the qualities of things and actions to the common apprehensions of men, abusing their minds with false notions, and so by this artifice making evil pass for good, and good for evil, in all the great concerns of life'.[253] Recurring in one of his later sermons to the image of 'seeing' moral truths, South adds that such redescriptions merely judge 'by a false light'.[254] As soon as we recognise that this is so, our duty becomes clear. 'Let strict, naked and undisguised truth take place in all things; and let not evil be dignified with the title of good, nor good libelled with the name of evil, by a false and fraudulent appellation of things.'[255]

John Locke appears to arrive at something like the same conclusion in Book 3 of his *Essay Concerning Human Understanding*. Locke first acknowledges (in a passage remarkably reminiscent of *Leviathan*) that the difficulty of relating moral terms to their corresponding ideas will always be especially acute. 'Men's Names, of very compound *Ideas*, such as for the most part are moral Words, have seldom, in two different Men, the same precise signification; since one Man's complex *Idea* seldom agrees with anothers, and often differs from his own, from that which he had yesterday, or will have to morrow.'[256] But whereas Hobbes had emphasised the dangers of paradiastolic redescription to which this gives rise, Locke appears to believe that the problem can readily be overcome. By way of illustration, he offers one of the standard examples of paradiastolic speech in the rhetorical literature: the case in which 'I apply the Name *Frugality* to that *Idea* which others call and signify by this sound, *Covetousness*'.[257] According to Locke, the right way to resolve this kind of difficulty is simply to recognise that these are instances in which 'I may have the *Ideas* of Vertues, or Vices, and Names also', but in which I proceed to 'apply them amiss'.[258] Locke's general solution is thus that, when we frame in our minds a moral idea – the example he takes is that of justice – we first need to consider the circumstances that must answer to that idea for the term to be properly applied. We then need to consider, in the case of any action appraised as just or unjust, whether it meets our definition of justice, and can therefore 'pass under that denomination'.[259] So long as we take care to provide such definitions, we can be sure that 'moral Knowledge' will result, since good definitions

---

[253] South 1823a, p. 108.   [254] South 1823b, p. 204.   [255] South 1823b, p. 263.
[256] Locke 1979, III. IX. 6, p. 478.   [257] Locke 1979, III. X. 33, p. 507.
[258] Locke 1979, III. X. 33, p. 507.   [259] Locke 1979, III. XI. 17, p. 517.

of words provide 'a way, whereby their Meaning may be known *certainly*, and without leaving any room for any contest about it'.[260] Once again, the suggestion seems to be that, so long as the terms expressing our ideas are brought into conformity with the facts of the case, this will enable us to rule out the possibility of the facts being rhetorically redescribed.[261]

VII

As a solution to the problem of paradiastole, the suggestion that we can always hope to 'see' whether our moral language has been applied correctly or amiss was widely taken up. Among the writers we have been considering, however, by no means everyone admitted the force of the argument. During the course of the sixteenth century, a number of sceptically-minded humanists began to raise serious doubts about its premises, thereby implying that the dangers of paradiastole remained stubbornly unresolved.

Some of these writers went so far as to question the fundamental assumption that the moral order forms an aspect of the order of nature. This certainly appears to be an implication of Machiavelli's argument in the notorious central chapters of *Il Principe*. It is true that Machiavelli usually concentrates on the paradiastolic claim that, while cruelty and parsimony are undoubtedly the names of vices, many of the actions we normally condemn as cruel or parsimonious ought not to be described in such unfavourable terms. Sometimes, however, he appears to mount a different and more radical line of argument. He sometimes seems willing to question whether the terms we employ to describe the vices really are the names of actions that deserve to be condemned. What we call liberality, he sometimes seems to suggest, may not in fact be the name of a virtue; similarly, what we call cruelty may not be the name of a vice.[262]

If we turn to Montaigne, we find an even clearer willingness to challenge the idea of eternal fitnesses. As we have seen, to a writer like Gentillet it appears indisputable that, if an action can rightly be described as theft, then it must automatically stand condemned. But Montaigne disagrees. In his *Apology* for Sebond he examines the attitude of the ancient Spartans towards the taking of other people's goods. The Spartans

---

[260] Locke 1979, III. XI. 17, p. 517.
[261] For a discussion of Locke's views about words signifying ideas, and a comparison with Hobbes, see Ayers 1991, pp. 248–56.
[262] For these suggestions see especially Machiavelli 1960, pp. 67, 68–9.

are represented as acknowledging that such behaviour can only be described as theft, and thus as an instance of injustice.[263] However, they preferred to emphasise 'the vivacitie, diligence, courage, and nimblenesse that is required in surprising or taking any thing from ones neighbour, and the commodity which thereby redoundeth to the common wealth, that every man heedeth more curiously the keeping of that which is his owne'.[264] They took these considerations to be of greater weight than the injustice resulting from the seizure of other people's property. As a consequence, they viewed such actions in an unfamiliar moral light. While conceding that they amounted to theft, they denied that they ought on that account to be condemned. For them, theft was not the name of a sin.

The premise on which the more sceptical humanists mainly train their doubts, however, is the optimistic assumption that there will always be a true way of 'seeing' any given action or state of affairs. We already find the figure of the Count in Castiglione's *Cortegiano* shaking his head over this assumption in a frankly incredulous way. As we have seen, the Count is more impressed by the fact that we live in a world in which it is all too easy to call 'him that is sawcye, bolde; him that is sober, drie', and so forth.[265] This makes it very hard to 'see' how people's behaviour ought best to be described and appraised. As the Count says of himself, although he likes to believe 'that eche thing hath his perfection', he is forced to admit that the truth 'is oftentimes hid', and is never easy to discern. The same thing can easily manifest itself in many different lights. 'Not onelye one thynge maie seme unto you, and an other to me, but also unto my self it may appere sometime one thing, sometime another.'[266]

Montaigne – who includes several admiring references to the *Cortegiano* in his *Essais*[267] – announces a similar scepticism in his *Apology* for Sebond. He begins, like Castiglione, by placing a strong emphasis on the way in which our passions enter and affect our sense of how best to describe and appraise social behaviour. This explains why we cannot treat the laws of our country as a pattern of justice. Such laws amount to nothing more than a 'waveing sea of a peoples or of a Princes opinions, which shall paint me forth justice with as many colours, and reform the same into as many visages, as there are changes and alterations of passions in them'.[268]

[263] Montaigne 1892–3, vol. 2, p. 305.   [264] Montaigne 1892–3, vol. 2, p. 304.
[265] Castiglione 1994, p. 37. On paradox in Castiglione see Ossola 1987, pp. 51–9. For Castiglione's views about the mutability of language see Rebhorn 1983.
[266] Castiglione 1994, p. 36.
[267] See, for example, Montaigne 1892–3, vol. 1, p. 338, vol. 2, p. 373.
[268] Montaigne 1892–3, vol. 2, p. 302.

Of even greater importance in shaping our appraisals are the customs and institutions by which our sensibilities are themselves formed. So powerful is the force of custom that different nations frequently 'see' the same thing in a completely different light. 'One nation vieweth a subject with one visage, and thereon it staies; an other with an other.'[269] Nor can we hope to appeal from custom to reason to gain a clearer sense of how the subject in question ought truly to be seen. For even reason is affected by custom, and 'yeeldeth appearance to divers effects'. It is a 'pitcher with two eares, which a man may take hold on, either by the right or left hand'.[270] There can be no end, in short, to arguing *in utramque partem*.

There is thus no possibility of appealing to incontestable facts as a foundation for moral arguments. To suppose otherwise is an illusion, Montaigne thinks, even in the case of the law. 'So infinite a science' can only give rise to 'an exceeding confusion of judgements'. Alluding to the Count's way of putting the point in the *Cortegiano*, Montaigne insists that 'what one company hath judged, another will adjudge the contrary, and the very same will another time change opinion'.[271] The illusion merely becomes the more obvious, Montaigne thinks, if we turn to 'philosophicall opinions concerning vice and vertue'. There our variations of judgement scarcely need any emphasis, and some of them are best not mentioned at all.[272]

Hobbes has recently been portrayed by a number of commentators as in some way 'replying' to Montaigne and other exponents of Pyrrhonian scepticism. There may be something to be said for this interpretation of Hobbes's philosophy of nature. But when it comes to the question of human custom and law, he appears to be largely in agreement with the lines of argument laid out by Montaigne in his *Apology*. Hobbes in fact constitutes a further example – and perhaps the most important – of a writer who is deeply troubled by the dangers of paradiastole, but who nevertheless insists that all existing attempts to neutralise the threat have fallen short of the mark.

He is notorious in the first place for denying that the moral order can be viewed as an aspect of the order of nature. In every version of his civil science he goes out of his way to repudiate any suggestion that the virtues, and hence the laws of nature, can be treated as a part of the eternal fitness of things. A thorough-going voluntarist, he directly

---

[269] Montaigne 1892–3, vol. 2, p. 304. [270] Montaigne 1892–3, vol. 2, p. 305.
[271] Montaigne 1892–3, vol. 2, p. 306. [272] Montaigne 1892–3, vol. 2, p. 306.

opposes any such conception of intrinsic essences.[273] The laws of nature, as he states most forcefully in chapter 15 of *Leviathan*, are improperly called laws. They are simply dictates of reason, prudential maxims relating to the attainment and preservation of peace.[274] They amount to nothing more than the names of those qualities, and hence those lines of conduct, that men are directed by their reason to follow when considering 'what conduceth to the conservation and defence of themselves'.[275]

Of greater importance for my present argument are Hobbes's views about evaluative language. Here he is even more emphatic about the impossibility of gaining any general agreement about the correct appraisals to be placed on individual actions or states of affairs. His philosophy of language is specifically directed against the belief that – as Robert South was to put it in restating the traditional theory – 'words stand for things'.[276] For Hobbes, words can only stand for our conceptions of things. He already makes the point in discussing 'the names or appellations of things' in chapter 5 of *The Elements of Law*. All such names, he insists, consist of nothing more than 'the voyce of a Man, arbitrarily imposed, for a mark to bringe to his minde some Conception concerning the thinge on which it is imposed'.[277] Later he relates the argument specifically to the question of evaluative 'naming', his fullest consideration appearing in the two main chapters on language in *Leviathan*. In chapter 4 he again declares that 'all names are imposed to signifie our conceptions'[278] and in chapter 6 he draws the strongly nominalist inference that 'these words of Good, Evill, and Contemptible, are ever used with relation to the person that useth them: There being nothing simply and absolutely so; nor any common Rule of Good and Evill, to be taken from the nature of the objects themselves'.[279]

Hobbes also seeks to explain why such variations in the use of evaluative terms are only to be expected. As we have already seen, he lays his main emphasis on the extent to which our individual passions and interests inevitably affect our sense of how to appraise particular actions and states of affairs. He advances this claim in every version of his political theory, summarising the argument in general terms at the end of

[273] For Hobbes's voluntarism and its connections with anti-Platonist arguments about making and naming see Malcolm 1983, pp. 1–132, a discussion to which I am greatly indebted.
[274] Hobbes 1996, ch. 15, p. 111.
[275] Hobbes 1996, ch. 15, p. 111. It is true that, according to Warrender 1957 and Hood 1964, Hobbes's moral theory possesses just the character with which I am contrasting it. But I have attempted to respond to Hood in Skinner 1964 and to Warrender in Skinner 1988.
[276] South 1823a, p. 122.   [277] Hobbes 1969a, p. 18.   [278] Hobbes 1996, ch. 4, p. 31.
[279] Hobbes 1996, ch. 6, p. 39.

chapter 4 of *Leviathan*. 'Seeing all names are imposed to signifie our conceptions; and all our affections are but conceptions; when we conceive the same things differently, we can hardly avoyd different naming of them.'[280]

Like Montaigne, however, Hobbes also believes that our affections are in turn determined by the shaping power of custom and habit. As a result, he sometimes seems to treat this further consideration as even more fundamental to an explanation of how it comes about that one and the same action can always be described in morally contrasting ways. He first puts forward the suggestion in *The Elements of Law*, where he expresses it in the form of a striking allusion to the terminology of the *Ars rhetorica*. 'Ratio', he declares, 'now, is but Oratio, for the most part', since 'Custome hath so great a power, that the minde suggesteth onely the first word, the rest follow habitually'.[281] Although he makes no further allusion to this way of putting the point, he reverts to the point itself in each of the later versions of his civil science. His account of the laws of nature in chapter 3 of *De Cive* strongly emphasises that differences in custom as well as individual sensibility will always affect the use of evaluative language,[282] while his account of the same issues in *Leviathan* largely reiterates his earlier remarks. As he himself summarises, '*Good* and *Evill*, are names that signifie our Appetites, and Aversions; which in different tempers, customes, and doctrines of men, are different.'[283]

For Hobbes, accordingly, it is altogether vain to hope that the threat of paradiastole can be overcome by rigidly designating particular actions by means of corresponding evaluative terms. On the contrary, he seems to have experienced a growing conviction that this familiar response entirely misses the point. As a result, the discussion of paradiastole in *Leviathan* ends on a note more pessimistic than any sounded in his earlier accounts. He begins by repeating that, in the case of moral appraisal, the way in which we 'see' particular actions will always be coloured by 'a tincture of our different passions'.[284] But he goes on to draw a new and almost nihilistic conclusion: that, in consequence of such disagreements, the names of the virtues and vices 'can never be true grounds of any ratiocination'.[285] He now appears to believe that, because of the unavoidability of paradiastolic redescription, genuine moral argument is actually impossible.

---

[280] Hobbes 1996, ch. 4, p. 31.
[281] Hobbes 1969a, p. 23. On this passage and its implications see Johnston 1986, pp. 56–7.
[282] Hobbes 1983a, III. XXXI, p. 119.   [283] Hobbes 1996, ch. 15, p. 110.
[284] Hobbes 1996, ch. 4, p. 31.   [285] Hobbes 1996, ch. 4, p. 31.

VIII

Hobbes is no less sceptical than Montaigne about the possibility of gaining any general agreement about the right way to 'see' normative questions and apply evaluative terms. But his attitude to the ineliminable variety of human customs and affections is a strongly contrasting one. For Montaigne, the moral is simply to accept and follow whatever may happen to be the local prejudices of one's tribe. As the essay *Of Custome* insists, such acquiescence is the mark of a truly wise man. We must acknowledge the good sense of those who 'cast themselves headlong into the libertie or sanctuarie of custome'.[286] We must never allow ourselves to be distracted 'from following the common guise'. We must recognise that, while our thoughts remain our own, our duty in 'outward matters' is 'absolutely to follow the fashions and forme customarily received'.[287]

For Hobbes, however, there can be no question of leaving our moral evaluations with no firmer foundations than those supplied by custom and prejudice. As he observes in *Leviathan*, so long as 'private Appetite is the measure of Good, and Evill', we shall find ourselves condemned to living 'in the condition of meer Nature' and not in a sociable condition at all.[288] For Montaigne, of course, such an implication held no terrors. As he makes clear in his essay *Of the Caniballes*, he finds deeply appealing the idea of a 'natural' society maintained with 'little art', a society in which there would be 'no kinde of traffike, no knowledge of Letters, no intelligence of numbers, no name of magistrate'.[289] But for Hobbes this is simply a recipe for chaos. When he describes 'the natural condition of mankind' in chapter 13 of *Leviathan*, he closely echoes Montaigne's account: it would be a condition in which there would be 'no Knowledge of the face of the Earth; no account of Time; no Arts; no Letters; no Society'.[290] But such a condition, he immediately adds, would also be marked by 'continuall feare, and danger of violent death'. The natural life of man would be 'solitary, poore, nasty, brutish, and short'.[291]

In explaining why the state of nature would inevitably be a state of war, Hobbes always places great emphasis on the conflicts that are bound to arise from differences in the application of evaluative terms.[292] As we have seen, he already draws this conclusion at the end of *The Elements of Law*, stressing that where each man 'differeth from other concerning the

---

[286] Montaigne 1892–3, vol. 1, p. 114.   [287] Montaigne 1892–3, vol. 1, p. 116.
[288] Hobbes 1996, ch. 15, p. 111.   [289] Montaigne 1892–3, vol. 1, p. 222.
[290] Hobbes 1996, ch. 13, p. 89.   [291] Hobbes 1996, ch. 13, p. 89.
[292] See Whelan 1981. The point is also stressed in Krook 1956, p. 20; Shapiro 1983, p. 151; Missner 1983, pp. 410–11; Sorell 1986, pp. 127–33; Tuck 1989, p. 55. For general observations see also Jones 1951, pp. 80–1.

names and appellations of thinges', this can only lead to 'quarrells and breach of Peace'.[293] Even more revealing is the fact that, in reverting to the same issue in *De Cive*, he specifically denounces the practitioners of the *Ars rhetorica* as among the most dangerous enemies of social stability. One reason why such creatures as ants and bees are capable of living sociably without government, whereas we can never hope to do so, is that 'such animals lack that art of words by means of which good can be represented to the mind as better, and evil as worse, than is truly the case'.[294] The corresponding passage in *Leviathan* is even more bitterly phrased. The 'art of words' is such that its adepts can 'augment, or diminish the apparent greatnesse of Good and Evill' whenever they like, 'discontenting men, and troubling their Peace at their pleasure'.[295]

For Hobbes, accordingly, the question of how to resolve the problem of paradiastole remains one of the major tasks facing any civil science worthy the name.[296] As a first step towards a new solution, Hobbes begins by insisting on the crucial importance of the fact that the moral virtues are at the same time the names of those qualities that conduce to peace. He hints at this equation in *The Elements of Law*,[297] but it is in chapter 3 of *De Cive* that he first states it unequivocally. 'Such qualities as *modesty, equity, trust, humanity* and *pity* are not merely *good customs* or habits, that is to say *virtues*; we have shown that they are at the same time necessary means to peace.'[298] The corresponding passage in *Leviathan* reiterates and extends the argument. 'All men agree on this, that Peace is Good, and therefore also the way, or means of Peace, which (as I have shewed before) are *Justice, Gratitude, Modesty, Equity, Mercy* & the rest of the Laws of Nature, are good; that is to say, *Morall Vertues*; and their contrarie *Vices*, Evill.'[299]

To this Hobbes adds – at first sight rather strangely – that the significance of this consideration has hitherto been entirely overlooked. 'The Writers of Morall Philosophie, though they acknowledge the same Vertues and Vices' have failed to see that they are at the same time 'the way, or means of Peace'.[300] It is true that this might be regarded as a

[293] Hobbes 1969a, p. 188.
[294] Hobbes 1983a, V. V, p. 133: 'animantia bruta … carent tamen illa verborum arte … qua Bonum, Melius; Malum Peius repraesentatur animo, quam revera est'.
[295] Hobbes 1996, ch. 17, pp. 119–20.
[296] There is thus a crucial sense in which, as Hobbes himself stresses, he is a theorist of the virtues. As he observes in Hobbes 1996, ch. 15, p. 111, his ambition in *Leviathan* is to construct a 'science of Vertue and Vice'. The implications have been fruitfully explored by several recent commentators, especially Boonin-Vail 1994.
[297] See Hobbes 1969a, p. 94.
[298] Hobbes 1983a, III. XXXI, p. 120: 'ideoque *modestiam, aequitatem, fidem, humanitatem, misericordiam*, (quas demonstravimus ad pacem esse necessarias) *bonos* esse *mores*, sive habitus, hoc est, *virtutes*'.
[299] Hobbes 1996, ch. 15, p. 111.   [300] Hobbes 1996, ch. 15, p. 111.

fair criticism of certain scholastic doctrines of virtue. Hobbes certainly
seems to think so, for he specifically targets those who follow Aristotle
and identify the virtues as consisting in nothing more than 'a mediocrity
of passions'.[301] It might seem, however, that Hobbes is simply reiterating
an account of the virtues that practically every humanist had already
emphasised. Ever since Petrarch, humanist writers on *virtus* had been
arguing, in the manner of Cicero's *De Officiis*, that the term itself must
be understood in two contrasting ways. They accept of course that it
denotes a set of praiseworthy qualities; but they also take it to refer to
a form of social power. Specifically, they take it to refer to that form of
power by 'virtue' of which the *bonum commune*, and especially the good of
peace, can alone be secured. By the time Hobbes was writing, this claim
had become a commonplace, one that even the most 'politic' humanists
continued to endorse. Lipsius, for example, still makes this view of *virtus*
central to the argument of his *Politickes*, declaring with direct reference
to Cicero's *De Officiis* that 'he which regardeth the societie and benefit of
men, doth alwayes that which he ought'.[302]

   As Hobbes makes clear, however, he thinks of himself as having a new
and crucial insight to add to this familiar line of thought. His suggestion
is that, if the implications of this way of thinking about the virtues are
properly pursued, the problem of paradiastole can be finally resolved.
It cannot be said that he presents his solution with complete clarity in
The Elements of Law, but if we turn to *De Cive* we find him laying out
the argument with full assurance, after which he largely repeats it in the
corresponding chapters of *Leviathan*. The key passage occurs at the end
of chapter 3 of *De Cive*, at the point where Hobbes is rounding off his
analysis of the moral virtues and vices. As we have already seen, it is at
this juncture that he explicitly raises the issue of paradiastole. Because of
the 'neighbourly' relationship between so many of the virtues and vices,
'a good action performed by someone which is displeasing to someone
else'[303] can always be redescribed with 'the name of some neighbouring
vice'.[304] By the same token, 'disgraceful actions which please people can
similarly be redescribed with the name of a virtue'.[305] 'The upshot is that
one and the same action can always be praised by some, and described
as a virtue, while others censure it and convert it into a vice.'[306]

[301] Hobbes 1996, ch. 15, p. 111.   [302] Lipsius 1594, p. 113.
[303] Hobbes 1983a, III. XXXII, p. 120 speaks of a *bona actio* which *cuiquam displicet*.
[304] Hobbes 1983a, III. XXXII, p. 120: 'ei actioni imponitur nomen alicuius vitii vicini'.
[305] Hobbes 1983a, III. XXXII, p. 120: 'similiter nequitiae quae placent, ad virtutem aliquam
    referuntur'.
[306] Hobbes 1983a, III. XXXII, p. 120: 'Unde evenit eandem actionem ab his laudari & virtutem
    appellari, ab illis culpari & vitio verti.'

Hobbes insists that 'no philosopher has hitherto been able to discover the means of remedying this difficulty'.[307] But the means are close at hand. They simply depend on recognising that the virtues are not merely the names of qualities that conduce to peace, but that this is what constitutes their goodness. 'The goodness of any action resides in the fact that it constitutes a means to preserve peace, whereas the evil in any action resides in the fact that it constitutes a means to produce discord.'[308] At the end of chapter 15 of *Leviathan* the same claim is reiterated. While moral philosophers have always acknowledged the virtues and vices, they have never properly understood 'wherein consisted their Goodnesse'. They have never recognised that their goodness resides in the fact that they form 'the meanes of peaceable, sociable and comfortable living'.[309]

Hobbes's contention is that, once we grasp this point, the way is open to solving the problem of paradiastole. We need only ask, of a given action whose moral quality may be in dispute, whether the effect of the action will or will not be conducive to the preservation of peace. As *De Cive* expresses it, we need only enquire into the 'cause' or end towards which the action in question may be said to contribute.[310] If the end is that of peaceable and sociable living, then we cannot rightly withhold from the action the name of virtue. For as Hobbes has just told us, 'the goodness of any action resides in the fact that it constitutes a means to preserve peace'.

Hobbes underlines his conclusion by way of re-examining a number of classic instances in which the possibility of paradiastolic redescription had always seemed especially hard to block off. One is that of someone performing an act of 'extreme daring', where the question is whether the behaviour deserves to be commended as an instance of true courage. Another is that of someone making a gift, where the question is whether this is necessarily to be appraised as an act of genuine liberality.[311] The problem can be solved in these and all other such cases, Hobbes declares, if we merely apply his simple scientific test. 'An act of daring is to be commended, and under the name of *courage* is to be taken for a virtue – however extreme the daring may have been – in any case in which

---

[307] Hobbes 1983a, III. XXXII, p. 120: 'Neque huic rei remedii quicquam a Philosophis hactenus inventum est.'

[308] Hobbes 1983a, III. XXXII, p. 120: What philosophers have failed to observe ('cum enim non observarent') is that 'bonitatem actionum in ea sitam esse, quod in ordine ad pacem; malitiam in eo quod in ordine ad discordiam essent'.

[309] Hobbes 1996, ch.15, p. 111.

[310] See Hobbes 1983a, III. XXXII, p. 120 on the dependence of the morality of actions upon our assessment of the *causa* for the sake of which they were performed.

[311] Hobbes 1983a, III. XXXII, p. 120.

the cause is approved.'[312] So too with liberality. 'It is not the quantity of anything offered as a gift – whether great, small or middling – that constitutes *liberality*, but the cause for the sake of which the gift was made.'[313] The cause, as Hobbes has already explained in sketching the argument in *The Elements*, must of course be that of peace. It follows that 'the summe of vertue is to be sociable with them that will be sociable, and formidable to them that will not'.[314]

As with the virtues, so with the vices. Hobbes adds this further point in the explanatory notes appended to the second edition of *De Cive* in 1647. He mentions the case of 'an act of revenge, in which there is no consideration for the future good', and explains why such an act can only be described as cruel and hence condemned as a vice.[315] The reason is that one cannot imagine 'how it could possibly contribute to peace or to the conservation of any individual man'.[316] The discussion in chapter 15 of *Leviathan* subsequently generalises the point. The reason why we are justified in saying that 'the Lawes of Nature are Immutable and Eternall' is that 'Injustice, Ingratitude, Arrogance, Pride, Iniquity, Acception of persons, and the rest, can never be made lawfull'. The reason is simply that 'it can never be that Warre shall preserve life, and Peace destroy it'.[317]

As Hobbes admits, however, the contention that a given action will in fact conduce to peace remains a judgement. Who, then, shall be judge? As he notes in *The Elements of Law*, and subsequently reiterates, it is commonly said that such judgements must be made according to right reason.[318] With this answer, he says, 'I should Consent, if there were any such thinge to be found or knowne in *rerum natura*', but the difficulty is that 'commonly they that call for right reason to decide any Controversie, do mean their owne'.[319] As he has already emphasised, however, this is simply to restate the problem, not to solve it. All reasoning depends on naming; but in moral reasoning all naming depends on individual passion and prejudice. The implication, as he points out in *Leviathan*

[312] Hobbes 1983a, III. XXXII, p. 120: 'Nam audere, laudatur, & nomine *fortitudinis* pro virtute habetur, quamquam extremum sit, si causa approbetur.'
[313] Hobbes 1983a, III. XXXII, p. 120: 'Quantitas item rei quae dono datur, sive magna, sive parva, sive media sit, non facit *liberalitatem*, sed donandi causa.'
[314] Hobbes 1969a, p. 95.
[315] See Hobbes 1983a, III. XXVII, p. 118, claiming that any 'vindicta quae futurum bonum non respicit' must be characterised as *crudelitas*.
[316] Hobbes 1983a, III. XXVII, p. 118: 'Nam quid...ad pacem vel conservationem cuiusquam hominis conferre potest, non intelligo.'
[317] Hobbes 1996, ch. 15, p. 110.
[318] Hobbes 1969a, p. 188. See also Hobbes 1983a, XIV. XVII, pp. 213–14 and Hobbes 1985, pp. 111–12, 322.
[319] Hobbes 1969a, p. 188.

with particular acerbity, is that those who call for the settlement of moral disputes by reason are merely calling for 'every of their passions, as it comes to bear sway in them, to be taken for right Reason, and that in their own controversies: bewraying their want of right Reason, by the claym they lay to it'.[320]

For Hobbes, accordingly, the only possible solution is to appoint some-one to make our judgements for us. We must institute some person or body of persons whom we agree in advance to accept as our final 'Arbitrator or judge'.[321] As *The Elements of Law* succinctly puts it, 'seeing right reason is not existent, the reason for some man, or men, must sup-ply the place thereof'.[322] Hobbes is particularly insistent that among the duties of such an Arbitrator must be the giving of ultimate judgements in all cases where the appropriate normative description of some particu-lar action or state of affairs may be in dispute, and where the dispute may be of such a kind as to endanger civic peace. The Arbitrator, as *The Elements of Law* declares, must determine not merely the definitions but also the proper uses 'of all names not agreed upon, and tending to Controversie'.[323]

By way of example, both in *The Elements of Law* and *De Cive*, Hobbes considers the case of a 'strange and deformed birth'.[324] He notes that, when a deformed infant is born, a question may arise as to 'whether the same be a man or noe'.[325] This is not of course a question about the definition of the word 'man'. 'No one doubts', as Hobbes puts it in *De Cive*, 'that a man is a rational animal.'[326] The question is whether the infant's deformation is such that it does or does not deserve to be described as a rational animal. As *De Cive* adds, much may depend upon whether this powerfully normative description is applied or withheld. For example, if it is decided that the infant is rightly to be described as a man, then it cannot lawfully be killed.[327] How, then, is the question to be resolved?

---

[320] Hobbes 1996, ch. 5, p. 33.
[321] Hobbes consistently yokes these terms. See Hobbes 1969a, pp. 90–1 and cf. Hobbes 1996, ch. 5 pp. 32–3, ch. 6, p. 39.
[322] Hobbes 1969a, p. 188. As Tuck 1989, p. 57 rightly stresses, Hobbes's claim is thus that moral consensus can only be created politically.
[323] Hobbes 1969a, p. 189.
[324] Hobbes 1969a, p. 189. See also Hobbes 1983a, XVII. XII, pp. 261–2.
[325] Hobbes 1969a, p. 189.
[326] Hobbes 1983a, XVII. XII, p. 261: 'Nemo dubitat…quod, Homo sit Animale rationale.' Hobbes's point is that, although this is Aristotle's definition, the question of what falls under it must be determined not by Aristotle or any other philosopher but by the state.
[327] Hobbes 1983a, XVII. XII, p. 261.

Hobbes repeats his earlier answer as bluntly as possible. We must give up the traditional belief that the issue can somehow be decided in a rational and non-arbitrary way. As he puts it in his last and gloomiest consideration of the issue in *Leviathan*, the truth is that all such arguments 'must either come to blowes, or be undecided, for want of a right Reason constituted by Nature'.[328] We must recognise instead that the appointment of an Arbitrator is the only possible way out. This is Hobbes's final word on the case of the strange birth and all cases of a like character. The decision of the Arbitrator will of course, *ex hypothesi*, be arbitrary; but we have no alternative but to agree in advance to treat it as beyond appeal if we wish to avoid coming to blows.

To say that the Arbitrator must be a unitary moral person whose judgements must be accepted in advance as beyond appeal is to say that the Arbitrator must be the sovereign. This is indeed Hobbes's view, as he makes clear in *The Elements of Law* and later confirms in *De Cive* and *Leviathan*.[329] In the words of *The Elements of Law*, the person whose reason supplies the place of right reason must be 'he, or they, that hath the Soveraigne power', from which it follows that 'the civill Lawes are to all subjects the measures of their Actions, whereby to determine, whether they be right or wronge, profittable or unprofittable, vertuous or vitious; and by them the use, and definition of all names not agreed upon, and tending to Controversie, shall be established'.[330] As Robert South was to observe with deep disgust, Hobbes's eventual answer to the problem of paradiastole accordingly took the simple and scandalous form of claiming that 'good and evil, honest and dishonest' are 'founded in the laws and constitutions of the sovereign civil power'.[331]

It would not be too much to say that one of the main motives we possess, according to Hobbes, for establishing such a unitary and absolute sovereign is to solve the problems raised by the fact that some names inevitably tend to controversy. It would be a mistake to think of Hobbes's sovereign as instituted merely to terrify his subjects into obedience. Rather he keeps the peace in two distinct ways: by threatening them with punishment, but also by adjudicating their disputes. It is true that, in the passage in *Leviathan* where Hobbes first speaks of the Mortal God, he lays all his emphasis on the fact that 'he hath the use of

---

[328] Hobbes 1996, ch. 5, p. 33.
[329] Hobbes 1969a, pp. 112, 188–9; Hobbes 1983a, III. XXIX–XXXII, pp. 119–21; VI. VIII–XI, pp. 139–41; XIV. XVI–XVII, pp. 213–14; XVII. XII, pp. 261–2; Hobbes 1996, ch. 5, pp. 32–3, ch. 6, p. 39, ch. 26, pp. 190–1, ch. 46, p. 469.
[330] Hobbes 1969a, pp. 188–9.   [331] South 1823a, p. 115.

so much Power and Strength conferred on him, that by terror thereof he is inabled to conforme the wills of them all, to Peace at home, and mutuall ayd against their enemies abroad'.[332] But when he summarises his theory of sovereignty at the end of *Leviathan*, he instead chooses to emphasise the strongly contrasting image of the sovereign as Arbitrator. The state of nature, as he defines it in this later passage, is that condition in which 'there can be no generall Rule of Good, and Evill Actions'. By contrast, the instituting of a sovereign establishes just such a rule. The distinguishing feature of a commonwealth is that 'not the Appetite of Private men, but the Law, which is the Will and Appetite of the State' as represented by the sovereign, becomes the measure of good and evil, virtue and vice.[333]

The position in which Hobbes ends up is thus a somewhat puzzling as well as ironic one. As we saw at the outset, the ambition he announces is that of creating a science of virtue and vice. He makes it clear, moreover, that such a science will in part be defined by its refusal to rely on mere authority. And he declares that, with the publication of *De Cive*, he has succeeded in laying out the principles of just such a science. Nevertheless, the very core of his argument, both in *De Cive* and *Leviathan*, takes the form of an appeal to authority. Although Hobbes undoubtedly provides a solution to the problem of paradiastole, he appears to do so only at the expense of sacrificing his own scientific ideal.

At the same time, however, his solution has the great merit of confronting the problem in a uniquely uncompromising way. His final word is that, if we wish to overcome the threat of paradiastole by fixing our moral language unambiguously onto the world, we can only hope to do so by fiat. His conclusion remains deeply sceptical, and does little to uphold the dignity of moral philosophy. For all that, however, he may be right.

---

[332] Hobbes 1996, ch. 17, pp. 120–1.   [333] Hobbes 1996, ch. 46, p. 469.

5

Hobbes and the classical theory of laughter

I

Nietzsche tells us at the end of *Beyond Good and Evil* that 'I would go so far as to venture an order of rank among philosophers according to the rank of their laughter.'[1] Nietzsche violently dislikes those philosophers who, as he puts it, have 'sought to bring laughter into disrepute'. He particularly singles out Hobbes for this offence, adding that such a puritanical attitude is just what you would expect from an Englishman. Nietzsche's accusation is based, as it happens, on a misquotation of what Hobbes says about laughter in philosophy. But Nietzsche was undoubtedly right to point out that Hobbes – in common with most thinkers of his age – took it for granted that laughter is a subject in which philosophers need to be seriously interested. My aim in what follows will be to investigate the grounds and origins of this belief, and then seek to explain it.

II

The suggestion that laughter matters to philosophy first began to be extensively explored in the early decades of the sixteenth century. A number of leading humanists took it upon themselves to enquire into the meaning and significance of laughter, the most important discussions being those of Baldassare Castiglione in his *Libro del Cortegiano* of 1528 and Juan Luis Vives in his *De Anima & Vita* of 1539. Later in the century, for the first time since antiquity, a specialised literature began to appear on the physiological as well as the psychological aspects of the phenomenon.[2]

This chapter is a revised and extended version of an article that originally appeared under the title 'Why Laughing Mattered in the Renaissance' in *History of Political Thought* 22 (2001), pp. 418–47.
[1] Nietzsche 1990, section 294, p. 218.
[2] For fuller lists of Renaissance theorists of laughter see Screech 1997, p. 58n., and especially Ménager 1995, pp. 7–11. Ménager's is an excellent study and I am much indebted to it.

Here the pioneer was Laurent Joubert, a physician from Montpellier, whose *Traité du ris* was first published in Paris in 1579.[3] Soon afterwards several comparable treatises appeared in Italy, including Celso Mancini's *De risu, ac ridiculis* in 1598,[4] Antonio Lorenzini's *De Risu* in 1603[5] and Elpidio Berrettario's *Phisici, et Philosophi Tractatus de Risu* of the same year.[6] Still more striking is the prominence accorded to the topic by many of the greatest exponents of the new philosophy. Descartes examines the place of laughter among the emotions in his final work, *Les Passions de l'ame*;[7] Hobbes raises many of the same questions in *The Elements of Law* and in several of his later texts; Spinoza defends the value of laughter in Book 4 of the *Ethics*;[8] and a number of Descartes' avowed followers exhibit a special interest in the phenomenon, one notable example being Henry More in his *Account of Virtue*.[9]

According to all these thinkers, the most important question to ask about laughter is what emotions give rise to it.[10] Some commentators approached the puzzle by way of considering the phenomenon of laughter in conjunction with the shedding of tears. Francisco Vallesio, one of Philip II's physicians, included a chapter entitled *De Risu et Fletu* in his *Controversiae* in 1582,[11] while Nicander Jossius published an entire treatise under the same title in 1580.[12] Timothy Bright, a London physician, similarly juxtaposes laughter and weeping in his *Treatise of Melancholie* in 1586,[13] as does Rodolph Goclenius the elder in his *Physica Commentatio De Risu & Lacrymis* in 1597.[14] Hobbes likewise links laughter and tears in his *Critique* of Thomas White's *De Mundo*, as does Descartes in *Les Passions de l'ame*.[15]

---

[3] See Joubert 1579 and on its publishing history Ménager 1995, pp. 7–8. On the place of Joubert's work in the medical literature see Machline 1998, pp. 251–64.

[4] Mancini 1598. According to Ménager 1995, p. 9, Mancini's text was originally published in 1591. But Ménager appears to confuse the publishing history of Mancini's book with that of Antonio Lorenzini (on which see note 5 below).

[5] Lorenzini 1606. Lorenzini's text had already been published, together with a reprint of Nicander Jossius's 1580 treatise on laughter, in Lorenzini 1603.

[6] Berrettario 1603.   [7] Descartes 1988.   [8] Spinoza 1985, IV. P. 45, pp. 571–2.

[9] More 1690, pp. 69–78, 227–8.

[10] This contrasts with some of the most interesting scholarship on the history of laughter, which has concentrated on genres of comedy and their potential for the subversion of elites. See, for example, Bakhtine 1970 and Thomas 1977.

[11] Vallesio 1582, V. IX, pp. 220–2.   [12] Jossius 1580, pp. 44–144.

[13] Bright 1586, ch. 28, p. 161: '*Howe melancholie causeth both weeping and laughing, and the reasons how.*'

[14] Goclenius 1597.

[15] See Hobbes 1973, p. 360 on the 'affectus ridentium & flentium' and cf. Descartes 1988, Article 128, p. 156 linking 'le Ris' and 'les larmes'.

Among the elements common to laughter and weeping, these writers single out the fact that they are peculiar to humankind,[16] that they are largely uncontrollable,[17] and that they seem to be almost unnaturally vehement reactions to some inner movement of the soul.[18] They find it easy to agree that the main emotion expressed by weeping must be dejection and sadness,[19] perhaps accompanied on some occasions by fear.[20] But as Bright explicitly concedes, the cause of laughter 'is of more difficultie to finde out, and the reason not so manifest'.[21] What passion of the soul could possibly be so complex and powerful as to make us 'burst out', as Vallesio puts it, in this 'almost convulsive' way?[22]

One of the feelings involved, everyone agreed, must be some form of joy or happiness. Among the humanist writers, Castiglione stresses in his *Cortegiano* that (in the words of Sir Thomas Hoby's translation of 1561) 'laughing is perceived onlie in man, and (in maner) alwaies is a token of a certein jocundenesse and meerie moode that he feeleth inwardlie in his minde'.[23] Vives similarly maintains in *De Anima & Vita* that 'laughter is born of happiness and delight',[24] and this doctrine was widely repeated by the humanists of the next generation and beyond.[25]

We encounter the same assumptions in the medical literature, the pioneer in this instance being the physician Girolamo Fracastoro in his *De Sympathia & Antipathia Rerum* of 1546.[26] The cause of mirth, Fracastoro declares, must always be some form of 'internal happiness'.[27] Laurent Joubert agrees, arguing that the passion moving us to laughter

---

[16] Jossius 1580, pp. 91, 94–5; Vallesio 1582, p. 220. See also Goclenius 1597, pp. 21, 37, 45, who anticipates a possible objection by adding (p. 54) that the tears of the crocodile are not real but 'quasi' tears.

[17] Jossius 1580, pp. 52, 57; Vallesio 1582, p. 220; Goclenius 1597, p. 22.

[18] For the claim that 'risus et fletus praeter naturam fiunt' see Vallesio 1582, p. 222. Cf. Jossius 1580, p. 52, on how laughter 'oritur . . . ob vehementem occasionem' and Goclenius 1597, p. 21, on the 'animi commotio' involved.

[19] Jossius 1580, p. 99 claims that 'dolor seu dolorificium esset subiectum & materia fletus'. Cf. Vallesio 1582, p. 222, on 'tristitia' as the cause. See also BL Harl. MS 6083, fo. 177, Hobbes's fragment *Of Passions*, in which he likewise observes (fo. 177ʳ) that 'sudden deiection, is the passion; that causeth weeping'.

[20] Vallesio 1582, p. 222 argues that weeping can arise out of 'tristitia aut timore'.

[21] Bright 1586, p. 162.

[22] Vallesio 1582, p. 222 speaks of the 'quasi motus quidam convulsionis' that accompanies laughter. Jossius 1580, p. 57 similarly speaks of the passions that 'erumpunt in risum'.

[23] Castiglione 1994, p. 154.

[24] Vives 1550, p. 206: 'ex laetitia & delectatione risus nascitur'.

[25] See, for example, Jossius 1580, p. 57; Lorenzini 1606, p. 95.

[26] Ménager 1995, p. 8 notes that Fracastoro was one of the physicians appointed by the Vatican to attend the Council of Trent. He was also well known as a poet, and received the praise of Sir Philip Sidney. See Sidney 1912, p. 35. On Hobbes as a reader of Fracastoro see Leijenhorst 1996.

[27] Fracastoro 1546, fo. 23ᵛ states that, when we laugh, 'laetitia interna in facie manifestetur'.

must always be related in some way to joy,[28] while Francisco Vallesio more straightforwardly affirms that 'it is my belief that men laugh whenever something joyful takes place'.[29] Within a generation, everyone writing on the topic had come to take this assumption for granted. Descartes simply notes in *Les Passions de l'ame* that 'the Laugh seems to be one of the principal signs of Joy',[30] while Hobbes still more briskly concludes in *The Elements of Law* that laughter 'is alwayes joy'.[31]

It was generally acknowledged, however, that this joy must be of a peculiar kind, since it appears to be connected in some way with feelings of scorn, contempt and even hatred. Among the humanists, Castiglione mounts one of the earliest arguments to this effect. Whenever we laugh, we are always 'mockinge and scorninge' someone, always seeking 'to scoff and mocke at vices'.[32] Thomas Wilson enlarges on the suggestion in his *Arte of Rhetorique* of 1554, the earliest full-scale neo-classical treatise on eloquence in the English language. Wilson includes a long section in Book 2 entitled 'Of delityng the hearers, and stirryng them to laughter' in which he maintains that we experience feelings of contempt whenever we perceive 'the fondnes, the filthines, the deformitee' of someone else's behaviour, with the result that we are prompted to 'laugh him to skorne out right'.[33]

If we turn to the medical writers, we find the same theory laid out at greater length. Perhaps the subtlest analysis is that of Laurent Joubert, although he acknowledges a debt to the earlier work of François Valleriola, a fellow physician from Montpellier.[34] Suppose we ask, Joubert writes in the opening chapter of his *Traité*, 'what is the subject matter of laughter?'[35] Drawing on Valleriola's discussion,[36] Joubert answers that we laugh at 'everything which is ridiculous, whether it is something done or something said'.[37] But anything we find ridiculous, Joubert goes on to explain in chapter 2, will always 'be something that strikes us as ugly, deformed, dishonest, indecent, malicious and scarcely decorous'.[38] So our laughter will always arise from the contemplation

---

[28] Joubert 1579, pp. 72–3, 87–8.
[29] Vallesio 1582, p. 220: 'sentimus, homines ridere quum occurrit res iocunda'.
[30] Descartes 1988, Article 125, p. 153: 'il semble que le Ris soit un des principaux signes de la Joye'.
[31] Hobbes 1969a, p. 41.   [32] Castiglione 1994, pp. 155–6.   [33] Wilson 1554, fos. 74^v, 75^r.
[34] Valleriola 1588, p. 134 in turn speaks warmly of Joubert's *Traité du ris*.
[35] Joubert 1579, p. 15: 'Quelle est la matiere du Ris?'
[36] Valleriola 1554, III, IX, pp. 212–24, esp. pp. 217–18.
[37] Joubert 1579, p. 16: 'tout ce qui est ridicule . . . an fait, ou an dit'.
[38] Joubert 1579, p. 16: 'Ce que nous voyons de laid, difforme, des-honeste, indessant, mal-feant, & peu convenable.'

of deeds or sayings 'which have an appearance of ugliness without being pitiable'.[39] This in turn means that the joy we experience can never be unalloyed. We can never avoid some measure of scorn or dislike for baseness and ugliness, so that 'the common style of our laughter is contempt or derision'.[40] Joubert goes further and adds that, in consequence of these complex feelings, laughter can never be wholly unconnected with sadness. 'Given that everything which is ridiculous arises from ugliness and dishonesty',[41] and given that we can never contemplate such unpleasantness with equanimity, it follows that 'anything ridiculous gives us pleasure and sadness combined'.[42]

Joubert's emphasis on *tristesse* was rarely taken up, but his contention that laughter is basically an expression of scorn for ridiculous things was much reiterated,[43] especially by those who aspired to connect the insights of the humanists with those of the burgeoning medical literature. Perhaps the most important writer to forge these links was Robert Burton, who declares in the Introduction to his *Anatomy of Melancholy* of 1621 that there has never been 'so much cause of laughter' as we encounter in our present distempered world. He goes on to explain that in laughing we 'contemne others, condemne the world of folly', and that the world has never been so full of folly to scorn and condemn, so full of people who are 'Fooles & ridiculous'.[44] Sir Thomas Browne, another physician steeped in humanist learning, speaks in comparable vein in his *Pseudodoxia Epidemica* of 1646. Discussing the passion of laughter in Book 7, he agrees that 'a laugh there is of contempt or indignation', adding that even God himself is described in the scriptures as laughing the wicked to scorn.[45]

A similar analysis is proposed by several leading exponents of the new philosophy, including both Descartes and Hobbes. Descartes's principal claim about laughter in *Les Passions de l'ame* is that 'although the Laugh may seem to be one of the principal signs of Joy, joy cannot be the cause of laughter unless the joy is only moderate, and is at the same time mixed with an element of hatred or wonderment'.[46] The point is one on which

---

[39] Joubert 1579, p. 16: the 'fais ou dis' that provoke laughter are those 'qui ont apparance de laideur, & ne sont pitoyables'.
[40] Joubert 1579, p. 30: '[le] commum geanre ... e[s]t le mepris ou derision'.
[41] Joubert 1579, pp. 87–8: 'pour ce que tout ridicule provient de laideur & meffeance'.
[42] Joubert 1579, p. 87: 'la chose ridicule nous donne plaisir & tristesse'.
[43] For a similar account see Goclenius 1597, ch. 2, pp. 9, 15.
[44] Burton 1989, pp. 37, 57, 101.
[45] Browne 1928–31, vol. 3, p. 312. But Browne believes that there can also be 'a laugh ... of mirth and Jocosity'.
[46] Descartes 1988, Article 125, p. 153: 'Or encore qu'il semble que le Ris soit un des principaux signes de la Joye, elle ne peut toutefois le causer que lors qu' elle est seulement mediocre, & qu' il y a quelque admiration ou quelque haine meslée avec elle.'

he lays particular emphasis, and he later returns to it in his discussion of *la moquerie*. 'Derision or Mockery is a kind of Joy mixed with Hatred, and when this feeling arises unexpectedly the result is that we burst out with laughter.'[47]

It is not surprising that Hobbes is equally attracted by this explanation of laughter. His basic view of human psychology is that, as he expresses it in *Leviathan*, we need to 'put for a generall inclination of all mankind, a perpetuall and restless desire of Power after power, that ceaseth onely in Death'.[48] Not only do we find that men 'naturally love Liberty, and Dominion over others'.[49] We also find that in man 'Joy consisteth in comparing himselfe with other men', so that men 'can relish nothing but what is eminent'.[50] According to the theory of laughter we are examining, however, we laugh both as an expression of joy and at the same time as a means of conveying a scornful and contemptuous sense of our own superiority. This suggests that Hobbes's special interest in laughter may well derive from the fact that, on this analysis, the phenomenon of laughter provides a perfect illustration of his more general views about the nature of humankind.

This is not to say that Hobbes's explanation of laughter is precisely the same as that of Descartes. When Hobbes turns to the phenomenon in *The Elements of Law* – his first and fullest treatment of the subject – he includes one interesting variation on the usual theme. He observes that we sometimes laugh not because we feel contempt for any particular person, but rather because we have been made aware of some general absurdity. This allows for the possibility of 'laughter without offence', which is said to take place when we laugh 'at absurdityes and infirmityes abstracted from persons, and where all the Company may laugh together'.[51] Such laughter will still be an expression of our scorn and contempt, but instead of mocking other people to their faces we join together in ridiculing some ludicrous feature of the world and its ways.

Curiously, however, Hobbes never recurs to this possibility in any of his later pronouncements on laughter, and his usual explanation of the phenomenon remains close to that of Descartes.[52] His oft-quoted definition, initially formulated in *The Elements of Law*, runs as follows:

---

[47] Descartes 1988, Article 178, p. 195: 'La Derision ou Moquerie est une espece de Joye meslée de Haine ... Et lors que cela survient inopinement ... on s'esclate de rire.'
[48] Hobbes 1996, ch. 11, p. 70.   [49] Hobbes 1996, ch. 17, p. 117.
[50] Hobbes 1996, ch. 17, p. 119.   [51] Hobbes 1969a, p. 42.
[52] Heyd 1982, in an otherwise excellent discussion, makes the questionable suggestion (p. 289) that this may be due to the direct influence of Descartes. But this is because Heyd supposes (p. 286) that Hobbes first discusses laughter in 1650, whereas his principal discussion (in *The Elements of Law*) in fact dates from 1640, eight years before the publication of Descartes's *Les Passions de l'ame*.

The passion of Laughter is nothyng else but a suddaine Glory arising from suddaine Conception of some Eminency in our selves by Comparison with the Infirmityes of others, or with our owne formerly.[53]

He proceeds to explain that these feelings of glory are always scornful and patronising, always a matter of glorying over others or our own former weaknesses. He puts the point most brutally in chapter 9 of *The Elements*, in which he presents his 'comparison of the life of man to a race' and explains the role in this competition of the different passions of the soul:

> To fall on the suddaine, is disposition to Weepe
> To see another to fall, disposition to Laugh[54]

As in the case of Descartes, Hobbes's basic suggestion is thus that laughter expresses a joyful sense of our own superiority.

Hobbes's analysis is more complex than that of Descartes, however, for he goes on to suggest that this sense of superiority can arise in one of two distinct ways. Sometimes people laugh when they find themselves performing some action 'beyond their owne expectation', thereby making the pleasing discovery that they are more superior than they had supposed.[55] But usually they laugh 'at the infirmityes of others by comparison of which their owne abilityes are sett off, and illustrated', and in particular 'at Jests, the witt whereof always consisteth in the Elegant discovering, and conveying to our mindes some absurdity of another'.[56] This explains why 'it is no wonder therefore that men take it heanously to be laughed at'. For this is to say that, in becoming objects of laughter, they are being 'derided, that is, tryumphed over' and scorned.[57]

Returning to the issue in his fragment *Of Passions* in 1650, Hobbes still more trenchantly concludes that 'sudden imagination of a mans owne abilitie, is the passion that moves laughter'.[58] As this observation makes clear, Hobbes does not think of laughter itself as a passion, although he speaks elliptically at one moment in *The Elements* of 'the passion of Laughter'.[59] Rather, as he already indicates at the outset of his discussion in *The Elements*, he regards the occurrence of laughter as the natural 'signe' of a passion.[60] He adds in *The Elements* that the passion in question 'hath noe name',[61] but in the manuscript of 1650 he goes on to name it with confidence, observing that it centres on a feeling of superior power.

---

[53] Hobbes 1969a, p. 42.   [54] Hobbes 1969a, p. 48.   [55] tHobbes 1969a, p. 41.
[56] Hobbes 1969a, pp. 41–2.   [57] Hobbes 1969a, p. 42.
[58] Hobbes, *Of Passions*, BL Harl. MS 6083, fo. 177ʳ.
[59] Hobbes 1969a, p. 42.   [60] Hobbes 1969a, p. 41.   [61] Hobbes 1969a, p. 41.

Hobbes's final pronouncements on laughter can be found in the two versions of *Leviathan*, although the relevant passage from the Latin version of 1668 amounts to little more than a translation of the English version of 1651. Hobbes begins by reverting to the definition he had already furnished in *The Elements of Law*. 'Sudden Glory', he again declares, 'is the passion which maketh those *Grimaces* called LAUGHTER.'[62] He likewise reverts to his earlier claim that the sense of superiority prompting people to laugh can arise in one of two ways. They may succeed in accomplishing something beyond their expectations, with the result that they laugh 'because of some sudden act of their own, that pleaseth them'.[63] Alternatively, their sense of superiority may stem more directly from their perception of some contemptible weakness or infirmity in someone else. Hobbes now passes over the interesting possibility he had earlier raised in *The Elements* to the effect that this may sometimes cause people to laugh at their own previous selves. Perhaps, as he sometimes seems to imply, he had come to believe that our previous selves are equivalent to different persons, so that there is no distinction to be made.[64] Or perhaps he had come to feel that such self-mockery is less common than he had earlier implied, especially as he stresses in *The Elements* that no one ever laughs 'at the follyes of themselves past' unless they can be sure of doing so without 'any present dishonour'.[65] But whatever the reason for the omission, the outcome is that in *Leviathan* Hobbes focuses exclusively on what he had always taken to be the principal cause of people's laughter, namely 'the apprehension of some deformed thing in another, by comparison whereof they suddenly applaud themselves'.[66]

We can summarise by saying that, in the view of the writers I have been considering, two things must have happened if you find yourself convulsed with mirth. You must have perceived some contemptible vice or weakness in someone else, or possibly in your own previous self. And you must have been made aware of it in such a way as to induce a joyful feeling of superiority. One implication worth noting is that, according to this tradition of thought, a strong contrast needs to be drawn between the

---

[62] Hobbes 1996, ch. 6, p. 43. Hobbes 1841a, p. 46 translates the definition, although without offering a rendering of 'grimaces'.

[63] Hobbes 1996, ch. 6, p. 43. Cf. Hobbes 1841a, p. 46.

[64] It seems to be Hobbes's view that, even when our laughter is directed at our own former infirmities, this is an instance of our present ascendancy over others.

[65] Hobbes 1969a, p. 42.

[66] Hobbes 1996, ch. 6, p. 43. Hobbes 1841a, p. 46 offers a translation of the passage, but adds that we laugh not merely at the apprehension of some deformed thing in another (*conceptum turpitudinis alieni*) but also at their indecorous actions (*facti indecori*).

laugh and the smile. While laughter is derisive, smiling is taken to be a natural sign of pleasure, and especially of affection and encouragement. Sir Thomas Browne refers to the distinction in his *Pseudodoxia Epidemica* in the course of addressing the scholastic conundrum as to whether Christ ever laughed. His response is that, even if we grant that he never did so, we cannot imagine that he never smiled, for his smiling would have been the surest proof of his humanity.[67]

This view of smiling as an expression of love serves to connect it with the sublime, and especially with Christian images of heaven as a state of eternal joyfulness.[68] We find an allusion to these ideas in one of the texts most frequently cited by the writers I am considering. The text in question is the apocryphal letter, probably dating from the first century of the Christian era, allegedly sent by the great physician Hippocrates to Damagetes.[69] Hippocrates writes of having received an invitation from the people of Abdera to attend the philosopher Democritus, who had taken to laughing so continually that his fellow citizens had begun to fear for his sanity. Hippocrates reports that Democritus was able to give a good explanation of his behaviour, after which he suddenly exchanged his laughter for a smile, 'and from that moment he seemed to me to have a divine countenance, having altered his appearance in this way'.[70] We encounter many such expressions of rapture in the art of the Renaissance, in which we are usually made aware – by gestures of the hand or eyes cast longingly upwards – that the object of the joy is indeed heavenly. But in the most celebrated instance, that of Leonardo's *La Gioconda*, the source of the inward joy that makes her smile remains a mystery, thereby lending the painting its endlessly enigmatic quality.[71]

The idea that smiling expresses love, while laughter reflects contempt, was destined to have a long history. The anonymous author of *Mirth in Ridicule* (1708) writes of the distinction in sternly moralistic tones:

> 'Tis basely mean, the Wretched to disdain,
> And argues want of Sense, to *laugh* at Pain.
> Oh! rather all your tend'rest Pity show,

---

[67] Browne 1928–31, pp. 311–12.

[68] For a particularly rapturous discussion see the closing chapter of More 1690, pp. 265–6.

[69] My quotations come from the version entitled 'La cause morale du ris' (a translation from the Greek by M. I. Guichard) printed as an appendix to Joubert 1579, pp. 355–75.

[70] Joubert 1579, p. 375: 'Ce disant, il sourioit: & adonc il me sambloit une face divine, ayant changé la sienne.'

[71] For a discussion of smiling, and especially the smile of *La Gioconda*, see Ménager 1995, pp. 200–6.

Your gentlest Smiles, and kindest Looks bestow,
On those you see, by sad Decree of Fate,
And Hand of Providence, unfortunate.[72]

If we allow ourselves to glance forward for a moment into the next century, we find a rather more gifted poet, Charles Baudelaire, expressing some not dissimilar sentiments. The theme of Baudelaire's essay of 1855, *De l'essence du rire*, is that laughter is nothing less than diabolical, rooted as it is in pride and scorn, the deadliest of the deadly sins.[73]

For all its influence, however, the claim that laughter expresses scorn and contempt is far from self-evident, and it seems natural to begin by asking about its provenance. When and where did this view of laughter arise, and how did it come to exert such a powerful grip on Renaissance and early-modern thought?

III

When the authors I have been discussing speak about the sources of their theory, they generally lay a good deal of emphasis on their own originality and perceptiveness. When Hobbes, for example, first turns to the topic of laughter in *The Elements of Law*, he begins with a remarkably strong declaration to this effect:

There is a passion, which hath noe name, but the signe of it, is that distortion of the Countenance we call LAUGHTER, which is always joy; but what joy, what we thinke, and wherein we tryumph when we laugh, hath not hitherto bene declared by any.[74]

The tone is typically assured, but the claim is so far from being justified that one is left wondering a little at Hobbes's sense of his audience. Few of Hobbes's original readers would have lacked the benefit of a classical education, and almost all of them would in consequence have known that virtually nothing in Hobbes's analysis was as novel as he pretended. On the contrary, almost everything that Hobbes and his humanist predecessors say about laughter arises out of two strands of ancient thinking about the phenomenon, both of which can ultimately be traced to the philosophy of Aristotle. It is with Hobbes's great foe, not with Hobbes himself, that the story begins.

Aristotle's most frequently quoted observation about laughter comes from the text known to Latin antiquity as *De Partibus Animalium*, in which

---

[72] *Mirth in Ridicule* 1708, p. 14.   [73] Baudelaire 1956, pp. 109–30, esp. pp. 115–17.
[74] Hobbes 1969a, p. 41.

he notes that human beings are the only creatures that laugh.[75] For my present purposes, however, his most relevant remarks can be found in his *Art of Rhetoric*, particularly in the passage from Book 2 in which he discusses the manners of youth. Hobbes was a profound student of this text, and as we saw in chapter 2 he made a Latin paraphrase of it in connection with his duties as tutor to the young William Cavendish in the 1630s.[76] It was from this paraphrase that someone (but not Hobbes)[77] produced the translation that was published in c.1637 as *A Briefe of the Art of Rhetorique*, the earliest version of Aristotle's text to appear in English.[78] If we turn to this version, we find Aristotle saying that one of the characteristics of young people is that they are 'Lovers of Mirth, and by consequence love to jest at others'.[79] This leads him to enquire into the feelings expressed by their mirth, to which he replies that '*Jesting* is witty Contumely', having earlier assured us that contumely 'is the disgracing of another for his own pastime'.[80]

Aristotle's basic suggestion is thus that the mirth induced by jesting is always an expression of contempt, a suggestion already present in his earlier observation that among the sources of pleasure are 'ridiculous Actions, Sayings and Persons'.[81] As he points out himself,[82] he had already pursued these implications in his *Poetics*, especially in the brief section in which he had discussed the type of mimesis manifested in comedy.[83] Comedy deals in the risible, and the risible is an aspect of the shameful, the ugly or the base. If we find ourselves laughing at others, it will be because they exhibit some fault or mark of shame which, while not painful, makes them ridiculous. Those who are chiefly risible are accordingly those who are in some way inferior, especially morally inferior, although not wholly vicious in character.[84]

It is possible that Aristotle was indebted for some of these observations to the remarks that Plato makes about laughter in several of his dialogues. In the *Philebus* Plato considers the nature of the ridiculous,[85] and in the

---

[75] Aristotle 1961, III. 10, p. 281. For a discussion see Screech 1997, pp. 1–5.

[76] See Hobbes MSS (Chatsworth) MS D. 1, pp. 1–143.

[77] I owe this fact to Karl Schuhmann. For further discussion see above, chapter 1 note 27 and chapter 2 note 79.

[78] [Hobbes (?)]1986, pp. 33–128.   [79] [Hobbes (?)]1986, p. 86.

[80] [Hobbes (?)]1986, pp. 70, 86.   [81] [Hobbes (?)]1986, p. 57.

[82] Aristotle 1926, I. XI. 28, p. 128, and III. XVIII. 7, p. 466.

[83] It may be, however, that Aristotle is referring to a fuller discussion in the now lost Book 2 of his *Poetics*.

[84] Aristotle 1995, 1449a, p. 44.

[85] See Plato 1925 48c–50b, pp. 332–40 and cf. Plato 1926, 935d–936a, vol. 2, pp. 462–4, where he discusses the need to regulate comic writers in their use of ridicule.

Republic he foreshadows the central principle of Aristotle's analysis when he declares that laughter is almost always connected with the reproving of vice.[86] It would be fair to say, however, that Plato's observations remain scattered and unsystematic by comparison with Aristotle's more direct engagement with the topic, and it is perhaps not surprising that it was Aristotle's analysis that exercised the greatest influence in antiquity.

We find Aristotle's theory taken up in two distinct but convergent strands of thought. One was medical, and appears to have originated with the apocryphal letter of Hippocrates about Democritus, the laughing philosopher. Hippocrates reports that, in the hope of understanding Democritus's apparent insanity, one of the citizens of Abdera paid him a visit and 'began to weep in a loud voice in the manner of a woman weeping at the death of her child'.[87] But even in the face of this seemingly tragic outburst Democritus merely laughed. Hippocrates writes that at first he took Democritus to task for his insensitivity, but Democritus explained that 'I am only laughing at mankind, full of folly and empty of any good actions'[88] and at a world in which men occupy themselves 'with matters of no value, and consume their lives with ridiculous things'.[89] Hippocrates was greatly impressed, and on leaving Abdera thanked the people for enabling him to talk with 'the very wise Democritus, who alone is capable of giving wisdom to everyone in the world'.[90]

The other group of writers who explored the connections between laughter and contempt were the rhetoricians, and in this case they drew their inspiration directly from Aristotle's texts. The most elaborate analysis is Cicero's in Book 2 of *De Oratore*, in which the figure of Caesar is persuaded to discourse about the concept of the laughable.[91] Caesar begins by offering a restatement and elaboration of Aristotle's argument:

The proper field and as it were the province of laughter is restricted to matters that are in some way either disgraceful or deformed. For the principal if not

---

[86] Plato 1930–5, 452d, vol. 1, p. 436.

[87] Joubert 1579, Appendix, p. 358: 'voulant ancor mieus expliquer sa follie, se mit à pleurer à haute vois, comme une fame qui pleure la mort de son anfant'.

[88] Joubert 1579, Appendix, p. 363: 'Je ne me Ris que de l'homme, plein de folie, & vide de toutes accions droites.'

[89] Joubert 1579, Appendix, pp. 363–4: 'choses de nulle valeur, consument leurs vies an choses ridicules'.

[90] Joubert 1579, Appendix, p. 375: 'le tres-sage Democrite, qui seul peut randre sages tous les hommes du monde'.

[91] Cicero 1942, II. LVII. 233, vol. 1, p. 370.

the sole cause of mirth are those kinds of remarks which note and single out, in a fashion not in itself unseemly, something which is in some way unseemly or disgraceful.[92]

Caesar goes on to explain that the unseemliness can be either moral or physical in nature. He first suggests, again in strongly Aristotelian vein, that 'materials for ridicule can be found in the vices observable in people's behaviour, provided that the people concerned are neither especially popular nor figures of real tragedy'.[93] To which he adds that 'further materials especially suitable for making jokes are provided by ugliness and physical deformity'.[94]

The other leading rhetorician to examine the relations between laughter and contempt is Quintilian in Book 6 of his *Institutio Oratoria*, a discussion that appears to be indebted in equal measure to Aristotle's and Cicero's accounts. Quintilian reiterates that laughter 'has its source in things that are either deformed or disgraceful in some way',[95] adding that 'those sayings which excite ridicule are often false (which is always ignoble), often ingeniously distorted and never in the least complimentary'.[96] Neatly juggling *ridere* and *deridere*, he concludes that 'our mirth is never very far removed from derision', since the overriding emotion expressed by it will generally be one of disdainful superiority.[97] When we laugh, we are usually glorying or triumphing over others as a result of having come to see that, by comparison with ourselves, they are suffering from some contemptible weakness or infirmity. As Quintilian summarises, 'the most ambitious way of glorying is to speak derisively'.[98]

It will by now be evident that the contribution made by the Renaissance writers to the theory of the laughable was considerably less original than they chose to admit. The humanists were overwhelmingly indebted to the ancient rhetorical literature, and above all to Cicero's analysis in *De Oratore*. As Hoby not unfairly points out in his translation of

---

[92] Cicero 1942, II. LVIII. 236, vol. 1, p. 372: 'Locus autem et regio quasi ridiculi . . . turpitudine et deformitate quadam continetur; haec enim ridentur vel sola, vel maxime, quae notant et designant turpitudinem aliquam non turpiter.'

[93] Cicero 1942, II. LIX. 238, vol. 1, p. 374: 'materies omnis ridiculorum est in istis vitiis quae sunt in vita hominum neque carorum neque calamitosorum'.

[94] Cicero 1942, II. LIX. 239, vol. 1, p. 374: 'est etiam deformitatis et corporis vitiorum satis bella materies ad iocandum'.

[95] Quintilian 1920–2, VI. III. 8, vol. 2, p. 442, quoting Cicero *De Oratore*, II. LVIII. 236, vol. 1, p. 372: '[Risus] habet sedem in deformitate aliqua et turpitudine.'

[96] Quintilian 1920–2, VI. III. 6, vol. 2, p. 440: 'ridiculum dictum plerumque falsum est (hoc semper humile), saepe ex industria depravatum, praeterea nunquam honorificum'.

[97] Quintilian 1920–2, VI. III. 8, vol. 2, p. 442: 'A derisu non procul abest risus.'

[98] Quintilian 1920–2, XI. I. 22, vol. 4, p. 166: 'Ambitiosissimum gloriandi genus est etiam deridere.'

Castiglione, 'this discourse of Jestes is taken out of Cicero *de Orat.* lib. ii'.[99] So too with the medical writers, who partly draw on the same sources, but even more on Hippocrates's report about the case of Democritus. Joubert not only makes use of Hippocrates's letter in his *Traité*, but prints it in its entirety as an appendix.[100] Burton in his *Anatomy of Melancholy* actually comes before his readers in the *persona* of 'Democritus Junior', beginning his Introduction by reproducing ('*verbatim* almost', as he says himself)[101] the whole of Hippocrates's letter and adding a commentary on it. Finally, the exponents of the new philosophy appear no less indebted to the same authorities. Hobbes's noisy protestations about his own originality seem especially disingenuous, since even his well-known definition of laughter as sudden glory[102] appears to be taken from Quintilian's account.

It would be misleading, however, to imply that the early-modern writers inertly reiterate the views of their classical authorities, for they go on to make at least two important additions to their inherited arguments. First of all, they place a new emphasis on the role of suddenness, and hence of surprise, in the provocation of mirth. Cicero in *De Oratore* had alluded to the significance of the unexpected,[103] but his Renaissance followers greatly embroider the point. Castiglione stresses that 'certein newlye happened cases' are particularly apt to 'provoke laughter', especially if we surprise our hearers by speaking 'contrary to expectacyon'.[104] Vives further elaborates the insight, arguing that our mirth 'arises out of a novel sense of delight', and that 'sudden and unexpected things have more effect on us and move us more quickly to laughter than anything else'.[105]

For a fuller analysis we need to return to the medical writers, who first introduce into the argument the key concept of *admiratio* or wonderment.[106] The pioneering discussion appears to be that of Girolamo Fracastoro in his *De Sympathia* of 1546. 'The things that generally move us to laughter', he begins, 'must have a certain novelty about

---

[99] Castiglione 1994, p. 150.   [100] Joubert 1579, Appendix, pp. 355–75.
[101] Burton 1989, p. 33.
[102] Hobbes 1969a, p. 41. The definition is repeated in Hobbes 1996, ch. 6, p. 43 and (as 'Gloriatio subita') in Hobbes 1841a, p. 46.
[103] Cicero 1942, II. LXIII. 255, vol. 1, p. 388; cf. also II. LXXI. 289, vol. 1, p. 418.
[104] Castiglione 1994, pp. 188, 190.
[105] Vives 1550, p. 207: 'insperata vera & subita plus afficiunt, citius commovent risum'. On this assumption see Skinner 1996, p. 392. The claim was frequently reiterated by humanist writers of the next generation. See, for example, Mancini 1598, p. 217, arguing that anything which causes laughter must always happen *statim*, suddenly and all at once.
[106] The point was quickly taken up by the humanist writers. See, for example, Jossius 1580, p. 58; Lorenzini 1606, p. 95.

them' and must appear before us 'suddenly' and 'unexpectedly'.[107] When this happens, we instantly experience a sense of wonderment, which in turn creates in us a feeling of delight. The emotional sequence is thus that 'the sudden and the unexpected give rise to *admiratio*, which in turn gives rise to *delectatio*, which in turn provokes the movement of the face we call laughter'.[108] Francisco Vallesio fulsomely acknowledges Fracastoro's analysis and goes on to appropriate it.[109] 'As a result of experiment', he reports, 'I am led to believe that men laugh when something happens which is at once pleasant and new; the novelty gives rise to *admiratio*, the pleasure gives rise to joy' and the combination is what makes us laugh.[110]

Fracastoro's emphasis on *admiratio* was quickly taken up by the humanists, and in particular by a number of commentators on Aristotle's *Poetics*. Here the pioneer seems to have been Vincento Maggi in his *In Aristotelis Librum de Poetica Communes Explicationes* of 1550.[111] Speaking in the special tone of vehemence that humanist scholars liked to affect, Maggi declares that 'I cannot sufficiently express my astonishment as to why it is that Cicero should have failed to say a single word about the subject of *admiratio*, which is one of the causes of laughter, when the fact is that in the absence of *admiratio* it is never possible for laughter to occur.'[112] The reason why the presence of *admiratio* is indispensable is that we laugh only when we encounter new and surprising things. It is the presence of *novitas* that induces wonderment, and it is our sense of wonderment that makes us laugh.[113]

The philosophers of the next generation were largely content to bring together these humanist and medical accounts. Descartes, for whom *admiratio* is a fundamental passion,[114] begins by stressing the importance of novelty and suddenness, arguing that we laugh only when something happens 'to cause the lungs suddenly to inflate' so that 'the air they contain is forced out through the windpipe with impetuosity, forming

---

[107] Fracastoro 1546, fo. 23ᵛ: 'Nova quoque ea sunt, quae risum movere solent.' See also fo. 24ʳ on the need for the *res* to be *subita* and *repentina*.
[108] Fracastoro 1546, fo. 24ʳ: 'Subitam & repentinam etiam admirationem ac repentinam etiam delectationem faciunt [et ex delectatione] . . . motum oris, qui risus dicitur.'
[109] Vallesio 1582, p. 220 acknowledges both Valeriola and Fracastoro.
[110] Vallesio 1582, p. 220: 'Experimento sentimus, homines ridere, quum occurrit res iocunda, & nova . . . nova faciunt admirationem, iocunda gaudium.'
[111] Maggi 1550, pp. 301–27.
[112] Maggi 1550, p. 305: 'Mirari satis non possum cur Cicero . . . de admiratione, quae est una risus causa, ne verbum quidem fecerit . . . cum risus nunquam sine admiratione fieri possit.'
[113] Maggi focuses on the importance of *novitas* in part 2 of Maggi 1550, pp. 310–22.
[114] On the place of wonder in Descartes's theory of the passions see James 1997, pp. 169–70, 187–9.

an inarticulate and uncontrolled voice'.[115] He adds that these distinctive
physiological changes take place only when a new and sudden event
is associated with feelings of wonderment. The blood coming from the
spleen must be 'pushed towards the heart by some light emotion of
Hatred, aided by the surprise of *l'Admiration*' if the outcome is to be the
form of dilation with which laughter is associated.[116]

This Cartesian analysis was closely followed by Henry More in
his *Account of Virtue*,[117] while Hobbes had earlier brought the same
features together in his discussion of laughter in *The Elements of Law*.
He too stresses the importance of novelty and surprise, arguing that
'for as much as the same thinge is noe more ridiculous, when it groweth
stale, or usuall. Whatsoever it be that moveth Laughter, it must be new
and unexpected.'[118] He likewise agrees that the cause of laughter must
be something that gives rise to admiration, especially in the form of
'a suddaine conception of some ability in himself that laugheth'.[119] It is
when we experience 'the suddaine Imagination of our owne odds and
eminence' that we find ourselves bursting out with mirth.[120]

The other important addition made by the Renaissance theorists to
the classical theory of laughter arose out of their perception of a lacuna
in Aristotle's original account. Aristotle's thesis in the *Poetics* had been
that laughter reproves vice by way of expressing and soliciting feelings
of contempt for those who conduct themselves ridiculously. As Maggi
points out in his commentary on the *Poetics*, however, Aristotle had un-
characteristically failed to supply a definition of the ridiculous,[121] and
had failed in consequence to indicate which particular vices are most
susceptible of being held up to derision and thereby laughed to scorn.

To the medical writers this issue was of little significance, but to the humanists it often seemed the most interesting question of all. They found a
clue to the answer in Aristotle's contention that wholly vicious characters
are not properly the subject of ridicule.[122] Castiglione enlarges on the
insight by suggesting that the vices specifically deserving of our contempt
are those which exhibit 'affectation' rather than outright wickedness, and

---

[115] Descartes 1988, Article 124, p. 153: 'enflant les poumons subitement...fait que l'air qu'ils
contienent, est contraint d'en sortir avec impetuosité par le sifflet, où il forme une voix inarticulée
& esclatante'.
[116] Descartes 1988, Article 124, p. 154: 'poussée vers le coeur par quelque legere émotion de Haine,
aydée par la surprise de l'Admiration'.
[117] More 1690, p. 69: '*Derision* is compounded of joy and hatred; and if the Evil, which is the Object
of it, happens on asudden, it produces Laughter.'
[118] Hobbes 1969a, p. 41.   [119] Hobbes 1969a, p. 41.   [120] Hobbes, 1969a, p. 42.
[121] Maggi 1550, part 3, esp. p. 325.   [122] Aristotle 1995, 1449a, p. 44.

especially those which 'passe the degree' and thereby lead to extravagant behaviour. 'Those Affectations and curiosities that are but meane, bringe a lothsomnesse with them, but whan they be done oute of measure they much provoke laughter.' Those people who visibly 'passe the degree' when behaving discreditably reduce themselves to absurdity, which is why they 'doe rather provoke laughter then lothsomnesse'.[123]

Among the vices resulting from a failure to observe this ideal of *mediocritas*, one of the most contemptible was generally agreed to be avarice. Nicander Jossius singles out this weakness as one of the most obvious 'characteristics of body and soul' in which 'matters of ridicule lurk'.[124] Celso Mancini ends his *De Risu, Ac Ridiculis* by specifying in similar vein that one of the failings 'most worthy of derision' is 'the miserliness of old men, because any man is deformed and rendered monstrous by avarice'.[125] So too Paolo Beni, who notes in his *Commentarii* on Aristotle's *Poetics* that the figure of the miser always makes one of the best subjects for comedy.[126] The suggestion was not lost on the comic dramatists of the age, as Ben Jonson's *Volpone* and Molière's *L'Avare* are there to remind us.

Of all the vices open to derision, however, the most flagrant were said to be hypocrisy and vaingloriousness. If we glance forward to post-Renaissance theories of comedy, we generally find the figure of the hypocrite singled out as pre-eminently worthy of contempt. This is Henry Fielding's argument in the theoretical essay prefacing his comic novel *Joseph Andrews* of 1742. Echoing Hoby's translation of Castiglione, Fielding begins by laying it down that the vices most open to ridicule are those which exhibit 'affectation'. He goes on to assert that 'affectation proceeds from one of these two causes, vanity or hypocrisy', and that 'from the discovery of this affectation arises the ridiculous – which always strikes the reader with surprize and pleasure'. But he adds that this happens 'in a higher and stronger degree when the affectation arises from hypocrisy, than when from vanity', and he concludes by noting that 'our Ben Johnson, who of all men understood the *ridiculous* the best, hath chiefly used the hypocritical affectation' in his comedies.[127]

Among Renaissance theorists, by contrast, we encounter a weightier emphasis on the affectations of pride and vaingloriousness. It is possible

---

[123] Castiglione 1994, pp. 163–4.

[124] Jossius 1580, p. 75, offers 'quodam avaritiae genus & actiones' as his first example of the fact that 'in moribus quoque corporis, atque animi latent ridicula'.

[125] Mancini 1598, pp. 22–30: 'Ridendo avaritiam senum [quod] ab avaritia hominem fieri deformem & monstrum.'

[126] Beni 1613, p. 162.   [127] Fielding 1985, pp. 28–9.

that they may have been directly influenced by Plato at this point, for when Socrates examines the nature of the ridiculous in the *Philebus* he not only argues that those who render themselves absurd must be suffering from some kind of vice, but adds that the vice in question will generally be a lack of self-knowledge, especially in the form of self-conceit.[128] It is more likely, however, that the Renaissance writers were drawing on a suggestion of Cicero's in Book 2 of *De Oratore*, in which the figure of Caesar begins his analysis of the ridiculous by declaring that the people most worthy of being laughed to scorn are 'those who act in a particularly boastful way'.[129]

Whatever the source, the suggestion was one that the humanist writers of the Renaissance developed at much greater length. It is when people 'bragg and boast of them selves and have a proude and haughtye stomake', Castiglione maintains, that we are justified 'in mockinge and scorninge such a one' to raise a laugh.[130] He offers the example of men who 'speake of their auntientrye and noblenesse of birth' and of women who praise their own 'beawtie and handsomenesse'.[131] Celso Mancini singles out 'the would-be glorious soldier' as yet another type of person 'whose boastings make us laugh' because 'we know that such vaingloriousness is ridiculous and because such lack of measure irritates us'.[132] Francis Bacon makes a similar observation in his essay *Of Boldness* when he notes that boldness can readily shade over into vanity and thereby become laughable. This is why 'to men of great judgement, bold persons are a sport to behold; nay, and to the vulgar also, boldness hath somewhat of the ridiculous. For if absurdity be the subject of laughter, doubt you not but great boldness is seldom without some absurdity.'[133] Speaking in a loftier register, Lodovico Castelvetro – yet another learned commentator on Aristotle's *Poetics* – suggests that the principal cause of laughter arises from the fact that our corrupted and fallen natures have left us 'stuffed with vanity and pride'.[134] Once again, these insights were not lost on the comic dramatists of the age, who often exhibit a special detestation of those who act without 'measure' and try to pass beyond their degree. The overweening self-love of Malvolio in Shakespeare's

---

[128] Plato 1925, 48c–49c, pp. 332–6.
[129] Cicero 1942, II. LVIII. 237, vol. 1, p. 374, singles out the absurdity of those who 'se forte iactant'.
[130] Castiglione 1994, p. 155.   [131] Castiglione 1994, p. 163.
[132] Mancini 1598, pp. 229–30: 'Provocat nos ad risum iactantia militis gloriosi [quod] cognoscimus dementiam esse illam inanem gloriam . . . carens mensura nos vexat.'
[133] Bacon 1996, pp. 362.
[134] Castelvetro 1570, fo. 53^v, speaks of 'la natura nostra corrotta per lo peccato originale' and the fact that 'si riempie d'alegrezza, & di superbia'.

Twelfth Night, the vainglorious boasting of Puntarvolo in Jonson's *Every Man Out of his Humour*, the ridiculous social climbing of M. Jourdain in Molière's *Bourgeois Gentilhomme* are all variations on the same satirical theme.

IV

Although the theory that laughter is basically an expression of contempt carried with it the authority of Aristotle, some of the writers I have been considering felt obliged to point out that there appears to be an obvious objection to it. Surely our laughter is not always so derisory? Surely some laughter – for example, the laughter of infants – is an expression of unalloyed delight?[135]

A number of the medical writers, no doubt anxious to throw off the weight of scholastic learning, particularly emphasise this point. Fracastoro insists that 'the things which are said about the ridiculous are not properly said', for the truth is that 'laughter is composed out of joy and wonderment combined'.[136] Vallesio refers us to Fracastoro's anti-Aristotelian analysis and proceeds to adopt it. He begins by declaring that 'men laugh when something happens which is at once pleasant and new', but adds that 'our mirth ceases either when the feeling of novelty, or else the feeling of pleasure, wears off'.[137] From this he infers that our laughter need have nothing to do with contempt, since it can equally well be a simple response to a pleasing and surprising event. Developing the insight more systematically, the Pisan physician Elpidio Berrettario in his *Tractatus de Risu* introduces a sharp distinction between what he takes to be two distinct *genera* of mirth.[138] One is the *genus* discussed by Aristotle in the *Poetics*, in which our laughter is provoked by seeing vices successfully held up to ridicule.[139] But the other is unconnected with derision, and

---

[135] One might expect to find in addition some *moral* objections to contemptuous laughter, and especially to its use (in accordance with Cicero's instructions) to mock other people's weaknesses and infirmities. But such scruples are rarely voiced in this period. Sir Thomas More is the only leading humanist to make this kind of anti-Aristotelian point. See More 1965, p. 192. But see Cockagne 2000, pp. 79–82, 89–91 for later moral anxieties about laughter as an expression of ridicule.

[136] Fracastoro 1546, fos. 23^v–24^r: 'Verum haec non proprie ea sunt, quae ridicula dicuntur . . . Est autem risus, compositus ex admiratione & letitia.'

[137] Vallesio 1582, p. 220: 'Homines ridere, quum occurrit res iocunda, & nova . . . atque quamprimum cessat aut iocunditas, aut novitas, cessare risum.'

[138] Berrettario 1603, fos. 7^r and 22^r also singles out the laughter provoked by tickling, insisting (against Fracastoro) that this too is 'real' and a distinct *genus* of the phenomenon.

[139] Berrettario 1603, fo. 7^r.

simply arises 'when we are enticed into laughter by something that is joyful or precious to us'.[140]

Nor were these doubts confined to the medical literature. Castelvetro in his commentary on Aristotle's *Poetics*[141] opens his analysis of the passage in which, as he translates it, Aristotle had argued that 'the laughable is a subdivision of the base'[142] by retorting that 'laughter can be provoked in us by purely pleasurable things'.[143] Beni in his still more comprehensive *Commentarii* on the *Poetics* similarly questions Aristotle's claim that comedy is always preoccupied with reproving vice, pointing out that 'it is not at all rare for comedy to portray good men and to represent them in a praiseworthy way'.[144]

These observations were sometimes underpinned by an anti-Aristotelian vision of the joy and delight out of which laughter can arise. The underlying emotion, some theorists argued, can often be simple *joie de vivre*, unconnected with any feelings of superiority or scorn. Fracastoro observes that 'we often laugh and show our joy when we meet our friends and acquaintances, or else our children, and more generally those who are dear to us'.[145] Castelvetro illustrates the same *mise-en-scène*, picturing a situation in which 'a father and mother receive their little children with laughter and festivity, while in a similar way a lover greets his beloved with a laugh'.[146] Referring with approval to Fracastoro's analysis,[147] Berrettario adds with a flourish that we laugh not only when we encounter our children and friends, but also when we contemplate a beloved mistress or a precious stone.[148]

A further way in which laughter can sometimes arise, according to these writers, is when we experience a sudden defeat of our expectations, whether in the form of a surprising juxtaposition or some other kind of incongruity. Perhaps surprisingly, no one ever suggests that another possible source of innocent mirth might be the enjoyment of

---

[140] Berrettario 1603, fo. 19^r: 'Alterum vero, quando iucunditate & caritate quadam allicimur ad risum.'

[141] See Ménager 1995, pp. 32–3 for a discussion of this text.

[142] Castelvetro 1570, fo. 50^v: 'Il ridevole è particella della turpitudine.'

[143] Castelvetro 1570, fo. 51^r: 'Il riso si muove in noi per cose piacentici.'

[144] Beni 1613, p. 103: 'Comoedia non raro bonos exprimit . . . [et] cum laude represente[n]t.' Cf. also pp. 162, 197.

[145] Fracastoro 1546, fo. 23^v: 'Quum aut amicis & familiaribus, aut filiis, & universaliter charis occurrimus . . . ridere solemus, & laetitiam ostendere.'

[146] Castelvetro 1570, fo. 51^r: 'Il padre & la madre con riso & con festa riceve I figlioletti piccioli . . . & parimente l'amante raccoglie la donna amata con riso.' See also the tabulation at the end of this section of Castelvetro's commentary, which is headed (fo. 54^v) 'cose piacenti che ci muovono a riso'. The first is said to be 'carita di persone prossime o amate o di cose desiderate'.

[147] Berrettario 1603, fo. 20^v. [148] Berrettario 1603, fos. 19^r, 21^v.

nonsense – especially surprising in view of the fact that the genre of nonsense poetry was to attain a considerable vogue in the seventeenth century.[149] But they certainly believe that purely innocent laughter can be provoked by actions that seem to make no sense. Nicander Jossius, although in general a close follower of Aristotle, illustrates the possibility at considerable length. He invites us to consider how we would react 'if a woman were to put on male attire, or gird herself with a sword and set out for the forum, or if a boastful soldier were to settle down with boys learning their grammar at school, or if a prince were to dress himself up as a peasant'.[150] We would certainly laugh, but the reason for our mirth would be the utter incongruity of it all, the failure to pay due respect 'to time, place, moderation or appropriateness'.[151] While these situations would undoubtedly be startling, perhaps even ridiculous, Jossius appears to suggest that we would laugh at them less in contempt than in sheer astonishment.

These insights were eventually developed in Augustan culture into a general defence of the claim that there can be purely good-natured laughter.[152] We encounter the suggestion in Joseph Addison's articles on laughter in the *Spectator* of 1711,[153] in Francis Hutcheson's explicitly anti-Hobbesian *Reflections upon Laughter* in 1725,[154] and perhaps most interestingly in Fielding's Preface to *Joseph Andrews*. As we have seen, Fielding's analysis at first sight looks thoroughly classical, for he accepts that comedy aims to ridicule certain types of affectation, and he agrees that the vices most susceptible to ridicule are avarice, hypocrisy and vanity. At the same time, however, he draws a strong distinction between the comic and what he describes as the burlesque. While the latter genre 'contributes more to exquisite mirth and laughter than any other', it never does so by seeking to arouse contempt. Rather it works by conveying a sense of the 'surprizing absurdity' of some situation, 'as in appropriating the manners

---

[149] On the origins of this genre see Malcolm 1997, esp. pp. 3–29.

[150] Jossius 1580, pp. 71–2: 'si mulier induat habitum virilem, aut accincta ense proficiscatur ad forum ... [aut si] miles gloriosus ... sedeat cum pueris in schola discens grammaticam ... [aut] si princeps ut rustica gens vestiat'.

[151] Jossius 1580, p. 71: 'ad locum, ad tempus, ad modum, aut occasionem'.

[152] On this development see Tave 1960, esp. pp. 43–87.

[153] [Addison] 1965, no. 249 (15 December 1711), vol. 2, pp. 465–9, refers us back to an earlier article (no. 49, 24 April 1711, vol. 1, pp. 200–4) about Hobbes's theory of laughter. Addison maintains (pp. 466, 468) that while Hobbes's account 'seems to hold in most cases' we need to recognise a form of laughter 'in it self both amiable and beautiful'.

[154] Hutcheson 1750, originally published as three articles in the *Dublin Review* for 1725. (For the printing history see Tave 1960, p. 56.) Hutcheson 1750, pp. 6, 29 denounces the 'palpable absurdity' of Hobbes's failure to recognise that laughter frequently 'evidences good nature'.

of the highest to the lowest' or by producing other 'distortions and exaggerations'. The effect, if successful, will be to make us laugh, but our mirth in these cases will be 'full of good-humour and benevolence'.[155]

If, however, we return to the exponents of the classical theory, we find them unrepentant in the face of these alleged counter-examples. The suggestion that laughter can be purely joyful strikes them not as an objection to Aristotle's theory but as an obvious mistake. The delighted laughter of infants they refuse to accept as an instance of genuine laughter at all. Laurent Joubert simply dismisses the possibility,[156] but Nicander Jossius – who takes pride in assuring us that 'I speak out of the mind of Aristotle'[157] – explains that 'for true laughter' it is essential 'that the person who laughs should be *aware* of something ridiculous'.[158] Antonio Lorenzini enlarges on the argument, claiming that 'it is necessary for the person who laughs to know that he laughs' and explaining that this is how it comes about that 'man alone is capable of laughter'.[159]

The suggestion that adults may be capable of purely joyful laughter is dismissed as still more obviously misconceived. Confronted with Fracastoro's contention that laughter arises from wonderment combined with sheer delight, François Valleriola somewhat irritably retorts in his *Enarrationum Medicinalium* that such an explanation is merely inept.[160] One reason is that, when we experience *admiratio*, our feelings will generally be too deep for laughter – a point developed by Joubert and later by Descartes.[161] But Valleriola's main argument is the purely Aristotelian one that, if we find ourselves laughing, this will not be due to *admiratio* – a response we reserve for great things – but rather to a feeling of scorn for something base and absurd.[162]

A further and subtler argument mentioned by several of these writers is that, if we suppose our laughter to be the product of pure delight, we are almost certainly deceiving ourselves. As Castiglione puts it, while 'a certein jocundenesse' will undoubtedly be present, the truth is that 'a man laugheth onlie at those matters that are disagreeing in themselves,

---

[155] Fielding 1985, pp. 26–8. On the evolution of the contrast between laughter produced by satire (contemptuous and ridiculing) and by the burlesque (sympathetic), see Paulson 1988.

[156] Joubert 1579, ch. 9, pp. 288–301.

[157] Jossius 1580, p. 69: 'ego tamen dico ex mente Aristotelis . . .'.

[158] Jossius 1580, p. 52, claims that, for the 'verus risus', it is essential 'quod ridicula cognoscit'. Emphasis added.

[159] See Lorenzini 1606, p. 74, where the Socratic figure of Cosmus declares that 'oportet eum, qui ridet, quod ridet, cognoscere', adding that 'etiam solus homo ad risum aptus sit'.

[160] Valleriola 1554, p. 218.

[161] Joubert 1579, p. 72; Descartes 1988, Article 125, p. 153.

[162] Valleriola 1554, p. 217.

and (to a mans seeminge) are in yll plight'.[163] Joubert carries the argument still further when he maintains that, if we reflect on what brings us joy and what arouses our mirth, we shall find that they have no connection with each other. 'The object or matter of rejoicing is something serious that brings pleasure, gain, profit, convenience or some other true contentment', whereas 'the nature of the emotion that makes us laugh is nothing but light, bantering, vain and often untruthful'.[164]

Among humanist writers, perhaps the most vehement attack on the idea of innocent mirth comes from Sir Philip Sidney in his *Defence of Poesie* of 1580. Sidney concludes by severely criticising the writers of comedy who mistakenly believe that 'delight should be the cause of laughter'. Rather, he insists, laughter and delight 'have as it were a kind of contrarietie'. We take delight 'in things that have a conveniencie to our selves', whereas laughter 'almost ever cometh of thinges moste disproportioned to our selves and nature'. Delight 'hath a joy in it either permanent or present', but laughter 'hath onely a scornfull tickling'. The emotion that 'stirreth laughter' is always scornfulness, never delight.[165]

There is something arrestingly alien about this insistence that laughter is always an expression of contempt, and thus that those who become objects of laughter automatically lower themselves in the eyes of others, an outcome to be avoided at all costs. Nowadays we are inclined to believe that the capacity to laugh at ourselves – not at our previous selves, but at our actual conduct – is praiseworthy and deserves to be encouraged. It is clear, however, that for the classical and Renaissance writers it would have been unthinkable to draw attention in such a way to what they evidently saw as pure loss of face. Horace explicitly makes the point in his opening *Satire* after seeking to amuse us with his contemptuous account of our natural avariciousness. 'What are you laughing at?' he suddenly asks. 'If you change the name, the story is told about yourself.'[166] The assumption is that, as soon as you see that this is so, this will instantly cut short your mirth.

---

[163] Castiglione 1994, pp. 154–5.
[164] Joubert 1579, p. 72: 'L'objet ou matiere de la rejouïssance, e[s]t chose serieuse qui apporte plaisir, gain, proufit, commodité, ou autre vray contantement. La matiere de l'affeccion faisant rire, n'et que sollatre, badine, vaine, & souvant mansongere.'
[165] Sidney 1912, p. 40.
[166] Horace 1929, I. I. lines 69–70, pp. 8–10:

> quid rides? mutato nomine de te
> fabula narratur.

v

As I have been stressing, for most of the writers discussed here it mattered a great deal to be able to insist – with polemical force if necessary – that laughter is basically an expression of scorn and contempt. But why was this felt to be so important? Why were so many of the medical as well as humanist writers so strongly committed to this belief?

For the physicians, the significance of the argument lay in the fact that it accorded a place to laughter in the promotion of good health. Joubert explains in detail that the encouragement of mirthfulness is exceptionally valuable in the case of those with cold and dry complexions, and hence with small and hard hearts.[167] Anyone cursed with this temperament suffers an excess of *atra bilis* or black bile in the spleen, which in turn gives rise to feelings of rage and, unless treated, to loss of *esprit* and eventual melancholia.[168] The example to which the physicians constantly recur is that of Democritus, whose bilious temperament made him so impatient and irritable that, as Burton reports in *The Anatomy of Melancholy*, he eventually became almost suicidally depressed.[169] Democritus's decision to cultivate the habit of laughter provided him with a remedy for this dangerous predicament.[170] By making himself a constant spectator of human absurdity, he was able to overcome his splenetic disposition by laughing at everything that excited his contempt. Not only did this improve the flow of his blood, thereby making him temporarily more sanguine; it also helped him to expel the black bile that would otherwise have brought a return of his melancholia. As Joubert confirms, we must be sanguine and light-hearted to remain 'civil', and the medical virtue of laughter stems from the fact that its violent action enables us to correct a threatening imbalance in our temperament.[171] What Hippocrates perceived in the case of Democritus was that his laughter, far from being a symptom of madness, was probably the chief means of keeping him sane.[172] 'Heart-easing Mirth', as Milton revealingly calls it in *L'Allegro*, was widely recognised as a powerful medicine.[173]

---

[167] Joubert 1579, pp. 251–4, 258–9.   [168] Joubert 1579, pp. 81–3, 273–6.
[169] Burton 1989, p. 2.
[170] Joubert 1579, Appendix, p. 363, speaks of this 'remede et cure'.
[171] Joubert 1579, p. 259, speaks of the value of laughter in helping to sustain 'la symmetrie & moderacion de la temperature ou complexion humaine'.
[172] For similar observations about the power of laughter to purge ill humours see Bright 1586, ch. 31, pp. 178–84, and Berrattario 1603, ch. 10, fos. 25^v–26^r.
[173] Milton 1998, p. 22, line 13.

If we turn by contrast to the humanists, and more particularly to the theorists of rhetoric, we encounter an entirely different line of argument. For the rhetoricians, the significance of the fact that laughter is an expression of scorn and contempt is essentially forensic in character. If it is true, they argue, that laughter is the outward manifestation of these particular emotions, we can hope to convert it into a uniquely powerful weapon of moral and political debate.

To see how they arrive at this conclusion, we need to begin by recalling perhaps the most basic assumption inherited by the philosophers of the Renaissance from the rhetorical culture of ancient Rome. To state it in the terms that eventually became proverbial, there will always be two sides to any question in the moral or civil sciences. As Quintilian explains in his chapter on the nature of rhetoric, if you argue about such questions you will find yourself in a situation 'in which two wise men may with just cause take up one or another point of view, since it is generally agreed that reason can lead even the wise to fight among themselves'.[174] It will always be possible 'to employ the weapons of powerful speech *in utramque partem*, on either side of the case', with the result that you can never hope to demonstrate beyond question that one or the other side is in the right.[175]

We have already seen in volume 2 chapter 10 what was taken to follow from this predicament. If there are two sides to the question, your aim must be to argue in such a way that – as we still say – you persuade your audience to come round to your side. The characters in Cicero's *De Oratore* repeatedly insist on the crucial importance of knowing how to speak 'winningly', how to move or sway your auditors into seeing things from your point of view.[176] The commitment is vividly conveyed by the figure of Antonius when he declares that, should you find yourself confronting an audience 'actively hostile to your cause and friendly to your opponent', your objective must be 'to try to swing them round as if by some kind of machinery'.[177] The image survives in modern times in the form of the judgement that the greatest feat of parliamentary oratory will always be to cause an adversary to 'cross the floor'.

How can this be done? Not by reason alone, because there may be equally good reasons on either side. Rather you must learn how to

---

[174] Quintilian 1920–2, II. XVII. 32, vol. 1, p. 338: 'duos sapientes aliquando iustae causae in diversum trahant (quando etiam pugnaturos eos inter se, si ratio ita duxerit, credunt)'.

[175] Quintilian 1920–2, II. XVII. 10, vol. 1, p. 322: 'in utramque partem valet arma facundiae'.

[176] Cicero 1942, I. VIII. 30, vol. 1, p. 22; II. XLII. 178, vol. 1, p. 324; III. VI. 23, vol. 2, p. 18; III. XIV. 55, vol. 2, p. 44.

[177] Cicero 1942, II. XVII. 72, vol. 1, p. 252: when the judge is 'amicus adversario et inimicus tibi', then 'tanquam machinatione aliqua . . . est contorquendus'.

supplement your reasoning with the passionate force of powerful speech. You must learn, in other words, how to arouse in your audience a purely emotional commitment to your side of the case. As the figure of Antonius in *De Oratore* puts it with cynical frankness, after attracting the attention of your auditors 'you must try to shift them so that they become ruled not by deliberation and judgement but rather by sheer impetus and perturbation of mind'.[178] As we saw in volume 2 chapter 10, a deliberate ambiguity in the use of the word *move* may thus be said to lie at the heart of the argument. One of your aims in moral or political debate must always be to shift or move your audience to adopt your own perspective. But the only means of attaining this goal will be to speak or write in such a way that they are not merely convinced but 'greatly moved'.[179] This is the power that prompts your adversaries to cross the floor: if and only if they feel sufficiently moved will they move.

These contentions leave the rhetoricians confronting a question of some practical importance. Are there any specific techniques we can hope to learn and deploy in such a way as to move the emotions of an audience? Cicero gives his answer in Book 3 of *De Oratore*, in which he explains that this brings us to the topic of *ornatus* – that is, the figures and tropes of speech – and their crucial place in the theory of eloquence. Here the figure of Crassus takes up the argument. 'The greatest praise for eloquence is reserved for the amplification of argument by means of *ornatus*', and it is by means of such amplification 'that we are able either to conciliate the minds of our listeners or else to excite them', arousing or calming their passions at will.[180] Quintilian later explores the argument at greater length in Books 8 and 9 of the *Institutio Oratoria*, where he ends by declaring that the figures of speech, correctly deployed, possess an unsurpassed power to rouse the emotions and move people to accept our point of view.[181]

We still need to know how this can be done. Here the classical rhetoricians have several suggestions to make, but one of the most important is

---

[178] Cicero 1942, II. XLII. 178, vol. 1, p. 324: 'Ipse sic moveatur, ut impetu quodam animi et perturbatione, magis quam iudicio aut consilio regatur.'

[179] As the figure of Antonius in *De Oratore* expresses it, the highest art is to argue in such a way that, while appearing merely to teach, 'you have the power to move the minds of your audience as much as possible'. See Cicero 1942, II. LXXVII. 310, vol. 1, p. 434: 'habere hanc vim magnopere debent, ut ad eorum mentes apud quos agetur movendas pertinere possint'.

[180] Cicero 1942, III. XXVII. 104, vol. 2, p. 82: 'Summa autem laus eloquentiae est amplificare rem ornando . . . vel cum conciliamus animos vel cum concitamus.'

[181] Quintilian 1920–2, IX. I. 21, vol. 3, p. 358: 'Plurimum tamen ad commendationem facit, sive in conciliandis agentis moribus sive ad promerendum actioni favorem.' On *figurae* as the chief means by which 'ornatur oratio', cf. Quintilian 1920–2, X. V. 3, vol. 4, p. 114.

that we can hope to deploy a particular range of figures and tropes in such a way as to excite laughter and thereby discredit our opponents. When Quintilian first introduces this suggestion in Book 6 he apologises for its seeming triviality.[182] But he later makes it clear that he is far from supposing that any such apology is genuinely required. Returning to the topic in Book 10, he declares that 'this use of humour, together with the ability to inspire pity, are undoubtedly the two means of stirring the emotions that have the greatest impact of all'.[183]

We can now see the special significance for these writers of the claim that laughter arises out of scorn and contempt. If a distinctive range of figures and tropes can be used to arouse laughter, and if laughter is invariably an expression of such hostile feelings of superiority, then we can hope to deploy these figures and tropes in such a way as to arouse these hostile feelings against our dialectical enemies. We can thereby hope to make them look ridiculous in the eyes of our audience, and in consequence make our own side of the case look correspondingly more impressive. This is the main promise held out by Cicero in Book 2 of *De Oratore*, in which the figure of Caesar declares that a talent for exciting laughter 'is not only of great value in replying to your opponent's arguments, but is of no less value in attacking them, since humour can be used to break up his case, to obstruct his arguments, to make light of his cause, to deter him from speaking and to turn aside what he has said'.[184]

It remains to explain the role of the figures and tropes in bringing about these dramatic results. We need to recall that, as Cicero had argued, we can hope to induce the specific and devastating effect of laughter only if we *suddenly* bring home to an audience that someone or something is deserving of contempt. The role of the figures and tropes arises from the fact that several of them are especially well adapted to producing this indispensable element of shock or wonderment. One such trope, Cicero explains, is that of irony, since ironic speakers characteristically say the opposite of what we expect, thereby surprising us and potentially making us laugh.[185] To which he adds that various forms of deliberate under-statement or overstatement (described by later writers as meiosis and hyperbole) possess a similar power to defeat our expectations, thereby

---

[182] Quintilian 1920–2, VI. III. 8, vol. 2, p. 442.

[183] Quintilian 1920–2, X. I. 107, vol. 4, pp. 60–2: 'Salibus certe et commiseratione, qui duo plurimum in adfectibus valent.'

[184] Cicero 1942, II. LVIII. 236, vol. 1, p. 372: 'maxime respondentis, nonnunquam etiam lacessentis; vel quod frangit adversarium, quod impedit, quod elevat, quod deterrret, quod refutat'.

[185] Cicero 1942, II. LXV. 261, vol. 1, p. 394, and esp. II. LXVII. 269–72, vol. 1, pp. 402–4.

inducing 'incredible levels of surprise' and corresponding opportunities for ridicule.[186]

The ancient writers find little more to say about the connections between *ornatus* and laughter, but in the hands of the Renaissance rhetoricians this aspect of the classical theory was very much elaborated. This development may have been due to the fact that the Renaissance writers place so much more emphasis on the element of *admiratio* in the provocation of laughter, which may in turn have made them more sensitive to the power of what they liked to describe as the mocking tropes. But whatever the cause, the result was that they succeeded in identifying, defining and illustrating a far broader range of these rhetorical techniques than any of their classical predecessors had done.

Among the mocking *tropi*, they lay particular emphasis on the device they describe as *asteismus*. Thomas Wilson assures us in his *Arte of Rhetorique* that this is one of the best means of producing a 'just occasion of muche laughter'.[187] Henry Peacham offers a helpful analysis in *The Garden of Eloquence*, explaining that we have a case of asteismus when 'a word having two significations is exprest in the one and understood in the other', or when 'a saying is captiously taken and turned to another sense'.[188] The required element of surprise is furnished by the fact that the words will seem entirely innocent if we only think of their ordinary meaning, but will suddenly lose their innocence as soon as the alternative meaning occurs to us.

Besides adding to the *tropi*, the Renaissance theorists considerably extend the list of mocking *figurae* of speech. Among the devices they single out is the one they usually call *synchoresis*. Dudley Fenner explains in his *Artes of Logike and Rethorike* of 1584 that this is the figure we employ 'when an argument is mockingly yeelded unto'.[189] Here the element of surprise is furnished by the fact that, expecting to find the argument countered, we instead find this expectation suddenly undermined. A second figure especially well suited to satirical use is said to be *aposiopesis*. Fenner informs us that this is the figure in play 'when the course of the sentence begun is so stayed, as thereby some part of the sentence not being uttered, may be understood'.[190] Henry Peacham adds that, if the unexpected silence additionally leaves 'the venome of some false suspicion behind it', the effect may be to hint at something contemptible, and hence worthy of

---

[186] Cicero 1942, II. LXVI. 267, vol. 1, p. 400: 'Etiam illa quae minuendi aut augendi causa ad incredibilem admirationem efferuntur.'
[187] Wilson 1554, fo. 76[v].   [188] Peacham 1593, p. 34.
[189] Fenner 1584, Sig. E, I[v].   [190] Fenner 1584, Sig. D, 4[v].

ridicule.[191] A further and still more blatantly ridiculing figure is said to be *tapinosis*. According to Henry Peacham, we make use of this device whenever 'the dignitie or majestie of a high matter is much defaced by the basenesse of a word'.[192] Here the use of inappropriate terminology occasions the required shock of surprise, while the replacement of a dignified description by a ludicrous one virtually guarantees a laugh.

These rhetorical techniques were widely deployed by the moral and political theorists of the Renaissance, who make full use of them to un-mask the vices of avarice, vanity and hypocrisy, the vices said to be especially deserving of our scorn and contempt. Erasmus relies on the device of ironic inversion throughout his *Encomium Moriae* to satirise the hypocrisies of the age,[193] while More in *Utopia* makes repeated use of rhetorical understatement to ridicule the avarice and vaingloriousness of the nobility and the rich.[194] Of all the Renaissance satirists, however, perhaps the most devastating in his use of these particular techniques is Hobbes, especially in Books 3 and 4 of *Leviathan*. Hobbes is no less a master of irony and mocking understatement,[195] but he is equally skilful at deploying the more rarified devices recommended by the rhetori-cians, especially in his attacks on the avarice, vanity and hypocrisy of the Roman Catholic church.[196]

Hobbes satirises clerical avarice in several ways, but one of the most memorable is undoubtedly by his use of the mocking trope of asteis-mus. When, for example, he turns to examine the Catholic doctrine of Purgatory, he plays on the fact that the word *profit* can either mean (as Cotgrave's *Dictionarie* of 1611 puts it) 'gaine, lucre' or else 'benefit, utilitie'.[197] We are told, Hobbes says, that the Doctors of the Church conducted lengthy debates about the location of 'the place which they were to abide in till they should be re-united to their Bodies in the Resurrection'. At first they supposed that 'they lay under the Altars', but 'afterward the Church of Rome found it more profitable to build for them this place of Purgatory'.[198]

Hobbes likewise takes every opportunity to ridicule the Church's hypocrisies, but never more successfully than when he uses the mock-ing figure of aposiopesis to satirise the doctrine of clerical celibacy.

---

[191] Peacham 1593, p. 118.   [192] Peacham 1593, p. 168.
[193] For an analysis of Erasmus's satirical techniques see Screech 1997, pp. 161–75, 188–90.
[194] A point perceptively made in McCutcheon 1971, pp. 114–16.
[195] For Hobbes's use of these techniques see Skinner 1996, pp. 404–5, 421–2.
[196] For a full account of these techniques (on which I draw in what follows) see Skinner 1996, pp. 413–25.
[197] Cotgrave 1611, Sig. Sss, vi[r].   [198] Hobbes 1996, ch. 44, p. 426.

He begins with a series of opprobrious comparisons between the Catholic priesthood and the fairies. The fairies acknowledge only one king; the priests acknowledge only the pope. The fairies live in enchanted castles; the priests have cathedral churches. The fairies cannot be made to answer for their crimes; the priests likewise vanish from the tribunals of justice. Then he adds his aposiopesis: 'The *Fairies* marry not; but there be amongst them *Incubi*, that have copulation with flesh and bloud. The *Priests* also marry not.'[199]

A good Renaissance rhetorician, Hobbes registers still greater indignation at the pride and vaingloriousness of the schoolmen, whose teachings he summarises under the heading of 'vain philosophy'.[200] He introduces them with a broadly satirical use of asteismus, turning against them the ambiguity inherent in the word *egregious*, which in seventeenth-century English (as Cockeram's *Dictionarie* of 1623 informs us) could mean either 'Excellent' or else 'vile, base'.[201] Hobbes scoffingly avails himself of the double meaning when he speaks of the whole tribe of scholastic theologians as 'Egregious persons'.[202] Most disparaging of all is Hobbes's deployment of the mocking figure of tapinosis to dismiss the attempts of the schoolmen to base the Christian religion on a combination of reason and faith. He retorts that, properly defined, religion is merely '*Feare* of power invisible, feigned by the mind, or imagined from tales publiquely allowed'. Nothing in his entire philosophy caused so much offence. Sir Charles Wolseley exclaimed in *The Reasonableness of Scripture-Belief* that the definition illustrates more clearly than anything the iniquity of those who, 'by an empty prophane sort of discourse, which themselves call Wit', have disgraced the age.[204]

VI

My principal aim in the foregoing analysis has been to expound a theory, but I have attempted at the same time to trace a narrative, a narrative that originates with Aristotle and reaches its climax with the new philosophy of the seventeenth century. By way of conclusion, I want finally to note that, as well as having a beginning and a middle, the story I have been recounting has a recognisable end.

The classical and Renaissance view of laughter as an expression of contempt was countered from two different directions by the end of

---

[199] Hobbes 1996, ch. 47, p. 481. [200] Hobbes 1996, ch. 46, p. 458.
[201] Cockeram 1968, Sig. D, 7ᵛ. [202] Hobbes 1996, ch. 8, p. 59.
[203] Hobbes 1996, ch. 6, p. 42. [204] Wolseley 1672, Sig. A, 3ʳ–4ʳ.

the seventeenth century. As we have seen, one challenge was mounted by those who wished to defend the anti-Hobbesian thesis that laughter can sometimes be an expression of unalloyed delight. But another arose from within the Hobbesian theory itself. A number of moralists began to suggest that, even though it may be true that laughter is always an expression of contempt, we must be very wary of expressing our contempt in the form of outright laughter.

Hobbes himself had a particular reason for issuing this warning. The disposition to laugh, he always maintains, is nothing other than a disposition to insist on our own superiority. But such aggression, he also believes, is an obvious threat to peace, and consequently an affront to the laws of nature. As he makes clear in his definitive account of these laws in chapters 14 and 15 of *Leviathan*, he sees the threat as directed in particular against the eighth and ninth laws. The ninth enjoins '*That every man acknowledge other for his Equall by Nature*', adding that 'the breach of this precept is *Pride*'.[205] Still more relevant is the eighth law, which Hobbes presents as follows:

And because all signes of hatred, or contempt, provoke to fight; insomuch as most men choose rather to hazard their life, than not to be revenged; we may in the eighth place, for a Law of Nature, set down this Precept, *That no man by deed, word, countenance, or gesture, declare Hatred, or Contempt of another.* The breach of which Law, is commonly called *Contumely*.

Having insisted that laughter is always an expression of contempt, Hobbes now insists that, since all such expressions lead to violence, we must avoid them altogether in the name of upholding 'the first, and Fundamentall Law of Nature; which is, *to seek Peace, and follow it*'.[206]

During the latter part of the seventeenth century, we also encounter a second and very different line of argument in favour of avoiding and even proscribing outright laughter. This further doubt arose as an aspect of what has been described as the civilising process.[207] An important part of this development was the growing demand for mutual respect and restraint, and more particularly for the control of various bodily functions that had previously been classified as involuntary.[208] Laughter came to be seen as a form of incivility, and at the same time as an obvious instance of an uncontrolled reaction that needed, in polite society, to be governed and preferably eliminated.

We encounter little of this animus against laughter even in the most exacting courtesy-books of the Renaissance. Castiglione is certainly anxious

[205] Hobbes 1996, ch. 15, p. 107.   [206] Hobbes 1996, ch. 14, p. 92.   [207] Elias 1994.
[208] Elias 1994, pp. 110–17; Thomas 1977, p. 79.

that our mirth should never be vulgar, nor of such a kind as to give rise to blasphemy or dangerous hostilities.[209] But he is so far from viewing laughter as inherently blameworthy that, in Book 2 of the *Cortegiano*, he makes the irreproachable figure of Lady Emilia call on M. Bernarde, after a particularly high-spirited exchange, to 'leave nowe makynge us laugh wyth practisynge of Jestes, and teache us howe we should use them'.[210] We find an even broader tolerance in Stefano Guazzo's *La Civile Conversazione*, the leading courtesy-book of the next generation. Guazzo's text is suffused with laughter, but none of his high-born ladies and gentlemen appears to find anything ill-bred or reprehensible in it. When the figure of Lord Hercules, in the course of the banquet described in Book 4, is persuaded to declaim his lover's complaint, we are told that 'everie one laughed apace'.[211] And when at an earlier stage of the banquet one of the lords tells a *risqué* anecdote, we are told that the entire company – including the Queen – 'burst out in such a laughing' that for some time no one was able to speak.[212]

If, however, we glance forward a century, we come upon a demand for decorum so greatly increased that laughter begins to be virtually debarred. We already encounter this demand in the courtly comedies of the later seventeenth century, in which we are regularly admonished that, as Lord Froth declares in Congreve's *Double-Dealer*, 'there is nothing more unbecoming a man of quality than to laugh; Jesu, 'tis such a vulgar expression of the passion!'[213] Yet more severe are the admonitions to be found in books of conduct intended for ladies. As Lord Halifax explains in his *Advice to a Daughter* of 1688, women have a special need to observe decorum and prudence, a requirement that obliges them wholly to avoid anything resembling 'a concert of senseless merriment'.[214] Halifax goes on to draw the moral with his habitual confidence:

> It is not intended by this that you should forswear laughing; but remember that, fools being always painted in that posture, it may fright those who are wise from doing it too frequently, and going too near a copy which is so little inviting; and much more from doing it loud, which is an unnatural sound and looketh so much like another sex that few things are more offensive. That boisterous kind of jollity is as contrary to wit and good manners as it is to modesty and virtue.[215]

Too much laughter is now seen as an offence not merely against good breeding but against morality itself.

[209] Castiglione 1994, pp. 155, 159–60.   [210] Castiglione 1994, p. 153.
[211] Guazzo 1925, vol. 2, p. 198.   [212] Guazzo 1925, vol. 2, p. 132.
[213] Congreve 1981, I. i, p. 25. For this and other comparable references see Tave 1960, p. 10 and notes.
[214] Halifax 1969, p. 298.   [215] Halifax 1969, p. 298.

Soon after this, we reach the point at which, at least among the genteel and the civilised, laughter is outlawed altogether. When Erasmus Jones's popular courtesy-book, *The Man of Manners*, reached its third edition in 1737, one of the warnings he inserted into the section entitled 'General Rules for a Genteel and Prudent Behaviour' was that 'it is not becoming to break out into violent loud Laughter upon any Occasion whatever'.[216] By the time we reach Lord Chesterfield's *Letters to his Son*, some ten years later, we find that laughter, that great vehicle of contempt, has become an object of contempt itself. Chesterfield repeatedly insists that 'there is nothing so illiberal, and so ill bred, as audible laughter', and that laughing is something that 'people of sense and breeding should show themselves above'. To laugh is 'low and unbecoming', especially in virtue of 'the disagreeable noise that it makes, and the shocking distortion of the face that it occasions' whenever we succumb to it.[217]

This is not of course to deny that laughter may be a natural expression of contempt, nor to deny that we should find the means to express our contempt when appropriate. It is merely to insist that something more controlled than scornful laughter is required. Moreover, the requirement can easily be met, according to Chesterfield, for we need only train ourselves to reduce our laughter to a sub-laugh – that is, to a *sorriso*, a *sourire*, a contemptuous smile. As Chesterfield duly concludes this part of his advice to his son, 'I could heartily wish, that you may often be seen to smile, but never heard to laugh while you live.'[218]

The imperative of decorum was undoubtedly the principal source of the growing movement in the early-modern period to outlaw laughter from civilised life. To anyone living in a post-Freudian culture, however, a further reason for wishing to avoid contemptuous laughter is bound to suggest itself. Such outbursts are liable to be interpreted not merely as highly aggressive, but at the same time as obvious strategies for dealing with feelings of inadequacy and self-doubt. To us these are familiar thoughts, but one might well wonder whether any of the moralists of the early-modern period had access to them. The answer, perhaps unsurprisingly, is that in general they seem not to have done. To this generalisation, however, there is at least one exception, and that is Hobbes.[219]

As early as *The Elements of Law*, we already find Hobbes observing that it is generally those who 'are greedy of applause, from every thinge they doe well' who enjoy laughing 'at their own Actions, performed never so

---

[216] [Jones] 1737, p. 37. For the ascription see Cockagne 2000.
[217] Chesterfield 1901, Letter 144, vol. 1, p. 212.   [218] Chesterfield 1901, Letter 144, vol. 1, p. 213.
[219] There is a hint of the same idea in Descartes 1988, Article 179, p. 196.

little beyond their owne expectation'.[220] He also notes that such laughter consists in effect of 'the recommending of our selves to our owne good opinion, by comparison with another mans Infirmityes or absurditie', and adds in more critical tones that 'it is vaine-glory, and an argument of little worth to thinke the Infirmityes of another sufficient matter for his tryumph'.[221]

For the explicit suggestion, however, that laughter betokens a lack of self-esteem we need to turn to Hobbes's *Answer* to Sir William Davenant's Preface to *Gondibert*, which Hobbes published in 1650:

Great persons that have their mindes employed on great designes, have not leasure enough to laugh, and are pleased with the contemplation of their owne power and vertues, so as they need not the infirmities and vices of other men to recommend themselves to their owne favor by comparison, as all men do when they laugh.[222]

Here Hobbes brings together two equally stern thoughts about laughter, namely that great minds will lack not merely any motive but any time to indulge in it.

If we turn to *Leviathan*, published a year later, we find Hobbes concentrating his main attention on the suggestion that laughter reveals a weakness of character, and expressing the thought in yet more forbidding tones:

[Laughter] is incident most to them, that are conscious of the fewest abilities in themselves; who are forced to keep themselves in their own favour, by observing the imperfections of other men. And therefore much Laughter at the defects of others, is a signe of Pusillanimity. For of great minds, one of the proper workes is, to help and free others from scorn; and compare themselves onely with the most able.[223]

Since this is Hobbes's last word on the subject, it is striking to find him introducing two entirely new elements into his basic theory of laughter as an expression of contempt. One is that, because it is appropriate for great minds to compare themselves only with the most able, they will have no occasion to entertain such feelings of superiority or scorn. His other and still more demanding suggestion is that gifted people have in addition a positive moral duty to help others to cultivate similar feelings of magnanimity and respect.

Although Hobbes had never previously expressed these ideas in print, they were by no means new commitments on his part. He had held these

---

[220] Hobbes 1969a, p. 41. [221] Hobbes 1969a, p. 42.
[222] Hobbes 1971b, p. 53. [223] Hobbes 1996, ch. 6, p. 43.

views for a considerable time, as is evident from a remarkable letter of admonition and advice he had addressed to Charles Cavendish, the younger son of the second earl of Devonshire, at the time when he had taken up residence in Paris in 1638:

> To encouradge inferiours, to be cheerefull with ones equalls & superiors, to pardon the follies of them one converseth withall, & to help men of, that are fallen into ye danger of being laught at, these are signes of noblenesse & of the master spirit. Whereas to fall in love with ones selfe upon the sight of other mens infirmities, as they doe that mock & laugh at them, is the property of one that stands in competition with such a ridiculous man for honour. They are much deceived that think mocking Witte. for those be few y^t cannot do it. And what witte is it to loose a frend though the meanest in the world for the applause of a jest.[224]

Here the duty to exhibit and help others to cultivate a proper sense of magnanimity is so much emphasised that Hobbes comes close to the traditional humanist claim that *virtus vera nobilitas est*.

These almost unrecognisably self-righteous observations are in obvious tension with the withering tones of scorn and contempt that Hobbes liked to visit upon his intellectual adversaries, in particular the schoolmen whom he mocks so relentlessly in Book 4 of *Leviathan*. Nor is it easy to believe that he took himself in these passages to be following his own advice and comparing himself only with the most able. Despite his own penchant for satire, however, Hobbes is clearly in earnest in counselling us to avoid derisive laughter whenever possible. We need to fear it not merely as a breach of the peace, not merely as a failure of magnanimity, but even more deeply as a lapse of self-control, a slipping of the mask of assurance with which we must always aim to confront the hostile world.

---

[224] Hobbes 1994, Letter 28, vol. 1, pp. 52–3.

6

Hobbes and the purely artificial person of the state

Hobbes prefaces *Leviathan* with a letter in which he dedicates the work to
Francis Godolphin and at the same time offers him a summary of the theory of public authority contained in the book. 'I speak', Hobbes explains,
'not of the men, but (in the Abstract) of the Seat of Power.'[1] This seat,
he adds in his Introduction, is occupied by 'that great LEVIATHAN
called a COMMON-WEALTH, or STATE'.[2] The essence of
Hobbes's theory of public power is thus that the person identifiable as
the true 'subject' of sovereignty in any lawful state must be the person of
the state itself.

Hobbes's opening remarks allude to what has proved to be one of the
most enduring puzzles in our inherited theories of government. On the
one hand, most contemporary political philosophers would agree with
Hobbes that the state is the seat of sovereignty.[3] As Hobbes expresses the
claim later in *Leviathan*, it is 'the Reason of this our Artificiall Man the
Common-wealth, and his Command, that maketh Law', so that civil
law is nothing other than 'the Will and Appetite of the State'.[4] But on
the other hand, most contemporary philosophers would also agree with
Hobbes when he adds that the state amounts to nothing more than an
artifice. To quote Hobbes's way of expressing this further point, the state
has no capacity 'to doe any thing'; it is 'but a word, without substance,
and cannot stand'.[5] There, then, is the puzzle. How can the state, an
apparent abstraction, nevertheless be the name of the person who makes
laws, punishes criminals, declares war and peace and performs all the

---

This chapter is a revised version of an article that originally appeared under the same title in *The
Journal of Political Philosophy* 7 (1999), pp. 1–29.
[1] Hobbes 1996, Epistle, p. 3.   [2] Hobbes 1996, Introduction, p. 9.
[3] For some recent examples see the contributions to Biersteker and Weber 1996.
[4] Hobbes 1996, ch. 26, p. 187 and ch. 46, p. 469.
[5] Hobbes 1996, ch. 26, p. 184 and ch. 31, p. 245.

other actions necessary for maintaining – in Hobbes's fine phrase – the safety of the people and their other contentments of life?[6]

One reason for wishing to focus on Hobbes's answer is a strictly exegetical one. He informs us in chapter 17 of *Leviathan* that the state can actually be defined as 'One Person'.[7] But it is far from clear what he means by this claim, and even less clear what he means by adding that this person is also the seat of power. Nor have these problems been very satisfactorily addressed in much of the critical literature. It is remarkable how many surveys of Hobbes's thought – even the best recent surveys[8] – tend to glide past these issues in silence. The exegetical task is accordingly that of trying to say something further about the meaning of Hobbes's claims about the person of the state.

My principal reason, however, for wishing to re-examine Hobbes's theory is a more philosophical one. As I have observed, we continue to organise our public life around the idea of the sovereign state. But it seems to me that we do not always understand the theory we have inherited, and that arguably we have never managed fully to make sense of the proposition that the person of the state is the seat of sovereignty. This encourages me to hope that an historical investigation of Hobbes's argument may turn out to be of more than purely historical interest.

II

Hobbes eventually worked out a distinctive and highly influential approach to the question of how it is possible for a state – or any other abstraction or collectivity – to perform actions and take responsibility for the consequences. The explanation, he proposed, depends on making sense of what he describes as the class of attributed actions. What we need to understand is how actions can be validly attributed to agents, and genuinely counted as theirs, even when the agents in question did not in fact perform the actions, and perhaps could not in principle have performed them.

Hobbes gives his answer without preamble in chapter 16 of *Leviathan*, the chapter entitled *Of Persons, Authors and Things Personated*. His proposed solution (already implicit in his title) is impressively if deceptively

---

[6] Hobbes 1996, ch. 30, p. 231.   [7] Hobbes 1996, ch. 17, p. 121.
[8] For example, Tuck 1989, Flathman 1993, Martinich 1997. But this lack of interest is especially marked among Anglophone commentators. By contrast, the French literature includes a number of important studies of the *personne* of the state. See, for example, Polin 1981, Tricaud 1982, Jaume 1986, Lessay 1992, Zarka 1995. For a valuable recent discussion in English see Sommerville 1992, pp. 57–63.

straightforward. It is possible, he argues, for an action genuinely to be attributed to a collectivity – or to an abstraction or even a thing – provided that one particular condition is met. The agent to whom the action is attributed must be represented by another agent who can validly claim to be 'personating' the first by way of acting on their behalf.[9]

The inspiration for this approach – along with so much else in the conceptual apparatus of *Leviathan* – appears to be drawn from the *Digest* of Roman law.[10] Book 14 of the *Digest* opens by considering the implications of the fact that owners of various kinds of property – specifically, owners of ships and shops – can appoint other persons to serve as their captains or managers.[11] The law describes a number of circumstances in which you may be liable for the consequences of whatever actions are performed on your behalf when you agree *praeponere* – that is, to appoint someone to serve as your agent.[12] Although you will not have performed the actions yourself, you will be legally obliged *praestare* – that is, to stand by the actions and accept responsibility for them as your own.[13]

There are several indications in Hobbes's early works that – in common with other constitutional theorists of the 1640[14] – he was aware of this theory and interested in developing it.[15] In his first treatise on civil

---

[9] Pitkin 1967 rightly stresses that representation is the basic concept. Although I disagree with Pitkin at several points, I am greatly indebted to her classic analysis.

[10] Brett 1997, pp. 205–35 examines the place of this legal tradition in Hobbes's thought. See also Springborg 1976 on Hobbes's 'incorporation' of the commonwealth and Lessay 1992, pp. 167–79 on Hobbes's invocations of the Roman law of corporations.

[11] *Digest* 1985, XIV. I. 1, vol. 1, p. 415 and XIV. III. 1, vol. 1, p. 422. Johnston 1995, esp. pp. 1517–24 discusses these passages and their implications for legal liability.

[12] *Digest* 1985, XIV. I. 5, vol. 1, p. 415 and XIV. III. 5, vol. 1, p. 422: even if I have put someone else in charge (*praeposui*) I may still be liable in full (*in solidum teneri*).

[13] *Digest* 1985, XIV. I. 5, vol. 1, p. 415: '*debeo praestare qui eum praeposui*' – 'I who have appointed that person ought to stand by their actions'.

[14] Among parliamentary writers, [Parker] 1933, p. 193 speaks of the need for 'Authors' to take responsibility for their 'Actors'; among royalists, [Digges *et al.*] 1642, p. 22 claims that acts performed by judges are in effect performed by the king, since 'they sustaine his person'. Thomas Thomason wrote on the title-page of his copy of [Digges] 1642: 'Falk.[land] Chilyw:[orth] Digges & ye rest of ye University'.

[15] The earliest of these intimations can be found in [Hobbes (?)] 1986, I. 14, p. 61, where he speaks of the need to know 'what a *publique Person*, or the *City* is; and what a *private Person*, or *Citizen* is'. This text is an English rendering of Hobbes MSS (Chatsworth) MS D. 1, Hobbes's Latin paraphrase of Aristotle's *Rhetoric*. For this manuscript see chapter 1 note 27 and chapter 2 note 79. Hobbes's paraphrase is in turn drawn from Goulston 1619, a Latin translation of Aristotle's *Rhetoric* published by Goulston alongside his edition of the Greek text. But the passage from chapter 14 is one of several that might lead one to doubt whether the English version in [Hobbes (?)] 1986 is in fact Hobbes's work. There is nothing in Goulston's text or Hobbes's Latin paraphrase corresponding to the suggestion that a city can be described as 'a *publique Person*', and elsewhere in his early works Hobbes always prefers to speak of 'civil' persons. I owe this point to Karl Schuhmann, who has persuaded me that the English version is almost certainly not by Hobbes.

science, *The Elements of Law*, the manuscript of which he circulated in 1640, he already isolates the category of 'civil persons'[16] and asks how 'a multitude of persons naturall' can become 'united by Covenants into one person Civil, or body politique'.[17] And in the earliest published version of his political theory, the *Elementarum Philosophiae Sectio Tertia De Cive* of 1642, he examines the same question at greater length,[18] defining a city or *civitas* as a *persona civilis* 'whose *will*, from the covenants of many men, is to be taken for the *will* of them all'.[19]

At the same time, Hobbes begins to raise the question of how it is possible for actions to be attributed to civil persons of this kind. In *The Elements* he asks how 'any action done in a multitude' can be 'attributed to the multitude, or truly called the action of the multitude'.[20] And in *De Cive* he begins to supply his answer. He introduces a distinction in chapter 7 between a *populus* considered as a collectivity and 'a disunited multitude to whom it is not possible for any *action* or any *right* to be attributed'.[21] The implication, duly pursued in chapter 12, is that a united body of people, by contrast with a mere multitude, may be capable of acting as a single person in the sense that 'it is possible for *one single* action to be attributed to it'.[22]

The weakness of these discussions is that they lack any account of how such attributions are to be made, and of how to distinguish between genuine attributions and those that may be counterfeited. It is only in the *Leviathan* of 1651 that these questions are properly addressed and a theory of attributed action is systematically laid out. This initial effort, however, was marred by some obscurity and even incoherence. Hobbes later recognised these defects himself, and took the chance to introduce a number of improvements when he published *De Homine* in 1658, in which he devoted his closing chapter to the theme of *De Homine Fictitio*. Still later he introduced yet further refinements when he revised *Leviathan* and reissued it in Latin in 1668. While it will be best to begin with the English *Leviathan* of 1651, which contains Hobbes's fullest statement of

---

[16] Hobbes 1969a, pp. 108, 117. Later, Hobbes adds (p. 174) that 'though in the Chapters of subordinate Corporations, a Corporation be declared to be one Person in lawe, yet the same hath not been taken note of in the body of a Commonwealth, or City'.

[17] Hobbes 1969a, p. 108.

[18] Hobbes 1983a, V. IX–X, p. 134 and VI. I, p. 136 describes the *civitas* as a *persona civilis*.

[19] Hobbes 1983a, V. IX, p. 134: 'cuius *voluntas*, ex pactis plurium hominum, pro *voluntate* habenda est ipsorum omnium'.

[20] Hobbes 1969a, p. 108.

[21] Hobbes 1983a, VII. V, p. 153: 'multitudo dissoluta cui nulla neque *actio* neque *ius* attribui potest'. Cf. Hobbes 1983a, VI. I, p. 136 on why it is impossible for an action to be attributed to a multitude.

[22] Hobbes 1983a, XII. VIII, p. 190: 'cui actio *una* attribui possit'.

his distinctions and arguments, it will be necessary at various points to take account of these later corrections and embellishments.

Hobbes introduces his attempt to analyse attributed action in terms of representation at the start of chapter 16 of *Leviathan*,[23] where he begins by unveiling his definition of the underlying concept of a person:

A PERSON, *is he*, whose words or actions are considered, either as his own, or as representing the words or actions of an other man, or of any other thing to whom they are attributed, whether Truly or by Fiction.[24]

To construe. A general theory of action will not only have to explain how individual persons can represent themselves, so that their words and actions can truly be attributed to them. Such a theory will also have to explain how it is possible for one person to represent someone else – or some *thing* else – in such a way that the words or actions of the representative can validly be attributed to the person (or thing) being represented. To put the point in a different way – as Hobbes himself does later in the chapter – a general theory of action will need to include an account of how it is possible for one person to act in the name of another. This is because 'to *Personate*, is to *Act*, or *Represent* himselfe, or an other; and he that acteth another, is said to beare his Person, or act in his name'.[25]

These phrases about 'bearing' and 'personating' fall strangely on modern ears, so it is worth recalling that Hobbes's usages were not at all uncommon at the time. It has lately been suggested that the peculiarities of his terminology stem from the fact that he was drawing on the vocabulary of covenanting theology.[26] But as Hobbes himself emphasises, his terminology is largely taken from the theatre.[27] By the time he was writing, the idea of 'bearing' or 'presenting' *dramatis personae* on the stage had become sufficiently familiar to be understood even by such unsophisticated thespians as the tradesmen in *A Midsummer Night's Dream*. Rehearsing the story of Pyramus and Thisbe, they find themselves beset by various problems of mimesis. One is how to convey the fact that the lovers met by moonlight. They decide that someone will have to enter 'with a bush of thorns and a lantern and say he comes to disfigure, or to present, the person of Moonshine'.[28] A further problem is that the lovers spoke through a chink in a wall, and that it will not be possible to

[23] Although Hobbes 1996, ch. 15, pp. 103–4 already introduces the concept when discussing the attribution of justice and injustice to actions and to men.
[24] Hobbes 1996, ch. 16, p. 111.   [25] Hobbes 1996, ch. 16, p. 112.
[26] See Martinich 1992, pp. 165, 384 and references there.
[27] Paganini 2001 also draws attention to Boethius's *De Persona* and Renaissance commentaries on it. On the place of theatricality in Hobbes's account see Pye 1984 and Runciman 1997, pp. 224–9.
[28] Shakespeare 1988, *A Midsummer Night's Dream*, III. i. 54–6, p. 320.

bring a wall on stage. Again they agree that 'some man or other must present Wall',[29] and when they later perform their play the wall is duly personated by the tinker Snout.[30]

The anxiety of Shakespeare's rustics to demonstrate their mastery of theatrical terminology is of course part of the comedy. But the passage reminds us that, in drawing on the same terminology in *Leviathan*, Hobbes was merely 'translating', as he puts it, a range of concepts long familiar in the playhouse to encompass 'any Representer of speech and action, as well in Tribunalls, as Theaters'.[31] The outcome, as he adds, is that in his theory 'a *Person*, is the same that an *Actor* is, both on the Stage and in common Conversation'.[32] As Hobbes's theory continually reminds us, *persona* is, in Latin, the ordinary word for a theatrical mask.

The term *attributed* was likewise a familiar piece of legal terminology, and was evidently chosen by Hobbes with some care. The Latin verb *attribuere* had always been used to convey the sense that something should be counted as belonging to someone. Furthermore, there was always the implication – as in the case of attributing an anonymous text to its rightful author – that the responsibility for a work may sometimes be hard to assign, and that appearances may often be deceptive. These considerations had already been highlighted by the ancient theorists of forensic eloquence. They had made it a principle that, whenever the wording of a text is in question in a court of law, you must seek to cast doubt on whatever attributions of meaning and authorship have been made by your adversaries.[33] The parallel with attributed action is close: while it may be evident who performed a given action, it may not be evident who should count as its true author, and hence as responsible for its consequences. These were exactly the parallels that Hobbes was concerned to bring out.

With the introduction of the key concept of an attributed action, Hobbes comes face to face with the principal problem he needs to address. What is to count as the valid representation of one person's words or actions by someone else, such that it will be proper to say of an action performed by a representative that it ought to be attributed to the person – or thing or collectivity – being represented? What, in a word, distinguishes representation from misrepresentation?

Hobbes grappled with this problem in every recension of his civil science, but it was only in *Leviathan* that he arrived at an answer that he

---

[29] Shakespeare 1988, *A Midsummer Night's Dream*, III. i. 62, p. 320.
[30] Shakespeare 1988, *A Midsummer Night's Dream*, V. i. 154–5, 160–1, p. 330.
[31] Hobbes 1996, ch. 16, p. 112.   [32] Hobbes 1996, ch. 16, p. 112.
[33] See, for example, *Ad C. Herennium* 1954, II. IX. 13, p. 80 on how a *sententia* should be *adtributa*.

seemed to find satisfactory.[34] Once again his solution wears an air of
remarkable simplicity, but it constitutes one of the most important theoretical advances he made between the publication of *De Cive* in 1642 and
Leviathan nearly a decade later, and arguably embodies his most original
contribution to the theory of the state.[35] His suggestion is that an action
can be validly attributed to one person on the basis of its performance
by a representative if and only if the representative has in some way
been duly authorised,[36] and hence instructed and commissioned, to perform the action concerned.[37] The crucial concept is accordingly that of
authorisation,[38] and more specifically that of being an author and hence
in a position to grant authority.[39] These terms make no appearance in *The
Elements* or *De Cive*. Although Hobbes gives some consideration in those
texts to the question of where authority may be said to reside, he never
considers how it comes to be authorised. In *Leviathan*, by contrast, he
deploys the concepts of authorisation and of 'being an author' to furnish
the entire theoretical grounding for his theory of the legitimate state.[40]

This terminology is introduced at an early stage in chapter 16 of
Leviathan. Hobbes first employs these terms when considering the sense
in which we can speak of actions, by analogy with possessions, as 'owned'
by particular individuals:

Then the Person is the *Actor*; and he that owneth his words and actions, is the
AUTHOR: In which case the Actor acteth by Authority. For that which in
speaking of goods and possessions, is called an *Owner*, and in latine *Dominus*, in
Greeke κύριος, speaking of Actions, is called an Author.[41]

---

[34] Although Hobbes made several changes in the Latin version of *Leviathan* to his theory about the
person of the state, his theory about authorisation remained unchanged.
[35] Rightly stressed in Gauthier 1969, p. 120 and Zarka 1995, p. 197.
[36] Note that 'duly' need not mean 'explicitly': implicit authorisation is a possibility for Hobbes.
[37] Hobbes does not say that the representative has to be authorised by the person being represented.
As we shall see in section III, he needs to leave space for the fact that this will sometimes be
impossible in principle.
[38] Hobbes 1996, ch. 17, p. 120 and ch. 21, p. 151 explicitly invokes this terminology. On Hobbes's
concept of authorisation see Copp 1980, pp. 582–95, a discussion to which I am particularly
indebted.
[39] On 'authors' and 'authority' in this period see Elsky 1989.
[40] My discussion is mainly confined to the basic case in which one natural person or body of persons
directly authorises another to act either on their behalf or on behalf of a third party. Hobbes adds
many possible refinements: conditional authorisation (Hobbes 1996, ch. 16, p. 115); authorisation
of Assemblies (Hobbes 1996, ch. 19, p. 129); and authorisation not by mutual covenant but by
covenant with a conqueror (Hobbes 1996, ch. 20, p. 141). A full analysis of Hobbes's theory would
need to take account of these refinements, but in the meantime there are several good reasons
for concentrating on the basic case. One is that Hobbes does so himself. Another is that he is not
always successful in explaining how the refinements fit on to the basic case. As we shall see, one
consequence is that sometimes there is insufficient textual basis for discussing them.
[41] Hobbes 1996, ch. 16, p. 112.

Hobbes is asking what allows an actor – that is, a representative – to claim that he is acting by authority. (I shall sometimes be obliged to follow him in writing as if all such actors are male.) The representative needs to be able to claim that he was duly authorised, in which case the person who granted him authority will count as the author of his action and will have to take responsibility for its consequences. The conclusion is guaranteed by the two stipulations underpinning Hobbes's argument. The first states that anyone who authorises an action can be identified as its author. The second adds that, when we speak about the authors of actions, we are equivalently speaking about their owners, since we are speaking about those who must 'own up' to whatever is done in their name.[42]

A dramatic implication underlies this analysis, as Hobbes immediately points out:

> From hence it followeth, that when the Actor maketh a Covenant by Authority, he bindeth thereby the Author, no lesse than if he had made it himselfe; and no less subjecteth him to all the consequences of the same.[43]

The implication is brought out still more forthrightly in *De Homine*: 'He is called an author who has declared that he wishes an action to be held as his own which another person has performed.'[44] Hobbes is now prepared unequivocally to state that the reason why authors must 'own up' to the actions they have authorised is that the actions in question will be theirs, not those of anyone else.

The significance of the implication is that it yields the required criterion for judging when an alleged author can validly claim to have been misrepresented. If you are impersonated by a purported representative without having antecedently granted him authority, you are under no obligation to 'own' his actions, since you cannot be said to have authorised their performance. It is only 'when the Authority is evident' that the author is obliged; if, by contrast, 'the Authority is feigned, it obligeth the Actor onely; there being no Author but himselfe'.[45]

To round off his exposition, Hobbes provides an account of the mechanism by which it is possible for one person to receive the kind of authority that enables them validly to represent another and act in their name. He

---

[42] I am indebted to Pitkin 1967, pp. 18–19 on owning and 'owning up'.

[43] Hobbes 1996, ch. 16, p. 112.

[44] Hobbes 1839d, XV. 2, p. 131: '*Author enim vocatur is, qui actionem quam facit alius pro sua habere se velle declaravit.*'

[45] Hobbes 1996, ch. 16, p. 113.

gives his explanation – again by analogy with the ownership of goods – in the same passage of chapter 16:

And as the Right of possession, is called Dominion; so the Right of doing any action, is called AUTHORITY.[46] So that by Authority, is alwayes understood a Right of doing any act; and *done by Authority*, done by Commission, or License from him whose right it is.[47]

To construe again. To be able to act by authority is to have been granted a commission or at least a licence to perform an action by some person or persons who must possess the right to perform the given action themselves. The grant must take the form of a voluntary transfer of right, since commissioning and licensing are names of voluntary acts. So the receipt of such a commission must be equivalent to the acquisition of the transferred right of performing the action involved.[48] Hobbes later summarises more clearly in *De Homine*. 'They are said to have authority who do something by the right of someone else',[49] so that 'unless he who is the author himself possesses the right of acting, the actor has no authority to act'.[50]

By signalling acceptance of such a covenant,[51] the authorising agent acquires two contrasting obligations towards his representative. One is a duty to take responsibility for the actions performed by the representative in his name. But the other is a duty of non-interference. The latter obligation follows from the fact that, whenever an authorising agent voluntarily transfers the right to perform an action, he thereby gives up the right to perform it himself. As Hobbes explains, 'To *lay downe* a mans Right to any thing, is to *devest* himselfe of the *Liberty*, of hindring another of the benefit of his own Right to the same.'[52] He goes on to trace the implications in his most minatory tones:

---

[46] Hobbes in BL MS Egerton 1910, p. 96 adds 'and sometimes warrant' at this point, but this is omitted from the 1651 text.

[47] Hobbes 1996, ch. 16, p. 112.

[48] This point is worth underlining, if only because it has sometimes been argued that (as Gauthier 1969, p. 124 puts it) although the act of authorisation seems to involve 'some translation of right', this is 'evidently not mere renunciation, nor is it transfer, in Hobbes's usual sense'.

[49] Hobbes 1839d, XV. 2, p. 131: 'Itaque authoritatem habere dicuntur, qui quid iure faciunt alieno.'

[50] Hobbes 1839d, XV. 2, p. 131: 'Nisi enim is, qui author est, ius habet agendi ipse, actor agendi authoritatem non habet.'

[51] Note that this is the form of the covenant only in what I am calling the basic case – what Hobbes 1996, ch. 16, p. 115 calls the case of being 'simply' as opposed to 'conditionally' authorised. Leyden 1982, pp. 89–95 discusses the special complexities attaching to conditional authorisation.

[52] Hobbes 1996, ch. 14, p. 92.

When a man hath in either manner abandoned, or granted away his Right; then is he said to be OBLIGED, or BOUND, not to hinder those, to whom such Right is granted, or abandoned, from the benefit of it: and that he *Ought*, and it is his DUTY, not to make voyd that voluntary act of his own: and that such hindrance is INJUSTICE, and INJURY, as being *Sine Jure*; the Right being before renounced, or transferred.[53]

Once you have covenanted, you must leave it to your representative, who is now in possession of your right of action, to exercise it at his discretion when acting in your name.

Before considering how Hobbes applies this general theory, we need to examine one allegedly knock-down objection to his entire line of thought.[54] One commentator to press the objection has been Joel Feinberg, who has raised it in discussing Hobbes's example in chapter 15 of *Leviathan* of a master who 'commandeth his servant to give mony to a stranger'.[55] The servant is acting as his master's representative, from which it follows, according to Hobbes, that the act of paying the stranger must be attributed to the master.[56] According to Feinberg this analysis is dangerously misleading. Although the 'pecuniary consequences' may be the same as if the master had acted himself, 'it is nevertheless true that *he* did not act'; what we have to say is that his servant acted for him.[57] The objection is thus that attributed actions are not actions.

One possible retort[58] would be to insist that, in spite of the obvious difference between attributed actions and actions performed at first hand, the two ought nevertheless to be classified together on the grounds of their numerous family resemblances.[59] While this raises some interesting questions about the concept of action, Hobbes himself makes no

53 Hobbes 1996, ch. 14, pp. 92–3.
54 Copp 1980, pp. 585–6 offers a more specific objection. I can validly be held accountable for an action performed by someone else if I coerce them into performing it. But coercing is not authorising; so I can validly be held accountable, *pace* Hobbes, for actions I have not authorised. Hobbes would not regard this as an objection. For him, coercion and freedom of action are compatible, so that even coercive acts of authorisation genuinely authorise. For a discussion of this aspect of Hobbes's theory of freedom see below, chapter 7 section III.
55 Hobbes 1996, ch. 15, p. 104; cf. Feinberg 1970, p. 227.
56 Hobbes 1996, ch. 16, pp. 112, 113; cf. also Hobbes 1996, ch. 22, p. 156.
57 Feinberg 1970, p. 227.
58 Copp 1979, pp. 177–8 suggests another possible retort: that the question of what it may be misleading to say in the case of the master and his servant depends on what is in question about the episode. Suppose that, although the servant duly hands over the money, a question later arises as to whether the stranger has been paid. What it will be misleading to say in these circumstances is that the master has *not* paid the stranger. He *has* paid him – by commanding and thereby causing his servant to make the payment.
59 Copp 1980, pp. 581–2 discusses Feinberg's objection to Hobbes's analysis and proposes this response.

attempt to mount this kind of defence, and he surely stands in no need of it. It is true that he likes to speak of attributed actions as if they are genuine instances of action. But it is sufficient for his purposes to defend the much less controversial claim he puts forward about 'ownership': the claim that, when someone acts as an accredited representative, the person being represented must 'own' the consequences of the action *as if* they had performed it themselves. The action counts as theirs, and is called their action,[60] not because they actually performed it, but because they are under an obligation to take responsibility for its occurrence.[61]

III

I have now laid out what I take to be the basic elements in Hobbes's theory of attributed action. But the plot is a great deal thicker than I have so far intimated. When Hobbes introduces his theory, he specifies that two distinct types of person are capable of performing attributed actions: natural persons and feigned or artificial persons:

A PERSON, is he, *whose words or actions are considered, either as his own, or as representing the words or actions of an other man, or of any other thing to whom they are attributed, whether Truly or by Fiction.*

When they are considered as his owne, then is he called a *Naturall Person*: And when they are considered as representing the words and actions of an other, then is he a *Feigned or Artificiall person.*[62]

To appreciate the scope of Hobbes's theory, and to locate the person of the state within his general scheme of things, we next need to consider these different types of person and the different ways in which it is possible for actions to be attributed to them.

Since the distinction between natural and artificial persons turns out to be fundamental to Hobbes's theory of the state, it is unfortunate that he introduces it in such an ambiguous way. In the second paragraph quoted above, strict grammar requires that the referent of the final 'he' should be 'an other', so that the artificial person must be the person represented. But the flow of the sentence suggests that the referent of 'he' must be the

---

[60] This phrase is actually invoked by Hobbes's friend Ben Jonson in *Catiline his Conspiracy*. See Jonson 1937, III. i. 38–9, p. 469, where Cicero, on his election as Consul, is made to declare:

> 'For every lapse of mine will, now, be call'd
> Your error, if I make such . . .'

[61] Runciman 1997 p. 7. I am much indebted to Runciman's analysis at this point.

[62] Hobbes 1996, ch. 16, p. 111. These paragraphs are unchanged in sense from Hobbes's manuscript version in BL MS Egerton 1910, pp. 95–6.

natural person mentioned at the start of the first paragraph, in which case the artificial person must be the representative.

Hobbes initially resolved the ambiguity by endorsing the latter alternative. Later in chapter 16 he explains that 'Of Persons Artificiall, some have their words and actions *Owned* by those whom they represent', thereby making it clear that the artificial person is the representative.[63] The artificiality of such representatives, he later makes clear, resides in the fact that they are acting as public persons rather than in their private capacity. This is explicitly brought out in chapter 35, where Hobbes declares that 'the King of any Countrey is the *Publique* Person, or Representative of all his own Subjects', to which he adds in chapter 42 that any such '*Publique Person*' will at the same time be 'the Representant of the Common-wealth'.[64]

It is still more unfortunate, however, that so many of Hobbes's interpreters have followed him at this point.[65] The subsequent deletion from the Latin *Leviathan* of the passage from chapter 16 in which Hobbes lays it down that representatives are artificial persons strongly implies that he had come to feel that he initially misstated his own argument. There are in any case conclusive reasons for preferring the alternative reading, reasons that seem especially conclusive in the case of the person of the state. If we adopt Hobbes's initial proposal and call representatives artificial persons, then sovereigns are artificial persons while states are not. This is bad enough in itself, since states are obviously not natural persons, while sovereigns obviously are. The problem is made worse when commentators infer that, since the state is neither a natural nor an artificial person, it must be a *persona ficta*. It is true that Hobbes occasionally uses the terms 'artificial' and 'fictitious' as synonyms in this context.[66] But as we shall see in section IV, it is crucial to his theory that, although the state is an artificial person, it is very far from being fictitious in the strict sense of being imaginary.[67]

---

[63] Hobbes 1996, ch. 16, p. 112.   [64] Hobbes 1996, ch. 35, p. 285; ch. 42, p. 399.

[65] The reason is that, insofar as Hobbes's commentators have examined his theory of persons, they have usually concentrated on chapter 16 of *Leviathan*. Some have gone so far as to claim that Hobbes's articulation of his theory is almost wholly confined to that chapter. See, for example, Pitkin 1967, pp. 14–15; Gauthier 1969, p. 121; Runciman 1997, pp. 7–8. As a result, it has come to be widely agreed that Hobbes's distinction between natural and artificial persons is equivalent to the distinction between represented persons and their representatives. See, for example, Hood 1964, pp. 147–8; Pitkin 1967, pp. 15–16; Gauthier 1969, pp. 121–3; Jaume 1986, pp. 95–104; Baumgold 1988, pp. 38, 45; Martinich 1992, p. 165; Tukiainen 1994, p. 46; Martinich 1995, pp. 228–30; Zarka 1995, pp. 208–18; Runciman 1997, pp. 7–8, 33. But for two correctives to which I am indebted see Tricaud in Hobbes 1971a, pp. 168–9 and Copp 1980, pp. 582–4.

[66] See Hobbes 1996, ch. 16, p. 113 and cf. Hobbes 1840d, p. 130.

[67] But Runciman 2000 counters that, although the state is not a fictional person, it is best understood as a 'person by fiction'.

The decisive point is that Hobbes himself subsequently makes it clear that his own considered preference is for using the terminology of artificial persons to describe persons who are represented. He first brings this out at a later stage in the English *Leviathan* in the course of explaining his intensely controversial theory about the three persons of the Holy Trinity. He describes Moses and Christ as natural persons who spoke in the name of God, thereby serving as His representatives on earth. But he adds that each represented God in his own way, Moses by preaching His word, Christ by 'Teaching, and Reigning' as his son.[68] The implication is that God converted Himself into an artificial person by virtue of authorising his representation in these contrasting ways. Hobbes underlines the suggestion by adding that the effect of these representations was to give God a number of different *personae*, since He became 'one Person as represented by Moses, and another Person as represented by his Sonne the Christ'.[69]

Hobbes indicates his change of mind yet more clearly in the course of restating his theory of attributed action in the final chapter of *De Homine*. Here he leaves little room for doubt that, when he speaks of artificial or fictitious persons, he means persons represented:

What concerns the civil use of the term person can be defined as follows. *A person is someone to whom the words and actions of men are attributed, whether they are his own or those of someone else.* If they are his own, then the person is a *natural* one. If they are those of someone else, then the person is a *fictitious* one.[70]

Returning to the same issue yet again in the Latin *Leviathan* ten years later, Hobbes appears to confirm this analysis:

A Person is *someone who acts either in his own name or in the name of someone else.* If he acts in his own name, then the Person is *his Own* or a Natural one; if he acts in the name of someone else, then the Person is *Representative* of the one in whose name he acts.[71]

Here the terminology of artificial or fictitious persons is dropped, while the persons whom Hobbes had initially classified as artificial are now described simply as representatives.

[68] Hobbes 1996, ch. 41, p. 338; ch. 42, pp. 339–41. [69] Hobbes 1996, ch. 41, p. 338.
[70] Hobbes 1839d, p. 130: 'Quod autem ad usum personae civilem attinet, definiri potest hoc modo; *persona est, cui verba et actiones hominum attribuuntur vel suae vel alienae*: si suae, persona *naturalis* est; si alienae, *fictitia* est.'
[71] Hobbes 1841a, p. 123: 'PERSONA est *is qui suo vel alieno nomine res agit*: si suo, persona *propria*, sive naturalis est; si alieno, persona est eius, cuius nomine agit *repraesentativa*.' (Note that, although Molesworth uses the 1668 edition of the Latin *Leviathan* as his copy-text, he does not hesitate, here as elsewhere, to alter spellings and weed out Hobbes's luxuriant use of capital letters.)

It would be unwise, however, to assume that Hobbes simply nodded when he initially claimed that representatives are engaged in a form of artifice. What he seems to have had in mind is that, when you serve as a representative, you act as the player of a legally or socially recognised role. You become a public person as opposed to an ordinary individual. Hobbes offers many examples: you can serve as a lieutenant, a vicar, an attorney, a deputy, a procurator, a rector, a master, an overseer, a guardian, a curator and the like.[72] To adopt one or other of these *personae* is to play a part in a world that Hobbes never ceased to describe as artificial: the world of civil society in which our behaviour is conditioned and regulated by the artificial chains of the civil law.[73] The insight he evidently wished to capture is that there is a sense in which all the world's a stage.

Perhaps one might go so far as to say that the best statement of Hobbes's theory is the one that he never explicitly gave. The suggestion is hermeneutically daring, to say the least, but perhaps both possible ways of reading Hobbes's theory are correct. Natural persons convert themselves into artificial persons – even into a variety of different *personae* – by agreeing to be represented in different ways. But natural persons who agree to serve as representatives also convert themselves into artificial persons, since the act of making such an agreement is at the same time the act of turning oneself from a private individual into a public person discharging a recognised role.

With these cautions and attempted clarifications, I am now in a position to lay out Hobbes's considered views about the defining characteristics of natural persons. A natural person is someone capable of representing him or herself. In the words of Hobbes's initial definition, it is when someone's words and actions are 'considered as his owne' that he can be described as 'a Naturall Person'. As we have seen, however, anyone capable of owning his actions in this way can also be described according to Hobbes as an author, and hence as capable of authorising other persons to serve as his representatives. A further defining characteristic of natural persons must therefore be that they are capable of converting themselves – for certain determinate purposes – into represented or artificial persons by way of commissioning others to act in their name.

We may say, then, that in isolating the category of natural persons Hobbes has two closely connected ideas in mind. One is that natural

---

[72] Hobbes 1996, ch. 16, pp. 112–13; cf. Hobbes 1841a, pp. 123–4, where he lists *deputati, procuratores* and *proreges*, and later adds *rectores, curatores* and *tutores*.

[73] Hobbes speaks of the civil society in which we live as artificial (*artificialis*) and as tied together by artificial chains (*vincula artificialia*) in the Latin as well as in the English *Leviathan*. For the English formulae see Hobbes 1996, Introduction, pp. 9–10 and Hobbes 1996, ch. 21, p. 147. For the Latin formulae see Hobbes 1841a, pp. 2, 161.

persons are those capable of autonomously choosing whatever roles or *personae* they may wish to assume in social life. Hobbes is very fond of quoting a remark of Cicero's to the effect that (as he translates it in *Leviathan*) it is possible to 'bear' a number of different persons simultaneously.[74] Hobbes's most interesting gloss on the dictum appears in his posthumously published *Answer* to John Bramhall's *The Catching of Leviathan*:

> Cicero, in an epistle to Atticus, saith thus: *Unus sustineo tres personas, mei, adversarii, et judicis:* that is, 'I that am but one man, sustain three persons; mine own person, the person of my adversary, and the person of the judge'. Cicero was here the substance intelligent, one man; and because he pleaded for himself, he calls himself his own person: and again, because he pleaded for his adversary, he says, he sustained the person of his adversary: and lastly, because he himself gave the sentence, he says, he sustained the person of the judge. In the same sense we use the word in English vulgarly, calling him that acteth by his own authority, his own person, and him that acteth by the authority of another, the person of that other. And thus we have the exact meaning of the word *person*.[75]

Hobbes's allusion here to the idea of 'being one's own man' as opposed to being the person (perhaps even the creature) of someone else points to his second and closely related thought: that a natural person is someone under no one else's sway. He is someone capable of voicing his own thoughts, making his own promises, agreeing the terms of his own contracts and covenants.

It is worth underlining these implications, since they have the effect of making the category of natural persons a remarkably narrow one.[76] Hobbes seems to have come to terms with this aspect of his theory only in the course of working it out. When he first speaks of 'men as persons natural' in *The Elements of Law*, he appears to treat all human beings as natural persons.[77] But in *Leviathan* he explicitly states that many people lack the required ability to act on their own behalf, including 'Children, Fooles, and Mad-men'.[78] On the one hand, such persons are undoubtedly capable of acting and of exercising rights, since they are capable of having actions attributed to them on the basis of their performance by guardians authorised to act in their name. But on the other hand, they 'can be no

---

[74] Hobbes 1996, ch. 16, p. 112. He also quotes the dictum in the corresponding passage of the Latin *Leviathan* (and again in the Appendix); in chapter 15 of *De Homine*; and in his *Answer* to Bramhall. See, respectively, Hobbes 1841a, pp. 123, 533; Hobbes 1839d, XV. 1, p. 130; Hobbes 1840b, p. 310.

[75] Hobbes 1840b, pp. 310–11.

[76] But as Tricaud 1982 notes, Hobbes also speaks of human beings as persons in familiar, non-technical ways. In Part 1 of *Leviathan* he consistently uses 'person' to refer to any man, woman or child. See Hobbes 1996, ch. 2, pp. 16, 17–19; ch. 7, pp. 48–9; ch. 8, pp. 51–2; ch. 12, pp. 80, 82–3. In Part 2 he uses the term to refer more specifically to the living bodies of men, women and children. See Hobbes 1996, ch. 20, p. 141; ch. 21, pp. 152, 154; ch. 30, pp. 236, 238.

[77] Hobbes 1969a, p. xiv.   [78] Hobbes 1996, ch. 16, p. 113.

Authors (during that time) of any action done by them', because they have no capacity to take responsibility for any actions their guardians may undertake.[79]

Nor does Hobbes even treat the class of natural persons as co-terminous with that of sane adult males. In Hobbes's England some 20 per cent of the latter class would have been servants,[80] and servants according to Hobbes are not to be counted as natural persons, or at least not for a considerable number of purposes.[81] This exclusion stems from the fact that the civil law takes lawful families to be united in 'the Father, or Master' as 'one Person Representative'.[82] But to say that a father is a representative is to say that he has the right to speak and act in the name of his entire family.[83] This in turn means that, insofar as the father chooses to exercise this right, his household servants (to say nothing of his wife and children) cannot be counted as natural persons, since they lack the required capacity to speak and act on their own behalf.[84]

I next need to examine Hobbes's contrasting concept of an artificial person, which is of still greater importance for his theory of the state. So far we have seen that some natural persons can be artificial at the same time. But Hobbes is principally interested in those artificial persons who are not natural persons at all. These are persons capable of being represented, but incapable of acting as authors in the distinctive manner of natural persons, and hence of authorising their own representatives. It follows that, while it is possible for such artificial persons to speak and act, it is possible for them to do so *only* if their words and actions can validly be attributed to them on the basis of their performance by some other person or collectivity licensed to act in their name.

Hobbes proposes no particular term to isolate this category, but it may be helpful to designate them as *purely* artificial persons to distinguish them from those who voluntarily take on this status by authorising others to represent them. As we have seen, Hobbes further lays it down that two

---

[79] Hobbes 1996, ch. 16, p. 113. The time to which Hobbes refers is the time of their childhood, folly or madness.

[80] I am greatly indebted to Keith Wrightson for making this computation on my behalf. His figure is derived from information in Wrigley and Schofield 1981 and Kussmaul 1981.

[81] The proviso is important, because Hobbes is here treading a very fine line. A servant ordered to walk to a neighbour's house with a message who instead chooses to run will apparently be running to the house (as opposed to somewhere else) as an artificial person, but running (as opposed to walking) as a natural one.

[82] Hobbes 1996, ch. 22, pp. 162–3.   [83] Hobbes 1996, ch. 20, p. 142.

[84] There is a remarkably close parallel with the Leveller refusal to include servants even in an extended franchise on the grounds that 'they are included in their masters'. See Woodhouse 1938, p. 83.

sub-classes of this category need to be anatomised: those whose words and actions can be 'truly' attributed to them, and those who can only have words and actions attributed to them 'by Fiction'.

Nothing further is said in *Leviathan* about the class of purely artificial persons who are also wholly fictitious. But in *De Homine* it emerges that what Hobbes has in mind are the characters impersonated by actors on the stage:

> For it was understood in the ancient[85] theatre that not the player himself but someone else was speaking, for example Agamemnon, namely when the player, putting on the fictitious mask of Agamemnon, was for the time being Agamemnon. At a later stage, however,[86] this was understood to be so even in the absence of the fictitious mask, namely when the actor declared publicly which person he was going to play.[87]

This is a dark passage, but the implications for my present argument can perhaps be spelled out as follows. If I play the part of Agamemnon on the stage, the actions I perform in the *persona* of Agamemnon will be taken by the audience to be Agamemnon's actions rather than mine. They will not 'truly' be taken to be Agamemnon's actions, however, but only 'by fiction', since the audience will remain aware of the fact that (as we put it in a knowingly ambiguous phrase) I am only playing. This will especially be the case, Hobbes implies, if I follow the convention of explicitly pointing out that I am merely engaged in a performance. For then it will be clear that I am only pretending to be an imaginary character, that there is no other person whom I am 'truly' representing, and thus that there is no one else to whom my actions can validly be attributed.[88]

Some commentators have taken exception to Hobbes's inclusion of stage characters in his account. As Hanna Pitkin emphasises, Hobbes lays it down that, if there is to be a valid act of representation, there must be some natural person or collectivity in possession of the right to authorise it. Pitkin adds that this requirement makes no sense in the

---

[85] I have added the adjective, since Hobbes makes it clear in the preceding sentence that he is referring to ancient Greece and Rome.

[86] A later stage, that is, in the evolution of theatrical conventions, when masks were no longer worn.

[87] Hobbes 1839d, XV. 1, p. 130: 'Intelligebatur enim in theatro loqui non ipse histrio, sed aliquis alius, puta Agamemnon, nimirum faciem fictitiam Agamemnonis induente histrione, qui pro illo tempore erat Agamemnon; quod tamen postea intelligebatur etiam sine facie ficta, nimirum profitente se actore quam personam acturus erat.'

[88] From the fact, however, that the action of a play does not 'truly' take place, it does not follow for Hobbes that a play might not create as powerful an impression as an action 'truly' performed. See Hobbes 1969a, p. 68, where he goes to the extreme of arguing that, because 'not truth, but Image, maketh passion', it follows that 'a Tragedie affecteth no lesse than a Murder, if well acted'.

case of actors in a play. 'No one has authorized their actions, neither the person(s) they represent nor any third party.'[89] But this is an unhistorical criticism. By 1640, the year in which Hobbes completed *The Elements of Law*, the compulsory licensing of theatrical productions had been a feature of English law for nearly a century. The official with the right to authorise the representation of fictional characters on the stage was the Master of the Revels, from whom a permit had to be purchased for every play intended for public performance.[90] Two years later, moreover, all the theatres in England were closed by Act of Parliament.[91] While it remained possible to impersonate Agamemnon on the stage, it was no longer legally permissible to do so, since it was no longer possible to obtain the necessary licence. It is, in short, anachronistic to suggest that Hobbes introduces any inconsistency into his general theory of persons by implying that theatrical representations have to be authorised. He was writing in a society in which the need for such authorisation was taken for granted.

I turn finally to Hobbes's other class of purely artificial persons: those who, while incapable of acting except through representatives, are nevertheless more than merely fictitious because they are capable of having words and actions 'truly' attributed to them. As we have seen, Hobbes regards some human beings (notably fools and madmen) as purely artificial in this sense. But he is more interested in the fact that various inanimate objects and even figments of the imagination can be classified in a similar way. Among inanimate objects he lists 'a Church, an Hospital, a Bridge'. Since these are 'things Inanimate' they 'cannot be Authors, nor therefore give Authority to their Actors'. Nevertheless, they can perfectly well be personated or represented 'by a Rector, Master, or Overseer' who can be commissioned and thereby given authority to act on their behalf.[92] Among imaginary objects he singles out the gods of the heathen. Such idols obviously cannot be authors, 'for an Idol is nothing'.[93] Nevertheless, in ancient times such deities were frequently recognised as having the ability not merely to own possessions but to exercise rights. As in the case of the hospital and the bridge, these capacities stemmed from the fact that authorised persons (in this case officiating priests) were assigned a legal right to act in their name.[94]

---

[89] Pitkin 1967, p. 25.   [90] Bentley 1971, pp. 145–50.   [91] Bentley 1971, p. viii.
[92] Hobbes 1996, ch. 16, p. 113.
[93] Hobbes 1996, ch. 16, p. 114. As he later points out (Hobbes 1996, ch. 45, p. 445), he is quoting St Paul.
[94] Hobbes 1996, ch. 16, pp. 113–14.

To classify bridges, hospitals and imaginary objects as persons may seem the merest abuse of language, and Hobbes in *Leviathan* undoubtedly baulks at expressing his argument in these terms. The most he is prepared to say is that 'there are few things, that are uncapable of being represented by Fiction'.[95] As he subsequently recognised, however, this is an unfortunate way of expressing his point. What he appears to be saying is that, like Agamemnon, the hospital and the bridge are purely fictitious entities. But this is not in the least what he believes. On the contrary, it is crucial to his argument that, if the hospital or the bridge is validly represented by an authorised overseer, then the actions of the overseer will 'truly' and not merely 'by fiction' count as the actions of the hospital or the bridge.

Eventually Hobbes resolved the confusion by biting the bullet. When he translated *Leviathan* into Latin, he rewrote the passage to say that, since there are few things incapable of being represented, 'there are few things incapable of being persons'.[96] This certainly clarifies the phrase in the English *Leviathan* about representation 'by Fiction'. The fiction is evidently that the bridge, the hospital and so forth are persons; if and only if we allow that fiction can they be validly represented. Meanwhile Hobbes had made the point explicitly in *De Homine*: 'even an inanimate thing can be a person, that is, can own possessions and other goods and be able to act at law', so long as it is capable of being validly represented.[97] Hobbes's final position is thus that the hospital and the bridge are indeed persons, albeit purely artificial ones, since there is no doubt that they can be validly represented.

The category of purely artificial persons leaves Hobbes with one last problem to solve. Who has the right to authorise their representation? We have seen that, in the case of entirely fictitious *personae*, the answer in Hobbes's time was fully determinate: the right was possessed by the Master of the Revels acting as an officer of state. But what of purely artificial persons who are not fictitious, but who possess (like the bridge) their own independent reality, or may even be able to count (like the child or the madman) as natural persons for certain purposes? We still need a test for judging whether a third party who lays claim to authorise

95 Hobbes 1996, ch. 16, p. 113.
96 Hobbes 1841a, p. 124: 'Paucae res sunt, quarum non possunt esse personae.'
97 Hobbes 1839d, XV. 4, p. 132: 'Etiam rei inanimatae persona esse potest, id est, possessiones et alia bona habere, et iure agere potest.' It is thus a mistake to infer, as does Runciman 1997, p. 21, that 'unrepresented "fooles" are not persons'. A person is anyone (or any thing) *capable* of being represented.

someone to represent such persons has a valid title to invite such a representative to act in their name.

The solution Hobbes puts forward is that the person performing such acts of authorisation must stand in some appropriate relationship of dominion or ownership with respect to the purely artificial person concerned.[98] One possibility, Hobbes suggests, would be for the relationship to be that of ownership in the strict sense. This applies to the case of the bridge: Hobbes specifically states that the person who authorises the overseer to procure its maintenance must be its proprietor.[99] A second possibility would be for the relationship to be that of a governor to his charge. This applies to the case of the church and the hospital, and equally to the fool, the madman and the child: all stand in need of governors with sufficient legal standing to authorise rectors or guardians to act on their behalf.[100] A third possibility would be for the dominion to be that of the state itself. When, for example, the gods of the heathen were represented by priests, their authority according to Hobbes 'proceeded from the State'.[101] Finally, Hobbes considers a fourth possibility to which he attaches particular importance, although he only mentions it explicitly when discussing family power later in *Leviathan*. This last form of dominion arises when the first party brings the third into existence.[102] Again Hobbes has in mind the case of children, and offers as an example the right of dominion over infants in the state of nature. Since it will always be the mother who brings the child into the world, 'the right of Dominion over the Child dependeth on her will, and is consequently hers'.[103] She can decide either to nourish it, or to abandon it, or to dispose of her rights in it to someone else.[104]

IV

I am now in a position to apply Hobbes's general theory to solve the puzzle I began by isolating about the person of the state. How can such a

---

[98] Weimann 1996, pp. 12–13 comments on this linkage of authority with ownership.

[99] Hobbes 1996, ch. 16, p. 113.

[100] It is not clear, however, why Hobbes appears to exclude the possibility that the owner of the bridge or the governor of the child might decide to commission himself. If I stand in a relation of dominion with respect to the bridge or the child, then according to Hobbes I can authorise anyone I wish to represent them. But if I can authorise anyone, then I can certainly authorise myself.

[101] Hobbes 1996, ch. 16, p. 114.

[102] But Hobbes 1996, ch. 17, p. 120 implicitly mentions this form of dominion, since it underlies his pattern of sexual imagery, especially his claim that Leviathan is engendered out of the union of the multitude.

[103] Hobbes 1996, ch. 20, p. 140.   [104] Hobbes 1996, ch. 20, p. 140.

seemingly insubstantial person be the holder of sovereignty and the seat of power?

First we need to see exactly where Hobbes places the person of the state on his general map. He begins in chapter 16 of *Leviathan* by considering the process by which the members of a multitude living in a condition of mere nature can manage, as he puts it, to 'institute' a legitimate commonwealth or state.[105] Before turning to his analysis, however, I need to note by way of preliminary that I shall be concerned only with Hobbes's account of sovereignty 'by Institution', not with sovereignty 'by Acquisition'. Hobbes introduces this distinction at the end of chapter 17 of *Leviathan*, thereafter devoting chapters 18 and 19 to 'institution' and chapter 20 to 'acquisition'.[106] Sovereignty is said to be 'acquired' when the members of a multitude covenant not with each other but with a conqueror to whom they individually submit themselves. Presumably Hobbes believed that the latter type of covenant also has the effect of converting the multitude into an artificial person with the conqueror as its sovereign representative. But he never says so, and his analysis of sovereignty by acquisition makes no mention of the person of the state. Although sovereignty by acquisition is in some ways the fundamental case,[107] it is not clear that Hobbes ever thought through his views about artificial persons in relation to it. For this reason it seems not merely preferable but essential to concentrate on the case of sovereignty 'by Institution', the subject of chapters 18 and 19.

The only means, according to Hobbes, by which a multitude can manage to 'institute' a commonwealth is by transforming themselves into an artificial person by way of authorising some natural person or persons to represent them. This is not in the least to say that the multitude acts in the manner of a single *persona* in agreeing to set up a government. This had been the view of the so-called 'monarchomach' or 'king-killing' writers of the French religious wars.[108] The author of the *Vindiciae, Contra Tyrannos*, for example, had argued in discussing the exemplary case of Israel that the king acted as one party to the covenant and the people as the other. Both were able to contract as single persons, the king because

---

[105] Hobbes 1996, ch. 17, p. 121.
[106] While this order seems logical, Hobbes must originally have placed what is now chapter 20 before chapter 19. The present chapter 20 makes two references (Hobbes 1996, pp. 139, 142) to the 'precedent chapter' which are in fact references to chapter 18, while chapter 21 makes a further reference (Hobbes 1996, p. 154) to 'the precedent chapter' which is in fact a reference to chapter 19.
[107] An argument persuasively developed in Hoekstra 1998.
[108] On these writers see Skinner 1978b, pp. 302–48.

he was a natural person, the people because they constituted a *universitas* and 'were therefore able to play the part of a single person'.[109] But it is precisely this monarchomach view of the people as a natural unity capable of acting as one person that Hobbes aims to discredit. 'The Multitude naturally is not *One*, but *Many*', he retorts, so that it is only 'the *Unity* of the Representer, not the *Unity* of the Represented, that maketh the Person *One*'. The only way in which 'a Multitude of men, are made *One* Person' is 'when they are by one man, or one Person, Represented'. There is, in short, no natural unity outside the state; unity and community are attained only with the appointment of a representative, and 'cannot otherwise be understood in multitude'.[110]

In chapter 17 Hobbes goes on to describe the mechanism by which this transformation takes place. It is as if each and every individual should agree with everyone else 'to conferre all their power and strength upon one Man, or upon one Assembly of men, that may reduce all their Wills, by plurality of voices, unto one Will'. When they perform this act of mutual covenanting, this is as much as to say that they 'appoint one Man, or Assembly of men, to beare their Person'. So the outcome 'is more than Consent, or Concord; it is a reall Unitie of them all, in one and the same Person', in consequence of which they are now able, through the agency of the person representing them, to act in the manner of a single person with one will and voice.[111]

What is the name of the artificial person brought into existence when a multitude forms itself into such a unity by instituting a representative? The name of the person thus engendered is the commonwealth or state. As soon as the members of the multitude agree, each with each, 'to appoint one Man, or Assembly of men, to beare their Person', the multitude 'so united in one Person, is called a COMMON-WEALTH, in latine CIVITAS'[112] – the term Hobbes also translates in *Leviathan* as 'state'.[113] This union or coupling together has the effect of engendering immediate issue in just the manner of a marital union blessed by God. (The one crucial difference, later emphasised by Hobbes, is that the offspring of the multitude has no determinate gender, for 'though *man* be *male* and *female, authority* is not'.)[114] Following out his metaphor of marriage and

---

[109] *Vindiciae* 1994, p. 38: '*universitas enim hominum unius personae vicem sustinet*'.
[110] Hobbes 1996, ch. 16, p. 114.   [111] Hobbes 1996, ch. 17, p. 120.
[112] Hobbes 1996, ch. 17, p. 120; cf. Polin 1981, p. 95; Tukiainen 1994, p. 48.
[113] Hobbes's preferred translation of *civitas* is 'commonwealth'. See, for example, Hobbes 1996, ch. 17, p. 120; ch. 26, p. 183. But when he uses 'state' as a translation, the word he is translating is almost always *civitas*. For the most striking instance see Hobbes 1996, Introduction, p. 9.
[114] Hobbes 1840d, p. 434.

procreation, Hobbes then proceeds to baptise the person of the commonwealth or state with its own specific name, informing us of it in his
gravest tones. 'This is the Generation of that great LEVIATHAN, or
rather (to speake more reverently) of that *Mortall God*, to which wee owe
under the *Immortal God*, our peace and defence.'[115]

We still need to know the name of the person appointed by the members of the multitude to act in their name when they take the decision to be
represented. Hobbes replies that the name of this person is the sovereign,
who is thereby given authority to 'bear' or 'carry' or act the part of the
purely artificial person of the state. The commonwealth or state 'is *One*
Person', and 'he that carryeth this Person, is called SOVERAIGNE, and
said to have *Soveraigne Power*'.[116] The same distinction is subsequently
drawn even more clearly in the Latin version of *Leviathan*. There the
holder of *summa potestas* or sovereign power is described, in a phrase
closely echoing Cicero's *De Officiis*, as 'he who bears the Person of
the State'.[117] The sovereign may in turn be a natural person, as in the
case of a monarchy, or else an assembly of natural persons, as in the case
of an aristocracy or democracy.[118] But in every case the legal standing
of the sovereign will be that of 'the absolute Representative of all the
subjects'.[119]

It is worth underlining the complexity of Hobbes's argument, if only
because so many commentators have oversimplified it. We are told that
the 'civil person' brought into existence by the union of the multitude
is the sovereign.[120] As we have seen, however, the name of the person engendered by the transformation of the multitude into one person
through their agreement to appoint a representative is not the sovereign
but the state. The sovereign is the name of the representative of the multitude united in one person, and is thus the name of the representative of
the state.

Armed with this analysis, we can now see how the apparently insubstantial person of the state can nevertheless be the holder of sovereignty
and the seat of power. Hobbes concedes of course that all the actions

---

[115] Hobbes 1996, ch. 17, p. 120.   [116] Hobbes 1996, ch. 17, p. 121.

[117] Hobbes 1841a, p. 131: 'Is autem, qui civitatis personam gerit, *summam habere* dicitur *potestatem*.' Cf.
Cicero 1913, I. XXXIV. 124, p. 126 on the office of magistrates: 'se gerere personam civitatis'.

[118] Hobbes 1996, ch. 19, p. 129. The question of how assemblies can act as representatives obviously
raises further questions, but I am concerned here only with the basic case. Copp 1980, p. 599
suggests that Hobbes must regard assemblies as their own representatives, but Hobbes himself
never pronounces on the point.

[119] Hobbes 1996, ch. 22, p. 156.

[120] See, for example, Baumgold 1988, pp. 38–9; Burgess 1990, p. 687; Fukuda 1997, p. 43; Martinich
1997, pp. 44–9. But see, by contrast, Jaume 1986, pp. 99–100 and Zarka 1995, pp. 212, 225.

performed by states will in fact have to be performed by sovereigns acting in their 'politique' capacity.[121] He is always careful to insist, however, that sovereigns are not the proprietors of their sovereignty. They are holders of offices with duties attached, their fundamental duty being to procure the safety and contentment of the people. Although they are granted the right to exercise complete sovereign power, this power is merely 'placed' and 'resideth' in them by virtue of the office they are asked to discharge.[122] The true status of all lawful sovereigns is thus that they are merely 'the Person representative of all and every one of the Multitude'.[123]

As I have shown, however, the central contention of Hobbes's theory of attributed action is that, whenever a person or collectivity agrees to appoint such a representative, whatever actions are thereafter performed by the representative in their name will be attributable not to the representative but rather to the person or collectivity being represented. Not only will those who appoint the representative be held accountable for the consequences of any actions undertaken on their behalf, but the actions in question will actually count as theirs, not as those of the representative who carries them out. It follows that, whenever our sovereigns exercise their powers in order to procure our safety and contentment, the acts they perform should not be regarded as their own but rather as those of the person whom they are representing, that is, the person of the state. This, then, is how it comes about that we can properly speak – and not by metaphor – of the commonwealth or state as the person who imposes the laws and thereby ensures that our safety and contentment are secured. Although the sovereign is always the legislator, the legislator 'is always the Representative of the Common-wealth'.[124] So 'the name of the person Commanding' is not the sovereign but the person whom the sovereign represents. And the name of that person, as Hobbes eventually declares in a further echo of Cicero, is '*Persona Civitatis*, the Person of the Common-wealth'.[125]

[121] Hobbes 1996, ch. 19, p. 131. For general claims to the effect that the only way in which the state can act is for the sovereign representative to act in its name, see also Hobbes 1996, ch. 19, p. 136; ch. 21, p. 149; ch. 24, p. 174; ch. 26, pp. 184, 186; ch. 31, p. 253.

[122] Hobbes 1996, ch. 18, p. 127; ch. 20, p. 144. On the sovereign as holder of an office of trust see Hobbes 1996, ch. 18, p. 126; ch. 20, p. 143.

[123] Hobbes 1996, p. 129. For other references to the fact that the sovereign is merely the representative of the state, see Hobbes 1996, ch. 17, p. 121; ch. 22, pp. 155–6; ch. 23, p. 167; ch. 26, p. 185; ch. 27, p. 212; ch. 29, p. 223. When we are instead told in Hobbes 1996, ch. 26, p. 187 that the sovereign is 'the Person of the Common-wealth' (rather than the representative of that Person), this appears to be either an ellipsis or perhaps a slip of the pen.

[124] Hobbes 1996, ch. 29, p. 223.

[125] Hobbes 1996, ch. 26, p. 183; cf. Cicero 1913, I. XXXIV. 124, p. 126. Lessay 1992, pp. 159–60 discusses the allusion.

It is important to emphasise Hobbes's route to this conclusion, if only because a number of commentators have claimed to find in his theory of the state an incipient or latent belief in the real personality of groups.[126] The will of the sovereign, we are told, comes to be identical with that of the commonwealth because Hobbes presents us with a vision 'of an organic community, whose will is the sovereign's will'.[127] It is certainly true according to Hobbes that there cannot fail to be an identity between the will of a lawful sovereign and the will of the commonwealth or state. As I have laboured to demonstrate, however, this is not in the least because Hobbes believes in any kind of organic unity between the two. It is simply because he insists that all lawful sovereigns are representatives, and thus that all their public actions must be attributed to the person whom they represent, namely the person of the state.

It remains for Hobbes to distinguish between the representation and misrepresentation of the state's authority. How are we to discriminate between lawful sovereigns and those who merely usurp the powers of the state without enjoying the standing of accredited representatives? To put the same question the other way round, who has the right to authorise the actions of the state?

It is not open to Hobbes to reply that sovereigns themselves possess this right. Sovereigns are merely representatives, and all representatives must themselves be authorised. Nor can the actions of the state be authorised by the state itself. If an agent is to authorise its own actions it must be a natural person, capable of exercising its own rights and acting in its own name. But the state is not a natural person; on the contrary, there is a sense in which it more closely resembles a fictitious person such as Agamemnon in Aeschylus's play of that name. Agamemnon has no existence, except as words on a page, until he is brought to life by the skills of an actor who impersonates him and speaks his lines. The state likewise amounts to little more than a verbal entity in the absence of a sovereign to represent it and play its part in the world.

This is not to say that Hobbes regards the state as a *persona ficta*, as some commentators have maintained.[128] As we have seen, the defining characteristic of such *personae* is that, when someone represents them, the acts performed by their representatives will be attributable to such

---

[126] Forsyth 1981, pp. 197–8. But for an excellent critique of the view that the unity of Hobbes's commonwealth is 'organic' see Kronman 1980, pp. 167–8.

[127] Baumgold 1988, p. 39.

[128] See, for example, Gierke 1957, pp. 44–7; Oakeshott 1975b, p. 204; Runciman 1997, pp. 14, 18, 29.

persons merely 'by fiction'. But it is of the utmost importance to Hobbes's theory that the acts performed by sovereigns are 'truly' attributable to the state, and are in fact the actions of the state in the real world.

While the state is not fictional, however, it is undoubtedly a member of the class of persons I have characterised as purely artificial, and bears a close resemblance to such exemplary members of the class as hospitals, bridges and so forth. Like such inanimate objects, the state is unquestionably capable of acting, since it is capable of being represented and of having actions 'truly' attributed to it. Like such objects, however, the state cannot give authority to anyone to represent it, and cannot therefore authorise its own representation. As Hobbes puts it, it has no capacity 'to doe any thing, but by the Representative'.[129] So shadowy, indeed, is its existence that it might be thought to bear a yet closer resemblance to such purely artificial persons as the gods of the heathen. Whereas hospitals and bridges remain things even when they are not being personated, the state in the absence of a sovereign 'is but a word', just as the gods of the heathen are 'nothing' in the absence of a priest to represent them.[130]

Who then is capable of authorising the actions of the state? We already know the answer in general terms from our examination of how it is possible for one person validly to authorise a second to represent a third – as in the case of the owner of a bridge who authorises an overseer to act on its behalf. As we have seen, two requirements must be met. One is that the natural person or persons authorising the representation must themselves possess the right to undertake whatever actions they intend to authorise. The other is that this right must in turn be owed to the fact that they stand in some appropriate relationship of dominion over the purely artificial person concerned.

According to Hobbes there is only one possible way in which these conditions can be satisfied in the case of the state. The public acts of a sovereign will count as valid acts of the state if and only if the sovereign has been authorised to perform them by each and every member of the multitude. With this contention, Hobbes is finally able to offer his formal definition of a commonwealth or state: it is '*One Person, of whose Acts a great Multitude, by mutuall Covenants one with another, have made themselves every one the Author, to the end he may use the strength and means of them all, as he shall think expedient, for their Peace and Common Defence*'.[131]

---

[129] Hobbes 1996, ch. 24, p. 171; ch. 26, p. 184.   [130] Hobbes 1996, ch. 16, p. 114; ch. 31, p. 245.
[131] Hobbes 1996, ch. 17, p. 121.

Hobbes makes good this central contention by pointing out in the first place that the individual members of the multitude undoubtedly possess the right to perform the actions undertaken by sovereigns as representatives of the state. When Hobbes describes the lines of conduct that sovereigns are authorised to pursue, he always makes it clear that their rights of action are merely those possessed by each one of us in the state of nature. These rights can be summarised as the blameless liberty of using our powers in any way that we judge necessary to defend our lives against others and to secure ourselves against threats by anticipating them.[132] Because the exercise of these equal rights brings war, we are led by reason to recognise that the best means of attaining peace and the other contentments of life will be to transfer our rights to a sovereign who will exercise them on our behalf. When we covenant to appoint such a sovereign, it is accordingly with the specific purpose of providing more effectively for our own peace and contentment. The sovereign is commissioned, in other words, merely to exercise those of our rights which, so long as we exercise them ourselves, will lead to war.[133]

Finally, Hobbes argues in addition that the individual members of the multitude stand – and alone stand – in an appropriate relationship of dominion with respect to the person of the state. The source of their dominion lies in the fact that the union of the multitude brings the state into existence. As a result, the relationship of the multitude to the state is analogous to that of the mother to her infant in the state of nature. Just as the mother brings her child into the world, thereby acquiring dominion over it, so the union of the multitude serves to procreate the state. Hobbes goes to the almost blasphemous extreme of drawing a parallel between this act of engendering and the work of God. 'The *Pacts* and *Covenants*, by which the parts of this Body Politique were at first made, set together, and united, resemble that *Fiat*, or the *Let us make man*, pronounced by God in the Creation.'[134]

As Malcolm has recently emphasised, however, the person whom we engender when we covenant to institute a sovereign representative needs to be simultaneously seen in two perspectives.[135] On the one hand, the person in question – the person of the commonwealth or state – is 'but

---

[132] Hobbes 1996, ch. 13, pp. 87–8, ch. 14, p. 91.

[133] Hobbes 1996, ch. 13, pp. 87–9; ch. 18, p. 124; ch. 19, p. 131.

[134] Hobbes 1996, Introduction, pp. 9–10. But does the artifice created by the multitude more closely resemble a man or a machine? See Tukiainen 1994 and Runciman 1997, pp. 16–24 for Hobbes's contrasting structures of imagery.

[135] Malcolm 1998, pp. 145–6.

a word' in the absence of a sovereign to act in its name. But on the other hand, it is important to Hobbes that the state is at the same time the name of a common power whose stature and strength are greater than those of any of its subjects and of all of them put together. While Hobbes aims to demystify sovereign power by showing it to be the outcome of a rational choice made by individual agents, he wishes at the same time to leave his great Leviathan invested with a certain mysterious force, if only as a guarantee that we shall in turn think of it, as we should, with a certain awe.

v

What prompted Hobbes to develop this novel and intricate theory of the state? The clue lies, I believe, in attending to what he says at the outset of *Leviathan* about his hopes for the work. He aspires, he says, to pass unwounded between the opposing swords of 'those that contend, on one side for too great liberty, and on the other side for too much Authority'.[136]

Those contending for too much authority are identifiable as the theorists of divine right, who rose to renewed prominence in the face of the parliamentary attack on the English crown in the early 1640s. All political power, these writers declare, is 'naturall'.[137] God is its 'immediate Author'[138] and all rulers acquire it from divine ordination rather than from the consent of the people, who have 'no more *possibility* in right to choose their *Kings*, then to choose their *Fathers*'.[139] Hobbes's vision of the state as an artificial person authorised by its own citizens has the effect of challenging every element in this argument. All political power, he replies, is 'Artificiall'.[140] The only source from which the authority of the state can validly flow is 'the consent of every one of the Subjects'.[141] The capacity of sovereigns to act as legitimate representatives of the state must therefore be 'derived originally from the consent of every one of those that are to bee governed'.[142] The state is a wholly human contrivance, not in the least an outcome of God's providence.

During the civil wars of the 1640s, this view of consent became one of the leading arguments used by the supporters of Parliament to question the powers of the crown. Drawing on the work of the monarchomachs,

---

[136] Hobbes 1996, Epistle, p. 3.   [137] Morton 1643, p. 3.
[138] Williams 1643, pp. 48, 49; Maxwell 1644, p. 19. See Sanderson 1989, p. 48 on Maxwell's authorship of this tract.
[139] Williams 1643, pp. 43, 48.   [140] Hobbes 1996, ch. 17, p. 120.
[141] Hobbes 1996, ch. 28, p. 219.   [142] Hobbes 1996, ch. 42, p. 395.

Henry Parker developed perhaps the most influential version of the argument in his *Observations* of 1642.[143] He begins by restating the monarchomach claim[144] that the only way in which lawful authority can arise is when 'a societie of men', acting in the manner of a *universitas*, agrees by 'common consent' to set it up.[145] One implication is that, since 'the fountaine and efficient cause' of all authority 'is the people', it follows that 'the King, though he be *singulis Major*, yet he is *universis minor*' – of lesser standing than 'the whole universality' from which his power is derived.[146] A further implication is that, if the king violates the terms of the covenant imposed by the *universitas* of the people in granting him power, they must retain the right to withdraw their consent and set down the authority they originally set up. As Parker summarises, 'the whole universality' of the people is not only the 'free and voluntary Author' of all sovereignty; it also retains its original sovereignty at all times, and accordingly remains 'the proper Subject of all power'.[147]

While Hobbes agrees that all lawful government arises from consent, he violently disagrees with the radical implications drawn from this argument by the supporters of Parliament. He seeks instead to demonstrate that these alleged implications embody a peculiarly dangerous plea for too great liberty. As before, moreover, the way in which he mounts his case is by invoking and applying exactly the theory of attributed action on which I have concentrated.

One way in which Hobbes applies his theory is by returning to his rival account of how it is possible for a multitude to act as 'one person'. A proper understanding of this process, he insists, will wholly defuse the Parliamentarian argument:

There is little ground for the opinion of them, that say of Soveraign Kings, though they be *singulis majores*, of greater Power than every one of their Subjects, yet they be *Universis minores*, of lesse power than them all together. For if by *all together*, they mean not the collective body as one person, then *all together*, and *every one*, signifie the same; and the speech is absurd. But if by *all together*, they understand them as one Person (which person the Sovereign bears,) then the power of all together, is the same with the Sovereigns power; and so again the speech is absurd.[148]

[143] See Sommerville 1992, pp. 60–3; Mendle 1995, pp. 70–89.
[144] The influence of monarchomach thought, in particular the *Vindiciae*, was noted by Parker's critics at the time. See Mendle 1995, pp. 123–5.
[145] [Parker] 1933, p. 167.
[146] See [Parker] 1933, pp. 168, 210, and cf. *Vindiciae* 1994, pp. 47–8, 78, 107, 157–8, 172 for the use of the *maior singulis, minor universis* formula.
[147] [Parker] 1933, pp. 167, 210.
[148] Hobbes 1996, ch. 18, p. 128; cf. Sommerville 1996, p. 262.

Hobbes's fiercely polemical message is thus that, since the people only transform themselves into a collective body by way of instituting a sovereign, it makes no sense to think of them as a collective body setting limits in advance to the exercise of sovereign power.

The main way, however, in which Hobbes applies his theory of attributed action to attack the Parliamentarian cause is by invoking his analysis of what it means to authorise a representative. If we understand this process aright, he insists, we shall see that it is the merest *non sequitur* to suppose that the theory of covenanting commits us to defending the sovereignty of the people. On the contrary, we shall see that the idea of consent as the only source of lawful government is fully compatible with a strong defence of absolute sovereignty and the duty of non-resistance.

As we have seen, Hobbes stipulates that, if an act of authorisation is to be validly performed, a transfer of right must take place. Once this covenant has passed, the authorising agent is left with two specific obligations towards his or her representatives. One is the duty to 'own' their actions and those of any third party for whom they may have been authorised to act. But the other is the duty not to interfere with the execution of their commission, since the right to act as they think best in discharging their task is precisely what has been voluntarily handed over to them.

In chapter 17 of *Leviathan* Hobbes argues that the covenant by which lawful states are instituted takes exactly this form. When the members of the multitude agree, each with each, to appoint a sovereign representative, theirs is a covenant of authorisation embodying a declaration that a set of rights has been transferred. They covenant 'in such manner, as if every man should say to every man, *I Authorise and give up my Right of Governing my selfe, to this Man, or to this Assembly of men*'.[149] At the same time Hobbes examines the precise character of the covenant involved. What the members of the multitude agree is 'to conferre all their power and strength upon one Man, or upon one Assembly of men'.[150] But as we have seen, this has the effect of producing two immediate consequences. It gives them a single will and voice, thereby converting them into one person, the person of the state. But it also creates a representative of that person in the figure of the sovereign, who is thereby given the job of 'bearing' or 'carrying' the person of the state. To say all this, however, is to say that the members of the multitude remain the authors of all the

[149] Hobbes 1996, ch. 17, p. 120.   [150] Hobbes 1996, ch. 17, p. 120.

actions of their sovereign, and at the same time remain the authors of all the actions of the person whom they have authorised their sovereign to represent, namely the person of the state. Each member of the multitude must now 'acknowledge himselfe to be Author of whatsoever he that so beareth their Person, shall Act, or cause to be Acted, in those things which concerne the Common Peace and Safetie'.[151]

Hobbes lastly turns, in chapter 18, to consider the implications of this political covenant. The members of the multitude have given up their right of using their own discretion to secure their safety and contentment. They have voluntarily ceded their right of self-government to be exercised by their sovereign on their behalf. It follows according to Hobbes's theory of authorisation that the members of the multitude must now be under an absolute obligation not to interfere with their sovereign in the exercise of the rights they have transferred to him. The sovereign acquires complete discretion and absolute power to decide what shall be done to preserve the safety and contentment of every subject under his charge.

Hobbes goes still further. Not only do the members of the multitude have no remaining right to question the actions of their sovereign; they have a positive duty to 'own' whatever actions their sovereign may undertake in seeking their safety and contentment. But this is to say, according to Hobbes's theory of attributed action, that the public acts of the sovereign, and hence of the state, are nothing other than the acts of the individual members of the multitude. So it will not merely be unjust for them to oppose their sovereign; it will actually be self-contradictory, for they will be opposing themselves.

This moral is finally drawn in a powerful summarising passage in chapter 18:

Because every Subject is by this Institution Author of all the Actions, and Judgments of the Soveraigne Instituted; it followes, that whatsoever he doth, it can be no injury to any of his Subjects; nor ought he to be by any of them accused of Injustice. For he that doth any thing by authority from another, doth therein no injury to him by whose authority he acteth: But by this Institution of a Common-wealth, every particular man is Author of all the Soveraigne doth; and consequently he that complaineth of injury from his Soveraigne, complaineth of that whereof he himselfe is Author; and therefore ought not to accuse any man but himselfe.[152]

Although Hobbes returns to this claim with evident satisfaction in a number of later passages, he stands in no need of such uncharacteristic

---

[151] Hobbes 1996, ch. 17, p. 120.   [152] Hobbes 1996, ch. 18, p. 124.

repetitiousness.[153] His account of attributed action already enables him to rest his case against the constitutionalist writers of his age. The concept of the political covenant is not a means of limiting the powers of the crown; properly understood, it shows that the powers of the crown have no limits at all. The theory of attributed action lies at the heart of the politics of *Leviathan*.

[153] Hobbes 1996, ch. 19, p. 136; ch. 24, p. 172.

7

Hobbes on the proper signification of liberty

I

'Civil philosophy', Hobbes declares in an oft-quoted boast at the start of *De Corpore*, is a science 'no older . . . than my own book *De Cive*'.[1] As he later explains in *Leviathan*, the failure of all previous efforts has been due to their 'want of Method'.[2] The method followed hitherto, especially in the universities, has been to rely on the authority of selected writers and books.[3] The universities, indeed, have come to rely so heavily on one particular writer that their teachings no longer deserve to be called philosophy, but merely Aristotelity.[4] This approach, however, is nothing but 'a signe of folly', one that is 'generally scorned with the name of Pedantry'.[5] The only scientific way of proceeding is to follow the methods of geometry, which requires its practitioners to 'begin at settling the significations of their words'.[6] Only by this means can we hope to avoid the insignificant speech of the schoolmen and lay the foundations for a genuine science of political life. For 'the foundation of all true Ratiocination, is the constant Signification of words'.[7]

As Hobbes turns to employ this approach in *Leviathan*, there is no case in which he is so anxious to insist on his own definitions, and to argue that all others are dangerously misleading, as he is in explicating the concept of liberty. It is striking, moreover, that his anxieties on this score increased as he progressively refined his theory of the state. In *The Elements of Law*, originally circulated in 1640, he voices no such concern and fails even to supply a formal definition of liberty.[8] Only in *De Cive*, first published in 1642, does he formulate the basic definition on which he

---

This chapter is a revised version of an article that originally appeared under the same title in *Transactions of the Royal Historical Society*, 5th series, 40 (1990), pp. 121–51.
[1] Hobbes 1839e, p. ix.   [2] Hobbes 1996, ch. 5, p. 34.   [3] Hobbes 1996, ch. 4, pp. 28–9.
[4] Hobbes 1996, ch. 46, p. 462.   [5] Hobbes 1996, ch. 6, p. 37.   [6] Hobbes 1996, ch. 4, p. 28.
[7] Hobbes 1996, ch. 34, p. 269.   [8] Hobbes 1969a, p. 134.

later relies.[9] Even at this stage, moreover, he still alludes only glancingly to the dangers of misunderstanding the term, while his application of his own formula is not free from ambiguity. By the time he came to publish *Leviathan* in 1651, however, all such equivocations had been removed, and the meaning of liberty had come to be one of his central themes. Not only does he devote a special chapter to discussing the liberty of subjects, but he constantly emphasises the importance of establishing 'the proper signification of the word', what it 'signifieth (properly)', its 'proper and generally received meaning', how to understand it 'in the proper sense'.[10]

These developments prompt two questions, both of which I shall seek to answer in sections IV and V of this chapter. Why does Hobbes become increasingly preoccupied with the idea of liberty? And why does he become increasingly anxious to insist that, as *Leviathan* puts it, 'it is an easy thing for men to be deceived' by its 'specious name'?[11] Before we can address these issues, however, we obviously need to be sure that we have understood what Hobbes means by the concept of liberty itself. This is a topic on which his commentators seem to me to have cast a considerable amount of darkness. So I shall first consider this purely textual problem in sections II and III, before turning to the more contextual and historical questions in which I am principally interested.

II

When Hobbes first introduces the topic of human freedom in *Leviathan*, it is in connection with his discussion of 'the right of nature' in chapter 14. This right is defined as 'the Liberty each man hath to use his own power as he will himselfe for the preservation of his own Nature'.[12] (Here as elsewhere Hobbes equates human freedom with the freedom of a man, a usage I shall sometimes be constrained to follow.) This freedom or liberty,[13] Hobbes at once stresses, must be defined in negative terms.[14] The presence of liberty is always marked, that is, by the absence of something. Specifically, it is marked by 'the absence of externall Impediments'.[15] And

---

9 Hobbes 1983a, IX. IX, p. 167.
10 Hobbes 1996, ch. 14, p. 91; ch. 21, pp. 145, 146, 147.
11 Hobbes 1996, ch. 21, p. 149.   12 Hobbes 1996, ch. 14, p. 91.
13 As Hobbes 1996, ch. 21, p. 145 makes clear when he speaks of what 'LIBERTY, or FREEDOME, signifieth' he makes no distinction between the two terms. I have followed him in using them interchangeably.
14 On Hobbes's general disposition to offer negative definitions see Pasquino 1994.
15 Hobbes 1996, ch. 14, p. 91.

by 'impediments', Hobbes adds, he means anything that can hinder a man from using his powers 'according as his judgement, and reason shall dictate to him'.[16]

This analysis is subsequently taken up and elaborated at the start of chapter 21, at which point Hobbes presents his formal definition of what it means to be a free man:

And according to this proper, and generally received meaning of the word, *A FREE-MAN, is he, that in those things, which by his strength and wit he is able to do, is not hindred to doe what he has a will to.*[17]

As this definition makes clear, Hobbes sees two essential elements in the concept of human freedom. One is the idea of possessing an underlying power or ability to act. As Hobbes had already observed in chapter 14, it is in relation to 'a man's power to do what hee would' that we speak of his being or not being at liberty.[18] The other is the idea of being unimpeded in the exercise of such powers. As Hobbes explains later in chapter 21, the freedom of a man 'consisteth in this, that he finds no stop in doing what he has the will, desire or inclination to doe'.[19]

Hobbes's basic doctrine can thus be very simply summarised. He already hints as much at the start of chapter 14 of *Leviathan*,[20] but he says so most clearly at the end of *The Questions Concerning Liberty, Necessity and Chance*, his final reply to Bishop Bramhall on the problem of free will. A free agent is someone who, in respect of his powers or abilities, 'can do if he will and forbear if he will'.[21]

As Hobbes acknowledges, however, this analysis is not yet a very illuminating one. We still lack an account of the kinds of limitations on human action that can count as impediments. To put the point another way, we still lack a criterion for distinguishing between inherent limitations of our powers themselves, and positive constraints upon our freedom to exercise or forbear from exercising those powers in accordance with our will and desires.

---

[16] Hobbes 1996, ch. 14, p. 91.   [17] Hobbes 1996, ch. 21, p. 146.

[18] Hobbes 1996, ch. 14, p. 91. Cf. Hobbes 1996, ch. 10, p. 62, where he defines 'The POWER *of a man*' as 'his present means, to obtain some future apparent Good'.

[19] Hobbes 1996, ch. 21, p. 146. The point is foreshadowed in Hobbes 1996, ch. 6, p. 44, where he argues that deliberation is so called 'because it is a putting an end to the *Liberty* we had of doing, or omitting, according to our own Appetite, or Aversion'.

[20] Hobbes 1996, ch. 14, p. 91 defines 'right' as 'liberty to do or to forbeare'.

[21] See Hobbes 1656, p. 301 and cf. Hobbes's opening formula, pp. 28–9. For a bibliography of Hobbes's debate with Bramhall see Macdonald and Hargreaves 1952, pp. 37–41. I quote from the original version of Hobbes's *Questions* (Hobbes 1656) but the text is also available in Molesworth's edition (Hobbes 1841b).

Turning to this further problem at the start of chapter 21, Hobbes distinguishes two ways in which a person's freedom may be hindered or impeded. The first is common to human and inanimate bodies.[22] It occurs when an agent encounters 'the opposition of some externall body' which operates in such a way that the agent is tied – or, as Hobbes also says, is bound[23] – so that 'it cannot move but within a certain space'.[24] Hobbes has just laid it down that to be free is to be unimpeded from doing or forbearing from doing something. But these are cases in which the agent is impeded from doing something. An action within the agent's powers is rendered physically impossible of performance. It follows that such agents 'are not at Liberty, to move in such manner, as without those externall impediments they would'.[25]

The other way in which a person can be hindered from using their powers at will is considered in the same passage. This happens when they are physically bound or obliged to act in some particular way by the operation of an irresistible external force.[26] Hobbes assumes that, if we are to describe a man as free, we must not only be able to say that he is free to act; we must also be able to say that, if he acts in a certain way, then he performs his action freely, in that he 'may refuse to doe it if he will'.[27] If, by contrast, he cannot forbear from acting, then his action will not be that 'of one that was *free*'.[28] As Hobbes had already noted in his preliminary discussion in chapter 14, obligation and liberty 'in one and the same matter are inconsistent'.[29]

This second type of impediment might seem to be of merely residual significance, especially as Hobbes largely confines himself to illustrating it with such simple instances as that of a criminal who is 'led to prison

---

[22] Hobbes 1996, ch. 21, pp. 145–6. Hobbes even claims (p. 145) that the concept of liberty can be applied to inanimate bodies (his example being a body of water) 'no less' than to rational creatures. If he means that the concept can be applied in exactly the same way this seems a slip, for his definition of human freedom makes essential reference to the will. Hobbes 1656, p. 209 explicitly distinguishes human freedom from wider notions of free action when he observes that 'I understand compulsion to be used rightly of living creatures only'.

[23] Hobbes 1996, ch. 14, pp. 91, 92–3.

[24] Hobbes 1996, ch. 21, p. 145. Hobbes also speaks in the same passage of the agent being 'restrained'.

[25] Hobbes 1996, ch. 21, p. 146.

[26] Note that Hobbes distinguishes with a fair degree of consistency between being 'forced' and being 'compelled'. I am compelled if my will is coerced. I am forced if it is rendered physically impossible for me to forbear from acting in a certain way. For Hobbes, compulsion is compatible with liberty but force is not. See Hobbes 1656, pp. 199–200, 208–9, 216–17. The point is well brought out in Wernham 1965, p. 123.

[27] Hobbes 1996, ch. 21, p. 146.   [28] Hobbes 1996, ch. 21, p. 146.

[29] Hobbes 1996, ch. 14, p. 91.

by force'.[30] But in fact the category of actions we cannot forbear from performing is of considerable theoretical importance for Hobbes, because he takes it to be the means of defining two forms of human bondage.

One is that of slavery. According to Hobbes's analysis, both in *De Cive* and *Leviathan*, the lack of liberty suffered by slaves is not simply due to the fact that they are 'kept in prison, or bonds'.[31] It is also due to the fact that 'their labour is appointed to them by another' in such a way that their bodies 'are not in their own power'.[32] A slave is thus defined as someone whose lack of freedom is due in part to the fact that he is, literally, a bondsman: someone who is bound or forced to act, and is not at liberty to forbear from acting.[33] The other way in which human freedom is similarly forfeited is among those who admit God's providence. This too is stressed in both *De Cive* and *Leviathan*, although in this case the earlier analysis is the fuller one. God's power, to those who recognise it, must appear irresistible.[34] When he issues a command to those who believe in him – for example through the Scriptures, which many believe to be the word of God – then 'they cannot forbear from obeying him'.[35] They are tied or bound to obey in such a way 'that their bodily liberty is forfeited'.[36] As Hobbes starkly summarises in chapter 45 of *Leviathan*, all religious believers 'are Gods Slaves'.[37]

---

[30] Hobbes 1656, pp. 216–17. Hobbes 1969a, p. 63 uses the same example. The reason why the category may appear residual, even empty, is that Hobbes sometimes speaks as though an action we cannot forbear from performing is a case in which we are acted upon, not a case in which we act. See, for example, Hobbes 1656, pp. 209, 216–17. But the implication that all actions are free by definition is one that Hobbes elsewhere rejects. See Hobbes 1996, ch. 21 p. 146, where he lays it down that it is only 'actions which proceed from the will' which 'proceed from *liberty*'.

[31] Hobbes 1996, ch. 20, p. 141.   [32] Hobbes 1996, ch. 45, p. 447.

[33] See Hobbes 1996, ch. 45, p. 447 for the explicit distinction between 'the service of Bondmen' and 'a voluntary Servant'. Except for discussing enslavement as a result of conquest in war, however, Hobbes does not explain how such bondage can arise. His discussion of slavery seems in tension with his stress on the implications of human equality.

[34] Hobbes 1983a, XV. V, p. 221.

[35] Hobbes 1983a, XV. VII, p. 223: 'non potest non obedire'. Orr 1987, pp. 58–9 interprets Hobbes as claiming that, although fear of our fellow-men does not take away liberty, fear of God does. What Hobbes seems to be saying, however, is that it is our fatalistic disbelief in our capacity to resist God's power that forces us to obey and so takes away our liberty. If we turn to Hobbes 1996, ch. 31, pp. 246–7 (the corresponding passage in *Leviathan*) we find all reference to fear deleted. Hobbes is now clear that the believer is forced to obey simply by the fact that God appears an irresistible force. Orr is right to point out, however, that there is something unsatisfactory about Hobbes's argument. As we have seen, Hobbes holds that liberty can only be taken away by external impediments to motion. It is clear that God's omnipotence will constitute such an impediment if it is a fact. But it is not clear how it can be said to do so if it is merely believed to be a fact. For further discussion see Goldsmith 1966, pp. 111–13 and appendix 4.

[36] Hobbes 1983a, XV. VII, p. 223: 'libertas . . . corporeis tollitur'.

[37] Hobbes 1996, ch. 45, p. 447.

The whole of Hobbes's analysis thus depends on his initial distinction between power and liberty.[38] An agent forfeits his liberty if an external force renders him either powerless to act or powerless not to act in some particular way. The distinction is I think clear, but is nevertheless worth underlining because, as Hobbes himself stresses, it is all too easy for the two concepts to become confused.[39] The danger arises from the fact that, if we follow a Hobbesian analysis, we are bound to say of someone capable of exercising the power to act in some particular way that they are also at liberty to act in that way. In this case, the agent's power and liberty amount to the same thing. This being so, there is a temptation – as Hobbes duly notes in his reply to Bramhall[40] – to add that, if someone analogously lacks the power to act, they must also lack the liberty.

This is certainly a temptation to which 'negative' theories of liberty have fallen prey in contemporary no less than in early-modern philosophy.[41] But as Hobbes rightly observes, it may or may not make sense to claim that an agent who lacks power also lacks liberty. It will not make sense 'when the impediment of motion is in the constitution of the thing itselfe'.[42] To take Hobbes's own example, a man 'fastned to his bed by sicknesse' lacks the power to move, but it makes no sense to say that he lacks liberty.[43] The reason why he cannot be said to be unfree is that nothing is impeding him from moving; he is simply incapable of movement. This contrasts with the predicament of someone 'imprisoned, or restrained, with walls, or chayns'.[44] His plight is similar to that of the sick man in that he is unable to leave. But the sick man would still be unable to leave even if the prison doors were to be opened, whereas the prisoner is only unable because the doors remain locked. He possesses an underlying power or ability to leave which has been taken away from him.[45] So while the sick man merely lacks ability, the prisoner lacks freedom.

If this interpretation is sound, it is worth adding that Hobbes's theory of human freedom seems to have been rather widely misunderstood. Hobbes is often singled out as the classic exponent of what is sometimes

---

[38] But for a different analysis of this distinction see Kramer 2001.

[39] Hobbes 1996, ch. 21, p. 146; cf. Hobbes 1656, p. 211.

[40] Hobbes 1656, pp. 209–11.

[41] See, for instance, Cassinelli 1966, p. 28, for a contrasting discussion of an example similar to the one considered in Hobbes 1996, ch. 21, p. 146. Oppenheim 1981, p. 87 offers a good criticism of Cassinelli's analysis.

[42] See Hobbes 1996, ch. 21, p. 146. I have supplied the word 'in', missing in Tuck's edition.

[43] Hobbes 1996, ch. 21, p. 146; cf. Hobbes 1656, p. 211.

[44] Hobbes 1996, ch. 21, p. 146.

[45] See Hobbes 1996, ch. 14, p. 91 and cf. Hobbes 1656, p. 285.

called the pure negative theory of liberty.[46] He is claimed, that is, to hold the view that a man is unfree if and only if his doing of some particular action has been rendered impossible.[47] But this appears to be untrue to his analysis in two distinct ways. Although Hobbes agrees that an agent lacks freedom if an action within his powers has been rendered impossible, he does not think that this is the only way in which unfreedom can be produced.[48] The agent will also lack freedom if he is tied or bound to act in such a way that he cannot forbear from acting. The other misunderstanding is that, even if no one is rendering it impossible for an agent to act in a given way, it still does not necessarily follow for Hobbes that the agent is free to perform the action concerned.[49] This is because, as we have seen, the action in question may be beyond the agent's powers. It is true that, given the lines along which Hobbes analyses the concept, he might be willing to admit that the agent is free to *try* to perform the action – although he does not pronounce on that question at any stage. But what is certain is that, for Hobbes, the question of whether the action is one that the agent is or is not free to perform simply does not arise.

Rather than being an instance of the pure negative theory of liberty, Hobbes's analysis serves to suggest that there may be something amiss with that theory itself. To state it in its positive and most widely accepted form, the theory holds that agents are free unless actions within their powers are subjected to 'preventing conditions'.[50] This formulation certainly avoids the awkwardness of claiming that agents remain free to perform actions that are beyond their powers. But it still appears to confuse the general concept of social freedom with the more specific notion of being free to act.[51] It overlooks the possibility that an agent's lack of freedom may derive not from being unfree to act, but rather from being unable to act freely.[52]

---

[46] See Taylor 1982, p. 142. As a paradigm of the pure negative theory Taylor cites Steiner 1974–5.

[47] This is to allude to the definition given in Steiner 1974–5, p. 33.

[48] As appears to be assumed, for example, in Day 1983, where Hobbes's analysis is treated as though he is concerned only with being free and unfree to act.

[49] As is assumed, for example, in Goldsmith 1989, p. 24, where it is claimed that according to Hobbes to be unfree means 'to be restrained from acting as one wishes to act'. This implies that we remain free so long as no one restrains us from performing an action we may wish to perform. As we have seen, however, Hobbes's view is that, if the action is beyond our powers, the question of freedom does not arise. But Goldsmith's is a valuable analysis, especially for its emphasis on the coherence of Hobbes's views.

[50] See, for example, MacCallum 1972, p. 176.

[51] See the excellent discussion in Oppenheim 1981, pp. 83–4.

[52] This distinction is well drawn, however, in McNeilly 1968, p. 171. See also Watkins 1965, pp. 120–2 and Raphael 1984, p. 30.

III

So far I have presented Hobbes's theory of human freedom as a simple and unambiguous one. But it must be admitted that this interpretation faces a difficulty. It is a difficulty, moreover, that has caused many of Hobbes's commentators to conclude that his theory is not only more complicated than I have been implying but is seriously confused.[53]

The main grounds for this accusation are furnished by the range of examples Hobbes uses to illustrate his theory at the start of chapter 21. One of the cases he considers is that of a free gift. 'When we say a Guift is Free', he maintains, 'there is not meant any Liberty of the Guift, but of the Giver, that was not bound by any law, or Covenant to give it.'[54] Hobbes's point is that the agent is free in the sense of being able to act freely as opposed to being bound or forced to act. But his chosen instance seems to presuppose a view much broader than I have so far been suggesting of the range of ties that can properly be said to take away our liberty to forbear from acting. As well as the purely physical constraints of slavery, he now appears to include not merely the bonds of law but also of our own promises.

The other example Hobbes discusses in the same passage is that of freedom of speech. 'When we *speak Freely*', the freedom we exercise 'is not the Liberty of voice, or pronunciation, but of the man, whom no law hath obliged to speak otherwise than he did'.[55] Here Hobbes is making the converse point that the agent is at liberty in the sense of being free to act as opposed to being stopped or prevented from acting. But again he appears greatly to expand his sense of the range of ties that are capable of stopping us, and hence of taking away our liberty. As well as the purely physical bonds on which he initially concentrated, he now appears willing to include the bonds of law as another such potential impediment.

In the light of such examples it is easy to see how the accusation of inconsistency arises. Hobbes first defines freedom as the absence of purely physical hindrances. But he then seems to allow that our liberty can also be limited by legal and moral ties. By passing, as one critic has put it, 'from physical impediments to obligations' as his criterion of unfreedom, he leaves his analysis muddled and confused.[56]

---

[53] For the accusation that Hobbes's discussion of liberty is confused see, for example, Pennock 1965, pp. 102, 116; Wernham 1965, pp. 120–1; Gauthier 1969, pp. 62, 65–6; Ross 1974, pp. 55–6; Raphael 1984, pp. 30–4. But for defences of Hobbes's consistency see Leyden 1982, pp. 45–50 and Goldsmith 1989.

[54] Hobbes 1996, ch. 21, p. 146.   [55] Hobbes 1996, ch. 21, p. 146.

[56] McNeilly 1968, p. 171. Note that, although *Leviathan* contains an extensive discussion of the concept of unfreedom, Hobbes never uses that word.

I cannot see that this criticism is justified. Consider first Hobbes's contention that we are tied or bound by our covenants and promises even 'in the condition of meer Nature'.[57] It is certainly true that he speaks as if the act of promising, and hence of laying aside a right, prevents me from acting contrary to my word. I am said 'to be OBLIGED, or BOUND, not to hinder those, to whom such Right is granted'.[58] He also speaks as though a promise or covenant can similarly tie or bind me to act. 'If I Covenant to pay a ransome' in the state of nature, I am said to be 'bound by it'.[59] Hobbes also supplies an unambiguous account of the means by which these ties operate. It is a law of nature, as the start of chapter 15 declares, '*That men performe their Covenants made*', and we are bound to obey the laws of nature.[60] Not only are we 'forbidden' and 'commanded' by their dictates, but they also 'bind to a desire they should take place'.[61]

Hobbes is no less clear, however, that these ties cannot be said to limit our liberty in the proper signification of the word. The laws of nature, as he repeatedly affirms, are 'improperly' called laws; they are nothing more than 'Conclusions, or Theoremes concerning what conduceth to the conservation and defence' of ourselves.[62] When we say, therefore, that we are tied or bound by these laws, we are merely saying that, if we desire peace and defence, we are bound or obliged to follow the dictates of reason. No such bonds, however, can ever restrict our liberty in the proper signification of the word. As Hobbes has explained, such limitations can only arise from the natural strength of external impediments. But as he almost wistfully puts it, the bonds of which he is now speaking have no strength at all 'from their own Nature', for 'nothing is more easily broken than a mans word'.[63] They have no power to 'bridle' us from acting as ambition, avarice and anger dictate, nor do they have any power to force us to act and thereby 'hold men to the performance of their Covenants'.[64] They leave us, in short, in full possession of our natural liberty.

---

[57] Hobbes 1996, ch. 14, p. 97.   [58] Hobbes 1996, ch. 14, p. 92.
[59] Hobbes 1996, ch. 14, p. 97.   [60] Hobbes 1996, ch. 15, p. 100.
[61] For these formulae see Hobbes 1996, ch. 14, pp. 91–2 and ch. 15, p. 110 respectively.
[62] Hobbes 1996, ch. 15, p. 111.
[63] Hobbes 1996, ch. 14, p. 93. Yet Hobbes 1996, ch. 21, p. 146 does say, in discussing the example of a free gift, that it will be free if the giver 'was not bound by any law or Covenant to give it'. The addition of 'or Covenant' may be a slip. The liberty of the giver can certainly be bound by law, in that the law constrains our liberty as subjects. But it cannot similarly be constrained by the donor's own covenants. As Hobbes 1996, ch. 17, p. 117 stresses, these 'are but Words', and in the absence of laws are 'of no strength to secure a man at all'. There are two possible ways of rescuing Hobbes's consistency. We can take him either to be referring to just those cases in which covenants are legally enforceable, or else to be speaking of what we are rationally bound or obliged to do even in the condition of mere nature.
[64] Hobbes 1996, ch. 14, pp. 96, 99.

Hobbes admittedly adds that, although the force of words is too weak to hold men, there are two possible ways of strengthening it. One is 'a Feare of the consequence of breaking their word', while the other is 'a Glory, or Pride in appearing not to need to breake it'.[65] However, it is Hobbes's contention that neither of these auxiliary strengths can ever be expected to suffice in the condition of mere nature. No reliance can be placed on pride, for this presupposes 'a Generosity too rarely found to be presumed on, especially in the pursuers of Wealth, Command, or sensuall Pleasure; which are the greatest part of Mankind'.[66] Nor can we rely on fear, because there is no reason to feel any alarm at the consequences of failing to keep our promises unless we have good grounds for fearing either the wrath of God or of our fellow-men. But there is no reason to entertain a sufficient fear of our fellow-men. For 'Nature hath made men so equall' in the condition of mere nature that they will have just as strong a reason for feeling intimidated by us.[67] Nor does the fear of being punished by God supply a rational person with a sufficient motive for keeping their promises. Any rational person is bound to confess that God is completely incomprehensible.[68] This being so, there can be 'no naturall knowledge of mans estate after death; much lesse of the reward that is then to be given to breach of Faith'.[69] Nor does it alter the case that the Scriptures appear to promise us punishments after death for failing to abide by our word. For while we may believe, we cannot possibly know that the Scriptures are the word of God.[70] It follows that, for all we know, there may be no such punishments. And it follows from this – at least if we reject

[65] Hobbes 1996, ch. 14, p. 99.

[66] Hobbes 1996, ch. 14, p. 99. As Oakeshott 1975a, pp. 119–25 emphasises, however, Hobbes leaves open the possibility that pride can be 'moralised', and thus that justice and the pursuit of glory need not be incompatible. See also Thomas 1965, pp. 202–7 on the place of 'generous natures' in Hobbes's theory.

[67] On natural equality see Hobbes 1996, ch. 13, pp. 86–7. For the fact that this will tend (in the absence of compulsive laws) to militate against our keeping of our promises, simply because no sufficient 'inequality of Power' will appear, see Hobbes 1996, ch. 14, p. 99. But if 'Nature hath made men so equall', how can one man get another so completely into his power as to enslave him? Hobbes does not directly address this point.

[68] This point is constantly reiterated in *Leviathan*, especially in the discussions of religion and of vain philosophy. See Hobbes 1996, ch. 12, pp. 77–8; ch. 46, pp. 466–8. This does not mean that Hobbes disbelieves in God, although it does mean that he sharply distinguishes knowledge from belief. On this point see Glover 1965.

[69] Hobbes 1996, ch. 15, p. 103. See Wootton 1983 on the fact that such a dismissal of the fear of God as a rational ground for obedience – by no means unknown to humanists of the Renaissance – had by this time become exceptional.

[70] For this claim see Hobbes 1996, ch. 33, p. 267 and ch. 43, p. 406. For the fact that we cannot hope to receive any supernatural revelation of God's will see Hobbes 1996, ch. 26, pp. 197–200. Hobbes thus distances himself from the claim that we can acquire knowledge of an omnipotent God. Cf. the valuable discussion in Halliday, Kenyon and Reeve 1983.

Pascal's wager, as Hobbes implicitly does – that 'Covenants, without the Sword, are but Words, and of no strength to secure a man at all'.[71]

So far we have been considering the status of our promises and covenants in the condition of mere nature. But a similar set of considerations applies if we turn to Hobbes's account of the manner in which human laws may be said to tie or bind us when we quit the state of nature and submit ourselves to the laws of a commonwealth. Again, there can be no doubt that Hobbes repeatedly speaks of our being bound, and thus apparently rendered unfree, by the force of the laws to which we submit. They are said to be capable of binding men from acting, as when they serve 'to tye their hands from rapine, and revenge'.[72] They are likewise said to be capable of binding men to act, as in the case where 'Subjects are bound to uphold whatsoever power is given to the Soveraign'.[73] But again, the question is whether these ties or bonds can be counted as impediments to freedom in the proper signification of the word.

To grasp Hobbes's answer, we need to begin by making a cardinal distinction that he himself draws in the passage of chapter 21 of *Leviathan* immediately following the one on which we have so far concentrated. On the one hand, there is the idea of liberty as he has so far been considering it, the idea of 'naturall *liberty*, which only is properly called *liberty*'. But on the other hand, we need to take note of a distinct concept he now introduces for the first time, a concept he labels 'the *Liberty* of *Subjects*'.[74]

Hobbes's distinction reminds us of the fact that, throughout *Leviathan*, he is interested in two separate 'conditions of mankind'.[75] There is the condition of mere nature, the condition in which we are free from legal constraints and at the same time possess our natural liberty to the extent that we are capable of exercising our powers without being physically prevented or compelled.[76] But there is also what Hobbes describes as our artificial condition, the condition we voluntarily take upon ourselves when we covenant to become the subjects of an 'Artificiall Man' and thereby load ourselves down with the 'Artificiall Chains' of the law.[77] It is in relation to this underlying duality between nature and artifice, and hence between natural liberty and our liberty as subjects, that we need to assess the coherence of Hobbes's views about the capacity of laws to

---

[71] Hobbes 1996, ch. 17, p. 117. But for a sharply contrasting account of the relationship between God's law and political obligation see Hood 1964, pp. 85–90, 135–7.

[72] Hobbes 1996, ch. 19, p. 128.   [73] Hobbes 1996, ch. 26, p. 200.

[74] Hobbes 1996, ch. 21, p. 147.

[75] For a full analysis of Hobbes's distinction between the worlds of nature and artifice see Rossini 1988.

[76] Hobbes 1996, ch. 13, pp. 86–90.   [77] Hobbes 1996, ch. 21, p. 147.

limit our freedom, and hence about the relationship between coercion and liberty.

Hobbes is emphatic that the force of law definitely limits our freedom as subjects. To say that someone is a subject is to say that they have covenanted to give up the condition in which everyone is naturally placed, the condition of mere nature in which 'every man holdeth this Right, of doing any thing he liketh'.[78] But to say that the state of nature can be defined as a condition in which everyone can do as they like is to say that it is a state in which, apart from our rational obligation to obey the laws of nature, we have no legal obligations at all. There is therefore a sense in which, in agreeing to give up our natural condition, we are agreeing to give up a form of liberty. Hobbes summarises the crucial contrast at the end of his chapter on civil laws:

> For *Right* is *Liberty*, namely that Liberty which the Civil Law leaves us: But *Civill Law* is an *Obligation*; and takes from us the Liberty which the Law of Nature gave us. Nature gave a Right to every man to secure himselfe by his own strength, and to invade a suspected neighbour, by way of prevention: but the Civill Law takes away that Liberty, in all cases where the protection of the Law may be safely stayd for.[79]

To insist on the rationality of giving up this freedom from human law is the fulcrum of Hobbes's theory of the commonwealth. Because everyone in the state of nature enjoys this freedom, and because 'Nature hath made men so equal' in power and strength, the state of nature can only be described as a condition of liberty in the most paradoxical sense.[80] It can equally well be described as a condition in which we all enjoy an equal liberty to master and enslave our neighbours, while they enjoy the same liberty 'to make themselves Masters' of our own 'persons, wives, children and cattell' if they can.[81] Hence the emphasis that Hobbes always places on 'that misery, which accompanies the Liberty of particular men'.[82]

Nevertheless, there remains a sense in which liberty is forfeited when we covenant to become subjects of a commonwealth. To live as a subject is, by definition, to live in subjection to law. To speak of the liberty of a subject is thus to speak essentially of 'the Silence of the Law'.[83] If there are 'cases where the Soveraign has prescribed no rule, there the Subject hath the Liberty to do, or forbeare, according to his own discretion'.[84]

---

[78] Hobbes 1996, ch. 14, p. 92. [79] Hobbes 1996, ch. 26, p. 200.
[80] Hobbes 1996, ch. 13, p. 86. [81] Hobbes 1996, ch. 13, p. 88.
[82] Hobbes 1996, ch. 13, p. 90. [83] Hobbes 1996, ch. 21, p. 152.
[84] Hobbes 1996, ch. 21, p. 152. Hence Hobbes defines a crime (ch. 27, p. 201) as 'the Committing (by Deed, or Word) of that which the Law forbiddeth, or the Omission of what it hath commanded'.

But where the law enjoins or forbids a certain course of action, there the subject is tied or bound to act or forbear from acting as the law and the sovereign command.

As Hobbes makes clear at the outset, however, these considerations apply only to the liberty of subjects. It remains to ask whether these considerations apply to liberty in the proper signification of the word. For only in that case will it be justifiable to claim that Hobbes's exposition is confused.

Before turning to that question, it is important to note that Hobbes allows one exception even to the doctrine that the form of liberty characteristic of the state of nature is cancelled by our obligation to obey the civil law. The exception is grounded on the nature of the reasons we possess for covenanting to take upon ourselves the bonds of a subject. 'The motive, and end for which this renouncing and transferring of Right is introduced, is nothing else but the security of a mans person, in his life, and in the means of so preserving life, as not to be weary of it.'[85] From this it follows that, since 'the end of Obedience is Protection', there must be certain natural rights – and hence liberties of action – that 'can by no Covenant be relinquished'.[86] Specifically, I cannot consistently agree to relinquish my freedom to act in protection of my life and bodily liberty. For my sole aim in agreeing to the covenant was to assure a better protection for precisely those rights than I could have hoped to achieve by my own efforts in the free but warlike condition of mere nature.[87]

However, the main point on which Hobbes wishes to insist is that, even in those cases where the freedom of the state of nature is undoubtedly abridged by our obligation to obey the civil laws, this does nothing to limit our liberty in the proper signification of the word.

Hobbes of course intends this conclusion to seem a paradoxical one. But the paradox can readily be dissolved if we turn to the account he gives of the distinctive way in which any system of law operates to ensure the obedience of those subject to it. There are two separate routes, according to Hobbes, by which a citizen can come to feel the force of a law and decide to obey it. One is that all rational persons will, *ex hypothesi*, recognise that obedience is in their interests. For the basic aim of law is to seek peace by protecting life and liberty, and these are the goals that all rational persons seek above all. So the liberty of such agents to act as their judgement and reason dictate will not in the least be infringed

---

[85] Hobbes 1996, ch. 14, p. 93.   [86] Hobbes 1996, ch. 21, p. 153.
[87] For this claim see Hobbes 1996, ch. 14, pp. 98–9. For the remarkably extensive range of things that a subject, 'though commanded by the Soveraign', may 'without Injustice refuse to do', see Hobbes 1996, ch. 21, pp. 150–3.

by their obligation to obey the law. The dictates of their reason and the requirements of the law will prove to be one and the same.

This expresses a traditional view about the compatibility of law and liberty, one that John Locke was classically to restate a generation later in his *Two Treatises of Government.*[88] '*Law*, in its true Notion, is not so much the Limitation as *the direction of a free and intelligent Agent* to his proper Interest.' Locke draws the inference that, when we submit to the direction of such laws, this will constitute an expression rather than a restriction of our liberty. 'That ill deserves the Name of Confinement which hedges us in only from Bogs and Precipices.'[89] This is not merely a doctrine that Hobbes appears to endorse, but one that he enunciates in the form of a simile later echoed by Locke with remarkable closeness. 'The use of Lawes', as Hobbes puts it in discussing the office of the sovereign in chapter 30, 'is not to bind the People from all Voluntary actions; but to direct and keep them in such a motion, as not to hurt themselves by their own impetuous desires, rashnesse, or indiscretion; as Hedges are set, not to stop Travellers, but to keep them in the way.'[90]

As Hobbes stresses, however, this is not the reason why the generality of men obey the law, moved as they are by mere considerations of wealth, command and sensual pleasure. The only mechanism by which they can be brought to obey is by making them more frightened of the consequences of disobedience.[91] As we have seen, there is admittedly no hope of employing this device outside the confines of the commonwealth. Covenants without the sword are but words, and of no strength to secure a man at all. But if a 'visible Power' is erected 'to keep them in awe, and tye them by feare of punishment to the performance of their Covenants', then there is every prospect of compelling them both to act in line with their obligations and at the same time to forbear from acting as partiality, pride and revenge would otherwise dictate.[92]

It is of course true that, where the mechanism of using fear to produce obedience works successfully, a subject will elect not to exercise his powers or abilities in various ways. The whole purpose of assigning the right of

---

[88] For Locke's views on political liberty see Tully 1993, pp. 315–23.

[89] Locke 1988, II, para. 57, p. 305.

[90] Hobbes 1996, ch. 30, pp. 239–40 puts the point in this way when discussing the extent to which laws are necessary. But the argument is a corollary of his earlier contention that we are bound by reason to obey the laws of nature.

[91] Hobbes occasionally seems to allow a more direct mechanism: subjects may be physically forced to act by authorised agents of the commonwealth. For passages in which this seems to be envisaged see Hobbes 1996, ch. 14, p. 96, where the state is said to be capable of compelling by force, and ch. 21, p. 151, where the sovereign is described as capable of authorising assault.

[92] Hobbes 1996, ch. 17, p. 117.

punishment to sovereigns is to form and direct the wills of their subjects in just this way. Hobbes's point, however, is that this does nothing to take away the continuing power or ability of a subject to act as his will and desires dictate. 'The Consent of a Subject to Sovaraign Power' is such that 'there is no restriction at all, of his own former naturall Liberty'.[93]

To see how Hobbes can consistently defend this crucial conclusion, we need only recall his account of the means by which we are alone capable of forfeiting our liberty in the proper signification of the word. An external impediment must intervene in such a way that we are either physically stopped from acting or physically forced to act. But neither fear nor any other passion of the soul can possibly count as such an impediment. Rather, a man who acts out of fear performs his action because he wills or desires to avoid various consequences which, he fears, will otherwise befall him. Of such a man we can certainly say that he acts as he does because his will has been 'formed' or 'compelled'.[94] But to compel someone's will is only to cause them to have a will or desire to act other than the will or desire for the sake of which they would otherwise have acted. When such a person acts, it will still be because they possess the will or desire to act in precisely the way in which they duly act. Even if the cause of their having this will is fear, the action they perform out of fear will remain a free action.

To illustrate his argument, Hobbes takes an example originally put forward by Aristotle at the start of Book 3 of the *Nicomachean Ethics*, the example of a man who 'throweth his goods into the Sea for *feare* the ship should sink'.[95] The man certainly acts out of fear; so we may say if we like that he felt compelled to act. But as Hobbes grimly adds – challenging Aristotle's analysis[96] – 'he doth it neverthelesse very willingly, and may refuse to doe it if he will: It is therefore the action, of one that was *free*'.[97]

Hobbes's basic argument is thus that 'Feare, and Liberty are consistent'.[98] If we speak of being tied or bound by the laws, we can only

[93] Hobbes 1996, ch. 21, p. 151.
[94] Because Hobbes distinguishes between bodily coercion, which takes away liberty, and coercion of the will, which does not, he has no objection to describing threats of punishment as coercing and compelling us to act, while insisting that the resulting actions will nevertheless be freely performed. See, for example, Hobbes 1996, ch. 14, pp. 96; ch. 15, pp. 100–1; ch. 28, pp. 220–1; ch. 42, pp. 391–2; ch. 45, pp. 449–50.
[95] See Hobbes 1996, ch. 21, p. 146 and cf. Aristotle 1934, III. 1, p. 118.
[96] According to Aristotle 1934, III. 1, p. 118, the action is 'mixed': voluntary and yet in a sense involuntary.
[97] See Hobbes 1996, ch. 21, p. 146 and cf. Hobbes 1656, pp. 199, 208.
[98] See Hobbes 1996, ch. 21, p. 146 and cf. Hobbes 1656, p. 209.

be speaking metaphorically. Hobbes is anxious to underline this implication, for he proceeds to describe the artificial character of these bonds
in a grotesque piece of imagery at odds with his usual expository style:

> But as men, for the atteyning of peace, and conservation of themselves there by,
> have made an Artificiall Man, which we call a Common-wealth; so also have they
> made Artificiall Chains, called *Civill Lawes*, which they themselves, by mutuall
> covenants, have fastned at one end, to the lips of that Man, or Assembly, to whom
> they have given the Soveraigne Power; and at the other end to their own Ears.[99]

Hobbes is alluding to Lucian's version of the fable of Hercules.[100] According to Lucian, the ancient Gauls thought of Hercules as a venerable
and exceptionally prudent orator, symbolising his gifts of persuasion by
picturing him as drawing men along by fetters attached at one end to his
tongue and at the other end to his followers' ears.[101] Hobbes's original
readers might perhaps have been surprised to come upon this classical
flourish, especially as Hobbes boasts in the Review and Conclusion that
he has deliberately left *Leviathan* unencumbered with such conventional
references to ancient authorities.[102] But Hobbes would undoubtedly have
expected his original readers to recognise the allusion and to grasp its relevance, especially as Lucian's claim that men can be 'led by the ears' had
already become a favourite *topos* among humanist writers on rhetoric by
the end of the sixteenth century.[103]

For Hobbes, the moral of the story is not in doubt. On the one hand, the
artificial chains by means of which we are persuaded to obey the laws are
of course sufficient to bind us as subjects. For the category of 'subject' is
itself an artificial one, the product of that indispensable piece of political
artifice, the Covenant, from which political obligation can alone be derived. But on the other hand, these chains are 'in their own nature but
weak'. They can be made to hold only 'by the danger, though not by
the difficulty of breaking them'.[104] We retain our natural liberty at all
times to break what Hobbes in a further classical allusion (this time to
Plutarch's life of Solon) calls the cobweb laws of our country.[105]

---

[99] Hobbes 1996, ch. 21, p. 147.
[100] For a discussion, with illustrations, see Bredekamp 1999, pp. 126–31.
[101] Lucian 1913, vol. 1, p. 65.   [102] Hobbes 1996, Conclusion, p. 490.
[103] See, for example, Montaigne 1946–7, I. 27, vol. 2, p. 55 on those who are 'subjects à estre menez
par les oreilles' and the further reference in Montaigne 1946–7, I. 51, vol. 2, pp. 229–30. See also
Sonnet 58 in Sidney 1962, p. 193, claiming that 'with his golden chaine/The Oratour so farre
men's harts doth bind'. Lucian's image of Hercules appears as Emblem 181 in Alciato 1621,
p. 751, although with the interesting variation that Hercules's strength is shown as overcome by
the force of eloquence.
[104] Hobbes 1996, ch. 21, p. 147.
[105] See Hobbes 1996, ch. 27, p. 204 and cf. Plutarch 1579, p. 89. For further discussion see chapter
2 section II above.

I cannot see, therefore, that there is any serious inconsistency in Hobbes's theory of human freedom. He does not contradict himself by saying first that liberty can only be constrained by external impediments and later that it can also be constrained by laws. Rather we can summarise his argument by observing that natural liberty and civil law belong, for Hobbes, to two different spheres. Liberty 'according to the proper signification of the word' belongs to the sphere of nature, the sphere in which everyone possesses an equal right, and thus a liberty, 'to use his own power, as he will himselfe, for the preservation of his own Nature; that is to say, of his own Life'.[106] This liberty can only be constrained by ties or bonds which are themselves natural – that is, physical – in character. But civil law belongs to the sphere of artifice, the sphere in which, as Hobbes's Introduction explains, 'by Art is created that great LEVIATHAN called a COMMON-WEALTH, or STATE, (in latine CIVITAS) which is but an Artificiall Man'.[107] The laws of such common-wealths undoubtedly limit our liberty as subjects, since the aim of the sovereign is to make us feel sufficiently frightened of the consequences of disobeying to feel tied or bound by his commands. But in this case the ties are purely artificial, and leave unimpaired our natural liberty to make use of our powers as we please. Summing up in chapter 21, Hobbes spells out this crucial implication as unambiguously as possible: 'generally all actions which men doe in Common-wealths, for *feare* of the law, are actions, which the doers had *liberty* to omit'.[108]

IV

I have now laid out what I take to be Hobbes's views about the proper signification of liberty. But I am far from supposing that I have said enough to enable his theory to be fully understood. As I indicated at the outset, it remains to explain why he should have been so anxious to insist that this explication of the concept is the only coherent one. Having followed the account he gives, it now becomes possible to rephrase my initial question more pointedly. Why should Hobbes have been so anxious to insist on such a restricted analysis of the circumstances in which we can legitimately claim that our liberty has been infringed?

We first need to recognise that Hobbes had a profound philosophical motive for drawing the boundaries of unfreedom in such a narrow way. On the one hand, a major concern of *Leviathan* is to explore the relationship between liberty and political obligation. Hobbes accordingly stands

---

[106] Hobbes 1996, ch. 14, p. 91.   [107] Hobbes 1996, Introduction, p. 9.
[108] Hobbes 1996, ch. 21, p. 146.

in need of a firm criterion for distinguishing between free and unfree actions. But on the other hand, Hobbes is a determinist. He cannot allow that anyone is ever free to will or not to will. To be free is to be unimpeded from moving according to one's will and desires. But since the will itself 'is not subject to Motion', it cannot be 'subject to Impediment'.[109] It follows that 'from the use of the word *Freewill*, no Liberty can be inferred to the will, desire or inclination' in any instance at all.[110]

It might seem that this leaves Hobbes with an insuperable difficulty. But by adopting the precise view of human freedom I have outlined, he is able to frame an elegant solution to it. On the one hand, he is able to maintain that the will is never free, always determined. 'Every act of mans will, and every desire, and inclination proceedeth from some cause', so that 'to him that could see the connexion of those causes, the *necessity* of all mens voluntary actions, would appear manifest'.[111] But on the other hand, he is able to mark a clear distinction between free and unfree actions. A man remains free provided that no external impediment obstructs him from acting according to his will or desires. He only ceases to be free if he is impeded in such a way that his will (which is itself caused) no longer functions as the cause of his actions.

As Bishop Bramhall acutely remarked, Hobbes is here reviving an essentially Stoic vision of the compatibility between liberty and necessity.[112] The effect is to enable him to speak of human freedom in a manner wholly consistent with his determinism. An agent's will is never free; but where the agent is unimpeded from acting at will, we may nevertheless speak of free action. As Samuel Pepys noted in his *Diary* for 20 November 1661, the solution is 'very shrewd'.[113]

As well as having these metaphysical commitments, Hobbes had at least two powerful reasons of a political nature for wishing to draw the boundaries of unfreedom in a restricted way. As we have already seen in volume 2 chapter 12, it is clear in the first place that he had come to feel an urgent need to respond to the dangers he associated with the classical republican theory of liberty espoused by so many of his fellow-countrymen. This attitude reflects one of the sharpest changes of direction to be found in the evolution of Hobbes's political

---

[109] Hobbes 1996, ch. 21, p. 146; cf. Hobbes 1656, p. 29.
[110] Hobbes 1996, ch. 21, p. 146; cf. Hobbes 1656, p. 289.
[111] Hobbes 1996, ch. 21, pp. 146–7.
[112] Modern commentators have been inclined to credit Hobbes with the invention of this 'compatibilist' doctrine. See, for example, Raphael 1984, p. 30. But cf. Bramhall's comments on Hobbes's evident debt to the Stoics as quoted in Hobbes 1656, pp. 192–4, 195–7.
[113] Pepys 1970–83, vol. 2, p. 217.

thought.[114] In *The Elements of Law* he had basically accepted the classical republican case, arguing that 'Liberty in a Common wealth' can only be said to be truly secured 'in the Popular State, or Democracy'.[115] Aristotle is warmly praised for having stressed this insight: he 'saith well' that 'the ground or intention of a Democracy, is Liberty'.[116] In *De Cive*, however, Hobbes begins to change his mind. Aristotle's contention that 'in the case of a commonwealth governed by its own citizens, liberty can be assumed' is now dismissed as a mere speech of the vulgar, and Aristotle is criticised 'for following the custom of his time in confusing dominion with liberty'.[117] By the time Hobbes came to publish *Leviathan*, he had acquired a further and more urgent reason for wishing to repudiate the classical republican theory of liberty. He now believed that 'by reading of these Greek, and Latine Authors, men from their childhood have gotten a habit (under a false shew of Liberty,) of favouring tumults, and of licentious controlling the actions of their Soveraigns'.[118] One consequence, he now maintains, was the civil war itself. The outcome of being 'made to receive our opinions concerning the Institution, and Rights of Common-wealths, from *Aristotle, Cicero*' and other defenders of popular states has been 'the effusion of so much blood; as I think I may truly say, there was never any thing so deerly bought, as these Western parts have bought the learning of the Greek and Latine tongues'.[119]

Hobbes is particularly exercised by two distinctive elements in the classical republican theory of liberty. One is the contention – which he again quotes from Aristotle's *Politics* – that '*in democracy*, Liberty *is to be supposed: for 'tis commonly held, that no man is* Free *in any other government*'.[120] The other is the connected doctrine that Greece, Rome and modern republics are worthy in some special sense to be described as 'free Commonwealths', whereas 'all manner of Common-wealths but the Popular' can be dismissed as tyrannies.[121]

Faced with these arguments, which he had come to regard as seditious, what Hobbes does is to deploy his distinctive analysis of liberty in such a way as to try to show that both of them are arbitrary and absurd. This is obvious, he thinks, in the case of the inflammatory contention 'that the Subjects in a Popular Common-wealth enjoy Liberty; but that

---

[114] A point excellently brought out in Gauthier 1969, pp. 145–6.
[115] Hobbes 1969a, pp. 169–70.   [116] Hobbes 1969a, p. 170.
[117] Hobbes 1983a, X.VIII, p. 176: 'Aristoteles . . . consuetudine temporis libertatem pro imperio nominans. Lib. 6. *Politicorum*, cap. 2. *In statu populari libertas est ex suppositione. Quod vulgo dicunt.*'
[118] Hobbes 1996, ch. 21, p. 150.   [119] Hobbes 1996, ch. 21, pp. 149–50.
[120] Hobbes 1996, ch. 21, p. 150.   [121] Hobbes 1996, ch. 46, p. 470 and ch. 21, p. 149.

in a Monarchy they are all Slaves'.[122] As Hobbes takes himself to have shown, to speak of the liberty of subjects is only to speak of the silence of the law. But all commonwealths have laws, and no subject can be free of them. 'They that live under a Monarch' may deceive themselves into thinking otherwise, but we never encounter this illusion among those who actually live under popular governments. For as Hobbes adds in his most forbidding tones, 'they find no such matter'.[123]

No less absurd, on the analysis Hobbes now gives, is the republican idea of the *vivere libero* or 'free commonwealth', the idea 'whereof there is so frequent, and honourable mention' in Greek and Roman writings on statecraft.[124] Given that freedom merely consists in the absence of impediments, the only sense we can assign to this concept is that such commonwealths must be free to act as they will or desire. But this form of natural liberty is obviously common to all states that are 'not dependent on one another', each of which 'has an absolute Libertie, to doe what it shall judge' to be 'most conducing to their benefit'. It makes no sense, therefore, to speak as if some particular types of commonwealth can uniquely be described as 'free states'. 'Whether a Common-wealth be Monarchicall, or Popular, the Freedome is still the same.'[125]

As I showed in volume 2 chapter 11, the ideals of classical republicanism suddenly acquired a new salience in the immediate aftermath of the regicide of 1649. So it is hardly surprising to find that Hobbes felt the need to denounce them with so much vehemence.[126] As I indicated in chapter 1 of the present volume, however, Hobbes also had a more immediate reason for wishing to insist on his distinctive analysis of liberty at the time when he began writing *Leviathan* in the autumn of 1649. By highlighting his views about the compatibility between freedom and coercion, he hoped to supply an answer to the most vexed question of conscience that had arisen at that precise juncture: the question of whether the new government of the Commonwealth 'without a King or House of Lords' could be lawfully obeyed.[127]

No sooner had the Rump Parliament and its Council of State installed themselves in power in February 1649 than they found their legitimacy questioned on all sides.[128] The most violent denunciations came from

---

[122] Hobbes 1996, ch. 29, p. 226.   [123] Hobbes 1996, ch. 29, p. 226.
[124] Hobbes 1996, ch. 21, p. 149.   [125] Hobbes 1996, ch. 21, p. 149.
[126] For the presence of classical republican arguments in the pamphlet literature following the regicide see Wallace 1964, pp. 384–5.
[127] The formula used in the Oath of Engagement, January 1650. See *Constitutional Documents*, p. 391. For the associated pamphlet literature see Wallace 1964.
[128] For the settlement and creation of the Council see Worden 1974, pp. 177–85.

surviving royalists, but the most dangerous opposition came from a number of groups that had hitherto supported the parliamentary cause. Among these, the most intransigent were the Levellers. But by far the most numerous were those who remained loyal to the authority of Parliament as it had been constituted before its purge by Colonel Pride in the name of the army leadership in December 1648.[129]

Both these latter groups denounced the government from the same basic standpoint. They agreed that, because liberty is a birthright, any regime must derive its legitimacy from a voluntary act of submission on the part of its own subjects. With the Levellers this took the form of a demand that the new regime should receive its powers from a formal Agreement of the People. With this goal in mind, John Lilburne, William Walwyn, Thomas Prince and Richard Overton issued the third and final *Agreement of the Free People of England* in May 1649.[130] But the leading writers in support of Parliament – Edward Gee, Edmund Hall, William Prynne, Nathaniel Ward and many others – were scarcely less emphatic about the indispensability of popular consent. As the author of *The Grand Case of Conscience* put it in June 1649, any regime that can lawfully call on the allegiance of its citizens must originate in 'the generall consent of the major part of the people'.[131]

As both groups went on to argue, however, the government of the Rump lacked any such basis in consent. The Levellers concentrated on the fact that, as John Lilburne fulminated in *Englands New Chains Discovered*, with its 'long plotted Council of State erected', the army leadership now 'threateneth tyranny'.[132] More sweepingly, the protagonists of Parliament maintained that the entire sequence of events from Pride's Purge to the execution of the king and the abolition of the House of Lords lacked any vestige of consent and hence of lawfulness. As William Prynne concluded in *Summary Reasons Against the New Oath and Engagement*, the new Commonwealth was 'forcibly and treasonably erected' by sheer military strength, 'without consent of Kingdome, People or Parliament'.[133]

Having fought for their liberty against the tyranny of Charles I, the people of England had thus been rewarded with a new form of slavery. By entitling his major pamphlet of February 1649 *Englands New Chains*

---

[129] See Underdown 1971, pp. 143–72 on the purge and pp. 173–207 on subsequent moves to execute the king and found the Commonwealth.
[130] See Lilburne *et al.* 1998.
[131] *Grand Case* 1649, p. 14. For the date of publication (22 June 1649) see Wallace 1964, p. 391.
[132] Lilburne 1964, pp. 165, 167. On the authorship and circumstances of composition see Aylmer 1975, p. 142.
[133] [Prynne] 1649, pp. 3, 13. For the attribution see Lamont 1963, pp. 187–8.

Discovered, John Lilburne registered his disgust as plainly as possible. Scarcely less violent was the language of the tracts written in support of summoning a new Parliament. Nathaniel Ward affirms in his *Discolliminium* that 'I believe, while the Parliament of England are the armies Servants, the People of England shall be very Slaves'.[134] William Prynne in his *Summary Reasons* even feels able to congratulate the late King Charles for his prophetic insight in seeing that the army would 'subject both King and People, Lawes and Liberties' and 'bring them into perpetuall slavery and bondage'.[135]

There can therefore be no duty to obey the new government. Edmund Hall puts the point as unambiguously as possible in his *Lazarus's Sores Licked*. The new regime owes its ascendancy to 'bare possession, without any right', which 'gives no true title to any power', and hence no basis for demanding allegiance.[136] Edward Gee goes even further in his *Exercitation Concerning Usurped Powers*, stressing that the people of England now have a positive duty of disobedience. The new government has come to power by sheer force in the manner of a conquering party usurping a lawfully established form of sovereignty.[137] But 'the right and title of Sovereignty is not built upon possession'; it can only be built 'upon the people's consent'.[138] Such 'violent intrusion into, and possession of the Seat of Authority gives no right to it, and consequently neither draws allegiance after it, nor evacuates it in relation to another'.[139] To yield obedience to such a conquering and usurping power is in consequence unlawful, and cannot be justified.[140]

Among supporters of the Rump, the initial response to these outbursts was in part a concessive one. They admitted that the new government was perhaps illegal in its origins, but argued that it ought nevertheless to be obeyed as a power ordained of God.[141] In the course of 1650, however, a much more positive line of defence emerged. A number of writers began to claim that, even though the government may have acquired its powers

[134] [Ward] 1650, p. 53. For the attribution see Wallace 1964, p. 398.
[135] [Prynne] 1649, p. 6.
[136] [Hall] 1650, p. 3. For the attribution see Wallace 1964, p. 401.
[137] [Gee] 1650, pp. 5–7, using the pretence that he is describing 'a nation in America'. For the attribution see Wallace 1964, pp. 394–5. For a yet more explicit reference to the new government as 'a conquering party' see *Grand Case* 1649, p. 7.
[138] [Gee] 1650, pp. 11–12.
[139] [Gee] 1650, p. 13. For the same claim see [Prynne] 1649, p. 12 and [Ward] 1650, p. 8.
[140] [Gee] 1650, p. 9. For the same conclusion see *Grand Case* 1649, pp. 7, 9 and [Prynne] 1649, p. 3.
[141] For the development of this argument see below, chapter 10 section II. See also Wallace 1968, pp. 43–7, 51–6.

The proper signification of liberty

only as a consequence of the army's victory, this ought not to be regarded as impugning either its legitimacy or its title to allegiance.

This suggestion appears to have originated with Anthony Ascham,[142] but was soon taken up in yet more forthright style by such publicists as George Wither and especially Marchamont Nedham in *The Case of the Commonwealth of England, Stated.*[143] The point on which these writers all agree is that conquest is simply one of the means (and historically the most usual means) by which political authority comes to be lawfully acquired.[144] Bodin and Grotius had already put forward this argument, as had a number of likeminded writers in England, including John Hayward, Alberico Gentili and Calybute Downing.[145] Nedham not only quotes both Bodin and Grotius,[146] but applies their doctrine (in defiance of common law sentiment)[147] directly to the history of England, claiming that William I and Henry VII both founded their dynasties on the right of conquest.[148]

It is thus a misconception, Nedham argues in his response to Gee's *Exercitation*, to suppose that 'only a call from the people' can 'constitute a lawful magistracy'.[149] This forgets that a king may 'by right of war lose his share and interest in authority and power, being conquered'. When this happens, 'the whole right of kingly authority' is 'by military decision resolved into the prevailing party'. This in turn means that 'what government soever it pleases them next to erect is as valid *de iure* as if it had the consent of the whole body of the people'.[150] 'For the sword creates a title for him or those that bear it, and installs them with a new majesty of empire, abolishing the old.'[151] As Richard Saunders summarised in the title of a sermon published shortly afterwards, 'plenary possession makes a lawful power'.[152]

---

[142] For Ascham's argument see below, chapter 9 section IV.
[143] For a biography of Nedham see Frank 1980. On the writing of *The Case* see Knachel 1969. On Nedham's changing political outlook see Worden 1994; on the question of his consistency see Worden 1995.
[144] For this claim see [Wither] 1650, p. 42; for the attribution see Wallace 1964, p. 401. See also Nedham 1969, pp. 15–29. A similarly forthright argument had earlier appeared in *The Constant Man's Character* 1650, pp. 64–70.
[145] See Sommerville 1986a; Sommerville 1986b, pp. 66–9; and Burgess 1992, pp. 82–6.
[146] Nedham 1969 cites Bodin (p. 32) and Grotius (p. 39).
[147] For common law hostility to conquest theory see Pocock 1957, pp. 42–55 and cf. Pocock 1987, pp. 293–305.
[148] Nedham 1969, pp. 25–9, 48–50. For further discussion of the use of historical arguments in the engagement controversy see below, chapter 8 section III.
[149] Nedham 1969, p. 37.   [150] Nedham 1969, p. 36; cf. also p. 40.   [151] Nedham 1969, p. 38.
[152] Saunders 1651. For the date of publication (28 July 1651) see Wallace 1964, p. 404.

V

It is against this background that Hobbes's analysis of political obligation in *Leviathan* needs to be understood.[153] I seek to develop this argument at greater length in chapters 9 and 10 below, although I now feel that my discussion assimilates Hobbes's analysis too closely to the defenders of *de facto* sovereignty.[154] There are important similarities, but this reading makes too little of the fact that, in the basic premises of his political theory, Hobbes stands closer to William Prynne, Edward Gee and other such enemies of the Rump than he does to such enthusiastic defenders of *de facto* powers as Anthony Ascham, Marchamont Nedham and their ilk. Hobbes agrees in the first place with the Parliamentarian writers that our natural condition is one of 'full and absolute Libertie in every Particular man'.[155] He likewise agrees that, because 'all men equally, are by Nature Free', there can be 'no Obligation on any man, which ariseth not from some Act of his own'.[156] He consequently agrees that conquest and victory can never in themselves yield any 'right of Dominion over the Vanquished' nor any obligation on the part of the conquered. When someone submits merely as a result of being made captive, their obedience will be due to the fact that they are 'kept in prison, or bonds' and cannot help themselves.[157] As we have seen, however, to be physically forced into submission in this way is, for Hobbes, to be in the condition not of a subject but a slave.[158] If, by contrast, a man's obligation is to be that of a true and conscientious subject, it is indispensable that his submission should take the form of an act of free consent. Right and obligation can never be derived simply from conquest or victory.[159]

The significance of Hobbes's intervention in the debates about the Commonwealth government is not best captured, therefore, by seeing him essentially as a defender of *de facto* powers. The importance of his argument stems rather from what the theorists of rhetoric would have called its dispositionally ironic character: familiar premises are adopted,

---

[153] This is not to deny that there are other contexts too. For valuable expansions of the argument see Burgess 1986 and Burgess 1990.

[154] This is also true, I now feel, of the discussions in Johnston 1986, p. 208 and Baumgold 1988, pp. 124–33.

[155] Hobbes 1996, ch. 21, p. 149.   [156] Hobbes 1996, ch. 21, p. 150.

[157] Hobbes 1996, ch. 20, p. 141.

[158] Hobbes 1996, ch. 27, p. 204 corroborates the point by saying that, although 'in all ages, unjust Actions have been authorised, by the force, and victories of those that have committed them', such actions have in all cases been unjust.

[159] See Hobbes 1996, Conclusion, p. 486 on the mistake of those who seek to 'justifie the War, by which their Power was at first gotten, and whereon (as they think) their Right dependeth'.

but they are then shown to yield surprising inferences.[160] Hobbes accepts the basic assumptions of the Rump's leading adversaries, but he seeks to show that the wrong conclusions have been drawn from them. Above all, he seeks to show that those who believe the government to be imposing a new form of bondage have simply failed to understand the proper signification of liberty.

In mounting this case, Hobbes develops two distinct lines of attack. The more general is aimed at the Levellers and other radical enemies of the new regime who, as he puts it, are clamouring for liberty and calling it their birthright.[161] Given his analysis of human freedom, Hobbes now feels able to dismiss their claims as totally confused. Suppose, he says, we take it that what these agitators are demanding is 'Liberty in the proper sense', that is, 'corporall Liberty' or 'freedome from chains, and prison'. Then it is 'very absurd for men to clamor as they doe' for this form of freedom, since they manifestly enjoy it already.[162] But suppose we instead take them to be calling for liberty in the sense of 'exemption from laws' – what Hobbes has been describing as the liberty of subjects. To ask for complete freedom in this sense is no less absurd. For this is to demand a return to the state of nature. But as Hobbes has already shown, to call for a return to this condition is to call in effect for our own servitude, since it is to ask for that form of unrestricted liberty 'by which all other men may be masters' of our goods and lives.[163]

Hobbes reserves his most detailed criticisms, however, for those who had been arguing about the rights of conquest. He mainly focuses on this issue in the Review and Conclusion of *Leviathan*, where he complains that 'divers English books lately printed' have made it evident that no one really understands 'what is Conquest' nor how it relates to the obligation of subjects.[164] But it is in chapter 20 that he first takes up the issue of 'Dominion acquired by Conquest, or Victory in war', and is thus led to examine the predicament of a man who, finding his sovereign vanquished, submits to his conqueror 'to avoyd the present stroke of death'.[165]

The first point that Hobbes makes about the liberty of a man in such a situation is that he is free to submit. If 'his life and corporall Libertie' are given to him 'on condition to be Subject to the Victor, he hath Libertie to

[160] Quintilian 1920–2, IX. II. 44–7, vol. 3, pp. 398–400.
[161] Hobbes 1996, ch. 21, pp. 147, 149. For evidence about the clamour for liberty see Lindley 1986.
[162] Hobbes 1996, ch. 21, p. 147.   [163] Hobbes 1996, ch. 21, p. 147.
[164] Hobbes 1996, Conclusion, pp. 484–5.   [165] Hobbes 1996, ch. 20, pp. 141.

accept the condition'.[166] Here in turn Hobbes has two claims to advance.
The first, which he takes for granted, is that such a man is free in the fundamental sense that nothing is stopping him. Although Hobbes observes
in his Conclusion that such impediments can certainly arise, the only instance he mentions is that of someone prevented from submitting through
being abroad at the time when his country is conquered.[167] Hobbes's
other and principal claim is that such a man is also free as a subject. He
is under no legal or moral obligation not to submit. This follows from
the fact that our obligations as subjects depend, as we have seen, upon
our sovereign's capacity to protect us. If our sovereign is conquered, we
lose any such protection and the commonwealth is thereby dissolved.
We thereupon cease to be subjects, and each of us is left 'at liberty to
protect himselfe by such courses as his own discretion shall suggest unto
him'.[168]

In his Review and Conclusion Hobbes clarifies and elaborates this
account of 'when it is that a man hath the liberty to submit'. He reiterates
that 'for him that hath no obligation to his former Soveraign but that of
an ordinary Subject', the moment arrives 'when the means of his life is
within the Guards and Garrisons of the Enemy'.[169] But he now adds the
topical observation that, if the man is not merely a subject but a soldier in
a civil war, the case becomes more complicated. 'He hath not the liberty
to submit to a new Power, as long as the old one keeps the field, and
giveth him means of subsistence.' Once that protection is lost, however,
he too is at liberty to 'seek his Protection wheresoever he has most hope
to have it; and may lawfully submit himself to his new Master'.[170]

The other point Hobbes makes specifically about the liberty of a man
in this predicament is also brought out in chapter 20, but is particularly
underlined in the Review and Conclusion. It is that such a man is not
merely free to submit; if he submits, he will also be acting freely. Here
again Hobbes has two claims to advance. The first and obvious one is
that such a man will be acting freely in the legal sense. He is clearly under
no legal obligation to submit, since his predicament is such that he has
no legal obligations at all. But Hobbes's chief claim – and the heart of
his eirenic reply to the enemies of the Commonwealth – is that such a
man will also be free according to the proper signification of the word.
If he submits, his act will be that of a free man voluntarily consenting to
a new sovereign power.

[166] Hobbes 1996, ch. 21, p. 154.   [167] Hobbes 1996, Conclusion, p. 486.
[168] Hobbes 1996, ch. 29, p. 230.   [169] Hobbes 1996, Conclusion, p. 484.
[170] Hobbes 1996, Conclusion, p. 485.

To see how Hobbes arrives at this central conclusion, we need only recall the conditions that would have to be met before it could properly be argued that such a man's freedom of action had been infringed. He would have to be physically tied or bound to submit in such a way that he could not forbear from submitting. As we have seen, this is of course a possible way of inducing obedience. It describes the manner in which a slave, someone 'not trusted with the libertie of his bodie', is forced into submission.[171] It is Hobbes's principal aim, however, to establish that this is not the position of the man who subjects himself to a conqueror in order to avoid imprisonment or death. The reason is that this describes the predicament of a man who, unlike the slave, is offered a condition of submission, and is thus at liberty to accept or refuse that condition 'if hee will'.[172] He is not forced to submit by being 'beaten, and taken'. On the contrary, he is presented with a clear choice, and accordingly acts freely in making it. He can either refuse to submit, or else he can agree to submit on condition that 'his life, and the liberty of his body is allowed him'.[173]

Hobbes's fundamental contention is thus that the man he is describing is someone who, far from being forced into subjection, freely consents to the terms of his submission and thereby enters into a covenant with a new sovereign.[174] 'Having liberty to submit to him, he consenteth, either by expresse words, or by other sufficient sign, to be his Subject.'[175] He may thus be said to 'contract with the Victor, promising Obedience, for Life and Liberty'.[176] Hobbes's reason for treating it as an error to suppose that plenary possession makes a lawful power is thus that 'it is not therefore the Victory, that giveth the right of Dominion over the Vanquished, but his own Covenant'.[177]

---

[171] Hobbes 1996, ch. 21, p. 154.   [172] Hobbes 1996, Conclusion, p. 485.

[173] Hobbes 1996, ch. 20, p. 141.

[174] Hobbes 1996, Conclusion, pp. 484–5. But if the man submits only on condition that his life and liberty are spared, this would appear to make the victorious sovereign a party to the covenant. This would be contrary to Hobbes's earlier contention (ch. 18, p. 122) that 'he which is made Soveraigne maketh no Covenant with his Subjects before-hand'. This raises no problems in the case of what Hobbes calls (ch. 17, p. 121) a 'Common-wealth by *Institution*', because the form taken by the Covenant in such cases is that each prospective subject agrees with everyone else who shall be sovereign. Ever since Pufendorf raised the doubt, however, critics have complained that Hobbes contradicts himself when he comes to what he calls (ch. 17, p. 121) 'a Common-wealth by *Acquisition*', and thus to the relationship of victor and vanquished. For there he explicitly states (ch. 20, p. 138) that those who covenant 'subject themselves, to him they are afraid of'. As Gauthier 1969, pp. 114–15 observes, however, Hobbes's consistency can be rescued if we interpret him as saying not that the conqueror covenants to allow life and liberty to those he has vanquished, but merely accepts their covenant by allowing them life and liberty while remaining free from any obligation to respect those terms.

[175] Hobbes 1996, Conclusion, p. 484.   [176] Hobbes 1996, Conclusion, p. 486.

[177] Hobbes 1996, ch. 20, p. 141.

In relating his theory of liberty to the debates about the legitimacy of the Commonwealth government, Hobbes appears to have acted with full self-consciousness. The best evidence lies in the fact that his conclusions are based not just on a clarification but on a revision of his earlier arguments. In *The Elements of Law* he still espouses the orthodox position he repudiates in *Leviathan*, contrasting the predicament of a man who 'submitteth to an Assaylant for feare of death' with that of someone who makes a 'Voluntary offer of Subjection'.[178] In *De Cive* his analysis is more ambiguous, and undoubtedly begins to shift in the direction later taken up in *Leviathan*.[179] But he still marks a distinction between states 'founded on contracts and on mutually given faith' and states 'acquired by power and natural force', and he still maintains that only in the former case can we say that the *civitas* has been 'founded on the consent of many men' who have 'willingly submitted themselves'.[180]

In *Leviathan*, by contrast, he unequivocally asserts that, when a man submits to a conqueror to avoid the present stroke of death, his act of submission is the willing act of a free man. As a result, he is able to make a novel and dramatic intervention in the arguments about conquest and allegiance. As we have seen, many enemies of the Rump had maintained that, because the new Commonwealth government was founded on conquest and usurpation, it lacked any basis in consent and condemned the people of England to a state of enslavement. Many of its defenders had retorted that, although the government was doubtless imposed without consent, the fact of its being founded on an act of conquest gave it a just title to be obeyed. By contrast with both these positions, Hobbes maintains that there is no need to invoke the supposed rights of conquerors to vindicate the present duty of allegiance. By deploying his distinctive analysis of liberty, he is able to insist that the concepts of conquest and consent are not in the least incompatible in the way that all parties to the debate had hitherto supposed.

This in turn enables Hobbes to draw the polemical conclusion in which he is clearly most interested. Since the act of submitting to a conqueror is based on consent and expressed in a covenant, a man who submits in this way cannot possibly be described as a slave, as the Levellers and the supporters of Parliament were both trying to insist. Rather he must be

---

[178] Hobbes 1969a, p. 127.

[179] See in particular Hobbes 1983a, VIII. I, p. 160, where he clearly states that conquest and consent are at least potentially compatible.

[180] Hobbes 1983a, VIII. I, p. 160 contrasts a *civitas* 'pactis & fide mutuo data ... inita est' with a *civitas* 'quae acquiritur potentia & viribus naturalibus', adding that only the *civitas* founded 'pactis & fide mutuo data' can be said to be based on the 'consensio' of men acting 'volentes'.

acknowledged to be a true subject with an absolute duty of obedience. This final conclusion is initially drawn at the end of the chapter on the liberty of subjects:

> If a Subject be taken prisoner in war; or his person, or his means of life be within the Guards of the enemy, and hath his life and corporall Libertie given him, on condition to be subject to the Victor, he hath Libertie to accept the condition; and having accepted it, is the subject of him that took him; because he had no other way to preserve himself.[181]

The suggestion that such a man has no obligation to obey, on the grounds that he has merely been compelled to submit out of fear, is scornfully dismissed at the end of the chapter on the dissolution of commonwealths as nothing more than a fraudulent pretence.[182] Finally, the same argument is triumphantly reiterated in the closing pages of the Review and Conclusion. A man who finds himself conquered is at liberty to 'submit himself to his new Master' and 'may do it lawfully, if hee will. If therefore he doe it, he is undoubtedly bound to be a true Subject: For a Contract lawfully made, cannot lawfully be broken.'[183]

---

[181] Hobbes 1996, ch. 21, p. 154.   [182] Hobbes 1996, ch. 29, p. 230.
[183] Hobbes 1996, Conclusion, p. 485.

8

History and ideology in the English revolution

I

Ideological arguments are commonly sustained by an appeal to the past, an appeal either to see precedents in history for new claims being advanced, or to see history itself as a development towards the point of view being advocated or denounced.[1] Perhaps the most influential example from British history of this prescriptive use of historical information is provided by the ideological arguments associated with the constitutional revolution of the seventeenth century. It was from a propagandist version of early English history that the 'whig' ideology associated with the Parliamentarians – the ideology of customary law, regulated monarchy and immemorial parliamentary right – drew its main evidence and strength.[2] The process by which this 'whig' interpretation of history was bequeathed to the eighteenth century has already been traced.[3] But it remains to analyse the various ways in which an awareness of the past became a politically relevant factor in the upheavals of the previous century. The acceptance of the whig view of early English history represented the triumph of one among several conflicting ideologies that had relied on the same historical support. And despite the resolution of the conflict by the widespread acceptance of the whig view, the whigs themselves were covertly influenced by the rival ideologies which their triumph might seem to have suppressed. It is the further investigation

---

This chapter is an abbreviated and extensively revised version of an article that originally appeared under the same title in *The Historical Journal* 8 (1965), pp. 151–78.

[1] The same ideology may of course draw on other sources, particularly on a society's less conscious reflections about its own structure. See Macpherson 1962 for a classic attempt to analyse this type of source.

[2] The classic study is Pocock 1957, now supplemented by Pocock 1987, pp. 255–387. But for contrasting analyses see Simpson 1973, Woolf 1990, Klein 1993. See also Burgess 1992; Cromartie 1995, pp. 11–29; Burgess 1996, pp. 165–208.

[3] Butterfield 1944. I assume familiarity in what follows with the ideological position which (following Butterfield) I label 'whig'.

of these historical and political commitments that will be attempted here.

II

The whig appeal to immemorial right was not without its own difficulties. The whig story contained an embarrassing anomaly in the fact
that the continuity of ancient liberties had evidently been rudely interrupted at the time of the Norman conquest in 1066. The need for the
whigs to dispose of this anomaly turned the question of the rights of
conquerors into the pivotal issue throughout the ensuing debate. The
Norman conquest was liable to appear at first blush as an obvious instance of legitimate rule founded on no better a title than the success
of military force. But the ingenuity of the whigs ensured that no such
inappropriate lessons about the uses of power were drawn. There came
in consequence to be enshrined in the accepted historiography a notable paradox: the whig interpretation of the Norman conquest – so
influential that it united in agreement the republican Algernon Sidney[4]
with the common lawyer Sir Edward Coke,[5] so important that it later
seemed to Sir William Blackstone[6] to reveal the cornerstone of English
liberties – depended on denying that any such conquest had ever taken
place.

The elaboration of this aspect of the whig historiography became a
preoccupation of English legal and political writers for over a century.[7]
The insistence of the Parliamentarians on the immemorial antiquity of
the House of Commons, together with their repudiation of any suggestion that the Norman conquest had brought about the destruction of Saxon laws and liberties, can be traced back into the reign of
Elizabeth[8] and forward into the eighteenth century.[9] As J. G. A. Pocock

---

[4] Sidney 1990, pp. 472–3 and pp. 491–3 denies that William the Conqueror abolished the laws of
the Saxons or their institutions of government.

[5] For Coke's formulation of the theory of continuity see Wilson 1777.

[6] Blackstone 1803, vol. 4, pp. 407–43 speaks of the 'gradual restoration of that antient constitution,
whereof our Saxon forefathers had been unjustly deprived'.

[7] On the evolution of historical scholarship see Douglas 1939 and Kliger 1952. On its ideological
implications see Hill 1958, pp. 50–122 and Pocock 1957. I disagree with Hill and Pocock on several
issues, but it will readily be seen how much I owe to their work.

[8] Elton 1955, p. 320 describes the imprisonment by the House of Commons in 1582 of Arthur Hall,
who had mocked their claim to be a 'new person in the Trinity', as 'perhaps the most significant
sign of the new spirit in parliament'.

[9] For example, it still seemed polemically worthwhile in 1714 to republish Sir John Fortescue's
Governance of England, originally written in the 1470s, and for the editor to underline in his Preface
the supremacy of the immemorial law. See Fortescue-Aland 1714, pp. i–lxxxii.

has observed, the 'unending denials' that the conquest 'had caused any
change in the essential character of the law' became the intellectual
backbone of the Parliamentarian revolution, and with the parliamentary triumph it came to be regarded as incontestable fact.[10]

Despite its tendentiousness, the whig interpretation was assured of its
success by the fact that it appealed to almost every shade of opinion.
No Parliamentarian could allow that William I had made a conquest
of England, since this would be to imply that the kings of England
had inherited an absolute form of sovereignty. But nor could any royalist
defend the legitimacy of conquest, since this would be to concede the right
of usurpers to allegiance, thereby leaving Charles I no case against Oliver
Cromwell.[11] What every Parliamentarian asserted, no royalist could
deny.[12] The attempt to construct a royalist counter-historiography was a
late and doomed development. It was to receive no systematic articulation until the 1680s, when the researches of Robert Brady, the staunchly
royalist Master of Gonville and Caius College, Cambridge, finally established that the origins of the Commons' writ could be traced no further
back than the feudal summonses of 1265. Even at that stage, however,
the promise of a royalist historiography was to be frustrated. Although
historically impeccable, Brady's conclusions gave comfort to the most
absolutist pretensions of the Stuart monarchy. The Parliamentarians'
bogus history thereby attained its final ascendancy, since any arguments
tending to absolutism were automatically outlawed with the conclusion
of the political revolution in 1688.[13]

This story, however, raises a further question – one that has remained unanswered in discussions about seventeenth-century historical
thought. As Christopher Hill phrases it, 'why did the Parliamentarians
find it necessary so regularly and consistently to attack a view which
nobody held?'[14] No royalist until late in the century made use of English

---

[10] Pocock 1957, p. 42.

[11] But in fact – and in spite of what is said in note 12 – my claim here is mistaken, as Wallace
1968, pp. 22–7 first pointed out: many royalists earlier in the century had made use of conquest
theory, including John Bramhall, John Maxwell and Griffith Williams. For further criticism of
my argument and additional evidence see Sommerville 1986a.

[12] Existing studies make an important mistake at this point in assuming that earlier royalists used
conquest arguments. Kliger 1952, p. 134 speaks of 'Royalists who urged that the monarch had
absolute power by title of conquest' but discusses only one, who did not do so. Hill 1958, pp. 61–3
and p. 87 picks up the error, but his own text remains misleading, and incorrect on Filmer. Pocock
1957, p. 54 corrects the mistake, but makes another in confusing the legitimists' with the *de facto*
theorists' use of the argument.

[13] Pocock 1951, pp. 202–3 discusses Brady and the political dangers inherent in his position after
1688.

[14] Hill 1958, p. 62n.

history to argue the rights of conquerors. Yet the leading anti-absolutist writers of the age continued to offer heated refutations of the conquest argument. John Locke still felt obliged to include in his *Second Treatise* a long chapter on the subject – an obligation that his editor has felt at a loss to explain.[15] In his *Discourses Concerning Government*, Algernon Sidney insisted on fathering on to Sir Robert Filmer the assertion (which Filmer had never made) that there had been a conquest, only in order to deny it.[16] The paradox remains. As Peter Laslett has expressed it, 'the English populist writers of the seventeenth century, including Milton, Locke and Sidney, all wrote as if the defenders of kingship and absolutism had argued from conquest, but in fact they did not'.[17]

To resolve the paradox, we first need to recognise that the historians I have cited arguably take too narrow a view of their theme. To say that the right of conquest was 'refuted times without number, but very seldom actually made'[18] is to oversimplify the structure of ideas within which the concept was employed. The debate between parliamentary and royalist history was only one of several divergent perspectives in which the significance of conquest was discussed. Most obviously, the question of what exactly happened at the time of the Norman invasion in 1066 was a subject of intense interest to the chroniclers and historians of medieval England, and these writers tended to take a very different view of those remote events.

Viewing the evidence in a less embattled spirit of enquiry, most of the chroniclers regard it as obvious that the English were conquered and subdued. As a result they tend to write in such a way as to undermine the twin pillars of the whig historiography. First of all, they generally accept that the coming of the Normans annulled the Saxon institutions of government, and that a new legal system was enforced by the will of William the Conqueror. Moreover, they deny that this process was in any way checked by the power of Parliament, since they can find no evidence that Parliament in its familiar form existed any earlier than the thirteenth or possibly the twelfth century. The presence of this strand of historical writing has tended to be overlooked. But the whigs themselves could scarcely have remained unaware of it: initially it took the form

---

[15] See Laslett's annotation in Locke 1988, p. 384n.
[16] Sidney 1990, pp. 220–1 discusses both Filmer and Hobbes. For Sidney's attack on conquest theory see Sidney 1990, pp. 32–3. For Filmer's views on conquest see Filmer 1991, pp. 12, 33–4, 48, 53–4.
[17] See Laslett's annotation in Locke 1988, p. 385n.   [18] Pocock 1957, p. 149.

of ignoring their version of early English history altogether, and later it developed into a self-conscious repudiation of it.

The later, self-conscious repudiation was chiefly the work of the eighteenth-century historians of the Scottish school, and above all of David Hume, John Robertson and John Millar. They treat the whig concept of the ancient constitution as a *locus classicus* of sociological in-eptitude in the analysis of a society. They maintain in particular that the attempt to foist the sophistications of representative democracy onto the age of the Anglo-Saxons reflects a failure of intellectual sympathy, while the attempt to insist on their continuity beyond the Norman conquest involves a failure of historical realism.[19] Hume is especially concerned to emphasise instead the 'complete subjection'[20] of the English in 1066, since he treats the conquest as the start of a new epoch, a point at which to mark off from each other two very different societies. The govern-ment of the Saxons, far from enshrining the liberties of the ancient constitution, was 'very little advanced beyond the rude state of nature'.[21] 'The pretended liberty of the times', Hume goes on, was no more than 'an incapacity of submitting to government'.[22] There was nothing at all distinctive about early English society. As Millar and Robertson likewise report, the Saxons acted 'with the same destructive spirit, which distin-guished the other barbarous nations'.[23] Millar also questions the whig contention that Saxon liberties survived the conquest by showing that no such liberties could ever have existed in so 'barren and rude'[24] an age, when most of the population were still 'either slaves, or tenants at will of their master'.[25] There was nothing in Saxon society or government in the least calculated 'to secure the liberty and the natural rights of mankind'.[26]

It was the Norman conquest itself, Hume declares, which for the first time 'put the people in a situation of receiving slowly, from abroad, the rudiments of science and cultivation'.[27] There can be no doubt, more-over, that the source of this change lay in a conquest 'entirely supported by arms' which rendered the invaders 'extremely absolute'.[28] William I 'totally subdued the natives' and 'pushed the rights of conquest' to 'the utmost extremity against them'.[29] Both Millar and Hume add that, although it is always possible to dispute about words, the conquest was a

---

[19] See Forbes 1954 and Forbes 1975.   [20] Hume 1826, vol. 1, p. 251.
[21] Hume 1826, vol. 3, p. 266.   [22] Hume 1826, vol. 3, p. 266.
[23] Robertson 1769, vol. 1, p. 197.   [24] Millar 1812, vol. 1, p. 6.   [25] Millar 1812, vol. 1, p. 376.
[26] Millar 1812, vol. 1, p. 376.   [27] Hume 1826, vol. 1, p. 204.
[28] Hume 1826, vol. 1, pp. 251, 99.   [29] Hume 1826, vol. 1, p. 251.

genuine one in the vital sense that it did not retain, but entirely changed, prevailing constitutional arrangements.[30]

It is true, however, that this form of sociological history was a much later development. The seventeenth-century chroniclers knew nothing of comparative history, and generally contented themselves with treating the Norman conquest as a brute historical fact. The best-known instance of this commitment can be found in Hobbes's *Behemoth*, his chronicle of the Long Parliament. Hobbes includes in the second of his four dialogues a consideration of 'the ground and originall of that Right' which the Lords and Commons were to 'pretend to' in the course of the civil wars.[31] Hobbes traces the source of existing constitutional arrangements mainly to the time of the Normans and their conquest of England. As he declares later in the work, 'King William the Conqueror had gotten into his hands by victory all the Land in England', as a result of which he was able to make such arrangements as he pleased.[32]

It has been supposed that Hobbes's treatment was unique, or at least exceptional, in seventeenth-century historical thought.[33] But in fact his views formed part of a well-marked and by no means particularly sophisticated historical tradition. Even the briefest chronicles of the period find space to mention that a conquest by 'a people fierce and valorous' took place in 1066. Far from confirming the existing system of land-holding, the invaders 'laid the foundation' for a new monarchy 'by changing laws, disinheriting of nobles, and bestowing the land revenues on the Normans'.[34] The supposed election of William I is dismissed as a 'pretence'.[35] William is said to have 'got his right by his Sword',[36] and it is variously pointed out that he 'behaved himself as a Conqueror indeed',[37] and that he 'practised the licentious power of an insolent Conqueror'.[38] As one chronicler confidently summarises, 'we all know' that 'the first *jus*, or right of his title' was 'by meer Conquest'.[39]

---

[30] Millar 1812, vol. 2, p. 9. Millar 1812, vol. 2, pp. 9–11 offers a historiography of the whig view. He is cautious about stating 'whether the accession of this monarch is to be considered in the light of a real conquest', but convinced of the 'considerable changes' it brought.

[31] Hobbes 1969b, p. 76.   [32] Hobbes 1969b, p. 119.   [33] See, for example, Hill 1958, p. 91.

[34] *Brief Chronology* (n.d.), single folio sheet.

[35] [Persons] 1655, p. 87. This text (as its publisher noted, p. 166) was a partial reissue of [Persons] 1594, to which Hayward 1603 had been a response.

[36] *True Portraiture* (n.d.), p. 13. Mendle 1995, pp. 166–8 assigns this text to Henry Parker.

[37] *True Portraiture* (n.d.), p. 17.   [38] Martyn 1615, p. 6.

[39] *The True Portraiture* (n.d.), p. 11. Christianson 1996, pp. 24–5, 34–6, 45–8, 52–6, 80–4 notes that John Selden speaks in similar terms in his *Titles of Honour* (1614), although in his *Historie of Tithes* (1618) he denies that William was a conqueror and argues that the Saxon code of law survived the alleged conquest in 1066.

William's status as a conqueror is said to be confirmed not merely by the fact that he ruled with a 'stiffe and rigorous hand',[40] as 'a Conqueror, with more Policie than by profitable Lawes',[41] but also by the fact that he abolished the existing constitution and system of government. The accounts of his rigour varied. Sir Richard Baker's *Chronicle* concedes that he used his conquest 'moderately'.[42] The *Breviary* attributed to Sir Walter Raleigh[43] similarly speaks of William's readiness to scrutinise existing laws, 'whereof some he abrogated, and some allowed'.[44] But most of the chroniclers offer a more direct (albeit innocent) challenge to the whig bastion of immemorial law at this point. Sir John Hayward's *The Lives of the III. Normans*, sometimes described as the first textbook on the conquest, gives a highly coloured account of the collapse of the ancient constitution in 1066.[45] The 'ancient lawes and policies of State were dashed to dust; all lay couched under the Conquerours sword, to bee newly fashioned by him, as should bee best fitting for his advantage'.[46] The histories of William Martyn and Lambert Wood offer similar accounts. According to Martyn in his *Historie* of 1615, William I became 'sole Lord and Soveraigne of each whole Kingdome', 'ruled it as a Conqueror', and 'erected sundrie Courts for the administration of his new Lawes'.[47] According to Wood in his *Florus Anglicanus*, published some forty years later, 'this King (which is the use for Conquerours to do) abolishing forthwith all the Customs of the English Nation, and the greatest part of their Laws, brought in immediately his own Countrey fashions'.[48]

None of these conclusions, however, leads the chroniclers to subscribe to the Leveller view that any legal system thus founded must be denounced as invalid, as nothing better than the will of a tyrant. William's original right may have been based on a 'pretence', but God none the less countenanced his rule and 'confirmed his off-spring in the Crown more than these Five hundred years'.[49] The author of the *Breviary* even suggests that the odium attaching to conquerors may have helped to

---

[40] [Hayward] 1613, p. 82. For the attribution see Douglas 1939, p. 149.

[41] Martyn 1615, p. 3.

[42] Baker 1643, p. 23. Powicke 1938, p. 260 describes this as 'the standard work' of its time on early English history. As London 1658 shows, the chronicles of Martyn and Baker remained popular in the 1650s.

[43] Raleigh 1693. But the attribution was doubted even at the time. Hearne 1885–1921, vol. 10, p. 198 remarks 'I do not look upon this Thing as Sir Walter Raleigh's'.

[44] Raleigh 1693, p. 57.

[45] For this description see Douglas 1946, p. 6. For a full analysis of Hayward's historical writings see Richardson 1998.

[46] [Hayward] 1613, p. 91.   [47] Martyn 1615, pp. 3–5.   [48] Wood 1657, p. 10.

[49] [Persons] 1655, p. 87.

obscure William I's signal merits. 'This name of Conquest (which ever imports Violence, and Misery) is of so harsh a sound, and so odious in nature, as a people subdued seldom gives the Conquerour his due, tho' never so worthy.'[50]

The Norman conquest was thus accepted as an act of absolute power, and as the basis for a new system of laws, by chroniclers through-out the seventeenth century. Even the triumph of the whig ideology and the rejection of Brady's history after 1688 did not immediately lead to the discrediting of their arguments. The anonymous *New History of the Succession*, published in 1690, lays particular emphasis on the conquest, and specifically targets Sir Henry Spelman for having cravenly retreated into arguing that William the Norman *non conquisivit* but rather *acquisivit* or purchased his right to the crown. No one doubted at the time, the author retorts, that William made himself 'King of the stout English by force, and Conqueror of them in War; which is far different from a Purchaser of the Nation; and consequently very opposite to Sir Henry Spelman's interpretation'.[51] Nor was this view an isolated phenomenon: a *Medulla Historiae Anglicanae* that went through three editions between 1679 and 1687 proclaims the same view of William as a conqueror who 'abrogated, for the most part, the ancient Laws of the Land';[52] a *Britanniae Speculum* of 1683 argues the same case.[53]

The contention that the Norman conquest was an act of absolute power was by no means loosely thrown off. The chroniclers underline their interpretation by the way in which they handle the other issue crucial to the whig interpretation, the dating of the origins of Parliament. It was essential to the anti-royalist case that the summoning of the entire Parliament, including the Commons, had been a right and custom time out of mind. Even those, like William Prynne,[54] who were inclined to dispute with the lawyers about the origins of the House of Commons agreed that the institution of Parliament itself must be immemorial. None of the chroniclers, however, exhibits much belief in any such theory of continuity. They all accept without question that Parliament was an invention of (at earliest) the twelfth century.

It is a remarkable fact that their treatment of this topic brings them close to the account given by the century's most learned commentator

[50] Raleigh 1693, p. 69.   [51] *New History* 1690, p. 32n.   [52] Howell 1687, p. 82.
[53] *Britanniae Speculum* 1683. The author attacks Hobbes in the preface and later cites Filmer with approval.
[54] Lamont 1963, pp. 177–80 discusses Prynne's *Plea for the Lords* in which Prynne makes use of Filmer's arguments to attack Coke.

on feudal society, Sir Henry Spelman. Spelman recognises 1066 as the starting-point of a new form of society and correlates the emergence of the modern Parliament (which he dates to the mid-thirteenth century) with the decay of feudalism in its pure form.[55] The chroniclers, without a tithe of Spelman's scholarship, arrive at very similar conclusions. Parliament, they agree, was simply a royal creation. This is Hayward's contention in 1613, copied almost word-for-word by Baker in 1643 and subsequently reiterated by Martyn and Wood. It was Henry I who 'devised' Parliament and 'ordered the manner and fashion' of it.[56] This was the first occasion of the 'convening of the several Orders, which is now called a Parliament'.[57] King Henry I 'first instituted the forme of the high Court of Parliament', since 'before his time, onely certaine of the Nobilitie and Prelats of the Realme were called to consultation about the most important affaires of the state'.[58]

Once again this is very similar to Hobbes's view in *Behemoth*. Just as Hobbes accepts the evidence for a conquest in 1066, so he questions the continuity of Parliament. 'I do not doubt', as he puts it, 'but that before the Conquest some discreet men, and known to be so by the King, were called by special Writ to be of the same Councell, though they were not lords; but that is nothing to the House of Commons.'[59] A Parliament in this full and proper sense never existed 'for ought that I know, till the beginning of the Raigne of Ed. I., or the latter end of the Raigne of Hen. III., immediatly after the misbehaviour of the Barons'.[60] Hobbes thus dates the emergence of the full Parliament to an even later time, thereby underlining his refusal to credit any theory of continuity. Again there is nothing *sui generis* about his argument;[61] again it is close to the views of the most popular chronicles of the time.

The conclusions of the chroniclers are obviously not grounded – as were Spelman's infinitely more learned investigations – on any knowledge of the comparative structures of feudal monarchies. They are simply based on recognising that 1066 represented a break in continuity and the coming of a new law. But this means that in one important detail the chroniclers are able to speak more accurately than Spelman himself. Spelman had still felt compelled to revert – anomalously enough, as we have seen – to the whig position of denying that there could ever have

---

55 Pocock 1957, pp. 108–14 discusses this aspect of Spelman's thought.
56 Martyn 1615, p. 23.   57 Wood 1657, p. 24.
58 [Hayward] 1613, pp. 283–4. His account is repeated word-for-word in Baker 1643, p. 40.
59 Hobbes 1969b, p. 77.   60 Hobbes 1969b, p. 77.
61 See, by contrast, Hill 1958, p. 91, who describes Hobbes as 'always *sui generis*' when discussing his views about English history.

been a 'real' conquest. He could visualise the origins of Parliament in the decline of feudalism, but never as the mere product of a monarch's will. It is a considerable irony that the chroniclers' lack of recognition of the issues at stake enabled them to reach a conclusion that was historically far more accurate.

The chroniclers thus brought down, with unintended violence, the twin pillars of the whig historiography. They made no denial of the conquest; they saw no continuity of Saxon institutions. And by thus failing to fall in with the whig interpretation, they silently wrote themselves into whig polemics. So long as they continued to accept the evidence for the conquest, it remained essential for the whigs to issue refutations to all possible readers. It was thus in the interests of absolutists and constitutionalists alike – as the writings of Filmer, Sidney and Locke sufficiently attest – to sink their other differences in converging on this point. It is a measure of the predominant influence of the whig ideology that their bogus history managed to displace disinterested historical enquiry so thoroughly that the continued existence of this alternative historical vision has itself been overlooked, even in works of modern scholarship.

III

Besides suppressing a number of historical narratives, the triumph of whig ideology helped to discredit two contrasting political groups whose spokesmen had drawn on the same body of historical evidence. One of these groups consisted of the Levellers and their allies, for whom the Norman conquest was at once the defining and the disastrous moment in the formation of the English legal system. The other group included a number of writers on the rights of *de facto* powers who anticipated, in effect, the ideological content of the later royalist historiography associated with Robert Brady.

The discussion of the Norman conquest in both these cases attained a new conceptual level. These writers no longer treat the historical evidence as carrying prescriptive force. They recognise instead that, as Hobbes was to put it, history can offer only 'examples of fact', never 'argument of Right'.[62] History still provides the framework for their political views, but only as a means of illustrating a number of arguments also capable of being more abstractly stated. The conquest remains

[62] Hobbes 1969b, p. 76.

important to these writers, however, in their accounts of both the rights of citizens and the obligations of the state. And in spite of the dogma that the whig denial of the conquest went virtually unchallenged, they all assume that a conquest must certainly have taken place.

This gives rise in the tracts of the Levellers to a political temper dramatically more radical than that of the Parliamentarians, although dependent on very much the same historical sources.[63] The Levellers use conquest theory as a means of denouncing all existing rule as an alien yoke laid on the English, and of proclaiming instead the natural rights of free subjects. Perhaps the classic instance of their invocation of an historical vocabulary to sustain this case is provided by Richard Overton in his *Remonstrance of Many Thousand Citizens* in 1646.[64] Due to the Norman conquest 'this Nation hath been held in bondage all along ever since'.[65] There was undoubtedly an 'unhappy conquest' in 1066 and 'Norman bondage' was its result.[66] The outcome was the arbitrary introduction of Norman laws and their 'litigious and vexatious way amongst us'.[67] The conquest is thus treated not merely as an unquestionable fact, but as the sullied source that effectively poisoned all subsequent government.[68]

The Levellers use this analysis to press home their demands for constitutional reform. The entire history of England since the conquest reveals that the English kings have been failing to derive their authority from its only legitimate source, 'the voluntary trust of the People'.[69] Even John Lilburne, the leading Leveller publicist, found himself criticised by his own supporters for excessive deference to the existing system of law. 'Magna Charta', William Walwyn admonished him, 'hath been more precious in your esteeme than it deserveth.'[70] History is relevant, Overton agrees, but only to denounce history. 'We remain under the Norman yoke of an unlawfull Power, from which wee ought to free our selves; and which yee ought not to maintaine upon us, but to abrogate.'[71] No government

---

[63] Little need be said of this here, since Hill 1958, pp. 75–82 provides a brilliant anatomy of the historical and rationalist elements in Leveller thought. See also Macpherson 1962, pp. 107–59. The fullest study is Brailsford 1961. Macpherson's analysis is convincingly challenged in Thomas 1972.

[64] See Overton 1933a, and for the attribution see Haller 1934, p. 111. For a discussion of other attributions see Zagorin 1954, p. 22n.

[65] Overton 1933a, p. 354.   [66] Overton 1933a, p. 369.   [67] Overton 1933a, p. 365.

[68] See Schenk 1948, pp. 67–9 on the widespread adoption of the same idea in radical news-sheets.

[69] Overton 1933a, p. 363.

[70] [Walwyn] 1933, p. 315. But Lilburne did use the conquest argument, although his views have usually been misleadingly assimilated to those of the common lawyers. Gibbs 1947, p. 131 assumes that Lilburne 'closely copied' Coke, but for a corrective see Brailsford 1961, pp. 96–142. For a valuable discussion of Lilburne's reliance on historical arguments see Seaberg 1981.

[71] Overton 1933a, p. 363. See also Overton 1933b for a restatement of the attack.

can be lawful until the marks of conquest have been washed away in an Agreement of the People.

The same historical vocabulary was employed to almost contradictory ends by the writers on *de facto* sovereignty. These theorists are less easy to identify as a self-conscious group or movement. They have indeed received almost no attention from historians, and will require proportionately more discussion here.[72] But they can be recognised by their use of conquest theory in the service of a distinctive argument about the concept of political power itself, an argument deployed above all in 1649–51 at the time of the controversy surrounding the oaths of 'engagement' demanded by the new Commonwealth government.

The defining commitment of these writers is that no government can hope to survive an examination of its original right to rule. This claim is emphatically made, for example, by Anthony Ascham, perhaps the most significant of these apologists for *de facto* power.[73] As he expresses it in his first treatise, his *Discourse* of 1648, the right to rule is 'a thing always doubtfull', and it 'would be ever disputable in all Kingdomes, if those Governours who are in possession should freely permit all men to examine their Titles'.[74] To put it more brutally – as Marchamont Nedham does in his *Case of the Commonwealth of England, Stated* in 1650 – 'the Power of the Sword Is, and Ever Hath Been, the Foundation of All Titles to Government'.[75] The history of every government since the time of Nimrod, the first politician, has been a history of conquest and subordination. But whereas the Levellers had used this claim to denounce all existing regimes, these theorists use it to insist that it would be pointless to look for the 'rightful' basis of any existing government.[76]

---

[72] But see now Wallace 1968, pp. 9–68; Gunn 1969, pp. 82–7; Tuck 1979, pp. 151–5; Burgess 1986.

[73] Ascham is the one member of the group who has received separate treatment. He is denounced in Coltman 1962, pp. 197–239 and is defended against Coltman in Wallace 1963. See also Zagorin 1954, pp. 64–7; Gunn 1969, pp. 82–7; Tuck 1979, pp. 123–4, 152–4. The present chapter considers only the historical elements in Ascham's thought. Chapter 9 examines his intellectual relations with Hobbes, while chapter 10 attempts to situate him more generally within the debates about *de facto* power in the early 1650s.

[74] Ascham 1648, p. 22. Re-issued in November 1649 with its title abbreviated and ten chapters added. See Ascham 1649c and cf. Wallace 1964, pp. 392–3. See also chapter 9 section III below.

[75] Nedham 1969, p. 15. Nedham had a proverbially chequered career as a pamphleteer, on which see Zagorin 1954, pp. 121–7; Frank 1980; Worden 1994. Nedham's numerous changes of front misled Kliger 1952, pp. 142–3 into assimilating his views to those of the anti-Normanists. I discuss Nedham further in chapters 9 and 10 below. As with Ascham, my aim in chapter 9 is to consider his use of Hobbes's theories, and in chapter 10 to situate him more generally within the debates about *de facto* power in the early 1650s.

[76] The doctrine they defend is thus stronger than that of a writer like Henry Ferne. Pocock 1957, pp. 149–50 maintains that Ferne uses the argument in the same way as Hobbes. But Ferne 1642, pp. 19–22 maintains that no right of conquest can be allowed against a legitimate ruler. It is this

History shows us that conquest is simply one of the most usual ways of acquiring political power. To appeal from the rights of conquerors to some higher right can never clarify the question of allegiance; it can only make it impossible to answer. As George Wither warns in his *Respublica Anglicana* of 1650, 'if this Plea therefore be admitted, no Government could lawfully have been obeyed' – a phrase strikingly echoed by Hobbes in *Leviathan*.[77] 'Few kingdomes in Europe', as the author of *The Exercitation Answered* agrees, 'have beene so begun, or indeed otherwise then by Conquest.'[78]

It is typical of these writers to dissemble the force of their scepticism under a cloak of conventional Christian obedience.[79] 'It is no part of our Christian Profession', as John Dury asserts in his *Considerations* of 1650, 'to become Judges of the great ones of this World, in respect of their Rights and pretentions to power.'[80] Even if 'the Sword or supreme power' is held by a usurper, the author of *The Exercitation Answered* agrees, this must still be regarded as 'truly the ordinance of God', for otherwise it could never have happened.[81] But their reliance on this providentialist vocabulary seems (as they would doubtless have wished) to have been overemphasised by their commentators.[82] It masks an essentially ratio- nalist conception of political obligation. To call for obedience to the powers that be is in effect to claim, as many of them put it, that there is a 'mutual relation of Protection and Allegiance' – another phrase strik- ingly echoed by Hobbes.[83] The point is strongly underlined by the anony- mous author of *Conscience Puzzel'd* in 1650. If a so-called legitimate power is conquered, and if its subjects are thereby rendered 'unable to maintain their former Government, and Governors, as the Governors to defend and protect their people', then 'we count it lawfull for a people to make the best conditions they can with the Conquerors, to desire protection

---

claim that the writers I am discussing attack. For example, Elcock 1651, p. 61 names Ferne as a holder of false principles of passive obedience.

[77] [Wither] 1650, p. 42; see also [Osborne] 1811, p. 157. Cf. Hobbes 1996, Conclusion, p. 486: 'there is scarce a Common-wealth in the world, whose beginnings can in conscience be justified'.

[78] *Exercitation Answered* 1650, p. 44 (*recte* p. 46).

[79] I have allowed this claim to stand, but the implicit accusation of deception now strikes me as unwarranted. More generally, my argument now seems to me to underestimate the theistic element in *de facto* theory. See State 1985 for a valuable critique along these lines.

[80] [Dury] 1650a, p. 11. See Batten 1944, pp. 213–22 for this attribution and a list of Dury's works.

[81] *Exercitation Answered* 1650, p. 30.

[82] Coltman 1962, p. 237, for example, speaks of Ascham as having a 'vision of man as a victim', which seems to me to ignore his preoccupation with calculations of advantage.

[83] *Discourse* 1650, p. 11. See also [Ascham] 1649b, p. 26 and Drew 1651, p. 23. Hobbes 1996, Conclusion, p. 491 similarly says of *Leviathan* that it was written 'without other designe, than to set before mens eyes the mutuall Relation between Protection and Obedience'.

from them, and promise subjection to them'.[84] This indeed is the only rule, Dury declares, 'agreeable to sense, to reason, and to Conscience'.[85] 'We must distinguish', John Rocket adds in his *Christian Subject* of 1651, 'betwixt what is humane, and what is divine' in God's ordinance.[86] As subjects we are committed to investigating whether our rulers are in fact maintaining 'those reciprocall acts of publike justice and protection, which are the fundamentall reason, of all such relative Obligations'.[87] The characteristic conclusion of these writers is thus that, although the right of governments to be obeyed may be based on the ordinance of God, the right of any particular government must be constituted and recognised by what Thomas White in his *Grounds of Obedience and Government* of 1655 calls 'the pure force of Rationality'.[88]

These writers invoke the evidence of history less as a form of proof than as a means of endorsing what one of them calls 'an everlasting Rule in politicks'.[89] As John Hall of Durham declares in his *Grounds and Reasons of Monarchy Considered* in 1650, historical evidence is useful only to prove 'matter of Fact', never to demonstrate 'matter of Right'[90] – yet another phrase soon to be echoed by Hobbes.[91] Many of these writers accordingly stop short at, or even retreat from, any specific mention of the Norman conquest. Prominent 'engagers' like Anthony Ascham and John Dury, as well as writers of the later 1650s like Richard Baxter and Thomas White, all discuss the rights of conquerors, but hardly ever refer to the most familiar instance from English history.[92] Ascham, for example, considers it sufficient to nod at history in passing. If one party's rights 'bee but one as good as anothers, then his is the best who hath possession: which generally is the strongest title that Princes have'.[93]

It is conceivable that some of these writers may have felt it prudent to exercise a certain caution in drawing such heterodox conclusions from English history. Henry Parker, for example, offers elaborate historical proofs of a conqueror's right and title to allegiance, but restricts his

---

[84] *Conscience Puzzel'd* 1650, p. 7.
[85] [Dury] 1650a, p. 13. Commentators have obscured a distinction between those who saw all power as a reflection of God's will and those who assumed that it was part of God's will that men should create their own political arrangements. See, for example, Zagorin 1954, p. 72. The first view, the substance of Jenkin 1651 and Carre 1651, does not begin to be a political argument, but the second recognises that there may sometimes be an argument about when not to submit.
[86] Rocket 1651, p. 74.
[87] [Dury] 1650b, p. 19. For this attribution see Batten 1944.
[88] White 1655, p. 122. A friend of Hobbes's, he dedicated his book to another, Kenelm Digby.
[89] Grey 1649, p. 40.   [90] Hall 1650, p. 27.
[91] Hobbes 1969b, p. 76: history yields no 'argument of Right, but onely examples of fact'.
[92] White 1655 (general remarks); Baxter 1994 (equivocal remarks, esp. pp. 35–7, 100–4).
[93] Ascham 1648, p. 23.

examples exclusively to ancient Roman history.[94] Samuel Eaton similarly begins his *Oath of Allegiance* in 1650 by admitting that 'the Kings Ancestors came by Conquest', but goes on to express the fear that the precedent may not be regarded as acceptable, and eventually decides 'nor dare I grant it'.[95]

Several of these writers, however, refer almost casually to the Norman conquest as a familiar instance of a still more familiar truth. As the author of *Englands Apology* points out, speaking of the recent alterations in government, 'if any be frighted at the change, as that which seems to be dangerous and unlawfull, and putting by the heire of the Crowne; I hope they are not ignorant, how many changes have been in England by the tyranny and usurpations of Kings, and of forraigne powers over us'.[96] John Rocket, seeking to defend the 'lawfulnesse of this present Authoritie' in *The Christian Subject*, similarly offers 'this Observation to any man that is but ordinarily read in our English Chronicles': that while 'the former power by which our Kings reigned, and under which our fore-fathers lived, was many times obtained by usurpation', everyone nevertheless 'yielded subjection, and swore allegiance' to them.[97] Similarly, a major assumption of Michael Hawke's *The Right of Dominion* of 1655 is 'that the Law of Armes, is above all Laws', and that all history corroborates the point.[98] Dominion is always 'first atchieved by valour, and Empires purchased by arms'. This is 'most apparent' in English history, in which power has followed 'the arms of the Romans, Saxons, Danes, Normans, and other particular forces'.[99]

When these writers seek to make good this principle, moreover, they sometimes emphasise the importance of 1066 as a leading illustration of their views about the nature of power. They leave no doubt that they regard the events of 1066 as a genuine conquest, and feel it important to stress the fact. As Francis Rous maintains in *The Lawfulness of Obeying the Present Government* in 1649, the Normans had 'no title at all by lineall descent and proximity of blood'. Although the nation 'doth yield subjection to their Lawes to this very day', their rule was founded on 'meere force without title of inheritance', since their first king, 'the Conqueror',

Parker 1651, p. 77. Mendle 1995 provides the best account of Parker's career. See also Jordan 1942, pp. 140–78, where Parker is credited (p. 173) with originating the 'modern' concept of sovereignty. His attitude to conquest theory is not discussed.
[95] Eaton 1650, p. 47.   [96] *Englands Apology* 1651, p. 33.   [97] Rocket 1651, pp. 108–9.
[98] Hawke 1655, ch. 7, chapter heading.
[99] Hawke 1655, pp. 42–3. Hawke has received no attention. He is unknown to the DNB, and Zagorin 1954, p. 93 was unable to discover anything about him. Yet he was an able and learned writer, who cites Ascham, de Moulin and Hobbes as well as a number of classical authorities.

undoubtedly 'came in by force'.[100] When Peter English, several years later, puts forward his first 'Assertion' in his *Survey of Policy* – 'Whether or not, is the power of the King absolute'[101] – he underscores the same point. 'The Conquerour came not to the Crown of England, by bloodright, but by meer Conquest, having the whole Kingdom of England against him.'[102] Marchamont Nedham provides a still more unequivocal formulation in his *Case of the Commonwealth*. Nedham undertakes to show 'that the power of the sword ever hath been the foundation of all titles to government in England both before and since the Norman Conquest'.[103] He refuses to accept the claims made for William I's right: 'he had none save a frivolous testamentary title'. Rather he 'established himself a title by conquest upon the destruction of King Harold and of the laws and liberties of the nation'.[104]

These conclusions, however, are not invoked – as they are by the Levellers – to repudiate the possibility of acquiring rights by usurpation or conquest.[105] Rather they are used to defend the rights of usurping powers against the claims of legitimists. When Ascham, for example, replies to the author of *The Grand Case of Conscience*, he criticises those who refuse to admit that 'the nature of politick justice of society and Religion is such that we may & ought to submit in obedience to those who plenarily possesse', claiming that they appear to have forgotten 'that there was ever such a man in England as William the Conquerour'.[106] We find the same attitude embodied soon afterwards in John Drew's tract entitled *The Northern Subscribers Plea, Vindicated*. Since the English freely allowed 'way or place to the Conquerour in England', it follows that 'if engaging in our case would be a participation in sinne, by consenting to, and establishing the change, theirs could not be without an accessarinesse'.[107] The same principle had in the meantime been more abstractly stated by Lewis de Moulin in *The Power of the Magistrate*. Not only does de Moulin argue that it is a just action to yield 'fealty or Homage to him that hath possession *de facto*, though not *de jure*'; he also points out that the whole of English history bears witness to this truth. The recognition of *de facto* power

---

[100] [Rous] 1649, pp. 46. On Rous see Zagorin 1954, pp. 67–8.
[101] English 1653, pp. 2–134.   [102] English 1653, p. 78.   [103] Nedham 1969, p. 25.
[104] Nedham 1969, p. 26.
[105] Several of these writers go out of their way to attack the Levellers. Nedham 1969, pp. 96–110 denounces them as licentious and unreasonable. The author of *Engagement Vindicated* 1650, p. 11 dismisses them as 'the dregges of the people'. [Osborne] 1811, p. 161 speaks of them as dangerously utopian.
[106] [Ascham] 1649b, p. 32. This tract has usually been ascribed to Francis Rous, but Wallace 1964, pp. 391–2 convincingly attributes it to Ascham.
[107] Drew 1651, p. 30.

'hath been always practised in England under all the Kings since the Conquest'. Despite the usurpation by the Normans, and despite the fact that 'they had no just title to the crown', the validity of their rule was never questioned.[108]

As J. G. A. Pocock has observed, the great objection to such a frank acceptance of the rights of conquerors was that it left the English constitution marked with an 'indelible stain' of absolute sovereignty.[109] It has been assumed that this was sufficient to forestall such arguments altogether. But the writers I am considering acknowledge the constitutional as well as the historical implications of their commitment. They explicitly accept that, in tracing the powers of the crown to the right of conquest, they are producing an argument in favour of absolutism.

The most celebrated formulation of this argument is owed to Hobbes in his *Dialogue* between the philosopher and the student of the common laws. Since the laws of England were originally 'assented to by submission made to the Conqueror here in England', they take the form of a *fiat* from an absolute power, a power which 'is all descended to our present king'.[110] Once again, it has been assumed that this acceptance of the implications of conquest theory must have been unique.[111] But similar views had been articulated by several theorists of *de facto* sovereignty long before Hobbes made these somewhat *ad hoc* remarks under the restored monarchy. Francis Osborne in his *Perswasive* of 1652 treats it as obvious that any conquest has the effect of conferring absolute power. He describes the Norman conquest as 'hitherto the fairest flower in the crowne of our Kings' until superseded by the more recent conquests of the army.[112] Like Hobbes, Osborne believes that an historical study of the recent wars may be helpful in teaching us to imitate our ancestors, 'who suffered the crown of England with more patience to be transferred from one strangers head to another'.[113] Osborne's conclusion was strongly reinforced a year later by Peter English in his *Survey of Policy*. 'We deny not but under the reigne of the Conquerour himself, Regall Government in England, was of a most absolute and arbitrary power.' He

---

[108] Moulin 1650, pp. 27–8. Lewis de Moulin (1606–80) was born in France, but was a graduate of both Oxford and Cambridge, and was (as his title-page says) 'History-reader of the University of Oxford'.

[109] Pocock 1957, p. 53.

[110] Hobbes 1840e, pp. 24, 21. On the *Dialogue* see Cromartie 1995, pp. 98–104.

[111] See, for example, Pocock 1957, p. 149, claiming that 'conquest struck few roots in royalist thought' and that 'for a systematic exposition of its meaning we must turn to so untypical and unpopular a thinker as Thomas Hobbes'.

[112] [Osborne] 1811, p. 158.   [113] [Osborne] 1811, p. 160.

even professes to believe – although he is unusually learned in historical citation – that 'very reason it-self teacheth the point: for he subdued England by strength of hand'.[114] By 1658 we find Peter Heylyn in his *Stumbling-Block of Disobedience and Rebellion* resting his entire demonstration of the claim that 'the power of making Laws' is 'properly and legally in the King alone' on a consideration of the Norman conquest. As Heylyn concludes, 'for the proof thereof, I shall thus proceed. When the Norman Conqueror first came in, as he wonne the Kingdom by the sword, so did he govern it by his power: His Sword was then the Scepter, and his will the Law.'[115]

The study of these writers on *de facto* power suggests two reflections of some historical importance. First of all, it is they who present us with a fully articulated and rationalist theory of sovereignty for the first time in the history of English political thought. Their acceptance of the right of conquest is no mere 'low level' articulation of a prejudice not found in the higher reaches of literacy, as Christopher Hill has suggested.[116] These were sophisticated writers, who had read and cited Machiavelli, Bodin and Grotius.[117] Moreover, they deploy their reading – especially their reading of Grotius[118] – in such a way as to fulfil exactly the threat that the whig apologists chiefly feared from the admission of conquest as a valid title to rule: the threat of 'the ill use the Champions of Absolutist Monarchy may be inclined to make of such a concession'.[119]

My other reflection is that these writers provide us with a means of throwing some light on the sources and ideological orientation of Hobbes's political thought. Hobbes has generally been treated as a figure of lonely heterodoxy, 'always *sui generis*' and increasingly 'the *bête noire* of his age'.[120] This understanding is due in large part to the methodology habitually employed by historians of ideas, who like to abstract major figures from their intellectual environment in such a way as to make them appear either representative or unique. But this approach seems to me historically misleading. As we have seen, Hobbes was neither the first

---

[114] English 1653, p. 77. English is unknown to the DNB, and has received no attention, but he is perhaps the most learned of all these writers.

[115] Heylyn 1658, p. 267. For Heylyn (1600–62) and for the attribution of this tract, see DNB.

[116] Hill 1958, p. 62n.

[117] The writers on the *ius gentium* may have provided an important source. They generally discuss the rights of conquerors, and when Filmer 1991, pp. 229–30 criticises the idea that supreme power can be acquired by victory in war he specifically refers to Grotius.

[118] Wallace 1968, pp. 32–8 was the first to stress that we encounter in these writers the earliest serious use of Grotius in English political thought.

[119] See Fortescue-Aland 1714, 'Preface', pp. i–lxxxii, and cf. Douglas 1939, p. 149n.

[120] Hill 1958, p. 91; Mintz 1962, p. vii.

nor the only political writer of the mid-seventeenth century to discuss
conquest as a means of acquiring political authority, nor was he the first
nor the only writer to draw absolutist lessons from the historiography.
He did not even provide the most original or systematic formulation of
the theory of *de facto* sovereignty. It is even open to us to suppose that
he may to some extent have adopted his conclusions from some of the
earlier writers I have singled out. His *Leviathan* of 1651 discusses conquest
only in general terms.[121] His *Behemoth*, with its account of the origins of
Parliament, remained unpublished until a pirated edition appeared in
1679, the year of his death.[122] And his *Dialogue*, in which he draws absolutist lessons from the historical evidence, was published only in 1681.[123]
The writers of a generation earlier had already made use of the same
historical vocabulary, in addition to sharing the rationalist assumptions
conventionally associated exclusively with Hobbes – a theme too large
to follow out here, but one that would repay some further research.[124]

IV

The defence of absolutism by means of conquest theory was attempted
only very occasionally in the latter part of the seventeenth century.[125]
Despite its bogus history, the contrasting whig ideology triumphed at
the very moment when the materials to undermine its historical foundations became fully available. For all his impeccable learning, Robert
Brady ended up as the hero only of the non-jurors.[126] Although absolutist attitudes were outlawed, however, they by no means disappeared.
By an extraordinary irony, the absolutist version of conquest theory
was covertly revived by the whigs themselves and took its place under

---

[121] Hobbes 1996, esp. pp. 484–6.   [122] Tönnies 1969b, pp. viii–ix.
[123] Macdonald and Hargreaves 1952, pp. 8–9.
[124] Nedham 1969, pp. 135–9 appeals to Hobbes's authority, and Hobbes is also cited and discussed
in Hall [of Richmond] 1654 and in Hawke 1655, both of whom echo some turns of phrase. As
Goldie 1991, p. 610 rightly remarks, Hall 1654 is 'extraordinarily faithful to Hobbes'. Tönnies
first spotted that Nedham published abstracts from Hobbes's *De Corpore Politico* in *Mercurius
Politicus*, the official newspaper he edited, in 1651. On this point see Tönnies 1969a, p. xi and cf.
chapter 9 section IV below. On Nedham as editor see Frank 1980, Worden 1994 and Worden
1995.
[125] But one encounters an enthusiastic defence – although never in print – in the writings of
Sir William Petty. See Petty 1927, vol. 1, pp. 16–21, a dialogue on Parliament in which Petty
accepts that William I ruled as a conqueror. See also Petty 1927, vol. 2, pp. 35–9, a commentary
on Hobbes's theory of sovereignty.
[126] See, for example, *British Liberty Asserted* 1714, p. 61, denouncing the non-juror George Harbin
for his reliance on Robert Brady, an historian 'refuted by Tyrrell and others in every thing
material'.

heavy camouflage within the eighteenth-century pantheon of Lockean liberalism.[127]

This intellectual sleight of hand seems to have passed off unnoticed by historians.[128] But the exposure of the stratagem can be traced to 1709,[129] the year in which the latter-day patriarchalist Charles Leslie launched his assault on the whig writer William Higden. Higden had published *A View of the English Constitution* in 1709, attempting to prove that 'the King, for the time being, hath, both by the Statute and Common Law, the Legislative Power of this Kingdom'.[130] Higden sought to substantiate this claim by means of a long disquisition on the succession to the English throne, arguing that 'the People of England always submitted, and took Oaths of Fidelity to the Thirteen Kings, who from the Conquest to Henry the VII. came to the Throne without Hereditary Titles, as well as to the Six Hereditary Kings, who Reigned in that Period'.[131] Higden's was a view that readily fitted into the ideological framework associated with the Glorious Revolution. His book went through four editions within six years, and his theory was taken up and elaborated by many prominent whigs, including Sir John Willes, one of the chief justices, and Benjamin Hoadly, the leader of the low church divines.

However, the opponents of the whigs did not fail to point to the monstrous irony underlying this defence of the rights of citizens – by the supposed liberals of the day – in terms of mere possession. Charles Leslie saw in Higden's account a covert elevation of the rights of conquest, and hence a solvent of all natural allegiances.[132] The implication, he warned, is to make rebellion 'an Injury only when it is little, and robs the King of a share', whereas 'if it takes all, it is no injury at all!'[133] Leslie later extended his campaign to include Hoadly as well as Higden

---

[127] On 'the triumph of *de facto* theory at 1688', see Kenyon 1977, pp. 21–34. It must be emphasised that in what follows I am far from wishing to adopt the suggestions of Strauss 1953 or Cox 1960 to the effect that Locke's political theory somehow covertly restates that of Hobbes. My whole point is that to insist on Hobbes as the inevitable point of departure is unhistorical.

[128] Except for the discussion in Douglas 1939, pp. 165–7 and Straka 1962. But see now Goldie 1980 for a comprehensive bibliographical study of the debate about allegiance sparked by the 1688 Revolution, and see also Thompson 1977.

[129] Or to 1689, when Ascham 1649c was anonymously re-issued as *A Seasonable Discourse*. See Goldie 1980, pp. 522–3.

[130] Higden 1709, p. 60. Hearne 1885–1921, vol. 2, p. 284 notes the publication and vol. 3, p. 93 its author's *Defence*. But Hearne is unsympathetic to Higden, because (as he says, vol. 2, p. 297) he 'resolves all into Possession'.

[131] Higden 1709, p. 1.

[132] Leslie replied anonymously to Hoadly in [Leslie] 1709a and [Leslie] 1709b; to Higden in [Leslie] 1709c; and to both of them in [Leslie] 1711. His authorship was immediately guessed. See Hearne 1885–1921, vol. 2, p. 297. On Leslie see Schochet 1975, esp. pp. 220–4.

[133] [Leslie] 1709c, p. 30.

in a dialogue optimistically entitled *The Finishing Stroke*. A Hottentot (an earlier incarnation of the noble savage) is innocently made to draw an unfavourable comparison between Hoadly's and Higden's schemes of government and no government at all. The crucial objection is put in a rhetorical question to Hoadly. 'Does not your Law turn with every Blast of Wind? Here are Two fighting for the Crown, the Law Stands by, and Waites the Success; and will Hang those that are Beaten, and recognise the Conquerour: And if the other Conquer him again, then the Law turns to his Side again.'[134]

A further irony, as the enemies of the whigs were not slow to observe, was that these arguments not only contradicted the vaunted principle of consent, but could also be traced to the writings of the philosopher most vilified by all good whigs – Thomas Hobbes. This was the opening shot fired by George Harbin in his folio of 1713, *The Hereditary Right of the Crown of England*, the most influential assault on the whigs to emerge from the controversy. Harbin claims to show, by an elucidation of the royal succession even more elaborate than Higden's, that the English monarchy has invariably rested on indefeasible hereditary right. This view was never challenged, he insists, until the subversive writings of the interregnum period produced by 'Thomas White *a Papist*, Dr Goodman, Baxter, Eaton, Ascham, Hobbes'.[135] 'The first Time that the Duty of Paying Allegiance to Powers in Possession began to be taught publickly in this Kingdom' was in the works of these 'Papists, Fanaticks, and Deists' whose heresies the whigs are attempting to revive.[136]

As Harbin had previously intimated, moreover, it was Hobbes with whom he chiefly associated this argument. On the title-page of his earlier attack on the whigs – his *English Constitution Fully Stated* – he had reproduced the passage from Thomas Tenison's *The Creed of Mr Hobbes Examined* in which Hobbes had been criticised for (amongst other things) allowing the right of conquest.[137] Harbin now insists on tracing this doctrine specifically to Hobbes, denouncing it at the same time as 'pernicious in its Consequences to all Nations'.[138] The same genealogy is traced by Charles Leslie, who declares that the original 'Assertors of the Pernicious Position' that 'Possession and Strength gives a title to Govern' were 'Hobbs, Owen, Baxter, Jenkins, etc.'[139] And in his denunciation of

[134] [Leslie] 1711, p. 132.
[135] [Harbin] 1713, p. 1, marginal gloss. Harbin's anonymity was the cause of a tragic muddle, on which see Douglas 1939, p. 167.
[136] [Harbin] 1713, p. 1.   [137] Tenison 1670, p. 4. See Mintz 1962, pp. 72–9.
[138] [Harbin] 1710, title-page, quoting Tenison 1670, p. 4. For the attribution see DNB.
[139] [Leslie] 1709c, p. 103.

Benjamin Hoadly for failing to see 'the Difference betwixt a Physical Power and a Legal Authority', Leslie simply exclaims 'this is Hobbs his State of Nature'.[140]

Of all these denunciations of the whigs, however, perhaps the most pointed was provoked by the publication of John Broughton's *Great Apostacy from Christianity* in 1718. Discussing the 'evil influence' of refusing to pay allegiance when due, Broughton cites with approval 'the late Dr Higden' and his claim that a subject's proper course of action is to maintain 'a strict Adherence to a Constitution, as it stands in Fact'.[141] This brought an immediate retort from the non-juring bishop George Smith, who savaged Broughton in *A Vindication of Lawful Authority* for having 'thought fit to revive this Monster' of 'Hobbism' in the discussion of allegiance.[142] The express aim of Smith's reply was to provide (in the words of his own subtitle) 'A Confutation of Hobbism in Politicks, as it is reviv'd by some Modern Doctors'.

The proponents of hereditary right were undoubtedly right to sense in the arguments used by Higden and his fellow whigs a strong whiff of Hobbesian thought. It would never of course have occurred to any of these modish whigs to refer to a writer with a reputation as old-fashioned and sinister as that of Hobbes. There is indeed nothing in what they say that would have necessitated a reading of Hobbes's own works. Under the guise of their constitutionalism, however, the parallels with the absolutist use of conquest theory are inescapable.

The disguise adopted by the whigs took the form of the claim that they were arguing in effect about tacit consent. The contention that all governments must be based on the consent of the governed had by then become axiomatic: it is 'so plain a Truth', according to Richard Venn, 'that it is not worth proving'.[143] When proof was offered, however, it was generally historical in character. It was 'a Fundamental of the Constitution under the Saxon Monarchy' that no monarch could rule without 'the Consent and Assent of the Lords Spiritual and Temporal, and the People of the Land'.[144] William the Norman thus came to the throne not by right of conquest but 'by virtue of his prior Parliamentary Title',[145] and 'founded his Right upon the Election of the People'.[146]

---

[140] [Leslie] 1709b, p. 22.   [141] Broughton 1718, pp. 142–3.
[142] [Smith] 1718, p. 4. For Smith (1693–1756) and for this attribution see DNB.
[143] Venn 1715, p. 18.   [144] *British Liberty Asserted* 1714, p. 5.
[145] *Parliamentary Right Maintain'd* 1714, p. 98. William III's title was held to be of the same kind. See also Venn 1715, p. 48.
[146] *Treason Unmask'd* 1713, p. 236.

As these writers recognise, however, they need to give an account of what it means to consent tacitly to government. One widely accepted answer (especially after James II's flight in 1688) was that the bounds of consent and the consequent duty of obedience are set by the capacity of our rulers to protect us. As Richard Venn explains, 'the care of the Nation being the true primary End, and first Design of Government itself; whenever a King does of himself relinquish the Care of the Nation, he does by a necessary Consequence relinquish the Government also, and so make void his own Right and Title'.[147] The basis, in other words, on which we are understood to give our consent is that we are being cared for and protected. As John Shute was later to explain, any doctrine opposed to the view that 'allegiance is only due for the sake of Protection' would be 'inconsistent with the happiness of Mankind'.[148]

This test, however, entailed a disquieting corollary. If the basis of allegiance is protection, then subjects will be justified in transferring their allegiance to any ruler better equipped than their existing government to care for them.[149] But this is simply to concede that subjects are bound to recognise the rights of conquerors. As John Shute puts it, 'since the Conqueror has Power to hinder them' from taking orders from anyone else, 'they for the sake of their own Preservation must be glad' to receive protection from him.[150] Several of Harbin's critics pause anxiously on the brink of this purely Hobbesian inference. 'Persons of great Reputation for their Learning and Integrity', as Richard Venn guardedly remarks, assure us that we ought not to inquire 'by what Right or Title a King ascends the Throne', since it is 'sufficient to constitute him the Object of their Obedience, that he has Possession'. But Venn only feels able to add that he finds 'considerable Probabilities' in this view.[151] Other critics, however, felt able to take the Hobbesian argument at a confident plunge. A summary of the conclusions to which this committed them can be found in John Shute's *Revolution and Anti-Revolution Principles Stated and Compared*. It is impossible, Shute concludes, to separate the right to govern from the power. On the one hand, an invader may have 'never so just a cause of War', but everyone will continue to support whatever authority 'retains the Power of Protecting them'. And on the other hand, a successful invader will find that everyone will 'think it their Duty to

---

[147] Venn 1715, p. 33.
[148] [Shute] 1714, p. 16. For Shute (1678–1734), see Robbins 1959, pp. 234–6.
[149] For the suggestion that this plunges a dagger into the heart of sovereigns, see the discussion of Hobbes's *Leviathan* in Jolley 1987.
[150] [Shute] 1714, pp. 11–12.   [151] Venn 1715, pp. 49, 53.

transfer their Allegiance to the Conqueror, tho' he had no just cause for making War'.[152]

The Norman conquest is thus invoked once again as the earliest and best example of a political truth to which the whole of English history is said to bear witness. Kings are owed allegiance not because of their right but because of their power to protect. Protection being 'the Cause of our Allegiance', as Chief Justice Willes proclaims, it must always be due 'to him that protects us; and not to him who is not able'.[153] It was thus entirely appropriate that 'Oaths of Fidelity were universally taken' to William the Conqueror 'after his Government was settled'.[154] Furthermore, it is not only clear that William created his own right to the succession, but that he possessed no other right. Any attempt, these writers agree, to trace an hereditary claim 'must be absolutely void in its own Nature'.[155] There is 'unquestionable Evidence of Duke William's having no Right to the Crown, but by the Sword'.[156] He was 'a stranger in blood' to the English crown; 'invasion by the Normans' broke up the established succession in the House of Egbert.[157] William was in short 'justly from his Victory and ensuing Fortunes stiled the Conqueror'.[158]

The irony was complete. Parliamentary right was sustained by an argument that, a generation earlier, would have been used to undermine it. The Parliamentarians who had stood for the rights of representative assemblies against absolute power succeeded in stealing and putting to work the arguments of their leading adversaries. The unfortunate Harbin found himself denounced for treason by the whigs for attempting to confute an argument associated above all with their greatest opponent, the infamous author of *Leviathan*, Thomas Hobbes.[159]

V

This chapter has attempted to present one case-history in the variety of uses of historical evidence. The uses in this instance were more complex and devious even than the protagonists themselves might have been

---

[152] [Shute] 1714, p. 21.
[153] [Willes] 1714, p. 45. For this attribution see Pargellis and Medley 1951, p. 76.
[154] Higden 1709, p. 2.   [155] [Willes] 1714, p. 20.
[156] *British Liberty Asserted* 1714, p. 14. See also [Shute] 1714, p. 59 for a similar denial.
[157] Asgill 1714, pp. 62, 64. John Asgill (1659–1738) wrote several such pieces, none of much value.
[158] *Treason Unmask'd* 1713, p. 235. These remarks are lifted without acknowledgement from *New History of the Succession* 1690, p. 32.
[159] The charge of treason was levelled by Asgill, Shute and the author of *Treason Unmask'd*, and in the preface to *British Liberty Asserted*.

ready to admit. The eventual acceptance of whig ideology was based on covert adaptations as well as suppressions of earlier and more complex structures of ideas. The resulting amalgam was extremely influential; but it can now be seen that the process was not without its casualties.

The most obvious casualty was the accurate investigation of the early English past. It so happened that the most ideologically acceptable version of the historical evidence was the least historically accurate. The whig interest in early English history was born of frankly propagandist needs. But the influence of whiggery became so pervasive that the partisan dismissal of the Norman conquest became enshrined in the accepted scholarly tradition. The error was manifest, but it has only been eradicated by the most polemical revisions of modern scholarship. Meanwhile the most popular histories all repeated with implicit faith the whig myth of an ancient constitution. The great exception, David Hume's *History*, was vilified at its first appearance and was later denounced by Macaulay himself.[160] Conversely, Macaulay viewed Henry Hallam with considerable esteem,[161] and Hallam's *View of the State of Europe* embodied the whig mythology in its most patriotic form.[162] According to Hallam the continuity of English liberty makes the constitutional history of England an 'object of superior interest' to that of other European nations. Although this continuity might appear to have been interrupted at 1066, English laws and liberties always survived, and 'became a tangible possession' once again with the grant of the Great Charter in 1215. The shocking view that the Charter merely sprang 'from the private ambition of a few selfish barons' can thus be dismissed with complete confidence.[163]

The same mythology received yet more formidable backing when Edward Freeman published his five enormous volumes on the Norman conquest some sixty years later.[164] Freeman uses his immense learning in effect to endorse the same whig propaganda. The intention of his entire account, the fullest ever conceived, is almost paradoxically to demonstrate that the Norman conquest was not after all a very significant event. 'I cannot too often repeat', he begins, 'for the saying is the very summing up of the whole history, that the Norman Conquest was not the wiping out of the constitution, the laws, the language, the national life of Englishmen'.[165] At the end of his last volume, in the chapter entitled 'The Political Results of the Conquest', he repeats once more that 'the

---

[160] For Macaulay on Hume see Macaulay 1866, vol. 5, p. 152.
[161] For Macaulay on Hallam see Macaulay 1866, vol. 5, pp. 162–6.
[162] On Hallam see Burrow 1981, pp. 30–5.   [163] Hallam 1819, vol. 2, pp. 375, 421, 447–55.
[164] On Freeman see Burrow 1981, pp. 193–228.   [165] Freeman 1867–76, vol. 1, p. 72.

final effect' of the conquest 'was to enable us to preserve more of the spirit and institutions of earlier times, to keep up a more unbroken continuity' with the ancient constitution of Saxon England.[166]

The other casualty of the whig hegemony proved to be nothing less than the submerging of any predominant rationalism in the English political tradition. This process itself embodied a notable irony, for while Sir Edward Coke's conception of immemorial right originally supplied the support for a revolutionary programme, its legacy proved to be a sceptical conservatism. History came to be seen as the embodiment of what is constitutionally proper, not to be questioned except at grave peril. This attitude was to become one of the most characteristic and influential voices in English political thought.[167] It was not to be Hobbes's view of history – as evidence to substantiate more abstract conclusions – but rather Sir Matthew Hale's reply to Hobbes – that we must hold fast to history itself – that went into the mainstream of the tradition. This has come to be regarded as pre-eminently the tradition of Edmund Burke. But Burke looked to Hale, and Hale looked to Coke, and so the tradition falls into place as one of the most potent legacies of the whig ideology.[168]

If we were to try, however, to trace the roots of English liberalism, we should hardly look for them in this whig attitude to political life. The insistence of Hobbes on human equality as the necessary point of departure, the insistence of the Levellers on a theory of natural rights as the appropriate political inference, the insistence of all the writers on sovereignty I have examined on some principle of utility as the proper measure of a government's value – these, the more systematically rationalist attitudes, are also the more recognisably liberal in temper.[169]

The whig ideology amounted neither to genuine history nor to systematic political theory. It was more like political propaganda in historical dress. Yet the whig mode of thought left the deepest mark not only on the theory and practice of politics but on the study of history itself. The great achievement of the whigs was to suppress or adapt the historical and theoretical views by which their own ideology might have been most severely damaged. This attempt to study the process may thus be said to endorse a familiar truism: the most accepted ideology is by no means always the one founded on the most acceptable evidence.

---

[166] Freeman 1867–76, vol. 5, p. 334.

[167] See Oakeshott 1962, pp. 111–36 for an eloquent restatement of the doctrine.

[168] For Burke's affinities with Hale see Pocock 1971, pp. 216–32. For Hale on Hobbes see Yale 1972 and Cromartie 1995, pp. 100–2.

[169] This claim is one of the themes of Macpherson 1962, esp. pp. 263–77.

9

The context of Hobbes's theory of political obligation

I

Two assumptions about the reception of Hobbes's political theory seem to be widely accepted.[1] The first is that the theory bore virtually no relationship to any other political ideas of its time.[2] It was 'an isolated phenomenon in English thought, without ancestry or posterity'.[3] The second is that it proved completely unacceptable. Hobbes's 'boldness and originality' provoked 'intense opposition',[4] so that 'no man of his time occupied such a lonely position in the world of thought'.[5] I want to suggest that both these claims stand in need of some reconsideration. One of my aims in presenting this argument will be to arrive at a more accurate picture of Hobbes's intellectual milieu. In particular, I shall argue that the intentions of his critics, as well as the ideological uses of his theory, have to some degree been misunderstood. But my main purpose is to suggest that a knowledge of Hobbes's intellectual milieu is not merely of historical but of exegetical significance for students of his thought. In particular, I shall argue that to recover the context in which his political theory was written is to be in a position to cast doubt on one prevailing interpretation of his theory of political obligation.

II

The belief that Hobbes was simply 'the *bête noire* of his age',[6] and made his impact 'almost entirely by rousing opposition'[7] appears to derive from

---

This chapter is a much altered and updated version of an article that originally appeared under the title 'The Ideological Context of Hobbes's Political Thought' in *The Historical Journal* 9 (1996), pp. 286–317.

[1] I have allowed this claim to stand, but the two assumptions I cite are nowadays much less widespread than when this chapter was originally written. For a nuanced and authoritative survey of Hobbes's reception see now Goldie 1991 and cf. also Parkin 1999.

[2] See, for example, Hill 1958, p. 91.   [3] Trevor-Roper 1957, p. 233.   [4] Mintz 1962, p. 155.

[5] Gooch 1915, p. 23.   [6] Mintz 1962, p. vii.   [7] Stephen 1961, p. 67.

placing too much emphasis on the fulminations of his many clerical adversaries. There is no doubt that Hobbes was particularly singled out for his originality, particularly denounced for his heterodoxy. But he also gained a serious and to some extent a sympathetic hearing as a philosopher of politics in his own time. As we shall see in detail in chapter 11, this was particularly true on the continent of Europe. By the end of the century we find Bayle saluting him in his *Dictionnaire* as 'one of the greatest minds of the seventeenth century'.[8] And within his own lifetime his political works were extensively translated,[9] were studied and discussed by a number of jurists,[10] and even began to acquire something of a popular following in Holland as well as France.[11] As Hobbes himself was fond of pointing out,[12] his influence 'beyond the seas' in his own lifetime was well-attested.[13]

Nor did Hobbes lack for a similar following in England. By the end of the century his works were beginning to be accepted as authoritative even by theorists of avowedly opposed temperament. He is hailed by Sir Peter Pett in *The Happy Future State of England* of 1688 as 'a great Enquirer into *humane Nature*' and Pett goes on to link him with Descartes as 'those two great Masters of Witt and Philosophy'.[14] Charles Blount similarly refers to him as 'the great Instructor of the most sensible Part of Mankind',[15] while even Shaftesbury acknowledges that 'Tom Hobbes I must confess a genius, and even an original among these latter leaders in philosophy'.[16]

This element of sympathetic as well as serious appraisal can be traced to the decade in which *Leviathan* was first published. As early as 1654, we find John Webster warning his readers in his *Academiarum Examen* against overrating ancient theories of statecraft, specifically on the grounds that 'our own Countreyman master Hobbs hath pieces of more exquisiteness, and profundity in that subject, than ever the Grecian wit was able to

---

[8] Bayle 1697, vol. 3, pp. 99–103: 'l'un des plus grans esprits du XVII. Siècle'.

[9] Charles Cotton translated *De Cive* into English (see Hobbes 1983b and for the attribution see Malcolm 2000); Samuel Sorbière and François du Verdus both translated it into French (see Hobbes 1649 and Hobbes 1660). Sorbière also made a French translation of *De Corpore Politico* (see Hobbes 1652).

[10] Pufendorf 1672, VII. I, pp. 862–70; VII. II, pp. 870–96; VII. VI, pp. 972–9; Beckman 1679, p. 7; Gundling 1706, pp. 16–17 (a discussion of *De Cive*); Textor 1916, vol. 2, pp. 9, 82.

[11] For Holland see Velthuysen 1651, p. 2; Court 1661 and for a discussion Blom 1995, pp. 101–28, 157–82. For France see Merlat 1685, pp. 219–22; Rothkrug 1965, pp. 116–30 (on Lartigne) and pp. 315–28.

[12] Hobbes 1840d, p. 435: 'as for his reputation beyond the seas, it fades not yet'.

[13] Sortais 1920–2, vol. 2, pp. 456–516.

[14] [Pett] 1688, pp. 21, 57. For the ascription, and a discussion, see Goldie 1984.

[15] Blount 1693, pp. 104–5.   [16] Shaftesbury 1900b, p. 414.

reach unto'.[17] John Selden and Francis Osborne, both of whom arguably reveal Hobbesian traits in their own political writings, can also be ranked amongst the earliest sympathetic students of Hobbes's political works. Selden is known to have sought Hobbes's acquaintance on the strength of reading *Leviathan*,[18] while Osborne speaks of Hobbes as one of those who have 'imbellished this doting Age'.[19] Similarly James Harrington, in working out his own political theory during the 1650s, treated Hobbes's *Leviathan* as the only serious rival to his own neo-classical conception of a balanced constitution.[20] And although, as he said himself, he could not accept the 'gothic' balance for which Hobbes had argued, he believed 'that Mr. Hobbes is and will in future ages be accounted the best writer, at this day, in the world'.[21]

   Hobbes's reputation amongst 'the solemn, the judicious' as John Eachard mockingly called them,[22] was conceded at the time even by his adversaries. It is clear, moreover, that what disturbed them was not merely the alarming content of Hobbes's doctrines but the no less alarming extent to which they seemed to be gaining in popularity. As early as October 1651 we find Henry Hammond writing to Matthew Wren to lament the fact that *Leviathan* 'takes infinitely among the looser sons of the Church'.[23] Within two years of its publication, Alexander Rosse claimed to be expecting to be denounced himself for denouncing so fashionable a work.[24] By 1657 George Lawson was noting how much *Leviathan* is 'judged to be a rational piece' by 'many Gentlemen' and by 'young Students in the Universities'.[25] By 1670 Thomas Tenison felt obliged to admit that 'there is certainly no man who hath any share of the Curiosity of this present Age' who remains 'unacquainted with his Name and Doctrine'.[26] Clarendon noted around the same time how readily Hobbes's reputation seemed to weather every storm, and how much his works continue 'to be esteem'd as well abroad as at home'.[27] By the time of his death Hobbes had grown 'so great in reputation', as John Whitehall irritably observed, that even apparently 'Wise and Prudent' men had come to accept his political views, which 'are daily undertaken to be defended'.[28]

   Doubtless Hobbes's opponents wished to emphasise the menace. But there is independent evidence of Hobbes's popularity. A catalogue of

[17] Webster 1654, p. 88.   [18] Aubrey 1898, vol. 1, p. 369.   [19] Osborne 1673, Sig. Pp, 6ʳ.
[20] For Harrington's critique of Hobbes see Fukuda 1997, pp. 75–90 and Skinner 1998, pp. 84–6.
[21] Harrington 1977, p. 423.
[22] [Eachard] 1673, The Author to the Reader, Sig. A, 4ᵛ. For the attribution see Ure 1958, p. x.
[23] 'Illustrations' 1850, p. 295.   [24] Rosse 1653, Sig. A, 4ᵛ.
[25] Lawson 1657, Sig. A, 2ᵛ. See Condren 1989 for Lawson and his critique of Hobbes.
[26] Tenison 1670, p. 2.   [27] Clarendon 1676, Sig. A, 3ʳ.   [28] Whitehall 1679, p. 3.

'the most vendible Books in England' which happens to survive for the year 1658 includes all his works on political theory, and shows him one of the most saleable of all the authors listed under 'Humane Learning', surpassed in the number of his entries only by Francis Bacon and Walter Raleigh.[29] The printing histories of his political works certainly bear this out.[30] By 1668, as Pepys noted in his *Diary*, *Leviathan* was 'so mightily called for' that he had to pay three times the original price to get a copy of it.[31] Ten years later, the figure of Hobbes in John Eachard's *Mr Hobbes's State of Nature Considered* is able to taunt his detractors with the reflection that, despite their fulminations, his works 'have sold very well, and have been generally read and admir'd'.[32]

The failure to stress this element of popularity has tended to give a misleading impression of the intentions of Hobbes's critics. They have been pictured as attacking a single source of heterodox opinion. Hobbes was attempting, we are told, 'to sweep away the whole structure of traditional sanctions', but this merely provoked 'a widespread re-assertion of accepted principles'.[33] This is not what his critics felt at the time. Rather they took themselves to be attacking the ablest presentation of a political outlook that was gaining dangerously in acceptability. To the more hysterical it even seemed possible to believe that 'most of the bad Principles of this Age are of no earlier a date then one very ill Book, are indeed but the spawn of the *Leviathan*'.[34] Certainly it was widely believed that 'Hobs his Leviathan hath corrupted the gentry of the nation'.[35] The fear that Hobbes had debauched a whole generation moved even his most statesmanlike critics. Richard Cumberland excused his long denunciation of Hobbes in his *De Legibus Naturae* of 1672 with the hope that his criticisms might go some way towards limiting the corrrupting influence of Hobbes's nefarious doctrines.[36] And even Clarendon, writing from the bitterness of his second exile, claimed to be able to trace 'many odious Opinions' back to *Leviathan*, 'the seed whereof was first sowed in that Book'.[37]

Other critics offered a different and perhaps more plausible explanation for the fact that, as Richard Baxter put it, Hobbes's works continued to be 'greedily sought and cryed up'.[38] As several commentators

---

[29] London 1658, Sig. T, 3^r to Sig. Z, 1^v.
[30] Macdonald and Hargreaves 1952, pp. 10–14, 16–22, 30–6, 76–7.
[31] Pepys 1970–83, vol. 9, p. 298.   [32] Eachard 1958, p. 14.   [33] Bowle 1969, pp. 13, 43.
[34] Wolseley 1672, Sig. A, 4^r.
[35] Clark 1891–1900, vol. 2, p. 472; cf. also vol. 2, p. 116.
[36] Cumberland 1672, 'Prolegomena', Sig. E, 1^v to Sig. E, 2^r. For Cumberland on Hobbes see Parkin 1999.
[37] Clarendon 1676, Sig. *, 3^r.   [38] Baxter 1680, p. 8.

explained, it was due to the scoffing and atheistic temper of the age that Hobbes's works had come to enjoy such an undeserved and dangerous popularity.[39] This was Gilbert Burnet's judgement on Hobbes in his *History of My Own Time*,[40] as well as Francis Atterbury's diagnosis when he came to reflect, a generation later, on Hobbes's malign influence.[41] The same point had already been made by several earlier adversaries. According to John Eachard, Hobbes's rudest and shrewdest critic, the age had thrown up so many people 'who were sturdy, resolved Practicants in *Hobbianism*' that they 'would most certainly have been so, had there never been any such man as *Mr. Hobbs* in the World'.[42] William Lucy summed up the general feeling in his attack on *Leviathan* in 1657:

This book I find admir'd by many Gentlemen of sharp wits, and lovers of learning; the reason I attribute first to the *Genius* that governs this age, in which all learning, with Religion, hath suffered a change, and men are apt to entertain new opinions in any Science, although for the worse, of which sort are Mr. Hobbs his writings.[43]

For these critics, Hobbes may not have been the sole cause, but he was certainly the leading symptom, of the increasingly sceptical and rationalist temper of the times.

The point on which all Hobbes's opponents agreed was that it was not merely Hobbes but the new and spreading malaise of 'hobbism' that needed to be counteracted. It is true that 'hobbism' was often applied as little more than a general epithet of alarm and abuse. The hobbist villain became a stock character on the Restoration stage: Vizard in *The Constant Couple*, for example, comes on reading what appears to be *The Practice of Piety*, but is in fact *Leviathan* under plain cover.[44] The term 'hobbism' in such contexts generally signified little more than a 'wild, Atheistically disposed' attitude to the powers that be, as one critic put it,[45] together with a presumed desire to 'subvert our Laws and Liberties, and set up Arbitrary Power'.[46] But the term was also used to describe a more specific moral and political outlook. When Isaac Newton, for example, confessed to John Locke that 'I took you for a Hobbist', it is evident that both of them attached a clear meaning to the charge, as

---

[39] For examples see Syfret 1950, pp. 235-8.   [40] Burnet 1897-1900, vol. 1, p. 334.
[41] Atterbury 1723, p. 66.
[42] [Eachard] 1673, 'The Author to the Reader', Sig. A, 3ᵛ.
[43] [Lucy] 1657, Sig. A, 3ᵛ. The text is signed 'William Pike', but Lucy himself supplies the attribution in Lucy 1663, his further and fuller attack on *Leviathan*.
[44] Farquhar 1700, p. 2. See Teeter 1936.   [45] *Sober Enquiry* 1673, p. 51.
[46] Crowne 1683, p. 49.

well as regarding it as a grave accusation, one for which Newton was subsequently anxious to apologise.[47]

When the term was applied in this way, it was generally used to refer to two specific doctrines. One was a view about moral and political obligation. The hobbist was recognised as someone for whom the duty to obey an established government derives not from religious sanctions, but merely from calculations of individual self-interest. To be a hobbist was to assume that everyone is concerned above all with their own self-preservation and to be willing in consequence to obey any power capable of affording them protection. As one anonymous critic complained, not only do 'the Hobbeans vainly fancy' that God has left it 'arbitrary to man' to institute political societies.[48] They also fancy that these societies should be governed 'according to the Principles of Equality and Self-preservation agreed to by the Hobbists'.[49] These are the terms in which John Locke in his *Essay Concerning Human Understanding* contrasts a hobbist with a Christian sense of obligation. The hobbist, as Locke puts it, justifies the keeping of compacts and promises not by saying 'because God, who has the Power of eternal Life and Death, requires it of us', but 'because the Publick requires it, and the *Leviathan* will punish you, if you do not'.[50] As Locke was to confide in his commonplace book in 1676, 'a Hobbist, with his principle of self-preservation, whereof himself is to be judge, will not easily admit a great many plain duties of morality'.[51]

The other doctrine regarded by contemporaries as distinctively hobbist was described by one critic as a particular 'scheme of human nature'.[52] To be a hobbist was to regard mankind as basically antisocial, and to believe that we are 'compelled into Society meerly for the advantages and necessities of life'.[53] According to the hobbists, as Shaftesbury sardonically remarked, the state of nature is peopled by 'dragons, leviathans, and I know not what devouring creatures'.[54] This view of our natural condition as equivalent to 'a State of War' passed into general currency as a typically hobbist belief.[55] In 1673, for example, John Dryden was censured for representing mankind in one of his plays 'in a Hobbian State of War'.[56] In 1691 William Sherlock upheld the right to change allegiance when a ruler becomes incapable of governing on the grounds that society would otherwise 'dissolve into a Mob,

---

[47] Newton 1961, p. 280.   [48] *Letter to a Friend* 1679, p. 6.   [49] *Great Law of Nature* 1673, p. 8.
[50] Locke 1979, I. III. 5, p. 68.   [51] King 1830, vol. 1, p. 191; Locke 1997, p. 371.
[52] *Animadversions* 1691, p. 16.   [53] *Confusion Confounded* 1654, p. 9.
[54] Shaftesbury 1900a, vol. 2, p. 83.   [55] *The Parallel* 1682, p. 12.
[56] *Censure of the Rota* 1673, p. 3.

or Mr. Hobbs's state of Nature'.[57] By 1694, James Lowde felt obliged to admit in his *Discourse Concerning the Nature of Man* that to write about the natural sociability of mankind might be thought old-fashioned, since the assumption was so much at odds with the views of learned persons, among whom he specifically mentions Hobbes.[58] Similarly, the whig writers on political obligation – Locke, Sidney, Tyrrell, Mead – frequently allude to the fact that 'some Men' (as Locke darkly puts it), and especially Hobbes (as the others mention) have popularised the view that man's condition without government would be a *bellum omnium contra omnes*.[59]

The extent to which these hobbist views were current in late seventeenth-century England has tended to be underestimated. When, for example, S. P. Lamprecht published his survey of 'Hobbes and Hobbism', he spoke of finding only one 'favourable' as opposed to fifty-one 'hostile' reactions to Hobbes's political theory during Hobbes's own lifetime.[60] It is clear that a good deal of information has been missed here. As I shall next seek to show, a considerable group of political writers, all contemporary with Hobbes, adopted precisely the so-called hobbist views that so disquieted Hobbes's more conventional critics. Moreover, several of these writers explicitly relied on Hobbes's authority in setting out their hobbist views, especially on the topic of political obligation.

III

The problem of political obligation became a major issue at two moments in the constitutional upheavals of the seventeenth century. The first was in 1649, immediately after the execution of Charles I and the establishment of the Commonwealth. The second was in 1689, immediately after the removal of James II and the acceptance of William and Mary. At both these junctures the new government raised the issue in an acute form by requiring oaths of allegiance to be sworn to its authority. This made the question of the grounds on which it might be appropriate to swear or withhold allegiance an inevitable topic of debate.

One suggested answer, put forward in 1649 and again in 1689, was that everyone should regard themselves as politically obliged on the

---

[57] [Sherlock] 1691a, p. 38. Locke quotes this remark in the commentary he wrote on Sherlock's book. See Locke 1997, p. 314.

[58] Lowde 1694, Sig. A, 5^r and Sig. A, 6^v.

[59] Locke 1988, II. 19, p. 280; Sidney 1990, pp. 55–6, 432; [Tyrrell] 1692–4, p. 777 (where he appears to agree); Mead 1689, Sig. B, 3^v–4^r.

[60] Lamprecht 1940, p. 32.

grounds that the new government was based on accepting the people's ultimate sovereign power, and stemmed from the removal of a ruler who had tyrannously sought to deny their rights. This was the direction of John Milton's thinking in his *Tenure of Kings and Magistrates* in 1649, and of John Locke's in his *Two Treatises of Government* in 1690. But a second and contrasting answer, also put forward in 1649 and 1689, claimed that the new government should be obeyed even if it could not be shown to reflect the will of the people or to have been rightfully instituted. This reaction has been much less studied, but was arguably of more importance at the time, since the adoption of the first answer – grounding political obligation on a theory of natural rights – was a sophisticated as well as a radical step to take in a society so widely committed to the belief that all political power is directly ordained by God.

The second suggestion was in turn defended in two different ways. One consisted of placing a strong emphasis on the providential origins of every kind of regime. The Pauline injunction to obey 'the powers that be' was taken to include all successfully constituted political authorities, whether or not they could be shown to possess a just or even a legal title to rule. Their title was taken to lie simply in their capacity to govern, for this capacity, it was said, must reflect the will and hence be the gift of God. The credit for originating this ingenious compromise between passive obedience and revolutionary change appears to be due to Francis Rous, a leading presbyterian member of the Long Parliament who went over to the independent party in 1649.[61] Rous's brief tract of April 1649, *The Lawfulness of Obeying the Present Government*, presents exactly this argument, and was followed by an extensive pamphlet literature devoted to examining whether or not one could in conscience swear allegiance to the new Commonwealth regime.[62] The revival of the same argument after 1689 was mainly the work of William Sherlock, the Dean of St Paul's, whose *Case of the Allegiance Due to Soveraign Powers* was published in 1691 in order to justify his decision, in common with many other clergymen, to take the new oaths of allegiance 'after so long a Refusal'. This too gave rise to an extensive pamphlet war, in which the merits of *de facto* theories of obligation were again debated at length.

This providentialist defence of *de facto* power was one of the arguments claimed to be hobbist in character. The accusation was acutely embarrassing, especially to Sherlock and his clerical supporters, and Sherlock

---

[61] Rous's contribution to the debate about *de facto* powers is discussed more fully in chapter 10 below.

[62] See Wallace 1964, p. 390 for Rous's tract and pp. 390–405 for the ensuing pamphlet war.

himself took some pains to counter it. As he admits, some claim 'that it is Hobbism' to defend the right of possessors to be obeyed.[63] But this calumny, he insists, can readily be answered:

Those who say this do not understand Mr. Hobbs, or me: for He makes Power, and nothing else, to give Right to Dominion; and therefore asserts, That God himself is the Natural Lord and Governour of the World, not because He made it; but because he is Omnipotent; but I say, That Government is founded in Right, and that God is the Natural Lord of the World, because He made it.[64]

Sherlock addressed the issue still more directly in a further pamphlet published later in the same year, in which he not only declared that 'their present majesties government' is 'thoroughly settled', but that 'we may submit to it, without asserting the principles of Mr. Hobbs'.[65]

Such disclaimers did not prevent the 'engagers' of the 1650s or the *de facto* theorists of the 1690s from being energetically charged with hobbism by their enemies. Sherlock and his followers may tell us, it was said, that they are endorsing the principles of the Church of England, but in fact they are reviving arguments from 'the Rebels in the Year '42 and from the Advocates of Cromwel's Usurpation'.[66] They may claim to be corroborating the doctrine of obligation found in the *Convocation Book*, but that text offers them 'but little service', whereas there are 'other Writings that would have done the trick to an hair, such as Hobs, Baxter, Owens, and Jenkins, etc.'.[67] Hobbes, moreover, is seen as the determining influence. Several of the assaults on Sherlock ('the Doctor' to his more sarcastic opponents) seek to establish by textual parallels that, long before the Doctor's time, 'Mr. Hobbes hath taught the same'. 'The question', as one critic puts it, 'is whether Mr. Hobbes and the Doctor teach not the same doctrine' about the legal right and possession of sovereignty, and the transferring of allegiance to usurpers? The answer is that, on the question of political obligation, Hobbes and Sherlock are '*fratres fratrerrimi*, and it is not within the power of metaphysics to distinguish them'.[68] A similar comparison was mounted by another critic who claimed to show that 'Mr. Hobbs makes Power, and nothing else, give Right to Dominion. And pray does not the Doctor do the same? I am much mistaken if this be not the design of his Whole Book.'[69] A more

[63] [Sherlock] 1691a, p. 15.   [64] [Sherlock] 1691a, p. 15.
[65] This is the full title of [Sherlock] 1691b. For the attribution see Goldie 1980, p. 558.
[66] *Answer* 1691, p. 1.
[67] [Richardson] 1691, pp. 4–5. For the attribution see Goldie 1980, p. 555.
[68] *Examination* 1691, pp. 14, 15.
[69] *Dr. Sherlock's Case of Allegiance* 1691, p. 73; cf. also pp. 80–2 for alleged parallels with *Leviathan*.

cynical critic concluded that Hobbes's principles had actually been sur-passed. For while 'Mr. Hobbes taught the Absolute Power of all Princes, only as a Philosopher, upon Principles of mere Reason', these latter-day hobbists 'by Adding the authority of Scripture' make themselves 'sure of as profitable an Office in the State'.[70]

Given that Sherlock was reviving the providentialist arguments orig-inally put forward by Francis Rous, it was manifestly unfair – although polemically irresistible – to press the charge of hobbism so vehemently. But there was another group of writers who developed a more authenti-cally hobbist line of thought, especially in the aftermath of the regicide of 1649, and it is on this group that I now wish to concentrate. According to these writers, submission is owed to any powers that be – including merely *de facto* powers – on the grounds of self-interest. The consequence of refusing allegiance to any government capable of protecting us will always be worse than the apparent inconvenience of ceding our rights to that government. The capacity of any government, regardless of its title to rule, to offer such protection is accordingly taken to be a sufficient reason for paying it allegiance. This was the rationalist and utilitarian form of *de facto* theory regarded by contemporaries both as Hobbes's own view of political obligation and as the view of a genuinely hobbist following.

It is true that the list of theorists who espoused this view, and thought of themselves as followers of Hobbes, is short and contains no writer of the first rank. But the only way to compile such a list is on the basis of direct quotation and sympathetic discussion of Hobbes's political works. It needs to be recognised at the outset that these are particularly rigor-ous tests to apply to the conventions of seventeenth-century debate. The trend of the times was towards informality, even anonymity. Hobbes was not much cited, but nor was any other contemporary political writer. The fashion was to treat too much quotation as slavish, too much read-ing as a waste of time. Hobbes himself boasted to Aubrey that 'if he had read as much as other men, he should have knowne no more then other men'.[71] Francis Osborne similarly argued that 'pregnant wits stifle their own natural fertility through a too long and frequent commerce with Books', and ridiculed the habit of constantly deferring to supposed authorities.[72] John Selden laid it down as a maxim that 'in quoting of Books' you should cite only 'such Authors as are usually read', advis-ing that 'others you may read for your own Satisfaction, but not name

---

[70] *Dr Sherlock's Two Kings* 1691, p. 13.   [71] Aubrey 1898, vol. 1, p. 349.
[72] Osborne 1673, p. 582.

them'.[73] Another of Hobbes's friends, Sir William Petty, offered similar advice in a hyperbolical letter of 1653 to Robert Boyle. Not only does he warn Boyle against 'continual reading', which 'weakens the brain', but roundly informs him that, if he occupies himself with contemporary scribblers, he will merely be 'corrupted with lies, disgusted with absurdities, and tired with impertinencies'.[74]

It seems likely, moreover, that even among those who may have felt Hobbes to be worthy of citing as an authority, the number may have been further diminished by considerations about Hobbes's dangerous reputation. A man who had been named in Parliament as the author of works that 'tend to Atheism, Blasphemy, or Profaneness' was not a writer to cite without good cause as an authority on anything.[75] This type of suppression is of course impossible to prove. But it was regarded at the time as beyond dispute that, among prudent writers who would 'scarce simper in favour or allowance' for Hobbes, there were many who were none the less hobbists for that.[76] It is certainly clear that in seventeenth-century England there were political opinions that one might entertain, even discuss, but much prefer not to see printed. Some argued that Hobbes himself had acted too boldly in publishing doctrines which 'though he thought them to be true' were 'too dangerous to be spoken aloud'.[77] There are several signs that those who sympathised with Hobbes's views felt able to say so more readily in private than in published form. We find 'Hobbism' anatomised without commentary only in personal commonplace books.[78] William Rand is one example of an early reader of *Leviathan* who confessed his admiration for Hobbes in glowing terms, but only in the pages of his private correspondence.[79] Sir William Petty provides another example of a contemporary who quoted Hobbes in his private memoranda and singled him out as a leading writer on political theory,[80] but never once mentioned Hobbes in any of his published works.

When such considerations are given due weight, it is by no means necessarily tendentious to suggest that there may have been more silent reliance on Hobbes by contemporary writers than appears in their published works. The Hobbesian premise, for example, that civil association

---

[73] Selden 1927, p. 24.   [74] Fitzmaurice 1895, pp. 45–6.   [75] *Journals* 1660–7, p. 636, col. 2.
[76] [Eachard] 1673, 'The Author to the Reader', Sig. A, 4^v.
[77] Pierce 1658, Sig. *, 3^v–4^r.   [78] BL Sloane MSS, 904, 1458.
[79] See, for example, Rand to Hartlib, 18 July 1651, Hartlib Papers (Sheffield) 62/30/4A, where Rand writes that Hobbes 'is the only protestant I know of whom for ingenious & free sparkish notions I dare compare to Sir Kenelme Digby, White or Des Cartes'.
[80] Petty 1927, vol. 1, pp. 122, 155, 219; vol. 2, p. 5.

must be based on the mediation of basically anti-social impulses can be found in several of the 'engagement' tracts of the early 1650s.[81] It can also be found in a number of treatises from the same period on the need for absolute power,[82] as well as in the works of Francis Osborne,[83] Thomas White[84] and Matthew Wren from later in the same decade.[85] The implication that, as Hobbes puts it in *Leviathan*, there is a 'mutuall Relation between Protection and Obedience'[86] is likewise echoed in several of the 'engagement' tracts.[87] We also encounter the argument in Lewis de Moulin's *Power of the Magistrate*, in which he claims that 'possession is the great condition required for the duty of Allegiance'.[88]

Among these writers, moreover, we do in fact find a number of explicit acknowledgements of Hobbes's authority. The earliest citations can be found in an anonymous tract of 1649 entitled *The Original & End of Civil Power*,[89] and in John Hall of Durham's treatise of 1650, *The Grounds and Reasons of Monarchy Considered*.[90] We also find Hobbes cited in a similar way by a number of writers from the later 1650s.[91] It is true that these citations tend to fall away after the Restoration, from which point we may perhaps date the beginnings of Hobbes's merely sinister reputation. But as late as 1660 we still find him invoked by John Heydon in *The Idea of the Law* as an authority on the law of nature and nations.[92]

The most significant of these appeals to Hobbes's authority can be found in the 'engagement' controversy of the early 1650s. One view that the engagers associate with Hobbes's name is that everyone is capable of reckoning the necessity of submission, since everyone shares a paramount desire for self-preservation and peace. On the one hand, as Michael Hawke maintains in *Killing Is Murder*, 'the natural State of man, before they were settled in a Society, as Master Hobbs truely saith, was a meer warre'.[93] But on the other hand, as Hawke had earlier argued in his *Right of Dominion*, the recognition of this fact means that 'every one hath sufficient power to rein, and moderate his outward demeanor', so that

[81] For example, in *Engagement Vindicated* 1650, pp. 5–6; in [Dury] 1650a, pp. 13–14 and in [Dury] 1650b, p. 20.
[82] For example, in *Confusion Confounded* 1654, p. 9; Hall [of Durham] 1654, pp. 13–14, 98.
[83] [Osborne] 1811, pp. 158–9.   [84] White 1655, pp. 44–5.   [85] Wren 1659, pp. 49–50.
[86] Hobbes 1996, Conclusion, p. 491.
[87] See, for example, *Conscience Puzzel'd* 1650, p. 7; *Discourse* 1650, p. 11; Eaton 1650, p. 8; Elcock 1651, p. 47.
[88] Moulin 1650, p. 29.   [89] Philodemius 1649, p. 15.   [90] Hall 1650, Sig. A, 4ʳ⁻ᵛ.
[91] For example, Scot 1650, p. 140; Harrington 1977, pp. 712, 716, 722, 724–5.
[92] Heydon 1660, pp. 125, 151. See also *Treatise of Human Reason* 1674, pp. 44–5. The discussion in Heydon 1660 is taken virtually word for word from Nathaniel Culverwell's *Discourse of the Light of Nature* (1652).
[93] Hawke 1657, p. 7.

'in this sense is Mr. Hobs saying true, that the law of nature is easily kept'.[94] The basic point, as an anonymous writer adds, is that in Hobbes's view political obligation arises because men are 'forced thereto by a kind of necessity for prevention of those evills, which would necessarily be the consequents of having all things common'.[95] In the *Right of Dominion* the same contention is expressed in even more hobbist terms. Citing 'Mr. Hobbes, *Philosophical Rudiments*' as his source, Hawke declares that 'it is the law of nature that men live peaceably, that they may tend the preservation of their lives, which whilst they are in war they cannot, and which is the first and fundamental law of nature'. To which he adds – again citing Hobbes as his authority – that what this shows us is that 'Humane nature it selfe' is 'the Mother of the natural law'.[96]

The 'Corollarie' of this view, Hawke goes on, is that 'possession is the great condition for our obedience and allegiance'. For 'as Master Hobbes saith', we cannot doubt that 'a sure and unresistable power conferres the Right of Dominion'.[97] The same inference had already been drawn by Albertus Warren in his *Eight Reasons Categorical* of 1653. According to Warren 'the question' during the revolution 'never was whether we or any other people ought to be governed by an Arbytrary power'. There must always be some such power in any state if its citizens are to be protected. To know who holds that power, moreover, is equivalent in Warren's view to knowing whom we ought to obey. It follows that 'our present Governours, I say, without more adoe, do not offend the letter of the Law in rationally providing for the people: because they are above the Law of men and (taken collectively) to those ends aforesaid; else we should be in an hostile condition, as Mr. Hobbs well observeth'.[98]

IV

As well as being cited by a number of avowed admirers, Hobbes's name is invoked by several contributors to the 'engagement' controversy who arrive at their conclusions independently of studying Hobbes's works. They quote him not as the source of their opinions, but rather in corroboration of a number of views they already hold. They provide the best evidence that Hobbes's theory was by no means 'an isolated phenomenon in English thought'.[99] Rather it represented a contribution (and was perhaps intended as a contribution) to a particular strand of

---

[94] Hawke 1655, p. 25.   [95] Philodemius 1649, p. 15.
[96] Hawke 1655, pp. 27, 29; cf. also p. 30.   [97] Hawke 1657, p. 12.
[98] Warren 1653, p. 5.   [99] Trevor-Roper 1957, p. 233.

debate about the rights of *de facto* powers at the climax of the English revolution.

The most important of these *de facto* theorists is Anthony Ascham, who published *A Discourse* in 1648, concerned (in the words of its subtitle) with *What is particularly lawfull during the Confusions and Revolutions of Governments*.[100] Ascham begins in hobbist vein by describing 'the cholericknesse of war' as a tempest continually threatening to overwhelm civil society.[101] His equally hobbist conclusion is that a willingness to 'owne' and obey whatever powers may be capable of protecting us provides us with the sole means of escaping from the mutability of things.[102] Part 1 of the *Discourse* argues for this conclusion from the almost parodically Hobbesian premise that 'there is nothing in the skin (as they say) which will not doe its best to save it'.[103] This leads to a discussion, in chapter 3, of 'first-Possessors', who were able 'without scruple of doing other wrong' to 'place their Bodies where they would'.[104] This account is then modified in chapter 4 – very much in the manner of Grotius – by positing a situation 'of extreame or naturall necessity' in which men were obliged to revert to a more communal system.[105] Two contrasting conclusions are then said to follow. On the one hand, appropriation has always been accepted since primitive times as a good enough basis for civil association. The best title, in short, has always been taken to be possession.[106] But on the other hand, even rights of possession can never be absolute, for they lose their priority, in times of emergency, to a basic Hobbesian right to life.

These assumptions lead, in part 2 of Ascham's *Discourse*, to a yet more hobbist argument about the mutual relations between protection and obedience. The specific issue on which Ascham unsurprisingly focuses is whether a true subject can fittingly take oaths and pay allegiance to a usurping power. Here he exhibits complete disregard for any questions about the rightful origins or the best form of government. For him the only question is whether the holders of power are capable of protecting our lives. If they cannot protect us, then our obligations are at an end. 'Nature commends me to myself for my own protection and preservation' when no one else is able to protect me, so that 'he who hath sworne Allegiance and fidelity to his Prince, is absolved, and set at liberty, if his Prince abandon his Kingdome'.[107] If, however, our government is capable of assuring our life and liberty, then we have a duty to obey

---

[100] Ascham 1648. [101] Ascham 1648, Sig. *, 4ʳ. [102] Ascham 1648, pp. 24–5, 87–8.
[103] Ascham 1648, p. 4. [104] Ascham 1648, pp. 10–14. [105] Ascham 1648, pp. 14, 16–17.
[106] Ascham 1648, pp. 22–3. [107] Ascham 1648, pp. 76–7.

it, regardless of any questions about the legal origins of its power. The touchstone throughout is necessity; and especially 'necessity of warre'. We must obey if we are protected, although we are released 'of all imaginable duty' when such protection fails.[108]

Ascham's view of the inescapably conditional nature of all political covenants might appear to be in contradiction to the other work he wrote on contractual relationships, his manuscript tract of 1647 entitled *Of Marriage*.[109] There he begins by stressing that, after a man 'hath engaged himself in that ffellowship of souls and bodies, which must last till death, hee is noe longer himself, and makes use of his Liberty but once; to loose it for ever after all his life'. But Ascham makes it clear that he regards the marriage contract as unique, arguing that 'all other' contracts may 'cease by mutual dissent'. It is only the connubial relationship, as he rather gloomily puts it, that 'represents the ffuneral of our Liberties'.[110]

The language as well as the assumptions of Ascham's *Discourse* are strongly hobbist in character. So is the language of his tract *Of Marriage* when he speaks about ordinary covenants. But Hobbes is never mentioned in either of these works, nor is his authority ever invoked. There is, in short, no evidence that at this stage Ascham had any knowledge of Hobbes's only published work of political theory, his *De Cive* of 1642. In 1649, however, Ascham reissued his *Discourse* in a second edition, its length augmented by ten chapters, its title shortened to *Of the Confusions and Revolutions of Goverments*.[111] Ascham now reverts (at the end of part 2) to his earlier discussion about the 'natural' state and character of man. Not only does he expand his earlier account, but he now corroborates it by reference to the authority of Hobbes. First he adds a justification of his views about political obligation by considering the origins of magistracy and civil government in a state of nature. He now deduces the obligation of subjects to obey whatever power is capable of affording them protection from the typically Hobbesian assumption that no civil society would otherwise be possible. Such liberty would be 'a great prejudice to us; for hereby we were clearly left in a state of warre, to make good this naturall free state of the world, which refer'd all to the tryall of force, and not of law, against which no one could offend'. The only solution is to submit to a single source of power, for 'Mr. Hobbs his supposition (if there be

[108] Ascham 1648, pp. 92–3.
[109] A[scham] *Of Marriage*, Cambridge University Library MS Gg. 1. 4, fo. 1. The tract is untitled, but I have used as a title its opening words.
[110] A[scham] *Of Marriage*, Cambridge University Library MS Gg. 1. 4, fos. 1, 4.
[111] Ascham 1649c. The title reads 'goverments' in all the copies I have seen.

two Omnipotents, neither would be oblig'd to obey the other) is very pertinent and conclusive to this subject'. Finally, Ascham adds further corroboration of his views about the mutual relation between protection and obedience. He repeats his earlier contention that any failure of our rulers to protect us automatically licenses a shift of allegiance. But he now calls in two greater authorities to underline his point. The change is justified whenever '(as Grotius and Mr. Hobbes say) there be a dereliction of command in the person of whom we speak, or if the country be so subdu'd, that the Conquerours can no longer be resisted'.[112]

A further use of Hobbes's authority to lend weight to an already completed argument can be found in the writings of Marchamont Nedham. So close indeed is Hobbes's account of political obligation to the arguments used by Nedham and other *de facto* theorists to justify the rule of the Rump that, in the pages of *Mercurius Politicus*, the official newspaper that Nedham edited, Hobbes's doctrine acquired the somewhat invidious status of propaganda for the new Commonwealth. During January 1651, all four of the editorials prefacing Nedham's weekly news-sheet consisted of unsigned extracts from Hobbes's *De Corpore Politico*.[113] Nedham started with the passage in which Hobbes had spoken of the lawfulness of subjecting ourselves to invading powers in the name of preserving our lives.[114] In the second week he printed Hobbes's defence of the reasonableness of relinquishing our rights in order to obtain protection and defence.[115] In the third week he added Hobbes's account of the need to transfer as much power as possible to our rulers if we are to receive security in return.[116] Finally he printed Hobbes's assurance that we cannot be said to be acting against our conscience if we obey existing laws, since in following the law we shall be following our conscience at the same time.[117]

Nedham illustrates in his own writings as well as in his journalism how readily his political stance can be supported by the authority of Hobbes. This can best be observed in his *Case of the Commonwealth of England, Stated*, which went through two editions in 1650. Nedham's aim is to provide (in part 1) a general account of the 'Necessity and Equity' of submission to the powers that be, and to vindicate (in part 2) the authority of the

---

[112] Ascham 1649c, pp. 108, 119.
[113] Frank 1961, pp. 257–8 notes that Hobbes's authority was also invoked on at least two other occasions in Nedham's newspaper.
[114] *Mercurius Politicus* 1651a, p. 503; cf. Hobbes 1650, pp. 57–8.
[115] *Mercurius Politicus* 1651b, p. 519; cf. Hobbes 1650, p. 64.
[116] *Mercurius Politicus* 1651c, pp. 535–6; cf. Hobbes 1650, pp. 66–7.
[117] *Mercurius Politicus* 1651d, pp. 551–2; cf. Hobbes 1650, pp. 140–1.

new Commonwealth regime. The central contention of his work, as of Ascham's, is the Hobbesian claim that all government stems from our need to protect ourselves from each other by way of yielding our rights to some common power. The maintenance of such a power is said to be the sole alternative to anarchy. In part 2 of the *Case* Nedham uses this claim to denounce the changes proposed by the royalists, the Levellers and all other enemies of the new regime. In the central chapter of part 1 he simply states it as axiomatic that 'there being a necessity of some government at all times for the maintenance of civil conversation and to avoid confusion, therefore such as will not submit, because they cannot have such a governor as themselves like, are in some sense mere anarchists'.[118]

Nedham is thus led, like Ascham, to the bleak conclusion that, since government is an absolute necessity, political obligation must be owed to any regime capable of sustaining political order. He has no qualms about the implication that allegiance may shift with events. The wheel of fortune, as his opening chapter observes, turns in unpredictable but irrevocable ways. Once it has turned against a particular government, its citizens will merely be building 'castles in the air against fatal necessity' if they try 'to maintain a fantasy of pretended loyalty'.[119] There can be no duty to remain loyal to a rightful as opposed to a successful *de facto* power. Nedham insists at the end of chapter 2 that no such distinction can usefully be upheld. On the one hand, 'the power of the sword ever hath been the foundation of titles to government'. And on the other hand, the people have 'never presumed to spurn at those powers', but have '(for public peace and quiet) paid a patient submission to them'.[120]

Nedham's defence of *de facto* power is mounted without reference to Hobbes. As in the case of Ascham, however, Hobbes's authority is subsequently invoked to corroborate the argument. When Nedham issued the second edition of his book later in 1650, he added an appendix explaining that, although he believed his conclusions to be 'sufficiently proved', he had decided 'to fasten them more surely upon the reader' by 'inserting some additions' from Salmasius and 'out of Mr. Hobbes, his late book *De Corpore Politico*'.[121] The closing pages of the appendix accordingly consist of extracts from Hobbes's book, from which a topical and wholly Hobbesian moral is duly drawn:

[118] Nedham 1969, p. 30.   [119] Nedham 1969, p. 14.
[120] Nedham 1969, pp. 27–8.   [121] Nedham 1969, p. 129.

It may plainly be inferred that since no security for life, limbs, and liberty (which is the end of all government) can now be had here by relinquishing our right of self-protection and giving it up to any other power beside the present, therefore it is very unreasonable in any man to put himself out of the protection of this power by opposing it.[122]

Stated positively, Nedham adds, the moral of Hobbes's account is that 'since there is no other possible way to preserve the well-being of this nation but by a submission to the present powers', it follows that 'we may pay subjection to them in order to our security'.[123] With these invocations of Hobbes's authority Nedham rests his case.

V

When Sir Robert Filmer came to write his shrewd critique of Hobbes's political theory, he thought of it not in isolation – as Hobbes's more recent commentators have tended to do – but rather as the expression of an outlook common to 'Mr. Selden, Mr Hobbes, Mr. Ascham and all others of that party'.[124] The appropriateness of linking these names – to which we may now add those of Nedham, Hawke, Warren and others – has, I hope, been sufficiently vindicated. But it remains to fulfil my promise at the outset and try to indicate how a failure to take account of this context has arguably had a damaging effect on the exegesis of Hobbes's political thought, and notably on the understanding of his theory of political obligation.

One recent trend[125] in the interpretation of Hobbes's theory of obligation has consisted of increasing the emphasis on his connections with a more traditional moral outlook. The suggestion has been that his theory can and ought to be detached from its 'scientific' premises and grounded instead on a doctrine of natural law. Howard Warrender, the most persuasive commentator to follow this path, has reformulated Hobbes's account of political obligation in the language of moral duty. A subject comes to feel obliged, on this reading, not primarily by making calculations of oblique self-interest, but rather by acknowledging a prior obligation to obey the laws of nature in virtue of recognising them to be the commands of God. Hobbes is thus treated as 'essentially a natural

---

[122] Nedham 1969, p. 136.　　　[123] Nedham 1969, p. 135.

[124] Filmer 1991, p. 281; cf. also p. 237.

[125] The trend is no longer recent, as it was when I originally wrote this chapter. Rather it can now be seen, as Tuck 1989, pp. 110–11 points out in his survey of the historiography, to be a phase of discussion particularly characteristic of the 1950s and 1960s, at the end of which period this chapter was first published.

law philosopher' who believes that 'the laws of nature are eternal and unchangeable' and that, 'as the commands of God, they oblige all men who reason properly, and so arrive at a belief in an omnipotent being whose subjects they are'.[126]

Warrender's reading has been endorsed by John Plamenatz[127] and further elaborated by F. C. Hood. According to Hood there is a dichotomy in Hobbes's theory between an 'artificial' and a 'real' system of obligation, a dichotomy only resolved when Hobbes 'goes behind his philosophic fiction of command without a commander to the reality from which the fiction was derived, when he says that the second law of nature is the law of the Gospel'.[128] The basic contention underlying these accounts can best be summarised in the words of A. E. Taylor, the first interpreter to put forward this view of Hobbes's theory of obligation. Hobbes, we have to assume, 'meant quite seriously what he so often says, that the "natural law" is the command of God, and to be obeyed *because* it is God's command'.[129]

I cannot myself find a single passage, at least in *Leviathan*, in which Hobbes presents the deontological argument that, according to Taylor, he 'so often' enunciates. But it is not my intention to ask directly, as a matter of textual exegesis, whether this interpretation offers the best account of Hobbes's meaning. What I want to suggest is that the relationship between Hobbes's argument and the context in which he wrote it bears on this issue more directly than has been supposed. For the view of Hobbes's intellectual relations implied by these accounts seems to me historically incredible. My suggestion is that the weight of this testimony is perhaps sufficient (somewhat as Hume argued in the case of miracles) for any such interpretation to stand discredited.

If Hobbes intended to ground political obligation on a prior duty to obey the commands of God, then it follows that every contemporary – every follower, every opponent, every sympathiser – equally missed the point of his theory. Furthermore, they were all mistaken in exactly the same way. Consider first the hobbist followers I have discussed. They all locate the grounds of political obligation in the paramount need for self-protection, and trace this paramount need to man's nasty and brutish nature. Many of them, moreover, specifically cite Hobbes as an authority on both these crucial points. This was also the popularly

---

[126] Warrender 1957, p. 322.
[127] See Plamenatz 1965, a partial endorsement, and see also Warrender 1965, a response to Plamenatz.
[128] Hood 1964, p. 97. For a critique of Hood's reading of *Leviathan* see Skinner 1964.
[129] Taylor 1965, p. 49.

received impression of Hobbes's intentions amongst his contemporaries. One commonplace book in which 'Mr. Hobs creed' is anatomised summarises him as having taught 'that the prime law of nature in the soul of man is that of temporal self-love' and 'that the law of the civil soveraign is the onely obliging rule of just and unjust'.[130] A further summary presents us with 'The Principles of Mr Hobs' under five headings:

1 Thatt all Right of Dominion is founded only in Power
2ly Thatt all Moral Righteoussnesse is founded only in the Law of the Civill Magistrate
3ly That the Holy Scriptures are made law only by civill Authority
4ly Thatt whatever the Civill Magistrate commands is to bee obeyed notwithstanding contrary to Divine Morrall laws
5ly That there is a Desireable Glory in Being and being reputed an Atheist.[131]

We encounter the same assumptions once again when Daniel Scargill, the 'penitent Hobbist', was forced to recant his views before the University of Cambridge in 1669. The tenets that he and his accusers both regarded as pre-eminently those of Hobbes were that 'all right of dominion is founded only in power', and that 'all moral righteousness is founded only in the positive law of the civil magistrate'.[132]

Consider next the position of Hobbes's contemporary critics. These writers were themselves Christian moralists, who might have been expected to be particularly attuned to seeing similar overtones in Hobbes's political works. Most of them, however, go out of their way to emphasise what Clarendon calls Hobbes's 'thorough novelty'.[133] They see in Hobbes no element of a traditional moral outlook. They see only a dangerous iconoclast, someone who (in John Bramhall's words) 'taketh a pride in removing all ancient land-marks, between Prince and subject, Father and child, Husband and Wife, Master and servant, Man and Man'.[134] All these critics agree, moreover, on the form that Hobbes's iconoclasm takes. They associate him with two particular doctrines, both of which (as Clarendon remarks) would 'overthrow or undermine all those Principles of Government, which have preserv'd the Peace of this Kingdom through so many ages'.[135]

They assume in the first place that Hobbes grounds political obligation on calculations of rational self-interest, and consequently believed that subjects become obliged to any power possessing the capacity to protect them. His point of departure, in the eyes of these critics, is not

---

[130] BL Sloane MS 1458, fo. 35^r.   [131] BL Sloane MS 904, fo. 14^r.
[132] See Axtell 1965 and refs. there.   [133] Clarendon 1676, Sig. A, 1^v.
[134] Bramhall 1658, p. 542.   [135] Clarendon 1676, Sig. A, 3^v.

with the requirements of natural law but with the fears and needs of natural man. When the University of Oxford issued its condemnation of heterodox books in 1683, Hobbes was mentioned and denounced by name as the writer who had invented the claim that 'Self preservation is the fundamental law of nature and supersedes the obligation of all others'.[136] This was also the view of Hobbes's contemporary readers. As Filmer, Warwick and others unhesitatingly declare, Hobbes believes that there is an equal 'right of nature' in everybody, and that civil society can only 'arise from necessity and fear' upon these 'Principles of Equality and Self-preservation'.[137]

The other doctrine that Hobbes's critics particularly associated with his name was that, when citizens are not adequately protected, their obligations automatically cease. Hobbes intended no less, as Clarendon maintains, than to give subjects 'leave to withdraw their obedience' from their sovereign at the very moment 'when he hath most need of their assistance'.[138] This was seen as final proof that, as Thomas Tenison puts it, Hobbes has no belief in the 'obligation laid upon us by Fedility (the Law of God Almighty in our nature) antecedent to all humane covenants'.[139] He instead makes 'civil laws the rules of good and evil'.[140] Far from seeing in Hobbes any element of their own natural law doctrine, these critics treat his account of political obligation as the most dangerous assault on it. 'Where these Principles prevaile', as Bramhall concludes, 'adieu honour, and honesty, and fidelity, and loyalty: all must give place to self-interest.'[141]

Some modern commentators have taken the heroic course of denying that any of this evidence matters, on the grounds that 'any modern reader can see the general irrelevance' of these critics.[142] But to concede this claim is to complete the paradox. Hobbes himself is turned into the least credible figure of all. He has to be represented as articulating a traditional theory of natural law in a manner so convoluted that it was everywhere taken for the work of a man prepared (in Bramhall's memorable phrase) to 'take his Soveraign for better, but not for worse'.[143] And despite his well-known predilection for the quiet life, despite his terror at being arraigned for heresy, he has to be represented as failing altogether to disown the alarmingly heterodox writers who cited his authority, or to disarm his innumerable critics by pointing out their complete misunderstanding of

---

[136] 'Judgement . . . of the University' in Wilkins 1737, vol. 4, pp. 610–12.
[137] Filmer 1991, pp. 187–8; Warwick 1694, p. 55; *Great Law of Nature*, p. 8.
[138] Clarendon 1676, p. 90.   [139] Tenison 1670, p. 147.   [140] *Examination of the Arguments*, p. 15.
[141] Bramhall 1658, p. 519.   [142] Brown 1962, p. 337n.   [143] Bramhall 1658, p. 519.

his arguments. It becomes extraordinary that Hobbes never did any of these things.

Hobbes's followers and critics are turned into scarcely less credible figures. It becomes difficult in the first place to understand why his opponents should have felt so threatened. A more careful reading of his works would have shown them, as Hood insists, that there is 'nothing that is original in Hobbes's moral thought'.[144] A reading of any of the writers who invoked his authority, however, would have revealed a highly original view of political and moral obligation of exactly the kind that they claimed (mistakenly, we are told) to find in Hobbes's own works. It becomes hard to understand why it should have been Hobbes, rather than these other writers, on whom they continued to focus their attacks.

Finally, it becomes even harder to understand why any of Hobbes's avowed followers should have troubled to cite his authority. All of them had worked out a view of political obligation of an avowedly anti-deontological character. All of them (we are assured) had in any case completely misunderstood the writer whom they all continued (without eliciting any protest) to cite as a leading exponent of their own belief that political obligation and protection are mutually related. It becomes clear, in short, that however plausible the deontological interpretation of Hobbes's theory of obligation may be as a reading of *Leviathan*, the price of accepting it is to remove most of the points of contact between Hobbes and the intellectual milieu in which he lived and worked.

VI

My intention, in this preliminary attempt to surround Hobbes's theory of political obligation with its appropriate ideological context, has been to argue a methodological as well as an historical case. I am suggesting that a knowledge of the sort of historical information I have provided is not merely desirable as 'background' to the study of a given writer. It can also be deployed as a further test of plausibility, apart from the evidence of a writer's own works, for any suggested interpretation of those works. I am suggesting, that is, that it has been a mistake to assume, in the case of Hobbes, that the 'question of what his theory is' (as Warrender puts it) can properly be regarded as 'prior' to, and separate from, the question of its intellectual relations and the climate of opinion in which it was formed.[145] Any interpretation must imply some links between a given theory and the

---

[144] Hood 1964, p. 13.   [145] Warrender 1957, p. ix.

circumstances in and for which it was produced. My general conclusion is that one of the conditions for accepting any suggested interpretation of a political theory should be that these links must themselves be of an historically credible kind. My particular conclusion is that this condition is so much lacking, in the case of the deontological reading of Hobbes's theory of political obligation, that the validity of this interpretation must for this reason alone be regarded as questionable.

10

Conquest and consent: Hobbes and the engagement controversy

The opening months of 1649 saw the climax of the English revolution: the king was executed, the monarchy and House of Lords abolished, the Commonwealth of England proclaimed. But this outcome was far more radical than most moderates in the presbyterian party had wanted, and far more revolutionary than the instinctive royalism of most English people could readily countenance. One of the immediate tasks of the new government was accordingly to persuade such moderate and hostile groups that the revolution was really over. They had to be given reasons for 'engaging' with the newly established Commonwealth, accepting and swearing allegiance to it rather than trying to continue the fight.[1] There was a need, in other words, for a theory of political obligation in terms of which the new government could be legitimated. And it was clear that any such theory would in turn have to satisfy two contrasting conditions. It would need to be couched in a sufficiently familiar form to be acceptable to presbyterian and even royalist opinion. But it would need at the same time to be capable of performing the revolutionary task of justifying the duty to obey a merely *de facto* and usurping political power.

The Council of State was plainly aware of the need, which it sought to meet in March 1649 with its own Declaration, 'expressing the grounds of their late proceedings, and of setling the present government in the way of a free state'.[2] The arguments of the Declaration echoed those of a number of government propagandists, notably John Milton in his *Tenure of Kings and Magistrates*, first published in February 1649.[3] The basic

---

This chapter is a revised and updated version of an essay that originally appeared under the same title in *The Interregnum: The Quest for Settlement*, ed. G. E. Aylmer (London, 1972), pp. 79–98.
[1] To 'engage' with the new government was to accept the oath of 'engagement' to its authority.
[2] See *Declaration* 1649, and for its significance in the ensuing controversy see Wallace 1968, pp. 44–5.
[3] For the date of publication (13 February 1649) see Dzelzainis 1991, p. xxvii.

claim on which they agree is that any lawful regime must originate in a
decision by the people to consent to its establishment.[4] The execution of
Charles I is thus represented as the removal of a tyrant and a reassertion
of the people's right to set limits to the powers of government.[5]

This type of justification, however, was of strictly limited value outside
the ranks of the Independent party. Such arguments could scarcely be expected to persuade any former royalists, since most of them derived their
views on political obligation from the simple assertion that kings enjoy
a God-given right to rule.[6] But nor could such arguments be expected
to persuade many members of the presbyterian party. They had admittedly supported the revolution up to the time of Colonel Pride's purge
of Parliament in December 1648, and many of them would doubtless
have been prepared to endorse the premises of the government's case.[7]
But the presbyterians had also sworn the Solemn League and Covenant,
which included an oath binding them 'to preserve and defend the King's
Majesty's person'.[8] It was difficult to see how any but the most cynical
could now justify taking oaths and paying allegiance to the very power
that had deprived the king of his life.[9]

It was at this juncture that a different defence of the new government
began to be urged by a studiously moderate (though mainly presbyterian)
group of political writers.[10] The basic contention put forward by these
theorists was that St Paul's injunction to obey the powers that be as ordained of God can validly be argued even in the case of usurping powers.
The claim is historically important, and worth examining in some detail,
for at least two reasons. It was this defence of *de facto* sovereignty that in
the event supplied exactly the type of argument needed to persuade the
presbyterians and even the royalists of their duty to 'engage' with the

---

[4] Milton 1991, pp. 8–11.   [5] Milton 1991, pp. 8, 32–3.
[6] On the prevalence of this assumption see Schochet 1975, Daly 1979 and Sommerville 1986b,
pp. 9–56.
[7] This is clear, for example, from the reactions of William Prynne and Edward Gee, both presbyterians who denounced the Commonwealth on the grounds that it was established without the
consent of the people. See above, chapter 7 section IV and cf. Prynne 1649, pp. 3, 13 and [Gee]
1650, pp. 11–12.
[8] *Constitutional Documents* Article 3, p. 269. For the anxiety of the presbyterians to achieve compatibility between their previous engagements and any new demands for allegiance see Dury 1650c
and *Memorandums* 1650, Sig. A, 3ᵛ.
[9] For the civil war as a case of conscience see Wallace 1968, pp. 9–12 and Thomas 1993,
pp. 43–6. On the place of apparently contradictory promises in the ensuing controversy see
Vallance 2001.
[10] For the pioneering treatment of these writers see Zagorin 1954, pp. 62–77. The two fundamental
studies remain Wallace 1964 and Wallace 1968. More recent contributions include Gunn 1969,
pp. 82–7; Baumgold 1988, pp. 125–32; Sommerville 1992, pp. 63–70.

new regime.[11] A further reason for studying these writers is that their arguments, and the conditions out of which they arose, provide a context within which the main aims and several of the most characteristic doctrines of Hobbes's political theory can best be understood.[12] In Hobbes's intellectual house there are of course many mansions. But the principal thesis of the present chapter is that one of Hobbes's aims in *Leviathan* was to contribute to precisely this debate about the rights of *de facto* powers at this critical juncture in the English revolution.

II

One justification for remaining passively obedient to the new Commonwealth, even if one disapproved of it, was provided by invoking the authority of Calvin. His *Institutes of the Christian Religion* had repeatedly emphasised the duty of private citizens not to meddle in affairs of state.[13] This sentiment was in turn echoed by many of the more religious-minded among the *de facto* theorists. The most indefatigable of these was John Dury, a presbyterian divine who spent much of his life travelling abroad in the interests of Protestant reunion. He returned to England in 1645, took the Covenant and turned himself into a vocal supporter of Parliament.[14] Dury limited himself exclusively to Calvin's argument in publishing what was in fact the first of the *de facto* defences of the Commonwealth, *A Case of Conscience Resolved*, which initially appeared in March 1649.[15] Dury simply declares that, even if questions arise about the legitimacy of our rulers, we 'ought not to apply' ourselves 'to intermeddle in their affairs'.[16] His later contributions to the debate all return to the same theme. 'All private men', as he puts it in his *Considerations* of 1650, 'ought to walk unblameably under the superior powers of the World', since 'it doth not belong to us to judge definitively of the Rights which the Supream Powers over us in the World, pretend to have unto their places'. The lesson, as he expresses it with his usual repetitiousness,

---

[11] Although they seldom go so far as to describe themselves as *de facto* theorists, they frequently make use of the distinction between *de iure* and *de facto* powers when discussing the crisis of 1649. See, for example, *Discourse* 1650, pp. 16, 22.

[12] When I originally put forward this claim, I ought perhaps to have made it clearer that I did not of course mean that these writers provide the *only* immediate context for understanding the character of Hobbes's theory of obligation. For corrections and developments of my argument see Burgess 1986, Baumgold 1988, Burgess 1990.

[13] For Calvin's insistence that only magistrates, never individuals, can question established powers see Skinner 1978b, pp. 219–21, 230–3.

[14] For these details see DNB *sub* Dury and cf. Turnbull 1947, pp. 249–51.

[15] [Dury] 1649; cf. Wallace 1968, p. 44.   [16] [Dury] 1649, p. 4.

is that it is 'no part of our Christian Profession to become Judges of the great ones of this World'.[17]

A more secularised version of this argument consisted, equally simply, of pointing out that there had already been too many disputes over matters of government, that these had led only to conflict and bloodshed, and that the time had come to settle for peace at any price. This line of thought proved especially attractive to surviving royalists, who later liked to insist that their own non-intervention in the affairs of the Commonwealth constituted the badge and guarantee of their political innocence. Something of the same attitude can be seen in the preoccupation of the royalist poets in the 1650s with the pleasures of pastoral retreat (as in Edmund Waller, Abraham Cowley and Henry Vaughan) and in the popularity of such encouragements to rustic retirement as Izaak Walton's *Compleat Angler*, first published in 1653.[18]

A similar outlook is reflected in several of the *de facto* defences of the Commonwealth. Anthony Ascham brings to a close his *Bounds & Bonds of Publique Obedience* in 1649 by expressing the earnest hope that his fellow-countrymen will now prevent anyone from 'coming on the Stage to Act our late Tragedy over againe'.[19] Marchamont Nedham in his *Case of the Commonwealth* of 1650 likewise seeks to vindicate not merely the 'necessity and equity' of submission to the new regime but its 'utility and benefit' as well. The greatest benefit to be gained, he adds, is that the Commonwealth will 'have leave to take breath a little in the possession of a firm peace' if everyone now agrees to 'close cordially in affection' and 'submit and settle'.[20] The same overwhelming desire for 'the preservation of a firm and lasting peace', the same hope for a 'unity of minds' and 'a restraining of the hands' provides a recurrent motif of *de facto* theory throughout the months following the regicide.[21]

There are many elements of the same temperament to be found in Hobbes's political works.[22] He frequently condemns ambitious subjects who meddle in affairs of state as one of the causes of the dissolution of commonwealths. 'The Popularity of a potent Subject', as he puts it in *Leviathan*, 'is a dangerous Disease', since the people are always liable to be

---

[17] [Dury] 1650a, p. 10. For the attribution see Wallace 1968, p. 394. As Wallace notes, Dury's tract went through four editions in as many months.

[18] For this theme see Røstvig 1954, pp. 19–22 and Thomas 1965, pp. 201–2.

[19] [Ascham] 1649b, pp. 36–7. For the attribution see Wallace 1964, p. 391.

[20] Nedham 1969, p. 127.

[21] See, for example, *Logical Demonstration* 1650, pp. 2–3; *Constant Man's Character* 1650, pp. 71–2; *Memorandums* 1650, p. 7.

[22] For this theme see Thomas 1965, an article of exceptional importance.

'seduced from their loyalty' by 'the flattery of Popular men' and thereby 'drawn away from their obedience to the Lawes'.[23] He also lays much emphasis on the value of being able to leave political matters for others to decide while one gets on with one's own life. He accordingly treats it as one of the disadvantages of democracy that everyone has a hand in public business. He assures us in a withering passage in *De Cive* that democratic assemblies merely encourage childish vanity, leading their members to neglect their families for more glamorous but less genuine duties.[24] Conversely, he regards it as a special virtue of monarchies that subjects are able to lead a retired life and keep out of trouble whoever may be in charge.[25] As he explains in the same chapter of *De Cive*, anyone under a monarchy 'who is prepared to live quietly' will be 'free of danger', for 'only the ambitious suffer', while 'the rest are protected from being wronged'.[26] Most insistently of all, he argues that the course of prudence in any civil society will always be to hold fast to whatever security has been achieved, and to prevent anyone from acting – even from the highest motives – in such a way as to endanger the peace. He admits in *Leviathan* that the need for such unconditional obedience may appear to bring with it many incommodities. But he retorts that the greatest incommodity that any government can bring will always be painless by comparison with the sole alternative, namely 'the miseries, and horrible calamities, that accompany a Civill Warre'.[27]

Such demands for submission in the name of peace doubtless had some effect. But they could scarcely be said to offer any new arguments to anyone still in doubt about the godliness or even the legality of paying allegiance to the new regime. The problem of persuading such persons of tender conscience remained the same. They needed to be convinced that it would not merely be beneficial to submit and obey, but in some way compatible with their existing oaths and covenants.

The credit for originating the main argument in terms of which this scruple was overcome seems to be due to Francis Rous. As I have already noted in chapter 9, Rous first outlined his argument in a brief but important tract of April 1649 entitled *The Lawfulness of Obeying the Present Government*.[28] A leading presbyterian, Rous had sat in the Parliaments of

---

[23] Hobbes 1996, ch. 29, p. 229; ch. 30, p. 234. See also Hobbes 1969a, pp. 141–2, 175–8 and Hobbes 1983a, XII. X–XIII, pp. 191–4.
[24] Hobbes 1983a, X. XV, p. 179; cf. Hobbes 1998, pp. 124–5.
[25] Hobbes 1983a, X. VII, pp. 174–5.
[26] Hobbes 1998, p. 120; cf. Hobbes 1983a, X. VII, pp. 174–5.
[27] Hobbes 1996, ch. 18, p. 128.
[28] [Rous] 1649. For the attribution see Wallace 1964, p. 390.

the 1620s as well as in the Long Parliament since its opening in 1640.[29] He had taken the Covenant in 1644, going over to the Independent party (like many other 'engagers') shortly before the execution of Charles I.[30] His pamphlet seeks to establish 'that though the change of a Government were beleeved not to be lawfull, yet it may lawfully be obeyed'.[31] He thus begins by offering a prudent and important concession: he makes no attempt to deny that the new regime is unlawful; he only attempts to show that it may not be unlawful to obey such a regime.

Rous's ensuing argument may be said to proceed in three simple steps. He begins by taking his stand squarely on 'the duty of submission and obedience to Authority' laid down by St Paul in the opening verses of chapter 13 of the Epistle to the Romans.[32] This was the most widely quoted text on the question of political obligation throughout the seventeenth century. It represented an inescapable authority, one that no presbyterian or even royalist opponent of the new regime could possibly fail to accept. Rous's next step is to ask precisely what powers were in fact accepted by St Paul, and were subsequently accepted throughout English history, as having a title to be obeyed. He answers that, even though 'in this Nation many persons have beene setled in supreme power and authority by meere force without title of inheritance', this consideration has never been regarded hitherto as a sufficient reason for refusing them the obedience that the apostle commands.[33] Rous's third step then follows readily. St Paul's injunction must be taken literally as a command to obey *whatever* powers are in a position to demand our obedience:

When a question is made whom we should obey; it must not be lookt at what he is that exerciseth the power, or by what right or wrong he hath invaded the power, or in what manner he doth dispence it, but onely if he have power. For if any man doth excell in power, it is now out of doubt, that he received that power of God; Wherefore without all exception thou must yield thyself up to him and heartily obey him.[34]

Rous's conclusion is thus that the possession of power is in every instance an indication of God's will and providence, and consequently a sufficient title to be obeyed.

Rous's argument was of the utmost importance throughout the ensuing debate, and many people clearly welcomed it immediately and with relief. To the most tender consciences, however, his ingenious transformation of passive obedience into a defence of the revolution must have seemed more shocking than persuasive, and no sooner had Rous

[29] Shaw 1900, vol. 1, p. 265.   [30] Wallace 1964, p. 385.   [31] [Rous] 1649, p. 1.
[32] [Rous] 1649, p. 1.   [33] [Rous] 1649, p. 4.   [34] [Rous] 1649, p. 7.

published his pamphlet than a series of counter-attacks began to appear. Rous's critics all focus on the same two vulnerable points in his argument. First they question his interpretation of St Paul's injunction to obey the powers that be. Rous, they object, introduces a dangerous confusion between the genuine authority that God ordains and the mere possession of power. The anonymous author of *The Grand Case of Conscience Stated*, whose tract appeared within two months of Rous's pamphlet, puts the objection with particular force.[35] While authority is undoubtedly 'ordained by God', our actual rulers are merely 'constituted by men' and have at most 'Gods permission', not his ordinance.[36] The moral is that 'Men in Authority' are 'to be obeyed no further than as acting according to that Authority'.[37] A large number of Rous's other opponents took up a similar stance. They agree that the crucial text from Romans 13 will yield the right answer 'if clearly opened and rightly understood'. But they insist that the correct interpretation must be that the Apostle is referring not to any 'powers that be' but only to lawfully constituted authority. This alone is ordained of God, although he may well permit (but never ordain) many forms of tyranny. And while the apostle commands us 'not to resist their power', he never commands us 'not to resist their Tyranny'.[38]

The other argument mounted by Rous's critics was a closely related one. The reason, they maintain, why St Paul must have intended a distinction between power and authority is that otherwise there could never be any justifiable resistance to tyrannous government. Once more the author of the *Grand Case* strongly emphasises the point. If we grant 'that men assuming to themselves the place and power of Magistrates, by what right or means soever they came by it, must be obeyed, surely it would be the greatest inlet to tyranny in the world, and the speediest means of destroying states that could be invented'.[39] Rous's later critics all concur. Rous's doctrine would 'open too wide a gap to rebels' powers and loyal subjects' misery' and would encourage 'intrusion into the seat of authority' by those without any lawful claim to it.[40]

To any but the most cynical, these responses must have seemed a serious challenge to Rous's case. Once the distinction between powers ordained and powers merely permitted by God was firmly drawn, the way was open first to insist that God never ordains but often permits the wicked to rule, and thence to infer that the rule of the Rump must be just

[35] For the date of publication (22 June 1649) see Wallace 1964, p. 391.
[36] *Grand Case* 1649, p. 3.   [37] *Grand Case* 1649, p. 3.
[38] See [Ward] 1649, p. 8 and *Enquiry* 1649, pp. 9–10.
[39] *Grand Case* 1649, p. 3.   [40] [Ward] 1649, p. 8; *Enquiry* 1649, p. 10.

such a wicked power, sent to vex but also to test sinful men. Meanwhile the royalists had arrived at the same conclusion. One poignant example is provided by John Wenlock, who records his reply to a soldier who assured him that the victories of Parliament over the king were a direct sign of God's providence:

Alas, friend, that is no good argument on your side, for we know that God doth many times permit wicked men to prosper in their ways, to their own destruction; and if you were an historian, you would know that God hath suffered the Turks so to prevail against the Christians for many hundred years because of their sins.[41]

The fact that God so often allows the wicked to prosper is, as these writers concede, one of the great mysteries. But this makes them all the more anxious to insist that, although such evils may be permitted, they are never positively ordained.

While Rous's position was being undermined by such doubts, the need for an effective defence of the new regime was becoming all the more urgent. The Rump found its authority increasingly called into question throughout 1649 by a strange but predictable coalition of royalist and Leveller arguments. The Levellers turned against the Commonwealth the weapons they had previously used against the king, declaring that the new government no less than the old was a tyranny based on ignoring the will of the people.[42] Meanwhile the royalists fanned the widespread hatred of the Rump with the publication of *Eikon Basilike*, their celebration of the tragic and appealing figure of 'Charles, King and Royal Martyr'.[43] At the same time they began to mount a series of highly emotive denunciations of the impiety as well as the illegality of the new regime. Bishop Juxon's *The Subjects Sorrow*, offering 'lamentations' for a king 'unjustly put to death by his owne people' appeared as early as March 1649.[44] Fabian Philipps's *King Charles the First no Man of Blood but a Martyr for his People* was in print by June.[45] By the end of the summer, the need for a convincing defence of the Commonwealth had become yet more urgent

[41] On Wenlock and his *Declaration* see Hardacre 1956, p. 83.
[42] This, for example, was one of John Lilburne's arguments as early as February 1649 in his *Englands New Chains Discovered*. See Lilburne 1964, pp. 165, 167.
[43] *Eikon Basilike* 1649. The title-page of Thomason's copy notes that the first impression appeared on 9 February 1649.
[44] [Juxon] 1649. The attribution and date of publication are given on the title-page of Thomason's copy. William Juxon (1582–1663) was Bishop of London, and after the restoration Archbishop of Canterbury.
[45] [Philipps] 1649. For the date of publication see the title-page of Thomason's copy and for the attribution see DNB.

as a result of the actions of the government itself. During October it took the aggressive step of requiring an oath of 'Engagement' to be sworn to its authority, and in the following January it demanded that the oath be taken by all men over the age of eighteen.[46] The question of political obligation was thus turned into a formal test of citizenship.

It was of course possible in this predicament simply to hold fast to the providentialist case in favour of engagement originally presented by Rous. This approach was duly followed by many defenders of the Commonwealth, and probably remained the most widely used argument in favour of subscribing to the new oaths of allegiance.[47] As the anonymous author of *The Engagement Vindicated* put it, writing in the opening week of 1650, 'every change' in 'great Bodies Politick' must be seen as 'a signal act of Providence' and must for that reason be seen as a direct reflection of God's will.[48] William Jenkin, writing as late as November 1651, likewise claims that all alterations of civil government reflect 'the wise and righteous providences of God', so that 'a refusal to be subject to this present Authority' is equivalent to 'a refusal to acquiesce in the wise and righteous pleasure of God'.[49]

The difficulty, however, was that Rous's opponents had made it hard to accept that this line of reasoning offered adequate grounds for actively paying allegiance to the new regime. Just as the invocations of providence continued, so the attacks continued on the interpretation of the Pauline injunctions upon which they depended.[50] The polemical situation was one of stalemate. New arguments in favour of submitting in conscience to the Commonwealth government were urgently required.

One argument floated at this juncture sought to vindicate the lawfulness of engagement by the principles of radical Independency. As we have seen, this had initially been the government's own line of defence, and it continued throughout the ensuing controversy to offer a means of claiming that *de facto* powers can be accepted *de iure* by their own subjects. Henry Parker and Henry Robinson both lent their support to the engagement with the claim that the new government reflects the will of the

---

[46] *Constitutional Documents*, p. 391.   [47] Wallace 1968, pp. 46, 48.

[48] *Engagement Vindicated* 1650, p. 3. For the date of publication (7 January 1650) see Wallace 1964, p. 395.

[49] Jenkin 1651, p. 3. For other providentialist defences of engagement see *Logical Demonstration* 1650, p. 5, in which the civil war is treated as an appeal to heaven, and *Engagement Vindicated* 1650, pp. 2–3, in which the outcome is ascribed to providence.

[50] For example, Rous's original pamphlet was attacked in this fashion in *Traytors Deciphered* 1650, while *Engagement Vindicated* was similarly attacked in *Arguments and Reasons* 1650. See too the criticism of Dury's numerous contributions to the debate in *Answer to Mr J. Dury*. Wallace 1964, pp. 397, 399, 402 has established that all these anti-engagement tracts can be dated to 1650.

people,[51] while the republication of Milton's *Tenure of Kings and Magistrates* at the end of 1649 suggests that this line of thought was felt to have continuing relevance.[52] Even Gerrard Winstanley, the leading spokesman for the Diggers, eventually wrote in defence of the engagement in similar terms.[53]

The most pressing ideological need, however, was for a more conservative defence of engagement, and it was clear what form this defence would have to take. The vulnerable feature of Rous's case had been his questionable interpretation of St Paul's injunction to obey the powers that be. What was needed was an argument in which less emphasis was placed on the need to understand God's purposes, and more on the practical reasons for obeying *de facto* powers. There was an existing tradition – deriving mainly from Grotius – in which the rights of *de facto* rulers (especially conquerors) had already been discussed, and in which the obligation to obey such powers had been vindicated less by invoking God's providence than by stressing the needs of civil society, and especially the paramount need for security and peace. I next wish to show how this line of thought was taken up and developed at this precise juncture in the English revolution. I want in particular to focus on a group of lay apologists for engagement whose specific aim was to rescue the providentialist defence of *de facto* powers from the vulnerable position in which Rous had left it, and to defend his position by means of these very different arguments.

III

The first writer to supply a more secularised defence of *de facto* powers was Anthony Ascham,[54] a protagonist of Parliament throughout the 1640s who was shortly to pay with his life for supporting the new regime when he was murdered on his arrival as ambassador to Spain in 1650.[55] As I have already noted in chapter 9, Ascham had published a *Discourse* at the end of 1648 treating the rights of conquerors in the manner of Grotius.[56] He now turned, in two pamphlets specifically directed against

[51] See Jordan 1942, pp. 140–202; Mendle 1995, pp. 164–5, 177–9.
[52] Dzelzainis 1991, p. xxvii notes that the second edition may have been in print as early as October.
[53] Winstanley 1968, p. 15.
[54] On Ascham see Zagorin 1954, pp. 64–7, Coltman 1962, pp. 197–239, Wallace 1968, pp. 30–68, Gunn 1969, pp. 82–7; Tuck 1979, pp. 123–4, 152–4.
[55] Bell 1990, p. 261. Ascham arrived on 26 May and was assassinated on the following day.
[56] Ascham 1648. Grotius provides the inspiration for Ascham's discussion in chapters 3 and 4, as Ascham himself (p. 10) points out.

Rous's critics, to show that this type of argument could be deployed to rescue Rous's defence of the Commonwealth. The first of these counterblasts appeared in July 1649 as *A Combate Betweene Two Seconds*,[57] and was shortly followed by a longer tract entitled *The Bounds & Bonds of Publique Obedience*.[58] By November 1649 Ascham had added ten new chapters to his original *Discourse* and reissued it, in a more polemical and topical form, under the title *Of the Confusions and Revolutions of Goverments*.[59]

These tracts reiterate Rous's suggestion that the new government can lawfully be obeyed even if it is not a lawful power.[60] They also contain something – although not very much – of Rous's invocations of God's providence as the touchstone for obedience.[61] But at the same time they introduce two new and contrasting lines of argument. One is the suggestion that an understanding of political obligation depends less on an awareness of God's providence than on a recognition of the needs of political life. The highest goal in any state is said to be the maintenance of what the *Combate* calls 'public peace and quietness' and 'the preservation of the commonwealth from destruction'.[62] 'The soul of a state', as *The Bounds & Bonds* explains, consists in 'the administration of publique justice and protection', while 'the end of all law and Government' is 'to preserve our persons and estates'.[63] The same assumptions recur in perhaps the most important of the chapters added to *Of the Confusions and Revolutions of Goverments*. The 'chief end' of government is now described as 'Security and Protection', and we are warned that we must be prepared to yield up 'much of our generall rights' in the name of attaining that end.[64]

Ascham corroborates these conclusions by considering the alternative to yielding up our rights. The sole alternative, the *Combate* maintains, is to lose 'all justice and order, give up all to power, and so bring confusion upon the whole'.[65] *The Bounds & Bonds* draws the same lesson still more emphatically. Unless we submit, we shall be resolving in effect that 'the Common-wealth were dead, and each man were left in his naturals,

---

57 [Ascham] 1649a. For the attribution see Wallace 1964, p. 391. Ascham's argument is mainly directly against [Ward] 1649.

58 [Ascham] 1649b. For the attribution see Wallace 1964, pp. 391–2. Ascham is here replying to *Grand Case* 1649 as well as to [Ward] 1649.

59 Ascham 1649c. Like the *Discourse*, this appeared under Ascham's own name.

60 [Ascham] 1649a, p. 6; [Ascham] 1649b, pp. 2–3; Ascham 1649c, pp. 31, 47.

61 See [Ascham] 1649a, p. 7; [Ascham] 1649b, pp. 22–3; Ascham 1649c, pp. 109–10, 115 and pp. 157–9, the conclusion of the *Confusions*, where Ascham reverts to a purely providentialist argument.

62 [Ascham] 1649a, p. 13.   63 [Ascham] 1649b, pp. 27, 31.

64 Ascham 1649c, p. 109.   65 [Ascham] 1649a, p. 14.

to subsist of himselfe, and to cast how hee could in such a state of warre, defend himselfe from all the rest of the world, every man in this State having an equall right to every thing'.[66] Both aspects of the argument are summarised in one of the new chapters added to the *Confusions*. 'He who would keep his Naturall Liberty without Relation to a State, shall loose that and everything else; and he who will resolve to loose that Liberty may conserve to himselfe the enjoyment of all necessary things.'[67]

The upshot is that Ascham insists on a duty to obey any power capable of providing us with protection and security. As the *Combate* puts it, there is already an obligation to obey if peace is being preserved, simply 'in regard of common good'.[68] In *The Bounds & Bonds* the argument is applied to the case in hand. With 'the whole Kingdome now receiving all law, protection and subordinate Magistracy' from the Commonwealth regime, we have a duty to obey it simply because 'we receive necessary protection' from it.[69] The *Confusions*, in its final additional chapter, reiterates the claim in consciously secular tones. 'It is but reasonable, just and Necessary, that we obey those, who in good and convenient things command and Plenarily possesse us.'[70]

The first change of emphasis introduced by Ascham is thus that he places his main stress on the needs of civil society. The vulnerable interpretation of the Pauline injunctions, on which Rous's case had rested, is effectively bypassed. The other change is that he begins in consequence to wobble over the question of whether it is necessary to concede (as Rous had done) that such powers are unjust. He begins, that is, to question the relevance of the distinction on which the counter-attack on Rous had relied, and thereby raises the possibility of bypassing the argument used by the presbyterians to dismantle Rous's case.

There is no suggestion of such a *démarche* in the *Combate*, but there is a distinct hint of it in *The Bounds & Bonds*. To say, Ascham complains, that those 'who have us in their full possessing may be obey'd in no lawful things' is tantamount to saying that no one has ever lived under a lawful power, since 'we and our forefathers for the most part, have live'd under no better Titles then Plenary possession'.[71] By the time we come to the additional chapters in the *Confusions*, Ascham is on the brink of concluding that the present regime is not unlawful after all. Why may we not regard a government as lawful, he rhetorically asks, even if it is not founded upon a 'formall succession of Persons', so long as it maintains

---

[66] [Ascham] 1649b, p. 27.   [67] Ascham 1649c, p. 138.   [68] [Ascham] 1649a, p. 15.
[69] [Ascham] 1649b, p. 24.   [70] Ascham 1649c, p. 157.   [71] [Ascham] 1649b, pp. 14–16.

'the same Law and Equity, which the Excluded Magistrates ought to have done, if they had succeeded'?[72]

Ascham's attempt to rescue and reformulate Rous's case was not at first taken up in the controversy about engagement. It is true that John Dury in his next pamphlet, his *Considerations* of December 1649, repeated Ascham's claim that 'we are bound to shew fidelity unto those of whom we desire protection'.[73] But Dury was always opportunistic in exploiting all available arguments, and although he mentions this doctrine he mainly continues to rely on the providentialist contention that 'it is not possible that any can attain to the height of power, without Gods disposall of it into his hands'.[74] It is also true that we encounter a tone more pragmatic even than Ascham's in Albertus Warren's *The Royalist Reform'd*, which was published within a month of Ascham's *Confusions and Revolutions of Goverments*. But Warren's tract is a genially cynical affair, with none of Ascham's careful attempts to meet the remaining scruples of moderates. He merely insists that, if we 'persevere in screwing rigor of general lawes up to the height of injury', we shall make ourselves 'a burden unto our fellow Subjects' and 'weaken the esteem of the commonlawes wholesome constitution'.[75]

Although it seemed at first that Ascham's argument might not be taken up, the situation began to alter as soon as he published his one further contribution to the debate. When he was denounced by the great Anglican casuist Robert Sanderson,[76] he responded in January 1650 with *A Reply to a Paper of Dr. Sandersons*, restating with greater confidence the new emphases he had introduced into the controversy.[77] He now sidesteps the question of providence at the outset by claiming that, although governments may have been 'ordeined sometimes and in some Places extraordinarily by God', yet they are 'ordinarily now' set up 'by man in his publique Necessities' with the aim of ensuring 'that nations may be conserved from Confusions and Private injuries'.[78] At the same time he comes even closer to withdrawing Rous's original concession that the new government is an unlawful power. A situation may properly

[72] Ascham 1649c, p. 137.
[73] [Dury] 1650a, p. 16. For the date and attribution see Wallace 1964, p. 394.
[74] [Dury] 1650a, p. 13.
[75] Warren 1649, p. 44. For the date of publication (26 November 1649) see Wallace 1964, p. 394.
[76] Sanderson replied to Ascham in [Sanderson] 1649. For the date of publication (1 December 1649) and the attribution see Wallace 1964, p. 394.
[77] [Ascham] 1650. For the date of publication (9 January 1650) and the attribution see Wallace 1964, p. 395.
[78] [Ascham] 1650, p. 2.

be described as lawful, he now suggests, even if it is not strictly legal, for we ought to accept that something can 'be Lawfull which is not so much Legall as Equitable'. Besides which, he adds, 'in this state of confus'd families, and uncertainty' the idea of providing a legal proof of anyone's right to rule is probably a moral impossibility.[79]

Ascham's mode of argument, concerned less to answer the immediate 'case of conscience' than to give a general account of political obligation, never commended itself to the casuists or presbyterian divines who mainly kept up the debate about engagement over the next two years. Among a group of lay theorists, however, this way of defending *de facto* powers had an immediate impact. The first signs of this influence can be traced in an anonymous tract entitled *A Discourse Concerning the Engagement*, which was published within a month of Ascham's *Reply* to Sanderson.[80] Thereafter the same line of thought reappears in a number of important tracts over the next two years: in the *Memorandums* of a conference held in London in early 1650 to discuss the engagement;[81] in Marchamont Nedham's *Case of the Commonwealth* and George Wither's *Respublica Anglicana* of the same year;[82] in John Drew's influential tract of 1651, *The Northern Subscribers Plea, Vindicated*;[83] and finally in Francis Osborne's *Perswasive to a Mutuall Compliance* of early 1652.[84]

All these lay defenders of engagement take up Ascham's two distinctive arguments. They manage, at least to some extent, to avoid questions about providence by concentrating instead on what political society is for, and answering that it is essentially a product of necessity and a means to secure protection and peace. This is first intimated in the *Discourse*, which speaks of the 'dismal confusion' that must 'unavoidably follow' any refusal of allegiance.[85] The same judgement is strongly underlined by Nedham, who opens his discussion by claiming that there is 'a necessity of some government at all times' to ensure 'the maintenance of civil conversation and to avoid confusion'.[86] The author of the *Memorandums* agrees that the purpose of government is to provide 'a mutual relation for safetie', a means to ensure 'that the Publick may be preserved in peace', so that the 'ruine of all' can be avoided.[87] Thereafter the same

---

[79] [Ascham] 1650, p. 4.
[80] *Discourse* 1650. For the date of publication (29 January 1650) see Wallace 1964, p. 396.
[81] *Memorandums* 1650. For the date of publication (21 August 1650) see Wallace 1964, p. 400.
[82] See Nedham 1969 and [Wither] 1650. For the first edition of Nedham's tract (May 1650) see Knachel 1969, p. ix. For the attribution of *Respublica Anglicana* to Wither see Wallace 1964, p. 401.
[83] Drew 1651. For the date of publication (August 1651) see Wallace 1964, p. 404.
[84] [Osborne] 1811. For the date of publication (18 February 1651) see Wallace 1964, p. 405.
[85] *Discourse* 1650, p. 5.   [86] Nedham 1969, p. 30.   [87] *Memorandums* 1650, pp. 12–13.

note is struck in several other tracts, perhaps most forcefully in Osborne's *Perswasive to a Mutuall Compliance*. Osborne ends with a warning that it would be 'an act of the highest indiscretion for people so long beaten by the cruell stormes of a civil warre to refuse for the present any harbour, though never so incommodious, and to venture againe the wrack of so sacred a vessel as the commonwealth'.[88]

We can appreciate, according to these writers, the compelling reason for these commitments if we reflect on the essentially anti-social nature of man. Here again they take up an argument that Ascham had particularly emphasised. Nedham traces the origins of government to the fact that the world 'grew more populous and more exceeding vicious', thereby generating a need for 'someone more potent than the rest that might restrain them by force' and prevent the 'grand enormities' that would otherwise have ensued.[89] The same pessimistic assumptions can be found in the *Memorandums*, in which we are told that men in civil society must be ruled with 'no intermission', since the need for absolute power to restrain them is 'absolutely necessarie for the preservation of humane societies'.[90] Once again Osborne offers an unusually forthright version of the same argument. Until our forefathers learned to submit to government, and not to oppose 'successful and irresistible powers', they condemned themselves to living in a state of war, with their births 'dated from some forraine conquest or their deaths from a civil dissention at home'.[91] The implication – as Sanderson had already pointed out in shocked tones in his critique of Ascham – is that self-preservation must be regarded not merely as the basic motive for political obedience but as 'the first and chiefest Obligation in the World'.[92]

The most notable feature of these discussions is that several of these writers corroborate these claims by making fully explicit the two further arguments that Ascham had only adumbrated. The view of political obligation at which Ascham had in effect arrived was that protection constitutes a sufficient title to allegiance. While he never explicitly states this doctrine, however, it was now enunciated by several of the writers I am considering in unequivocal terms. As the author of the *Discourse* proclaims, there is simply a 'mutual relation of Protection and Allegiance'.[93] Marchamont Nedham repeats that 'protection implies a return of obedience', and adds in more minatory tones that 'it cannot in reason be expected that those who refuse obedience to their authority should receive

---

[88] [Osborne] 1811, p. 157. [89] Nedham 1969, p. 15. [90] *Memorandums* 1650, p. 7.
[91] [Osborne] 1811, p. 157. [92] [Sanderson] 1649, p. 6. [93] *Discourse* 1650, p. 11.

the benefit of protection' from it.[94] Thereafter we find the same commitment endorsed by all the writers I have singled out. The author of the *Memorandums* declares that 'Protection and Allegiance are relatives'.[95] George Wither agrees that 'I am bound to give subjection in all lawful things, where I receive protection'.[96] John Drew applies the maxim to the case in hand by arguing that 'the mutuall relation of protection and Allegiance presseth us to an owning and realliance with them (our present Powers) as our actuall Protectours'.[97]

The other conclusion at which Ascham had only hinted was that, since protection constitutes a sufficient title to allegiance, the original concession made by Rous can perhaps be withdrawn. Again this suggestion is enthusiastically taken up by the writers I am considering, all of whom explicitly deny that the distinction between powers ordained and powers merely permitted by God has any force. All of them in consequence repudiate the counter-attack mounted by Rous's opponents by declaring that the new government not only has a just title to rule, but a title no less just than that of any other government. The author of the *Discourse* already permits himself this conclusion, albeit hesitantly. Some people object, he admits, that only 'lawful powers, a power of right' are ordained of God and ought to be obeyed. But perhaps, he goes on, 'our present Powers may fall within that compass'.[98] Marchamont Nedham exhibits no such hesitation at all. 'It is undeniably evident', he declares, 'that the present prevailing party in England have a right and just title to be our governors.'[99] Nedham's note of confidence was soon to be echoed more widely. According to the *Memorandums*, there can be no doubt that 'a full possession of the place of Government doth give a title to govern'.[100] And according to George Wither, there is no reason to deny that the existing government of England is no less 'just and pious' than many other governments whose legality has never been called in doubt.[101] Francis Osborne brings his *Perswasive* to a close by reiterating once more that 'the duty of obedience' to the newly established government 'cannot in justice be denied'.[102]

IV

During 1650 and 1651, when the debate about political obligation reached its height, the insights initially explored by Anthony Ascham

[94] Nedham 1969, p. 30.   [95] *Memorandums* 1650, p. 8.   [96] [Wither] 1650, Sig. A, 3[r].
[97] Drew 1651, p. 23.   [98] *Discourse* 1650, p. 8.   [99] Nedham 1969, p. 40.
[100] *Memorandums* 1650, p. 12.   [101] [Wither] 1650, pp. 42–3.   [102] [Osborne] 1811, p. 161.

were eventually converted into a full-scale secular defence of the Commonwealth government. The way in which Ascham's argument was taken up, however, was not perhaps as clear-cut a process as the above account may tend to suggest. Although the lay defenders of engagement presented a similar theory of obligation, none of them argued for it in a very systematic way, and few of them stated, except in fragmentary form, the pessimistic view of human nature on which it was based. And although they made use of purely secular arguments, most of them continued to invoke God's providence as a supplementary argument – and sometimes a prominent argument – in favour of the same conclusion. This is true even of Nedham and Osborne,[103] and true to an even greater degree of the other theorists who followed Ascham's perhaps somewhat equivocal lead.[104] Of all the writers who contributed to the debate about *de facto* powers, only one eliminated all invocations of God's providence and grounded a theory of obligation entirely on an account of the political nature of mankind. This was Thomas Hobbes, to whose place in the controversy I now wish to turn.[105]

It was exactly at this juncture that Hobbes published – for the first time in England, and for the first time in English – his major works on civil science. His *Elements of Law*, the manuscript of which he had circulated in 1640, was now put into print, the epistemological sections in February 1650 under the title *Humane Nature*,[106] the political sections three months later as *De Corpore Politico*.[107] Next there appeared an English translation of the one work on politics that Hobbes had already published, his *De Cive* of 1642, which was issued in March 1651 as *Philosophicall Rudiments Concerning Government and Society*.[108] Finally, only a few weeks later, Hobbes published the masterpiece on which he had been working intensively throughout the previous year, *Leviathan*.[109]

As soon as this remarkable sequence of texts appeared, they were immediately recognised by the lay defenders of engagement as offering an authoritative presentation of a theory of political obligation at which

---

[103] See Nedham 1969, pp. 47–50 and [Osborne] 1811, p. 159, both discussing St Paul's injunction to obey the powers that be.

[104] *Discourse* 1650, pp. 3–9; *Memorandums* 1650, Sig. A, 2ᵛ.

[105] For other aspects of Hobbes's connection with the controversy see Sampson 1990 and Burgess 1990.

[106] For the date of publication (2 February 1650) see 'Illustrations' 1848, pp. 170–1 and cf. Tönnies 1969a, p. v and note.

[107] For the date of publication (4 May 1650) see Wallace 1964, p. 398.

[108] For the date of publication (12 March 1651) see the title-page of Thomason's copy, British Library.

[109] For the date of publication of *Leviathan* (late April or early May 1651) see above, chapter 1 section III.

they had already arrived. As I noted in chapter 9, this was explicitly acknowledged by Ascham, and soon afterwards by Nedham, Osborne and Warren. This is not to say that they were pointing to Hobbes's direct influence on their own political works. Ascham, Warren and Nedham had all produced their defences of *de facto* power before they could have read *De Corpore Politico*, and there is good reason to doubt whether any of them knew at that stage of *De Cive*, which had only been published in Latin in Paris and Amsterdam.[110] The striking fact is that they appear to have come upon Hobbes's treatises after publishing their own works, at which juncture they recognised, and took the opportunity to say, that Hobbes had articulated their own view of political obligation in a more systematic and comprehensive style.

Anthony Ascham seems to have read *De Cive* between the appearance of the first and second version of his *Discourse*. He thereupon included a new chapter on the state of nature and political obligation, referring to Hobbes's views in corroboration of his own conclusions and quoting Hobbes (together with Grotius) as one of his authorities.[111] Marchamont Nedham never seems to have read *De Cive*, but he evidently came upon *De Corpore Politico* immediately after publishing his own *Case of the Commonwealth*. (The two works appeared in the same week.) This prompted him to add an appendix to the second edition of *The Case* in which he quotes Hobbes's views and uses them, like Ascham, to underpin the position he had already taken up.[112] Both Albertus Warren and Francis Osborne appear to have read *Leviathan* soon after it came out in the following year. Although neither of them refers to Hobbes in writing about the engagement, both of them quote him in later works by way of underpinning their own distinctly Hobbesian views about political authority.[113]

The point that needs to be stressed is that these defenders of *de facto* powers were undoubtedly right to see in *De Corpore Politico* and *Leviathan* a theory of political obligation similar to their own. Hobbes's account of man's anti-social nature, especially in *Leviathan*, offers a highly coloured version of an argument that several of them had already expressed. As Hobbes puts it in a celebrated summary, the nature of mankind is such that, 'during the time men live without a common Power to keep them all in awe', they will be 'in that condition which is called Warre; and such a warre, as is of every man, against every man'.[114] Hobbes also gives

[110] Warrender 1983a, pp. 5, 8–13.   [111] Ascham 1649c, pp. 108, 119.
[112] Nedham 1969, pp. 135–9.   [113] Warren 1653, p. 5; Osborne 1673, Sig. Pp, 6ʳ.
[114] Hobbes 1996, ch. 13, p. 88.

a more extended account of the implications already drawn from this argument by a number of *de facto* theorists, in particular the implication that we need to transfer our natural rights to a common power if there is to be any prospect of civil peace. As Hobbes explains, I must 'give up my Right of Governing my selfe' to a sovereign authority endowed with 'the use of so much Power and Strength' as to make it capable of enforcing peace equally on everyone.[115] Civil society is thus viewed in Hobbes's analysis, as in that of the other *de facto* theorists, as the sole alternative to anarchy and the indispensable means by which we can hope to protect ourselves from the anti-social behaviour of our fellow-citizens.

Hobbes is thus led to restate a number of the most distinctive arguments of the *de facto* theorists I have discussed. He agrees in the first place that conquest can give a valid title to allegiance.[116] He even systematises this claim by deriving all political authority from the 'Naturall force' of conquest when it is not derived from an act of 'institution' on the part of those covenanting to set up a government.[117] One of his main polemical aims in *Leviathan*, as he explains in the Conclusion, is to show 'what is Conquest' and 'how it comes about, that it obliges men to obey'.[118] The obligation arises, he maintains, when a man has 'liberty to submit' to a conqueror and 'consenteth, either by expresse words, or by other sufficient sign, to be his Subject'.[119] A subject is in turn said to possess this liberty when 'the means of his life is within the Guards and Garrisons of the Enemy', for it is then that his lawful ruler no longer has the capacity to protect him.[120]

Hobbes agrees in consequence with the *de facto* theorists that subjects are released from their oaths of allegiance as soon as their lawful rulers are conquered. 'If a Monarch subdued by war, render himself Subject to the Victor; his Subjects are delivered from their former obligations, and become obliged to the Victor.'[121] This leads him to endorse the further *de facto* claim that no valid distinction can be drawn between powers 'ordained' and powers merely 'permitted'. Any power with the capacity to protect us must be regarded as legitimate and entitled to obedience. It is an axiom in *Leviathan* that, in all discussions about government, 'the present ought alwaies to be preferred, maintained, and accounted best'.[122] To which Hobbes adds in his Conclusion – very much in the

---

[115] Hobbes 1996, ch. 17, p. 120.
[116] I have allowed this claim to stand, but I would not now wish to put the point in quite this way, for reasons I have given above in chapter 7 section V.
[117] Hobbes 1996, ch. 17, p. 121.   [118] Hobbes 1996, Conclusion, p. 484.
[119] Hobbes 1996, Conclusion, p. 484.   [120] Hobbes 1996, Conclusion, p. 484.
[121] Hobbes 1996, ch. 21, p. 154.   [122] Hobbes 1996, ch. 42, p. 379.

spirit of the engagers – that any attempt to ground political obligation on right rather than possession will leave 'no tie of the Subjects obedience to their Soveraign at this day in all the world'.[123]

Like other *de facto* theorists, Hobbes grounds these conclusions on the assumption of a mutual relationship between the duty of our sovereigns to protect us and our duty as subjects to obey. As he argues in chapter 21 of *Leviathan*, 'the Obligation of Subjects to the Soveraign, is understood to last as long, and no longer, than the power lasteth, by which he is able to protect them'.[124] Anyone who enjoys protection 'is obliged (without fraudulent pretence of having submitted himselfe out of fear,) to protect his Protection as long as he is able'.[125] But if there is 'no farther protection of Subjects in their loyalty; then is the Common-wealth DISSOLVED, and every man at liberty to protect himselfe by such courses as his own discretion shall suggest unto him'.[126] The basic idea, as Hobbes summarises in his Conclusion, is that anyone who agrees to submit to the powers that be and 'live under their Protection openly' is thereby 'understood to submit himselfe to the Government'.[127]

Hobbes's *Leviathan* can thus be represented as a slightly belated but uniquely important contribution to the lay defence of engagement. It might still be doubted, however, whether this accurately reflects Hobbes's intentions in writing the work. But there can be little doubt that it does. When Hobbes replied in the 1660s to the criticisms made by John Wallis of his loyalty during the revolution, it was his proudest boast about *Leviathan* that it had 'framed the minds of a thousand gentlemen to a conscientious obedience to present government, which otherwise would have wavered in that point'.[128] And when he published *Leviathan* he made it clear that he intended his treatise as a contribution to the debate about the rights of *de facto* powers. It goes without saying that *Leviathan* is much else besides. But when Hobbes speaks in his Conclusion about what he has tried to accomplish, it is this aspiration that he emphasises himself. His book, he says, was 'occasioned by the disorders of the present time'.[129] It was motivated by the discovery 'that the Civill warres have not yet sufficiently taught men, in what point of time it is, that a Subject becomes obliged to the Conquerour'.[130] And it was written 'without other designe, than to set before mens eyes the mutuall Relation between Protection and Obedience'.[131]

[123] Hobbes 1996, Conclusion, p. 486.   [124] Hobbes 1996, ch. 21, p. 153.
[125] Hobbes 1996, ch. 29, p. 230.   [126] Hobbes 1996, ch. 29, p. 230.
[127] Hobbes 1996, Conclusion, p. 485.   [128] Hobbes 1845j, p. 336.
[129] Hobbes 1996, Conclusion, p. 491.   [130] Hobbes 1996, Conclusion, p. 484.
[131] Hobbes 1996, Conclusion, p. 491.

As we have seen, the idea of such a mutual relation had already been enunciated by several of the *de facto* theorists. Hobbes was clearly aware of this fact, and even appears to have recast his own argument to echo the formula they had popularised. The contention that protection and obedience are mutually related is arguably implicit in *De Cive*. But it is never explicitly stated, and although it is again implicit in the *De Corpore Politico* of 1650 it is not announced openly until the final paragraph of *Leviathan*. It is only at that moment – at the height of the controversy about engagement – that Hobbes employs the formula of 'mutuall Relation' for the first time.

These family resemblances between Hobbes's account of political obligation and that of the *de facto* theorists suggest two reflections about the place of Hobbes's political theory in the ideological contests of the English revolution. First of all, it is a mistake to suppose (as many commentators have done) that Hobbes's theory was an isolated phenomenon in the intellectual world of its time. We shall misunderstand his achievement if we try to give an account of his special status as a political philosopher mainly in terms of the alleged novelty of his doctrines. Hobbes's claim to originality lies to a greater degree at the epistemological level, in the reasons he gave for holding his political beliefs, than in his beliefs themselves. It was in his attempt to deduce his political system from an account of human nature, and in his emancipation from the confines of the providentialist vocabulary, that Hobbes made his most original contributions to the political theory of his age. It was this achievement that was barely hinted at by the other *de facto* theorists, even though several of them, independently of Hobbes, articulated a number of political doctrines that have since been associated exclusively with Hobbes's name.

11

Hobbes and his disciples in France and England

I

When Hobbes arrived in France at the end of 1640, 'the first of all that fled' from the growing threat of civil war in England,[1] he began an exile that was to last eleven years, an exile that was also to prove the most intellectually fruitful period of his long life. In Paris he reached the height of his polemical powers, conducting his debates with Descartes about the existence of secondary qualities[2] and with Bishop Bramhall about the freedom of the will.[3] At the same time he brought to fruition a lifetime of speculation about the science of politics, completing *De Cive* and writing the whole of *Leviathan*.[4] He also became active in what he described as a 'good company' of scientists and philosophers gathered round the figure of Marin Mersenne,[5] and spent much of his time in mathematical speculation and the conduct of optical research.

It may not have been pure chance that Hobbes in exile reached the zenith of his creative powers. For it is an ironic but revealing fact about his biography that in Paris he found exactly the kind of congenial intellectual company that he always lacked at home. On his return to England in 1651 he became an isolated figure. He was isolated for much of the time in the remote wilds of Derbyshire, where 'the

---

This chapter is an abbreviated and extensively revised version of an article that originally appeared under the same title in *Comparative Studies in Society and History* 8 (1966), pp. 153–67.

[1] Hobbes 1840d, p. 414.
[2] The best way to follow this dispute is in Hobbes 1994, pp. 54–80, 86–114, 116–20.
[3] For a discussion, see Robertson 1886, pp. 163–7. For a bibliography of the debate with Bramhall see Macdonald and Hargreaves 1952, pp. 37–41.
[4] For the composition and publication of these works see above, chapter 1 section III.
[5] Hobbes to Payne, 'Illustrations' 1848, p. 171. Hobbes provides a fine description of the Mersenne circle in his verse *Vita*. See Hobbes 1839b, p. xci, where he speaks of Mersenne as 'my faithful friend, and a learned man, wise and outstandingly good'. ('Mersennus, fidus amicus / Vir doctus, sapiens, eximieque bonus.')

want of learned Conversation', as he confessed to John Aubrey 'was a great inconvenience'.[6] He was isolated too in much of his political and mathematical speculation, provoking many quarrels with the orthodox scientists and divines.[7] He took no part in the scientific societies of the Restoration period and he published no further treatises of political philosophy.

Nevertheless, it would be a mistake to infer – as many commentators have done – that Hobbes became a complete outcast, a writer who was read only to be confuted.[8] This is to ignore the significance of his links with the more sympathetic intellectual community he found in France, and to overlook the fact that, even after his return to England, he remained closely in touch with a number of these scientific and philosophical friends. There is evidence that he continued to exchange views with them about his political works, and that they kept him up to date with new developments in the academies of Paris. Furthermore, it is clear from their correspondence that Hobbes left an abiding impact and an avowed following in France. Neither the extent nor the significance of these links have received any attention,[9] but they provide us with important new evidence about the preoccupations of the republic of letters at the time, as well as about the immediate impact of Hobbes's own works.

II

It is possible to reconstruct, from studying their correspondence, a list of most of the members of the Mersenne circle whom Hobbes met in Paris and got to know well. Some of this information can be gleaned from Mersenne's own newsletters, as well as from those of Samuel Sorbière and other likeminded *savants* who made it their business to keep the circles of the learned in touch with each other. But most of the evidence comes from the archive of Hobbes's own correspondence at Chatsworth,

---

[6] Aubrey 1898, vol. I, p. 338.
[7] For these disputes see Robertson 1886, pp. 167–85; Mintz 1962, pp. 63–109; and especially the very fine account in Jesseph 1999.
[8] Mintz 1962, p. 147.
[9] This was true at the time when I wrote this chapter, but the situation has been transformed by the appearance of Noel Malcolm's definitive edition of Hobbes's correspondence. This contains a 'Biographical Register' of Hobbes's correspondents (Malcolm 1994c), in which the links between Hobbes and his French disciples are fully disclosed. I have relied extensively on this superb piece of scholarship to correct and supplement my own account.

which has hitherto remained largely unexamined.[10] It is on this source that my ensuing discussion will largely be based.[11]

The weekly meetings held by Mersenne at his convent near the Place Royale provided Hobbes with an opportunity to meet several of the most important representatives of continental scientific thought.[12] Mersenne introduced him to Pierre Gassendi, a prominent member of his circle and of the later 'academy' *chez* Montmor.[13] Hobbes also seems to have met Pierre Fermat,[14] perhaps the leading French mathematician of the age, who later wrote some observations on Hobbes's own mathematical works.[15] And he encountered several of the other giant figures mentioned by de Coste as friends of Mersenne,[16] including Descartes,[17] Christiaan Huygens[18] and Gilles de Roberval, with whom he engaged in a debate about geometry at one of Mersenne's meetings in 1644.[19]

Hobbes made his closest friends, however, among a number of lesser luminaries associated with this group. These included several other English expatriates who had settled into Parisian intellectual life.[20] One of these was Sir Kenelm Digby, a friend of Mersenne's since the 1630s,[21] who had written to Hobbes from Paris as early as 1637 to send him a copy of Descartes's newly published *Discours de la méthode*.[22] Hobbes also

---

[10] I have allowed this claim to stand, if only to explain my own original motivation for writing this essay, but these materials have now been studied and published in full by Noel Malcolm in his edition of Hobbes's correspondence (Hobbes 1994). I have been happy to correct and supplement my own transcriptions and translations by reference to Malcolm's work.

[11] These manuscripts, formerly housed at Hardwick, have previously been made available to three scholars, none of whom made any use of the correspondence. Robertson 1886, p. 236n. mentions du Verdus, but cites no letters and dismisses the rest of the correspondence as 'of no account'. Tönnies 1912, p. 45 refers to the manuscripts, but again makes no use of the correspondence. So too Strauss 1963, p. xiii. But see now Hobbes 1994, Noel Malcolm's edition of the entire correspondence.

[12] Malcolm 1994c, p. 862.

[13] Malcolm 1994c, pp. 835–6. They subsequently corresponded with each other. See Hobbes 1994, Letter 62, pp. 178–9 and Letter 66, pp. 184–5.

[14] Lenoble 1943, p. xxxviii. I have allowed this claim to stand, but it was with Fermat's son Samuel that Hobbes became closely acquainted. See Malcolm 1994c, pp. 832–3.

[15] Hobbes 1994, p. 614; cf. Sorbière 1709, p. 96.

[16] See [Coste] 1649, pp. 30 and 89 for lists of some of Mersenne's friends, including Descartes, Fermat, Galileo, Gassendi and Hobbes himself.

[17] Hobbes first met Descartes in Paris in 1648, although they had already corresponded (with Mersenne acting as intermediary) in 1641. See Hobbes 1994, pp. 54–80, 86–114, 116–20 and cf. Malcolm 1994c, p. 827.

[18] Hobbes definitely met Huygens after returning to England, but may have encountered him at an earlier date. See Malcolm 1994c, pp. 842–3.

[19] Malcolm 1994c, p. 908.

[20] Brown 1934, pp. 59–63 rightly stresses this point.

[21] Coste 1649, p. 92; cf. Malcolm 1994c, p. 830 and note.

[22] Hobbes 1994, Letter 25, pp. 42–9.

made the acquaintance of Dr John Bramhall, a Laudian bishop in exile from the puritan revolution in England, who was later to prove one of his most effective controversial opponents.[23] Soon afterwards he befriended the young William Petty, just qualified as a doctor at Leiden, who was sent to Paris by John Pell with a letter of introduction to Hobbes.[24] Petty began to attend Mersenne's gatherings towards the end of 1645,[25] and subsequently worked with Hobbes on his *Minute or First Draught of the Optiques*, the surviving fair copy of which is in Petty's hand.[26] Charles Cavendish speaks of Petty in a letter of 1648 as a friend of Hobbes,[27] and Benjamin Worsley reports around the same time that Hobbes had made a present to Petty of a valuable lens for a microscope.[28]

Hobbes also counted among his close acquaintances a number of French philosophers and scientists whom he encountered *chez* Mersenne. One was Henri de Montmor, a rich virtuoso and patron of both Descartes and Gassendi, whose house became a regular meeting-place of the learned after Mersenne's death in 1648.[29] Another was Charles du Bosc, who had already stayed with Hobbes in London during the 1620s, and whom Hobbes was later to describe as 'a very dear friend'.[30] Du Bosc appears to have attended Mersenne's meetings on a regular basis in the early 1640s, and Sorbière later recollected that it was on one of these occasions that he himself encountered both du Bosc and Hobbes.[31] Claude Mylon, a pupil of Roberval's, similarly seems to have been introduced to Hobbes by Mersenne,[32] and in the first of his surviving letters to Hobbes he speaks warmly of their time together in Paris.[33] Thomas de Martel, another young associate of Mersenne's,[34] was similarly encouraged by

---

[23] Skinner 1996, pp. 378–80.

[24] Fitzmaurice 1895, p. 7; Strauss 1954, pp. 26, 28–9. Cf. Hobbes 1994, p. 752n.

[25] See Fitzmaurice 1895, pp. 7–8, a letter of November 1645 from Petty to Pell in which Petty speaks of holding discussions with Mersenne, Hobbes and Sir Charles Cavendish. See also Brown 1934, pp. 60–2.

[26] BL Harl. MS 3360. Cavendish to Pell, 11 November 1645, BL Add. MS 4278, fo. 223ʳ includes a postscript saying of this treatise that 'Mʳ: Petit hath writ it faire'. Cf. Aubrey 1898, vol. 1, pp. 367–8 and Fitzmaurice 1895, pp. 5–6.

[27] Charles Cavendish to William Petty, 17 April 1648, Hartlib Papers (Sheffield) 8/29/1A: 'I shewed Mr Hobbes your Letter who liked it soe well that he desired me to lend it to him which I did knowing him to be yowr friend.'

[28] Benjamin Worsley to an unidentified correspondent, 22 June 1648, Hartlib Papers (Sheffield) 42/1/1A.

[29] Brown 1934, pp. 64–90; cf. Hobbes 1994, p. 497 note 2.

[30] Pintard 1943, p. 627. For Hobbes's encomium see Hobbes 1994, Letter 140, p. 513.

[31] Malcolm 1994c, p. 796.

[32] Mylon certainly knew Mersenne by this time. See Malcolm 1994c, p. 868. But it may be that Mylon met Hobbes through du Verdus or their teacher Roberval.

[33] Hobbes 1994, Letter 81, pp. 272–6.   [34] Brown 1934, p. 59; cf. Pintard 1943, p. 332.

Mersenne to put himself in touch with Hobbes, and we find him writing to assure Mersenne in November 1643 that they had duly met.[35] Finally, it was through de Martel that Hobbes in turn encountered Sorbière, who had become well known to Gassendi as well as Mersenne in the course of 1641.[36] De Martel visited Sorbière in Holland in 1642, and introduced him to Hobbes soon after Sorbière's return to Paris in 1645.[37]

There were two other *habitués* of Mersenne's gatherings whom Hobbes appears to have met only towards the end of his stay in Paris, but who quickly became his intimate friends. One was Abraham du Prat, who had been an acquaintance of Sorbière's at least since 1640.[38] Sorbière later recalled that it was in du Prat's company that Mersenne showed him the manuscript of Hobbes's *De Cive* shortly before it was published in 1642.[39] Du Prat travelled extensively in the 1640s, but he returned to Paris in 1650 and it seems to have been in that year that he finally met and was befriended by Hobbes.[40] Similarly, it was almost at the end of his time in France that Hobbes made the acquaintance of François du Verdus, considered by Mersenne to be the most gifted of Roberval's pupils in mathematics.[41] Although he was more than thirty years younger than Hobbes, du Verdus became one of Hobbes's closest friends and subsequently his most indefatigable correspondent after Hobbes's return to England in 1652.

These were the men who kept Hobbes in touch with the world of continental science in his later life. Mylon, du Bosc and du Prat all corresponded with him in the 1650s, but it was Sorbière, de Martel and du Verdus with whom he retained the closest intellectual as well as personal links. Sorbière was to perform some signal services for Hobbes shortly after their initial encounter in Paris in 1645. First he agreed to see through the press the revised and extended version of *De Cive*, which was duly published in Amsterdam by the firm of Elzevir in 1647.[42] Next he made his own translation of the book, which appeared as *Elemens philosophiques du citoyen* in 1649.[43] Later he agreed to act once again as intermediary when the Amsterdam firm of Johan Blaeu published Hobbes's *Opera Philosophica* in 1668.[44] Hobbes rewarded Sorbière with

---

[35] Malcolm 1994c, p. 851.   [36] Malcolm 1994c, p. 893.   [37] Malcolm 1994c, p. 895.

[38] Malcolm 1994c, p. 879.   [39] Malcolm 1994c, pp. 879, 893–4.   [40] Malcolm 1994c, p. 880.

[41] Malcolm 1994c, p. 905. On the relations between Roberval's and du Verdus's mathematical work see Cantor 1880–1908, vol. 2, pp. 800–6.

[42] For Sorbière's involvement in this project see above, chapter 1 section III.

[43] See Hobbes 1649 and cf. Macdonald and Hargreaves 1952, p. 20.

[44] Malcolm 1994c, p. 897. For some indication of the extent of Sorbière's negotiations on Hobbes's behalf see Hobbes 1994, pp. 557, 564, 574, 586, 701.

the dedication of his *Dialogus Physicus*, in which he speaks of Sorbière as a most learned and beloved friend, and praises him for his unwavering commitment to the public good.[45]

Thomas de Martel was another correspondent of Hobbes's in his later years who seems to have been a particularly close friend in Paris. When Hobbes decided in 1646 to retreat from the city with the aim of trying to complete his *De Corpore*, it was to de Martel's family estates in Languedoc that he arranged to withdraw.[46] As we saw in chapter 1, Hobbes's plans were forestalled by the arrival of the English Court in Paris and his appointment as mathematics tutor to the Prince of Wales. But Hobbes remained closely in touch with de Martel, who wrote to him in England on a number of occasions in the 1650s,[47] always expressing his veneration and his gratitude for Hobbes's many kindnesses.[48]

Of all these friends, however, the closest seems to have been François du Verdus. When Hobbes came to write his verse autobiography, the *Vita Carmine Expressa*, he addressed it to 'my candid du Verdus, who understands my ways'.[49] The two men always professed the highest regard for each other. This prompted du Verdus to make a translation of Hobbes's *De Cive*, which he issued as *Les Elemens de la politique de Monsieur Hobbes* in 1660.[50] Hobbes's admiration prompted him to respond by dedicating one of his works to du Verdus, the mathematical *Examinatio et Emendatio*, which also appeared in 1660. Although they never met again after Hobbes's return to England in 1652, they continued to exchange letters for the next twenty years.[51]

III

If we now turn to the correspondence between Hobbes and these various friends, we begin to see the significance of the links he maintained with them after his return to England. One of their aims was to keep him informed – and to seek his advice – about their continuing efforts to place their scientific meetings on a firmer institutional base. We find Abraham du Prat writing in 1656 to tell Hobbes about the new Montmor 'academy'

[45] Hobbes 1985, pp. 346, 348.
[46] Hobbes 1994, Letter 40, p. 127. Hobbes also mentions the episode in his prose *Vita*. See Hobbes 1839a, p. xv, where he refers to de Martel as his noble friend from Languedoc.
[47] See Hobbes 1994, Letters 69, 72, 124, 129, 130, pp. 198–203, 208–10, 461–4, 479–84.
[48] See for example Hobbes 1994, Letter 69, pp. 198–203.
[49] Hobbes 1839b, p. xcix: 'Ipse meos nosti, Verdusi candide, mores.'
[50] See Hobbes 1660 and cf. Macdonald and Hargreaves 1952, pp. 21–2.
[51] Du Verdus sent his first surviving letter to Hobbes in 1653, his last in 1674. See Hobbes 1994, pp. 181–2, 736–43.

in which a number of their mutual friends had become involved.[52] When the academy was eventually incorporated in 1657, taking on a formal existence with Sorbière as its secretary, we find Sorbière himself writing to Hobbes to explain how this had come about, and to send him the constitution which he and du Prat had drawn up.[53] Sorbière was at first optimistic about this new *Assemblée*, as he called it, and boasted that 'it would be hard to put together a comparable gathering' anywhere else for discussing 'questions of natural science'.[54] But by the early 1660s we find him admitting that they are no longer foregathering *chez* Montmor, and that their new meeting-place has proved such a failure that 'in a short while there will be nobody at all wanting to go there'.[55] He also reports somewhat enviously that they have just heard about the incorporation of the Royal Society in London, adding the fervent hope that Hobbes will keep them in touch with its activities.[56]

Hobbes's friends were still more concerned to keep him up to date with the progress of their own research. Hobbes accordingly continued to hear reverberations throughout the 1650s of discussions he had held in Paris a decade earlier. Pierre Guisony[57] wrote in 1659 to inform him that 'at M. de Montmor's academy M. du Prat led us to hope that you would explain to us the phenomenon of the rising of the water in the small siphon'. He begged Hobbes not merely to supply the explanation but 'never to tire of instructing us'.[58] Soon afterwards Sorbière sent Hobbes some reflections about his dispute with Robert Boyle, in the course of which he expressed some doubts about Hobbes's contention that the universe is wholly filled with matter.[59] Hobbes also continued to receive a number of letters about mathematics, one of the leading interests of the Montmor group.[60] Claude Mylon wrote to him on several occasions in the mid-1650s about the dimensions of the circle,[61] although his letters express increasing frustration at Hobbes's inability to see that

---

[52] Hobbes 1994, Letter 106, pp. 393–4.   [53] Hobbes 1994, Letter 133, pp. 491–7.
[54] Hobbes 1994, Letter 133, pp. 494, 496.
[55] Hobbes 1994, Letter 150, p. 542. Cf. Brown 1934, pp. 117–34.
[56] Hobbes 1994, Letter 142, p. 519.
[57] An occasional member of the Montmor group, he was regarded as an expert on 'physical speculations'. See the letter from Chapelain to Huygens, 20 August 1659, in Huygens 1888–1950, vol. 2, p. 468 and note.
[58] Hobbes 1994, Letter 136, p. 503.   [59] Hobbes 1994, Letter 147, pp. 527–30.
[60] See Brown 1934, p. 99, noting that Henry Oldenburg described the Montmor group in 1659 as chiefly concerned with mathematics, specifically mentioning Abraham du Prat and Claude Mylon.
[61] Hobbes 1994, Letter 81, pp. 272–6; Letter 92, pp. 314–16; Letter 128, pp. 476–9; Letter 131, pp. 485–7; Letter 132, pp. 488–90.

his aspiration to square the circle was a futile one and that his calculations were 'absolutely false'.[62]

Hobbes was never regarded, however, merely as an ordinary corresponding member of the Montmor academy. He was treated with the special deference due to a 'very great philosopher', as du Verdus called him, someone who reasons from 'true principles which you alone have discovered'.[63] 'Your mind', as du Prat similarly assured him, is 'the absolute ruler of my own – and of my heart also'.[64] Letters from several strangers speak of their wish to come to England specifically in order to meet him. Paris is said to be 'full of such worthy people' (according to one letter of introduction) 'who ask me every day what you are doing, and enquire whether we can have any hope of receiving some new product of your genius'.[65] Another writer who proposed coming to England specifically to hold discussions with Hobbes said of his *De Corpore* that 'I have seen the works of Descartes, Gassendi, Galileo, and Mersenne, but they all amount to nothing in comparison with what I learn every day from your book', which 'will live and be read and admired by the most distant of future generations'.[66]

The letters Hobbes received from members of the Montmor group frequently express a similar deference – without the fatuity, but with no less seriousness. An introduction to Hobbes was clearly regarded as essential for any member visiting England. When Guisony arrived at Oxford in 1659, he had instructions from both du Prat and Sorbière to get in touch with Hobbes, and immediately wrote to tell him that no one 'has any right to challenge you for the first rank' among 'the great intellects' now living in England.[67] When Sorbière himself came to England four years later, he began by seeking out Hobbes as one of the scholars he principally needed to consult in his quest for instruction 'in matters of Literature, and the Sciences'.[68] And when he wrote to Hobbes immediately after his visit he saluted him as 'my dear master, my reverend Father' and assured him of his unfailing discipleship.[69]

Hobbes's connections with these friends from his Paris days went much further than the exchanges of such civilities. It is evident that, as the author of *Leviathan*, Hobbes also had an immediate and powerful influence on their ways of thought. It happens, moreover, that on this issue his

---

[62] Hobbes 1994, Letter 128, p. 478; cf. also Letter 131, pp. 485–7.
[63] Hobbes 1994, Letter 172, pp. 672–3.   [64] Hobbes 1994, Letter 70, p. 205.
[65] Hobbes 1994, Letter 173, p. 675.   [66] Hobbes 1994, Letter 85, p. 291.
[67] Hobbes 1994, Letter 136, p. 502.   [68] Sorbière 1709, p. 26.
[69] Hobbes 1994, Letter 154, p. 557.

correspondence is a particularly revealing source. One reason is that Hobbes's return to England virtually coincided with the publication of the book. The friends with whom he had discussed it in Paris were thus left to put into writing all the questions that their reading of it raised in their minds. A further reason is that *Leviathan* quickly acquired such a sinister reputation that public avowals of admiration for the work became difficult to make. As a result, the printed sources tend to suggest that Hobbes remained a figure in complete intellectual isolation. But in the privacy of his correspondence we can see more clearly the positive appeal of his arguments, perhaps especially to those who – like du Verdus in Bordeaux – had recently suffered from the upheavals associated with the Fronde.[70]

One development to which Hobbes's correspondence bears witness is that *Leviathan* aroused an immediate and extensive following in France. Copies were circulated (according to du Bosc) among most of Hobbes's friends in the Montmor academy.[71] There was also (according to du Prat as well as du Bosc) a widespread demand for a French version of the work.[72] The Parisian booksellers were even prepared at one stage to raise a fund among themselves to finance a translator.[73] We find du Prat writing in 1656 to complain to Hobbes about the continuing lack of a French edition,[74] while his nephew François later proposed to take the matter in hand himself:

I have this very day spoken to a bookseller about ye printing of y^r Leviathan here, who did open his eares to y^t proposition. & answer'd y^t y^r de Cive in French is sold publickly & y^t you were an author so well knowne as he made no doubt but ye booke would sell away. For my part, I have such a minde to ye worke, as y^t I shall never be satisfi'd till I come to an end of it.[75]

The younger du Prat was by no means alone in his enthusiasm. Charles du Bosc had already written to Hobbes that 'all ye learned men I know desire that Leuiathan were in french or Latine'.[76] Samuel Sorbière likewise urged the importance of arranging for a translation to be made.[77]

Hobbes's friends eventually went some way towards supplying the need for a translation themselves. As we have seen, Sorbière had already

[70] On this point see Malcolm 1994c, p. 908.
[71] Hobbes 1994, Letter 137, p. 504. Du Bosc mentions that he has already circulated copies to Sorbière, de Martel and du Prat.
[72] See Hobbes 1994, Letter 74 (du Prat to Hobbes), p. 214; Hobbes 1994, Letter 137 (du Bosc to Hobbes), p. 504.
[73] Hobbes 1994, Letter 74, p. 214.
[74] Hobbes 1994, Letter 77, p. 246: 'shall we never see your *Leviathan* in Latin or French? Will England have the enjoyment of this excellent work all on her own . . . ?'
[75] Hobbes 1994, Letter 155, p. 559.   [76] Hobbes 1994, Letter 137, p. 504.
[77] Hobbes 1994, Letter 162, p. 586.

published a French version of *De Cive*, while du Verdus was to issue a further translation in 1660.[78] Abraham du Prat wrote to Hobbes a year later to say that he and Sorbière were now meditating the more ambitious scheme of translating *Leviathan*, and that he proposed to undertake the project himself.[79] Nothing seems to have come of the venture, but in the meantime François du Verdus had contacted Hobbes to announce with characteristic hyperbole that he was learning English with the sole purpose of translating Hobbes's masterpiece.[80] He got as far as sending Hobbes a long set of queries about specific arguments[81] together with a specimen translation of chapter 4, *Du Langage*,[82] before evidently abandoning the task.

Hobbes's French disciples regarded him not merely as the greatest but as the most convincing political philosopher of the age. Hobbes's vaunted 'demonstration' of the need for absolute sovereignty, so troubling to his English contemporaries, seems to have struck his admirers in France as his finest achievement. Du Verdus's pupil François Peleau (who told Hobbes in 1656 that he had read *De Cive* thirty times)[83] wrote of *Leviathan* that 'I have never seen anything so fine', adding that it had given him the ambition of travelling to England 'purely in order to see you and listen to you', for 'in that way, I think, I shall draw philosophy and truth from their very source'.[84]

A year earlier, du Verdus had offered an even more explicit endorsement of Hobbes's basic argument:

You are the only person to have demonstrated, from the nature of civil society, that the authority of the state is absolute and indivisible. That is something which it is absolutely necessary for subjects to be well convinced of, and which they cannot truly understand without hating civil war and without being content to live in peace among themselves under the power of the state.[85]

Soon afterwards we find Sorbière writing to Hobbes in strikingly similar and even more fulsome terms:

You are indeed the father of politics and its leading expert, the person who, like Galileo in physics, put an end to empty quibbling on that subject; and what others had put forward in a desultory, ill-grounded, and obfuscating way, you with your lucid intelligence organised into a tightly ordered formation. So

---

[78] Macdonald and Hargreaves 1952, pp. 13, 20–22.
[79] Hobbes 1994, Letter 144, p. 523.
[80] Hobbes 1994, Letter 67, p. 190 and Letter 108, p. 413.
[81] Hobbes 1994, enclosure with Letter 100, pp. 345–58.
[82] Hobbes 1994, enclosure with Letter 108, pp. 402–10.
[83] Hobbes 1994, Letter 85, pp. 290–1.   [84] Hobbes 1994, Letter 93, pp. 318–19.
[85] Hobbes 1994, Letter 75, p. 228; cf. also Hobbes 1994, Letter 172, p. 673.

henceforth no seeker after truth, and no one who has learned from his own experience, will be able to doubt that what you have asserted about the state of nature and the state of dominion is absolutely certain and proven.[86]

Hobbes's own pupil William Petty later expressed a similar admiration for Hobbes's theory of sovereignty. His memoranda on the topic make it evident that he not only admired but agreed with Hobbes's basic argument. Petty not only hails him as 'the illustrious Hobbes, who invariably penetrates the nature of everything he discusses to the utmost depth'.[87] He also accepts that 'the Words *Soveraignty & Empire* doe signify even as Large a Power as Mr. Hobs attributes to his *Leviathan*; That is to say, a Power & Right of doing all things that are naturally possible'.[88]

It is true that this willingness to accept *Leviathan* as (in du Verdus's words) the only 'true, good political philosophy'[89] was largely confined, during Hobbes's own lifetime, to his private circle of friends. But they also made determined efforts to spread the word of Hobbes's genius to a wider audience. When Sir Samuel Tuke of the Royal Society visited the Montmor 'academy' in 1661, Henri de Montmor assured him that they regarded Hobbes as one of the *savants* most capable of 'the advancement of all sorts of learning in England' – a view that Tuke duly conveyed back to the Society-men in London.[90] Sorbière likewise made a number of efforts to popularise Hobbes's work. When he issued his translation of the *De Corpore Politico* in 1652, he began by assuring his readers that 'I can vouch for the fact that all the works which have come from the pen of this excellent Author up to the present time have been masterpieces.'[91] Sir William Petty similarly remained loyal to his youthful enthusiasm, continuing to urge Hobbes on his correspondents and even his children as the only modern writer worth reading on the theory of government.[92]

Admittedly Hobbes's disciples mainly spoke and wrote of his work in this rather crude spirit of propaganda. But some of them also studied his political system in a more critical and even creative way. Although no printed evidence has survived of such sympathetic efforts to evaluate Hobbes's conception of a 'geometry' of politics, several discussions among the unpublished letters and memoranda of du Verdus and Petty are concerned with exactly this central theme of Hobbes's work.

---

[86] Hobbes 1994, Letter 141, p. 517.
[87] Petty 1927, vol. 2, p. 35: 'Clarissimus Hobbius qui eorum quae tractat omnium naturam penitissimi scrutari solet.'
[88] Petty 1927, vol. 1, p. 219.   [89] Hobbes 1994, Letter 172, p. 673.
[90] Birch 1756–7, vol. 1, p. 267.
[91] [Sorbière] 1652, Sig. A, 3ᵛ: 'Tous les ouvrages qui jusqu'a present sont sortis de la plume de cet excellent Auteur sont des chef-d'oeuvres je t'avoüe.'
[92] Petty 1927, vol. 2, p. 5; cf also Petty 1928, Letter 181, p. 305.

Although their remarks are scattered and few, they provide the first evidence that has come to light about the immediate influence of Hobbes's hopes and schemes for a properly scientific theory of government. Both du Verdus and Petty agree with Hobbes that his most epoch-making and fruitful suggestion is that a science of politics must be constructed by a method analogous to geometrical demonstration. They endorse Hobbes's contention in *Leviathan* that geometry is 'the onely Science that it hath pleased God hitherto to bestow on mankind'.[93] Du Verdus agrees that 'the true philosophy' must be 'a geometrical philosophy', since 'it is not possible to be a philosopher without also being a geometer'.[94] Sir William Petty writes in almost identical terms. 'I think that the best Geometricians were the most Sagacious men, or that the most Sagacious men did ever make the Best Geometricians.'[95] Furthermore, it is clear that what Petty has in mind is not so much a specific mathematical skill as a capacity for thought that (as he remarks elsewhere in speaking of 'Geometry') 'takes in a great number of Principles'.[96] The best evidence of what he has in mind is supplied by the remarkable list of English writers who are said to embody the capacity most notably: 'Sir Thos Moore, Sir Fra Bacon, Dr Donne, Mr Hobbes'.[97]

Du Verdus and Petty also agree with Hobbes about the way in which 'geometrical' demonstrations need to be introduced into political argument. As du Verdus declares, quoting the Wisdom of Solomon, the method is a natural one, and is given by the fact that 'God made all things by number, weight, and measure'.[98] The same idea is pivotal to Petty's method of arriving at what he too describes as political demonstrations. He offers a particularly strong statement of his commitment in the Epistle to his unpublished 'Political Pastimes and Paradoxes', a work he had intended to dedicate to James II:

When I find out puzling & perplext matters that may bee brought to termes of Number Weight & Measure & consequently be made demonstrable and When I find Things of vast & generall concernment, which may bee discusst in a few Words, I willingly engage upon such undertakings, especially, when they tend to your Majesty's glory & greatness, & the happiness of your people, being Myselfe One of them.[99]

As he was later to put it in the Preface to his *Political Arithmetick*, which appeared posthumously in 1690, 'the Method I take' is to use 'Terms of Number, Weight, or measure', in such a way as to arrive at political

[93] Hobbes 1996, ch. 4, p. 28.   [94] Hobbes 1994, Letter 75, p. 224.
[95] Petty 1928, Letter 86, p. 158.   [96] Petty 1927, vol. 2, p. 199.   [97] Petty 1928, Letter 86, p. 158.
[98] Hobbes 1994, Letter 75, p. 224.   [99] BL Add. MSS 72886, vol. 37, item 1.

conclusions no less 'true, certain and evident' than in any of the other sciences.[100]

The hope that politics might be reduced to a science was crucial to Petty and Hobbes alike. Hobbes's hope was that an understanding of individual psychology might lead to the deduction of certain irreducibly necessary political consequences.[101] Petty aimed instead to investigate social and political life by essentially statistical means, with the eventual hope of grounding public policy on more accurate information about 'Lands and Hands'.[102] But their aims were certainly analogous, and Petty no less than du Verdus shared Hobbes's aspiration to construct what Hobbes describes in *Leviathan* as a 'Morall and Civill Science'.[103] As Petty was later to put it to the Royal Society, 'there is a Political Arithmetic, and a Geometrical Justice to be yet further cultivated in the World'.[104] Finally, both writers fully acknowledge the debt that this vision owed to Hobbes. As du Verdus told him in a letter of 1655, 'I find, Sir, that you are the only person to have constructed a body of philosophy in such a way that, like a true geometer, you begin with definitions which are completely clear in themselves.' The outcome, du Verdus goes on, is that 'you are the only person to have given us a true system of metaphysics' and 'the only person to have shown, by the definitions you have given and by the subsequent demonstrations which you draw from them, that you have indeed considered things in themselves'.[105]

IV

The evidence I have assembled is I think chiefly of value for the new light it sheds on Hobbes's immediate influence. Many of the *savants* he encountered in Paris came to think of him as the writer who had definitively shown what form a modern system of philosophy should take. As François Peleau declared in his first letter to Hobbes, 'it is thanks to you, Sir, that we can look clearly, and with unclouded vision, into the darkness of the sciences'.[106] This is hardly the kind of contemporary response to Hobbes's philosophy we have been taught to expect. The leading studies of Hobbes's immediate influence have focused almost exclusively on 'the intense opposition' his theories provoked. His impact, we are told, was almost entirely 'negative'; 'he left no disciples' and 'founded no school'.[107]

---

[100] Petty 1899, vol. I, p. 244.   [101] Hobbes 1996, Introduction, pp. 10–11.
[102] Petty 1927, vol. I, esp. pp. 171–200.   [103] Hobbes 1996, ch. 18, p. 129.
[104] Petty 1674, Epistle, Sig. A, 10ᵛ.   [105] Hobbes 1994, Letter 75, p. 227.
[106] Hobbes 1994, Letter 85, p. 290.
[107] Mintz 1962, p. 147; cf. also Bowle 1969, pp. 13, 43.

The discovery of so many avowed disciples suggests that some reappraisal of these assumptions is overdue.

There are grounds for suggesting, moreover, not merely that the conventional account of Hobbes's total rejection is false, but that it has arisen from a partial view of the evidence, from excessive concentration on a parochial English reaction. Hobbes was widely denounced in England, but he seems to have been widely accepted abroad. We have to square his unthinking rejection by many English critics with the equally unthinking discipleship implied by many of his foreign correspondents. Hobbes's English critics typically made little attempt to understand his system of thought. As has rightly been pointed out, they generally conducted their attacks at a level of generality at which it became possible to charge him with 'atheism' and thereby condemn him out of hand.[108] But again this does not seem to have been typical of his reception in continental Europe, where many of his followers fully sympathised with his most ambitious aspirations for a science of politics. The case of native genius failing to carry weight abroad is familiar; it may be that Hobbes to some extent provides an example of the converse case.

The evidence I have presented is also of interest for what it tells us about Hobbes's reactions to his avowed disciples. He was not only aware of the reverent spirit in which they took his pronouncements, but he seems to have treated them with marked civility and seriousness. When, for example, Sir William Petty published his 'discourse' to the Royal Society *Concerning the Use of Duplicate Proportion* in 1674, with its 'new hypothesis of springing or elastic motions' as well as its promise of a 'geometrical justice', he drew from Hobbes one of his rare acknowledgements of the value of a contemporary writer. Writing to John Aubrey, Hobbes declares that if he had seen Petty's book before publication 'I would not (as he thinks) have hindred it, but done as the Society did, that is, urg'd him to print it. For the doctrine is easy to be demonstrated. The last Chap: which is of Elasticity is different from the Principle which I have taken for Naturall Philosophie; but I am of opinion that his Supposition is very true, and will goe a great way.'[109] When other disciples wrote to Hobbes about his own work, he seems to have answered them in no less encouraging terms. This is especially clear in the case of du Verdus, who sent Hobbes a number of detailed questions about specific doctrines in

[108] Mintz 1962, p. 45.
[109] BL Add. MSS 72850, fo. 134. Cf. Hobbes 1994, Letter 198, p. 751. For an explanation of how this MS ended up in the Bowood archives (now lodged in the British Library) see Aubrey 1898, vol. 1, p. 368.

Leviathan at the time when he was first reading and interleaving the work, and appears to have received from Hobbes a point-by-point response.[110] There are even signs that Hobbes submitted with good grace to having *Leviathan* criticised by his correspondents. François Peleau, for example, wrote to query his view that man can be regarded as basically anti-social, and later wrote again to thank Hobbes for taking so much trouble to elaborate his argument and set his doubts at rest.[111]

These glimpses into the nature of Hobbes's contemporary influence undoubtedly provide his correspondence with its chief historical importance. It is also important, however, for providing us with an incidental but revealing insight into the sociology of science at the time. The interest displayed in Hobbes's idea of a science of politics by the mathematicians and scientists of his acquaintance bears out the view that, in spite of the trend towards specialised research, the age was still one in which the discussion of broad strategies of scientific enquiry remained of major importance.[112]

It has been said, no doubt correctly, that both the Mersenne and Montmor 'academies' confined their attention almost exclusively to mathematical and experimental science. The Mersenne circle undoubtedly gained its chief notoriety from publicising Galileo's discoveries, and its chief following from popularising the system of Descartes. The Montmor *Assemblée* similarly owed its fame to the fact that its members were among the first to hear about Christiaan Huygens's discovery of Saturn's rings. It is perhaps not surprising that, when the *Academie des Sciences* was officially incorporated in 1666,[113] the same interests – and to a large extent the same men – won an immediate ascendancy over it.

These developments, however, were not entirely in line with the aspirations of those who originally fostered these scientific societies. When du Prat and Sorbière drew up their constitution for the Montmor academy in 1657, they specifically laid it down that the *Assemblée* should include practitioners of 'the liberal arts' as well as 'people who have an interest in natural science, medicine, mathematics' and kindred subjects.[114] When Sorbière wrote to Colbert six years later to ask him for official patronage, he continued to argue in favour of the same broadly based approach, specifically warning against encouraging those who were merely

---

[110] See Hobbes 1994, Letter 94, pp. 325–6, in which du Verdus raises a number of queries, and cf. Hobbes 1994, Letter 108, p. 414, in which he thanks Hobbes for fully responding to them.
[111] Hobbes 1994, Letter 95, pp. 329–32 and Letter 110, pp. 422–5.
[112] On this point see Hall 1952, p. 163.
[113] On its formal incorporation see Hamel 1698, pp. 1–4.
[114] Hobbes 1994, Letter 133, p. 495.

interested in conducting experiments.[115] When the *Academie* was finally incorporated, the original intention was that 'it should consist not merely of those concerned with geometry and physics, but also those learned in history and in the more polite forms of literature'.[116]

All the evidence suggests that Hobbes shared with his French disciples a sense that this more inclusive and humanistic approach was the one that deserved to be encouraged and sustained. None of those who corresponded with Hobbes about the details of his *scientia civilis* were themselves students of political science. Mylon and du Verdus were both mathematicians, active in specialised controversy and research.[117] Sorbière and du Prat had both trained in medicine, and the latter evidently continued to practise.[118] Yet it seemed important to all of them to study Hobbes's political works as soon as they appeared, and it even seemed worthwhile to du Verdus and Sorbière to go to the considerable effort of translating them.

The concern to establish a science of politics had not yet lost its place in the general strategy of enquiry into the philosophy of nature. Although the main achievements of the Montmor academy were in mathematics and the physical sciences, the group continued to encourage a wider and more eclectic set of interests. And while the specialised researches of the *Academie des Sciences* quickly superseded their broadly based approach, this appears to have reflected not the prevailing mood of the *savants* but rather a conscious effort to limit and direct their enquiries. Like his disciples, Hobbes clearly felt more at home in the period just before this transition took place. In his contacts with the scientific academies, as well as in his own enquiries into the nature of man and society, he belongs to that phase of the scientific revolution which had not yet relinquished the hope of taking all knowledge for its province.

---

[115] Brown 1934, p. 126.
[116] Hamel, 1698, p. 3: 'non ex Geometris modo & Physicis, sed etiam ex iis constaret viris, qui a politioribus Litteris, & ab historia imprimis essent instructi'.
[117] See Malcolm 1994c, pp. 868–9 (on Mylon); pp. 905–6 (on du Verdus).
[118] Malcolm 1994c, pp. 836, 838 (on Guisony); pp. 850, 853–4 (on de Martel); p. 895 (on Sorbière).

12

Hobbes and the politics of the early Royal Society

I

Why was Hobbes never elected a Fellow of the Royal Society? The question has been asked and answered in nearly all the intellectual biographies and other such studies of Hobbes, as well as in several histories of the early Royal Society itself. Since I wish to discuss the same question again, it is worth pausing at the outset to neutralise two possible doubts about the value of the exercise. It might seem in the first place that, since Hobbes was in his old age by the time the Society was formally incorporated in 1662,[1] the question of his membership could scarcely have arisen. But in fact both Hobbes and his contemporary biographer John Aubrey viewed his exclusion as a deliberate and hostile act on the part of the Society-men. Hobbes went so far as to complain to Aubrey that the Society should not only have 'forborn to do me injury' but should have 'made me reparation afterward'.[2] 'All these people', he publicly declared in 1668, 'have wounded me and are my enemies.'[3]

A second and more cogent objection might be that the question I have asked, and whatever answer may be given to it, can scarcely be of great historical importance. But I want to suggest that there are at least two reasons for raising the question anew. One is that some comments on the issue by Hobbes himself indicate that the explanations usually given for

This chapter is a much revised and extended version of an article that originally appeared under the title 'Thomas Hobbes and the Nature of the Early Royal Society' in *The Historical Journal* 12 (1969), pp. 217–39.

[1] For the first charter (15 July 1662) see Birch 1756–7, vol. 1, pp. 88–96; for the second (1663) see note 123 below. On the significance of Charles II's patronage of the Society see Purver 1967, pp. 128–42.

[2] Hobbes 1994, Letter 198, p. 751. For the original see note 4 below. Many modern scholars have echoed these judgements. See, for example, De Beer 1950, p. 195; Peters 1956, pp. 41–2; Jones 1961, pp. 127–8.

[3] Hobbes 1845a, p. 237: 'Hi mihi omnes inimici sunt [et] ... laeserunt.' Hobbes is addressing Samuel Sorbière in the Dedication of the second edition (1668) of his *Dialogus Physicus de Natura Aeris* (1661).

his exclusion from the Society have been wide of the mark.[4] Hobbes's own reactions have received little attention, but they alter the usual picture of his relations with the Society-men. The other reason stems from the fact that Hobbes's exclusion has frequently been invoked to help substantiate a number of broader claims about the internal politics and general character of the early Society itself. The evidence I shall present implies that several of these claims likewise stand in need of being reconsidered.

II

Aubrey, in his *Life* of Hobbes, viewed Hobbes's exclusion from the Royal Society as a matter for comment, but certainly as no great mystery:

> The Royall Societie (generally) had the like for him: and he would long since have been ascribed a member there, but for the sake of one or two persons, whom he tooke to be his enemies. Dr. Wallis (surely their Mercuries are in opposition), and Mr. Boyle. I might adde Sr Paul Neile, who disobliges every body.[5]

Aubrey has often been criticised for the alleged unreliability of his *Brief Lives*. But there seem no grounds for doubting this particular explanation, and there is no reason why Aubrey should have been mistaken on the point. Since he himself was an early Fellow of the Society,[6] he was in a good position to know the views of other members throughout the first two decades of the Society's existence, the period during which Hobbes might in principle have been elected to the Fellowship. And since Aubrey wrote his *Lives* in the form of private notes, there is no reason why he should not have been wholly candid in giving his account of the episode.

It is clear, moreover, from a letter of February 1675[7] that Hobbes discussed the matter of his exclusion with Aubrey, and that he took the same view of it himself. Hobbes was prompted to write by the fact

---

[4] Letter from Hobbes to Aubrey, 24 February 1675. For the original [in the Petty Papers, vol. 6, pt. 2] see BL Add. MSS 72850, fo. 134. Transcript in Bodleian Library, Aubrey MS 12, fos. 166–7. For Aubrey's reply to Hobbes (24 June 1675) see BL Add. MSS 32533, fos. 37–8 and cf. Hobbes 1994, Letter 199, pp. 753–4.

[5] Bodleian Library, Aubrey MS 9, fos. 53^v–54^r. Cf. Aubrey 1898, vol. 1, p. 372. For a discussion of this passage see Shapin and Schaffer 1985, pp. 130–1, who take Aubrey to be engaged in 'an exercise in posthumous reconciliation' between Hobbes and the Society.

[6] Birch 1756–7, vol. 1, p. 172 notes that Aubrey was elected in January 1663.

[7] Hobbes to Aubrey, 24 February 1675. See note 4 above and cf. Hobbes 1994, Letter 198, pp. 751–2.

that Aubrey had evidently been asked by his friend Robert Hooke[8] to find out if Hobbes had any unpublished work he might be willing to send to the Society. Hobbes in reply first assures Aubrey that he has 'no Treatises of Philosophie or Mathematiques, but what are Printed', and that only William Crooke (Hobbes's publisher) 'can lawfully Print, the Copyes being his Propriety'. But Hobbes goes on to insist that, even if he did have 'any thing now in my hands towards the advancement of that Learning which the Society pretendeth to', he would not be prepared to send it to them. This is not, he adds, because of any hard feelings about Hooke, since Hobbes professes 'a great esteeme both of his good nature, and of his judgement in all manner of Philosophie'. Still less is it due to any surviving feelings of hostility towards the body of the Fellows or the aims of the Society as a whole. Hobbes declares that if he had anything to offer he 'could be content it should be published by the Society much rather then any other'. And yet he must refuse, he repeats, for two reasons. First, 'does M[r] Hooke think it fit that any thing of mine should passe through the hand of D[r] Wallis (that is not only no Philosopher at all nor Geometrician but also my enemy) or of any of his admirers?' Secondly, Hobbes is offended that the Society has failed to dissociate itself, as he feels it could and should have done, from 'the evil words and disgraces put upon me by Dr. Wallis' which 'are still countenanced, without any publique Act of the Society to do me right'. And so, he concludes, 'if Mr Hooke consider this, I hope he will not take it ill that his Motion is not entertayned by me'.

There are at least three points worth stressing about this 'very fine letter', as Aubrey called it.[9] It is clear in the first place that the initiative in these negotiations lay not with Hobbes – although he had previously sent some of his work to the Society[10] – but rather with Hooke, the Society's own curator of experiments.[11] This is worth noting in itself, especially in view of the hostility Hooke is alleged to have felt for Hobbes,[12] as well as

[8] Hobbes 1994, Letter 198, pp. 751–2 mentions 'Mr Hooke's design' to Aubrey. Cf. Hobbes 1994, Letter 199, pp. 753–4, in which Aubrey assures Hobbes in reply that Hooke 'approves very well of your reasons'. For Aubrey's friendship with Hooke see Britton 1845, p. 60 and Hunter 1975, pp. 97–8.

[9] Aubrey 1898, vol. 1, p. 368.

[10] Hobbes issued his *Lux Mathematica* in the form of 'a public memorial to the Royal Society' and dedicated it to that 'most noble and erudite' body. See Hobbes 1845d, pp. 91–2. For the discussion of Hobbes's mathematical work at meetings of the Society see Birch 1756–7, vol. 1, pp. 42, 78, 106. On the dedication of the *Lux Mathematica* see *Philosophical Transactions* 1963, vol. 7, pp. 5047–8.

[11] Birch 1756–7, vol. 1, p. 123 records that Hooke was appointed curator of experiments in November 1662.

[12] 'Espinasse 1956, pp. 121–2; cf. Gunther 1920–45, vol. 6, p. 139.

the contempt the Society is supposed to have felt for Hobbes's scientific work. Secondly, the ambiguity in Aubrey's explanation for Hobbes's exclusion is clarified in a surprising way. One reason why Hobbes was never 'ascribed a member' appears to have been that, in consequence of feeling ill-used by the Society-men, he eventually decided to refuse their overtures.[13] Finally, the letter corroborates Aubrey's straightforward account of why Hobbes was originally excluded. The truth seems to be that he initially incurred the enmity of three of the founding Fellows, who managed to keep him out, and that he came to feel sufficiently slighted by this treatment to insist on holding aloof.

There is no particular mystery, moreover, about the causes of the enmity between Hobbes on the one hand and Wallis, Boyle and Neile on the other. Some mystery does perhaps attach to the figure of Sir Paul Neile, who remains the most shadowy of the twelve founding Fellows of the Society.[14] But Aubrey's remark seems in any case to be offered more as a comment on Neile's general character than on his attitude to Hobbes. Certainly it does not fit the only surviving piece of evidence about Neile's relations with Hobbes, which appear to have been friendly enough. It was Neile who, on 4 September 1661, 'delivered into the society' a mathematical proposition from Hobbes, caused it to be registered and prompted the president, Lord Brouncker, to supply a solution to it.[15]

There can be no doubt, however, about the accuracy of Aubrey's report on the central issue, Hobbes's bad relations with John Wallis and Robert Boyle. Hobbes not only sought in his *Dialogus Physicus* of 1661 to cast doubt on Boyle's theories about the vacuum, but also made some 'severe' remarks, as Boyle complained, about the experiments conducted by the Society and about the value of experimental philosophy itself.[16] It is evident from the studiously moderate but fairly patronising *Examen* of Hobbes's *Dialogus* that Boyle published in 1662 that, while he did not take Hobbes's objections very seriously, he was nettled by Hobbes's

[13] Hobbes may have misunderstood the extent to which it was possible for the Society, under its own rules, to dissociate itself from the views of individual Fellows who had been 'assigned' a work on which to comment. Birch 1756–7, vol. 1, p. 106 quotes a minute of 27 August 1662 to the effect that 'no books presented to the censure of the society shall receive a public approbation from them'.

[14] Birch 1756–7, vol. 1, p. 3 lists the twelve original Fellows. For the small amount of information available on Neile see Ronan and Hartley 1960.

[15] Birch 1756–7, vol. 1, p. 42.

[16] Boyle 1744, vol. 1, p. 119a; cf. also p. 120a, where Boyle describes Hobbes's criticisms as 'provoking though unprovoked'. For a full analysis of Hobbes's dispute with Boyle see Shapin and Schaffer 1985.

conceited and disparaging style of argument.[17] He was also worried, as he admitted, lest Hobbes's 'fame and confident way of writing might prejudice experimental philosophy in the minds of those, who are yet strangers to it'.[18]

With Wallis Hobbes had a more protracted and bitter dispute, marked on both sides by a good deal of personal as well as professional animosity. There is no doubt that at the personal level Wallis behaved badly (as was widely conceded at the time)[19] and left Hobbes with an opening to defend himself and score some palpable hits.[20] But there is equally no doubt that on the mathematical issues Wallis's mounting irritation against Hobbes was fully justified. Hobbes's reckless assault on Wallis's *Arithmetica Infinitorum* in 1656[21] was completely routed by Wallis, first in Latin in his *Elenchus Geometriae Hobbianae*, and then in English in his *Due Correction for Mr Hobbes*.[22] As Wallis emphasised in the latter work, his first response had been sufficient to convince everyone capable of judging the issues except for Hobbes himself.[23] After one further exchange in the following year the debate lapsed.[24] Wallis was only drawn into repeating his criticisms when Hobbes in the *Dialogus Physicus* widened his campaign to include both Boyle and the experimental method more generally. Wallis then issued his *Hobbius Heauton-timorumenos*, more out of a regard for Boyle's reputation, as he wrote,[25] and to counter the fact that Boyle's

---

[17] Boyle 1744, vol. 1, pp. 118b, 119a, 120b.

[18] Boyle 1744, vol. 1, p. 119a.

[19] On this point Aubrey and Sorbière were agreed. See Sorbière 1664, pp. 95–6: 'ce Docteur ne l'a pas traitté comme il devoit'. Cf. Aubrey to Hobbes, 24 June 1675 (BL Add. MSS. 32533, fos. 37–8; Hobbes 1994, Letter 199, pp. 753–4) in which Aubrey describes Wallis as 'a most ill-natured man, an egregious lyer and back-biter'.

[20] See Hobbes 1840d for Hobbes's main defence. Wallis 1662, p. 5 had incautiously charged Hobbes with having written *Leviathan* 'in Defense of Olivers Title'. Hobbes 1840d, pp. 416–17 riposted by reminding Wallis that he had used his mathematical abilities to decode royalist despatches captured after the battle of Naseby. Subsequently, however, Hobbes likewise descended, especially in Hobbes 1845k, into vitriolic abuse.

[21] Hobbes 1845j, pp. 211–330.

[22] Wallis's *Elenchus* (Wallis 1655) was a reply to Hobbes 1839c, Hobbes's original defence of his geometry in *De Corpore*. Wallis added his *Due Correction* (Wallis 1656) after Hobbes included in the English edition of *De Corpore* (Hobbes 1839e) his *Six Lessons* addressed to Ward and Wallis. For these and other details see the authoritative survey in Jesseph 1999.

[23] Wallis 1656, p. 20 begins by maintaining that it will be easy for any learned person to 'see to how little purpose all is that you have said'.

[24] Hobbes replied to Wallis 1656 in Hobbes 1845k, to which Wallis responded in Wallis 1657. After this Hobbes was undoubtedly the aggressor, especially in Hobbes 1845a, his criticism of Boyle as well as Wallis. For these and other details see Jesseph 1999 and for a complete bibliography see Macdonald and Hargreaves 1952, pp. 41–51.

[25] Wallis 1662 takes the form (in the words of its title-page) of 'An Epistolary Discourse, Addressed, to the Honourable Robert Boyle, Esq.'.

mildness made him a poor controversialist,[26] than out of any sense that the least danger to 'any part of real learning' was likely to result from Hobbes's further offensive.[27]

It is also clear from Wallis's tone in his last extended reply[28] that by then it was not so much Hobbes's ignorant aspersions on his mathematical work that he took to be the chief offence. Wallis was even prepared to concede that at one time Hobbes had probably known quite a lot of geometry, and had merely 'forgotten much of what once he knew' in his old age.[29] The real offence was rather that Hobbes refused to accept, even in the face of repeated demonstrations, that his criticisms were groundless. For Wallis, as for Boyle, it was Hobbes's 'highly Opinionative and Magisterial' manner, the fact that he was 'wholly Impatient of Contradiction', that he showed such a complete 'incapacity, to be Taught, what he doth not know',[30] that constituted their main professional complaint.

The issue that needs explaining, however, is not why the disputes with Boyle and Wallis caused them to dislike Hobbes so much. For that is clear enough. The problem is to explain how it came about that their hostility was sufficient to persuade the inchoate body of the Royal Society that Hobbes should be excluded. For as Aubrey observed (echoing Hobbes himself), Hobbes not only had a high opinion of the Society and most of its members, which he publicly expressed in his *Behemoth*,[31] 'but they (generally) had the like for him' as well.[32]

Here again, however, there is no particular mystery, for the answer is suggested by the manner in which Hobbes chose to conduct his disputes with Wallis and Boyle. There was every reason for the Fellows to resent such a dogmatic controversialist, and to fear that such dogmatism might be prejudicial to the Society itself.[33] They had made it an article of faith to repudiate what Joseph Glanvill was to describe in 1661 as the vanity of

---

[26] Boyle 1744, vol. 5, p. 119a speaks of his own 'indisposedness to quarrel' in referring to his dispute with Hobbes.

[27] Wallis 1662, p. 4.

[28] After publishing Wallis 1669, Hobbes's adversary wearied of repeating his demonstrations. At first he contented himself with brief replies in the *Philosophical Transactions*, but he even stopped publishing these after 1672, although Hobbes produced two further books on the subject. For Wallis's final riposte (a critique of Hobbes 1845d) see *Philosophical Transactions* 1963, vol. 7, pp. 5067–73.

[29] Wallis 1662, pp. 7–8. [30] Wallis 1662, pp. 3–4; cf. also p. 7.

[31] See Hobbes 1969b, p. 148, where the Hobbesian figure of 'A' in the dialogue declares that 'natural philosophy' has been 'removed from Oxford and Cambridge to Gresham College in London', where several founding members of the later Royal Society first foregathered.

[32] Aubrey 1898, vol. 1, p. 372, refers to the passage from Hobbes 1969b quoted in note 31 above.

[33] Sprat 1959, pp. 28–32 particularly stresses the Society's aversion to 'Modern Dogmatists'. See Hunter 1981, pp. 178–9 for a discussion of this point.

dogmatising,[34] and they liked to insist that (as Glanvill himself declared) 'Confest Ignorance' is the only 'way to Science'.[35] Even Hooke, who subsequently changed his mind about Hobbes, initially found himself repelled, as he reported to Boyle, by Hobbes's disposition 'to undervalue all other men's opinions and judgments' and to display such 'an high conceipt of his own abilityes & performances though never soe absurd & pittifull'.[36] Both Wallis and Boyle clearly found Hobbes's dogmatism and conceitedness the most infuriating feature of the whole episode.

This was also the explanation for Hobbes's exclusion offered in the only independent testimony about his relations with the Royal Society, Samuel Sorbière's account in his *Relation d'un voyage en Angleterre* of 1664:

> It remains the general view that, if only Hobbes could have managed to be a little less dogmatic, he would have been very necessary to the Royal Society, for there are few people who look into things more closely than he does, and who have applied themselves for such a long time to Physics. He is in effect the heir of Bacon, under whom he served as an amanuensis in his youth.[37]

Thomas Sprat in his *Observations* on Sorbière subsequently impugned the comparison with Bacon[38] – as he impugned virtually everything in Sorbière's account[39] – but he never questioned this account of Hobbes's relations with the Fellowship. Rather he chose to repeat Sorbière's observation that Hobbes was generally considered 'too dogmatical in his Opinions' and was rightly 'censur'd for Dogmatical'.[40]

The reason, then, for Hobbes's exclusion from the Royal Society seems to amount to no more than this: that he antagonised, personally as well as professionally, two of the most influential founding members, and that his overbearing demeanour was such as to persuade the rest of the Society-men that, although he was (as Sprat conceded) a 'great wit',[41] they would prefer not to have to put up with his excessively 'disparaging'

---

[34] Glanvill 1661. See Talmor 1981, p. xv on this propagandising effort, which helped to win Glanvill a Fellowship of the Society in 1664.

[35] Glanvill 1665, title-page. On the two versions of Glanvill's text see Talmor 1981, p. ix.

[36] See the letter of 'about the year 1664' from Hooke to Boyle in BL Add. MS 6193, fos.68ᵛ–69ʳ. But 'Espinasse 1956, p. 122 is mistaken (as the letter cited in note 4 above shows) in assuming that this was consistently Hooke's view, or that the remark cited in Aubrey 1898, vol. 1, p. 30 is the only 'other record of communication' between Hooke and Hobbes.

[37] Sorbière 1664, p. 97: 'l'on demeura d'accord, que s'il [sc. Hobbes] eust esté un peu moins dogmatique, il eust esté fort necessaire à l'Academie Royale: Car il y a peu de gens qui regardent les choses de plus prés que luy, & qui ayent apporté une aussi longue application à la Physique. Il est en effect un reste de Bacon, sous lequel il a escrit en sa jeunesse.' Cf. Sorbière 1709, p. 40, in which (as Malcolm 1988, p. 49 observes) the anti-Hobbesian sentiment is intensified.

[38] Sprat 1708, pp. 163–4.

[39] On Sorbière's visit and his account of it see Guilloton 1930.

[40] Sprat 1708, pp. 162–3.   [41] Sprat 1708, p. 163.

and 'dogmatical' ways. This explanation is neither particularly novel nor particularly significant in itself.[42] The reason for wishing to underline it, however, is that it provides us with a starting point for reconsidering some more general claims about the nature of the early Royal Society itself. Moreover, there is a special reason for treating the information about Hobbes as a suitable point of departure. For it happens that the most prevalent theories about the politics of the early Society presuppose that Hobbes must have been excluded not because the Fellows preferred on balance not to have him as a member, but rather because the nature of the Society was such that he could not conceivably have been elected.

III

The first assumption I want to reconsider is that the early Royal Society was a body in which religious (and especially puritan) commitments were not only of personal importance to a number of leading Fellows, but were also significant in the motivation of their scientific work.[43] It is 'hardly surprising', we are told, that Hobbes was never elected a Fellow, given that the Society 'had a predominantly Puritan membership'.[44] Hobbes's exclusion has frequently been used to corroborate this general characterisation of the Society as a whole.[45] Hobbes was 'dangerous as an enemy', but he would have been 'far more insidiously dangerous as a friend'.[46] The early Fellows were 'on the defensive' about religious orthodoxy, and 'their first step was to keep Hobbes out'.[47] By shunning his company they 'were expressing their opinion that science did not challenge Christianity'.[48] This is why Hobbes was one of those 'conspicuous by their absence' from the new Society.[49]

One reason why this sounds so plausible is that, during the first five years of its formal existence, the Royal Society gained the services of two notable propagandists, Joseph Glanvill and Thomas Sprat, both of whom made it their business to propagate exactly these beliefs. The charge most frequently levelled against the early Fellows was that their

---

[42] Stephen 1961, p. 54 offers a similar explanation.
[43] For the classic statement of this assumption see Merton 1938. Christopher Hill went on to elaborate the argument, but more recently it has been extensively challenged. For bibliographies see Shapiro 1968, p. 16n.; Hunter 1981, pp. 214–16; Hunter 1989, pp. 359–60, 362–3.
[44] Peters 1956, pp. 41–2.   [45] See, for example, Syfret 1950, pp. 237–8.
[46] Bredvold 1956, p. 58; cf. Bredvold 1928, p. 422.
[47] Jones 1949, p. 107.   [48] Westfall 1958, pp. 20–1.
[49] Shapiro 1969, p. 192. Shapiro offers Samuel Hartlib as a further example of someone excluded because their views on religion 'were thought dangerous'.

'fault of *Sceptical doubting*', as Sprat delicately put it,[50] posed a threat to religious faith, a threat rendered all the more serious by their acceptance of the mechanical philosophy.[51] In 1669 the assembled *savants* at Oxford heard these accusations publicly hurled at them at the opening of the Sheldonian Theatre (designed by one of the Fellows) by the University's own Orator, Dr Robert South.[52] Still more disquieting, as Glanvill conceded, was that many of the *virtuosi* had proved 'willing to accept Mechanism upon Hobbian conditions'.[53] It is not surprising, therefore, that Thomas Sprat was specifically commissioned in his *History* of 1667 'to make a defence of the *Royal Society*, and this new *Experimental Learning*, in respect of the *Christian Faith*'.[54] Nor is it surprising that the Society should have rewarded Joseph Glanvill with a Fellowship for insisting in his *Scepsis Scientifica* (dedicated to the Society) that 'the meanest intellects may perceive' from the work of the Society 'that Mechanick Philosophy yields no security to irreligion'.[55]

It may be doubted, however, whether these facts serve to establish what has so often been alleged, namely that the early Society was consciously motivated by religious considerations in its scientific work. This is not to deny that the defence of religion by science was a matter of importance to some of the individual Fellows.[56] Robert Boyle specifically refers in his *Examen* of Hobbes to the need to confute 'the dangerous opinions about some important, if not fundamental, articles of religion I had met with in his *Leviathan*'.[57] But Boyle's attitude does not seem to have been representative of the active Fellowship as a whole. It is striking in the first place that John Wallis, Hobbes's other leading adversary, never sought to make capital out of Hobbes's religious heterodoxy. In public controversy Wallis made light of the issue,[58] and in a long reply to a request from

[50] Sprat 1959, p. 106.
[51] For example, Stubbe 1671, p. 48 complained that the members of the Society 'undermine the Foundations of our Religion and Monarchy'. See Jacob 1983, pp. 83–108 on Stubbe's denunciations and for other critics see Hunter 1981, pp. 136–8.
[52] On South see Reedy 1992. South's oration does not seem to have survived, but it was much discussed at the time. See, for example, Evelyn 1955, vol. 3, p. 531, speaking of South's 'malicious & undecent reflections on the *Royal Society* as underminers of the University'. See also Boyle 1744, vol. 5, pp. 514b–515b, a letter from Wallis to Boyle of July 1669 in which Wallis complains of South's 'satyrical invectives' against 'the Royal Society and new philosophy'.
[53] See the dedicatory 'Address' to the Royal Society in Glanvill 1665, Sig. A, 3^r to Sig. C, 4^v, at Sig. B, 1^{r-v}.
[54] Sprat 1959, p. 345. There has been a tendency to suppose that Sprat's *History* can in consequence be taken as an expression of the 'ideology' of the early Society. For a convincingly sceptical reappraisal see Hunter 1989, pp. 45–71.
[55] Glanvill 1665, Sig. B, 1^r.
[56] On this theme see Anderson 1933 and Cope 1956.
[57] Boyle 1744, vol. 1, p. 119a.
[58] Wallis 1662, p. 6: Hobbes merely 'thought it a piece of Wit to pretend to Atheism'.

Thomas Tenison to set out his views on Hobbes's character he remained remarkably untroubled. Hobbes, he suggests, merely had 'the confidence to talk profanely, which Atheistical persons call Witt'. However, Wallis goes on, he 'can hardly believe' that Hobbes 'was so much an Atheist, as he would fain have been'. Rather, he concludes, Hobbes's posturing amounted to little more than an 'affectation of singularity'.[59]

It is worth recalling in addition that several of the founding Fellows were themselves of questionable religious orthodoxy. Robert Merton has admittedly claimed in his classic study of the 'nuclear group' of five active Fellows – John Wilkins, John Wallis, Jonathan Goddard, Robert Boyle and William Petty – that their ascendancy points to the 'singularly strong influence' of religious and specifically puritan allegiances within the early Society.[60] But even Merton's list can be used to make the opposite point. The case of Boyle must be conceded, and perhaps that of Goddard too, on whom there is little relevant evidence. But Wallis, as we have seen, does not seem to have been greatly troubled even by Hobbes's notorious heterodoxy, while Wilkins was so opposed to any kind of zealotry that he found himself denounced as an atheist and widely charged 'with Hobbism, and everything that is bad'.[61] As for Sir William Petty, he was educated by the Jesuits[62] and published his first work in collaboration with John Graunt,[63] who managed to combine being a Roman Catholic convert with his Fellowship of the Society.[64] Another of Petty's collaborators was Hobbes himself,[65] for whom Petty always professed the highest regard.[66] And although Merton declares that Petty 'evinced clearly the influences of Puritanism',[67] the fact is that in later life (while vice-president of the Royal Society) he privately transcribed many of his religious opinions out of Hobbes's *De Cive* and *Leviathan*, which he also urged on his son as the only modern works on politics worth studying.[68]

We also need to reflect on the negative evidence about the Royal Society's alleged religious allegiances. If the early Society had indeed been anything like a puritan academy, this would certainly have

---

[59] Wallis to Tenison, draft letter, 30 November 1680, Bodleian Library MSS Add. D. 105, fos. 70ff.
[60] Merton 1938, pp. 471–2.
[61] For this accusation see DNB *sub* Wilkins and cf. Shapiro 1968, pp. 21–3.
[62] Fitzmaurice 1895, pp. 3–4.   [63] Glass 1964, pp. 63–9.
[64] Birch 1756–7, vol. 1, p. 77 records that Graunt was admitted to the Society in February 1662.
[65] See above, chapter 11 section II, and cf. Fitzmaurice 1895, pp. 7–8.
[66] See, for example, Hobbes 1994, Letter 199, pp. 753–4 in which Aubrey informs Hobbes that Petty 'alwaies asks for you with much affection'. Cf. also the reference to Hobbes in Petty 1674, Sig. A, 8ᵛ–9ʳ.
[67] Merton 1938, p. 472.
[68] Petty 1927, vol. 1, pp. 113–45; vol. 2, p. 5. On Petty as Fellow of the Royal Society see Strauss 1954, pp. 112–13, 118–19.

constituted a sufficient reason for keeping Hobbes out. But it is striking that neither Aubrey nor Sorbière gives any hint that Hobbes might
have been excluded on these grounds. Aubrey in particular might have
been expected to offer such an explanation, if only because he often
speaks elsewhere in his *Life* of Hobbes about the disadvantages under
which Hobbes laboured in consequence of his supposed atheism.[69] Still
more striking is the fact that Hobbes himself, in writing to Aubrey about
his exclusion, never hints at this explanation. Yet he above all might
have been expected to do so, especially as a rejection on such frankly
ideological grounds would have provided a rather more face-saving
story than the admission of mutual animosity that he felt obliged to
make.

IV

A second and contrasting suggestion has been that Hobbes was excluded
from the Society because of his views about the character of science
itself. While the Fellows aspired, as Sprat's *History* explains, to refine
and develop Bacon's experimental programme,[70] Hobbes despised this
approach and held fast to an older and more rationalist conception of
the sciences. This made him, we are told, an 'enemy' of Restoration
science and the protagonist of a strongly contrasting and increasingly
discredited world-view.[71] His exclusion from the Society is thus held to
be 'an accurate indication of his separation from the scientific opinion
of the day'.[72]

It is of course true that Hobbes was sceptical about the value of
purely experimental science.[73] Although he conducted numerous experiments himself,[74] some of which (as he pointed out) were 'approved
for probable' by the Royal Society itself, he was certainly contemptuous
of those who merely 'get engines made' and 'try conclusions', arguing
that 'they are never the more philosophers for all this'.[75] This difference of allegiance certainly marked him off from some at least of the
more prominent Society-men. One reason why Boyle published such an
extensive reply to Hobbes's critique of his own experiments about the
weight of air was that, as he explained, he feared that Hobbes's strategy

---

[69] Aubrey 1898, vol. I, pp. 334–5, 339, 353, 357, 360–1.
[70] Sprat 1959, pp. 35–6.   [71] Greene 1962, p. 462.
[72] Goldsmith 1966, p. 38. Malcolm 1988, an article of exceptional importance, offers a modified
restatement of this explanation.
[73] Shapin and Schaffer 1985, pp. 110–54.   [74] Malcolm 1988, pp. 46–8.
[75] Hobbes 1840d, p. 436.

might serve to 'discourage others' from making 'unobvious experiments' altogether.[76]

It is one thing, however, to note that Boyle and others disagreed with Hobbes's conception of scientific enquiry, and quite another to show that this made Hobbes appear as an alien or hostile figure to the Royal Society as a whole. The fact is that a number of the early Fellows shared his doubts about the value of the Society's experimental work.[77] They were highly sensitive to the charge – which Pepys mentions[78] and which Petty and Glanvill tried to rebut[79] – that many of the Society's projects looked useless or even (as Stubbe and Shadwell were to insist) wholly absurd.[80] Furthermore, the Society included from the outset a number of members whose interests lay entirely in theoretical as opposed to experimental pursuits. Speaking as secretary, Henry Oldenburg stressed in his Preface to the *Philosophical Transactions* for 1667 that the Society had always been willing to accept the contributions of 'famous Philosophers, learned Philologers and *Antiquaries*; whose Disquisitions, Readings, and Reasonings, have extended farther than their Experiences'.[81] As a number of these disquisitions reveal, moreover, several of the early Fellows were exponents of Cartesian natural philosophy rather than adherents of anything resembling the Baconian approach trumpeted by Sprat in his *History*[82] and in so many modern commentaries.[83] Henry Power's *Experimental Philosophy*[84] and John Mayow's *Tractatus Quinque*[85] are both works by avowed Cartesians who were also Fellows of the Society.[86] Finally, it would scarcely be an exaggeration to insist that much of the most distinguished work presented to the early Society was of this more

[76] Boyle 1744, vol. i, p. 118b. See Shapin and Schaffer 1985, pp. 169–207.
[77] Hunter 1981, p. 89.
[78] Pepys 1970–83, vol. 5, p. 32 writes (February 1664) of the king 'laughing at Sir W Petty' and the absurdities of the Royal Society, 'at which poor Petty was I perceive at some loss'.
[79] Petty 1674, pp. 1–2; Glanvill 1668, pp. 83–110 attempts to reply to the question (cited at pp. 83 and 90) mockingly posed by Robert Crosse: 'What have they done?'
[80] Stubbe 1670 Sig.*, 3r mocks these '*Airy* wits and *Drolls*' whose aim is merely to 'divert their idle hours'. Shadwell 1966, esp. p. 110 satirises Boyle's experiments through the character of Sir Nicholas Gimcrack. For other contemporary denunciations see Spiller 1980, pp. 15–32.
[81] *Philosophical Transactions* 1963, vol. 2, p. 410; cf. Jones 1950, p. 218.
[82] Sprat 1959, esp. pp. 35–8 constructs Bacon as the patron saint of modern experimental philosophy.
[83] Purver 1967 contains the fullest defence of the claim that the Royal Society aimed to implement a Baconian philosophy.
[84] Power 1664, Preface, Sig. C, 1r, explains that he plans to follow a number of principles 'of the ever-to-be-admired Des-Cartes'. On Power see Webster 1967a. See also Webster 1967b on the early Fellowship.
[85] Mayow 1674, p. 70 speaks of 'ingeniosissimus Cartesius' and makes use of Descartes's theories and observations at pp. 131, 184, 197, 302, *et passim*.
[86] Boas 1952, p. 452. Charleton, Digby and Glanvill also exhibit strong Cartesian influences. See Laudon 1966, Webster 1967a.

theoretical character – including, of course, the mathematics and astro-
nomical calculations of John Wallis.

The most important point, however, is that to set Hobbes against the
Royal Society, and to treat each as the enemy of the other's interests, is
to mistake the nature of the opposition faced by the Society at the outset
of its career.[87] During the 1660s its most powerful enemies remained the
divines in the universities and the proponents of the 'old learning' more
generally.[88] The major dispute was not about the rarified question of
which scientific strategy to follow, but rather about the value of scientific
enquiry itself. Consider, for example, Meric Casaubon's criticisms in his
Letter to Peter du Moulin of 1669, in which he replies to Glanvill's and Sprat's
propaganda on behalf of the Society.[89] Casaubon's chief fear is that the
search for purely mechanistic explanations will be liable 'to degenerate
into *Atheism*' by way of devaluing 'the mysteries of our faith'.[90] He is
opposed, that is, not merely to 'mechanism upon Hobbian conditions'
but to mechanism upon any conditions at all. He treats the very idea of
experimental philosophy as 'not merely prejudicial, but very destructive
to true Religion and Christianity'.[91] For him the differences between
Hobbes and the Society-men are of far less interest than their obvious
resemblances.[92]

It is true that the grounds on which a self-styled 'Christian virtuoso'
like Robert Boyle was able to insist that his researches underpinned
rather than undermined his religious faith were that his experiments provided evidence about the intended 'design' of the Universe. *L'horloge, donc
l'horlogier.* During the seventeenth century, however, this familiar trope
of the Enlightenment was still widely believed to carry alarming religious consequences. Casaubon, for example, in opposing the 'braggings
and boastings' of the early Royal Society,[93] correctly pointed to the subversive implications of their arguments for the fundamental belief that

---

[87] For a survey of this opposition see Syfret 1951.
[88] See, for example, Casaubon 1669, pp. 6–13, a defence of scholastic learning and in particular of
Aristotle. The significance of the scholastic assault on the new science had not been sufficiently
emphasised when I first wrote this chapter, but has now been excellently discussed in Spiller
1980; Goldie 1984, pp. 258–62; Gascoigne 1989, pp. 27–39.
[89] For these criticisms see Spiller 1980, p. 38, who notes that Casaubon addressed himself in part
to John Dury and Thomas Sprat, but more immediately to Joseph Glanvill's *Plus Ultra* of 1668.
[90] Casaubon 1669, p. 30.   [91] Casaubon 1669, p. 19.
[92] But Malcolm 1988, pp. 57–66 argues that it was this very congruence between Hobbes's views
and those of the Society-men that led the latter, in view of the former's increasingly sinister
reputation, to do their best to distance themselves from him. See also Jesseph 1999, pp. 274–81
and Parkin 1999, pp. 114–39 for two important discussions of this argument and its implications
for the relations between religion and Restoration science.
[93] Casaubon 1669, p. 25.

faith in God's providential 'will and pleasure' is essential for salvation. Casaubon quotes the Society-men's claim that 'most of our religious controversies, may be as well decided by plain reason', and that the best way to 'magnifie and discover' God is by 'the study of Gods great book, universal nature'.[94] He is horrified at the blasphemy of treating God's laws as a mere text to be studied and interpreted. 'This I do not understand', he retorts, for although 'the sense is obvious enough', it is 'a sense so amazing, that it is not credible'.[95] He not only objects that this is to forget that 'every thing hath its proper time, and that time is a secret of Gods dispensation', which must be left to God.[96] He also adds a very plain hint to the effect that this is nothing other than the doctrine of Hobbes and his followers, who have 'taken some pains to attemperate Christianity to the laws of every countrey, and commands of Supreme Powers'.[97] Casaubon's response is that God's 'greatest secrets' are on no account to be 'extorted' from him with such 'violence and presumption', for 'God must be left to his own will and pleasure'.[98] The pursuit of science is dismissed as little better than a form of blasphemy.

It is thus a serious mistake to suppose that only 'dogmatic theologians' opposed the religious arguments of the Society-men, and that this opposition was of no general significance.[99] The belief that God must be left to his own will and pleasure was no mere piece of dogmatic theology in mid-seventeenth century England; it was a cardinal article of religious faith.[100] But it was precisely this article which, as Casaubon and other critics observed, was being undermined by the efforts of the *savants* to show that God's inscrutable will is nothing more than a matter of natural laws and statistical probabilities. As the puritan divine Robert Crosse made clear in his dispute with Joseph Glanvill, this meant that for him experimental philosophy was simply atheism under another name.[101] The more conservative divines were, in short, fully justified in fearing that the new sciences would prove a solvent of this form of religious faith, and were correspondingly justified in seeing little difference between Hobbes and the Society-men in their willingness to question these established verities.

Once we recognise that, in the broad strategies of mid-seventeenth century science, Hobbes and the Society-men stood on the same 'side' throughout, a number of otherwise inexplicable details about Hobbes's

---

[94] Casaubon 1669, pp. 17, 20, quoting Glanvill 1668, Sig. B, 5ᵛ.
[95] Casaubon 1669, p. 17. [96] Casaubon 1669, p. 26. [97] Casaubon 1669, p. 17.
[98] Casaubon 1669, p. 27. [99] Merton 1938, p. 443 and note.
[100] See Spiller 1980, pp. 122–37 on Casaubon's handling of this point.
[101] For Crosse's charge and Glanvill's response see Glanvill 1668, Preface, Sig. A, 6ʳ to Sig. A, 8ᵛ.

relations with individual members of the Society fall into place. It need no longer seem 'rather odd'[102] that Samuel Hartlib should have lent Hobbes a letter from Boyle about his experimental work.[103] It need no longer seem 'curious'[104] that, when Henry Oldenburg wrote the earliest letter in which he discloses any interest in scientific matters, it should have been to Hobbes that he wrote in order 'to know the best authors' to be reading.[105] It need no longer seem surprising that, when Sorbière visited England in 1663, 'in order to inform myself about matters of science', it appeared to him that 'the first thing I needed to do in London was to seek out Mr Hobbes'.[106] Nor need it surprise us that Aubrey should have felt it appropriate in 1670 to present the Royal Society with a portrait of Hobbes, nor that the Society should have felt it appropriate to hang the picture in their meeting room.[107] Finally, it is perhaps no longer surprising to find Hooke writing in 1675 to enquire whether Hobbes has any new findings to report and send to the Society.

V

I want finally to consider a more extreme version of the thesis I have just discussed. Some commentators have argued that Hobbes was excluded from the Royal Society not because he espoused a rival scientific strategy, but rather because he failed the test of being a genuine scientist at all. He was 'the charlatanical but dreaded enemy' of Restoration science.[108] His 'extraordinary views about science' had been 'discredited in discerning circles' long before the Royal Society was founded.[109] His scientific as well as his religious beliefs were such that he was simply 'not respectable enough for the Royal Society'.[110] Here then, we are told, is a reason for his exclusion 'which, unfortunately, can only be called good: Hobbes was no scientist'.[111]

It is true that Hobbes's competence in the sciences became increasingly open to doubt in his later years. Boyle makes it painfully clear in the Preface to his *Examen* that he finds it impossible to regard Hobbes's

---

[102] Boas 1958, p. 17.
[103] Hartlib to Boyle, May 1648, in Boyle 1744, vol. 5, pp. 256b–257a; cf. Boas 1958, pp. 17–18.
[104] See the comments by the editors in Oldenburg 1965–86, vol. 1, p. 75.
[105] Oldenburg to Hobbes, June 1655, in Oldenburg 1965–86, Letter 32, vol. 1, pp. 74–5. For a discussion see Skinner 1967, pp. 286–93.
[106] Sorbière 1664, p. 65: 'pour m'informer des affaires des science, ... la premiere chose que je fis dés que je sus à Londres ce fut de chercher M. Hobbes'.
[107] Aubrey 1898, vol. 1, p. 372. On the significance of these facts see Shapin and Schaffer 1985, p. 132.
[108] Bredvold 1956, p. 58.   [109] Bredvold 1956, p. 57; Stephen 1961, p. 54.
[110] Goldsmith 1966, p. 38n.   [111] De Beer 1950, p. 197.

objections to his experiments as a serious scientific challenge.[112] Seth Ward (Hobbes's original mathematical opponent)[113] as well as John Wallis (who took over the battle from Ward) likewise found little difficulty in exposing not merely Hobbes's frequent mistakes in geometry but the inherent absurdity of many of his assumptions, especially about the limitations of algebraic geometry and the prospects of squaring the circle.[114] For the purposes of my present argument, however, the important point is not that Boyle and Wallis thought Hobbes an incompetent man of science, nor even that they may have been right to do so.[115] It is rather that, in assuming that this is why Hobbes was excluded from the Royal Society, we are presupposing that the Society's own image of itself was that it constituted a strictly professional body of accredited scientists.

This assumption is central to the most recent study[116] of the 'concept and creation' of the Royal Society. The Society was 'deliberately incorporated', we are told, with the 'central purpose' of 'building up new sciences'.[117] But at least two problems arise if we read the evidence in this way. One is that this characterisation makes it hard to explain the presence in the Society of a large number of 'Gentlemen free and unconfin'd', as Sprat called them,[118] whose professional credentials were in most cases far less convincing than those of Hobbes. Their influx has to be dismissed as 'a degree of dilettantism', even a regrettable 'failure of some Fellows to grasp the essential principles' of the Society's basic 'concept of science'.[119] And when the most professional of the Society's Fellows, such as Robert Boyle, are found discussing with these dilettantes such an 'absurdity' as the causal relationship between coffee-drinking and paralysis, this has to be seen as one of Boyle's 'occasional aberrations' and in any case nothing to do with 'the serious purpose of the Society'.[120]

To speak in this way, however, is to invest the Society with an anachronistic sense of its 'true nature'[121] which not even the most professional of

---

[112] Boyle 1744, p. 118a begins his *Examen* by remarking that he has been informed by learned acquaintances that there is no need to trouble himself with Hobbes's objections.
[113] See Shapiro 1969, pp. 98–111 for Ward's criticisms of Hobbes.
[114] Wallis 1662, p. 9 ridicules Hobbes's refusal to recognise that his 'profound speculations' on how to square the circle are completely fallacious. Huygens to Moray, July 1662 in *Correspondence of Scientific Men* 1841, vol. 1, p. 92, expresses astonishment that Wallis should have expended so much energy on disproving Hobbes's 'frivolous' arguments.
[115] Morgan 1872, p. 67 doubts whether they were right, declaring that Hobbes 'was not the ignoramus in geometry that he is sometimes supposed'.
[116] Purver 1967 was 'the most recent' discussion at the time when this chapter was originally published.
[117] Purver 1967, pp. 5 and 235–7.   [118] Sprat 1959, p. 67.   [119] Purver 1967, p. 238.
[120] Purver 1967, p. 84.   [121] Purver 1967, p. 5.

its Fellows would have been in a position to grasp at the time. It is clearly anachronistic in the first place to think of the Society as embodying some 'deliberately-conceived ideal' from which the dilettantes were excluded for lack of 'serious' professional expertise'.[122] It would always have been open to the small and highly professional group meeting at Oxford during the 1650s to continue their meetings on a similar scale and with a similar character. But instead they admitted so many gentlemen that by the time of the second charter of 1663[123] their numbers had risen from under thirty to over a hundred.[124] By the time of Sprat's *History*, only four years later, their numbers had swollen to over two hundred.[125] Birch's *History* for this period records no case of a candidate's being rejected on what would nowadays be regarded as professional grounds. And it is clear from Sprat's *History* that the Society-men considered it essential to their purposes to be 'so numerous', and would have regarded it as a mistake if they had 'onely requir'd *perfect Philosophers*'.[126] Sprat is actively worried lest the Society fall into the hands of mere experts, fearing that they would prove less disinterested and might even 'corrupt' the Society by tending 'to consult *present profit* too soon'.[127]

It seems a further anachronism to imply that, when the more expert Fellows took part in discussions with the gentlemen free and unconfined, the serious purposes of the Society were in some way compromised. Doubtless their arguments would strike us nowadays as 'occasionally simply silly'.[128] No doubt it was silly to spend so much time examining such curiosities as unicorns' horns,[129] or such questions as whether wounds can be 'sympathetically' healed,[130] or whether animal life can be 'equivocally' generated directly out of vegetable matter.[131] Had these questions seemed absurd at the time, however, it is hard to understand why Boyle, Charlton, Goddard, Glisson, Wilkins and other leading members of the

---

[122] Purver 1967, pp. 84, 239.
[123] See Birch 1756–7, vol. 1, p. 214 for the second charter, which received the royal signature on 22 April 1663.
[124] *Record of the Royal Society* 1940, pp. 375–8. Cf. Hall 1962, pp. 192–9.
[125] Sprat 1959, pp. 431–3 gives a list of Fellows.   [126] Sprat 1959, pp. 71–2.
[127] Sprat 1959, p. 67. The social (and epistemological) assumptions underlying the kind of anxiety expressed by Sprat have been fascinatingly explored in Shapin 1994, pp. 65–125.
[128] Purver 1967, p. 84.
[129] Birch 1756–7, vol. 1, p. 83 records that Boyle, Wilkins and Wallis were present when a unicorn's horn was presented and discussed at a meeting of May 1662.
[130] Birch 1756–7, vol. 1, p. 25 records that Boyle and Charlton were present when 'sympathetic cures' were discussed at a meeting of June 1661.
[131] Birch 1756–7, vol. 1, pp. 117–18, 212–13 records that the issue was discussed at meetings in October 1662 and March 1663, with Charlton, Glisson and Goddard being appointed to oversee the required experiments.

Society continued to play such a prominent part in discussing them.[132] If we assume, in short, that when the original Fellows failed to talk seriously by our standards of scientific enquiry, this must mean that they cannot have been intending to talk seriously at all, we shall merely prevent ourselves from understanding what conception of serious scientific enquiry they actually held.

I turn to the other problem that arises if we treat the founding of the Royal Society as the 'deliberate inauguration' of 'a new philosophy and a new scientific attitude'.[133] Such a characterisation makes it impossible to explain the apparent 'exclusion' not merely of Hobbes but of many other prominent practitioners of the established sciences. These further 'exclusions' have received little attention.[134] But even if we limit ourselves to the first two decades of the Society's existence, and even if we limit ourselves within that period to the names of leading exponents of the major scientific disciplines, it is clear that to think of the Society as dedicated to the promotion of 'a new system of sciences'[135] is a serious misconception of its character. Not only did many Fellows come to feel in the course of this period that it was professionally pointless to be a member[136] but a large number of leading scientists never happened to become members at all.

One of the principal interests of the early Fellows lay in the study of chemistry.[137] When Joseph Glanvill presented his defence of the Society in his *Plus Ultra* of 1668, he took as his first topic 'the Advantages this Age hath from the great advancements of Chymistry'.[138] Yet Josiah Pullen, who was working in Oxford throughout the seminal period of the 1650s, and was one of the founding members of the Oxford Chemical Society, was never made a Fellow of the Royal Society.[139] Nor was Edmund Dickinson, although he was a 'famous Chymist' and 'a very learned person', according to John Evelyn[140] (himself an early Fellow),[141] and

---

[132] See Hunter 1975, pp. 135–40 for a development of this point.
[133] Trevor-Roper 1967, p. xi; Purver 1967, p. 3.
[134] But see now the valuable remarks in Hunter 1982, pp. 5–10.
[135] Purver 1967, p. 3.
[136] Stubbe 1670, Sig.* 3[r] levels the charge that 'many of the *Nobility*, most of the *Physicians*, and other *understanding* and *serious* persons have either totally deserted the *Society*, or *discontinued* their presence at their *Assemblies*'. Cf. Birch 1756–7, vol. 3, p. 127, a report from Sir John Lowther in 1674 to the effect that members were complaining 'that they had been drawn into the Society contrary to their inclination'.
[137] Birch 1756–7, vol. 1, p. 406 records that the Society established a special committee to promote the subject as early as 1664.
[138] Glanvill 1668, p. 9.   [139] See DNB *sub* Pullen.   [140] Evelyn 1955, vol. 5, p. 599.
[141] Evelyn 1955, vol. 3, p. 266 records that he was elected to the Fellowship in January 1661.

even though his experiments with earth and water were discussed at a meeting of the Society in 1664.[142]

Another leading interest of the early Society – thanks in part to John Evelyn, but more especially to John Ray – lay in the study of botany. Yet Sir Robert Sibbald, who was mainly responsible for setting up the first botanical garden in Edinburgh,[143] was never made a Fellow, although some of his findings were published in the *Philosophical Transactions* of the Society.[144] Nor was Leonard Plukenet, although Ray himself in his *Historia Plantarum* described Plukenet as 'an outstanding man, and second to none in his knowledge of plants'.[145] Nor was Robert Morison, although he received a warm encomium from Ray,[146] was consulted by the Society,[147] and became Professor of Botany at the University of Oxford in 1669.

The most striking 'exclusions', however, are to be found among the physicians, especially when we recall that they more than any other profession helped to set up the Royal Society, with Thomas Willis, Thomas Millington, Jonathan Goddard and Walter Charleton all being numbered among the original Fellows.[148] Consider, for example, the case of Thomas Sydenham, 'England's Hippocrates'. His *Methodus Curandi Febres*, his classic study of acute diseases, was discussed in the *Philosophical Transactions* as soon as it appeared in 1666.[149] Sydenham had many admirers within the Society, including Sir Hans Sloane, his former pupil,[150] and Robert Boyle, to whom his book was dedicated.[151] Yet Sydenham was never elected to the Fellowship. Consider, similarly, the case of Sir Thomas Browne, who was saluted in the *Philosophical Transactions* as 'that deservedly famous physician'.[152] Browne corresponded with Power, Evelyn and several other members of the Society,[153] and many of his scientific observations, which Boyle himself referred to as 'faithful and

---

[142] Birch 1756–7, vol. 2, p. 68.   [143] Sibbald 1833, pp. 21–3.

[144] *Philosophical Transactions* 1963, vol. 19, pp. 321–5; vol. 20, pp. 264–7; vol. 22, pp. 693–4; vol. 25, pp. 2314–17.

[145] Ray 1686–1704, vol. 2, *Praefatio*, Sig. A, 3^r: 'praeclarus vir, & in stirpium cognitione nulli secundus'. Cf. Raven 1942, pp. 231–2.

[146] Ray 1686–1704, vol. 1, *Praefatio*, Sig. A, 3^r.

[147] Birch 1756–7, vol. 1, p. 212. Evelyn 1955, vol. 4, p. 68 records that he went to hear Morison lecture in 1675.

[148] Clark and Cooke, 1964–72, vol. 1, pp. 309–12.

[149] *Philosophical Transactions* 1963, vol. 1, pp. 210–13. Cf. Stimson 1935, p. 332; Clark and Cooke 1964–72, vol. 1, pp. 319, 334.

[150] Brooker 1954, pp. 44–5.

[151] Sydenham 1666, Sig. A, 2^r, Dedication to 'the most illustrious and excellent' Robert Boyle.

[152] *Philosophical Transactions* 1963, vol. 5, p. 1159.

[153] For Browne's correspondence with Power see Chalmers 1936, p. 29; with Evelyn, see Evelyn 1955, vol. 3, p. 594. Raven 1942, pp. 116–17 records that Ray made use of some of Browne's drawings. On Browne and Power see Post 1987, esp. p. 10.

candid',[154] were made available to the Society.[155] Yet he too was never elected to the Fellowship.

The list of prominent yet 'excluded' physicians can easily be extended. Samuel Collins was never made a Fellow, although he was the leading comparative anatomist of the day,[156] and corresponded with several of the Society-men.[157] Nor was Peter Barwick, although his treatment of smallpox brought him widespread fame and his method of combating the plague was discussed by the Society.[158] Nor was Nathaniel Hodges, although his observations on the symptoms of plague were likewise discussed by the Society in advance of their publication in 1672.[159] Nor was Arthur Dacres, although he was briefly Professor of Geometry at Gresham College as well as being a Fellow of the Royal College of Physicians.[160] Nor was William Briggs, although his discoveries about the anatomy of the eye were originally announced in the *Philosophical Transactions*[161] and were praised by Sir Isaac Newton for their accuracy and ingenuity in the prefatory Epistle he contributed to Briggs's *Nova Visionis Theoria* in 1685.[162] Nor, finally, were the three best-known royal physicians of the period, Richard Wiseman, Sir John Hinton and Sir Charles Scarburgh, although all of them enjoyed the highest professional repute, and Wiseman's pioneering experiments on the staunching of blood were reported in the Society's *Philosophical Transactions* in 1673.[163]

There are hints in the case of one or two of these figures that the explanation for their 'exclusion' may be as simple as it appears to have been in the case of Hobbes.[164] It is suggestive that Sydenham appears to have given mortal offence to Henry Oldenburg, the secretary of the Society.[165] And it is possible that Robert Morison was excluded because

---

[154] Boyle 1744, vol. 1, p. 345.   [155] Chalmers 1936, p. 30.
[156] Clark and Cooke 1964–72, vol. 2, pp. 455, 468.
[157] Munk 1878, vol. 1, p. 356. For Collins's correspondence with the Society see Birch 1756–7, vol. 1, p. 163 and vol. 2, pp. 156–7.
[158] Birch 1756–7, vol. 2, p. 99.
[159] Birch 1756–7, vol. 2, p. 76; cf. Hodges 1672. Clark and Cooke 1964–72, vol. 1, p. 322 note that Hodges was elected a Fellow of the Royal College of Physicians in the plague year.
[160] Birch, 1756–7, vol. 1, p. 435.   [161] *Philosophical Transactions* 1963, vol. 13, pp. 171–82.
[162] Briggs 1685; for Newton's *Epistola* see Sig A, 3^r to Sig. A, 4^v.
[163] *Philosophical Transactions* 1963, vol. 8, pp. 6052–3. For Wiseman's own account see Wiseman 1672 and 1676; cf. also Ogg 1956, vol. 2, pp. 725–7.
[164] As More 1934, p. 56 notes, the most dramatic parallel comes from the next generation, when Sir Isaac Newton managed to exclude his own successor in the Lucasian Professorship, William Whiston, on what appear to have been purely personal grounds.
[165] See Boyle 1744, vol. 5, pp. 377b–378a, a letter from Oldenburg to Boyle of 24 December 1667. Oldenburg apologises for refusing to see Sydenham, who has 'thought fit (God knows without cause) to rail against me and that was such a coward, as afterwards to disown it, although undeniable. I confess, that with so mean and unmoral a spirit I cannot well associate.'

of his quarrel with John Ray,[166] and Ralph Cudworth because of his quarrel with Henry More.[167] The crucial point, however, is that in most cases there appears to have been no particular reason for the 'exclusion' at all. Not only were these men prominent in well-established sciences, but there is no suggestion – to take up the other issue I have discussed – that they had in common any religious barrier to their being elected to the Fellowship. Some, indeed, were notable for their piety: Josiah Pullen was an active preacher; Peter Barwick was the brother of the Dean of St Paul's (whose biography he wrote) and was prominent in London as a churchman himself.[168] Few, if any, seem to have been 'excluded' from the Royal Society for any reason at all; rather they merely seem not to have been included.

VI

What, then, is the appropriate way to think about the character of the early Royal Society and Hobbes's relations with it? On the one hand, the inclusion of several Fellows of doubtful orthodoxy, together with the 'exclusion' of so many professional scientists, casts doubt on the idea that the early Society was a body of a self-consciously religious or a self-consciously professional kind. But on the other hand, the exclusion of Hobbes – if it was motivated neither by religious nor by professional susceptibilities – suggests that personal feelings must have been allowed to play a decisive role. Together, these facts perhaps suggest a different way of thinking about the early Society: not as a puritan academy, not as a professional gathering, but as something more like a gentlemen's club. The exclusion of Hobbes can then be readily explained: no one wants to encourage a club bore.[169] And the apparent exclusion of so many professional scientists can be explained no less readily: they happened not to belong to the particular social group that formed the club.[170] As for the undeniable fact that the club happened to include among its earliest members several scientists of genius, this looks less like the outcome of a deliberate plan to include the ablest *savants* and more like a prodigious stroke of luck.

---

[166] Raven 1942, p. 186 claims that because of Morison's quarrel 'the Royal Society ignored him'.
[167] See Passmore 1951, pp. 16–27 for their dispute.
[168] For these details about Barwick and Pullen see DNB.
[169] But see Malcolm 1988, pp. 48–51 for a reconsideration of this assessment of Hobbes's character.
[170] For a partial endorsement of this interpretation see Hunter 1979, pp. 189–90 and Hunter 1981, pp. 178–9.

To return to Sprat's *History* is I think to feel the force of this explanation. There is nothing in his account that reads like the expression of a plan to inaugurate 'a new system of sciences'.[171] But there is certainly a hope that, if the gentlemen continue to talk, something may come of it. It is clear that many of the Society's potential Fellows – including the young Isaac Newton – saw little point in entertaining such hopes.[172] It is worth recalling that, in consequence of their increasing doubts, the Society nearly foundered within ten years of its incorporation.[173] The arrival of Newton at that point, and the fact that he soon changed his mind about the value of the Society, constituted a further stroke of luck that no one had any right to expect.

[171] Purver, 1967, p. 3.

[172] Webster 1966 emphasises the importance of local groups. Boyle, Mayow, Power, Ray, Wallis and Willis all continued to do their main work at Oxford. Flamsteed worked in Derbyshire, Christopher Towneley's group in Lancashire. The latter was of particular importance, although Towneley himself was never elected a Fellow of the Royal Society.

[173] See Birch 1756–7, vol. 3, p. 135 on the decision of the Society ('considering the small number of members') to adjourn fixed meetings and to 'consider of a better way ... to provide good entertainment'. See Hunter 1982, pp. 33–9, 51–2 on the near collapse of the Society in the 1670s.

Bibliographies

MANUSCRIPT SOURCES

BIBLIOTHEQUE NATIONALE, PARIS

Fonds Latin MS 6566A: *Hobs* [Name on spine; no title-page]

BODLEIAN LIBRARY, OXFORD

Add. MS D. 105, fos. 70ff. [Wallis to Tenison, 30 November 1680, draft]
Aubrey MS 9: *The Life of Mr. Thomas Hobbes, of Malmesburie.*
Aubrey MS 12, fos. 166–7 [Hobbes to Aubrey, 24 February 1675, transcript]

THE BRITISH LIBRARY

Add. MS 4278, fo. 205^r to 206^v: Cavendish to Pell, 11 May 1645
Add. MS 4278, fo. 223^r to 224^v: Cavendish to Pell, 11 November 1645
Add. MS 4278, fo. 259^r to 260^v: Cavendish to Pell, 19 July 1646
Add. MS 4278, fo. 263^r to 263^v: Cavendish to Pell, 12 October 1646
Add. MS 4278, fo. 265^r to 266^v: Cavendish to Pell, 7 December 1646
Add. MS 4278, fo. 273^r to 274^v: Cavendish to Pell, 2 August 1648
Add. MS 4278, fo. 291^r to 292^v: Cavendish to Pell, 5 October 1649
Add. MS 4280, fo. 136^r to 136^v: Pell to Cavendish, 26 May 1649
Add. MSS 6193, fo. 68^v to 69^r: Hooke to Boyle, c1664 [transcript]
Add. MSS 32533, fos. 37–8: Aubrey to Hobbes, 24 June, 1675.
Add. MSS 72850: The Petty Papers, vol. 6, pt. 2, fo. 134 [Hobbes to Aubrey, February 1675, Letter in hand of James Wheldon]
Add. MSS 72886: The Petty Papers, vol. 37, item 1 (previously vol. 4, item 36): *Politicall pastimes and paradoxes* [Draft Epistle Dedicatory in hand of Sir William Petty, signed and dated 1687]
Egerton MS 1910: Thomas Hobbes, *Leviathan Or the Matter, Forme, and Power of A Commonwealth Ecclesiastical and Civil*
Harl. MS 3360: Thomas Hobbes, *A Minute or first Draught of the Optiques In two parts The first of Illumination second of Vision*
Harl. MS 4235: Thomas Hobbes, *The Elements of Law, Naturall and Politique*

Harl. MS 6083, fo. 177^r–177^v: Thomas Hobbes, *Of Passions* [MS in hand of Sir Charles Cavendish, endorsed 'parte of M^r: Hobbes his answear to my brothers quaeres'.]
Harl. MS 6796, fos. 193–266: [Thomas Hobbes, Latin optical treatise]
Harl. MS 6796, fos. 297–308: [*A Short Tract on First principles*]
Sloane MS 904, fo. 14^r: *The Principles of Mr. Hobs*
Sloane MS 1458, fo. 35^r: *Mr Hobs creed, called also the Hobbish Creed*

CAMBRIDGE UNIVERSITY LIBRARY

MS Gg. 1. 4: A[nthony] A[scham], [*Of Marriage*]. [56 folio sheets, preceded by unnumbered table of contents and two ascriptions of authorship: (1) 'By A A Gent London 1647'. (2) (in a different hand): 'Written By master Askham that was afterwards killed in Spaine being agent for the Parliament of England there.']

CHATSWORTH, DERBYSHIRE

Hardwick MSS:

Hardwick MS 29: *Book of Accounts: Begining 1608. Ending 1623*
Hardwick MS 70: Untitled. [Exercise book in hand of 3rd Earl of Devonshire, 53 fos., unpaginated, signed 'William Cavendysshe' on inside front and back covers, 'William Devoshier' on inside back cover.]

Hobbes MSS:

Hobbes MS A. 1: *Ad Nobilissimum Dominum Gulielmum Comitem Devoniae etc. De Mirabilibus Pecci, Carmen Thomas Hobbes*
Hobbes MS A. 2. B: *The Elementes of Law, Naturall and Politique*
Hobbes MS A. 5: Untitled. [Draft in scribal hand of ch. 3 and part of ch. 2 of *De Homine*, 15 quarto pages]
Hobbes MS A. 6: Untitled. [MS of *Vita Carmine Expressa*, mainly in hand of James Wheldon, with corrections by Hobbes, 10 folio pages]
Hobbes MS A. 8 (1): *Aristotelis Parva Moralia, sive de Ethicis virtutibus* in Hobbes MS A. 8: *Three Digests* [Bound folio MS volume, title on spine], pp. 1–39.
Hobbes MS D. 1: *Latin Exercises* [Bound MS volume: *Ex Aristot: Rhet.*, pp. 1–143; extracts from Florus's epitome of Livy's history, pp. 160–54 *rev.*]
Hobbes MS D. 2: Untitled. [Mathematics exercise book in hand of third earl of Devonshire with corrections by Hobbes]
Hobbes MS D. 3: *Essayes of 1 Arrogance 2 Ambition 3 Affectation 4 Detraction 5 Selfe=will 6 Masters and Servants 7 Expences 8 Visitations 9 Death 10 Readinge of Histories* [Bound MS volume, vi+78pp.]
Hobbes MS D. 5: *Questions relative to Hereditary Right. Mr Hobbes.* [Single quarto sheet]

Hobbes MS E. 1. A: [Library catalogue]
Hobbes MS G. 2: *The Lord Shaftsburys Speech in the House of Lords March. 25. 1679* [3 folio pages]
Hobbes MS G. 3: *A Copy of the Bill concerning the D: of York* [7 folio pages]
Hobbes MS 73. Aa: *Translations of Italian Letters* [Bound MS volume, 248pp., 34pp. blank at end. 76 letters from Fulgenzio Micanzio. Flyleaf inscription in Hobbes's hand: 'Translated out of the originall Italian Letters by Th: Hobbes, secretary to ye Lord Cavendysh'.]

ST JOHN'S COLLEGE, OXFORD

MS 13: *Behemoth or the Long Parliament. By Thomas Hobbes of Malmsbury.* [Fair copy in hand of James Wheldon, with additions and excisions in hand of Hobbes.]

SHEFFIELD UNIVERSITY LIBRARY

Hartlib Papers 42/1/1A–2B: Worsley to unidentified correspondent, 22 June 1648.
Hartlib Papers 8/29/1A–2B: Cavendish to Petty, 17 April 1648.
Hartlib Papers 62/30/1A–4B: Rand to Hartlib, 18 July 1651.

PRINTED PRIMARY SOURCES

Act for Subscribing the Engagement, An (1986). In *Divine Right and Democracy*, ed. David Wootton, London, pp. 357–8.
Ad C. Herennium de Ratione Dicendi (1954). Ed. and trans. Harry Caplan, London.
[Addison, Joseph] (1965). *The Spectator*, ed. Donald F. Bond, 4 vols., Oxford.
Alciato, Andreae (1621). *Emblemata cum Commentariis*, Padua.
Alessandria, Benzo d' (1890). *De Mediolano Civitate*, ed. L. A. Ferrai in *Bullettino dell' Istituto Storico Italiano* 9, pp. 15–36.
Animadversions on a Discourse Entitled, God's Ways of Disposing of Kingdoms (1691). London.
Answer to a Late Pamphlet, An (1691). London.
Answer to Mr J. Dury, An (1650). N.p.
Arguments and Reasons to Prove the Inconvenience & Unlawfulness of taking the new Engagement (1650). N.p.
Aristotle (1926). *The 'Art' of Rhetoric*, ed. and trans. J. H. Freese, London.
    (1934). *The Nicomachean Ethics*, ed. and trans. H. Rackham, London.
    (1961). *Parts of Animals*, ed. and trans. A. L. Peck, revised edn, London.
    (1995). *Poetics*, ed. and trans. Stephen Halliwell, London.
Ascham, Anthony (1648). *A Discourse: Wherein is examined, What is particularly lawfull during the Confusions and Revolutions of Governments*, London.
[Ascham, Anthony] (1649a). *A Combate Betweene Two Seconds*, London.
    (1649b). *The Bounds & Bonds of Publique Obedience*, London.
Ascham, Anthony (1649c). *Of the Confusions and Revolutions of Goverments*, London.

[Ascham, Anthony] (1650). *A Reply to a Paper of Dr. Sandersons*, London.

Asgill, John (1714). *The Protestant Succession Vindicated*, London.

Atterbury, Francis (1723). *Maxims, Reflections and Observations*, London.

Aubrey, John (1898). *'Brief Lives', chiefly of Contemporaries, set down by John Aubrey, between the years 1669 & 1696*, ed. Andrew Clark, 2 vols., Oxford.

Bacon, Francis (1857). *De Dignitate et Augmentis Scientiarum Libri IX* in *The Works of Francis Bacon*, ed. James Spedding, Robert Ellis and Douglas Heath, 14 vols., London, vol. 1, pp. 423–837.

  (1859). *Of the Colours of Good and Evil* in *The Works*, ed. James Spedding, Robert Ellis and Douglas Heath, 14 vols., London, vol. 7, pp. 73–92.

  (1996). *The Essays or Counsels, Civil and Moral* in *Francis Bacon*, ed. Brian Vickers, Oxford, pp. 341–456.

Baker, Sir Richard (1643). *A Chronicle of the Kings of England*, London.

Baudelaire, Charles (1956). *The Essence of Laughter (De l'essence du rire)* in *The Essence of Laughter and Other Essays, Journals, and Letters*, ed. Peter Quennell, New York, pp. 109–30.

Baxter, Richard (1680). *The Defence of the Nonconformists Plea for Peace*, London.

  (1994). *A Holy Commonwealth*, ed. William Lamont, Cambridge.

Bayle, Pierre (1697). *Dictionnaire Historique et Critique*, 4 vols., Rotterdam.

Beacon, Richard (1594). *Solon his Follie, or a Politique Discourse, Touching the Reformation of Common-weales Conquered, Declined or Corrupted*, Oxford.

Beckman, J. C. (1679). *Meditationes Politicae*, Frankfort.

Beni, Paolo (1613). *In Aristotelis Poeticam Commentarii*, Padua.

Berrettario, Elpidio (1603). *Phisici, et Philosophi Tractatus de Risu*, Florence.

[Béthune, Philippe de] (1634). *The Counsellor of Estate*, trans. Edward Grimeston, London.

Birch, Thomas (1756–7). *The History of the Royal Society of London for Improving of Natural Knowledge*, 4 vols., London.

Blackbourne, Richard (1839). *Vitae Hobbianae Auctarium* in *Thomae Hobbes Malmesburiensis Opera Philosophica Quae Latine Scripsit Omnia*, ed. Sir William Molesworth, 5 vols., London, vol. 1, pp. xxii–lxxx.

Blackstone, Sir William (1803). *Of the Rise, Progress and Gradual Improvement of the Laws of England* in *Commentaries on the Laws of England*, ed. Edward Christian, 4 vols., London.

Blount, Charles (1693). *The Oracles of Reason*, London.

Blount, Thomas (1971). *The Academie of Eloquence* [1656], ed. R. C. Alston, Menston.

Boyle, Robert (1662). *A Defence of the Doctrine Touching the Spring and Weight of the Air* in *New Experiments Physico-Mechanical Touching the Air. The Second Edition. Whereunto is added A Defence of the Authors Explication of the Experiments, Against the Objections of Franciscus Linus, And, Thomas Hobbes*, London.

  (1744). *An Examen of Mr. T. Hobbes his Dialogus Physicus de Natura Aeris* in *The Works of the Honourable Robert Boyle*, ed. Thomas Birch, 5 vols., London, vol. 1, pp. 118a–154b.

Bracciolini, Poggio (1964–9). *De Avaritia* in *Opera Omnia*, ed. Riccardo Fubini, 4 vols., Turin, vol. 1, pp. 1–31.

[Braham, Humfrey] (1555). *The Institucion of a Gentleman*, London.

Bramhall, John (1658). *The Catching of Leviathan*, London.

Brief Chronology of Great Britain, A (n.d.). N.p.

Briggs, William (1685). *Nova Visionis Theoria*, London.

Bright, Timothy (1586). *A Treatise of Melancholie*, London.

Britanniae Speculum (1683). London.

British Liberty Asserted, The (1714). London.

Broughton, John (1718). *The Great Apostacy from Christianity, with its Evil Influence on the Civil State*, London.

Browne, Sir Thomas (1928–31). *Pseudodoxia Epidemica* [1646] in *The Works of Sir Thomas Browne*, ed. Geoffrey Keynes, 6 vols., London, vols. 2 and 3.

Bruni, Leonardo (1968). *Laudatio Florentinae Urbis* [1403–4] in Hans Baron, *From Petrarch to Leonardo Bruni*, Chicago, pp. 217–63.

Burnet, Gilbert (1897–1900). *History of My Own Time*, ed. Osmund Airy, 2 vols., Oxford.

Burton, Robert (1989). *The Anatomy of Melancholy* [1621], Vol. 1: *Text*, ed. Thomas C. Faulkner, Nicholas K. Kiessling and Rhonda L. Blair, Oxford.

Butler, Charles (1629). *Rhetoricae Libri Duo*, London.

Cantor, Moritz (1880–1908). *Vorlesungen über Geschichte der Mathematik*, 4 vols., Leipzig.

Carmen de Figuris vel Schematibus (1863). In *Rhetores Latini Minores*, ed. Carl von Halm, Leipzig, pp. 63–70.

Carre, Thomas (1651). *A Treatise of Subiection to the Powers*, London.

Casaubon, Meric (1669). *A Letter of Meric Casaubon, D. D. etc. to Peter du Moulin, D. D. . . . Concerning Natural experimental Philosophie*, Cambridge.

Castelvetro, Lodovico (1570). *Poetica d'Aristotele vulgarizzata et sposta*, Vienna.

Castiglione, Baldassare (1994). *The Book of the Courtier*, trans. Thomas Hoby, ed. Virginia Cox, London.

[Cavendish, William] (1611). *A Discourse Against Flatterie*, London.

[Cavendish, William and Hobbes, Thomas] (1620). *Horae Subsecivae. Observations and Discourses*, London.

Censure of the Rota, The (1673). Oxford.

Chesterfield, Earl of (1901). *The Letters of the Earl of Chesterfield to his Son*, ed. Charles Strachey and Annette Calthrop, 2 vols., London.

Cicero (1913). *De Officiis*, ed. and trans. Walter Miller, London.

(1942). *De Oratore*, ed. and trans. E. W. Sutton and H. Rackham, 2 vols., London.

(1949). *De Inventione*, ed. and trans. M. M. Hubbell, London, pp. 1–346.

Clarendon, Edward, Earl of (1676). *A Brief View and Survey of the Dangerous and pernicious Errors to Church and State, in Mr. Hobbes's Book, Entitled Leviathan*, Oxford.

Cockeram, Henry (1968). *The English Dictionarie*, ed. R. C. Alston, Menston.

Confusion Confounded (1654). London.

Congreve, William (1981). *The Double-Dealer*, ed. J. C. Ross, London.

Conscience Puzzel'd, about subscribing the new Engagement (1650). N.p.

Constant Man's Character, The (1650). London.

Constitutional Documents of the Puritan Revolution 1625–1660, ed. Samuel Rawson Gardiner (1906), 3rd edn, Oxford.

Correspondence of Scientific Men of the Seventeenth Century (1841). Ed. Stephen J. Rigaud, 2 vols., Oxford.

[Coste, F. Hilarion de] (1649). *La Vie du R. P. Marin Mersenne*, Paris.

Cotgrave, Randle (1611). *A Dictionarie of the French and English Tongues*, London.

Court, Johan de la (1661). *Consideratien van Staat*, n.p.

Crowne, John (1683). *City Politics*, London.

Cumberland, Richard (1672). *De Legibus Naturae Disquisitio Philosophica*, London.

Day, Angel (1967). *The English Secretary or Method of Writing Epistles and Letters* [1592], ed. R. O. Evans, Gainesville, Florida.

Declaration of the Parliament of England, Expressing the Grounds of their Late Proceedings, and of Setling the Present Government in the Way of a Free State, A (1649). London.

Dee, John (1571). Preface to Euclid, *The Elements of Geometrie*, trans. Henry Billingsley, London, Sig. iiii^v to Sig. A iiii^r.

De Laude Civitatis Laudae [c.1250], ed. Georg Waitz in *Monumenta Germaniae Historica* (1872) vol. 22, Hanover, pp. 372–3.

Descartes, René (1988). *Les Passions de l'ame*, ed. Geneviève Rodez-Lewis, Paris.

Digest of Justinian, The, ed. Theodor Mommsen and Paul Krueger (1985), trans. Alan Watson, 4 vols., Philadelphia, Penn.

[Digges, Dudley *et al.*] (1642). *An Answer to a Printed Book*, Oxford.

Discourse concerning the Engagement: or the Northern subscribers plea, A (1650). London.

Dr. Sherlock's Two Kings of Brainford Brought Upon the Stage (1690). London.

Dr. Sherlock's Case of Allegiance Considered (1691). London.

Drew, John (1651). *The Northern Subscribers Plea, Vindicated*, London.

[Dury, John] (1649). *A Case of Conscience Resolved: Concerning Ministers Medling with State-Matters in their Sermons*, London.

(1650a). *Considerations concerning the present Engagement, whether it may lawfully be entered into; yea or no?* 4th edn, London.

(1650b). *A Disengag'd Survey of the Engagement*, London.

(1650c). *Just Re-proposals to Humble Proposals*, London.

[Eachard, John] (1673). *Some Opinions of Mr. Hobbs Considered in a Second Dialogue Between Philautus and Timothy*, London.

Eachard, John (1958). *Mr. Hobbs's State of Nature Considered*, ed. Peter Ure, Liverpool.

Eaton, Samuel (1650). *The Oath of Allegiance and the National Covenant Proved to be Non-obliging*, London.

Eikon Basilike. The Pourtraicture of His Sacred Majestie in his Solitudes and Sufferings (1649). N.p.

Elcock, Ephraim (1651). *Animadversions on a Book, Called, A Plea for Non-scribers*, London.

Elyot, Sir Thomas (1962). *The Book Named the Governor*, ed. S. E. Lehmberg, London.

Engagement Vindicated, The (1650). London.

Englands Apology, for its late change (1651). London.

English, Peter (1653). *The Survey of Policy*, Leith.

Enquiry after further satisfaction concerning obeying a change of government beleeved to be unlawfull, An (1649). London.

Euclid (1571). *The Elements of Geometrie*, trans. Henry Billingsley, London.

Evelyn, John (1955). *The Diary of John Evelyn*, ed. E. S. De Beer, 6 vols., Oxford.

Examination of the Arguments Drawn from Scripture and Reason, in Dr. Sherlock's Case of Allegiance, and His Vindication of It, An (1691). London.

Exercitation Answered, The (1650). London.

Farnaby, Thomas (1970). *Index Rhetoricus* [1625], ed. R. C. Alston, Menston.

Farquhar, George (1700). *The Constant Couple*, London.

Fenner, Dudley (1584). *The Artes of Logike and Rethorike*, n.p.

Ferne, Henry (1642). *The Resolving of Conscience*, Cambridge.

Fielding, Henry (1985). *Joseph Andrews*, ed. R. F. Brissenden, London.

Filmer, Sir Robert (1991). *Patriarcha and Other Writings*, ed. Johann Sommerville, Cambridge.

Fortescue-Aland, John (1714). *Preface to The Difference Between an Absolute and a Limited Monarchy*, London, pp. i–lxxxii.

Foster, Joseph (ed.) (1891–2). *Alumni Oxonienses: The Members of the University of Oxford, 1500–1714*, 4 vols., Oxford.

Fracastoro, Girolamo (1546). *De Sympathia & Antipathia rerum*, Venice.

Fraunce, Abraham (1950). *The Arcadian Rhetorike*, ed. Ethel Seaton, Oxford.

Freeman, Edward A. (1867–76). *The History of the Norman Conquest of England*, 5 vols., Oxford.

Gassendi, Pierre (1658). *Opera Omnia*, 6 vols., Lyon.

[Gee, Edward] (1650). *An Exercitation Concerning Usurped Powers*, n.p.

[Gentillet, Innocent] (1602). *A Discourse upon the Meanes of Wel Governing and Maintaining in Good Peace, a Kingdome, or other Principalitie . . . Against Nicholas Machiavell the Florentine*, trans. Simon Patericke, London.

Glanvill, Joseph (1661). *The Vanity of Dogmatizing*, London.

    (1665). *Scepsis Scientifica: Or, Confest Ignorance, the way to Science*, London.

    (1668). *Plus Ultra: Or, The Progress and Advancement of Knowledge Since the Days of Aristotle*, London.

Goclenius, Rodolph [the elder] (1597). *Physica Commentatio De Risu & Lacrymis*, Marburg.

Goulston, Theodore (1619). *Aristotelis de Rhetorica seu arte Dicendi Libri tres*, London.

Grand Case of Conscience Stated, about Submission to the New and Present Power, The (1649). N.p.

Great Law of Nature, The (1673). N.p.

Grey, Enoch (1649). *Vox Coeli, Containing Maxims of Pious Policy*, London.

Guazzo, Stefano (1925). *The Civile Conversation*, trans. George Pettie and Bartholomew Young, ed. Sir Edward Sullivan, 2 vols., London.

Gundling, Nicolas (1706). *Schediasma de Iure Oppignorati Territorii*, Magdeburg.

Halifax, Marquis of (1969). *The Lady's New Year's Gift; Or, Advice to a Daughter* [1688] in *Halifax: Complete Works*, ed. J. P. Kenyon, Harmondsworth.

[Hall, Edmund] (1650). *Lazarus's Sores Licked*, London.

Hall, John [of Durham] (1650). *The Grounds and Reasons of Monarchy Considered*, Edinburgh.

Hall, John [of Richmond] (1654). *Of Government and Obedience*, London.

Hallam, Henry (1819). *A View of the State of Europe during the Middle Ages*, 3 vols., London.

Hamel, Joanne-Baptista du (1698). *Regiae Scientiarum Academiae Historia*, Paris.

[Harbin, George] (1710). *The English Constitution Fully Stated: With Some Animadversions on Mr. Higden's Mistakes about it*, London.

(1713). *The Hereditary Right of the Crown of England Asserted*, London.

Harrington, James (1977). *The Political Works of James Harrington*, ed. J. G. A. Pocock, Cambridge.

Hawke, Michael (1655). *The Right of Dominion, and Property of Liberty*, London.

(1657). *Killing Is Murder*, London.

[Hayward, John] (1613). *The Lives of the III. Normans, Kings of England*, London.

Haywood, Sir John (1603). *An Answer to the First Part of a Certaine Conference, Concerning Succession*, London.

Hearne, Thomas (1885–1921). *The Remarks and Collections of Thomas Hearne*, 11 vols., Oxford.

Heydon, John (1660). *The Idea of the Law*, London.

Heylyn, Peter (1658). *The Stumbling-Block of Disobedience and Rebellion*, London.

Higden, William (1709). *A View of the English Constitution*, London.

Hobbes, Thomas (1629). *Eight Bookes of the Peloponnesian Warre Written by Thucydides . . . Interpreted . . . By Thomas Hobbes*, London.

[Hobbes, Thomas (?)] (c.1637). *A Briefe of the Art of Rhetorique*, London.

Hobbes, Thomas (1642). *Elementarum Philosophiae Sectio Tertia De Cive*, Paris.

(1649). *Elements philosophiques du citoyen*, trans. Samuel Sorbière, Amsterdam.

(1650). *De Corpore Politico. Or The Elements of Law, Moral & Politick*, London.

(1651). *Leviathan, or The Matter, Forme, & Power of a Common-wealth Ecclesiasticall and Civill*, London.

(1652). *Le Corps politique*, trans. Samuel Sorbière, Amsterdam.

(1656). *The Questions Concerning Liberty, Necessity, And Chance. Clearly Stated and Debated Between Dr. Bramhall Bishop of Derry, And Thomas Hobbes of Malmesbury*, London.

(1660). *Les Elemens de la politique de Monsieur Hobbes*, trans. François du Verdus, Paris.

(1839a). *T. Hobbes Malmesburiensis Vita* in *Thomae Hobbes Malmesburiensis Opera Philosophica Quae Latine Scripsit Omnia*, ed. Sir William Molesworth, 5 vols., London, vol. 1, pp. xiii–xxi.

(1839b). *Thomae Hobbes Malmesburiensis Vita Carmine Expressa* in *Opera Philosophica*, ed. Sir William Molesworth, London, vol. 1, pp. lxxxi–xcix.

(1839c). *Elementorum Philosophiae Sectio Prima de Corpore* in *Opera philosophica*, ed. Sir William Molesworth, London, vol. 1, pp. i–xii and 1–431.

(1839d). *Elementorum Philosophiae Sectio Secunda De Homine* in *Opera Philosophica*, ed. Sir William Molesworth, London, vol. 2, pp. 1–132.

(1839e). *Elements of Philosophy. The First Section, Concerning Body* in *The English Works of Thomas Hobbes of Malmesbury*, ed. Sir William Molesworth, 11 vols., London, vol. 1, pp. v–xii, 1–532.

(1840a). *Of Liberty and Necessity* in *The English Works*, ed. Sir William Molesworth, London, vol. 4, pp. 229–78.

(1840b). *An Answer to a Book Published by Dr. Bramhall . . . Called the "Catching of the Leviathan"* in *The English Works*, ed. Sir William Molesworth, London, vol. 4, pp. 279–384.

(1840c). *An Historical Narration concerning Heresy, and the Punishment thereof* in *The English Works*, ed. Sir William Molesworth, London, vol. 4, pp. 385–408.

(1840d). *Considerations upon the Reputation, Loyalty, Manners, and Religion, of Thomas Hobbes of Malmesbury* in *The English Works*, ed. Sir William Molesworth, London, vol. 4, pp. 409–40.

(1840e). *A Dialogue Between a Philosopher & a Student of the Common Laws of England* in *The English Works*, ed. Sir William Molesworth, London, vol. 6, pp. 1–160.

(1841a). *Leviathan, sive De Materia, Forma, & Potestate Civitatis Ecclesiasticae et Civilis* in *Opera Philosophica* ed. Sir William Molesworth, London, vol. 3, pp. v–viii and 1–569.

(1841b). *The Questions Concerning Liberty, Necessity, And Chance* in *The English Works*, ed. Sir William Molesworth, London, vol. 5, pp. 1–455.

(1844a). *Concerning the Virtues of an Heroic Poem*, in *The English Works*, ed. Sir William Molesworth, London, vol. 10, pp. iii–x.

(1844b). *The Travels of Ulysses* in *The English Works*, ed. Sir William Molesworth, London, vol. 10, pp. 382–427.

(1844c). *The Iliads and Odysses of Homer* in *The English Works*, ed. Sir William Molesworth, London, vol. 10, pp. 1–301, 303–536.

(1845a). *Dialogus Physicus de Natura Aeris* in *Opera Philosophica*, ed. Sir William Molesworth, London, vol. 4, pp. 233–96.

(1845b). *De Principiis et Ratiocinatione Geometrarum* in *Opera Philosophica*, ed. Sir William Molesworth, London, vol. 4, pp. 385–484.

(1845c). *Rosetum Geometricum* in *Opera Philosophica*, ed. Sir William Molesworth, London, vol. 5, pp. 1–88.

(1845d). *Lux Mathematica* in *Opera Philosophica*, ed. Sir William Molesworth, London, vol. 5, pp. 89–150.

(1845e). *Principia et Problemata Aliquot Geometrica* in *Opera Philosophica*, ed. Sir William Molesworth, London, vol. 5, pp. 151–214.

(1845f). *De Mirabilibus Pecci, Carmen* in *Opera Philosophica*, ed. Sir William Molesworth, London, vol. 5, pp. 325–40.

(1845g). *Historia Ecclesiastica* in *Opera Philosophica*, ed. Sir William Molesworth, London, vol. 5, pp. 341–408.

(1845h). *Decameron Physiologicum* in *The English Works*, ed. Sir William Molesworth, London, vol. 7, pp. 69–177.

(1845j). *Six Lessons to the Professors of the Mathematics* in *The English Works*, ed. Sir William Molesworth, London, vol. 7, pp. 181–356.

(1845k). *Marks of the Absurd Geometry, Rural Language, Scottish Church Politics, and Barbarisms of John Wallis* in *The English Works*, ed. Sir William Molesworth, London, vol. 7, pp. 357–400.

(1969a). *The Elements of Law Natural and Politic*, ed. Ferdinand Tönnies, 2nd edn, introd. M. M. Goldsmith, London.

(1969b). *Behemoth or the Long Parliament*, ed. Ferdinand Tönnies, 2nd edn, introd. M. M. Goldsmith, London.

(1971a). *Léviathan: traité de la matière, de la forme et du pouvoir de la république ecclésiastique et civile*, trans. François Tricaud, Paris.

(1971b). *The Answer of Mr. Hobbes to Sir Will. D'Avenant's Preface Before Gondibert* in *Sir William Davenant's Gondibert*, ed. David F. Gladish, Oxford, pp. 45–55.

(1971c). *A Dialogue Between a Philosopher and a Student of the Common Laws of England*, ed. Joseph Cropsey, Chicago, Ill.

(1973). *Critique du De Mundo de Thomas White*, ed. Jean Jacquot and Harold Whitmore Jones, Paris.

(1975a). *Hobbes's Thucydides*, ed. Richard Schlatter, New Brunswick, N.J.

(1975b). *Of the Life and History of Thucydides* in *Hobbes's Thucydides*, ed. Richard Schlatter, New Brunswick, N.J., pp. 10–27.

(1983a). *De Cive: The Latin Version*, ed. Howard Warrender, Oxford: The Clarendon Edition, vol. 2.

(1983b). *De Cive: The English Version*, ed. Howard Warrender, Oxford: The Clarendon Edition, vol. 3.

(1985). *A Physical Dialogue of the Nature of the Air* (1661), trans. Simon Schaffer in Steven Shapin and Simon Schaffer, *Leviathan and the Air-Pump: Hobbes, Boyle, and the Experimental Life*, Princeton, N.J., Appendix, pp. 346–91.

[Hobbes, Thomas (?)] (1986). *A Briefe of the Art of Rhetorique* in *The Rhetorics of Thomas Hobbes and Bernard Lamy*, ed. John T. Harwood, Carbondale and Edwardsville, Ill., pp. 33–128.

[Hobbes, Thomas (?)] (1988). *Court traité des premiers principes: Le Short Tract on First Principles de 1630–1631*, ed. and trans. Jean Bernhardt, Paris.

Hobbes, Thomas (1993). *Textes sur l'hérésie et sur l'histoire*, ed. Franck Lessay, Paris.

(1994). *The Correspondence*, ed. Noel Malcolm, 2 vols., Oxford: The Clarendon Edition, vols. 6 and 7.

[Hobbes, Thomas (?)] (1995). *Three Discourses* in *A Critical Modern Edition of Newly Identified Work by the Young Hobbes*, ed. Noel B. Reynolds and Arlene W. Saxonhouse, Chicago, Ill.

Hobbes, Thomas (1996). *Leviathan, or The Matter, Forme, & Power of a Commonwealth Ecclesiasticall and Civill*, ed. Richard Tuck, Cambridge.

(1998). *On the Citizen*, trans. Michael Silverthorne, ed. Richard Tuck, Cambridge.

Hodges, Nathaniel (1672). *Loimologia, sive Pestis Nuperae apud Populum Londinensem*, London.

Horace (1929). *Satires, Epistles and Ars Poetica*, ed. and trans. H. Rushton Fairclough, London.

Howell, William (1687). *Medulla Historiae Anglicanae*, 3rd edn, London.

Hume, David (1826). *The History of England*, 8 vols., Oxford.

Hutcheson, Francis (1750). *Reflections upon Laughter*, Glasgow.

Huygens, Christian (1888–1950). *Œuvres complètes de Christian Huygens*, 22 vols., The Hague.

'Illustrations of the State of the Church During the Great Rebellion' (1848). *The Theologian and Ecclesiastic* 6, pp. 161–75, 212–26.

'Illustrations of the State of the Church During the Great Rebellion' (1850). *The Theologian and Ecclesiastic* 9, pp. 288–98.

Isidore of Seville (1911). *Etymologiarum sive Originum Libri XX*, ed. W. M. Lindsay, 2 vols., Oxford.

Jaggard, William (1941). *A Catalogue of such English Bookes, as lately have bene, and now are in Printing for Publication* [1611], ed. Oliver M. Willard in *Stanford Studies in Language and Literature*, Stanford, Calif.

Jenkin, William (1651). *M. Jenkin's Recantation*, London.

[Jones, Erasmus] (1737). *The Man of Manners*, 3rd edn, London.

Jonson, Ben (1937). *Catiline his Conspiracy* in *Ben Jonson*, ed. C. H. Herford, Percy and Evelyn Simpson, 11 vols., Oxford, vol. 5, pp. 409–549.

Jossius, Nicander (1580). *De risu et fletu* in *Opuscula*, Rome, pp. 44–144.

Joubert, Laurent (1579). *Traité du ris, contenant son essance, ses causes, et mervelheus essais, curieusemant recherchés, raisonnés & observés*, Paris.

Journals of the House of Commons (1660–7). Vol. 8, London.

[Juxon, William] (1649). *The Subjects Sorrow: or Lamentations upon the Death of Britaines Josiah, King Charles, unjustly put to Death by His owne people*, London.

Lawson, George (1657). *An Examination of the Political Part of Mr. Hobbes his Leviathan*, London.

[Leslie, Charles] (1709a). *The Best Answer Ever Was Made*, London.

(1709b). *Best of All. Being the student's thanks to Mr Hoadly*, London.

(1709c). *The Constitution, Laws and Government of England Vindicated*, London.

(1711). *The Finishing Stroke*, London.

Letter to a Friend, A (1679). London.

Lilburne, John (1964). *Englands New Chains Discovered* and *The Second Part of Englands New Chains Discovered* in *The Leveller Tracts, 1647–53*, ed. William Haller and G. Davies, repd. Gloucester, Mass., pp. 157–70, 172–89.

Lilburne, John, Walwyn, William, Prince, Thomas and Overton, Richard (1998). *An Agreement of the Free People of England* in *The English Levellers*, ed. Andrew Sharp, Cambridge, pp. 168–78.

Lipsius, Justus (1594). *Six Bookes of Politickes or Civil Doctrine*, trans. W. Jones, London.

Livy (1929). *Livy: Books XXI–XXII*, ed. and trans. B. O. Foster, London.

Locke, John (1979). *An Essay Concerning Human Understanding*, ed. Peter H. Nidditch, Oxford.

(1988). *Two Treatises of Government*, ed. Peter Laslett, Cambridge.

(1997). *Political Essays*, ed. Mark Goldie, Cambridge.

Logical Demonstration of the Lawfulness of Subscribing the New Engagement, A (1650). London.

London, William (1658). *A Catalogue of the Most Vendible Books in England,* London.

Lorenzini, Antonio [*alias* Poliziano] (1603). *Tractatus Novus, Utilis et Iucundus,* Frankfurt.

(1606). *Dialogus Pulcherrimus et Utilissimus, de risu: eiusque causis et consequentibus,* Marburg.

Lowde, James (1694). *A Discourse Concerning the Nature of Man,* London.

Lucian (1913). *Heracles* in *Lucian,* ed. and trans. A. M. Harmon *et al.,* 8 vols., London, vol. 1, pp. 61–70.

[Lucy, William] (1657). *Examinations, Censures, and Confutations of Divers Errours in the Two first Chapters of Mr. Hobbes his Leviathan,* London.

Lucy, William (1663). *Observations, Censures, and Confutations of notorious Errours in Mr Hobbes his Leviathan and other his bookes,* London.

Macaulay, Thomas Babington (1866). *The Works of Lord Macaulay,* ed. Lady Trevelyan, 8 vols., London.

Machiavelli, Niccolò (1960). *Il Principe e Discorsi Sopra la Prima Deca di Tito Livio,* ed. Sergio Bertelli, Milan.

(1988). *The Prince,* trans. Russell Price, ed. Quentin Skinner, Cambridge.

Maggi, Vincento (1550). *De Ridiculis* in *In Aristotelis Librum de Poetica Communes Explicationes,* Venice, pp. 301–27.

Mancinelli, Antonio (1493). *Carmen de Figuris* in *Carmen de Floribus, Carmen de Figuris. De Poetica Virtute. Vitae Carmen,* Sig. E, VIII^r to Sig. H, I^v, Venice.

Mancini, Celso (1598). *De Risu, Ac Ridiculis* in *Moralis Philosophi Libri III,* Frankfurt, pp. 160–231.

Marsilius of Padua (1928). *Defensor pacis,* ed. C. W. Previté-Orton, Cambridge.

Martial (1919–20). *Epigrams,* ed. and trans. Walter C. A. Ker, 2 vols., London.

Martyn, William (1615). *The Historie, and Lives, of Twentie Kings of England,* London.

Maxwell, John (1644). *Sacro-sancta Regum Majestatis: Or, The Sacred and Royall Prerogative of Christian Kings,* Oxford.

Mayow, John (1674). *Tractatus Quinque Medico-Physici,* Oxford.

Mead, Samuel (1689). *Oratio Pro Populo Anglicano,* Trajecti ad Rhenum.

Memorandums of the Conferences held between the Brethren scrupled at the Engagement; and others who were satisfied with it (1650). London.

Mercurius Politicus (1651a). Number 31, 2 to 9 January 1651, London.

Mercurius Politicus (1651b). Number 32, 9 to 16 January 1651, London.

Mercurius Politicus (1651c). Number 33, 16 to 23 January 1651, London.

Mercurius Politicus (1651d). Number 34, 23 to 30 January 1651, London.

Merlat, Élie (1685). *Traité du pouvoir absolu des souverains,* Cologne.

Mersenne, Marin (1980). *Correspondance,* vol. 14, ed. Cornélis de Waard and Armand Beaulieu, Paris.

(1983). *Correspondance,* vol. 15, ed. Cornélis de Waard and Armand Beaulieu, Paris.

Millar, John (1812). *An Historical View of the English Government,* 4 vols., London.

Milton, John (1991). *The Tenure of Kings and Magistrates* [1649] in *Political Writings*, ed. Martin Dzelzainis, Cambridge, pp. 1–48.

(1998). *L'Allegro*, in *The Complete Poems*, ed. John Leonard, London, pp. 21–5.

Mirth in Ridicule: Or, A Satyr against immoderate Laughing (1708). London.

Montaigne, Michel de (1892–3). *The Essays of Montaigne done into English by John Florio Anno 1603*, ed. George Saintsbury, 3 vols., London.

(1946–7). *Essais*, ed. Jean Plattard, 6 vols., Paris.

More, Henry (1690). *An Account of Virtue*, trans. Edward Southwell, London.

More, Thomas (1965). *Utopia* in *The Complete Works of Sir Thomas More*, vol. 4, ed. Edward Surtz and J. H. Hexter, New Haven, Conn.

Morton, Thomas (1643). *The Necessity of Christian Subjection*, Oxford.

Moulin, Lewis de (1650). *The Power of the Magistrate in Sacred Things . . . With . . . a digression concerning allegiance*, London.

Munday, Anthony (1593). *The Defence of Contraries*, London.

Nedham, Marchamont (1969). *The Case of the Commonwealth of England, Stated*, ed. Philip A. Knachel, Charlottesville, Va.

New History of the Succession of the Crown of England, A (1690). London.

Newton, Isaac (1961). Letter to John Locke, 16 September 1693 in *The Correspondence of Sir Isaac Newton*, vol. 3, ed. W. H. Turnbull, Cambridge.

Nicholas, Edward (1886). *The Nicholas Papers: Correspondence of Sir Edward Nicholas*, ed. George F. Warner, vol. 1, 1641–1652, London.

Nietzsche, Friedrich (1990). *Beyond Good and Evil*, trans. R. J. Hollingdale, rev. edn, Harmondsworth.

Oldenburg, Henry (1965–86). *The Correspondence of Henry Oldenburg*, ed. A. Rupert Hall & Marie Boas Hall, 13 vols., Wisconsin and London.

Osborne, Francis (1673). *A Miscellany of Sundry Essaies, Paradoxes, and Problematical Discourses* in *The Works of Francis Osborn Esq.*, London, Sig Pp, 2^r to Sig Qq, 5^r and pp. 549–695.

[Osborne, Francis] (1811). *A Perswasive to a Mutuall Compliance under the Present Government* in *A Collection of Scarce and Valuable Tracts*, vol. 6, ed. Walter Scott, 2nd edn, London, pp. 153–77.

Overton, Richard (1933a). *A Remonstrance of many Thousand Citizens* in *Tracts on Liberty in the Puritan Revolution 1638–1647*, ed. William Haller, 3 vols., New York, vol. 3, pp. 349–70.

(1933b). *The Commoners Complaint* in *Tracts on Liberty in the Puritan Revolution 1638–1647*, ed. William Haller, 3 vols., New York, vol. 3, pp. 373–95.

Ovid (1979). *Ars Amatoria*, ed. and trans. J. H. Mozley, 2nd edn, London.

(1988). *Tristia*, ed. and trans. A. L. Wheeler, revised G. P. Goold, London.

Parallel, The (1682). London.

Parker, H[enry] (1651). *Scotlands Holy War*, London.

[Parker, Henry] (1933). *Observations upon some of His Majesties late Answers and Expresses* in *Tracts on Liberty in the Puritan Revolution 1638–1647*, ed. William Haller, 3 vols., New York, vol. 2, pp. 167–213.

Parliamentary Right Maintain'd (1714). N.p.

Pascal, Blaise (1960). *Les Provinciales* in *Oeuvres complètes*, ed. Jacques Chevalier, Paris, pp. 667–904.

Patin, Gui (1846). *Lettres*, ed. J.-H. Reveillé-Parise, 3 vols., Paris.

Peacham, Henry (1593). *The Garden of Eloquence . . . corrected and augmented*, London.

(1971). *The Garden of Eloquence*, ed. R. C. Alston, Menston.

Pepys, Samuel (1970–83). *The Diary*, ed. Robert Latham and William Matthews, 11 vols., London.

[Persons, Robert] (1594). *A Conference about the Next Succession to the Crowne of Ingland*, n.p.

(1655). *A Treatise Concerning the Broken Succession of the Crown of England*, London.

[Pett, Sir Peter] (1688). *The Happy Future State of England*, London.

Petty, Sir William (1674). *A Discourse . . . Concerning the Use of Duplicate Proportion*, London.

(1899). *Political Arithmetick* in *The Economic Writings of Sir William Petty*, ed. Charles Henry Hull, 2 vols., Cambridge, vol. 1, pp. 232–313.

(1927). *The Petty Papers: Some Unpublished Writings of Sir William Petty*, ed. Marquis of Lansdowne, 2 vols., London.

(1928). *The Petty–Southwell Correspondence 1676–1687*, ed. Marquis of Lansdowne, London.

[Philipps, Fabian] (1649). *King Charles the First, no Man of Blood: but a Martyr for his People*, London.

Philodemius, Eutactus (1649). *The Original & End of Civil Power*, London.

Philosophical Transactions: Giving Some Account of the Present Undertakings, Studies, and Labours of the Ingenious in Many Considerable Parts of the World (1963), 70 vols., New York.

Pierce, Thomas (1658). *Autocatachresis, or, Self-Condemnation, exemplified*, London.

Piot, Lazarus (1596). *The Orator: Handling a Hundred Severall Discourses, in Forme of Declamations*, London.

Plato (1925). *Philebus*, ed. and trans. Harold N. Fowler, London.

(1926). *Laws*, ed. and trans. R. G. Bury, 2 vols., London.

(1930–5). *The Republic*, ed. and trans. Paul Shorey, 2 vols., London.

Plutarch (1579). *The Lives of the Noble Grecians and Romanes, Compared together*, trans. Thomas North, London.

Power, Henry (1664). *Experimental Philosophy, In Three Books*, London.

[Prynne, William] (1649). *Summary reasons against the new oath and Engagement*, n.p.

Pufendorf, Samuel (1672). *De Iure Naturae et Gentium*, Lund.

Puttenham, George (1970). *The Arte of English Poesie* [1589], ed. Gladys Willcock and Alice Walker, Cambridge.

Quintilian (1920–2). *Institutio Oratoria*, ed. and trans. H. E. Butler, 4 vols., London.

Rainolde, Richard (1564). *A Booke called the Foundacion of Rhetorike*, London.

Raleigh, Sir Walter (1693). *An Introduction to a Breviary of the History of England*, London.

Ray, John (1686–1704). *Historia Plantarum*, 3 vols., London.

Record of the Royal Society of London, The (1940), 4th edn, London.

Records of the Virginia Company of London, ed. Susan Kingsbury (1906–35), 4 vols., Washington, D.C.

Registers of the Company of Stationers of London, 1554–1640 AD, A Transcript of the, ed. Edward Arber (1875–94), 5 vols., London and Birmingham.

[Richardson, John] (1691). *Providence and Precept*, London.

Riva, Bonvesin de la (1974). *De Magnalibus Mediolani* [1288], trans. Giuseppe Pontiggia, ed. Maria Corti, Milan.

Robertson, William (1769). *A View of the Progress of Society in Europe* in *The History of the Reign of the Emperor Charles V*, 3 vols., London, vol. 1, pp. 1–192.

Rocket, John (1651). *The Christian Subject*, London.

Rosse, Alexander (1653). *Leviathan Drawn out with an Hook*, London.

[Rous, Francis] (1649). *The Lawfulness of Obeying the Present Government*, London.

Rufinianus, Julius (1533). *De Figuris Sententiarum & Elocutionis Liber* in *De Figuris*, fos. 23^r–35^v, Venice.

Rutilius Lupus, P. (1970). *De Figuris Sententiarum et Elocutionis*, ed. Edward Brooks Jr., Leiden.

Sallust (1931). *Bellum Catilinae* in *Sallust*, ed. and trans. J. C. Rolfe, London, pp. 2–128.

[Sanderson, Robert] (1649). *A Resolution of Conscience, (by a learned divine) in answer to a letter sent with Mr Ascham's book*, n.p.

Saunders, Richard (1651). *Plenary Possession Makes a Lawful Power*, London.

Scot, Philip (1650). *A Treatise of the Schism of England*, London.

Selden, John (1927). *Table Talk of John Selden*, ed. Sir Frederick Pollock, London.

Seneca (1917–25). *Epistulae Morales*, ed. and trans. R. M. Gummere, 3 vols., London.

Shadwell, Thomas (1966). *The Virtuoso*, ed. Marjorie Hope Nicolson and David Stuart Rodes, London.

Shaftesbury, Anthony Ashley Cooper, Earl of (1900a). *Characteristics of Men, Manners, Opinions, Times, etc.*, ed. John M. Robertson, 2 vols., London.

(1900b). *The Life, Unpublished Letters and Philosophical Regimen of Anthony, Earl of Shaftesbury*, ed. Benjamin Rand, London.

Shakespeare, William (1988). *The Complete Works*, ed. Stanley Wells and Gary Taylor, Oxford.

[Sherlock, William] (1691a). *The Case of the Allegiance Due to Soveraign Powers, Stated and Resolved*, London.

(1691b). *Their Present Majesties Government Proved to be Thoroughly Settled, and That We May Submit to It, without Asserting the Principles of Mr Hobbs*, London.

[Shute, John] (1714). *The Revolution and Anti-Revolution Principles Stated and Compared*, 2nd edn, n.p.

Sibbald, Sir Robert (1833). *Autobiography*, Edinburgh.

Sidney, Algernon (1990). *Discourses Concerning Government*, ed. Thomas G. West, Indianapolis, Ind.

Sidney, Sir Philip (1912). *The Defence of Poesie* [1580] in *The Prose Works of Sir Philip Sidney*, ed. Albert Feuillerat, 4 vols., Cambridge, vol. 3, pp. 1–46.

(1962). *The Poems of Sir Philip Sidney*, ed. William A. Ringler, Jr, Oxford.

[Smith, George] (1718). *A Vindication of Lawful Authority*, London.

Smith, John (1969). *The Mysterie of Rhetorique Unvail'd* [1657], ed. R. C. Alston, Menston.

Sober Enquiry, A (1673). London.

[Sorbière, Samuel] (1652). *Le libraire au lecteur* in *Le corps politique ou les elements de la loy morale et civile*, n.p., Sig. A, 3^r–4^v.

Sorbière, Samuel (1664). *Relation d'un voyage en Angleterre*, Paris.

(1709). *A Voyage to England*, London.

South, Robert (1823a). *The Fatal Imposture and Force of Words: set forth in a sermon preached on Isaiah V. 20* in *Sermons Preached upon Several Occasions*, 7 vols., Oxford, vol. 4, pp. 108–38.

(1823b). *The Second Discourse on Isaiah V. 20* in *Sermons Preached upon Several Occasions*, 7 vols., Oxford, vol. 4, pp. 203–88.

Spinoza, Benedict de (1985). *Ethics* in *The Collected Works of Spinoza*, ed. Edwin Curley, vol. 1, Princeton, N.J.

Sprat, Thomas (1708). *Observations on Mons. De Sorbiere's Voyage into England*, London.

(1959). *History of the Royal Society*, ed. Jackson I. Cope and Harold W. Jones, St Louis, Mo.

Stubbe, Henry (1670). *Legends no Histories: Or, A Specimen Of some Animadversions Upon the History of the Royal Society*, London.

(1671). *A Reply to a Letter of Dr. Henry More*, Oxford.

Susenbrotus, Johannes (1562). *Epitome Troporum ac Schematum et Grammaticorum & Rhetorum*, London.

Sydenham, Thomas (1666). *Methodus Curandi Febres*, London.

Tacitus (1925). *The Histories, Books I–III*, ed. and trans. Clifford H. Moore, London.

(1970). *De Vita Julii Agricolae*, ed. and trans. M. Hutton and R. M. Ogilvie, London.

Tenison, Thomas (1670). *The Creed of Mr. Hobbes Examined*, London.

Textor, J. W. (1916). *Synopsis of the Law of Nations*, ed. Karl von Bar, Washington, D.C.

Traytors Deciphered in an Answeare to a Shameless Pamphlet (1650). N.p.

Treason Unmask'd (1713). London.

Treatise of Human Reason, A (1674). London.

True Portraiture of the Kings of England, The (n.d.). London.

[Tyrrell, James] (1692–4). *Bibliotheca Politica*, London.

Valerius Maximus (1966). *Factorum et Dictorum Memorabilium Libri Novem*, ed. Charles Kempf, Stuttgart.

Valleriola, François (1554). *De Risus Natura, & Causis* in *Enarrationum Medicinalium Libri Sex*, Lyon, pp. 212–24.

(1588). *Observationum Medicinalium Libri VI*, Lyon.

Vallesio, Francisco (1582). *De risu et fletu* in *Controversiarum Medicarum et Philosophicarum Libri Decem*, Frankfurt, pp. 220–2.

Velthuysen, Lambert van (1651). *Epistolica Dissertatio*, Amsterdam.

Venn, Richard (1715). *King George's Title Asserted*, 2nd edn, London.
Vindiciae, Contra Tyrannos (1994). Ed. and trans. George Garnett, Cambridge.
Virgil (1999–2000). *Aeneid*, ed. and trans. H. Rushton Fairclough, revised G. P. Goold, 2 vols., London.
Vives, Juan Luis (1550). *De Anima & Vita Libri Tres* ('ex ultima autorum eorundem recognitione'), Lyon.
Wallis, John (1655). *Elenchus Geometriae Hobbianae*, Oxford.
[Wallis, John] (1656). *Due Correction for M^{r}Hobbes*, Oxford.
Wallis, John (1657). *Hobbiani Puncti Dispunctio*, London.
   (1662). *Hobbius Heauton-timorumenos*, Oxford.
   (1669). *Thomae Hobbes Quadratura Circuli*, Oxford.
[Walwyn, William] (1933). *Englands Lamentable Slaverie* in *Tracts on Liberty in the Puritan Revolution 1638–1647*, ed. William Haller, 3 vols., New York, vol. 3, pp. 311–18.
[Ward, Nathaniel] (1649). *A Religious Demurrer, Concerning Submission to the Present Power*, n.p.
   (1650). *Discolliminium. Or, a most obedient reply to a late book, called, Bounds & Bonds*, London.
Warren, Albertus (1649). *The Royalist Reform'd*, London.
   (1653). *Eight Reasons Categorical*, London.
Warwick, Philip (1694). *A Discourse of Government*, London.
Webster, John (1654). *Academiarum Examen*, London.
Whichcote, Benjamin (1698). *Sermon 3* in *Select Sermons of Dr. Whichcot*, ed. Anthony, 3rd Earl of Shaftesbury, London, pp. 79–117.
White, Thomas (1655). *The Grounds of Obedience and Government*, London.
Whitehall, John (1679). *Leviathan Found Out*, London.
Wilkins, David (ed.) (1737). *Concilia Magnae Britanniae et Hiberniae a Synodo Verolamiensi A.D. 446 ad Londinensem A.D. 1717*, 4 vols., London.
[Willes, Sir John] (1714). *The Present Constitution, and the Protestant Succession Vindicated*, London.
Williams, Gr[iffith] (1643). *Vindiciae Regum; or The Grand Rebellion*, Oxford.
Wilson, George (1777). Preface to the Eighth Report in *The Reports of Sir Edward Coke*, rev. edn, 7 vols., London.
Wilson, Thomas (1554). *The Arte of Rhetorique, for the use of all suche as are studious of Eloquence*, n.p.
Winstanley, Gerrard (1968). *England's Spirit Unfoulded, or an Incouragement to take the Engagement*, ed. G. E. Aylmer in *Past and Present* 40, pp. 3–15.
Wiseman, Richard (1672). *A Treatise of Wounds*, London.
   (1676). *Severall Chirurgicall Treatises*, London.
[Wither, George] (1650). *Respublica Anglicana*, London.
Wolseley, Charles (1672). *The Reasonableness of Scripture-Belief*, London.
Wood, Anthony (1691–2). *Athenae Oxonienses*, 2 vols., London.
   (1892–1900). *The Life and Times of Anthony Wood, antiquary, of Oxford, 1632–1695, described by Himself*, ed. Andrew Clark, 5 vols., Oxford.
Wood, Lambert (1657). *Florus Anglicanus*, London.
Wren, Matthew (1659). *Monarchy Asserted*, London.

SECONDARY SOURCES

Adams, Robert M. (1962). *The Better Part of Valor: More, Erasmus, Colet, and Vives, on Humanism, War, and Peace, 1496–1535*, Seattle.

Anderson, Paul R. (1933). *Science in Defense of Liberal Religion*, New York.

Anglo, Sydney (1990). 'A Machiavellian Solution to the Irish Problem: Richard Beacon's *Solon his Follie* (1594)' in *England and the Continental Renaissance*, ed. Edward Chaney and Peter Mack, Woodbridge, pp. 153–64.

Axtell, James L. (1965). 'The Mechanics of Opposition: Restoration Cambridge v. Daniel Scargill', *Bulletin of the Institute of Historical Research* 38, pp. 102–11.

Ayers, Michael (1991). *Locke*. Vol. 1: *Epistemology*, London.

Aylmer, G. E. (ed.) (1975). *The Levellers in the English Revolution*, New York.

Bakhtine, Mikhaïl (1970). *L'Oeuvre de François Rabelais et la culture populaire au Moyen Age et sous la Renaissance*, trans. Andrée Robel, Paris.

Baldwin, T. W. (1944). *William Shakspere's 'Small Latine & Lesse Greeke'*, 2 vols., Urbana, Ill.

Barnouw, Jeffrey (1988). 'Persuasion in Hobbes's *Leviathan*', *Hobbes Studies* 1, pp. 3–25.

Barton, Anne (1984). *Ben Jonson, Dramatist*, Cambridge.

Batten, J. M. (1944). *John Dury*, Chicago.

Battista, Anna Maria (1966). *Alle Origini del Pensiero Politico Libertino: Montaigne e Charron*, Milan.

(1980). 'Come Giudicano la "Politica" Libertini e Moralisti nella Francia del Seicento', in *Il Libertinismo in Europa*, Milan, pp. 25–80.

Baumgold, Deborah (1988). *Hobbes's Political Theory*, Cambridge.

Beal, Peter (ed.) (1987). *Index of English Literary Manuscripts*. Vol. 2. *1625–1700. Part 1: Behn–King*, London.

Bec, Christian (1967). *Les Marchands écrivains: affaires et humanisme à Florence 1375–1434*, Paris.

Bell, Gary M. (1990). *A Handlist of British Diplomatic Representatives 1509–1688*, London.

Bentley, Gerald Eades (1971). *The Profession of Dramatist in Shakespeare's Time, 1590–1642*, Princeton, N.J.

Bernhardt, Jean (1988). *Essai de commentaire* in *Thomas Hobbes, Court traité des premiers principes: Le Short Tract on First Principles de 1630–1631*, ed. and trans. Jean Bernhardt, Paris, pp. 59–274.

Biersteker, Thomas J. and Weber, Cynthia (eds.) (1996). *State Sovereignty as Social Construct*, Cambridge.

Bloch, O. R. (1971). *La Philosophie de Gassendi*, The Hague.

Blom, Hans W. (1995). *Morality and Causality in Politics: The Rise of Naturalism in Dutch Seventeenth-Century Political Thought*, The Hague.

Boas, Marie (1952). 'The Establishment of the Mechanical Philosophy', *Osiris* 10, pp. 412–541.

(1958). *Robert Boyle and Seventeenth Century Chemistry*, Cambridge.

Boonin-Vail, David (1994). *Thomas Hobbes and the Science of Moral Virtue*, Cambridge.

Bowle, John (1969). *Hobbes and his Critics: A Study in Seventeenth Century Constitutionalism*, 2nd edn, London.
Brailsford, H. N. (1961). *The Levellers and the English Revolution*, London.
Brandt, Frithiof (1928). *Thomas Hobbes' Mechanical Conception of Nature*, London.
Bredekamp, Horst (1999). *Thomas Hobbes Visuelle Strategien*, Berlin.
Bredvold, Louis I. (1928). 'Dryden, Hobbes and the Royal Society', *Modern Philology* 25, pp. 417–38.
    (1956). *The Intellectual Milieu of John Dryden*, Ann Arbor, Mich.
Brennan, J. X. (1960). 'The *Epitome Troporum ac Schematum*: The Genesis of a Renaissance Rhetorical Text', *Quarterly Journal of Speech* 46, pp. 59–71.
Brett, Annabel S. (1997). *Liberty, Right and Nature: Individual Rights in Later Scholastic Thought*, Cambridge.
Briggs, John C. (1989). *Francis Bacon and the Rhetoric of Nature*, London.
Britton, John (1845). *Memoir of John Aubrey F.R.S.*, London.
Brooker, E. St. J. (1954). *Sir Hans Sloane*, London.
Brown, Harcourt (1934). *Scientific Organisations in Seventeenth Century France (1620–1680)*, Baltimore, Md.
Brown, K. C. (1962). 'Hobbes's Grounds for Belief in a Deity', *Philosophy* 37, pp. 336–44.
Burgess, Glenn (1986). 'Usurpation, Obligation and Obedience in the Thought of the Engagement Controversy', *Historical Journal* 29, pp. 515–36.
    (1990). 'Contexts for the Writing and Publication of Hobbes's *Leviathan*', *History of Political Thought* 11, pp. 675–702.
    (1992). *The Politics of the Ancient Constitution: An Introduction to English Political Thought, 1603–42*, London.
    (1996). *Absolute Monarchy and the Stuart Constitution*, London.
Burrow, J. W. (1981). *A Liberal Descent: Victorian Historians and the English Past*, Cambridge.
Butterfield, Herbert (1944). *The Englishman and his History*, Cambridge.
Canny, Nicholas (1987). 'Identity Formation in Ireland: The Emergence of the Anglo-Irish', in *Colonial Identity in the Atlantic World, 1500–1800*, ed. Nicholas Canny and Anthony Pagden, Princeton, N.J., pp. 159–212.
Cantalupo, Charles (1991). *A Literary Leviathan: Thomas Hobbes's Masterpiece of Language*, Lewisburg, Ky.
Caplan, Harry (1954). Introduction to *Ad C. Herennium de Ratione Dicendi*, London, pp. vii–xl.
Cassinelli, C. W. (1966). *Free Activities and Interpersonal Relations*, The Hague.
Chalmers, Gordon K. (1936). 'Sir Thomas Browne, True Scientist', *Osiris* 2, pp. 28–79.
Charlton, Kenneth (1965). *Education in Renaissance England*, London.
Christianson, Paul (1996). *Discourse on History, Law, and Governance in the Public Career of John Selden, 1610–1635*, Toronto.
Clark, Andrew (1891–1900). *The Life and Times of Anthony Wood*, 5 vols., Oxford.
Clark, George and Cooke, A. M. (1964–72). *A History of the Royal College of Physicians of London*, 3 vols., Oxford.

Cockagne, Emily Jane (2000). *A Cultural History of Sound in England 1560–1760*, PhD thesis, University of Cambridge.

Colie, Rosalie L. (1966). *Paradoxica Epidemica: The Renaissance Tradition of Paradox*, Princeton, N.J.

Coltman, Irene (1962). *Private Men and Public Causes: Philosophy and Politics in the English Civil War*, London.

Condren, Conal (1989). *George Lawson's Politica and the English Revolution*, Cambridge.

(1990). 'On the Rhetorical Foundations of *Leviathan*', *History of Political Thought* 11, pp. 703–20.

Cope, Jackson I. (1956). *Joseph Glanvill, Anglican Apologist*, St Louis, Mo.

Copp, David (1979). 'Collective Actions and Secondary Actions', *American Philosophical Quarterly* 16, pp. 177–86.

(1980). 'Hobbes on Artificial Persons and Collective Actions', *Philosophical Review* 89, pp. 579–606.

Cox, R. H. (1960). *Locke on War and Peace*, Oxford.

Cox, Virginia (1989). 'Rhetoric and Politics in Tasso's *Nifo*', *Studi Secenteschi* 30, pp. 3–98.

(1997). 'Machiavelli and the *Rhetorica ad Herennium*: Deliberative Rhetoric in *The Prince*', *Sixteenth-Century Journal* 28, pp. 1109–41.

Cromartie, Alan (1995). *Sir Matthew Hale 1609–1676*, Cambridge.

Curley, Edwin (1978). *Descartes Against the Skeptics*, Oxford.

Daly, James (1979). *Sir Robert Filmer and English Political Thought*, Toronto.

Danford, J. W. (1980). 'The Problem of Language in Hobbes's Political Science', *Journal of Politics* 42, pp. 102–34.

Day, J. P. (1983). 'Individual Liberty' in *Of Liberty*, ed. A. Phillips Griffith, Cambridge, pp. 17–29.

De Beer, G. R. (1950). 'Some Letters of Thomas Hobbes', *Notes and Records of the Royal Society* 7, pp. 195–206.

Dear, Peter (1984). 'Marin Mersenne and the Probabilistic Roots of Mitigated Scepticism', *Journal of the History of Philosophy* 22, pp. 173–205.

(1988). *Mersenne and the Learning of the Schools*, London.

Douglas, D. C. (1939). *English Scholars*, London.

(1946). *The Norman Conquest and British Historians*, Glasgow.

Dzelzainis, Martin (1991). Introduction to John Milton, *Political Writings*, Cambridge, pp. ix–xxv.

(1995). 'Milton's Classical Republicanism' in *Milton and Republicanism*, ed. David Armitage, Armand Himy and Quentin Skinner, Cambridge, pp. 3–24.

Elias, Norbert (1994). *The Civilising Process*, trans. Edmund Jephcott, Oxford.

Elsky, Martin (1989). *Authorising Words: Speech, Writing, and Print in the English Renaissance*, London.

Elton, G. R. (1955). *England under the Tudors*, London.

'Espinasse, Margaret (1956). *Robert Hooke*, London.

Feinberg, Joel (1970). *Doing and Deserving: Essays in the Theory of Responsibility*, Princeton, N.J.

Fitzmaurice, Lord Edmond (1895). *The Life of Sir William Petty*, London.

Flathman, Richard E. (1993). *Thomas Hobbes: Skepticism, Individuality, and Chastened Politics*, London.

Forbes, Duncan (1954). '"Scientific" Whiggism: Adam Smith and John Millar', *Cambridge Journal* 7, pp. 643–70.

(1975). *Hume's Philosophical Politics*, Cambridge.

Forsyth, Murray (1981). 'Thomas Hobbes and the Constituent Power of the People', *Political Studies* 29, pp. 191–203.

Frank, Joseph (1961). *The Beginnings of the English Newspaper*, Cambridge, Mass.

(1980). *Cromwell's Press Agent: A Critical Biography of Marchamont Nedham, 1620–1678*, Lanham, Md.

Fukuda, Arihiro (1997). *Sovereignty and the Sword: Harrington, Hobbes, and Mixed Government in the English Civil Wars*, Oxford.

Gabrieli, Vittorio (1957). 'Bacone, La Riforma e Roma nella Versione Hobbesiana d'un Carteggio di Fulgenzio Micanzio', *English Miscellany* 8, pp. 195–250.

Garnett, George (1994). Editor's Introduction to *Vindiciae, Contra Tyrannos*, ed. and trans. George Garnett, Cambridge, pp. xix–lxxvi.

Garver, Eugene (1980). 'Machiavelli's *The Prince*: A Neglected Rhetorical Classic', *Philosophy and Rhetoric* 13, pp. 99–120.

Gascoigne, John (1989). *Cambridge in the Age of the Enlightenment: Science, Religion and Politics from the Restoration to the French Revolution*, Cambridge.

Gauthier, David P. (1969). *The Logic of Leviathan: The Moral and Political Theory of Thomas Hobbes*, Oxford.

Gibbs, M. A. (1947). *John Lilburne the Leveller*, London.

Gierke, Otto von (1957). *Natural Law and the Theory of Society 1500 to 1800*, trans. Ernest Barker, Beacon edn, Boston, Mass.

Glass, D. V. (1964). 'John Graunt and his Natural and Political Observations', *Notes and Records of the Royal Society* 19, pp. 63–100.

Glover, William B. (1965). 'God and Thomas Hobbes' in *Hobbes Studies*, ed. K. C. Brown, Cambridge, Mass., pp. 141–68.

Goldie, Mark (1980). 'The Revolution of 1689 and the Structure of Political Argument: An Essay and an Annotated Bibliography of Pamphlets on the Allegiance Controversy', *Bulletin of Research in the Humanities* 83, pp. 473–564.

(1984). 'Sir Peter Pett, Sceptical Toryism and the Science of Toleration in the 1680s' in *Persecution and Toleration*, ed. W. J. Sheils, Oxford, pp. 247–73.

(1991). 'The Reception of Hobbes' in *The Cambridge History of Political Thought 1450–1700*, ed. J. H. Burns and Mark Goldie, Cambridge, pp. 589–615.

Goldsmith, M. M. (1966). *Hobbes's Science of Politics*, New York.

(1989). 'Hobbes on Liberty', *Hobbes Studies* 2, pp. 23–39.

(1991). 'The Hobbes Industry', *Political Studies* 39, pp. 135–47.

Gooch, G. P. (1915). *Political Thought in England: Bacon to Halifax*, London.

Grafton, Anthony and Jardine, Lisa (1986). *From Humanism to the Humanities: Education and the Liberal Arts in Fifteenth- and Sixteenth-Century Europe*, London.

Gray, Floyd (1974). 'Montaigne and Sebond: The Rhetoric of Paradox', *French Studies* 28, 134–45.

Greene, Robert A. (1962). 'Henry More and Robert Boyle on the Spirit of Nature', *Journal of the History of Ideas* 23, pp. 451–74.

Greenslade, B. D. (1975). 'The Publication Date of Hobbes's "Leviathan"', *Notes and Queries* 220, July, p. 320.

Guilloton, Vincent (1930). *Autour de la Relation du voyage de Samuel Sorbière en Angleterre 1663–4*, Northampton, Mass.

Gunn, J. A. W. (1969). *Politics and the Public Interest in the Seventeenth Century*, London.

Gunther, R. W. T. (1920–45). *Early Science at Oxford*, 14 vols., Oxford.

Hall, A. Rupert (1952). *Ballistics in the Seventeenth Century*, Cambridge.

(1962). *The Scientific Revolution*, 2nd edn, London.

Haller, William (1934). Commentary in *Tracts on Liberty in the Puritan Revolution 1638–1647*, ed. William Haller, 3 vols., New York, vol. 1.

Halliday, R. J., Kenyon, Timothy and Reeve, Andrew (1983). 'Hobbes's Belief in God', *Political Studies* 31, pp. 418–33.

Hampsher-Monk, Iain (1992). *A History of Modern Political Thought: Major Political Thinkers from Hobbes to Marx*, Oxford.

Hampton, Jean (1986). *Hobbes and the Social Contract Tradition*, Cambridge.

Hanson, Donald W. (1993). 'Science, Prudence, and Folly in Hobbes's Political Theory', *Political Theory* 21, pp. 643–64.

Hardacre, Paul H. (1956). *The Royalists during the Puritan Revolution*, The Hague.

Hardison, O. B., Jr. (1962). *The Enduring Monument: A Study of The Idea of Praise in Renaissance Literary Theory and Practice*, Chapel Hill, N.C.

Harwood, John T. (1986). Introduction to *The Rhetorics of Thomas Hobbes and Bernard Lamy*, Carbondale and Edwardsville, Ill., pp. 1–32.

Hervey, Helen (1952). 'Hobbes and Descartes in the Light of some Unpublished Letters of the Correspondence between Sir Charles Cavendish and Dr. John Pell', *Osiris* 10, pp. 67–90.

Heyd, David (1982). 'The Place of Laughter in Hobbes's Theory of the Emotions', *Journal of the History of Ideas* 43, pp. 285–95.

Hill, Christopher (1958). *Puritanism and Revolution*, London.

Hoekstra, S. J. (1998). The Savage, The Citizen and the Foole: The Compulsion for Civil Society in the Philosophy of Thomas Hobbes, DPhil thesis, University of Oxford.

Hood, F. C. (1964). *The Divine Politics of Thomas Hobbes: An Interpretation of Leviathan*, Oxford.

Howell, W. S. (1956). *Logic and Rhetoric in England, 1500–1700*, Princeton, N.J.

Hunter, Michael (1975). *John Aubrey and the Realm of Learning*, London.

(1979). 'The Debate over Science' in *The Restored Monarchy, 1660–1688*, ed. J. R. Jones, London, pp. 176–95.

(1981). *Science and Society in Restoration England*, London.

(1982). *The Royal Society and its Fellows 1660–1700: The Morphology of an Early Scientific Institution*, Chalfont St Giles.

(1989). *Establishing the New Science: The Experience of the Early Royal Society*, Woodbridge.

Hyde, J. K. (1965). 'Medieval Descriptions of Cities', *Bulletin of the John Rylands Library* 48, pp. 308–40.

Jacob, James R. (1983). *Henry Stubbe, Radical Protestantism and the Early Enlightenment*, Cambridge.

Jacob, James R. and Raylor, Timothy (1991). 'Opera and Obedience: Thomas Hobbes and *A Proposition for Advancement of Moralitie* by Sir William Davenant', *The Seventeenth Century* 2, pp. 205–50.

Jacoby, E. G. (1974). 'Thomas Hobbes in Europe', *Journal of European Studies* 4, pp. 57–65.

Jacquot, Jean and Jones, Harold Whitmore (1973). Introduction to *Thomas Hobbes: Critique du De Mundo de Thomas White*, Paris, pp. 9–102.

James, Susan (1986–7). 'Certain and Less Certain Knowledge', *Proceedings of the Aristotelian Society* 87, pp. 227–42.

(1997). *Passion and Action: The Emotions in Seventeenth-Century Philosophy*, Oxford.

Jardine, Lisa (1974). *Francis Bacon: Discovery and the Art of Discourse*, Cambridge.

Jardine, Lisa and Stewart, Alan (1998). *Hostage to Fortune: The Troubled Life of Francis Bacon*, London.

Jaume, Lucien (1986). *Hobbes et l'Etat représentatif moderne*, Paris.

Javitch, Daniel (1972). 'Poetry and Court Conduct: Puttenham's *Arte of English Poesie* in the Light of Castiglione's *Cortegiano*', *Modern Language Notes* 87, pp. 865–82.

Jesseph, Douglas M. (1999). *Squaring the Circle: The War between Hobbes and Wallis*, Chicago, Ill.

Johnston, David (1986). *The Rhetoric of Leviathan: Thomas Hobbes and the Politics of Cultural Transformation*, Princeton, N.J.

(1995). 'Limiting Liability: Roman Law and the Civil Law Tradition', *Chicago Kent Law Review* 70, pp. 1515–38.

Jolley, Nicholas (1987). 'Hobbes's Dagger in the Heart', *Canadian Journal of Philosophy* 17, pp. 855–73.

Jones, H. W. (1950). 'La Société Royale de Londres au XVIIe siècle', *Revue d'Histoire des Sciences* 3, pp. 214–21.

Jones, Richard F. (1949). 'The Background of the Attack on Science in the Age of Pope' in *Pope and his Contemporaries*, ed. James L. Clifford and Louis A. Anda, Oxford, pp. 96–113.

(1951). *The Seventeenth Century*, London.

(1961). *Ancients and Moderns*, 2nd edn, St Louis, Mo.

Jordan, W. K. (1942). *Men of Substance*, Chicago, Ill.

Kahn, Victoria (1985). *Rhetoric, Prudence and Skepticism in the Renaissance*, Ithaca, N.Y.

Kenyon, J. P. (1972). *The Popish Plot*, London.

(1977). *Revolution Principles: The Politics of Party, 1689–1720*, Cambridge.

King, Peter (1830). *The Life of John Locke*, 2 vols., 2nd edn, London.

Klein, William (1993). 'The Ancient Constitution Revisited' in *Political Discourse in Early Modern Britain*, ed. Nicholas Phillipson and Quentin Skinner, Cambridge, pp. 23–44.

Kliger, Samuel (1952). *The Goths in England*, Cambridge, Mass.

Knachel, Philip A. (1967). *England and the Fronde*, Ithaca, N.Y.

(1969). Introduction to Marchamont Nedham, *The Case of the Commonwealth of England, Stated*, Charlottesville, Va., pp. ix–xlii.

Kowalski, Georgius (1928). 'Studia Rhetorica II: Ad Figurae Paradiastole Historiam', *Eos* 31, pp. 169–80.

Kramer, Matthew (2001). 'Freedom, Unfreedom and Skinner's Hobbes', *Journal of Political Philosophy* 9, pp. 204–16.

Kristeller, Paul Oskar (1979). 'Humanism and Scholasticism in the Italian Renaissance' in *Renaissance Thought and its Sources*, ed. Michael Mooney, New York, pp. 85–105.

Kritzman, L. D. (1980). *Destruction/Découverte: Le fonctionnement de la rhétorique dans les Essais de Montaigne*, Lexington, Mass.

Kronman, Anthony (1980). 'The Concept of an Author and the Unity of the Commonwealth in Hobbes's *Leviathan*', *Journal of the History of Philosophy* 18, pp. 159–75.

Krook, Dorothea (1956). 'Thomas Hobbes's Doctrine of Meaning and Truth', *Philosophy* 31, pp. 3–22.

Kussmaul, Ann (1981). *Servants in Husbandry in Early Modern England*, Cambridge.

Lamont, William (1963). *Marginal Prynne*, London.

Lamprecht, Sterling P. (1940). 'Hobbes and Hobbism', *American Political Science Review* 34, pp. 31–53.

Laslett, Peter (1988). Introduction to *John Locke: Two Treatises of Government*, Cambridge, pp. 3–122.

Laudon, Laurens (1966). 'The Clock Metaphor and Probabilism', *Annals of Science* 22, pp. 73–104.

Leijenhorst, Cees (1996). 'Hobbes and Fracastoro', *Hobbes Studies* 9, pp. 98–128.

Lenoble, Robert (1943). *Mersenne ou la naissance du méchanisme*, Paris.

Lessay, Franck (1992). 'Le vocabulaire de la personne' in *Hobbes et son vocabulaire*, ed. Yves-Charles Zarka, Paris, pp. 155–86.

(1993a). Introduction to *Sur les lois relatives à l'hérésie* in Thomas Hobbes, *Textes sur l'hérésie et sur l'histoire*, Paris, pp. 57–63.

(1993b). Introduction to *De la Liberté et de la nécessité*, Paris, pp. 29–54.

Leyden, Wolfgang von (1982). *Hobbes and Locke: The Politics of Freedom and Obligation*, London.

Lindley, Keith (1986). 'London and Popular Freedom in the 1640s', in *Freedom in the English Revolution*, ed. R. C. Richardson and G. M. Ridden, Manchester, pp. 111–50.

MacCallum, Gerald C. (1972). 'Negative and Positive Freedom' in *Philosophy, Politics and Society*, 4th series, ed. Peter Laslett, W. G. Runciman and Quentin Skinner, Oxford, pp. 174–93.

Macdonald, Hugh and Hargreaves, Mary (1952). *Thomas Hobbes: A Bibliography*, London.

Machline, Vera Cecília (1998). 'The Contribution of Laurent Joubert's *Traité du Ris* to Sixteenth-Century Physiology of Laughter' in *Reading the Book of Nature: The Other Side of the Scientific Revolution*, ed. Allen G. Debus and Michael T. Walton, Kirksville, Mo., pp. 251–64.

Macpherson, C. B. (1962). *The Political Theory of Possessive Individualism: Hobbes to Locke*, Oxford.

Malcolm, Noel (1981). 'Hobbes, Sandys, and the Virginia Company', *Historical Journal* 24, pp. 297–321.

   (1983). Thomas Hobbes and Voluntarist Theology, PhD thesis, University of Cambridge.

   (1984). *De Dominis (1560–1624): Venetian, Anglican, Ecumenist and Relapsed Heretic*, London.

   (1988). 'Hobbes and the Royal Society' in *Perspectives on Thomas Hobbes*, ed. G. A. J. Rogers and Alan Ryan, Oxford, pp. 43–66.

   (1990). 'Hobbes's Science of Politics and His Theory of Science' in *Hobbes Oggi*, ed. Andrea Napoli and Guido Canziani, Milan, pp. 145–57.

   (1994a). General Introduction to *The Correspondence of Thomas Hobbes*, ed. Noel Malcolm, 2 vols., Oxford, vol. 1, pp. xxi–xli.

   (1994b). Textual Introduction to *The Correspondence of Thomas Hobbes*, ed. Noel Malcolm, 2 vols., Oxford, vol. 1, pp. xlii–lxxii.

   (1994c). 'Biographical Register of Hobbes's Correspondents' in *The Correspondence of Thomas Hobbes*, ed. Noel Malcolm, 2 vols., Oxford, vol. 2, pp. 777–919.

   (1996). 'A Summary Biography of Hobbes' in *The Cambridge Companion to Hobbes*, ed. Tom Sorell, Cambridge, pp. 13–44.

   (1997). Introduction to *The Origins of English Nonsense*, London, pp. 3–124.

   (1998). 'The Titlepage of *Leviathan*, Seen in a Curious Perspective', *The Seventeenth Century* 13, pp. 124–55.

   (2000). 'Charles Cotton, Translator of Hobbes's *De Cive*', *Huntington Library Quarterly* 61, pp. 259–87.

Martinich, A. P. (1992). *The Two Gods of Leviathan: Thomas Hobbes on Religion and Politics*, Cambridge.

   (1995). *A Hobbes Dictionary*, Oxford.

   (1997). *Thomas Hobbes*, London.

Mathie, William (1986). 'Reason and Rhetoric in Hobbes's *Leviathan*', *Interpretation* 14, pp. 281–98.

McCutcheon, Elizabeth (1971). 'Denying the Contrary: More's Use of Litotes in the *Utopia*', *Moreana* 31, pp. 107–21.

McManamon, John M. (1989). *Funeral Oratory and the Cultural Ideals of Italian Humanism*, Chapel Hill, N.C.

McNeilly, F. S. (1968). *The Anatomy of Leviathan*, London.

Ménager, Daniel (1995). *La Renaissance et le rire*, Paris.

Mendle, Michael (1995). *Henry Parker and the English Civil War: The Political Thought of the Public's "Privado"*, Cambridge.

Merton, Robert K. (1938). 'Science, Technology and Society in Seventeenth Century England', *Osiris* 4, pp. 360–632.

Mintz, Samuel I. (1962). *The Hunting of Leviathan*, Cambridge.

  (1968). 'Hobbes on the Law of Heresy: A New Manuscript', *Journal of the History of Ideas* 29, pp. 409–14.

Missner, Marshall (1983). 'Skepticism and Hobbes's Political Philosophy', *Journal of the History of Ideas* 44, pp. 407–27.

Monfasani, John (1988). 'Humanism and Rhetoric', in *Renaissance Humanism: Foundations, Forms, and Legacy*, 3 vols., ed. Albert Rabil Jr., Philadelphia, Penn., vol. 3, pp. 171–235.

More, Louis T. (1934). *Isaac Newton, a Biography*, New York.

Morgan, Augustus de (1872). *A Budget of Paradoxes*, London.

Munk, William (1878). *The Roll of the Royal College of Physicians*, 3 vols., 2nd edn, London.

Murphy, James J. (1981). *Renaissance Rhetoric: A Short-Title Catalogue of Works on Rhetorical Theory from the Beginning of Printing to AD 1700*, New York.

Oakeshott, Michael (1962). *Rationalism in Politics and Other Essays*, London.

  (1975a). *Hobbes on Civil Association*, Oxford.

  (1975b). *On Human Conduct*, Oxford.

Ogg, David (1956). *England in the Reign of Charles II*, 2 vols., 2nd edn, London.

Oppenheim, Felix (1981). *Political Concepts: A Reconstruction*, Chicago, Ill.

Orr, Robert (1987). 'Thomas Hobbes on the Regulation of Voluntary Motion' in *Lives, Liberties and the Public Good*, ed. George Feaver and Frederick Rosen, London, pp. 45–60.

Ossola, Carlo (1987). *Dal 'Cortegiano' all' 'Uomo di mondo'*, Turin.

Overhoff, Jürgen (2000). *Hobbes's Theory of the Will: Ideological Reasons and Historical Circumstances*, Lanham, Md.

Pacchi, Arrigo (1965). *Convenzione e Ipotesi nella Formazione della Filosofia Naturale di Thomas Hobbes*, Florence.

Paganini, Gianni (1999). 'Thomas Hobbes e Lorenzo Valla: Critica umanistica e filosofia moderna', *Rinascimento* 39, pp. 515–68.

  (2001). 'Hobbes, Valla e i Problemi Filosofici della Teologia Umanistica: la riforma "dialettica" della trinità' in *Dal Necessario al Possibile: Determinismo e Libertà nel Pensiero Anglo-olandese del XVII Secolo*, ed. L. Simonutti, Milan, pp. 11–45.

Pargellis, Stanley and Medley, D. J. (1951). *Bibliography of British History, the Eighteenth Century*, Oxford.

Parker, Patricia (1990). 'Metaphor and Catachresis' in *The Ends of Rhetoric: History, Theory, Practice*, ed. John Bender and David E. Wellberg, Stanford, Calif., pp. 60–73.

Parkin, Jon (1999). *Science, Religion and Politics in Restoration England: Richard Cumberland's De Legibus Naturae*, Woodbridge.

Pasquino, Pasquale (1994). 'Thomas Hobbes: La condition naturelle de l'humanité', *Revue française de science politique* 44, pp. 294–307.

Passmore, J. A. (1951). *Ralph Cudworth, An Interpretation*, Cambridge.

Paulson, Ronald (1988). *Don Quixote in England: The Aesthetics of Laughter*, Baltimore, Md.

Peck, Linda Levy (1996). 'Hobbes on the Grand Tour: Paris, Venice, or London?' *Journal of the History of Ideas* 57, pp. 177–83.

Peltonen, Markku (1995). *Classical Humanism and Republicanism in English Political Thought 1570–1640*, Cambridge.

Pennock, J. Roland (1965) 'Hobbes's Confusing "Clarity" – The Case of "Liberty" ' in *Hobbes Studies*, ed. K. C. Brown, Oxford, pp. 101–16.

Percival, W. Keith (1983). 'Grammar and Rhetoric in the Renaissance' in *Renaissance Eloquence*, ed. James J. Murphy, Berkeley, Calif., pp. 303–30.

Peters, R. S. (1956). *Hobbes*, Harmondsworth.

Pintard, René (1943). *Le Libertinage érudit dans la première moitié du XVIIe siècle*, Paris.

Pitkin, Hanna Fenichel (1967). *The Concept of Representation*, Berkeley, Calif.

Plamenatz, John (1965). 'Mr. Warrender's Hobbes' in *Hobbes Studies*, ed. K. C. Brown, Cambridge, Mass., pp. 73–87.

Pocock, J. G. A. (1951). 'Robert Brady, 1627–1700', *Cambridge Historical Journal* 10, pp. 186–204.

(1957). *The Ancient Constitution and the Feudal Law: English Historical Thought in the Seventeenth Century*, Cambridge.

(1971). *Politics, Language, and Time: Essays on Political Thought and History*, New York.

(1987). *The Ancient Constitution and the Feudal Law: A Reissue with a Retrospect*, Cambridge.

Polin, Raymond (1981). *Hobbes, Dieu et les hommes*, Paris.

Popkin, Richard H. (1979). *The History of Scepticism from Erasmus to Spinoza*, Berkeley, Calif.

Post, Jonathan F. S. (1987). *Sir Thomas Browne*, Boston, Mass.

Powicke, F. M. (1938). 'Notes on Hastings Manuscripts', *The Huntington Library Quarterly* 1, pp. 247–76.

Prins, Jan (1996). 'Hobbes on Light and Vision' in *The Cambridge Companion to Hobbes*, ed. Tom Sorell, Cambridge, pp. 129–56.

Pritchard, Allan (1980). 'The Last Days of Hobbes: Evidence of the Wood Manuscripts', *The Bodleian Library Record* 10, pp. 178–87.

Prokhovnik, Raia (1991). *Rhetoric and Philosophy in Hobbes's Leviathan*, London.

Purver, Margery (1967). *The Royal Society: Concept and Creation*, London.

Pye, Christopher (1984). 'The Sovereign, the Theater, and the Kingdome of Darknesse: Hobbes and the Spectacle of Power', *Representations* 8, pp. 84–106.

Railton, Peter (1986). 'Moral Realism', *Philosophical Review* 95, pp. 163–207.

Raphael, D. D. (1977). *Hobbes: Morals and Politics*, London.

(1984). 'Hobbes', in *Conceptions of Liberty in Political Philosophy*, ed. Zbigniew Pelczynski and John Gray, London, pp. 27–38.

Raven, Charles (1942). *John Ray, Naturalist*, Cambridge.

Raylor, Timothy (2001). 'Hobbes, Payne, and *A Short Tract on First Principles*', *The Historical Journal* 44, pp. 29–58.

Rayner, Jeremy (1991). 'Hobbes and the Rhetoricians' in *Hobbes Studies*, 4, pp. 76–95.

Rebhorn, Wayne A. (1983). 'The Enduring Word: Language, Time and History in *Il Libro del Cortegiano*' in *Castiglione: The Ideal and the Real in Renaissance Culture*, ed. Robert W. Hanning and David Rosand, London, pp. 69–90.

Reedy, Gerard (1992). *Robert South (1634–1716): An Introduction to his Life and Sermons*, Cambridge.

Reik, Miriam M. (1977). *The Golden Lands of Thomas Hobbes*, Detroit, Mich.

Reynolds, Noel B. and Hilton, John L. (1993). 'Thomas Hobbes and Authorship of the *Horae Subsecivae*', *History of Political Thought* 14, pp. 361–80.

Reynolds, Noel B. and Saxonhouse, Arlene W. (1995). 'Hobbes and the *Horae Subsecivae*' in *Thomas Hobbes, Three Discourses: A Critical Modern Edition of Newly Identified Work by the Young Hobbes*, ed. Noel B. Reynolds and Arlene W. Saxonhouse, Chicago, Ill., pp. 3–19.

Rhodes, Neil (1992). *The Power of Eloquence in English Renaissance Literature*, London.

Richardson, L. J. (1998). Sir John Hayward and Early Stuart Historiography, 2 vols., PhD thesis, University of Cambridge.

Robbins, Caroline (1959). *The Eighteenth-Century Commonwealthman*, Cambridge, Mass.

Robertson, George Croom (1886). *Hobbes*, Edinburgh.

Rogow, Arnold A. (1986). *Thomas Hobbes: Radical in the Service of Reaction*, New York.

Ronan, C. A. and Hartley, Sir H. (1960). 'Sir Paul Neile, F.R.S. (1613–1686)', *Notes and Records of the Royal Society* 15, pp. 159–65.

Ross, Ralph (1974). 'Some Puzzles in Hobbes' in *Thomas Hobbes in his Time*, ed. Ralph Ross, Herbert W. Schneider and Theodore Waldman, Minneapolis, Minn., pp. 42–60.

Rossini, Gigliola (1988). *Natura e Artificio nel Pensiero di Hobbes*, Bologna.

Røstvig, M.-S. (1954). *The Happy Man: Studies in the Metamorphoses of a Classical Ideal*, Oslo.

Rothkrug, Lionel (1965). *Opposition to Louis XIV*, Princeton, N.J.

Runciman, David (1997). *Pluralism and the Personality of the State*, Cambridge.

  (2000). 'What Kind of Person is Hobbes's State? A Reply to Skinner', *Journal of Political Philosophy* 8, pp. 268–78.

Sabbadini, Remigio (1967). *Le Scoperti dei Codici Latini e Greci ne' secolo XIV e XV*, ed. Eugenio Garin, Florence.

Sacksteder, William (1984). 'Hobbes' Philosophical and Rhetorical Artifice', *Philosophy and Rhetoric*, 17, pp. 30–46.

Sampson, Margaret (1990). '"Will You Hear What a Casuist He Is?" Thomas Hobbes as Director of Conscience', *History of Political Thought* 11, pp. 721–36.

Sanderson, John (1989). *'But the People's Creatures': The Philosophical Basis of the English Civil War*, Manchester.

Sarasohn, L. T. (1982). 'The Ethical and Political Philosophy of Pierre Gassendi', *Journal of the History of Philosophy* 20, pp. 239–60.

(1985). 'Motion and Morality: Pierre Gassendi, Thomas Hobbes and the Mechanical World-View', *Journal of the History of Ideas* 46, pp. 363–79.

Saunders, H. W. (1932). *A History of the Norwich Grammar School*, Norwich.

Schenk, Wilhelm (1948). *The Concern for Social Justice in the Puritan Revolution*, London.

Schlatter, Richard (1975). Introduction to *Hobbes's Thucydides*, New Brunswick, N.J., pp. xi–xxviii.

Schochet, Gordon J. (1975). *Patriarchalism in Political Thought*, Oxford.

Schuhmann, Karl (1984). 'Francis Bacon und Hobbes' Widmungsbrief zu *De Cive*', *Zeitschrift für Philosophische Forschung* 38, pp. 165–90.

(1990). 'Hobbes and Renaissance Philosophy' in *Hobbes Oggi*, ed. Andrea Napoli, Milan, pp. 331–49.

(1995). 'Le *Short Tract*, première oeuvre philosophique de Hobbes', *Hobbes Studies* 8, pp. 3–36.

(1996). 'Thomas Hobbes, Oeuvres', *British Journal for the History of Philosophy* 4, pp. 153–64.

(1998). *Hobbes: une chronique: Cheminement de sa pensée et de sa vie*, Paris.

Screech, M. A. (1997). *Laughter at the Foot of the Cross*, London.

Seaberg, R. B. (1981). 'The Norman Conquest and the Common Law: The Levellers and the Argument from Continuity', *Historical Journal* 24, pp. 791–806.

Seigel, Jerrold E. (1968). *Rhetoric and Philosophy in Renaissance Humanism: the Union of Eloquence and Wisdom, Petrarch to Valla*, Princeton, N.J.

Shapin, Steven (1994). *A Social History of Truth: Civility and Science in Seventeenth-Century England*, Chicago, Ill.

Shapin, Steven and Schaffer, Simon (1985). *Leviathan and the Air-Pump: Hobbes, Boyle, and the Experimental Life*, Princeton, N.J.

Shapiro, Barbara J. (1968). 'Latitudinarianism and Science', *Past and Present* 40, pp. 16–41.

(1969). *John Wilkins 1614–1672: An Intellectual Biography*, Berkeley, Calif.

(1983). *Probability and Certainty in Seventeenth-Century England*, Princeton, N.J.

Shapiro, Gary (1980). 'Reading and Writing in the Text of Hobbes's *Leviathan*', *Journal of the History of Philosophy* 18, pp. 147–57.

Shaw, W. A. (1900). *History of the English Church . . . 1640–1660*, 2 vols., London.

Simon, Joan (1979). *Education and Society in Tudor England*, Cambridge.

Simpson, A. W. B. (1973). 'The Common Law and Legal Theory' in *Oxford Essays in Jurisprudence*, ed. A. W. B. Simpson, 2nd series, Oxford, pp. 77–99.

Skinner, Quentin (1964). 'Hobbes's *Leviathan*', *Historical Journal* 7, pp. 321–33.

(1965). 'Hobbes on Sovereignty: An Unknown Discussion', *Political Studies* 13, pp. 213–18.

(1967). 'Science and Society in Restoration England', *Historical Journal* 10, pp. 286–93.

(1978a). *The Foundations of Modern Political Thought*. Vol. 1: *The Renaissance*, Cambridge.

(1978b). *The Foundations of Modern Political Thought*. Vol. 2: *The Age of Reformation*, Cambridge.

(1988). 'Warrender and Skinner on Hobbes: A Reply', *Political Studies* 36, pp. 692–5.

(1996). *Reason and Rhetoric in the Philosophy of Hobbes*, Cambridge.

(1998). *Liberty before Liberalism*, Cambridge.

Sommerville, Johann (1986a). 'History and Theory: the Norman Conquest in Early Stuart Political Thought', *Political Studies* 34, pp. 249–61.

(1986b). *Politics and Ideology in England, 1603–1640*, London.

(1992). *Thomas Hobbes: Political Ideas in Historical Context*, New York.

(1996). 'Lofty Science and Local Politics' in *The Cambridge Companion to Hobbes*, ed. Tom Sorell, Cambridge, pp. 246–73.

Sorell, Tom (1986). *Hobbes*, London.

(1990a). 'Hobbes's UnAristotelian Political Rhetoric', *Philosophy and Rhetoric* 23, pp. 96–108.

(1990b). 'Hobbes's Persuasive Civil Science', *The Philosophical Quarterly* 40, pp. 342–51.

(1993). 'Hobbes without Doubt', *History of Philosophy Quarterly* 10, pp. 121–35.

Sortais, Gaston (1920–2). *La philosophie moderne*, 2 vols., Paris.

Southgate, Beverley (1993). *'Covetous of Truth': The Life and Work of Thomas White, 1593–1676*, Dordrecht.

Spiller, Michael R. G. (1980). *"Concerning Natural Experimental Philosophie": Meric Casaubon and the Royal Society*, The Hague.

Springborg, Patricia (1976). *'Leviathan*, the Christian Commonwealth Incorporated', *Political Studies* 24, pp. 171–83.

State, Stephen A. (1985). 'Text and Context: Skinner, Hobbes and Theistic Natural Law', *Historical Journal* 28, pp. 27–50.

Steiner, Hillel (1974–5). 'Individual Liberty', *Proceedings of the Aristotelian Society* 75, pp. 33–50.

Stephen, Leslie (1961). *Hobbes*, Ann Arbor edn, Mich.

Stimson, Dorothy (1935). 'Puritanism and the New Philosophy in Seventeenth-Century England', *Bulletin of the Institute of the History of Medicine* 3, pp. 321–34.

Straka, G. M. (1962). 'The Final Phase of Divine Right Theory in England', *English Historical Review* 305, pp. 638–58.

Strauss, Erich (1954). *Sir William Petty: Portrait of a Genius*, London.

Strauss, Leo (1953). *Natural Right and History*, Chicago, Ill.

(1963). *The Political Philosophy of Hobbes: Its Basis and Its Genesis*, trans. Elsa M. Sinclair, Phoenix edn, Chicago, Ill.

Syfret, R. H. (1950). 'Some Early Reactions to the Royal Society', *Notes and Records of the Royal Society of London* 7, pp. 207–58.

(1951). 'Some Early Critics of the Royal Society', *Notes and Records of the Royal Society of London* 8, pp. 20–64.

Talmor, Sascha (1981). *Glanvill: The Uses and Abuses of Scepticism*, Oxford.

Tave, Stuart M. (1960). *The Amiable Humorist*, Chicago, Ill.

Taylor, A. E. (1965). 'The Ethical Doctrine of Hobbes' in *Hobbes Studies*, ed. K. C. Brown, Cambridge, Mass., pp. 35–55.

Taylor, Michael (1982). *Community, Anarchy and Liberty*, Cambridge.

Teeter, Louis (1936). 'The Dramatic Uses of Hobbes's Political Ideas', *E.L.H.* 3, pp. 140–69.

Thomas, Keith (1965). 'The Social Origins of Hobbes's Political Thought' in *Hobbes Studies*, ed. K. C. Brown, Cambridge, Mass., pp. 185–236.

(1972). 'The Levellers and the Franchise' in *The Interregnum: The Quest for Settlement*, ed. G. E. Aylmer, London, pp. 57–78.

(1977). 'The Place of Laughter in Tudor and Stuart England', *Times Literary Supplement*, 21 January, pp. 77–81.

(1993). 'Cases of Conscience in Seventeenth-Century England' in *Public Duty and Private Conscience in Seventeenth-Century England*, ed. John Morrill, Paul Slack and Daniel Woolf, Oxford, pp. 29–56.

Thompson, Martyn P. (1977). 'The Idea of Conquest in Controversies over the 1688 Revolution', *Journal of the History of Ideas* 38, pp. 33–46.

Tinkler, John F. (1988). 'Praise and Advice: Rhetorical Approaches in More's *Utopia* and Machiavelli's *The Prince*', *Sixteenth Century Journal* 19, pp. 187–207.

Tönnies, Ferdinand (1912). *Thomas Hobbes, der Mann und der Denker*, Stuttgart.

(1969a). Preface to Thomas Hobbes, *The Elements of Law Natural and Politic*, ed. Ferdinand Tönnies, 2nd edn, introd. M. M. Goldsmith, London, pp. v–xiii.

(1969b). Preface to Thomas Hobbes, *Behemoth or the Long Parliament*, ed. Ferdinand Tönnies, 2nd edn, introd. M. M. Goldsmith, London, pp. vii–xi.

(1975). *Studien zur Philosophie und Gesellschaftslehre im 17. Jahrhundert*, ed. E. G. Jacoby, Stuttgart.

Trevor-Roper, H. R. (1957). 'Thomas Hobbes', in *Historical Essays*, London, pp. 233–8.

(1967). Introduction to Margery Purver, *The Royal Society: Concept and Creation*, London, pp. xi–xvii.

Tricaud, François (1982). 'An Investigation Concerning the Usage of the Words "Person" and "Persona" in the Political Treatises of Hobbes' in *Thomas Hobbes: His View of Man*, ed. J. G. van der Bend, Amsterdam, pp. 89–98.

(1985). 'Éclaircissements sur les six premières biographies de Hobbes', *Archives de philosophie* 48, pp. 277–86.

Tuck, Richard (1979). *Natural Rights Theories: their Origin and Development*, Cambridge.

(1989). *Hobbes*, Oxford.

Tukiainen, Arto (1994). 'The Commonwealth as a Person in Hobbes's *Leviathan*', *Hobbes Studies* 7, pp. 44–55.

Tully, James (1993). *An Approach to Political Philosophy: Locke in Contexts*, Cambridge.

Turnbull, G. H. (1947). *Hartlib, Dury and Comenius*, Liverpool.

Underdown, David (1971). *Pride's Purge: Politics in the Puritan Revolution*, London.

Ure, Peter (1958). Introduction to John Eachard, *Mr Hobbs's State of Nature Considered*, Liverpool, pp. ix–xxiv.

Vallance, Edward (2001). 'Oaths, Casuistry, and Equivocation: Anglican Responses to the Engagement Controversy', *Historical Journal* 44, pp. 59–77.

Vickers, Brian (1968). 'King Lear and Renaissance Paradoxes', *Modern Language Review*, 63, pp. 305–14.
(1981). 'Rhetorical and Anti-rhetorical Tropes: On Writing the History of *Elocutio*', *Comparative Criticism* 3, pp. 105–32.
(1988). 'Rhetoric and Poetics' in *The Cambridge History of Renaissance Philosophy*, gen. ed. C. B. Schmitt, Cambridge, pp. 715–45.
(1989). *In Defence of Rhetoric*, rev. edn, Oxford.
(1990). 'The Recovery of Rhetoric: Petrarch, Erasmus, Perelman', *History of the Human Sciences* 3, pp. 415–41.
Viroli, Maurizio (1998). *Machiavelli*, Oxford.
Wallace, John M. (1963). 'The Cause Too Good', *Journal of the History of Ideas* 24, pp. 150–4.
(1964). 'The Engagement Controversy 1649–1652: An Annotated List of Pamphlets', *Bulletin of the New York Public Library* 68, pp. 384–405.
(1968). *Destiny his Choice: the Loyalism of Andrew Marvell*, Cambridge.
Warrender, Howard (1957). *The Political Philosophy of Hobbes: His Theory of Obligation*, Oxford.
(1965). 'A Reply to Mr Plamenatz' in *Hobbes Studies*, ed. K. C. Brown, Cambridge, Mass, pp. 89–100.
(1983a). Introduction to Thomas Hobbes, *De Cive: The Latin Version*, ed. Howard Warrender, Oxford, pp. 1–67.
(1983b). Introduction to Thomas Hobbes, *De Cive: The English Version*, ed. Howard Warrender, Oxford, pp. 1–18.
Watkins, J. W. N. (1965). *Hobbes's System of Ideas*, London.
Watson, R. A. and Force, J. E. (1988). 'Publications of Richard H. Popkin 1950–1986 inclusive', in *The Sceptical Mode in Modern Philosophy*, ed. R. A. Watson and J. E. Force, Dordrecht, pp. 151–62.
Webster, Charles (1966). 'Richard Towneley, 1629–1707, and the Towneley Group', *Transactions of the Historical Society of Lancashire and Cheshire* 118, pp. 51–76.
(1967a). 'Henry Power's Experimental Philosophy', *Ambix* 14, pp. 150–78.
(1967b). 'The Origins of the Royal Society', *History of Science* 6, pp. 106–28.
Weimann, Robert (1996). *Authority and Representation in Early Modern Discourse*, Baltimore, Md.
Wernham, A. G. (1965). 'Liberty and Obligation in Hobbes', in *Hobbes Studies*, ed. Keith C. Brown, Oxford, pp. 117–39.
Westfall, Richard S. (1958). *Science and Religion in Seventeenth Century England*, New Haven, Conn.
Whelan, Frederick G. (1981). 'Language and its Abuses in Hobbes' Political Philosophy', *The American Political Science Review* 75, pp. 59–75.
Whigham, Frank (1984). *Ambition and Privilege: The Social Tropes of Elizabethan Courtesy Theory*, Berkeley, Calif.
Wildermuth, M. E. (1989). 'The Rhetoric of Wilson's *Arte*: Reclaiming the Classical Heritage for English Protestants', *Philosophy and Rhetoric* 22, pp. 435–8.

Wilkins, David (1737). *Concilia Magnae Britanniae et Hiberniae*, 4 vols., London.

Willcock, Gladys and Walker, Alice (1970). Introduction to George Puttenham, *The Arte of English Poesie*, Cambridge, pp. ix–cii.

Willman, Robert (1970). 'Hobbes on the Law of Heresy', *Journal of the History of Ideas* 31, pp. 607–13.

Wolf, Friedrich O. (1969). *Die Neue Wissenschaft des Thomas Hobbes... Mit Hobbes' Essayes*, Stuttgart.

Woodhouse, A. S. P. (ed.) (1938). *Puritanism and Liberty*, London.

Woolf, D. R. (1990). *The Idea of History in Early Stuart England: Erudition, Ideology and 'The Light of Truth' from the Accession of James I to the Civil War*, London.

Wootton, David (1983). 'The Fear of God in Early Modern Political Theory', *Canadian Historical Association Historical Papers*, pp. 56–80.

Worden, Blair (1974). *The Rump Parliament*, Cambridge.

(1994). 'Marchamont Nedham and the Beginnings of English Republicanism, 1649–1656' in *Republicanism, Liberty and Commercial Society 1649–1776*, ed. David Wootton, Stanford, Cal., pp. 45–81.

(1995). 'Milton and Marchamont Nedham' in *Milton and Republicanism*, ed. David Armitage, Armand Himy and Quentin Skinner, Cambridge, pp. 156–80.

Wrigley, E. A. and Schofield, R. S. (1981). *The Population History of England 1541–1871: A Reconstruction*, Cambridge.

Yale, D. E. C. (1972). 'Hale and Hobbes on Law, Legislation and the Sovereign', *The Cambridge Law Journal* 31, pp. 121–56.

Zagorin, Perez (1954). *A History of Political Thought in the English Revolution*, London.

(1993). 'Hobbes's Early Philosophical Development', *Journal of the History of Ideas* 54, pp. 505–18.

Zappen, James P. (1983). 'Aristotelian and Ramist Rhetoric in Thomas Hobbes's *Leviathan*: Pathos versus Ethos and Logos', *Rhetorica* 1, pp. 65–91.

Zarka, Yves-Charles (1985). 'Personne civile et représentation politique chez Hobbes', *Archives de philosophie* 48, pp. 287–310.

(1995). *Hobbes et la pensée politique moderne*, Paris.

Index

379